Drugs in Society

Online Instructor and Student Resources

Thank you for selecting Anderson Publishing's *Drugs in Society: Causes, Concepts, and Control*. To complement the learning experience, we have provided a number of online tools to accompany this edition. Two distinct packages of interactive resources are available: one for instructors and one for students.

Please consult your local sales representative with any additional questions. You may also e-mail the Academic Sales Team at textbook@elsevier.com.

For the Instructor

Qualified adopters and instructors can access valuable material for free by registering at: http://textbooks.elsevier.com/web/manuals.aspx?isbn=9781455731879

- **Test Bank** Compose, customize, and deliver exams using unique multiple-choice and true-or-false questions created for *Drugs in Society: Causes, Concepts, and Control*.
- **PowerPoint Lecture Slides** Reinforce key topics with focused PowerPoint slides, which provide a visual outline with which to augment your lecture. Each individual book chapter has its own dedicated slide show.
- **Lesson Plans** Design your course around customized lesson plans. Each individual lesson plan contains content synopses, key terms, and other aids designed to spur class discussion.

For the Student

Students can access all the resources below by simply following this link: http://store.elsevier.com/product.jsp?&isbn=9781455731879

- **Self-Assessment Question Bank** Enhance review and study sessions with the help of this online self-quizzing asset. Each question is presented in an interactive format that allows for immediate feedback.
- **Case Studies** Apply what is on the page to the world beyond with the help of topic-specific case studies, each designed to turn theory into practice and followed by interactive scenario-based questions that allow for immediate feedback.

Drugs in Society
Causes, Concepts, and Control
Seventh Edition

Michael D. Lyman

Columbia College
Columbia, MO, USA

AMSTERDAM • BOSTON • HEIDELBERG • LONDON
NEW YORK • OXFORD • PARIS • SAN DIEGO
SAN FRANCISCO • SINGAPORE • SYDNEY • TOKYO

Anderson Publishing is an imprint of Elsevier

Acquiring Editor: Shirley Decker-Lucke
Development Editor: Ellen S. Boyne
Project Manager: Julia Haynes
Designer: Tin Box Studio, Inc.

Anderson Publishing is an imprint of Elsevier
225 Wyman Street, Waltham, MA 02451, USA

Library of Congress Cataloging-in-Publication Data
A catalogue record for this book is available from the Library of Congress.

British Library Cataloguing-in-Publication Data
A catalogue record for this book is available from the British Library.

ISBN: 978-1-4557-3187-9

For information on all Anderson publications
visit our website at http://store.elsevier.com

Typeset by TNQ Books and Journals

Printed in the United States of America

14 15 16 17 18   10 9 8 7 6 5 4 3 2

 Working together
to grow libraries in
developing countries

www.elsevier.com • www.bookaid.org

Contents

Preface

Despite decades of widespread enforcement, interdiction, prevention efforts, and treatment initiatives, the problems of drug abuse and trafficking continue to flourish in communities and neighborhoods across the United States. The extent of the problem has accelerated to the point that most of us know of someone who has been affected in some way by substance abuse.

One of the many lessons to learn from studying the United States drug problem is that change is an inevitable part of the drug abuse crisis. We cannot develop a sound drug control policy unless we first become students of history. Things are different now in the twenty-first century than they were in the mid-1980s, when crack cocaine first appeared on the nation's drug scene. Drugs and those who produce and sell them are notably different than their counterparts of 20, 30, and 50 years ago.

In 2012, for example, the social waters continued to remain muddied as "marijuana bars" were established in certain states. In one case, a New Year's Eve party in December 2012 enabled marijuana smokers to smoke freely in Club 64, a private "marijuana-specific social club" in Denver, named after Colorado's recently passed marijuana law, Amendment 64. To join, people filled out an online application and paid a $30 fee to become members. Members were advised of a private location in downtown Denver where they could attend a New Year's Eve party with other smokers.

Not only do the drugs of abuse themselves change, but patterns and trends of drug abuse also shift from one decade to the next. For example, over the decades, the focus of the nation's drug abuse problem shifted from opium to marijuana to LSD to PCP to cocaine; today, many look at methamphetamine as one of the prevailing national threats to human health and public safety. Furthermore, people who traffic drugs are also keenly aware of the element of change in the drug business. When factors such as competition from rival criminal groups or effective law enforcement measures place pressures on criminal trafficking organizations, their methods of manufacturing, transportation, and marketing must also be modified. Many of today's drug-trafficking organizations have become extremely resourceful in adjusting to political, economic, and social changes in the drug trade.

Indeed, domestic political agendas greatly affect the manner in which our government and society deal with the drug problem, and clearly such changes vary from one presidential administration to the next. One of the ironies of the drug problem is that, for the most part, people want the same things: safe neighborhoods, safe highways, drug-free workplaces, drug-free schools, addiction-free babies, and so forth. However, individual politics and values often dictate different ways of achieving these goals. Political agendas affect the philosophies of dealing with both drug abuse and drug offenders, which in turn dictate which and how many resources will be made available to deal with the nation's drug problem. So, with all these variables at work, it is little wonder why finding a resolution to the U.S. drug problem is so difficult.

This brings us to the purpose of this book. *Drugs in Society: Causes, Concepts, and Control*, Seventh Edition, deals with the three most pivotal areas of today's drug problem: drug abuse; drug trafficking; and drug control policy. We should acknowledge that the preparation of any book is a considerable undertaking, and this one has been no exception. Furthermore, any text dealing with drug abuse necessitates periodic updating because it is a diverse subject that encompasses numerous disciplines such as sociology, politics, psychology, medicine, criminal justice, public policy, and law.

Many social, political, and private policy changes have set the stage for this text, and this is precisely the premise of this seventh edition—change. It is a book about drugs, addictions, dealers, corrupt officials, drug cops, the courts, personal and public values, public policy, the laws, and the rising numbers of ruined communities and families throughout the country. Put simply, it is designed to give the reader insight into formulating possible solutions to the United States drug dilemma.

Drug abuse is a sensitive public issue. Discussions typically generate the political volatility of other heated social issues such as abortion, gun control, and capital punishment. It is therefore one of our primary goals to address the subject in a realistic fashion, with objective consideration given to both liberal and conservative social perspectives. This book, designed to offer a logical flow of information, is organized in three parts: "Understanding the Problem," "Gangs and Drugs," and "Fighting Back." Each part contains chapters that focus on the many critical areas of the United States drug problem, and give the reader a foundation for critical thinking and rational decision-making within this complex multidisciplinary field.

We would like to extend a sincere thank-you to the many individuals who assisted in the preparation of this project. Specifically, thanks is most offered to the many friends and associates in the drug enforcement profession, our colleagues in criminal justice and higher education, and the always helpful people at the National Institute of Justice, the National Center for Drugs and Crime Control, the Office of National Drug Control Policy, the Drug Enforcement Administration, the Federal Bureau of Investigation, and the Bureau of Justice Statistics. A special thanks is well deserved by the good people at Anderson Publishing (Elsevier) and their capable management, editorial, and production staff. Their belief in our work helped make this seventh edition of *Drugs in Society: Causes, Concepts, and Control* a reality.

In an effort to ensure accuracy and readability of the book's organization and content, we would like to encourage any and all comments about this text for use in future editions. Please feel free to contact us at any time in this regard. Again, we would like to thank you for adopting this textbook, and we hope that it provides you with a meaningful learning tool for understanding drugs in society.

Michael D. Lyman
Columbia College

Introduction

For many Americans, the drug problem is an abstract one involving other people and occurring somewhere else: heroin and crack are abused by the poor in outlying ghettos, cocaine and pharmaceuticals are used by the very rich, and other drugs are consumed by fast-trackers in the entertainment industry. Even drug busts on local television feature characters from neighborhoods on the far side of town—certainly not where *we* live. However, as responsible citizens living in a modern society, we can no longer adopt an out-of-sight, out-of-mind mentality with regard to drug abuse. We must begin by being honest with ourselves about the realities of drug abuse, and assume a more proactive attitude. For example, most of us are very well acquainted with the most abused drug in the country: alcohol. Statistics show that the fatal consequences of alcohol abuse outweigh those associated with any other drug. In addition, the scores of people involved with the illicit drug trade, from members of organized crime groups to casual dealers, have little respect for United States laws, legitimate forms of commerce, or a safe and prosperous society.

Perhaps accepting the problem—that is, not assuming that it is someone else's problem—is the first step in identifying workable solutions. This is the primary focus of Part I, "Understanding the Problem," which addresses the history of drug abuse and the development of drug control policy, drug pharmacology, theories of drug abuse, and the role of source countries in drug trafficking. Part I also focuses on drug-related crimes that support the illicit drug industry and are at the core of many senseless acts of violence in neighborhoods around the country.

Organized gangs bankrolled by the lucrative drug trade not only are rooted in major American cities, but also have long since expanded to communities of all sizes. Involved in drug trafficking are not only traditional organized crime groups such as the Mafia, but also nontraditional gangs that include many inner-city youth groups, as well as newly emerging Asian youth gangs. Such gangs have become reliant on the drug trade for fast money and local control of criminal enterprises in their communities.

In many American cities, widespread violence from competing Mexican Cartels has spilled over the Mexican border into America as they strive for control of the methamphetamine and cocaine markets. Outlaw motorcycle gangs such as the Hells Angels have added the drug trade to their many other criminal endeavors. These organizations and others are the focus of Part II of this book, "Gangs and Drugs," which discusses the involvement of organized crime in the drug trade.

As Americans accept the reality of drug abuse, we are faced with many questions: how have things gotten so far out of hand? What do we do now? Do solutions to the problem lie in the area of public health, culture, sociology, education, or criminal justice? Each of these areas offers some explanation. Part III, "Fighting Back," considers what is being done and what can be done to best deal with the problem. In doing so, its chapters discuss the role of federal drug enforcement organizations, drug laws, and drug enforcement initiatives. Additionally, critical issues such as drug courier profiling, covert police initiatives, legalizing medical marijuana, needle exchange programs, drug testing in the workplace and at home, and drug abuse in sports are all examined.

As an aid to readers of this book, numerous critical thinking questions have been provided throughout each chapter. These are designed to promote thought and discussion about some of the more important dynamics of the United States drug abuse problem. We have also provided reading objectives at the beginning of each chapter, along with important terms at each chapter's conclusion. All these features are created to provide the student of drug abuse with a means not only to understand the problem, but also to formulate realistic public policy responses.

Today, drugs in society present a myriad of social problems. Drugs threaten our standard of living and the quality of our neighborhoods. Drugs can ruin not only the lives of drug users, but also the lives of those who love them. They drain society of precious public resources that could be put to work elsewhere. Society has responded by passing criminal and civil laws, as well as implementing myriad social programs, each designed to deal with some aspect of the nation's drug abuse problem. Some of these initiatives have proved more successful than others, but limited as any initiative is, we can only hope that we can rise as a nation to meet the challenge.

Understanding the Problem

One of the assumptions of this book is that an educated society is better prepared to respond to the problem of drug abuse than one that is ill informed. To that end, the first six chapters are designed to give the reader the essentials regarding the nation's drug abuse crisis. To begin, we discuss the social and health consequences of drug use. Next is an in-depth review of the drugs most commonly abused in our schools and neighborhoods, followed by an overview describing how drugs of abuse emerged in modern society and what circumstances led to their gradual social control. We then offer an overview of the international and domestic drug-trafficking problem, providing an understanding of the origins of illicit drugs. Finally, drug-related crime is discussed in the context of predatory, political, and white-collar criminal behavior related to the drug trade. Each of these areas will prepare the reader for a discussion of organized criminal activity in the illicit drug trade, which is discussed in Part II.

1

The Nature of the Drug Problem

This chapter will enable you to:

- Learn the social and individual consequences of drug abuse
- Understand the reasons why people use drugs
- Realize the extent of the drug abuse problem in the United States
- Consider the various theories and explanations of drug abuse

With so many local and national governmental resources focusing on terrorism in 2013, the problem of drug abuse and addiction still remains a constant in every community across the nation. Experts agree that too many Americans need treatment for substance use disorders but do not receive it and that prescription drug abuse continues to ruin countless lives. Moreover, those who take drugs and drive threaten safety on our nation's streets and highways.

Research shows that perceptions of the risks of drug use by young people have declined over the past decade and that this is often a predictor of future increases in drug use. Still, a considerable amount of work is needed to reform our justice system and address drug use and drug-related crime.

Drug abuse is costly on all fronts. For example, in 2012, the Office of National Drug Control Policy (ONDCP) reported that illicit drug use in the United States contributed to an estimated $193 billion in crime, health, and lost productivity costs in 2007, the year for which the most recent estimate is available. But between 2008 and 2011, some degree of progress was seen in the reduction of drug abuse in the nation [1]. However, experts still see a need for improvement in the areas of prevention, early intervention, treatment, recovery support, criminal justice reform, law enforcement, and international cooperation.

Nearly every citizen across the country not only is aware of the nation's drug problem, but also most likely knows someone impacted by it. Family members, coworkers, friends, and neighbors all have the potential to become drug abusers or victims of drug abuse in one fashion or another.

One of the best ways to understand the nature of the drug problem is by considering statistics depicting the extent of drug abuse. For example, according to the World Drug Report, in 2010 between 155 and 250 million people, or 3.5–5.7 percent of the population ages 15–64, had used illicit substances at least once in the previous year [2]. Cannabis users made up the largest number of illicit drug users, 129–190 million people. Amphetamine-type stimulants were the second most commonly used illicit drugs, followed by opiates and cocaine. However, in terms of harm associated with use, opiates would be ranked at the top [3]. While the extent of the worldwide drug problem will be discussed in greater detail in upcoming chapters, drug abuse here in the United States remains an ongoing concern.

For example, in 2010, the United States government estimated the economic cost of the war on drugs to be roughly $215 billion [4]. Additionally, the United States government reports that the cost of incarcerating drug law offenders was $30.1 billion—$9.1 billion for police protection, $4.5 billion for legal adjudication, and $11.0 billion for state and federal corrections. In total, in 2005 roughly $45.5 billion was spent on these efforts [5]. The socioeconomic costs as well as the individual costs (i.e., the personal disadvantages in income and career) caused by the incarceration of millions of people are not included in this number.

This Book's Theme

This text is based on the understanding that drugs have been a part of society since the beginning of recorded history and will continue to be infused in society, one way or another, for the foreseeable future. While many drugs are beneficial to society, others cause considerable problems for communities and pose serious threats to the stability of an otherwise happy and functional family. In that regard, for generations, drugs have been responsible for the destruction of countless human lives. The ability of the scientific community to understand the true effects, benefits, and dangers of drugs on the human body remains a perennial challenge. Moreover, the drug abuse and the global manufacturing and trafficking mechanisms that support drug abuse continue to burden all aspects of the criminal justice system.

The book is designed to give the reader a realistic overview of the nation's drug problem, as well as to discuss what society is doing about it. Information is presented from historical, medical, legal, public policy, and practical points of view that will help the reader formulate informed opinions.

Overview of the Drug Crisis

The social effects of drug trafficking are accentuated and reinforced by their direct and indirect economic impacts. The sums spent on drugs represent resources lost to legitimate productive enterprises, and the money laundered by drug traffickers seems to corrupt all who come into contact with it. Consequently, drug traffickers who purchase legitimate businesses have learned that it is easy to integrate dealers into society. Drug traffickers who make use of existing legitimate businesses know that where such vast sums of money are involved, even "respectable citizens" can be induced to overlook the source of the money. In addition, the economic effect carries over into the workplace, where drug-using workers increase the costs of production, raise the levels of absenteeism, and raise the incidence of accidents on the job, all of which compel employers to implement expensive antidrug abuse programs.

Severe health problems are also created when drug abuse prevails. These problems include drug overdoses and poisonings from "street" drugs, as well as improperly consumed pharmaceutical drugs. Even marijuana can have devastating long-term effects. Not only is marijuana the drug with which many users begin drug abuse, but also marijuana cigarettes have many times the tar and carcinogens found in tobacco cigarettes. Additional problems include drug-addicted mothers who give birth to addicted babies, as well as the spread of diseases such as hepatitis and AIDS through drug users sharing contaminated needles. In the 1980s and 1990s, the proliferation of crack houses contributed to the financing of violent gangs, as well as related issues such as the spread of the AIDS virus. Today, crack houses are still a problem, and in many of them prostitution flourishes in the common sex-for-drugs transaction.

Drug abuse also has the ability to affect society on a much greater level—in terms of national security. Many larger drug organizations, particularly the South American and Southeast Asian cartels, have already become so powerful that they wield as much influence as many Latin and Central American governments. Drug money from these organizations has corrupted government officials, many of whom are themselves charged with the responsibility of drug control. In fact, the immense power and financial reserves of some of the largest drug-trafficking organizations have made them attractive partners in intelligence operations (such as those conducted during the Vietnam War and in Central America), thereby rendering United States policy confused and contradictory at times. Other drug-source countries that are hostile to the United States view drugs as a weapon to use against American society.

Drugs and the Family

It is easy to see that the drug user can have a residual effect on the lives of family members. A portrait of the drug user is provided in Chapter 14, but experience has shown that the dependent drug abuser will lie and steal if necessary to support his or her habit. In many cases, an occurrence called *backstabbing* takes place in families in which a member uses drugs. Here, young and middle-aged drug users who have depleted their own resources will turn to family members for drug money. In some cases, the family is unaware of the seriousness of the situation and provides money to the user, only to realize that more will be required soon. Many families cease to continue providing money, whereas others continue in an effort to "help" their dependent family member. This phenomenon gradually depletes the family's financial and emotional resources to the point at which family members lose faith in the drug user and begin to view him or her as troublesome, untrustworthy, or weak. In time, the person begins stealing items of value from the household to sell for drug money.

Sadly, in many cases, parents are part of the problem. Drug-dealing children who come home with hundreds of dollars are sometimes not disciplined by parents because that money, although obtained illegally, is needed to pay bills and buy food. The parents tend to rationalize their child's behavior by thinking that they will deal drugs anyway, or that society has somehow failed to provide them with sufficient means to earn a legitimate income. When this occurs, the parents tend to take on a childlike role, leaving the major decisions up to the primary breadwinner—the drug-dealing child. In other cases, parents who are drug users themselves will often fail to provide adequate attention, care, and financial support for their family, resulting in many children being taken in by grandparents, other relatives, or the state social service system.

Studies have also shown that unemployment and frequent drug use have been major contributors to the demise of the two-parent household, whereas stable employment and low drug use are associated with high rates of forming a "traditional" two-parent family. Research has shown that although drug abuse adversely affects all ethnic groups, the hardest hit are poor and minority families, and those with single female heads of households. Without help, many of these mothers experience great difficulty in controlling the actions of their young ones, who are charmed by drug dealing and other forms of street crime. Involvement in the drug culture also places youths in other types of jeopardy, including arrest, street violence, drug overdose, incarceration, and truancy.

Drugs and Teens

Young people feel the greatest pressure to use drugs, primarily from their peers. This pressure is often reinforced through popular culture, creating the mistaken belief that "everyone is doing it," and that drug use is "cool" and free of consequences. This "social norm" effect creates the mistaken belief among some young people—and sometimes even their parents—that more kids use drugs than actually do. In the past year, the majority of 12- to 17-year-olds talked at least once with one or more parents about the dangers of substance abuse. These discussions were helpful: rates of current substance use were lower for youths who did talk with parents than for those who did not.

Statistics from the Monitoring the Future (MTF) study published by the National Institute on Drug Abuse (NIDA) provided some insight as to drug abuse by teens. The study focused on the three substances most widely used by adolescents—cigarettes, alcohol, and marijuana (see Figure 1.1).

According to the 2011 MTF study, while illicit drug use among teens did not change significantly between 2010 and 2011, there have been significant increases in past-month use since 2006; however, it is mostly driven by increasing rates of marijuana use. For example, according to the ONDCP, between 2006 and 2011, "past-month" use of any illicit drug among 10th graders increased from 16.8 percent to 19.2 percent. During the same time period, past-month use of marijuana among 10th graders increased from 14.2 percent to 17.6 percent [6].

Marijuana use, which had been rising among teens for the past 3 years, continued to rise in 2011 in all prevalence periods for 10th and 12th graders. The recent rise in use stands in stark contrast to the long, gradual decline that had been occurring over the preceding decade. As mentioned in this chapter, it is significant that perceived risk for marijuana has been falling for the past 5 years, and disapproval declined for the past 3 to 5 years. In fact, some researchers argue that the decline in perceived risk may be related to the increased public discussions concerning medical marijuana [7].

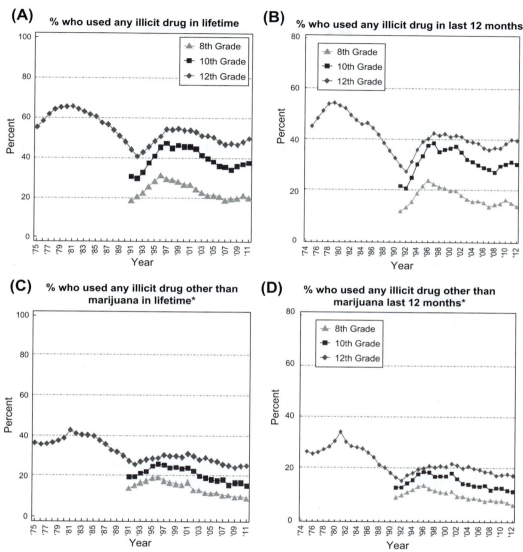

(A) % who used any illicit drug in lifetime

(B) % who used any illicit drug in last 12 months

(C) % who used any illicit drug other than marijuana in lifetime*

(D) % who used any illicit drug other than marijuana last 12 months*

*Beginning in 2001, a revised set of questions on other hallucinogen use and tranquilizer use were introduced. Data for "any illicit drug other than marijuana" were affected by these changes.

FIGURE 1.1 Graphs of trends in lifetime and annual use for 8th, 10th, and 12th graders. *Source: University of Michigan. (2011). Monitoring the Future Survey. Found in NIDA Research Report Series, Tobacco Addiction, (July 2012).*

Of particular importance, *daily marijuana use* increased significantly in all three grades in 2010, rising further in all three grades in 2011, though the one-year increase was not statistically significant. Daily use now stands at 1.3, 3.6, and 6.6 percent in grades 8, 10, and 12 [8]. That means that roughly one in 15 high school seniors today is a current daily, or near-daily, marijuana user [9].

Recent evidence in the abuse of synthetic drugs by teens is a growing concern. For example, in 2011, one in nine high school seniors had used *synthetic marijuana* (synthetic cannabinoids commonly marketed as "herbal incense" in products such as Spice or K2) during 2010; this means that as of the writing of this book, synthetic cannabinoids are the second most frequently used illicit drug, after marijuana, among high school seniors [10].

Research has shown that these substances can cause serious adverse health effects. For example, according to the ONDCP, calls to Poison Control Centers relating to synthetic cannabinoids reached 6890 in 2011—more than double the number received in 2010 [11]. *Synthetic marijuana* is an herbal drug mixture that usually contains designer chemicals that fall into the cannabinoid family. Until March 2011, these drugs were not scheduled by the Drug Enforcement Administration (DEA), so they were readily available on the Internet and in head shops, gas stations, and so on. The DEA did schedule them under its emergency authority for one year, beginning March 1, 2011, making their possession and sale no longer legal. MTF first addressed the use of synthetic marijuana in its 2011 survey, asking 12th graders about use in the prior 12 months, which would have covered a considerable period of time prior to the drugs being scheduled. Some 11.4 percent indicated use in the prior 12 months [12].

Ecstasy. After a decline of several years in perceived risk regarding, and disapproval of, ecstasy use—which MTF had been warning could presage a rebound in use—ecstasy use does now appear to be rebounding, primarily among older teens.

Alcohol use, including *binge drinking*, continued its longer term decline among teens, reaching historically low levels in 2011 in all three grades under study. Use has been in a long-term pattern of decline since about 1980, with the exception of a few years in the early 1990s during which alcohol use increased, along with the use of cigarettes and almost all illicit drugs [13].

Cigarettes. In 2012, NIDA reported that tobacco use kills approximately 440,000 Americans each year, with one in every five deaths the result of smoking [14]. Smoking harms nearly every organ in the body, causes many diseases, and compromises smokers' health in general. Nicotine, a component of tobacco, is the primary reason why tobacco is addictive, although cigarette smoke contains many other dangerous chemicals, including tar, carbon monoxide, acetaldehyde, nitrosamines, and more.

According to the 2010 National Survey on Drug Use and Health (NSDUH), an estimated 69.6 million Americans aged 12 or older use various forms of tobacco—58.3 million (23.0 percent of the population) were current cigarette smokers, 13.2 million (5.2 percent) smoked cigars, 8.9 million (3.5 percent) used smokeless tobacco, and 2.2 million (0.8 percent) smoked pipes, confirming that tobacco is one of the most widely abused substances in the United States [15]. Although the numbers of people who smoke are still unacceptably high, according to the Centers for Disease Control and Prevention (CDC) there has been a decline of almost 50 percent since 1965 [16]. See Figure 1.2.

Tobacco use among youth is also an ongoing concern. Research shows that after decelerating considerably in recent years, the long-term decline in *cigarette* use, which began in the mid-1990s, appeared to come to a halt in the lower grades in 2010. Indeed, both 8th and 10th graders showed evidence of a slight increase in smoking in 2010, though the increases did not reach statistical significance. Perceived risk and subsequently disapproval had both leveled off some years ago. In 2011, however, the decline in teen smoking resumed in the lower grades (there was a significant drop in use among the 10th graders), and also continued among 12th graders. Perceived risk and disapproval rose in all three grades, significantly among 10th graders. Availability also dropped significantly among 8th and 10th graders, but more than half of the 8th graders and nearly three-quarters of the 10th graders still say it would be "fairly easy" or "very easy" for them to get cigarettes if they wanted some [17].

Part of what might account for the decline in drug use among youth is an increased awareness of the dangers of drugs. Survey data show that drug use is inversely correlated with perceptions of the harmful effects of drugs. The better young people understand the risks of drug use, the more likely they are to choose not to use drugs. Clearly, parental involvement, education, and community action are keys to preventing drug use among youths.

The Cost of Combating Drugs

As stated in this chapter, drug abuse results in a considerable financial burden on families and communities. In 2012, the ONDCP reported that illicit drug use in the United States contributed to an estimated $193 billion in crime, health, and lost productivity costs [18].

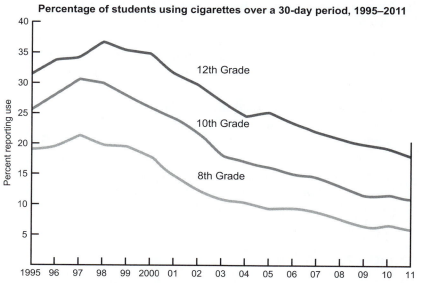

FIGURE 1.2 Graph of trends in prevalence of cigarette use for 8th, 10th, and 12th graders. *Source: University of Michigan. (2011). Monitoring the Future Survey. Found in NIDA Research Report Series, Tobacco Addiction, (July 2012).*

FIGURE 1.3 Many states have implemented drug-free school zones—areas extending 1,000 feet away from a school within which penalties for drug crimes are enhanced. *Source: Ellen S. Boyne.*

The damage caused by drug abuse and addiction is reflected in an overburdened justice system, a strained health care system, lost productivity, and environmental destruction.

The drug war plays a significant role in these increased expenditures. At the federal level, back in 1969, the Nixon administration spent $65 million on the war against drugs; by 1982, the Reagan administration had increased that figure to $1.65 billion; and by 2000, the Clinton administration had increased the price tag to $17.9 billion for the federal government ([19]). In 2012, the Obama administration requested, for Fiscal Year (FY) 2013, $25.6 billion to reduce drug use and its consequences in the United States. This represents an increase of $415.3 million (1.6 percent) over the FY 2012 enacted level of $25.2 billion [20]. See Table 1.1.

Spending at the state level, although more difficult to track, has similarly escalated dramatically due to draconian drug war policies. In 1998, for example, states spent $39.7 billion for adult and juvenile corrections and their court systems; 77 percent of those expenditures were directly related to the war on drugs [21]. Of the $29.8 billion spent by the states on incarceration, probation, and parole, 81 percent is spent on drug war–related programs. It costs $8.6 billion a year to simply incarcerate convicted drug offenders [22]. State spending on law enforcement–related policies in the drug war amounts to more than 10 times the spending on prevention, treatment, and education [23].

The Economics of Drug Control

Drug Prices

Our intense law enforcement campaign against drugs is supposed to make drugs more expensive for the consumer. After all, a law enforcement strategy built around interdiction,

Table 1.1   Federal Drug Control Spending by Function (Budget Authority in Millions)

Function	FY 2011 Final	FY 2012 Enacted	FY 2013 Requested
Treatment	$8,953.9	$8,747.5	$9,150.5
Percentage	35%	34.2%	36.3%
Prevention	$1,478.1	$1,400.5	$1,387.6
Percentage	5.8%	5.5%	5.5%
Domestic law enforcement	$9,143.0	$9,357.5	$9,418.9
Percentage	35.7%	36.6%	37.4%
Interdiction	$3,977.1	$3,591.6	$3,680.9
Percentage	15.5%	14.0%	14.6%
International	$2,027.6	$2,087.6	$1,962.0
Percentage	7.9%	8.2%	7.8%
Total	$25,579.7	$25,184.7	$25,599.9

Source: Office of National Drug Control Policy (2012).

asset forfeiture, and arrest and seizure ought to make the drug business more costly. However, once again, the data clearly show that the drug war is an astounding failure. Consider the case of heroin.

The conversation about drug economics must be had in the context of drug availability versus drug prices. This is because there is a direct correlation between drug availability and the price of drugs on the street (also see Chapter 4). A case in point is the way the price of cocaine has changed with its decreased availability. As of the writing of this text, based on numerous cocaine availability data indicators (seizures, price, purity, workplace drug tests, etc.), cocaine was considerably less prevalent in 2009 than in 2006. (Reasons for cocaine's decline in availability are discussed in Chapter 9 of this book.) According to United States government statistics, federal cocaine seizures decreased by 25 percent from 2006 (53,755 kg) to 2008 (40,449 kg), and remained low in 2009. Accordingly, the price per pure gram of cocaine increased from $94.73 in the third quarter of 2006 to $174.03 in the third quarter of 2009, whereas the purity of the drug decreased from 68.1 percent to 46.2 percent [24].

Drug Profits

Critics of the drug war argue that drug enforcement has failed to reduce use, has resulted in lower drug prices for both dealers and consumers, and has increased the quality and potency of drugs available for purchase in the United States. Despite the enormous expenditure of taxpayer dollars, the large number of arrests and subsequent incarcerations, and a proactive law enforcement strategy, the war on drugs has resulted in even greater profits for drug cartels. In fact, it can be argued that by the 1990s, the drug war had failed so miserably that the drug trade had become a major component of international trade, commerce, and economics. The international drug trade generates about $400 billion in international trade, and constitutes 8 percent of all international commerce annually [25]. Drug profits have been so inflated by the failed war on drugs that three-quarters of all drug shipments would have to be interdicted and seized in order to reduce the present profitability of the drug trade.

Some experts argue that it is the flawed logic of a law enforcement approach to drugs that directly results in this profitability. For example, a kilogram of coca base in Colombia costs about $950. The same kilogram, when it reaches wholesale distributors in the United States, sells for $25,000. A kilogram of heroin produced in Pakistan costs about $2,270 and sells for $129,380 in the United States. As political scientist Herbert Packer pointed out almost 40 years ago, efforts at prohibition lead directly to a "crime tariff" on prohibited substances, which is essentially a state-imposed tax that goes directly to organized crime. Colombian drug cartels bring $7 billion in drug profits into the Colombian economy annually; for comparison, Colombia's legal exports return profits of $7.6 billion annually [26]. Almost all (98 percent) of Bolivia's foreign exchange earnings from international trade come directly from the coca market [27]. In essence, the drug war subsidizes drug production and distribution.

The Availability of Drugs

It is all but impossible to estimate with certainty the amount of drugs available in the United States. As such, the determination as to whether the availability of a particular drug is increasing or decreasing is based on analysis of available data. Such data give us an indication of the price and purity of drugs, as well as trends in their transportation and distribution. For example, national data show that in 2009, cocaine availability was decreasing, whereas heroin, marijuana, methamphetamine, and MDMA (3,4-methylene-dioxy-*N*-methylamphetamine, also called "ecstasy" is discussed in greater detail in Chapter 3) were readily available [28].

Cocaine

The NSDUH estimates that in 2008, there were 1.9 million current (past-month) cocaine users, of which approximately 359,000 were current crack users. Adults aged 18–25 years have a higher rate of current cocaine use than any other age group, with 1.5 percent of young adults reporting past-month cocaine use. Overall, men report higher rates of current cocaine use than women [29].

The 2009 MTF survey, which annually surveys teen attitudes and drug use, reports a significant decline in 30-day prevalence of powder cocaine use among 8th-, 10th-, and 12th-graders from peak use in the late 1990s, as well as significant declines in past-month use among 10th and 12th graders from 2008 to 2009 [30].

Heroin

Heroin is widely available, and, if anything, its availability is on the increase. This is evidenced by its high wholesale purity, low prices, increasing levels of abuse, and number of overdose deaths. For example, according to DEA Heroin Signature Program data, the wholesale purity of Mexican heroin in 2008 was 40 percent. Moreover, Mexican heroin represented 39 percent of all heroin seized in the United States. In comparison, the purity of South American heroin was reported at 57 percent in 2008 [31].

In spite of record heroin and opium production in Afghanistan, the United States remains a secondary market for Southwest Asian heroin. This is because most heroin from that region is consumed regionally in Southeast Asia. Organizations that traffic in Southwest Asian heroin are generally based in Afghanistan, Pakistan, and India [32].

Methamphetamine

The availability of methamphetamine is currently increasing. According to some government estimates, the increased availability of methamphetamine in the United States is based somewhat on increased production of the drug in Mexico—the primary source of methamphetamine consumed in the United States [33]. The decreased availability of methamphetamine from Mexico in 2007–2008 was attributed to restrictions placed on precursor chemicals. In 2007, for example, prohibitions were placed on the importation of both pseudoephedrine and ephedrine into Mexico, and there was a ban on the use of both chemicals by 2008. By late 2008, however, Mexican traffickers adapted their trafficking process in a number of ways. These included using new smuggling routes for moving restricted chemicals, importing nonrestricted chemical derivatives instead of precursor chemicals, and establishing alternative production methods. For example, Mexican traffickers moved ephedrine and pseudoephedrine from sources in China and India using discreet smuggling routes through Central Africa, Europe, and South America [34]. Furthermore, packages containing such chemicals are purposely mislabeled as other items during transit, to avoid inspection by law enforcement in airports and seaports in Mexico.

A CLOSER LOOK: RESTRICTIONS ON THE RETAIL SALE OF PSEUDOEPHEDRINE

In September 2006, the federal Combat Methamphetamine Epidemic Act (CMEA) of 2005 became effective nationwide, setting restrictions on the retail sale of pseudoephedrine products. As of December 2009, 45 states had passed measures establishing or enhancing restrictions on over-the-counter sales or purchase of pseudoephedrine products, in addition to those set forth by the CMEA. Of those states, 20 made pseudoephedrine a scheduled drug, 43 imposed point-of-sale restrictions, and 26 enacted pseudoephedrine tracking laws.

Source: National Drug Intelligence Center (2010).

Marijuana

Marijuana has remained widely available in the United States, largely because of increasing production in Mexico. Statistics show that marijuana production in Mexico increased 59 percent between 2003 and 2009. To make things worse, there is an ongoing decrease in marijuana eradication in Mexico. This reduction is the result of the Mexican military's focus on antiviolence measures rather than crop cultivation. This differs from marijuana production in the United States, which has been hindered largely because of successful and increasing eradication efforts domestically. In fact, eradication of both indoor and outdoor plants more than doubled between 2004 and 2009. That said, more growers are establishing indoor sites to produce better marijuana and avoid the detection of outdoor growing operations [35].

Drug-Related Deaths

Illegal drug use is responsible for the deaths of thousands of Americans annually. The Substance Abuse and Mental Health Services Administration's (SAMHSA) Drug Abuse Warning Network (DAWN) collects data on drug-related deaths for medical examiners in 41 major metropolitan areas. DAWN found that drug-related deaths steadily climbed throughout the 1990s and the first decade of the twenty-first century [36].

According to the CDC, in 2006 a total of 38,396 persons died of drug-induced causes in the United States. This category includes not only deaths from dependent and nondependent use of legal or illegal drugs, but also poisoning deaths from medically prescribed and other drugs [37]. In addition, other causes of death, such as HIV/AIDS, are sometimes partially due to drug abuse. In 2010, DAWN identified specific drugs that were particularly dangerous and that often resulted in deaths. These include the following:

- Illegal or illicit drugs, such as heroin, cocaine, marijuana, and ecstasy;
- Prescription drugs, such as Prozac®, Vicodin®, OxyContin®, alprazolam, and methylphenidate;
- Over-the-counter medications, including aspirin, acetaminophen, ibuprofen, and multi-ingredient cough and cold remedies;
- Dietary supplements, including vitamins, herbal remedies, and nutritional products;
- Psychoactive, nonpharmaceutical inhalants;
- Alcohol in combination with drugs; and
- For those under age 21, alcohol alone without any other drug [38].

Health Complications

Many health-related complications are associated with drug abuse. Users can die from overdose; medical reactions can result from taking certain types of drugs; users are exposed to HIV infection, hepatitis, tuberculosis, and other diseases; injuries can result from accidents caused by intoxication; injuries can result from violence incurred while obtaining drugs or from associating with persons with violent criminal backgrounds; dependence can form with certain drugs; and chronic physical problems can develop in some drug users. Some of these effects, such as overdose, are directly related to drug use; others, such as violence stemming from illegal drug transactions, are indirectly associated with drug use behavior.

A brutal fact in the illicit drug industry is that some drugs sold on the streets are simply not what they are purported to be. This is sometimes due to increased purity of the drug over that to which the user has been accustomed, but another reason is that impurities are also commonly placed in drug solutions to either enhance or dilute the potency of the drug. Other times, drugs are misrepresented as something completely different from what they actually are. For example, during the late 1970s, powdered PCP (phencyclidine), known as "angel dust", acquired such a bad reputation on the street that dealers chose to rename it THC (an abbreviation for the active ingredient in marijuana – Tetrahydracannabinol), or cannabinol. In actuality, THC is one of the active ingredients in marijuana, giving it its intoxicating effects, but it has no connection whatsoever with the hallucinogen PCP. Dealers simply believed that THC sounded better than angel dust to potential drug buyers.

Use of certain drugs can result in specific physical reactions. For example, cocaine use can result in convulsions, or even cardiovascular failure, because it creates changes in heart rate and blood pressure. The reaction often occurs quickly and under circumstances in which medical treatment is not readily available. As we will see in Chapter 2, the myth that cocaine is a harmless drug has been replaced with the realization that it may be more harmful than other so-called hard drugs, including heroin. In addition, the reinforcing properties of cocaine often lead to binge consumption, which in turn increases the chances for dependence, overdose, withdrawal-like symptoms, or more serious cardiovascular complications, including death. Residual physical problems for cocaine abusers can include a ruptured aorta, central nervous system problems, and intestinal and obstetrical problems.

Specific reactions to other drugs can also be noted. Heroin, for instance, is a central nervous system depressant that can leave the user with acute toxic reactions resulting from overdose. More often than not, this occurs because users may not be aware that the purity of the heroin they inject is higher than what their system can tolerate. Other depressants and stimulants also can produce health complications, especially regarding drug-induced psychosis, in which users lose contact with reality and experience a rapid pulse and elevated blood pressure.

Attitudes about Drugs

Perhaps the varying attitudes that people harbor about drug abuse and control create confusion about the issue. Many positions about substance abuse or control are no longer clear-cut. Some drug users and former drug users have spoken out forcefully against drugs; others have urged a reconsideration of prohibition policies. Many parents, although strongly antidrug themselves, have ambivalent feelings about drug laws when their sons or daughters are drug users. Drug use, which in the past was more neatly confined to particular groups in society, has now taken root in all social strata. This means that virtually all of us have friends, relatives, or associates who are or have been drug users.

Drug control policy is discussed in Chapter 13, but it might be helpful here to review the basis of some attitudes behind drug use and control. From earliest recorded time, society has exhibited conflict over such heated issues as religion and politics, the latter of which is afforded greater attention in this book. One's willingness to criticize or accept public consensus frequently hinges on one's political attitudes. Such attitudes will most likely lean at least somewhat toward the conservative (right) or the liberal (left) view. Those holding conservative views tend to be more traditional and resistant to change, whereas those holding liberal views tend to be more open-minded about change and willing to try the hitherto untried. Excesses in either of these convictions tend to foster unrealistic views and attitudes. The issues of drug use and control have, however, blurred even these familiar political distinctions. Most conservatives, for example, favor tough laws, more police, and refined due process procedures for accused criminals, but some leading conservatives are actually arguing for repeal of the drug laws. They base their positions on two fundamental conservative tenets: first, the belief that the free market is self-regulating and will reduce drug abuse if allowed to operate; and, second, the traditional conservative position put forward by John Stuart Mill that government should interfere with individual freedoms as little as possible. Liberals, on the other hand, have traditionally stressed due process rights, non–law enforcement approaches to crime, and the belief that crime is rooted in a myriad of social problems. Yet leading liberal legislators, such as United States Representative Charles Rangel (D-NY) and the late United States Senator Edward Kennedy (D-MA), have been among the strongest supporters of unyielding antidrug efforts.

Why Do People Get High?

Whether it is caffeine, nicotine, alcohol, or another drug, abuse is an everyday part of our lives. So, several essential questions about drug abuse can be asked. For example, why do people willingly engage in behavior that might be dangerous, illegal, or unhealthy? Furthermore, many drugs fail to have obvious effects on the user, which makes us wonder why they are popular in the first place. For example, cigarette smokers generally do not appear to be in a state of euphoria when they smoke. The same is true for people who drink caffeine-based soft drinks. But what about harder drugs like heroin?

We think we know why a heroin user uses the drug: for its euphoric effect. However, the initial effects of many of today's popular drugs, like heroin, are in fact downright unpleasant. Stated differently, if 100 people were selected from the population and administered heroin, many would probably get sick and never want to see the drug again. So what's the point of taking the drug in the first place? The same could be said for alcohol or cocaine. One's first drink of whiskey or first experience with crack cocaine is not always pleasant. Given this premise, perhaps it is true that the more pleasant a drug's effects are on users, the more attractive that drug is to them. However, if this is so, then why do people smoke without any noticeable effect from the nicotine? As you see, we have now come full circle in our quandary.

Although numerous explanations have been offered on the subject, another glaring question still remains unanswered: is drug abuse representative of a universal human need? Some would argue that this is precisely the case, and that one of today's great challenges is for society to develop a drug that is completely safe for recreational consumption. Although this is a controversial premise, it inspires thought. Some people are lifelong abstainers, whereas others use drugs on a regular basis. Whether it is our daily fortification of coffee, tea, or cigarettes, or a reliance on prescription painkillers or antidotes for minor ailments, some form of drug use is an everyday part of living for most Americans.

Explanations for drug abuse are in constant debate. For example, some experts claim that there is a genetic basis for dependence and addiction, but others argue that it stems from a learned behavior. However, if a genetic propensity for drug abuse does exist, what created it? Alcohol abuse is a good example. Experts suggest that an insensitivity to the effects of this drug results in excessive drinking. Therefore, the insensitivity of some drinkers causes them to feel only slightly drunk when they are actually very intoxicated. As a result, they tend to drink more than others do. Some have suggested that this hypothesis extends to drug use in general.

■ ■ Critical Thinking Task ■

Create the "perfect" recreational drug for American society. (Remember: your creation must be free of harmful physiological or psychological effects.) Describe its ingredients, methods of consumption, social applications, price, and method of distribution.

In opposition to the genetic theory of dependence, other experts, such as Benjamin Stein, have argued that a syndrome known as the *addictive personality* exists [39]. Under this theory, a drug user consumes drugs because the drugs help organize an otherwise disordered life. The theory suggests that drug abusers are lonely, sad, and frightened people who possess a character flaw for which drugs offer a crutch. In comparison, other experts have suggested that drug abuse is simply learned behavior whereby the abuser fails to act responsibly with the drugs that he or she abuses.

Social explanations stress the influence of society, culture, and peers in a person's life. Some drugs are more likely to be abused by certain classes of people; other types of drugs are more available in specific areas of a city and, therefore, are more widely abused there. In addition, it has been argued that in many social circles, it is more socially acceptable for men to drink heavily than women. In some societies, drug consumption takes place in social, religious, or family settings. In any case, social explanations should be considered along with others when searching for answers to the question of why people use drugs.

The "Usefulness" of Drugs

As suggested in this chapter, to best deal with this perplexing issue, it is important to abandon our stereotypes that people use drugs for their pleasurable effects. For the sake of discussion, let's accept the proposition that people do not necessarily use a drug for its reputed pleasurable effects. Rather, let's assume that some drugs are used because people find them useful for less exotic reasons [40]. For example, hard-core heroin users generally do not use the drug for its euphoric effects, but rather to help them get through the day—to survive. The same is also true for many smokers and coffee drinkers. So, for many, drug use allows people to function on a day-to-day level. After all, the ability to perform a job successfully and receive a regular paycheck is a powerful motivator for many people.

In an attempt to better understand reasons for drug use, let's take a closer look at the reasons for wanting to alter one's physical or mental state. Research has shown that, as a rule, people take illicit drugs for the effects they produce. These effects may include mood change, pleasure, stimulation, sedation, or enhanced physical or psychological performance. In fact, more so than for their physical results, illicit drugs are taken for their mind-altering effects. As we will discuss in this chapter, drugs such as heroin have limited accepted medical use but may be taken for the relief of pain. Others, such as stimulants and sedatives, have distinct medical applications but may be taken to produce excitement, alertness, or feelings of relaxation. Given the many different variables of human nature—personal values, morals, beliefs, habits, and lifestyles—it is logical to assume that different people use drugs for different reasons. As we will see in the "Drug Abuse Forums" section, some reasons are rational, and others are more enigmatic.

Drug Abuse Forums

It is probably safe to generalize that millions of people abuse drugs for a number of reasons. Young people in junior high and high school, career people, and even the elderly from time to time use drugs unwisely or illegally. Therefore, many different reasons exist to explain drug abuse behavior; accordingly, there are many circumstances under which drug abusers engage in their activity. Next, we will consider some of the most common social forums of drug abuse.

The Natural High

The term *natural high* refers to a desirable euphoric feeling naturally produced by the body. A multitude of studies by experts in social behavior suggest that people naturally want to alter their state of consciousness at certain times throughout their lives. For example, children may help illustrate the innate desire to alter consciousness by the very manner in which they play. For all their innocence, they sometimes spin themselves into dizziness or ride on the roller coaster at the local amusement park to achieve a thrill and the corresponding physical exhilaration. Many adults also enjoy adrenaline-inducing rides for the mere excitement of the experience. Such an indulgence in and of itself may raise or distort perceptions of reality while generating endocrine drug reactions, such as the production of adrenaline and noradrenaline. These "highs" are particularly appealing because they are produced naturally, without the interference of external chemical stimuli. However, the endocrine-producing glands in our bodies do not always produce "uppers" like adrenaline. In fact, the body also manufactures its own "downers", such as serotonin and gamma-amino butyric acid.

Chemicals such as these are called *endogenous*; that is, they are produced in the body. Endogenous chemicals produced by the brain and various glands change our moods and actions, and even resemble some drugs taken by people for recreational purposes. For example, a group of endogenous chemicals called *endorphins*, discovered in 1975, closely resemble heroin or morphine in their chemical makeup, but they are naturally produced by the human body and act to relieve pain.

The Runner's High

The *runner's high* is a state of euphoria that is experienced by not only runners, but also anyone engaged in a vigorous workout. It is typically characterized by an obsessive-compulsive disorder-like compulsion to exercise to the exclusion of all other activities. Boxers and bikers have reported similar states of being, as have weight lifters, cross-country skiers, and rugby players.

The high itself has been described as a feeling of well-being or of being one with the world, or as a total out-of-body experience. It is typically related to longer periods of vigorous exercise rather than shorter, easier workouts, possibly due to the stress the body undergoes as the major muscle groups begin to run short on glucose. The experience of the high also seems to rely on the makeup of the individual runner: some experience it after running 5 miles, while others must run 20 before the euphoric feelings kick in.

The exact mechanisms underlying the runner's high have been debated for years. Endorphins (as discussed here) were assumed to be the basis for the good feelings associated with the runner's high, but a variety of other chemicals have been put forth as possible causes.

This debate has seemingly been brought to an end by the results of a 2008 German study of long-distance runners. The study showed that not only did periods of robust exercise produce endorphins, but also the degree of euphoria reported by the runners correlated to a surprising degree with the endorphin levels seen in their brains. In essence, the study found that the higher the endorphin levels, the greater the degree of euphoria experienced.

Happy Hour

The term *happy hour* does not refer to a reason why people become intoxicated, but rather to a social forum in which ritualistic recreational chemical use occurs in groups. Millions of people look forward to the traditional bar happy hour after a long day or week of work. The altering of one's mental state, or "attitude adjustment", through alcohol consumption is lawful, socially acceptable, and even commonplace. Such indulgence, however, is regulated through each state's criminal code because of the potential for accidents or criminal behavior if drinkers become intoxicated.

Although it is legal, alcohol can drastically change one's psychological and physiological condition. For this reason, most states have established limits for alcohol consumption in ways such as (1) restricting where liquor can be purchased, (2) increasing penalties for driving while under the influence (of alcohol and illicit drugs alike), (3) establishing special criminal provisions for crimes committed while intoxicated, (4) criminalizing the transportation of liquor out of bars in groups, and (5) regulating open liquor containers in motor vehicles.

Medicinal Use

Ingesting "harder" and more dangerous drugs under certain circumstances is lawful if prescribed by a medical practitioner who has identified a physical or psychological requirement for such medication. Morphine, for example, is a dangerous and highly addictive narcotic drug, but when taken under a doctor's supervision, it can be an extremely effective painkiller during surgery and recovery. The lawful distribution of dangerous drugs mandates their legal manufacture by legitimate pharmaceutical companies. The highly controlled circumstances in the manufacturing, distribution, and storage of dangerous substances will be discussed in greater length in Chapter 5.

Religious Use

Although some modern-day religions incorporate mind-altering substances such as wine in their ceremonies, few religions condone using enough of the substance for participants to become intoxicated. Exceptions to this rule, however, exist in certain cultures. For example, since the 1700s, North American Indian cultures have used peyote cactus, which produces a psychoactive drug, in religious ceremonies. Eating or smoking peyote was embraced in elaborate ancient ceremonies as a means to gain "oneness" with the spirits and with nature.

Today, peyote use by Native American Church members is legal in the United States under a specific exemption under law. This exemption from federal criminalization is as old as the origin of federal law creating peyote-related offenses. The law has been codified as a statute under the American Indian Religious Freedom Act of 1978, and it was made part of the common law in *Peyote Way Church of God v. Thornburgh* (1991); it is also in administrative law in the Code of Federal Regulations (CFR) at 21 CFR 1307.31, which deals with "special exempt persons":

Section 1307.31 Native American Church. The listing of peyote as a controlled substance in Schedule I does not apply to the nondrug use of peyote in bona fide religious ceremonies of the Native American Church, and members of the Native American Church so using peyote are exempt from registration. Any person who manufactures peyote for or distributes peyote to the Native American Church, however, is required to obtain registration annually and to comply with all other requirements of law.

Ironically, those Indian cultures that embrace the use of peyote in their religious practices also consider alcohol a curse. In a similar vein, followers of traditional Coptic Christianity, whose most recognizable United States denomination is the Rastafarians, use marijuana in their religious observations in much the same way other churches use wine.

To Alter Moods and Metabolism

When people are depressed, anxious, or bored, it is reasonable for them to desire a change in their mental state. Drugs are sometimes used both legally and illegally to create a shift in personality, attitude, and mood. Such measures might include the consumption of stimulants (uppers), depressants (downers), or even psychoactive drugs (hallucinogens that are either organic or clandestinely manufactured). In those cases in which the undesirable mood is due to a natural physiological chemical imbalance, physicians may lawfully prescribe certain drugs to help offset the body's chemical deficiencies. Excessive use of Valium and Librium, for example, was common in the 1950s to uplift a patient's depressed feelings.

These drugs were commonly prescribed because most doctors believed they were safe. In reality, not only can the drugs be dangerous by themselves, but also they can be particularly dangerous if combined with other drugs. Polydrug use is common in situations in which drug users ingest amphetamines in the morning as a "pick-me-up," and then take barbiturates in the evening to help "wind down." This creates a classic abuse cycle in which one type of drug is required to counteract another. Another common example of polydrug use, particularly among people taking depressants for medical purposes, is combining barbiturates and tranquilizers with alcohol, a combination that heightens inebriation and is potentially deadly.

To Inspire Creativity

Throughout the years, musicians, poets, and novelists have hailed the effects of certain drugs that supposedly promote creativity. Many artists have believed that drugs (often those belonging to the hallucinogen family) can release inhibitions and unleash the creative thought process. These individuals include American short-story writer and poet Edgar Allan Poe (1809–1849), who had a weakness for laudanum (tincture of opium); British writer Aldous Huxley (1894–1963), who experimented extensively with mescaline in the 1950s (and was quoted as stating that "pharmacology antedated agriculture"); the nineteenth-century author Oliver Wendell Holmes (1809–1894), who indulged in ether; and popular comedian Lenny Bruce (1926–1966), whose physical addiction to morphine ultimately cost him his life.

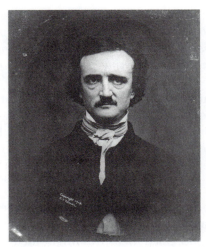

FIGURE 1.4 Edgar Allan Poe is a well-known writer who was thought to use drugs such as alcohol and laudanum (tincture of opium) to inspire creativity.

Measuring Drug Abuse

Considerable information exists regarding the extent of drug abuse throughout the country. However, most methods focus on households, high school seniors, and arrestees and offenders, and do not give any indication about other groups that are more difficult to reach. For instance, many members of the homeless population may be involved in some form of drug abuse. These people are missed in the household surveys, just as high school dropouts are not surveyed in high school senior surveys. Surveys have also revealed other aspects of the drug abuse problem. For example, an alarmingly high number of young adults have used illicit drugs, and the most commonly abused drug is marijuana. In addition, one-third of the United States population knows someone who uses crack cocaine. Today, most of what we know about drug abuse is derived from the following surveys:

- *NSDUH.* Formerly known as the National Household Survey on Drug Abuse (NHSDA), this survey has been conducted periodically since 1972 but is now an annual survey that randomly interviews people living in households and in specified group residences throughout the United States.
- *High School Survey.* Also referred to as Monitoring the Future, this survey was first developed in 1975. Results of the MTF survey offer indications of drug abuse frequency and drug abuse trends by high school–aged drug abusers.
- *Worldwide Survey of Substance Abuse and Health Behaviors among Military Personnel.* This survey is conducted annually and involves active-duty military personnel surveyed at military bases across the world.
- *Survey of Jail Inmates.* This survey comprises interviews of inmates who are awaiting trial or serving sentences in local jails. It is conducted annually.

- *Survey of State Prison Inmates.* This survey is conducted every 5–7 years. On average, an estimated 14,000 inmates are interviewed in 275 facilities.

Who are the Drug Users?

The surveys have also provided information regarding who the drug users are. For example, the *NIDA Household Survey on Drug Abuse* reports several interesting findings about drug users:

- Males are more likely than females to use drugs, but among youths aged 12–17, the rate of substance dependence or abuse was higher among females than males.
- People between the ages of 18 and 20 are more likely to have used illicit drugs in the past month [41].

Of course, as drug patterns and trends change over time, these statistics will also change. Also, as people get older, drug use rates shift. For instance, in 1995, lifetime rates of use became the highest among people aged 31 through 39, reflecting the peak drug-using years of the late 1970s [42].

David Musto, professor of psychiatry at Yale University, has written that we have moved to a "two-tier system" of drug consumption, marked by declining use among middle-class whites and increasing use among poor minorities. In *The American Disease: Origins of Narcotic Control*, he states that American society is repeating an earlier cycle of drug use. Musto points out that at the turn of the twentieth century, drugs were readily available and widely tolerated. As the incidences of abuse grew and people gained increased awareness, consumption dropped off and social attitudes became sterner. He further states that as the two-tier effect becomes more pronounced and minorities become more associated with drug abuse, public support for treatment might begin to wane. The result could be more public support for increased police and prisons and harsher sentences, reactions that are considered futile. "My concern is that as drug use declines among middle-class Americans, they will refuse to invest in the long-term needs of the inner city, like education and jobs" [43]. A primary task facing the ONDCP is harnessing the current antidrug energy and making it productive.

Geographical Differences

Trends of drug use in 20 major United States cities have been monitored by the Community Epidemiology Workgroup. Findings reveal that the types of drugs used in different cities vary. Availability and pricing of drugs determine the extent of use in most areas, but in other cases, cocaine has remained the major drug of abuse. Heroin use has declined in some cities, but has shown increased use in others. Stimulants, on the other hand, were most prevalent in Western cities. Furthermore, the NSDUH has shown that drug use varies across urban and rural areas, with higher instances of use in the larger metropolitan areas [44]. In contrast, high school senior surveys have shown that use rates of stimulants, inhalants, and sedatives were similar in both rural and nonrural areas, with marijuana and cocaine being used more often in urban areas than in rural areas.

The Social Costs of Drug Abuse

As we have indicated, law enforcement initiatives against drug abuse and trafficking are a financially exhausting proposition. Drug abuse also costs society billions of dollars in many other ways. These are seen in drug treatment and prevention programs, lost productivity on the job caused by impaired drug users, and the cost of other federal programs. The President's Fiscal Year (FY) 2011 National Drug Control Budget requested $15.5 billion to reduce drug use and its consequences in the United States. This represented an increase of 3.5 percent over the FY 2010 enacted level of $15 billion [45].

In addition to the financial burden imposed on Americans by drug abuse, there is an even greater price to pay: the effects of drugs on our youth. Studies have revealed that most drug users began to use drugs as adolescents, or even as preteens. Some reasons commonly offered are peer pressure, few legitimate means of income, and disordered homes. Adolescent drug abuse also impairs the learning capabilities of children, and in some cases can cause severe emotional problems. Additionally, one should remember that most drug abuse is illegal activity, and when drugs are indiscriminately used around children, a message is sent to them that gives legitimacy to this activity, particularly when their parents are the drug users. Statistics vary, but studies have shown that many child maltreatment cases involve substance abuse by parents or guardians.

Violence

The proliferation of drug-trafficking groups operating in the United States has increased substantially over the past 20 years. With the propagation of drug gangs interested in their share of the drug profit pie, drug-related crime has also spread to ancillary areas, where the profit motive outweighs the motivation of the addict to stay "well." Drug-trafficking gangs wage turf wars and calculated acts of revenge to establish control over neighborhoods. These gangs also recruit members as young as 8 years old to deal drugs or act as spotters. Although drug markets seemed to stabilize in the 1990s, the potential for competitive violence still remains.

The pursuit of higher education and legitimate work is no longer considered by many of these individuals to be the best way to get ahead in life. The allure of gold chains, fast cars, status, and parties has affected the traditional maturation process for many gang members. Indeed, drugs represent a set of already stifling environmental factors that create a social gauntlet between children and their education and legitimate employment. The violence associated with drugs poses one of the greatest social concerns. In numerous recent polls, respondents consider drug trafficking to be one of the greatest national concerns, and in many cases a serious threat to national security.

Addicted Babies

In Memphis, Tennessee, on January 17, 2013, Juanita Hardin was arrested after her baby was born addicted to drugs. Prosecutors reported that Hardin had given birth to not one, but four, babies addicted to cocaine in the last 5 years [46]. The problem of drug-addicted babies is so serious in Memphis that in 2010 the prosecutor's office created a special program, Born Addicted, for mothers of newly born drug-addicted babies [47].

Studies have shown that drug use can affect the development of a child even before birth. Research has shown that marijuana and cocaine use during pregnancy are associated with substantial reductions in fetal growth. Moreover, infants exposed to drugs, especially heroin, are prone to exhibiting withdrawal symptoms. Exposure to cocaine has been linked to various neurobehavioral and circulatory complications, including major congenital malformations. In 1996, a report by NIDA showed that between 1992 and 1993, 5.5 percent of women (about 221,000) in the United States used an illicit drug at least once during their pregnancy. Infants born to mothers who use drugs often go through withdrawal or have other medical problems at birth [48]. Health problems arising from drug abuse are a principal concern in drug control efforts. One particular issue is the problem of infants whose mothers have demonstrated a pattern of heavy cocaine use, especially in combination with alcohol.

Cocaine use by pregnant mothers can be detected only within 24–48 hours after use. Problems exist because the symptoms of a pregnant woman who suffers from cocaine addiction may not always be apparent to hospital officials. In many cases, pregnant addicts may not even visit hospitals until they are in labor.

Much attention was focused on the issue of cocaine-addicted babies during the late 1980s, because of the serious health-related risks facing unborn children. Such hazards include strokes *in utero*, physical malformations, and increased risk of death during infancy. In addition, because of the practice of "sex for drugs" (mentioned in this chapter) by some pregnant woman, many babies are born with ancillary health problems, including sexually transmitted diseases.

Dr Gordon B. Avery of the Children's National Medical Center in Washington, DC, stated that it is typical for cocaine babies to be born prematurely. He added, "In addition to the medical complications facing otherwise normal premature babies, cocaine babies face special hardships such as hydrocephaly (water on the brain), poor brain growth, kidney problems, and apnea (an unforeseen stoppage of breathing)" [49]. Confusion regarding this area of drug abuse exists partly because as recently as 1982, some medical textbooks on high-risk obstetrics still stated that cocaine had no harmful effects on the fetus. However, most sources agree that a fetus is particularly vulnerable to cocaine for several reasons:

- Although the placenta shields the uterus from many large, complex molecules (particularly those that cannot diffuse across fatty cell membranes), it is an open door to cocaine. This is true because cocaine is attracted to fatty compounds, and once the drug enters the blood and tissues of the fetus, it remains there longer than it does in an adult.

- The effects of cocaine on the mother-to-be also pose threats to the fetus. That is, when a woman addicted to crack becomes pregnant, the well-being of the fetus and of her own body is not her primary concern.
- An estimated 40–50 percent of cocaine-addicted pregnant women have been exposed to the AIDS virus.
- Among cocaine-addicted babies, the average birth weight is approximately 21 ounces lower than normal, while the average head circumference is about three-quarters of an inch smaller than that of normal babies. These differences may lead to future learning difficulties and an increased risk of infant mortality.

Demographically, the problem of cocaine-addicted babies extends beyond the inner city and across the national social spectrum. In many large cities such as New York, hospitals report that their obstetric and pediatric wards are overburdened, and that drug-related costs contribute greatly to the overall cost of health care.

An emerging problem is children who were born to cocaine-using mothers but who survive for a few years: "They operate on an institutional level; they eat and sleep, and eat and sleep. Something has been left out" [50]. Social workers and hospital professionals claim that these cocaine children may have difficulty playing or relating with other children, because they display symptoms of paranoia and distrust toward others. It has become a sobering reality that even if drug abuse were halted today, society would still be forced to deal with its effects in one way or another for decades (see Chapter 11).

Drugs and HIV

Drug use is a major factor in the spread of HIV infection. According to recent statistics, more than 34 million people are living with HIV worldwide, including 2.7 million new cases in 2010 alone. For the United States, the latest numbers indicate that 1.2 million Americans are living with HIV, and one in five of them does not know it [51]. Behaviors associated with drug abuse are among the main factors in the spread of HIV infection in the United States. Drugs can change the way the brain works, disrupting the parts of the brain that people use to weigh risks and benefits when making decisions.

Shared drug-using equipment can carry HIV and hepatitis, and drug use is linked with unsafe sexual activity. Alcohol and other drug use can also be dangerous for people who are taking *antiretroviral medications* (ARVs). Drug users are less likely to take all of their medications, and street drugs may have dangerous interactions with ARVs.

Again, HIV infection spreads easily when people share drug-using equipment. Sharing equipment also spreads hepatitis B, hepatitis C, and other serious diseases. Infected blood can be drawn up into a syringe and then get injected along with the drug by the next user of the syringe. This is the easiest way to transmit HIV during drug use, because infected blood goes directly into someone else's bloodstream. Even small amounts of blood on one's hands, cookers, filters, tourniquets, or in rinse water, can be enough to infect another user. Research has shown that HIV can survive in a used syringe for at least 4 weeks.

Drug Use and Unsafe Sex

For a lot of people, drugs and sex go together. Drug users might trade sex for drugs, or for money to buy drugs. Some people associate having unsafe sex with their drug use. In many cases, drug use, including use of methamphetamine or alcohol, increases the chance that people will not protect themselves during sexual activity. Someone who is trading sex for drugs might find it difficult to set limits on what they are willing to do. In other words, drug use can reduce a person's commitment to use condoms and practice safer sex.

Often, substance abusers have multiple sexual partners. This increases their risk of becoming infected with, and carrying, HIV or another sexually transmitted disease.

Lost Productivity

Drugs affect not only friends and families but also, logically, the workplace. Employees who use drugs may miss more work and be late for work more often than those who do not use them. In addition, illness, injury, encounters with the justice system, and related family problems may result. It is common for alcohol and other drugs to be used in combination, resulting in seriously affected coordination, concentration, risk taking, and other factors. Exactly how drugs affect each individual user depends largely on the user's dosage level, the rate of consumption, and the person's experience in using the drug. The extent of the drug use problem in the workplace was illustrated in a study of 2,500 postal workers, which found that postal workers who had used marijuana were:

- 1.6 times as likely as nonusers to have quit their jobs or have been fired.
- 1.5 times as likely to have had an accident and nearly twice as likely to have been injured.
- 1.5 times as likely to have been disciplined by a supervisor.
- 1.8 times as likely to be absent from work [52].

Concerns about safety mainly concentrate on high-precision or high-risk occupations such as those in transportation (e.g., airline pilots, air traffic controllers, railroad engineers, and truck drivers). Other concerns are shoddy manufacturing of products, bad business decisions, slow-moving business services, drug-related absenteeism, sickness, and employee turnover. Furthermore, employee interaction can be negatively affected by drug-using employees' mood changes. Many people employed in the nation's public and private sectors are drug users. According to a SAMHSA report, of the 20.3 million adults classified with drug dependence or abuse in 2008, 12.5 million (61.5 percent) were employed full-time [53]. Drug users tend to be less dependable than other workers, and they decrease workplace productivity. An earlier SAMHSA report noted that they are more likely to have taken unexcused absences in the past month—12.1 percent do so, compared to 6.1 percent of drug-free workers. Furthermore, illegal drug users get fired more often (4.6 percent) than their non-drug-using counterparts (1.4 percent) [54].

Drug Consumerism

The clandestine methamphetamine and crack market has created a new type of "consumerism" (for lack of a better term) that accompanies trafficking ventures. The new consumerism can be viewed from two angles: drug user consumerism and drug dealer consumerism. Because of drug user consumerism, many supermarkets have noticed increased sales of items such as scouring pads, cough syrup, and over-the-counter bronchial inhalers. The sales of these and similar items illustrate their greater worth in a clandestine market than in a legitimate market. Scouring pads and steel wool are used for cleaning drug pipes and for holding crack at the bottom of the pipe bowl. Grain alcohol is commonly used to ignite crack, and inhalers give drug users an added euphoric feeling, or *rush*, while under the influence of stimulants.

Theft is a common means for drug users to get money for drugs. Studies have shown that car parts, such as "T-tops" from the roofs of sports cars, high-end wheels and tires, are commonly stolen and then bartered or sold for drugs. Other favorites include virtually anything electronic, such as digital recorders, iPads and tablet computers, smart phones, and video games. At the opposite end of the consumerism spectrum is the drug-dealing side. Purchases of cellular phones, personalized license plates, jewelry, firearms, and automobiles for illegal purposes have actually boosted the legitimate market of these products. Cell phones and pagers are commonly used to arrange drug transactions, deliver supplies, and arrange for money pickups. Personalized license plates have emerged as a type of status symbol. Plates bearing variations of "boof" and "sling", for example, may refer to smoking and selling crack. Expensive rings, gold chains and watches are commonly used in bartering for drugs because such items are easily carried into crack houses and many dealers see them as status symbols.

Weapons such as the 9 mm semiautomatic gun have become popular with many drug dealers. The 9 mm, commonly referred to as a "muscle gun", is compact and has an intimidating appearance. Automobiles are also one of the most sought-after status symbols. Luxury vehicles have been seized by law enforcement agents when the vehicles have been purchased with cash earned from illicit sources. Expensive athletic shoes are also desired. In view of this connection, in 1998, the athletic shoe manufacturer Converse scrapped plans to launch a basketball shoe with the potentially controversial moniker "Young Guns", which was designed to attract urban teen males [55].

These buying trends pose serious ethical, moral, and legal dilemmas for retail merchants, who may be suspicious of some customers but may not have firm grounds for refusing to do business with them. Problems arise when customers present merchants with large sums of cash in exchange for goods. While merchants should not morally judge people because they possess large amounts of cash or because they are from a certain part of town, they should realize that the money they receive from any transaction may ultimately be subject to forfeiture under federal law if the customer turns out to be a drug dealer.

Theories of Drug Abuse and Crime

The search for solutions for reducing drug abuse and crime has baffled law enforcement authorities, social scientists, and criminal justice academicians alike. Although many proposed solutions to the problem are discussed throughout this book, several widely accepted social theories explain why people use drugs and under what circumstances they become lured into criminal lifestyles. First, however, we will address the concepts of vice and victimless crime, terms commonly associated with drug crimes and drug abuse.

Vice and "Victimless" Crime

Although *vice* in normal parlance refers to any bad habit or evil conduct, in legal jargon it specifically refers to the supplying of any illicit good or service. For example, smoking cigarettes may be a vice in the ordinary sense, but only activities that have been specifically outlawed are considered *vice crimes*: for example, drug trafficking, loan sharking, gambling, and prostitution. Some vice crimes are actually legal under carefully regulated circumstances. Gambling, for instance, is legal in some states under some circumstances. Nonetheless, illegal gambling activity thrives on the skirts of controlled gambling institutions. Through uncontrolled illegal organizations, profits may exceed those that can be realized through legitimate channels.

Enforcement techniques, especially for vice crimes such as drug trafficking, can be controversial because a police officer's professional code of conduct and the letter of the law with regard to criminal investigations are sometimes compromised in order to obtain information. Enforcement is particularly difficult in these cases because there is usually no complainant or victim, as there are in other types of criminal violations. Therefore, law enforcement officers must rely on a high degree of surreptitiousness and ingenuity to make arrests. This can be illustrated, for example, by a drug investigator's tolerance of a certain amount of drug use on the part of his or her informant while other people are under investigation for drug use activity similar to that of the informant.

In a study of drug law enforcement, Peter K. Manning and Lawrence John Redlinger listed the questionable and corrupt practices that have been associated with narcotics agents. These included taking bribes, using drugs, buying and selling drugs, arrogating stolen property, conducting illegal searches and seizures, protecting informants and their drug-trafficking activities, and committing acts of violence. In contrast, drug enforcement professionals, although willing to admit that there is a certain degree of corruption in all law enforcement agencies, defend their profession by pointing to several factors. First, because of the accessibility of federal grant money in the early 1990s, professional training is more readily available to drug enforcement officials than ever before [56]. Second, the adoption of a field training officer program for drug enforcement personnel in larger departments has helped weed out individuals who are not considered competent for the job. Third, because of an increase in drug-testing programs within law enforcement agencies, administrators have a new tool to check officers for drug abuse.

Regarding the term *victimless crimes*, another distinction must be made. A crime is usually characterized by an act that hurts someone or something, or by the potential for the act to hurt someone or something. The case of drug abuse is an exception because the primary victims (the drug abusers themselves) are willing participants in the activity. In addition, there are generally no complainants in vice crimes, for the reasons discussed here. So when charges are filed in vice cases, the state (or government) is the complainant. However, although the term *victimless crime* came into use to describe these crimes, this does not change the fact that innocent people are also commonly victimized by drug abuse.

Why do people choose drug abuse as a social lifestyle? What fuels one's ambition to become involved in a criminal drug-trafficking organization or in a behavior that is considered criminal? These questions will be addressed by sociological theories that attempt to explain the social nature of the drug problem.

Social Disorganization Theory

One popular explanation of drug abuse, social disorganization theory, addresses its links with poverty, *social disorganization*, and a feeling of hopelessness. The correlation between drug abuse and young minority group members has often been tied to factors such as racial prejudice, low socioeconomic status, lack of positive self-esteem, and uncharitable urban surroundings. As a result, the link between drug use, poverty, and race has been associated with high levels of mistrust and defiance common to lower-class urban areas [57]. In spite of a strong suggestion that drug abuse is linked with social disorganization, the relationship between class status and crime in general remains unclear. Today, social disorganization theory is most closely associated with the work of Chicago sociologists Clifford Shaw and Henry McKay.

Cultural Transmission

Shaw and McKay's study, first published in the early 1940s, developed the theory of *cultural transmission* and focused on crime within the context of a changing urban environment. Shaw and McKay examined criminality, particularly among young people, in Chicago during the 1920s and 1930s. They concluded that the popular concepts of body build and IQ were no longer accurate predictors of criminality, but that environmental factors in the cities were better predictors. Shaw and McKay saw criminality as a product of decaying "transitional neighborhoods" that were deteriorating from affluence to poverty. They examined certain areas that were consistently "high-crime" neighborhoods over several decades. Research revealed that although the ethnic composition of these neighborhoods changed over time, the level of criminality in these so-called *zones of transition* remained the same [58]. As a result of this study, it has been suggested that the attitudes, values, and norms of these areas are not only conducive to crime, but also transferred over time from one ethnic group to another. According to this theory, children become indoctrinated into a life of crime at an early age. This occurs particularly in males who associate regularly with criminals and drug dealers and look to them as role models.

Anomie

In 1938, Robert Merton introduced the concept of *anomie* to explain an individual's motive for involvement in deviant social behavior or crime [59]. In his theory, Merton attempted to adapt the abstract concept of anomie to living conditions in United States society. Earlier, French criminologist Emile Durkheim had applied the term to explain a feeling of "normlessness" that results in a breakdown of social rules and order. Merton later adapted the concept to fit living conditions in United States society. In this theory, Merton argued, the ends become more important than the means, and an individual will resort to deviant means if no legitimate means (e.g., education and employment opportunities) are available. Merton went on to emphasize that modern American society is goal oriented, with wealth and material goods being the most desired goals. The cultural goal of financial success is highly valued by the individual, but if that individual finds that (1) less value is attached by society to how that success is achieved, and (2) legitimate routes to financial success are blocked, he or she may opt for illegal means to achieve that particular end. For example, owning a home is generally considered one of the "great American dreams", but for many low-income families, this dream cannot be obtained through legitimate means. As a result, people from these families often "become estranged from a society that promises them in principle what they are deprived of in reality" [60].

To illustrate his theory, Merton cited a preoccupation with material success, or *pathological materialism*, endemic in American culture. A legitimate profit motive may be channeled through deviant means (e.g., drug dealing) when social barriers preclude legitimate channels such as good schooling, quality jobs, and higher income. The result may be the creation of a person willing to commit crimes to reach his or her goals. Merton further explained that there are five modes of individual adaptation to the contradiction between promised goals and available means: (1) conformity, (2) ritualism, (3) rebellion, (4) retreatism, and (5) innovation [61].

It is the first and third modes, conformity and rebellion, that may offer the most intelligible explanation of society's involvement in drug use. The fifth mode, innovation, creates one of the fundamental social infrastructures for involvement in organized crime. For example, the crime phenomenon of California youth gangs that spread to many major cities in the mid-1980s suggests that Merton's philosophy has contemporary validity. Such gangs represent thousands of inner-city youths from the Los Angeles area who have become extremely organized, targeting large cities and realizing hundreds of thousands of dollars of drug money (see Chapter 8).

Opportunity Theory

Opportunity theory is another popular theory that parallels Merton's theory of anomie; it attempts to explain that not only are legitimate social opportunities unequally distributed throughout society, but also even some illegitimate criminal opportunities are blocked for some youths. Richard A. Cloward and Lloyd E. Ohlin wrote that many male adolescents experience extreme deprivation of opportunity [62]. Therefore, many feel that their position within society is somewhat fixed, and that there are few legitimate ladders to success. In fact, they argue that criminal opportunities are available only for youths who have grown up in areas where collusion exists between members of the underworld and the general society. In these areas, adult criminals have worked out arrangements (through corruption) among businesses, politicians, and the police that leave them all but immune from prosecution. Their criminal enterprises (drug trafficking, gambling, and so forth) offer a stable income and an alternative to legitimate economic success. Fostered by adult criminals, youths fit right into this model and create a criminal subculture, preparing to join adult crime organizations by first running with criminally active street gangs. Cloward and Ohlin identified three types of delinquent subcultures: (1) the retreatist subculture (in which drug use is the primary focus), (2) the conflict subculture (in which gang activities are dedicated to destruction and violence as ways of gaining status), and (3) the criminal rackets subculture (in which gang activity is devoted to utilitarian or profit-motivated criminal pursuits) [63].

Essentially, Cloward and Ohlin view crime as a function of different opportunities provided to youths to attain both legitimate and illegitimate goals. When avenues for legitimate goals are blocked, illegitimate avenues are then pursued.

Differential Association

Some researchers embrace learning theories in which *differential association* attempts to explain a person's involvement in criminal activity. This theory, first formulated by Edwin Sutherland in 1939, suggests that a principal part of learning criminal behavior occurs within intimate groups [64]. This occurs in two ways. First, individuals, particularly those living in economically depressed areas, identify with the financially successful role models in their communities (e.g., drug dealers, pimps, and gamblers). Second, individuals are exposed to the lifestyle and techniques of criminal behavior in their communities. The specifics of what is learned are based on the frequency of contacts and the intensity and duration of each association. According to Sutherland, the individual learns specialized techniques, attitudes, justifications, and rationalizations. Sutherland offered nine basics of differential association:

1. Criminal behavior is learned.
2. The fundamental basis of learning criminal behavior is formed in intimate personal groups (e.g., gangs).
3. Criminal behavior is acquired through interaction with other persons in the process of communication.
4. The learning process includes the techniques of committing the crime, and specific rationalizations and attitudes for criminal activity.
5. General attitudes regarding respect (or lack of respect) for the law are reflected in attitudes toward criminal behavior.

6. A person becomes delinquent or criminal by accepting an excess of definitions favorable to violation of the law over definitions unfavorable to violation of the law.
7. Differential association may differ in duration, frequency, and intensity.
8. The processes for learning criminal behavior parallel those of any other type of learning.
9. Criminal behavior is an expression of general needs and values (as with noncriminal behavior), but it is not explained by those needs and values [65].

Sutherland believed that it is through the learning of these traits that a favorable predisposition to criminal lifestyles is developed.

Summary

Today's drug situation is a result of complex social interactions affecting many different people, places, and things. It is referred to in a number of different ways by public speakers, politicians, the media, and private citizens. Terms used to describe the situation include the *drug crisis*, the *drug problem*, the *drug dilemma*, the *drug epidemic*, and the *war on drugs*. However people choose to refer to the issue, drugs have remolded the social fabric of communities, the work environment, the learning environment of schools, the criminal justice system, and the drug treatment industry, to name just a few. From all indications, drug abuse in one form or another is here to stay.

There is no single drug abuse problem. Drug problems are related to both health and public safety, and much controversy exists around the best solution for the problem. The existence of drugs in our communities poses a considerable financial burden for society. Costs include the financial expense of street crimes such as robbery and burglary, criminal justice system costs, medical costs for victims, and the loss of productivity in the workplace. Other hidden costs include the moral cost of corrupt public officials, and family strife for drug users and their loved ones.

The very nature of the drug problem creates an element of criminality and comes with the violence associated with that element. Organized crime groups, such as the Jamaican posses and the California-based Crips and Bloods, have emerged since the "drug culture" materialized, and their presence has become well known in many United States communities. Long-established crime organizations have also flourished since the drug epidemic gained momentum.

The reasons why people take drugs are numerous. For example, some people desire a stimulation of the endocrine chemicals within the body. These internal chemicals tend to emulate the effects of morphine and give a feeling of euphoria. Other people use drugs to alter their moods in the traditional "happy hour" forum. Still others use certain drugs for the legitimate treatment of medical or mental health conditions. Drug trafficking and related drug activity are referred to by many as a "vice" crime. Additionally, many tend to refer to this type of behavior as "victimless", because all participants willingly engage in the act. For that reason, many feel that the enforcement of such crimes is the equivalent of government attempting to police morals and personal values, and that such crimes should be decriminalized, regulated, and taxed.

Several social theories have been posited to explain the criminal behavior that commonly accompanies drug abuse. Included are theories of social disorganization, anomie, cultural transmission, and differential association. Each of these theories adds to our understanding of drug abuse and criminality, and can be applied to the study of modern-day criminal behavior.

Do you recognize these terms?

- addictive personality
- anomie
- backstabbing
- cultural transmission
- differential association
- endogenous
- endorphins
- opportunity theory
- pathological materialism
- rush
- social disorganization
- vice crimes
- victimless crime
- zones of transition

Discussion Questions

1. What is meant by the term *drug abuse*?
2. Other than drug users themselves, who are the victims of drug abuse in our society?
3. Discuss some of the reasons why the drug problem is considered such a major social problem in the United States.
4. Discuss some of the health-related problems inherent in drug abuse.
5. What are some social factors that contribute to a climate of drug abuse?
6. What are the distinctions between the terms *vice* and *victimless crime*?
7. List the ways that cocaine in addicted pregnant mothers affects the fetus.
8. What are endorphins, and how do they relate to drug abuse?

Class Project

1. Discuss with fellow classmates or friends their perception of the country's drug problem and what can be done to solve it.

References

[1] Office of National Drug Control Policy (ONDCP). (2012). *2012 National drug control strategy: FY-2013 budget and performance summary.* Washington, DC: U.S. Department of Justice. Executive Office of the President of the United States, April.
[2] United Nations Office on Drugs and Crime (UNODC). (2010). *The globalization of crime: A transnational organized crime threat assessment.* New York: UNODC; United Nations Office on Drugs and Crime (UNODC). (2011). *World drug report.* New York: UNODC.
[3] Ibid.

[4] National Drug Intelligence Center. (2010). *National drug threat assessment 2010.* February, Washington, DC: U.S. Department of Justice.

[5] Office of National Drug Control Policy. (2001). *The National Drug Control Strategy, 2001 Annual Report.* Washington, DC: U.S. Government Printing Office.

[6] Office of National Drug Control Policy. (2012). *2012 National Drug Control Strategy: FY-2013 Budget and Performance Summary.* U.S. Department of Justice. Washington, DC: Executive Office of the President of the United States, April.

[7] National Institute on Drug Abuse. (2012). *Monitoring the future (MTF): National results on adolescent drug abuse.* Overview of Key Findings 2011. February.

[8] MTF (2012).

[9] Ibid.

[10] Office of National Drug Control Policy. (2010). *National drug control strategy 2010.* Washington, DC: U.S. Department of Justice. Executive Office of the President of the United States. p. 2.

[11] Ibid.

[12] MTF (2012).

[13] Ibid.

[14] National Institute on Drug Abuse. (2012). *Tobacco addiction.* U.S. Department of Health and Human Services. Publication Number 12-4342, July.

[15] Ibid.

[16] Ibid.

[17] MTF (2012).

[18] Office of National Drug Control Policy. (2012). *2012 National Drug Control Strategy: FY-2013 Budget and Performance Summary.* U.S. Department of Justice. Washington, DC: Executive Office of the President of the United States, April.

[19] Office of National Drug Control Policy. (2001). *The National Drug Control Strategy, 2001 Annual Report.* Washington, DC: U.S. Government Printing Office.

[20] ONDCP. (2012)

[21] National Center on Addiction and Substance Abuse. (2001). *Shoveling up: The impact of substance abuse on state budgets.* New York: Columbia University.

[22] Clingermayer, J., Hecker, J., & Madsen, S. (2005). Asset forfeiture and police priorities: The impact of program design on law enforcement activities. *Criminal Justice Policy Review, 16,* 319–335.

[23] Ibid.

[24] National Drug Intelligence Center. (2010). *National Drug Threat Assessment 2010.* February. Washington, DC: U.S. Department of Justice, p. 27.

[25] United Nations Office for Drug Control and Crime Prevention. (2000). *Opening statement to the tenth United Nations Congress on the Prevention of Crime and the Treatment of Offenders,* Found at: www.uncjin.org/Documents/10thcongress/10cStatements/arlacchi14.pdf.

[26] Trade and Environment Database (TED). (1997). *TED case studies: Colombia coca trade.* Washington, DC: American University.

[27] Office of Technology Assessment. (1990). *Protecting the Borders.* Washington, DC: United States Congress, U.S. Government Printing Office.

[28] National Drug Intelligence Center. (2010). *National Drug Threat Assessment 2010.* February. Washington, DC: U.S. Department of Justice.

[29] U.S. Department of Health and Human Services National Institute on Drug Abuse. (2010). *Research report: Cocaine abuse and addiction.* NIH. Publication Number 10-4166, September.

[30] Ibid.

[31] Ibid.

[32] Ibid.

[33] National Drug Intelligence Center. (2010). *National Drug Threat Assessment 2010.* February. Washington, DC: U.S. Department of Justice.

[34] Ibid.

[35] Ibid.

[36] Office of National Drug Control Policy. (2009). *The President's national drug control policy: 2009 Annual report.* Washington, DC: Executive Office of the President of the United States.

[37] Heron, M. P., Hoyert, D. L., Murphy, S. L., Xu, J. Q., Kochanek, K. D., & Tejada-Vera, B. (2009). Deaths: final data for 2006. *National vital statistics reports* (Vol. 57, No. 14). Hyattsville, MD: National Center for Health Statistics.

[38] Drug Abuse Warning Network (DAWN) DAWN Mortality Data. (2010). Located at: http://www.samhsa.gov/data/2k12/DAWNMEAnnualReport2010/DAWN-ME-AnnualReport2010.htm#Data1. Accessed March 2, 2013.

[39] Stein, B. (1988). The lure of drugs: They organize an addict's life. *Newsday.* (December 4), 6.

[40] Krogh, D. (1992). Smoking: Why is it so hard to quit? *Priorities.* (Spring), 29–31.

[41] Ibid.

[42] National Institute on Drug Abuse. (1996c). *1992–93 National Pregnancy and Health Survey: Drug Use Among Women Delivering Live Births.* Rockville, MD: U.S. Department of Health and Human Services.

[43] Musto, D. (1973). *The American disease: Origins of narcotic control.* New Haven: Yale University Press.

[44] National Institute on Drug Abuse. (2010). *National household survey on drug abuse.* Rockville, MD: U.S. Department of Health and Human Services.

[45] Office of National Drug Control Policy. (2010). *2009 National Drug Control Strategy. U.S. Department of Justice.* Washington, DC: Executive Office of the President of the United States.

[46] Found at: http://wreg.com/2013/01/17/woman-gives-birth-to-fourth-drug-addicted-baby/. Accessed March 9, 2013.

[47] Ibid.

[48] National Institute on Drug Abuse. (2009). *Monitoring the future: National results for adolescent drug use – overview of key findings 2008.* National Institutes of Health. U.S. Department of Health and Human Services.

[49] Kantrowitz, B., & Gonzalez, D. L. (1990). Still shocking after a year. *Newsweek.* (July 29), 48–49.

[50] Ibid.

[51] National Institute on Drug Abuse. (2013). *Drugs & HIV > learn the link.* Found at: http://hiv.drugabuse.gov/english/learn/overview.html. Accessed January 5, 2013.

[52] Zwerling, C., Ryan, J., & Endel, J. (1990). The efficacy of pre-employment drug screening for marijuana and cocaine in predicting employment outcome. *Journal of the American Medical Association.* (November), 264.

[53] U.S. Department of Health and Human Service. Found at: www.oas.samhsa.gov/nsduh/2k8nsduh/2k8Results.cfm#1.1 accessed March 15, 2010. National Youth Violence Prevention Resource Center. (2007). *Youth Gangs.* Found at: www.safeyouth.org/scripts/teens/gangs.asp.

[54] National Institute on Drug Abuse. (1997). *National household survey on drug abuse: Preliminary results for 1996.* Rockville, MD: U.S. Department of Health and Human Services.

[55] Wells, M. (1998). Converse cans 'Young Guns' shoes. *USA Today.* (April 15), 1B.

[56] Manning, P. K., & Redlinger, L. J. (2006). Invitational edges of corruption: some consequences of narcotic law enforcement. In P. E. Rock (Ed.), *Drugs and politics* (pp. 279). New Brunswick, NJ: Transaction.

[57] Winick, C. (1965). *Epidemiology of narcotics use.* New York: McGraw-Hill.

[58] Shaw, C. R., & McKay, H. D. (1942). *Juvenile delinquency in urban areas.* Chicago: University of Chicago Press.

[59] Merton, R. K. (1938). Social structure and anomie. *American Sociological Review, 3,* 672–682.

[60] Merton, R. K. (1967). *On theoretical sociology: Five essays old and new.* New York: The Free Press.

[61] Ibid.

[62] Cloward, R. A., & Ohlin, L. E. (1960). *Delinquency and opportunity.* New York: Free Press.

[63] Ibid.

[64] Sutherland, E. H. (1939). *Principles of criminology* (3rd ed.). Philadelphia: J. B. Lippincott Company.

[65] Ibid.

2

The History of Drug Abuse

This chapter will enable you to:

- Understand the beginnings of the world's drug abuse problem
- Realize the many social implications of drug abuse
- Compare developments in drug control legislation during recent decades
- Appreciate the development of the national drug control policy

Public perceptions of drugs and drug abuse have shifted dramatically over the past 200 years. Twice, Americans have accepted and then rejected drugs in our society. Understanding these striking historical swings helps us understand our current reactions to drug use. The United States' recurrent enthusiasm for recreational drugs, and the resulting campaigns for abstinence, present resounding problems for public policy makers as well as for the public they serve. Because the peaks of these episodes occurred about a generation apart, citizens rarely have an accurate picture (much less a recollection) of the latest wave of drug use. Criminologist David Musto argues that fear and anger have been the primary causes of society's intolerance for drugs, and such emotions have distorted public memory so grotesquely that it becomes useless as a point of reference for policy formation [1]. The lack of knowledge concerning our earlier encounters with drugs impedes the task of establishing a workable public policy toward dealing with the problem.

Due to the notoriety of drug use during the 1960s, many people assume that this decade was most responsible for our nation's current drug problem. Indeed, as we will see, the 1960s played a significant role in the development and propagation of certain drugs of abuse, but the roots of the problem go back much further in history.

History Repeats Itself

Humankind's drug abuse legacy began thousands of years ago in such diverse areas as China, Egypt, India, the Middle East, and the Americas, where cannabis, ephedra, and opium were used for medicinal purposes and as general health tonics. In many cases, the medicinal use of these plants turned to recreational use, creating a pattern of progression from use to abuse that has continued to the present. Seven thousand years ago, the Sumerians left records of a "joy plant," presumably the highly addictive opium poppy (*Papaver somniferum*). The euphoric effects of medicinal use of the plant led to recreational abuse of opium in Sumerian society.

The Chinese discovered alkaloid ephedrine (*Ephedra sinica*), an inhalant, as far back as 3000 B.C.E. and marijuana (*Cannabis sativa*) by 2000 B.C.E. Chinese emperors in the third millennium B.C.E. ate or brewed cannabis in tea. Later on, the custom of drying and smoking cannabis was imported from India. Within a few centuries, alcohol abuse in Babylonia was significant enough to inspire legal controls. In 1700 B.C.E., the Code of Hammurabi included censure of public intoxication. Likewise, opium abuse in ancient Egypt increased to such an extent that by 1500 B.C.E., Egyptian scriptures had censured the practice. Again, opium use, which had medicinal origins as a pain reliever in surgery, had become opium abuse.

In South America, the Incas chewed the coca leaf, the plant from which cocaine is derived. By 1000 B.C.E., the Incas believed that the coca leaf (*Erthroxylon coca*) aided in the digestion of food and the suppression of their appetites. So highly valued was the coca leaf that it was used instead of gold or silver to barter for food and clothing. Coca chewing is even reflected in the art of that period. For example, a ceramic statue now housed in a museum in Ecuador portrays an Indian with the characteristic chewer's bulge in the cheek.

Greek literature in the first millennium B.C.E. records an awareness of both opium and alcohol. Odysseus, the hero of Homer's epic tale *The Odyssey*, forbids his sailors from eating the lotus flowers when visiting the African land of the Lotus Eaters. This imaginative tale about the lotus-eating dreamers suggests Homer's familiarity with opium use among North African cultures. Later, in 400 B.C.E., Hippocrates, the father of modern medicine (for whom the Hippocratic Oath is named), recommended drinking the juice of the white poppy mixed with the seed of nettle. Yet another myth deals with Dionysus, the god of wine—and drunkenness. Under the influence of alcohol, the followers of Dionysus ran amok, killing people and destroying property. So, although wine festivals were an important part of Greek culture, they were surrounded by a legend that inspired laws restricting the excessive use of alcohol.

In still another early culture, hallucinogens were commonly used. Around 100 B.C.E., the Aztec Indians of North America used dried peyote cactus buttons in religious ceremonies. Tribal people believed they would get closer to the gods and nature if they consumed this magical plant. Magic mushrooms (also known as *psilocybin* mushrooms) and morning glory seeds (also known as *ololiuqui*) were other organic hallucinogens commonly used by the Indians.

Ancient cultures all around the world established customs of drug use quite independently. However, with improved ships, more extensive sea travel, and political and military expansion, cultures began to influence each other. For instance, the Roman conquest of the eastern Mediterranean in the first century C.E. contributed to the spread of opium use. Whether the drugs were imported or indigenous to a culture, drug use continued to flourish.

Drug use was so established in India, for both recreational and commercial purposes, that the Susruta treatise of C.E. 400 cataloged with unprecedented detail various types of cannabis preferred by the Indians. For example, *bhang*, a strain of cannabis generally considered weak in strength, was brewed into tea. *Ganja*, a more potent type of cannabis, was usually smoked. The high-grade *charas*, similar to hashish or sinsemilla, was commonly eaten by affluent Indians. In the ninth century, Arab traders introduced opium to China.

Within a few centuries, opium smoking in China (nicknamed "chasing the dragon") would become a major public health threat.

Drugs even entered military rituals in several parts of the world. Some eleventh-century Persian warriors smoked hashish to prepare for battle and for their fate as martyrs. Al-Hassan-ibn-al Sabbah ("The Old Man of the Mountains") led such a band of Shiite Muslim warriors. (The word *assassin*, which later evolved through European use to mean the murderer of a political figure, comes from Al-Hassan's name.) On the other side of the world, Incan warriors commonly chewed coca leaves. Some historians partially attribute Pizarro's defeat of the Incan Empire in 1532 to the fact that many Incan warriors were so inebriated that they were mentally and physically unable to fight.

As we'll discuss in Chapter 3, in North America, Native American Indians have a long tradition of smoking tobacco, a custom that was eventually introduced to European sailors. Magellan took tobacco to parts of Africa, while the Portuguese carried it to Polynesia. In the 1600s, Sir Walter Raleigh introduced pipe smoking to England. Jean Nicot, who first took tobacco to France, claimed that it had great medicinal properties. In fact, the stimulant nicotine, the most dangerous chemical in tobacco, is named after him. The popularity of tobacco spread so rapidly in many Asian and European countries that some governments began to censure it. Japan, for example, prohibited smoking in the mid-1650s, and at about the same time, in parts of Europe, smoking tobacco was punished by disfigurement or death.

The age of exploration contributed greatly to the spread of culture, colonialism, commerce—and drugs. Whether mildly stimulating or dangerously addictive, drugs and the drug trade flourished. Explorers introduced some African cultures to tobacco and borrowed other drugs from them. In 1621, the Ethiopian coffee bean was introduced in England, and by the 1650s, coffee houses were well established in London and elsewhere.

The Opium Menace of the 1800s

Opium addiction established itself as a major health threat in China. During the 1800s, the Qing (Manchu) Dynasty tried to restrict opium use through legislation focusing on trade. The main target of such legislation was the East India Company of Great Britain, which supplied China with opium from India, which was then a colony of the British Empire. In fact, the British forced their colonial subjects into a widespread system of opium production that gave the British a virtual monopoly on the opium trade. Today's opium cultivators in Southeast and Southwest Asia are the descendants of farmers who were forced to participate in the British opium trade. Despite legal controls, the opium problem in China became so great that hostilities broke out between Great Britain and China.

In the early 1800s, the Manchu government passed a standing order for its army to detain and search any British vessel suspected of carrying opium. This led to the first of two great *opium wars* between China and Britain (1839–1842). The first war resulted in the defeat of China. The victorious British quickly claimed that opium consumption was harmless, encouraged its use, and reaped the profits from its trade. Chinese officials continued their objections, and a second war (1856–1860) broke out. In this second opium war (also called the *Anglo-French War*), a joint offensive by Britain and France resulted in the second defeat of China. Presumably, profit from the opium trade was more important than the welfare of the Chinese people to those warring countries (France, Britain, Russia, and the United States) that imposed the Tientsin Treaty (1858) on China. China at first refused to ratify the treaty, but by 1860 the defeated nation was forced to agree to key provisions: the legalization of opium and the opening of 11 more ports to Western ships.

Opium use had naturally spread to Britain and continental Europe, where decades earlier the Romantic poet Samuel Taylor Coleridge had fought addiction to the drug. Aiding in the perpetuation of the English addiction cycle was the manufacture of many over-the-counter preparations and tonics containing opium, morphine (an opium derivative), and laudanum (tincture of opium), each with harmless-sounding names such as Mother Bailey's Quieting Syrup and Munn's Elixir. Other over-the-counter cures had cocaine as their only active ingredient. Such "cures" were typically sold by street peddlers, mail order houses, retail grocers, and pharmacists. At the time, users could also gain unrestricted access to opium in opium dens, and to morphine through retailers.

Throughout the eighteenth and nineteenth centuries, advances in chemistry led to derivatives from opium and new chemical preparations. German chemists developed anodyne, a liquid form of ether, in 1730. The British chemist Joseph Priestley, best known for his discovery of oxygen, held laughing gas parties in his home after he discovered nitrous oxide gas in 1776. During the early 1800s, chloroform gained popularity as an anesthetic. In 1804, German pharmacist Friedrich Sertürner developed morphine, which he named after Morpheus, the Greek god of dreams and sleep. Codeine, another opium derivative, discovered in 1832, was used as a cough suppressant. Morphine use in surgery led to the invention of the hypodermic needle in 1853. Ironically, doctors at that time believed patient addiction to morphine could be avoided if the drug were injected rather than swallowed.

During this time, because of a peculiarity of the U.S. Constitution, the powerful new forms of opium and cocaine were more readily available in the United States than in most nations [2]. Under the Constitution, individual states assumed responsibility for health-related issues. This included the regulation of medical practice and the availability of pharmaceutical drugs. In actuality, the United States had as many laws regarding health professions as it had states. For much of the nineteenth century, many states chose to have no controls at all; instead, lawmakers reacted to the free-enterprise philosophy that gave physicians freedom to practice medicine virtually as they saw fit. In comparison, nations with a less restricted central government, such as Great Britain, had a single, all-encompassing pharmacy law controlling the availability of drugs that were considered dangerous. So, when we consider drug abuse in the nineteenth-century United States, we are looking at an era of unbridled availability and limitless advertising of drugs.

Changes During the Late Nineteenth Century

In the 1860s, the American Civil War literally triggered a drug epidemic, resulting in hundreds of thousands of morphine addicts—400,000 in the Union Army alone [3]. The indiscriminate use of morphine and commercially available opium-based drugs prevailed on the battlefields, in prisons, and even on the home front. Self-medication for grief and pain often resulted in high dosages and, eventually, addiction. Meanwhile, opium use increased on the West Coast, and many Americans quickly associated opium smoking with Chinese immigrants, who were lured to California by the promise of work on the railroads. Chinese opium smoking was tolerated and even encouraged while the Chinese laborers worked for low wages, performing backbreaking tasks in jobs that few white Americans wanted. However, when a series of economic depressions in the late 1800s made jobs, even low-paying ones, a scarce commodity, nativist white anger was turned loose on the Chinese and their practice of opium smoking. This linking of drug abuse with a particular culture was one of the earliest examples of a powerful theme in the American perception of drugs: an association of drugs with a feared or rejected group within society. Similarly, cocaine would be linked with blacks, and marijuana with Mexicans, during the first part of the twentieth century.

Opium dens were so commonplace in San Francisco that the city passed an ordinance in 1875 to ban opium smoking in opium dens. This was considered the first antidrug law in the United States, and it resulted in a series of state and local legislative actions. (By 1912, nearly every state and many municipalities had regulations controlling the distribution of certain drugs.) However, the absence of any federal control over interstate commerce in habit-forming and other drugs, the absence of uniformity among state laws, and a lack of effective drug enforcement had one important implication: the rising tide of legislation directed at opiates (and later cocaine) was more a reflection of changing public attitudes toward these drugs than an effective strategy to reduce supplies to users [4]. The reality is that the reduction of opiate use around 1900 was probably due more to a fear of addiction, particularly among physicians, than to any successful campaign to reduce drug abuse [5].

More newly discovered drugs contributed to the pattern from use to abuse. Around 1870, Oscar Liebreich developed one of the first sedative hypnotics, chloral hydrate. In combination with alcohol, it was commonly abused as a recreational drug, as well as for more nefarious purposes such as the famous "Mickey Finn," a knockout cocktail used by muggers and robbers. Meanwhile, in 1878, cocaine was first isolated in an alkaloid form in an attempt to cure many of the postwar morphine addicts in the United States. Early on, its retail price was exceedingly high (compared to industrial wages of the time)—$5 to $10 per gram—but it soon fell to 25 cents a gram and stayed there until price inflation after World War I [6]. Although problems with cocaine were apparent almost from the beginning, by the 1880s this "cure" was used recreationally on a widespread basis. This was partly because popular opinion and leading medical "experts" touted cocaine as being both a beneficial and a benign stimulant. In fact, the crack cocaine epidemic that struck the United States during the mid-1980s was not the first cocaine epidemic. The nation's original cocaine epidemic occurred within roughly a 35-year period from the mid-1880s to 1920.

The History of Cocaine

Contributing to the spread of cocaine use was the considerable support of its use by the European medical community and, later, American medical professionals. In the absence of national legislation controlling the use of cocaine, its abuse spread. Initially, cocaine was offered as a cure for opiate addiction, an asthma remedy (the official remedy of the American Hay Fever Association), and an antidote for toothaches. In 1886, Atlanta-born John Styth Pemberton introduced the soft drink Coca-Cola, which, for the next 20 years, had a cocaine base. The soft drink was introduced as having the advantages of coca but lacking the dangers of alcohol.

Although cocaine failed as a cure for morphine addiction, it was still erroneously hailed as a cure for other problems. One report in 1883 explained how Bavarian soldiers given cocaine experienced renewed energy for combat. Sigmund Freud, inspired by American and German medical literature, first used cocaine as an aid in therapy in the 1880s. He used the "magical substance" in the treatment of depression, and believed it to be helpful with asthma and certain stomach disorders. Freud's professional use led to his own secret habit that was known to only a few close friends and associates during the later years of his life.

As medicinal cocaine use spread throughout Europe, so did its commercial and recreational appeal. A popular European elixir called Vin Mariani (named after its inventor, Angelo Mariani) surfaced in Paris and consisted of red wine and Peruvian coca leaf extracts. Historians believe that in the 1880s, Vin Mariani was probably the most widely

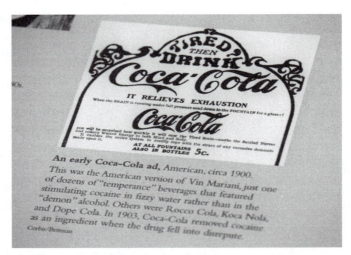

FIGURE 2.1 An early Coca-Cola ad, featuring cocaine as an ingredient, is part of an exhibit at the Drug Enforcement Administration Museum and Visitors Center in Arlington, Virginia. *Source: Associated Press.*

used medical prescription in the world, used even by popes, kings, queens, and other rulers. At the same time, William A. Hammond, a prominent American neurologist, hailed cocaine as being no more habit-forming than coffee or tea. After all, how could any substance that makes the user feel so good be so bad? Within one year of the discovery of cocaine, the Parke-Davis Company was marketing coca and cocaine in 15 different forms, including coca cigarettes, cocaine for injection, and cocaine for sniffing. Cocaine kits were sold by Parke-Davis, as well as by other companies. These kits even offered syringes for convenient injections. The company proudly announced that cocaine "can supply the place of food, make the coward brave, the silent eloquent and … render the sufferer insensitive to pain" [7]. Musto further points out that several reports from the years before the *Harrison Narcotics Act* of 1914 suggest that both the profit margin and street price of cocaine were unaffected by the legal availability of cocaine from a physician. He suggests that "perhaps the formality of medical consultation and the growing antagonism among physicians and the public toward cocaine helped to sustain the illicit market" [8].

Although peyote use was confined primarily to Native American religious ceremonies, at the turn of the twentieth century alcohol abuse was spreading throughout society to all social classes and racial groups. Epidemic alcohol addiction in the United States finally led to the controversial Eighteenth Amendment, which was ratified in 1919 and ushered

THE HISTORY OF COCAINE

1844	Cocaine, the principal alkaloid in coca leaves, is isolated.
1863	A preparation of coca leaves and wine called Vin Mariani gains popularity in Europe.
1878	Cocaine is used for morphine addiction.
1884	Sigmund Freud studies cocaine as a psychoactive drug to treat depression and fatigue.
1884	Karl Koller uses cocaine as a topical anesthetic in eye operations.
1886	Coca-Cola, a soft drink containing coca extract, comes on the market.
1906	The U.S. Pure Food and Drug Act prohibits interstate shipment of food and soda water containing cocaine.
1906	The Coca-Cola Company switches to "decocainized" coca leaves.
1914	The U.S. Harrison Narcotics Act lists cocaine as a narcotic.
1922	Congress prohibits most importation of cocaine and coca leaves.
1970	The U.S. Controlled Substances Act classifies cocaine as a Schedule II Stimulant.
1970s	Cocaine use becomes popular as a glamor drug with affluent segments of society.
1985	Crack cocaine is introduced and replaces phencyclidine (PCP) as the inner-city drug of choice.
2013	The availability of cocaine in the United States is greatly reduced due to the demise of many cocaine cartels.

in the era of Prohibition. Prohibition limited only the legal consumption of alcohol; illegal markets thrived. Alcohol—and even marijuana, which served as an inexpensive substitute for costly black-market alcohol—was easily available in (among other places) secret bars called *speakeasies*. Many famous jazz musicians performing in such speakeasies were thought to be drug abusers.

Twentieth-Century Developments

As the twentieth century unfolded, so did the introduction of many new drugs. In 1903, barbiturates were discovered in Germany, and in 1912 amphetamines were mass produced as an antidote for asthma. Benzedrine inhalers were introduced for the first time in 1932 for treatment of adverse respiratory conditions, and in 1938 the painkiller Demerol, which is today a highly prized substitute for heroin on the streets, was synthesized and placed on the market. Thus, drug abuse in the early twentieth century was nothing new or unusual. What was relatively new was the variety of drugs abused, and the extent to which each decade since 1900 can be characterized by particular drug fads, especially in the United States.

As early as 1887 and in the absence of federal laws, some states had begun regulatory procedures. Finally, because of growing concern over opiate addiction and the nonmedical use of drugs at the turn of the twentieth century, several important federal legislative actions were taken. The first was a federal prohibition of the importation of opium by Chinese nationals in 1887, and a restriction of opium smoking in the Philippines in 1905. These actions were followed by the passing of the federal Pure Food and Drug Act in 1906, which required over-the-counter medicine manufacturers to correctly label the inclusion of certain drugs. However, the act failed to restrict the use of these drugs. In the following seven years, the United States government participated in several international conventions designed to motivate other nations to pass domestic laws dealing with drug control. In 1909, the Shanghai Opium Convention strongly supported such controls, but its recommendation generated little actual legislation among the nations involved, including the United States.

By 1910, President William Howard Taft presented Congress with a State Department report stating that cocaine was more appalling in its effects than any other habit-forming drug in the United States. A year earlier, President Theodore Roosevelt had led the effort to ban drugs in the nation's capital when he was informed by local police of their suspicions that the use of cocaine predisposes the user to commit criminal acts. Failure to pass the proposed Foster Anti-Narcotic Bill led to a debate at the famed 1911 International Conference at The Hague, which deliberated the issue of whether the United States would actually enact such legislation. Resulting from The Hague conference, the Senate's ratification of the convention in 1913 committed the United States to enact laws to suppress the abuse of opium, morphine, and cocaine. The goal was a world in which narcotics were restricted to medicinal use. Both producing and consuming nations would have control over their own boundaries.

Returning from The Hague was the State Department's opium commissioner, Hamilton Wright, who began to structure a comprehensive federal antidrug law. Blocking his efforts was the specter of states' rights. The major cause of addiction was thought to be the indiscriminate prescription of dangerous drugs by health professionals, yet how could the federal government interfere with the prescribing practices of physicians, or demand that pharmacists keep records? To Wright, the answer was obvious: the governmental power to tax. After extensive negotiations with pharmaceutical, export, import, and other medical interests, the Harrison Narcotics Act was passed in December 1914 and became the hallmark of federal drug control policy for the next 65 years. Many people viewed the Harrison Narcotics Act as a rational way to limit addiction and drug abuse through taxation and regulation. It was a regulatory device that, according to the American Opium Commission, "would bring the whole traffic and use of these drugs into the light of day and, therefore, create a public opinion against the use of them that would be more important, perhaps, than the act itself." The act was heralded as a method of drug abuse control and as a public awareness tool.

The success of the enforcement of the act was directly attributed to the chosen source of authority and constitutional power to collect taxes. Because it was basically a tax revenue

DEVELOPMENT OF THE HARRISON NARCOTICS ACT

1909	At the Shanghai Opium Convention, representatives of 13 nations met to discuss ways of controlling illicit drug traffic.
1912	At the International Opium Convention, the first binding international instrument governing the shipment of narcotic drugs was signed at The Hague, Netherlands.
1914	The Harrison Narcotics Act was passed and became the hallmark of United States federal drug control policy for the next 65 years.
1920	The First Assembly of the League of Nations established an Advisory Committee on Traffic in Opium and Other Dangerous Drugs. Under League auspices, three main drug conventions were developed over the next two decades.
1925	The Second International Opium Convention established a system of import certificates and export authorizations for licit international trade in narcotics.
1931	The Convention for Limiting the Manufacture and Regulating the Distribution of Narcotic Drugs introduced a compulsory estimation system aimed at limiting the amount of drugs manufactured to those needed for medical and scientific purposes.
1936	The Convention for the Suppression of the Illicit Traffic in Dangerous Drugs was the first international instrument that called for severe punishment for illegal traffickers.
1946	Drug control responsibilities formerly carried out by the League of Nations were transferred to the United Nations. The Division of Narcotic Drugs was also created to act as the secretariat for the commission, and to serve as the central repository of UN expertise in drug control.

(Continued)

DEVELOPMENT OF THE HARRISON NARCOTICS ACT—Cont'd

1961 The Single Convention on Narcotic Drugs codified all existing multilateral treaty laws. It placed under control the cultivation of plants grown as raw material for narcotic drugs. Controls were continued on opium and its derivatives, and the coca bush and cannabis were placed under international control, obliging governments to limit production to amounts needed for scientific and medical use.

1971 Until 1971, only narcotic drugs were subject to international control. The Convention on Psychotropic Substances extended controls to include a broad range of man-made, mood-altering substances that could lead to harmful dependencies. These included hallucinogens such as lysergic acid diethylamide (LSD) and mescaline, stimulants such as amphetamines, and sedative-hypnotics such as barbiturates.

1981 The International Drug Abuse Control Strategy was formed and implemented a five-year program. It included measures for wider adherence to existing treaties, coordinating efforts to ensure a balance between the supply and demand for drugs for legitimate use, and steps to eradicate the illicit drug supply and reduce traffic.

1984 In its Declaration on the Control of Drug Trafficking and Drug Abuse, the UN General Assembly characterized drug traffic and abuse as "an international criminal activity" that constituted "a grave threat to the security and development of many countries and peoples."

1987 The International Conference on Drug Abuse and Illicit Trafficking focused on developing long-term drug control strategies, policies, and activities to attack at the national, regional, and international level drug abuse and trafficking.

measure, it required people who prescribed or distributed certain drugs to register with the government and buy tax stamps. In addition, the law stipulated that possession of drugs by an unregistered person was unlawful unless prescribed by a physician in good faith. The responsibility of enforcement rested with the Department of the Treasury.

Because of so many ambiguities in the Harrison Act, conflict erupted between the medical community and law enforcement officials. From the beginning, the Treasury Department insisted that medical maintenance of opiate addicts (treatment through declining usage) was unlawful, but physicians opposed this belief. Lower courts of law initially upheld the practice of drug maintenance of addicts, but a series of U.S. Supreme Court decisions, including the 1919 ruling in *Webb et al. v. United States*, stated that maintaining addicts on narcotic drugs, even by prescription, was illegal.

Early enforcement of the Harrison Narcotics Act resulted in mass arrests of physicians, pharmacists, and unregistered users. In fact, some 30,000 physicians were arrested during this period for dispensing narcotics, and about 3,000 actually served prison sentences. Consequently, doctors all but abandoned the treatment of addicts for nearly half a century in the United States. Furthermore, although private sanitariums that claimed to cure addiction had existed since the mid-1800s, they were unable to serve all the remaining addicts when physicians became wary of prescribing opiates for maintenance. To respond

SELECTED PROVISIONS OF THE HARRISON NARCOTICS ACT

Section 1—Any person who was in the business of dealing in the specified drugs was required to pay a special annual tax of one dollar. In 1918, the Revenue Act increased the special annual tax on importers, manufacturers, producers, and compounders to $24, on wholesalers to $12, on retailers to $6, and on practitioners to $3.

Section 2—The selling or giving away of any specified drugs was prohibited except pursuant to the written order of the person to whom the drug was being given or sold. The written order was required to be on a special form issued by the Commissioner of Internal Revenue.

Section 4—It was unlawful for anyone who had not previously registered to engage in interstate trafficking of the specified drugs.

Section 8—The possession of any of the specified drugs was illegal with the exception of employees of registrants and patients of physicians.

Section 9—The punishment for any violation of the act was to be not more than $2,000, not more than five years in prison, or both.

Section 10—The Commissioner of Internal Revenue was given responsibility for enforcing the act.

to this need, between 1919 and 1921, 44 cities opened municipal clinics to provide temporary maintenance for addicts. Such clinics soon found themselves aggressively targeted for investigation by agents of the Narcotics Division. By 1925, all these clinics had been closed. Despite popular criticism of the prohibition of narcotic drugs during this period, the Harrison Narcotics Act proved to drastically reduce the consumption of narcotics in the United States. This conclusion is evident when we observe the reduction of the number of addicts during a 25-year period: in 1920, there were an estimated 500,000 addicts, and in 1945, the addict population was roughly 40,000–50,000.

Prohibition: A Public Policy Disaster

Although moderate drinking was generally accepted during the eighteenth century, by the early nineteenth century some people began to perceive an increase in the abuse of alcohol, and they began the *temperance movement* to promote total abstinence from alcohol. The American Temperance Society, founded in 1826, began gathering pledges of abstinence. Within three years, more than 200 antiliquor organizations were active, and by 1830, temperance reform "constituted a burgeoning national movement" [9]. In the 1840s, the Washington Temperance Societies conducted revival-style meetings to encourage similar pledges. These groups viewed the nation's growing cities, filled with newly arriving Irish, Jewish, and Italian immigrants, as centers of deterioration and wickedness. The alleged propensity of these immigrants to drink heavily was viewed as the driving force behind their supposedly deviant lifestyle. As early as 1846, the state of Maine was persuaded to outlaw alcohol; similar attempts followed elsewhere. However, these efforts were hampered by the Civil War, and despite the passage of many liquor laws, the sale and use of alcohol remained widespread.

The national *Prohibition movement*, also known as the Noble Experiment, was spear-headed by Prohibitionists, who felt that alcohol was a dangerous drug that destroyed lives and disrupted families and communities. Consequently, they believed it was the responsibility of the government to prohibit its sale. Between 1880 and 1890, a new wave of prohibition sentiment swept the evangelical Protestant churches. Organized by the Women's Christian Temperance Union (WCTU), the Anti-Saloon League of America, and the National Prohibition Party, prohibitionists put pressure on their local politicians for an amendment to the U.S. Constitution.

In January 1919, the *Eighteenth Amendment* was passed, outlawing the manufacture and sale of alcohol except for industrial use. Prohibition marked a triumph of morality of middle- and upper-class Americans over the threat posed to their culture by the new Americans [10]. Nine months after the Eighteenth Amendment was passed, it was followed by the passage of the Volstead Act, which provided an enforcement mechanism. The law was sporadically enforced and met with considerable public opposition. In fact, Erich Goode wrote that most Prohibitionists were extremely naïve about both the feasibility of enforcing Prohibition and the impact the Volstead Act would have on drinking and related problems (1993). Soon, bootlegging, speakeasies, and smuggling flourished under the direction and dominance of local gangsters. It was estimated that Chicago had approximately 10,000 speakeasies in operation at any given time during the Prohibition era. Opponents of the law claimed that it was ineffective and that it represented an unnecessary restriction of personal choice. As a result, a massive campaign was mounted to repeal the amendment, which became a reality in 1933 with the ratification of the *Twenty-First Amendment*. Thereafter, the *temperance movement* faded. In Chapter 13, we discuss the policy lessons learned as a result of the Prohibition experience.

Prohibition created a virtual gold mine for crime that made millionaires out of criminals such as Meyer Lansky, Waxey Gordon, Owney Madden, Al Capone, Dutch Schultz, and many others. It affected the lives of many people throughout the country. It tainted politics and corrupted police officers. The stage was now set for one of the most lawless periods in the history of the United States: the *Roaring Twenties*. Despite the newly passed law, no one went thirsty during this period. Flappers, bobbed hair, the Charleston, coonskin coats, the hip flask, and other memorabilia combined to give this period its distinct tone.

It soon became clear to many entrepreneurial criminals that there was a need for an organized infrastructure to handle public demand for alcohol. Factories were needed to produce liquor; a transportation system was needed to deal with bulk shipments; and an importation system capable of dealing with large bulk shipments from England, Cuba, and Canada had to be constructed. This market demand for more complex organization combined with advances in electronic technology that would revolutionize communications to drastically revamp gambling and bring what we now know as organized crime into the modern age.

The Roaring Twenties set the stage for clandestine abuse of alcohol and marijuana in the shadow of Prohibition. Interestingly, the opiate problem—in particular, morphine and heroin—declined in the United States during the 1920s and 1930s until most of the problem was confined to individuals labeled by law enforcement and the powerful as social outcasts in urban areas. After World War I, America's international antidrug efforts continued as both the British and American governments proposed adding The Hague Convention to the Versailles Treaty. The result would mean the addition of domestic laws controlling narcotics. This incorporation resulted in the passing of the British Dangerous Drugs Act of 1920, a law often portrayed as a response to a bustling narcotics problem in Britain. During the 1940s, some Americans suggested that by adopting a medical model and supplying heroin to addicts (rather than relying on law enforcement efforts for drug control), the opiate problem in Britain had almost been eradicated. In fact, Britain had no such problem to begin with. This example illustrates how the desperate need to solve the drug problem in the United States creates misconceptions about a foreign drug predicament.

In the 1930s, partly due to the popularity of marijuana and amphetamines, the Federal Bureau of Narcotics (FBN) was created within the Department of the Treasury. Under the direction of Commissioner Harry Anslinger, the FBN separated the enforcement of alcohol laws from those dealing with other drugs. The FBN was charged with enforcing the Harrison Narcotics Act, among other drug laws, but the responsibility of interdiction remained with the Bureau of Customs. Although marijuana was not included in the Harrison Narcotics Act, the FBN did include an optional provision in the Uniform Narcotic Drug Act, which it extended to the states. During his tenure as bureau commissioner,

THE HISTORY OF HEROIN	
1874	Heroin is isolated from morphine.
1898	The Bayer Company of Germany commercially produces heroin, which is later found to be more potent than morphine.
1900	Heroin is determined to be highly addictive, even though it was originally believed to be a cure for opium addiction.
1914	In the United States, the Harrison Narcotics Act is passed, which restricts the manufacture, importation, and distribution of heroin.
1924	Heroin becomes readily available on the black market, as its manufacture is prohibited.
1930	The French Connection becomes the primary international supplier of heroin to the United States.
1964	The controversial methadone maintenance program is launched to treat opiate addicts.
1970	In the United States, heroin is classified as a Schedule I Narcotic by the Controlled Substances Act.
1985	The United States government estimates that there are 500,000 to 750,000 heroin addicts in the country.
2010	Heroin purity increases as the warring between powerful drug cartels in Mexico escalates.

Anslinger regularly issued reports and wrote books and articles for popular magazines, claiming that while under the influence, marijuana users rob, kill, rape, and chop up their families in a drug-induced frenzy [11]. Consequently, concern about violent crime and the dangers of marijuana grew, and many states passed legislation prohibiting its use.

Post-Prohibition Drug Abuse

By the mid-1930s, national awareness about marijuana use resulted in it being placed on the FBN's enforcement agenda. Unlike opiates and cocaine, marijuana was introduced during a time of intolerance; consequently, it was not until the 1960s (40 years later) that it was widely used. Marijuana was not included in the 1914 Harrison legislation, because at the time it was not considered a particularly dangerous drug.

In an effort to avoid assuming additional responsibilities at the federal level, the FBN had minimized the dangers of marijuana use and failed to support federal marijuana control measures. Instead, in its 1932 annual report, it urged the states to adopt a Uniform State Narcotics Law, which was implemented in 1932. By 1937, the FBN had changed its position. The desire to expand its power, budget, and personnel allocations led the FBN to engage in a scare campaign against marijuana and to support federal controls. Even scientific publications during the time fearfully described marijuana's alleged ominous side effects.

Due to public concern over its increasing popularity for recreational use during Prohibition, when marijuana was a cheap alternative to alcohol, states began passing legislation against its use or possession. Many of the early antimarijuana laws were passed in the western states, where marijuana was linked with Mexican laborers and seen as part of the "Mexican problem." Like the earlier Chinese immigrants, Mexicans had been brought into the United States to work on the farms and ranches of the Southwest in difficult, low-paying jobs not wanted by the white majority. However, as the Great Depression of the 1930s settled over the United States, immigrants became an unwelcome minority linked with violence and the smoking of marijuana. By 1931, "all but two states west of the Mississippi and several more in the east had enacted prohibitory legislation against it" [12].

As a result of increasing public pressure, the FBN supported the federal *Marijuana Tax Act*, which was passed in 1937. This congressional measure was basically a nominal revenue measure patterned after the Harrison Narcotics Act. At the time, however, marijuana had some commercial use in the manufacture of hemp rope, hemp twine, veterinary medicines, and other products. In fact, at the time of the act's passage, it was estimated that there were more than 10,000 acres of marijuana being cultivated in the United States. The Marijuana Tax Act required a substantial transfer tax for all marijuana transactions. The act required that any person whose business was related to marijuana pay a special tax. Additionally, the transference of marijuana had to be pursuant to a written order on a special form issued by the Secretary of the Treasury. The person transferring

THE HISTORY OF MARIJUANA	
c. 2000 b.c.e.	Reference to marijuana found in India.
1545	Hemp is introduced to Chile.
1611	Hemp is cultivated by early settlers in Virginia.
1856	*Putnam's Magazine* publishes an account of Fitzhugh Ludlow's marijuana-consuming experiences.
1875	"Hashish houses" appear and are modeled after Chinese opium dens.
1920	Marijuana use for recreational purposes increases during Prohibition.
1937	The Marijuana Tax Act is passed and outlaws untaxed possession or distribution of marijuana.
1950–1960	Recreational marijuana use spreads on college campuses and in high schools.
1970	The Controlled Substances Act lists marijuana as a Schedule I hallucinogen.
1990	Alaska "recriminalizes" marijuana after 15 years of relaxed marijuana laws.
2012	As of December 2012, 16 states have passed legislation that allows the use of medical marijuana, but they continue to receive national criticism. Also in 2012, the states of Colorado and Washington legalized the recreational use of marijuana.

the marijuana was then required to pay a tax of $1 per ounce if registered, and $100 per ounce if not registered.

The Postwar Era

In addition to marijuana, amphetamines, which were originally prescribed to curb obesity and depression, became popular among students, professionals, and even homemakers who sought the euphoric effects of the drugs. The popularity of amphetamines continued through World War II, partly because they were so easily obtained with a doctor's prescription. As soon as the user market for amphetamines surpassed the legitimate sources of supply, an illicit market was created to meet the demand.

LSD was popularized during the 1940s and 1950s in certain communities. It was initially discovered in 1938 by Albert Hoffman and W.A. Stoll, Swiss chemists who were experimenting with ergot fungus, a parasitic fungus that grows on rye. The use of LSD for mental disorders was widely researched in the 1940s, and was praised by the psychiatric community in the 1950s. Soon, many members of the psychiatric community used LSD for both therapy and recreation. In 1962, Harvard professor Timothy Leary and Richard Alpert began treating inmates at the Massachusetts Correctional Institute with LSD. One year later, under a cloud of scandal, they were relieved of their positions at Harvard. LSD was also tested by the Central Intelligence Agency (CIA) as part of its efforts to find the ultimate "truth serum," and again later in an attempt to find a "mind control" drug. In fact, the CIA administered LSD to unsuspecting, nonconsenting victims, at least one of whom committed suicide.

Use of LSD through most of this time was restricted to a small part of the United States population. More common in the 1950s was the use of marijuana, tranquilizers, and various combinations of drugs. The coffee houses frequented by members of the 1950s' Beat Generation often served as clearinghouses for these drugs. Tranquilizers, ranging from the minor benzodiazepines to more dangerous barbiturates, can produce intoxication similar to that produced by alcohol. Again, the easy availability of tranquilizers via prescription contributed to their abuse. Like many amphetamines, tranquilizers have been available through both legitimate and illicit markets. Mixed drug use, or *polydrug* use, such as taking "uppers" in the morning for energy and "downers" at night to induce sleep, also became more commonplace during the 1950s and 1960s. In addition, some adolescents at this time began experimenting with such drug trends as sniffing glue or paint, occasionally with lethal consequences.

During the 1950s, two major laws were passed: the Boggs Act of 1951 and the Narcotics Control Act of 1956. Essentially, these laws severely increased the penalties for violations of the import-export laws and internal revenue laws relating to marijuana and narcotics. These penalties included mandatory minimum prison sentences along with expanded fines for drug violations.

THE HISTORY OF LSD

1938	LSD is first produced in Basel, Switzerland.
1943	Dr Albert Hoffman accidentally ingests a lysergic acid compound and experiences "fantastic visions." Hoffman later takes LSD purposely to study its effects.
1949–1953	LSD is researched for treatment of mental disorders, alcoholism, and epilepsy.
1962	Drs Timothy Leary and Richard Alpert of the Harvard Center for Research in Human Personality use LSD on inmates at the Massachusetts Correctional Institute.
1963	The illicit market for LSD begins, and different types of LSD appear.
1965	New York is the first state to outlaw LSD.
1967	LSD is reported to damage white blood cells in laboratory studies.
1968	Negative effects of LSD, such as "flashbacks" and "bad trips," are reported.
1968	The popularity of LSD peaks and stabilizes in the late 1960s.
1970–1995	Different forms of LSD, such as blotter, microdot, and windowpane acid, appear on the illicit market.
2002	LSD enjoys a relative stable user market with no notable increases or decreases in use.
2010	LSD remains a Schedule I hallucinogen under United States federal law.

The Turbulent 1960s

The 1960s are notorious for the celebration of drug abuse among youths. This proved to be a watershed decade. The use of most illegal drugs was greeted with increased tolerance, as were a wide range of unconventional behaviors, including the growth of movements opposing the war in Vietnam as well as challenging mainstream American culture; the popularization of rock music and its related lifestyle; the creation of psychedelic art; and enormous media publicity devoted to drugs, drug users, and drug proselytizers. A vigorous drug subculture came into existence. During this time, some social groups viewed drug use in positive terms, evaluated individuals on the basis of whether they used illegal drugs, and believed it a virtue to "turn on" someone who did not use drugs. This subculture proved to be a powerful force in recruiting young people into the use of illegal psychoactive drugs. Never before had drug abuse reached such a large, youthful audience.

In Vietnam, United States soldiers became addicts by the thousands, as had their counterparts in the Civil War. Heroin, marijuana, and hashish were widely available to the armed forces, many of whom, once addicted, turned to drug trafficking. Since the Vietnam War, recreational use of heroin has escalated in the United States, especially in economically depressed inner cities. Controversial methadone clinics opened in 1964 to treat opiate addicts. Although methadone is effective, it is itself a highly addictive narcotic drug (see Chapter 14).

Soon there was a shifting of drugs of choice in the American drug scene. The use of psychedelic substances—such as LSD, MDA (methylenedioxyamphetamine), DMT (*N*-diethyltryptamine), heroin, and marijuana—began in the 1960s and continued to be popular through the early 1970s. By the early 1970s, cocaine was gaining popularity as

FIGURE 2.2 Two American soldiers exchange vials of heroin. Despite an antidrug crackdown, drug use was rampant among American soldiers in Vietnam. *Source: Copyright Bettmann/Corbis/AP Images.*

a recreational drug, but was affordable only to affluent consumers. Despite the end of the Vietnam conflict in the early 1970s and the subsequent calming of the social and political waters, drug abuse failed to wane. The already popular use of PCP increased during this time, along with the newly developed depressant Quaalude (methaqualone). Cocaine was still growing in popularity to the point at which small gold cocaine spoons on necklaces were the rage in some social circles. In fact, during the 1970s, New York's exclusive disco, Studio 54, displayed a dance floor that was decorated with a huge coke spoon. It was rumored that preferred clientele were furnished free samples of the drug. By the end of the 1970s, use of cocaine and its close cousin, methamphetamine, was still gaining momentum. Methamphetamine and other domestic drugs—PCP and LSD—were illegally produced in the United States in an increasing number of clandestine laboratories.

Because of the growing epidemic of drug abuse across the nation, many drug laws were passed in an attempt to control the problem. In 1961, the United Nations adopted the Single Convention on Narcotics Drugs. The Single Convention established regulatory schedules for psychotropic substances and quotas to limit the production and export of licit pharmaceuticals. In 1963, the President's Advisory Commission on Narcotics and Drug Abuse (also known as the Prettyman Commission) recommended a larger role by the federal government in the treatment of drug addicts. Accordingly, the 1963 Community Mental Health Centers Act became law, and provided for federal assistance to nonfederal treatment centers. In 1965, the Drug Abuse Control Amendments were also passed. These brought the manufacture and distribution of amphetamines and barbiturates under federal control, and imposed criminal penalties for illegally manufacturing these drugs. In addition, it created the Bureau of Alcohol and Drug Abuse Control within the Department of Health, Education, and Welfare (HEW), while enabling the HEW secretary to add substances to the controlled list (LSD was added the following year). Toward the end of the 1960s, the 1966 Narcotic Addict Rehabilitation Act created

THE HISTORY OF PCP

1959	PCP is first developed as a disassociative anesthetic for use in surgery.
1960	Medical use of PCP on human patients is discontinued because of violent side effects. Veterinary medicine adopts the use of PCP as an animal tranquilizer.
1965	Recreational use of PCP spreads because of illicit production of the drug.
1970	PCP is sold as "THC" and "cannabinol" on the streets, because people are beginning to associate the drug with negative experiences.
1978	President Jimmy Carter enacts special legislation against PCP.
1980	Clandestine laboratory technology spreads in the manufacture of PCP.
1985	The use of PCP drastically declines with the popularity of crack cocaine.
1990	Criminal cases involving PCP all but disappear from the criminal courts.
2002	PCP begins to re-emerge in larger American cities.
2013	PCP's popularity is moderate at best, but it retains its Schedule II status under United States federal law.

a federal compulsory treatment program and gave financial support to community-based treatment programs. Finally, in 1968, the FBN was transferred to the Justice Department and merged with the Bureau of Drug Abuse Control to form the Bureau of Narcotics and Dangerous Drugs (BNDD).

Late Twentieth-Century Developments

Although media attention to drugs and drug use declined between the late 1960s and late 1970s, the actual use of drugs did not. Numerous surveys point to a strong increase during this period. The late 1970s and early 1980s probably represent another turning point in the recreational use of marijuana, hallucinogens, sedatives, and amphetamines. However, as seen in the previous chapter, studies have shown a considerable drop in the use of most drug types through the 1990s and beyond.

The shift in drug control policy was finalized in 1970 with the passing of the *Controlled Substances Act*, which created a common standard of dangerousness to rank all drugs rather than concentrating on specific substances. It also allowed the scheduling of substances to be done administratively. The year 1970 continued to be an eventful year for drug control legislation, with the passing of the federal Racketeer-Influenced and Corrupt Organizations (RICO) and Continuing Criminal Enterprise (CCE) laws, which were designed to focus on the leaders of large criminal organizations. As discussed in greater detail in Chapter 11, this decade was the catalyst for many modern drug control policy issues and debates.

Finally, in 1972, the issue of decriminalization of marijuana as a policy option was debated by the Presidential Commission on Marijuana and Drug Abuse. This debate sprang from the rising number of persons arrested on marijuana charges during the 1960s

---

PROVISIONS OF THE 1970 CONTROLLED SUBSTANCES ACT

The legal infrastructure to the federal drug control effort is the 1970 Comprehensive Drug Abuse Prevention and Control Act, Title II, which is also known as the Controlled Substances Act (CSA). This federal measure updated all previously existing drug laws and gave uniformity to federal drug control policy. Generally speaking, the CSA's four provisions consist of the following:

- mechanisms for reducing the availability of dangerous drugs;
- procedures for bringing a substance under control;
- criteria for determining control requirements; and
- obligations incurred by international treaty arrangements.

The CSA placed all substances that were in some manner regulated under existing federal law into one of five schedules. The criteria by which drugs are placed in these schedules are theoretically based on the medical use of the substance, its potential for abuse, and safety or addiction (dependence) liability. These five schedules are listed below:

(Continued)

PROVISIONS OF THE 1970 CONTROLLED SUBSTANCES ACT—Cont'd

Schedule I
- The drug or other substance has a high potential for abuse.
- The drug or other substance has no currently accepted medical use in treatment in the United States.
- There is a lack of accepted safety for use of the drug or other substance under medical supervision.

Schedule II
- The drug or other substance has a high potential for abuse.
- The drug or other substance has a currently accepted medical use in treatment in the United States or a currently accepted medical use with severe restrictions.
- Abuse of the drug or other substance may lead to severe psychological or physical dependence.

Schedule III
- The drug or other substance has a potential for abuse less than the drugs or other substances in Schedules I and II.
- The drug or other substance has a currently accepted medical use in treatment in the United States.
- Abuse of the drug or other substance may lead to moderate or low physical dependence or high psychological dependence.

Schedule IV
- The drug or other substance has a low potential for abuse relative to the drugs or other substances in Schedule III.
- The drug or other substance has a currently accepted medical use in treatment in the United States.
- Abuse of the drug or other substance may lead to limited physical dependence or psychological dependence relative to the drugs or other substances in schedule III.

Schedule V
- The drug or other substance has a low potential for abuse relative to the drugs or other substances in Schedule IV.
- The drug or other substance has a currently accepted medical use in treatment in the United States.
- Abuse of the drug or other substances may lead to limited physical dependence or psychological dependence relative to the drugs or other substances in Schedule IV.

In addition, the law imposes nine control mechanisms on the manufacturing, purchasing, and distribution of controlled substances.

and 1970s. This, in conjunction with a growing scientific debate about the dangers of marijuana, generated pressure to reduce penalties for marijuana violations. In fact, not only did the Comprehensive Drug Abuse Prevention and Control Act of 1970 reduce federal penalties for marijuana violations, but also the Carter administration formally advocated legalizing marijuana in amounts up to one ounce. In addition, during the 1970s, 11 states decriminalized penalties for possession of marijuana, although some small penalties were retained. Gallup Polls conducted over several years on relaxation of laws against marijuana are instructive. In 1980, 53 percent of Americans favored legalization of small amounts of marijuana; by 1986, only 27 percent supported that view. At the same time, those favoring penalties for marijuana rose from 43 percent to 67 percent. As a result, many states revised or "recriminalized" their laws relating to marijuana violations, indicating a newfound concern about the potential hazards of the drug, a trend that began in the late 1970s and continues today.

■ ■ Critical Thinking Task ■

Project yourself 35 years into the future. Predict the incidence of drug use, both legal and illegal, in the United States. Discuss the type and availability of drugs in the 2040s and 2050s, any interdiction efforts, internal efforts to deal with the drug problem, and the effects of drugs on future society. Base your prediction on past and current trends.

Hallmarks of drug abuse in the 1980s included the synthesis of drugs and the lifestyles of some music and sports celebrities. Designer drugs such as China White heroin and ecstasy (MDMA) are potentially deadly synthetic substances similar to opiates and hallucinogens. However, in some areas, they may be technically legal because they can be produced without certain illegal chemical analogs. Crack, a freebase form of cocaine, was developed around this time and provided a potent but cheap alternative to cocaine. The crack and methamphetamine markets of the 1980s spawned an upsurge in organized crime. Newcomers to the drug trade included such youth gangs as the Crips and Bloods, as well as Jamaican gangs known as *posses*. Many cities across the United States are now terrorized by the drug-related violence of such gangs. This in turn provided a basis for much media and entertainment industry attention. One example is the 1988 film *Colors*, which portrays the violence of inner-city youth gangs involved in the drug trade.

Meanwhile, many top athletes were turning to anabolic steroids, which build muscle, to maintain a competitive edge. Mass disqualification of athletes thought to be using steroids dominated the coverage of the Pan Am games in Caracas, Venezuela, in 1983. In 1988, Ben Johnson gained notoriety but lost an Olympic gold medal due to his use of steroids. Other drugs ruined the lives of other celebrities. Comedian John Belushi died in 1983 as a result of respiratory complications from the use of cocaine mixed with heroin, a concoction called a *speedball*. The deaths of two athletes in June 1985 helped bring home the tragedy of cocaine. Len Bias had been drafted by the Boston Celtics; he celebrated his draft by using cocaine and died of cardiac arrest as a result of the drug and a pre-existing heart ailment. Football star Don Rogers also died that month from cocaine poisoning.

As drug use increased among American youths, so did drug education programs aimed at curbing the problem. Former First Lady Nancy Reagan's "Just Say No" campaign was subjected to ridicule by those who accused it of being simplistic and unrealistic, while supporters defended it as a commonsense prevention strategy that focused on potential first-time users rather than hardcore street addicts. Despite lukewarm support for programs such as "Just Say No," the public became more intolerant of drug-related tragedies. This public outrage finally resulted in the controversial drug testing of air traffic controllers, train engineers, bus drivers, and other employees whose jobs were associated with public safety.

The medical cover story of the 1990s—acquired immune deficiency syndrome (AIDS)—helped clarify the association between drug use and public safety. Among the high-risk groups for AIDS, a lethal, infectious disease for which there is currently no cure, are intravenous drug users such as heroin addicts. Because of the nature of heroin abuse and the illegality of heroin, activity commonly takes place in secluded settings, such as urban "shooting galleries" where the sharing of hypodermic syringes (also illegal in most jurisdictions) has become commonplace. American recreational drug use thrived in the 1980s, but not as a result of ignorance about the drugs themselves. Indeed, no society has been more aware of the tragic price paid for substance abuse.

As of 2000, the number of drug abusers had declined by almost 50 percent from the 1979 high of 25 million—a decrease that represents an extraordinary change of behavior [13]. Despite that drop, statistics reveal that almost one-third of all Americans aged 12 and older have used an illicit drug. As of the preparation of this book, the primary drugs of abuse are marijuana, cocaine, heroin, and methamphetamine. However, club drugs such as MDMA (ecstasy) and OxyContin have achieved considerable popularity, especially among youths.

Although in 2013 drug abuse is still at an unacceptably high level, it does not approach the emergency situation of the 1970s and 1980s. As drug use declined during the 1990s, national attention also faded. Consequently, disapproval of drugs and the perception of risk by young people have also declined over the last three decades [14]. On the forefront, a number of drug abuse challenges are becoming more and more prevalent. These include the abuse of drugs such as bath salts, K2 and Spice, Ritalin, nitrous oxide (which is administered with balloons, known as "whippets"), the hallucinogen DMT, and antienergy drinks such as *Four Loko* that advocate "relaxation in a can" but can contain sedatives. As with all things in the realm of drug abuse, once one trend subsides, predictably, another presents itself.

The Twenty-First Century and Beyond

It is difficult to speculate about the future of recreational drug use in our society because of the ever-changing social climate. As history has proven, the basis for social acceptance of some drugs and not others is neither rational nor consistent. Should certain drugs be authorized by law for recreational use? If lawfully sanctioned, under what circumstances should drug use be permitted? Given the high incidence of drug-related crime and drug-related health problems, can we responsibly consider the legalization of any dangerous substance? Or have the health problems associated with drug abuse and the ancillary crime associated with drug trafficking in the illicit market become so dangerous that a post-Prohibition (focus on treatment and prevention) approach is required?

It appears that the customary use of products containing legal drugs, such as coffee and tobacco, as well as certain over-the-counter drugs, will continue indefinitely. Alcohol use will undoubtedly continue despite initiatives on community, state, and national levels for curbing many of the dysfunctional aspects of alcohol abuse. Illicit consumption of substances such as marijuana and cocaine will most likely continue, but to what extent is questionable. Perhaps public education and prevention programs in the future will meet the challenge of informing drug users and prospective drug users of the dangers of these substances. In addition, it is likely that continued research will provide insight into the psychological and physiological effects of these drugs. Based on the advances in chemical technology, clandestine drug manufacturers will probably conceive new ways to increase the potency of drugs and reduce the retail price.

Responsibility for combating the drug problem in the future will rest with governmental functions such as law enforcement, treatment and prevention programs, as well as the court and correctional systems. Others who must share in this responsibility include parents, teachers, and community leaders. Only through this multidisciplinary approach can the incidence of drug abuse and drug-related crime be reduced and ultimately abolished.

Summary

Of all the social phenomena affecting public health and safety, it is clear that drug abuse has superseded all other forms of widespread social deviance. There is much agreement that drugs can cause severe social problems, and that some drugs are less harmful than others. However, there is little agreement as to which drugs are less harmful and to what extent they should be tolerated.

Cannabis and the opium poppy have been generally accepted as the oldest mind-altering drugs of abuse, since historic records of their use date back some 7,000 years. Further, these two drugs have been associated with both medical treatment and recreational uses. Regional origins include South America for the coca plant; North America for alcohol, tobacco, and peyote; and Mexico, Southeast Asia, Southwest Asia, and China for opium and cannabis.

Before the late 1800s, drugs were, for the most part, legal and readily available. During and after the Civil War, morphine was widely used and abused as a painkiller. Toward the end of the nineteenth century, "cures" for morphine addiction were developed. For example, cocaine (1878) and heroin (1898), both thought to be nonaddictive antidotes for morphine addiction, were synthesized during the last quarter of the century. Other drugs, such as barbiturates and amphetamines, were also developed around the turn of the twentieth century and have proven to be some of the most widely abused drugs in history. Concern about the use of opiates led to the passing of several pieces of federal legislation, such as the 1914 Harrison Narcotics Act. This comprehensive act exemplified national concern over the abuse of coca- and opiate-based drugs. The Harrison Act marked one of the first laws to break away from the era of legalized drugs into a period of regulation. The public perception of drugs grew increasingly negative while drug abuse expanded during the early to mid-1900s, leading public policy into an attitude of prohibition. Although Prohibition (1920–1933) was designed to reduce alcohol consumption, it inadvertently resulted in an increase of marijuana use. Along with this increase was an escalation in the clandestine abuse of other drugs, such as cocaine and heroin. Although alcohol prohibition failed to last, other drugs became controlled more often, as evidenced by the passing of the Marijuana Tax Act in 1937.

PCP was synthesized in the late 1950s. The drug ultimately proved to be harmful to human patients, but was successful as a general anesthetic for animals. Shortly thereafter, LSD, originally developed in 1938, was studied by Harvard professor Timothy Leary and became one of the first widely used recreational "psychedelic" drugs. Much social and political unrest—civil rights protests, race riots, the women's liberation movement, and demonstrations against 3,4-methylenedioxy-N-methylamphetamine involvement in Vietnam—marked the era of the 1960s. Abuse of drugs, including cocaine, marijuana, amphetamines, LSD, and PCP, continued to flourish during this period, resulting in the passing of the 1970 Controlled Substances Act, which specified all drugs that were to be considered unlawful.

As the 1970s approached, however, the harmful effects of illicit drugs were downplayed by the media and entertainment industry as certain drugs such as cocaine achieved an elevated status among drug users. To supply the growing numbers of drug users, many entrepreneurial drug chemists began to cook their own batches of drugs, including methamphetamine and PCP. By the early 1980s, there was a significant increase in clandestine laboratory technology, which continues to spread across the United States. Designer drugs such as China White heroin and MDMA (ecstasy) are illicit drugs that were popularized during the 1980s. Each of these also represents innovative clandestine laboratory advances by domestic criminals entering the illicit drug market.

The drug-using population of the 1980s also witnessed the genesis of crack—a potent, freebase form of cocaine. The popularity of crack created a great profit margin, which lured many new organized crime groups into the drug trade. Competition over cities and neighborhoods as sales turf by street gangs and organized crime groups has thus become a primary concern of policy makers in the twenty-first century.

Do you recognize these terms?

- Controlled Substances Act
- Eighteenth Amendment
- Harrison Narcotics Act
- Marijuana Tax Act
- opium wars
- polydrug use
- Prohibition
- Roaring Twenties
- temperance movement
- Twenty-First Amendment

Discussion Questions

1. Discuss China's role in global drug addiction and how that country attempted to deal with its own opium problem.
2. Discuss the early historical (both medical and recreational) use of cannabis.
3. How has the historical use of opium in China affected drug abuse in the United States today?
4. Discuss the American Civil War's unique association with the drug morphine.
5. Discuss the first antidrug law passed in the United States and the circumstances surrounding it.
6. Compare the drug abuse climate in the United States before and after the passage of Prohibition.
7. List the elements of the 1960s and early 1970s that possibly accelerated drug use during that time.

References

[1] Musto, D. (1991). Opium, cocaine, and marijuana in American history. *Scientific American.* (July), 40–47.
[2] Ibid.
[3] O'Brien, R., & Cohen, S. (1984). *The encyclopedia of drug abuse.* New York: Facts on File.
[4] Musto, D. (1991). Opium, cocaine, and marijuana in American history. *Scientific American.* (July), 40–47.
[5] Ibid.
[6] Ibid.
[7] Ibid.
[8] Ibid.
[9] Lender, M. E., & Martin, J. K. (1987). *Drinking in America: A history.* New York: Free Press.
[10] Gusfield, J. R. (1963). *Symbolic crusade: Status politics and the American Temperance Movement.* Urbana: University of Illinois Press.
[11] Goode, E. (1993). *Drugs in American society* (4th ed.). New York: McGraw-Hill.
[12] President's Commission on Organized Crime. (1986). *America's habit: Drug abuse, drug trafficking and organized crime.* Washington, DC: U.S. Government Printing Office.
[13] Office of National Drug Control Policy. (2001). *The national drug control strategy, 2001 annual report.* Washington, DC: U.S. Government Printing Office.
[14] Luntz Research. (1996). *National survey on American attitudes on substance abuse II, teens and their parents.* New York: Center on Addiction and Substance Abuse.

3

Drug Abuse and Pharmacology

This chapter will enable you to:

- Understand the meaning of the term *drug abuse*
- Discover reasons why people take drugs
- Realize the various social forums in which drugs are taken
- Learn the pharmacology of popular drugs of abuse
- Identify the effects of drugs on the drug user

The literature on drug identification and pharmacology is rich with varying opinions, but not much is really known about drugs' effects on the human physiology. For example, drugs such as alcohol and cocaine often affect different users in different ways. Not only do the user's moods differ from one drug to another, but the development of tolerance and addiction differs from one user to the next as well. In this chapter, we examine those drugs that are currently not only popular, but also potentially hazardous in society. We also study legal distinctions and categories of drugs, as well as the effects those drugs have on those who use them.

Defining Drugs

To some, attempting to define the word *drug* might seem absurd, since it is such a commonly used word in our everyday lives. Today, though, the word seems to serve as a catch-all for just about any medicinal or chemical substance. In fact, it refers to both dangerous substances, such as lysergic acid diethylamide (LSD), which is illegal to possess and has no medicinal use, and more benign substances, such as aspirin and nonprescription cold remedies. *Webster's Dictionary* attempts to define the word *drug* in a general sense as "a substance used by itself or a mixture in the treatment or diagnosis of disease." Although somewhat comprehensive, this definition still fails to recognize the use of drugs for applications other than the treatment of disease, such as recreational use. Therefore, at the risk of oversimplification, a more practical definition might be as follows:

> *A drug is any chemical you take that affects the way your body works. Alcohol, caffeine, aspirin, and nicotine are all drugs. A drug must be able to pass from your body into your brain. Once inside your brain, drugs can change the messages your brain cells are sending to each other, and to the rest of your body. They do this by interfering with your brain's own chemical signals: neurotransmitters that transfer signals across synapses.*

Certainly, most drug use in accordance with a legitimate medical problem is not only lawful but also appropriate, yet the word *drug* actually encompasses a much broader scope of definition. We could, therefore, recognize as a drug any substance that alters the user's physiological or psychological state, whether that substance is used for medicinal or nonmedical use.

Drug abuse is another term randomly discussed in substance abuse literature. Just exactly what does it mean? To some, drug abuse may refer to the taking of any illicit drug or the overuse of prescribed drugs. For others, drug abuse is illicit drug use that results in social, economic, psychological, or legal problems for the drug user. The Bureau of Justice Statistics (1991) describes drug abuse as the use of prescription-type psychotherapeutic drugs for nonmedical purposes or the use of illegal drugs.

Why Study Drug Abuse and Addiction?

As we learned in Chapter 1, abuse and addiction to alcohol, nicotine, and illegal substances cost Americans upward of half a trillion dollars a year, considering their combined medical, economic, criminal, and social impact. Every year, abuse of illicit drugs and alcohol contributes to the deaths of more than 100,000 Americans, while tobacco is linked to an estimated 440,000 deaths per year [1]. The Centers for Disease Control reported that in 2008 more than 36,000 people died as a result of prescription drug overdoses (Centers for Disease Control, 2011). People of all ages suffer the harmful consequences of drug abuse and addiction. These include the following:

- *Babies* exposed to legal and illegal drugs in the womb may be born premature and underweight. This drug exposure can slow the child's intellectual development and affect behavior later in life.
- *Adolescents* who abuse drugs often act out, do poorly academically, and drop out of school. They are at risk of unplanned pregnancies, violence, and infectious diseases.
- *Adults* who abuse drugs often have problems thinking clearly, remembering, and paying attention. They often develop poor social behaviors as a result of their drug abuse, and their work performance and personal relationships suffer.
- *Parents*' drug abuse often means chaotic, stress-filled homes, and child abuse and neglect. Such conditions harm the well-being and development of children in the home, and may set the stage for drug abuse in the next generation.

Drugs, the Brain, and Addiction

We know generally in what ways drugs affect the user. However, the pharmacological mechanisms through which some drugs exert their effects are only partially understood.

Doctors call a drug addictive if it makes the user dependent on the drug. Unpleasant withdrawal symptoms appear unless the drug is taken. Addictive drugs also make the user crave them—there is an overwhelming urge to continue taking the drug, even after withdrawal symptoms have disappeared. Addiction is similar to other diseases, such as heart disease, in that both disrupt the normal, healthy functioning of the underlying organ; have serious harmful consequences; are preventable and treatable; and, if left untreated, can last a lifetime.

Researchers have identified locations and substances in the brain that are closely associated with the effects of drugs and their reinforcement properties. Although the process is complex, the so-called neurotransmitter *dopamine* appears to play an important role in determining the effects of drugs such as cocaine and heroin. For example, cocaine acts on the pleasure center of the brain to the extent that in some people, particularly those with personality disorders already in place, cocaine becomes more important and pleasurable than some of the most basic human needs such as food, sex, or exercise. Normally, dopamine is released by nerve centers and is then withdrawn. In the case of cocaine, dopamine continues to be transmitted, significantly raising the blood pressure and increasing the heart rate.

How central is dopamine's role in the brain? Scientists are still trying to find an answer to that question, but what they do know is that it is no accident that people are attracted to drugs. Simply stated, when some drugs of abuse are taken, they can release 2–10 times the amount of dopamine that natural rewards do. In some cases, this occurs almost immediately (as when drugs are smoked or injected), and the effects can last much longer than those produced by natural rewards. The resulting effects on the brain's pleasure circuit dwarf those produced by naturally rewarding behaviors such as eating and sex [2]. The effect of such a powerful reward strongly motivates people to take drugs again and again. This is why scientists sometimes say that drug abuse is something we learn to do very, very well.

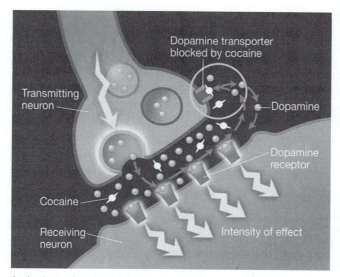

FIGURE 3.1 Cocaine in the brain: In the normal communication process, dopamine is released by a neuron into the synapse, where it can bind to dopamine receptors on neighboring neurons. Normally, dopamine is then recycled back into the transmitting neuron by a specialized protein called the dopamine transporter. If cocaine is present, it attaches to the dopamine transporter and blocks the normal recycling process, resulting in a buildup of dopamine in the synapse, which contributes to the pleasurable effects of cocaine. *Source: NIDA Research Report Series, Cocaine Abuse and Addiction, September 2010.*

The major drugs of abuse—such as narcotics (such as heroin) or stimulants (such as cocaine or methamphetamine)—mimic the structure of neurotransmitters, the most powerful mind-altering drugs the human body creates. Neurotransmitters underlie every thought, emotion, memory, and learning process. They carry the signals between all the nerve cells (or neurons) in the brain. Among some 50 neurotransmitters discovered to date, at least six, including dopamine, are known to play a role in addiction [3].

At a purely chemical level, every experience that people find enjoyable—whether listening to music, embracing a lover, or savoring chocolate—amounts to little more than an explosion of dopamine. Dopamine, though, like most biologically important molecules, must be kept in strict bounds. Too little dopamine in certain areas of the brain triggers the tremors and paralysis of Parkinson's disease. Too much causes the hallucinations and bizarre thoughts of schizophrenia [4]. Probably the most significant breakthrough in addiction came in 1975, when psychologists Roy Wise and Robert Yokel at Montreal's Concordia University reported on the behavior of drug-addicted rats. One day the rats were placidly dispensing cocaine and amphetamines to themselves by pressing a lever attached to their cages, and the next they were banging at the lever with frantic persistence. The reason was that the scientists had injected the rats with a drug that blocked the action of dopamine. In the years following, evidence has mounted regarding dopamine's role in drug addiction.

We also know that drug abuse may be a symptom of a larger problem. For example, people with certain psychiatric disorders may be prone to drug abuse. Alcohol and other drug problems often occur along with other psychiatric disorders. Those with drug problems frequently have affective, anxiety, or personality disorders. Sometimes, however, the reverse is also true. One example of this is the self-medication hypothesis. In this case, a person who is depressed may use drugs to elevate his or her mood, or a person who is suffering severe anxiety may seek relief through the relaxing effects of certain drugs. In other cases, people who are addicted to one drug may seek to counter that drug's effects by taking another drug with opposite effects. This polydrug use may result in an overdose, or even the death of the user, depending on the mixture of drugs taken.

Side Effects

Adding to the dangers of substance abuse is the reality that drugs alter people's behavior. Psychoactive drugs alter people's moods, perceptions, attitudes, and emotions. As a result, concern is often expressed about the impact of drug use on work, family, and social relations. Another concern is that many drugs provide the user with unintended side effects. Although some of these side effects may be short-term and relatively harmless in nature, some have just the opposite effect. Heroin users, for example, initially take the drug for its euphoric effects, but they soon discover that euphoria is also accompanied by nausea, constricted pupils, and respiratory depression. Cannabis products such as marijuana and hashish can result in memory loss and disorientation. Users of hallucinogens such as LSD often complain of bad hallucinations and imagined flashbacks. Just exactly what constitutes the effects of any particular drug depends on a number of factors, such as the mood of the user and how the drugs are taken. A good example is cocaine, a drug that usually elevates one's mood. In users who are depressed prior to drug consumption, however, a deeper depression may result. In addition, after the initial effects of the drug wear off, cocaine users experience anxiety, depression, fatigue, and an urge for more cocaine. Drug users will often look to drugs such as those in the stimulant family to enhance their intellectual or physical performance. Because these drugs increase one's alertness, there is a perception of improved performance, but in reality the user experiences severe fatigue and a reduced capacity for learning, which can offset any physical improvements caused by the drugs.

How Drugs Work in the Brain

Drugs are chemicals. They work in the brain by tapping into the brain's communication system and interfering with the way that cells normally send, receive, and process information. Some drugs, such as marijuana and heroin, can activate neurons because their chemical structure mimics that of a natural neurotransmitter. This similarity in structure "fools" receptors and allows the drugs to lock onto and activate the nerve cells. Although these drugs mimic brain chemicals, they do not activate nerve cells in the same way as a natural neurotransmitter, and they lead to abnormal messages being transmitted through the network.

Other drugs, such as amphetamine or cocaine, can cause the nerve cells to release abnormally large amounts of natural neurotransmitters or prevent the normal recycling of these brain chemicals. This disruption produces a greatly amplified message, ultimately disrupting communication channels. The difference in effect can be described as the difference between someone whispering into your ear and someone shouting into a microphone.

Brain reward (dopamine) pathways

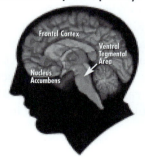

These brain circuits are important for natural rewards such as food, music, and sex.

Drugs of abuse increase dopamine

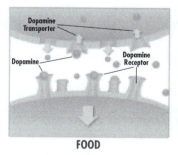
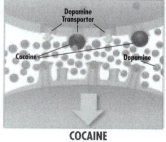

Typically, dopamine increases in response to natural rewards such as food. When cocaine is taken, dopamine increases are exaggerated, and communication is altered.

FIGURE 3.2 Drugs of abuse target the brain's pleasure center. *Source: NIDA Research Report Series,* Drugs, brains, and behavior: The science of addiction, *August 2010.*

Most drugs of abuse directly or indirectly target the brain's reward system by flooding the circuit with dopamine. Dopamine is a neurotransmitter present in the regions of the brain that regulate movement, emotion, cognition, motivation, and feelings of pleasure. Overstimulation of this system, which rewards our natural behaviors, produces the euphoric effects sought by people who abuse drugs and teaches them to repeat the behavior.

Effects of Drug Abuse

To best understand the many different drugs abused on our streets, we should first consider some clinical terms commonly associated with drug abuse. These terms define the predominant effects of drugs and are generally associated with the most dangerous drugs of abuse:

- *Physical dependence (or physiological dependence).* A growing tolerance of a drug's effects so that increased intake of the drug is needed in order to prevent withdrawal symptoms.
- *Psychological dependence.* A controversial term that generally means a craving for or compulsive need to use drugs, because they provide the user with a feeling of well-being and satisfaction. However, attempts to equate physical dependence or addiction with psychological dependence are highly questionable because psychological dependence may be developed for any activity, from listening to rock music to enjoying sex.
- *Tolerance.* A situation in which the user continues regular use of a drug and must administer progressively larger doses to attain the desired effect, thereby reinforcing the compulsive behavior known as drug dependence.
- *Withdrawal.* The physical reaction of bodily functions that, when a body is deprived of an addictive drug, causes increased excitability of the bodily functions that have been depressed by the drug's habitual use.

We should note that psychological dependence is subjective and difficult to define, but is characterized by a person's compulsive need to use drugs. Furthermore, the extent to which drugs produce physical dependence will vary. Heroin, for instance, has an extremely high potential for physical dependence. In comparison, cocaine is not addictive in the same way as heroin, but its potential for psychological dependence is high in some people, particularly those with obsessive personality traits—especially when the cocaine used is in the form of crack, because of the intense initial dose in the vapor. This variation in the potential for physical dependence is one reason for the scheduling of drugs under federal and state laws (see Chapter 11).

Factors Contributing to Addiction

At first, people may perceive what seem to be positive effects with drug use. They also may believe that they can control their use; however, drugs can quickly take over their lives.

Consider how a social drinker can become intoxicated, put himself behind a wheel, and quickly turn a pleasurable activity into a tragedy for him and others. Over time, if drug use continues, pleasurable activities become less pleasurable, and drug abuse becomes necessary for abusers to simply feel "normal." Drug abusers reach a point where they seek and take drugs despite the tremendous problems caused for themselves and their loved ones. Some individuals may start to feel the need to take higher or more frequent doses, even in the early stages of their drug use.

The initial decision to take drugs is mostly voluntary. However, when drug abuse takes over, a person's ability to exert self-control can become seriously impaired. Brain-imaging studies from drug-addicted individuals show physical changes in areas of the brain that are critical to judgment, decision-making, learning and memory, and behavior control. Scientists believe that these changes alter the way the brain works, and may help explain the compulsive and destructive behaviors of addiction.

No single factor determines whether a person will become addicted to drugs. The overall risk for addiction is impacted by the biological makeup of the individual—it can even

A CLOSER LOOK: ENVIRONMENTAL FACTORS THAT INCREASE THE RISK OF ADDICTION

Research has shown that a number of factors can contribute to one's susceptibility to become addicted to a drug. These include the following:

- *Home and Family.* The influence of the home environment is usually most important in childhood. Parents or older family members who abuse alcohol or drugs or who engage in criminal behavior can increase children's risks of developing their own drug problems.
- *Peer and School.* Friends and acquaintances have the greatest influence during adolescence. Drug-abusing peers can sway even those without risk factors to try drugs for the first time. Academic failure or poor social skills can put a child further at risk for drug abuse.
- *Early Use.* Although taking drugs at any age can lead to addiction, research shows that the earlier a person begins to use drugs, the more likely they are to progress to more serious abuse. This may reflect the harmful effects that drugs can have on the developing brain; it also may result from a constellation of early biological and social vulnerability factors, including genetic susceptibility, mental illness, unstable family relationships, and exposure to physical or sexual abuse. Still, the fact remains that early use is a strong indicator of problems ahead, among them substance abuse and addiction.
- *Method of Administration.* Smoking a drug or injecting it into a vein increases its addictive potential. Both smoked and injected drugs enter the brain within seconds, producing a powerful rush of pleasure. However, this intense "high" can fade within a few minutes, taking the abuser down to lower, more normal levels. It is a starkly felt contrast, and scientists believe that this low feeling drives individuals to repeated drug abuse in an attempt to recapture the high pleasurable state.

Source: National Institute on Drug Abuse (2010). *Drugs, brains and behavior: The science of addiction.* U.S. Department of Health and Human Services, August.

be influenced by gender or ethnicity, his or her developmental stage, and the surrounding social environment (e.g., conditions at home, at school, and in the neighborhood). Scientists estimate that genetic factors account for between 40 and 60 percent of a person's vulnerability to addiction, including the effects of environment on gene expression and function. Adolescents and individuals with mental disorders are at greater risk of drug abuse and addiction than the general population.

Dependence versus Abuse

When addressing the task of understanding the many different drugs that have been popularized on the street, perhaps we should first consider certain clinical terms and definitions commonly associated with drugs and drug use. These terms define certain predominant effects of drugs, and are generally associated with those drugs that are considered the most dangerous.

To begin, we should note that drug abuse can be described in many different ways. Generally, however, the pathological use of substances that affect the central nervous system (CNS) falls into two main categories: substance dependence and substance abuse. Let's look closer at these two terms. The fourth edition of the *Diagnostic and Statistical Manual of Mental Disorders* (DSM-IV-TR), published by the American Psychiatric Association in 2000, outlines the criteria for *substance dependence* as the presence of three or more of the following symptoms occurring at any time in the same 12-month period:

1. *Tolerance*, as defined by either of the following:
    (a) A need for markedly increased amounts of the substance to achieve intoxication or the desired effect
    (b) A markedly diminished effect with continued use of the same amount of the substance
2. *Withdrawal*, as manifested by either of the following:
    (c) The characteristic withdrawal syndrome for the substance
    (d) The same, or a closely related, substance is taken to relieve or avoid withdrawal symptoms.
3. The substance is often taken in larger amounts or over a longer period than was intended.
4. There is a persistent desire or unsuccessful efforts to cut down or control substance use.
5. A great deal of time is spent in activities necessary to obtain the substance (e.g., visiting multiple doctors or driving long distances), use the substance (e.g., chain smoking), or recover from its effects.
6. Important social, occupational, or recreational activities are given up or reduced because of substance use.
7. The substance use is continued despite knowledge of having a persistent or recurrent physical or psychological problem that is likely to have been caused or exacerbated by the substance (e.g., current cocaine use despite recognition of cocaine-induced depression, or continued drinking despite recognition that an ulcer was made worse by alcohol consumption) [5].

Substance abuse is another term commonly used both in conversation and in the literature of drug abuse. It has also been defined by the DSM-IV-TR. Substance abuse differs from substance dependence in that it is a less severe version of dependence. In short, abuse is diagnosed when the person's use of a substance is maladaptive, but not severe enough to meet the diagnostic criteria for dependence [6]. Understanding these terms helps us not only categorize drugs, but also recognize abnormal behavior that often accompanies drug use.

Drug Categories

To better understand the various types of drugs and their effects, a system of categories has been generally recognized. Each of these seven categories (stimulants, depressants, hallucinogens, narcotics, cannabis, steroids, and inhalants) may contain both legal and controlled substances. Each substance possesses unique characteristics. We discuss these categories next.

Stimulants

Stimulants, also known as *uppers*, reverse the effects of fatigue on both mental and physical tasks. Two commonly used stimulants are nicotine, which is found in tobacco products, and caffeine, an active ingredient in coffee, tea, some soft drinks, and many nonprescription medicines. Used in moderation, these substances tend to relieve malaise and increase alertness. Although the use of these products has been an accepted part of American culture, the recognition of their adverse effects has resulted in a proliferation of caffeine-free products and efforts to discourage cigarette smoking.

A CLOSER LOOK: DEPENDENCE VERSUS ADDICTION

Physical dependence occurs because of *normal* adaptations to chronic exposure to a drug, and it is not the same as addiction. Addiction, which can include physical dependence, is distinguished by compulsive drug seeking and use, despite sometimes devastating consequences.

Someone who is physically dependent on a medication will experience withdrawal symptoms when use of the drug is abruptly reduced or stopped. These symptoms can be mild or severe (depending on the drug), and can usually be managed medically or avoided by using a slow drug taper.

Dependence is often accompanied by tolerance, or the need to take higher doses of a medication to get the same effect. When tolerance occurs, it can be difficult for a physician to evaluate whether a patient is developing a drug problem or has a real medical need for higher doses to control his or her symptoms. For this reason, physicians need to be vigilant and attentive to their patients' symptoms and level of functioning to treat them appropriately.

Source: National Institute of Justice (2011). U.S. Department of Health and Human Services, and National Institute on Drug Abuse, October.

A number of stimulants, however, are under the regulatory control of the U.S. Controlled Substances Act (CSA) of 1970. Some of these controlled substances are available by prescription for legitimate medical use in the treatment of obesity, narcolepsy, and attention deficit disorders. As drugs of abuse, stimulants are frequently taken to produce a sense of exhilaration, enhance self-esteem, improve mental and physical performance, increase activity, reduce appetite, produce prolonged wakefulness, and "get high." They are among the most potent agents of reward and reinforcement that underlie the problem of dependence.

Stimulants are diverted from legitimate channels and are clandestinely manufactured exclusively for the illicit market. They are taken orally, sniffed, smoked, and injected. Smoking, snorting, or injecting stimulants produces a sudden sensation known as a *rush* or a *flash*. Abuse is often associated with a pattern of binge use—sporadically consuming large doses of stimulants over a short period of time. Heavy users may inject themselves every few hours, continuing until they have depleted their drug supply or reached a point of delirium, psychosis, and physical exhaustion. During this period of heavy use, all other interests become secondary to recreating the initial euphoric rush. Tolerance can develop rapidly, and both physical and psychological dependence occur. Abrupt cessation, even after a brief 2–3-day binge, is commonly followed by depression, anxiety, drug craving, and extreme fatigue known as a *crash*.

Therapeutic levels of stimulants can produce exhilaration, extended wakefulness, and loss of appetite. These effects are greatly intensified when large doses of stimulants are taken. Physical side effects, including dizziness, tremor, headache, flushed skin, chest pain with palpitations, excessive sweating, vomiting, and abdominal cramps, may occur as a result of taking too large a dose at one time, or taking large doses over an extended period of time. Psychological effects include agitation, hostility, panic, aggression, and suicidal or homicidal tendencies. Paranoia, sometimes accompanied by both auditory and visual hallucinations, may also occur. Overdose is often associated with high fever, convulsions, and cardiovascular collapse. Because accidental death is partially due to the effects of stimulants on the body's cardiovascular and temperature-regulating systems, physical exertion increases the hazards of stimulant use.

Caffeine

Caffeine plays an important role in understanding drug abuse in many societies around the world. It is a bitter-tasting, odorless chemical that can be either manufactured synthetically or derived from coffee beans, tea leaves, or cola nuts. It was first extracted from coffee in 1820 and from tea leaves in 1827, and it is currently found in cola drinks, cocoa, and some diet pills. As a rule, it acts as a mild stimulant and is generally harmless to people, except for its addictive nature. In larger doses, caffeine is known for causing insomnia, restlessness, and anxiety in users. Physical effects of caffeine include an increase in heart rate and possible irregularities in the heart. In fact, some researchers maintain that heavy coffee drinkers are more prone to develop coronary heart disease [7]. Because caffeine is associated with insomnia, it has been used by many people to postpone fatigue. However, not all the effects of caffeine have proven to be negative. For example, because caffeine decreases blood flow to the brain, it has been used in treating migraine headaches, and physicians have used it to treat poisoning caused by depressants such as alcohol and morphine. Furthermore, studies suggest that it somewhat increases the effectiveness of common analgesics such as aspirin, and helps relieve asthma attacks by widening bronchial airways [8]. Caffeine has probably become the most popular drug in the world and has etched a niche in everyday American life.

Coffee

Of the caffeine drinks that have gained popularity over the centuries, coffee has become an American (and even a global) icon. In 2013, coffee shops and coffee houses proliferate in every community across the nation, and even in many around the world, and serve as popular meeting places for social gatherings. The word *coffee* was derived from the Arabic word *gahweh* (pronounced *kehevh*). People drink it as a morning pick-me-up, as a midday break drink, and as a means to stay alert late at night. As a result of its popularity, the coffee industry is one of the most profitable in the world. In fact, the coffee bean is thought to be the world's most valuable agricultural commodity. Today, the United States remains the top global importer of coffee, although United States per capita coffee consumption ranks only in the top 10, behind most countries in Western Europe and Scandinavia [9].

Coffee, which is native to Ethiopia, has been cultivated and brewed in Arab countries for centuries. The drink was introduced into Europe in the mid-seventeenth century, and plantations in Indonesia, the West Indies, and Brazil soon made coffee cultivation an important element of colonial economies. Today, Latin America and Africa produce most of the world's coffee, with the United States the largest importer and consumer. Coffee's unique flavor is determined not only by the variety, but also by the length of time the green beans are roasted. After roasting, the beans are usually ground and vacuum-packed in cans. Because the flavor of coffee deteriorates rapidly after it is ground or after a sealed can is opened, many coffee drinkers today buy whole roasted beans and grind them at home. Instant coffee, which makes up about one-fifth of all coffee sold, is prepared by forcing an atomized spray of very strong coffee extract through a jet of hot air, evaporating the water in the extract and leaving dried coffee particles that are packaged as instant coffee. Another method of producing instant coffee is freeze drying. Decaffeinated coffee is another popular form of coffee. To make decaffeinated coffee, the green bean is processed in a steam or chemical bath to remove the caffeine, the substance that produces coffee's stimulating effect.

Nicotine

Nicotine is another stimulant found in most societies around the world. Since colonial times, nicotine has maintained a large and prosperous tobacco industry, and despite evidence of its ill effects on health, today it is consumed almost as fast as it is produced.

In the early 1900s, cigarettes were the most common form of taking nicotine. This trend occurred after a series of public health warnings about the dangers of chewing tobacco and its link to tuberculosis. Unaware of the high risks to the lungs, heart, blood, and nervous system, people switched to smoking cigarettes instead of chewing tobacco. In addition, the cigarette industry utilized automatic rolling machines for cigarette production, making them more affordable, and relied on extensive advertising campaigns for mass sales. In 1964, the first surgeon general's report on smoking was issued, titled *Report of the Surgeon General's Advisory Committee on Smoking and Health*. It received mass media coverage and convinced many Americans of the dangers of smoking. In subsequent years, manufacturers produced low-tar and filtered cigarettes, which were touted as being "safer." Finally, during the 1990s, many antismoking campaigns emerged, rallying support for increased numbers of no-smoking areas in public places. In many cities today, smoking has been completely outlawed in stores, restaurants, and workplaces.

■ ■ Critical Thinking Task ■

Assume that you are an attorney whose client, a nonsmoker dying of lung cancer, is suing the tobacco industry for damages inflicted from secondhand smoke. Submit your summation speech to the jury.

In addition to the discomfort experienced by nonsmokers, nicotine has been proven to be an addictive substance creating physical dependence on the part of the smoker. Those who have developed nicotine dependence often must seek specially designed programs to aid them in gradually cutting back on smoking. Nicotine, a colorless, extremely poisonous liquid alkaloid, turns brown on exposure to air. As the most potent ingredient of the tobacco plant, *Nicotiana tabacum*, nicotine is found mainly in the leaves. Nicotine, the addictive substance in the tobacco plant, was named for Jean Nicot, a French ambassador who sent tobacco from Portugal to Paris in 1560. Nicotine's effects on the human body after prolonged use can be devastating. It can affect the human nervous system, causing respiratory failure and general paralysis. It may also be absorbed through the skin. Interestingly, only two or three drops (less than 50 milligrams [mg]) of the pure alkaloid placed on the tongue are rapidly fatal to an adult [10]. A typical cigarette contains 15–20 mg of nicotine, but the actual amount that reaches the bloodstream—and hence the brain—through normal smoking is only about 1 mg. Nicotine is believed to be responsible for most of the short-term effects and many of the long-term effects of smoking, as well as for tobacco smoking's addictive properties. Because of the popularity of filter-tipped cigarettes, nicotine yields have declined by about 70 percent since the 1950s. Nicotine is also produced in quantity from tobacco scraps and is used as a pesticide. When converted to nicotinic acid, a member of the vitamin B group, it is used as a food supplement.

Smoking

Smoking is a common practice in many societies and typically refers to the inhaling of tobacco smoke. Smoking implements include cigarettes, pipes, cigars, bidis, hookahs, vaporizers, and bongs. It has been suggested that smoking-related disease kills one-half of all long-term smokers, but these diseases may also be contracted by nonsmokers. A 2007 report states that about 4.9 million people worldwide each year die as a result of smoking [11].

Despite a 1989 report issued by the United States surgeon general concluding that cigarettes and other forms of tobacco are addictive, and that nicotine is the drug that causes addiction, in 2009 the National Survey on Drug Use and Health reported that an estimated 70.9 million Americans aged 12 or older were current (past-month) users of a tobacco product. More specifically, 59.8 million persons (23.9 percent of the population) were current cigarette smokers, 5.3 percent smoked cigars, 3.5 percent used smokeless tobacco, and 0.8 percent smoked tobacco in pipes [12].

The history of smoking is vast, and concerns about it have existed for years. Native Americans smoked pipes, and European explorers had introduced the practice into the Old World by the early sixteenth century. Controversy over the health effects of smoking have stemmed from that time. Much of this concern is with good cause; cigarette smoke consists of more than 4700 compounds, 43 of which are carcinogens, such as tar [13]. Nicotine is considered the addicting agent that makes quitting smoking so difficult.

By the early 1960s, numerous clinical and laboratory studies on smoking and disease had been conducted. In 1964, a committee appointed by the surgeon general of the U.S. Public Health Service issued a report based on the critical review of previous studies on the effects of smoking. The report concluded that nearly all lung cancer deaths are caused by cigarette smoking, which was also held responsible for many deaths and much disability from various illnesses such as chronic bronchitis, emphysema, and cardiovascular disease. The *Journal of the American Medical Association* has reported that more than 400,000 people die every year from smoking-related diseases—more than from alcohol,

---

HOW COCAINE IS PROCESSED

1. Coca farmers, known as *campesinos*, cultivate plants throughout the Andean region of South America.
2. Depending on the method and variety of coca used, coca plants may take up to 2 years to mature fully.
3. Once harvested, coca leaves are sometimes allowed to dry in the sun to keep the leaves from rotting.
4. Cocaine base processors stomp the coca leaves to macerate the leaves and help extract desired alkaloids.
5. The solution is transferred by bucket to a plastic-lined pit, where lime or cement is added.

crack, heroin, murder, suicide, car accidents, and AIDS combined [14]. A 1984 report by the U.S. Public Health Service also suggested that passive inhalation of smoke by non-smokers (secondhand smoke) could be harmful. Although considered controversial at the time, studies have since confirmed many of these charges [15]. Some experts estimate that passive smoke kills as many as 50,000 Americans a year, and it is the third leading preventable cause of death, behind smoking and drinking. Studies have shown that children are particularly sensitive to passive smoke, and that smoking by pregnant women may harm the fetus [16].

Since 1964, tobacco advertising has been restricted, and health warnings have been mandated for advertisements. Most states in the United States have also passed laws to control smoking in public places such as restaurants and workplaces, where nonsmoking areas may be required. Most American airlines have prohibited smoking on flights lasting 6 hours or less, whereas others have prohibited smoking on all flights. Among the military, the U.S. Army has been particularly strict in imposing smoking restrictions. The tobacco industry and many smokers regard antismoking measures as harassment, whereas many nonsmokers defend the measures on the grounds that the government has a duty to discourage unhealthful practices, that public funds in one form or another become involved in treating diseases caused by smoking, and that smokers pollute the air for nonsmokers.

Quitting smoking is thought to be extremely difficult, especially for chronic smokers. In fact, the Centers for Disease Control and Prevention (CDC) report that 70 percent of regular smokers try to quit, but only 8 percent succeed [17]. In recent years, smoking-withdrawal clinics have become popular, although most people who quit smoking are thought to do it on their own. Nicotine gum and skin patches may be useful tools for quitting the habit. Nicotine gum, which has been around for years, tends to lessen early withdrawal symptoms. Nicotine patches, which are available by prescription, are yet another way to allow the smoker to deal with the behavioral aspects of quitting before confronting the physical effects of nicotine withdrawal.

Cocaine

Cocaine is an intense, euphoria-producing stimulant drug with strong addictive potential. Also called coca, coke, crack, flake, snow, and soda cot, cocaine is usually distributed as a white, crystalline powder. Cocaine is often diluted ("cut") with a variety of substances, the most common of which are sugars and local anesthetics. It is cut to stretch the amount of the product and increase profits for dealers. In contrast, cocaine base (crack) looks like small, irregularly shaped chunks (or rocks) of a whitish solid.

Cocaine is the active alkaloid that is extracted from the leaves of the *Erythroxylum coca* plant, which contains between 0.5 and 1.0 percent cocaine. *Erythroxylon coca* grows in the high Andes region of South America. Chewing the leaves of the plant as a remedy for fatigue, nausea, and altitude sickness has been a custom in the region for as long as written records of human practice exist [18].

EXPOSING TOBACCO ADDICTION: A TIMELINE

1964	The United States surgeon general releases reports concluding that smoking causes lung cancer.
1965	Federal law requires the surgeon general's warnings on cigarette packs.
1980	The surgeon general reports that smoking is a major threat to women's health.
1988	The surgeon general reports that nicotine is an addictive drug.
1990	Smoking is banned on all domestic flights lasting 6 hours or less.
1994	Executives of the seven largest United States tobacco companies swear in congressional testimony that nicotine is not addictive.
1994	Tobacco company executives deny allegations that they manipulate nicotine levels in cigarettes.
1995	President Bill Clinton announces United States Food and Drug Administration (FDA) plans to regulate tobacco for minors.
1997	Tobacco company Liggett concludes a landmark settlement with states that insulates the company from tobacco litigation in return for admitting that cigarettes are addictive.
1997	A federal judge rules that the government can regulate tobacco.
1998	Attorneys general and tobacco companies settle a lawsuit for $246 billion over a 25-year period.
2010	Smoking bans (either state, county, or local) have been enacted covering all bars and restaurants in each of the 60 most populated cities in the United States except for these 16: Arlington, Texas; Atlanta, Fort Worth, Jacksonville, Memphis, Las Vegas, Nashville, New Orleans, Oklahoma City, Philadelphia, St. Louis, Tampa, Tulsa, and Virginia Beach.

The actual word *coca* comes to us from the Aymara Indians, a local tribe living in the area now known as Bolivia, and translates as *plant*. The Aymara were conquered by the Inca in the tenth century. Coca received elevated religious status in the Incan Empire, being used prominently in religious ceremonies, marriages, rites of prophecy, and initiation rituals for *haruaca*, young Incan noblemen. Production and use of coca were tightly regulated in Incan society. Incan rulers restricted production to state-owned plantations, and restricted its use to rituals and as a special gift bestowed on the favored only by Incan royalty. Use among the general population was heavily regulated and restricted [19].

The use of coca was introduced to the general populace only after the Spanish conquest of the Incan Empire. Under an edict issued by King Philip II, coca was made available as a labor-enhancing substance, a food substitute, and an ameliorative for hunger. Social norms that regulated its use among the Inca disappeared with the passage of time under Spanish rule [20].

Coca use and production remained restricted because the plant does not grow in Europe and the harvested leaves lost their efficacy during the long voyage from South America to Europe; it was not until 1750 that botanist Joseph de Tussie able to successfully transfer the first plants to Europe. Nonetheless, coca was highly praised in writings by visitors to South America for its stimulant attributes and its usefulness in easing breathing difficulties at high altitudes [21].

HOW COCAINE WORKS

The exact effects of cocaine on the human body are not quite clear. Research suggests, however, that the physical cyclical effects of cocaine are as follows:

- Upon ingestion, cocaine first enhances, then later interferes with, the transmission of the pleasure signals of the brain. A message is carried across the synapse between the axon of one nerve cell and the body of another by chemicals called *neurotransmitters*.
- Of the neurotransmitters released by cocaine, the most important is *dopamine*. Dopamine fills receptors on the body of the next cell and sparks a continuation of the message.
- Normally, pumps reclaim the dopamine, but according to a leading theory, cocaine blocks this process. Dopamine remains in the receptors, sending an enhanced message before breaking down. Prolonged cocaine use may also deplete dopamine, rendering the sensation of pleasure impossible for the user.

Cocaine as a drug was not isolated from the plant until the mid-nineteenth century. Dr Theodor Aschenbrant, a Bavarian army physician, initiated the first recorded use of cocaine as a medicine, treating asthenia and diarrhea with the drug. In 1859, the Italian physician Dr Paolo Mantegazza published what is probably the earliest tract on cocaine, praising its widespread potential for medical use [22].

It was at about the same time that cocaine began appearing in nonmedicinal substances as well. As discussed in Chapter 2, Angelo Mariani patented the formula for and produced Vin Mariani, a wine containing 6 mg of cocaine per serving. Vin Mariani was used medicinally by some people but was also popular at social events, and it was the preferred drink served at social gatherings hosted by Pope Leo XIII and King William III of England. Another contemporary example of nonmedical use was the inclusion of cocaine in the original formula for Coca-Cola, which was patented in 1886 [23].

Use of cocaine among the literati was common. Sir Arthur Conan Doyle used the drug and made his fictional hero Sherlock Holmes a user who found cocaine useful in sharpening his powers of deduction. Robert Louis Stevenson, it is believed, wrote his novel about Dr Jekyll and Mr Hyde under the influence of the drug. In addition, Alexander Dumas, Jules Verne, and Thomas Edison were acknowledged cocaine users who praised the drug's qualities [24].

Dr W. H. Bentley brought cocaine to the United States as a drug to cure opium, morphine, and alcohol addiction in 1878. Sigmund Freud was both a user and an advocate of cocaine, arguing it was effective in treating depression and morphine addiction. One of Freud's students, Dr Koller, introduced the use of cocaine as a local anesthetic in 1884. The major pharmaceutical firm Parke-Davis was selling cocaine as an additive in cigarettes, an ingredient in an alcohol-based drink called Coca Cordial, a nose spray, a tablet, and an injectable fluid by 1890 [25].

The first signs of medical resistance toward cocaine use appeared between 1885 and 1890. Reports on the negative psychological and physical reactions associated with using cocaine as an antidote to morphine addiction surfaced in the medical literature. Because common medical practice at the time was to treat morphine addiction by combining cocaine and morphine, it is unclear whether these reports actually reflected problems with cocaine, the results of reducing morphine doses to addicts, or problems with combining two drugs with such antagonistic pharmacological properties. An unfortunate side effect of this confusion was the linking of cocaine and morphine in international attempts to control addictive or dangerous drugs, despite their almost opposite qualities and effects. This confusion is one of the reasons why early efforts to regulate cocaine were undertaken.

By 1890, snorting cocaine was quite fashionable among the wealthy and among artists and writers in the United States. Several policies and practices implemented over the next several decades impacted use rates. For instance, in 1906, cocaine was removed as an active ingredient in Coca-Cola, and Novocain was developed and used as a local anesthetic, which led to a reduction in the medicinal use of cocaine. The passage of the Pure Food and Drug Act of 1906 and the Harrison Narcotics Act in 1914 instituted controls on over-the-counter medicines that limited cocaine's availability. Around the same time, personal use of cocaine was criminalized in Europe, but medical use continued until the introduction of amphetamines in the 1930s.

It was not until the 1970s that cocaine resurfaced in the United States, Canada, and Europe as a recreational drug. While very popular, increases in cocaine's use were slowed by its prohibitive price: it sold in the United States for between $100 and $150 per gram. The growth of cocaine use began to accelerate in the mid-1970s and extended into the early 1980s. The legal suppression of amphetamine use, failed United States drug control policies in South America, and the activities of the Central Intelligence Agency-backed paramilitary groups in Central and South America combined to increase availability and reduce the consumer price. By the end of the 1980s, the supply of cocaine in the United States had increased by more than 400 percent, the purity of imported cocaine had more than doubled, and the wholesale price at a port of entry had declined by about 500 percent. Use, while relatively stable in terms of numbers, spread to all strata of American society [26].

In the 1980s, United States intelligence agents working with the Nicaraguan contras in an attempt to overthrow the Nicaraguan government (1) solicited funds for the operation from the Medellín cartel; (2) provided logistical air support for cocaine flights to the United States and allowed the cartels the use of contra landing strips in Costa Rica; (3) arranged State Department payments to companies owned by drug traffickers, ostensibly as part of a humanitarian relief operation; and (4) allowed the contras to deal in large quantities of cocaine themselves. Recent investigations have revealed that a sizeable portion of the cocaine being sold to Los Angeles–based street gangs for the production of crack came from the contras [27].

The principal routes of cocaine administration are oral, intranasal, intravenous, and inhalation. Snorting, or intranasal administration, is the process of inhaling cocaine powder through the nostrils, where it is absorbed into the bloodstream through the nasal tissues. The drug also can be rubbed onto mucous tissues. Injecting, or intravenous

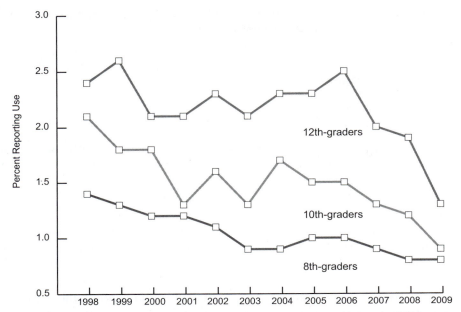

FIGURE 3.3 Trends in 30-day prevalence of cocaine abuse among 8th, 10th, and 12th graders, 1998–2009. *Source: NIDA Research Report Series,* Cocaine abuse and addiction, *September 2010.*

use, releases the drug directly into the bloodstream and heightens the intensity of its effects. Smoking involves inhaling cocaine vapor or smoke into the lungs, where absorption into the bloodstream is as rapid as by injection [28]. This rather immediate and euphoric effect is one of the reasons why crack became enormously popular in the mid-1980s.

Research has led to a clear understanding of how cocaine produces its pleasurable effects, and why it is so addictive. Scientists have discovered regions within the brain that are stimulated by all types of reinforcing stimuli such as food, sex, and many drugs of abuse. One neural system that appears to be most affected by cocaine originates in a region of the midbrain called the ventral tegmental area (VTA). Nerve fibers originating in the VTA extend to a region known as the nucleus accumbens, one of the brain's key areas involved in reward [29]. Animal studies show that rewards increase levels of the brain chemical (or neurotransmitter) dopamine, thereby increasing neural activity in the nucleus accumbens. In the normal communication process, dopamine is released by a neuron into the synapse (the small gap between two neurons), where it binds to specialized proteins (called dopamine receptors) on the neighboring neuron and sends a signal to that neuron. Dopamine is then removed from the synapse to be recycled for further use [30]. Drugs of abuse can interfere with this normal communication process. For example, scientists have discovered that cocaine acts by blocking the removal of dopamine from the synapse, which results in an accumulation of dopamine and an amplified signal to the receiving neurons. This is what causes the initial euphoria commonly reported by cocaine abusers.

Cocaine's effects appear almost immediately after a single dose and disappear within a few minutes to an hour. Taken in small amounts, cocaine usually makes the user feel euphoric, energetic, talkative, and mentally alert, especially to the sensations of sight, sound, and touch. It can also temporarily decrease the need for food and sleep. Some users find that the drug helps them perform simple physical and intellectual tasks more quickly, although others experience the opposite effect.

The duration of cocaine's euphoric effects depends upon the route of administration. The faster the drug is absorbed, the more intense the resulting high, but also the shorter the duration. The high from snorting is relatively slow to arrive, but it may last from 15 to 30 minutes; in contrast, the effects from smoking are more immediate but may last only 5–10 minutes [31].

The short-term physiological effects of cocaine use include constricted blood vessels, dilated pupils, and increased body temperature, heart rate, and blood pressure. Large amounts of cocaine may intensify the user's high, but can also lead to bizarre, erratic, and violent behavior.

Cocaine is derived from coca leaves grown in Bolivia, Peru, and Colombia. The cocaine-manufacturing process takes place in remote jungle laboratories where the raw product undergoes a series of chemical transformations. Colombia produces about 90 percent of the cocaine powder reaching the United States. According to the 2005 Colombia Threat Assessment, 90 percent of the cocaine shipped to the United States comes from the Central America–Mexico corridor [32].

Methamphetamine

Methamphetamine (meth) is a stimulant; its FDA-approved brand name medication is Desoxyn. Methamphetamine continues to be second only to alcohol and marijuana as the drug used most frequently in many western and Midwestern states. Seizures of dangerous laboratory materials have increased dramatically—in some states, fivefold. In response, many special task forces and local and federal initiatives have been developed to target methamphetamine production and use. Legislation and negotiation with earlier source areas for precursor substances have also reduced the availability of the raw materials needed to make the drug.

Methamphetamine comes in many forms and can be smoked, snorted, injected, or orally ingested. The preferred method of methamphetamine abuse varies by geographical region and has changed over time. Smoking methamphetamine, which leads to very fast uptake of the drug in the brain, has become more common in recent years, amplifying methamphetamine's addictive potential and adverse health consequences. Regular meth is available as a pill or powder. Crystal meth resembles glass fragments or shiny blue-white "rocks" of various sizes. On the street, it is referred to as batu, biker's coffee, black beauties, chalk, chicken feed, crank, crystal, glass, go-fast, hiropon, ice, meth, methlies quick, poor man's cocaine, shabu, shards, speed, stove top, Tina, trash, tweak, uppers, ventana, vidrio, yaba, or yellow bam.

A CLOSER LOOK: THE EFFECTS OF MATERNAL COCAINE ABUSE

The full extent of the effects of prenatal cocaine exposure on a child is not completely known, but many scientific studies have documented that babies born to mothers who abuse cocaine during pregnancy are often born prematurely, have low birth weights and smaller head circumferences, and are shorter in length than babies born to mothers who do not abuse cocaine.

Nevertheless, it is difficult to estimate the full extent of the consequences of maternal drug abuse and to determine the specific hazard of a particular drug to the unborn child. This is because multiple factors—such as the amount and number of *all* drugs abused (including nicotine), the extent of prenatal care, possible neglect or abuse of the child, exposure to violence in the environment, socioeconomic conditions, maternal nutrition, other health conditions, and exposure to sexually transmitted diseases—can all interact to impact maternal, fetal, and child outcomes.

Some may recall that "crack babies," or babies born to mothers who abused crack cocaine while pregnant, were at one time written off as a lost generation. They were predicted to suffer from severe, irreversible damage, including reduced intelligence and social skills. It was later found that this was a gross exaggeration. However, the fact that most of these children appear normal should not be overinterpreted to indicate that there is no cause for concern. Using sophisticated technologies, scientists are now finding that exposure to cocaine during fetal development may lead to subtle, yet significant, later deficits in some children, including deficits in some aspects of cognitive performance, information processing, and attention to tasks—abilities that are important for the realization of a child's full potential.

Source: National Institute of Drug Abuse (2009). *Cocaine abuse and addiction*. Washington, DC: U.S. Department of Health and Human Services.

The drug also alters the mood in different ways, depending on how it is taken. Immediately after smoking the drug or injecting it intravenously, the user experiences an intense rush or "flash" that lasts only a few minutes and is described as extremely pleasurable. Snorting or oral ingestion produces euphoria—a high but not an intense rush. Snorting produces effects within 3–5 minutes, and oral ingestion produces effects within 15–20 minutes [33].

As with similar stimulants, methamphetamine most often is used in a "binge-and-crash" pattern. Because the pleasurable effects of methamphetamine disappear even before the drug concentration in the blood falls significantly, users try to maintain the high by taking more of the drug. In some cases, abusers indulge in a form of binging known as a "run," forgoing food and sleep while continuing abuse for up to several days.

As a powerful stimulant, methamphetamine, even in small doses, can increase wakefulness and physical activity, and decrease appetite. Methamphetamine can also cause a variety of cardiovascular problems, including rapid heart rate, irregular heartbeat, and increased blood pressure. Hyperthermia (elevated body temperature) and convulsions may occur with methamphetamine overdose, and, if not treated immediately, can result in death.

Most of the pleasurable effects of methamphetamine are believed to result from the release of very high levels of the neurotransmitter dopamine. Dopamine is involved in motivation, the experience of pleasure, and motor function, and it is a common mechanism of action for most drugs of abuse. The elevated release of dopamine produced by methamphetamine is also thought to contribute to the drug's deleterious effects on nerve terminals in the brain.

Long-term methamphetamine abuse has many negative consequences, including addiction. Addiction is a chronic, relapsing disease, characterized by compulsive drug seeking and use, accompanied by functional and molecular changes in the brain. In addition to being addicted to methamphetamine, chronic abusers exhibit symptoms that can include anxiety, confusion, insomnia, mood disturbances, and violent behavior. They also can display a number of psychotic features, including paranoia, visual and auditory hallucinations, and delusions (e.g., the sensation of insects creeping under the skin). Psychotic symptoms can sometimes last for months or years after methamphetamine abuse has ceased, and stress has been shown to precipitate spontaneous recurrence of methamphetamine psychosis in formerly psychotic methamphetamine abusers [34].

With chronic abuse, tolerance to methamphetamine's pleasurable effects can develop. In an effort to intensify the desired effects, abusers may take higher doses of the drug, take it more frequently, or change their method of drug intake. Withdrawal from methamphetamine occurs when a chronic abuser stops taking the drug; symptoms of withdrawal include depression, anxiety, fatigue, and an intense craving for the drug.

Chronic methamphetamine abuse also significantly changes the brain. Specifically, brain-imaging studies have demonstrated alterations in the activity of the dopamine system that are associated with reduced motor speed and impaired verbal learning. Recent studies in chronic methamphetamine abusers have also revealed severe structural and functional changes in areas of the brain associated with emotion and memory, which may account for many of the emotional and cognitive problems observed in chronic methamphetamine abusers.

Differences between Cocaine and Methamphetamine

Methamphetamine is structurally similar to amphetamine and the neurotransmitter dopamine, but it is significantly different from cocaine. Although these stimulants have similar behavioral and physiological effects, there are some major differences in the basic mechanisms of how they work. In contrast to cocaine, which is quickly removed and almost completely metabolized in the body, methamphetamine has a much longer duration of action and a larger percentage of the drug remains unchanged in the body.

This results in methamphetamine being present in the brain longer, which ultimately leads to prolonged stimulant effects. And although both methamphetamine and cocaine increase levels of the brain chemical dopamine, animal studies reveal much higher levels of dopamine following the administration of methamphetamine due to the different mechanisms of action within nerve cells in response to these drugs. Cocaine prolongs dopamine actions in the brain by blocking dopamine reuptake. Although, at low doses, methamphetamine blocks dopamine reuptake, methamphetamine also increases the release of dopamine, leading to much higher concentrations in the synapse, which can be toxic to nerve terminals [35].

Methcathinone

Methcathinone, known on the streets as "cat," is a structural analog of methamphetamine and cathinone. Clandestinely manufactured, methcathinone is almost exclusively sold in a stable and highly water-soluble hydrochloride salt form. It is most commonly snorted, although it can be taken orally by mixing it with a beverage or diluting it in water and injecting it intravenously. Methcathinone has an abuse potential equivalent to that of methamphetamine, and it produces amphetamine-like effects. It was placed in schedule I of the CSA in 1993.

Methylphenidate

Methylphenidate, a schedule II substance, has a high potential for abuse and produces many of the same effects as cocaine and amphetamines. Unlike other stimulants, methylphenidate has not been produced in clandestine labs, but abuse of this substance has been documented among addicts who dissolve the tablets in water and inject the mixture. Complications arising from this practice are commonly due to the insoluble fillers used in the tablets. When injected, these materials block small blood vessels, causing serious damage to the lungs and retina of the eye. Binge use, psychotic episodes, cardiovascular complications, and severe psychological addiction have all been associated with methylphenidate abuse.

Methylphenidate is used legitimately in the treatment of excessive daytime sleepiness associated with narcolepsy, as is the newly marketed schedule IV stimulant, modafinil (Provigil). However, the primary legitimate medical use of methylphenidate (Ritalin, Methylin, and Concerta) is to treat attention deficit hyperactivity disorder (ADHD) in children. The increased use of this substance for the treatment of ADHD has paralleled an increase in its abuse among adolescents and young adults who either take the tablets orally or crush them and snort the powder to get high. Abusers have little difficulty obtaining methylphenidate from classmates or friends who have been prescribed it.

Anorectic Drugs

A number of drugs have been developed and marketed to replace amphetamines as appetite suppressants. These *anorectic drugs* include benzphetamine (Didrex), diethylproprion (Tenuate and Tepanil), mazindol (Sanorex and Mazanor), phendimetrazine (Bontril and Prelu-2), and phentermine (Lonamin, Fastin, and Adipex). These substances are in schedule III or IV of the CSA and produce some amphetamine-like effects. Of these diet pills, phentermine is the most widely prescribed and the most frequently encountered on the illicit market. Two schedule IV anorectics often used in combination with phentermine—fenfluramine and dexfenfluramine—were removed from the United States market because they were associated with heart valve problems.

Khat

For centuries *khat,* the fresh young leaves of the *Catha edulis* shrub, has been consumed where the plant is cultivated, primarily East Africa and the Arabian Peninsula. There, chewing khat predates the use of coffee and is used in a similar social context. Chewed in moderation, khat alleviates fatigue and reduces appetite. Compulsive use may result in manic behavior with grandiose delusions or in a paranoid type of illness, sometimes accompanied by hallucinations. Khat has been smuggled into the United States and other countries from its source countries for use by immigrants. It contains a number of chemicals, among which are two controlled substances, cathinone (schedule I) and cathine (schedule IV). As the leaves mature or dry, cathinone is converted to cathine, which significantly reduces its stimulatory properties.

Depressants

Historically, people of almost every culture have used chemical agents to induce sleep, relieve stress, and allay anxiety. Though alcohol is one of the oldest and most universal agents used for these purposes, hundreds of substances have been developed that produce central nervous system (CNS) depression. These drugs have been referred to as downers, sedatives, hypnotics, minor tranquilizers, anxiolytics, and antianxiety medications. Unlike most other classes of drugs of abuse, depressants are rarely produced in clandestine laboratories. Generally, legitimate pharmaceutical products are diverted to the illicit market. A notable exception is a relatively recent drug of abuse, gamma hydroxybutyric acid (GHB).

Chloral hydrate and paraldehyde are two of the oldest pharmaceutical depressants still in use today. Other depressants, including gluthethimide, methaqualone, and meprobamate, have been important players in the milieu of depressant use and abuse. However, two major groups of depressants have dominated the licit and illicit market for nearly a century—first barbiturates and now benzodiazepines.

Barbiturates were very popular in the first half of the twentieth century. In moderate amounts, these drugs produce a state of intoxication that is remarkably similar to alcohol intoxication. Symptoms include slurred speech, loss of motor coordination, and impaired judgment. Depending on the dose, frequency, and duration of use, one can rapidly develop tolerance of, as well as physical and psychological dependence on, barbiturates. With the development of tolerance, the margin of safety between the effective dose and the lethal dose becomes very narrow. That is, to obtain the same level of intoxication, the tolerant abuser may raise his or her dose to a level that could result in coma or death.

Although many individuals have taken barbiturates therapeutically without harm, concern about the addictive potential of barbiturates and the ever-increasing number of fatalities associated with them led to the development of alternative medications. Today, fewer than 10 percent of all depressant prescriptions in the United States are for barbiturates.

Benzodiazepines were first marketed in the 1960s. Touted as much safer depressants with far less addiction potential than barbiturates, today these drugs account for about one out of every five prescriptions for controlled substances. Although benzodiazepines produce significantly less respiratory depression than barbiturates, it is now recognized that benzodiazepines share many of their undesirable side effects. A number of toxic CNS effects are seen with chronic high-dose benzodiazepine therapy, including headaches, irritability, confusion, memory impairment, and depression. The risk of developing oversedation, dizziness, and confusion increases substantially with higher doses of benzodiazepines. Prolonged use can lead to physical dependence, even at doses recommended for medical treatment.

Unlike barbiturates, large doses of benzodiazepines are rarely fatal unless combined with alcohol or other drugs. Although primary abuse of benzodiazepines is well documented, abuse of these drugs usually occurs as part of a pattern of multiple drug abuse. For example, heroin or cocaine abusers will use benzodiazepines and other depressants to augment their "high," or alter the side effects associated with overstimulation or narcotic withdrawal.

There are marked similarities among the withdrawal symptoms seen with most drugs classified as depressants. In the mildest form, the withdrawal syndrome may produce insomnia and anxiety, usually the same symptoms that initiated the drug use. With a greater level of dependence, tremors and weakness are also present, and in its most severe form the withdrawal syndrome can cause seizures and delirium. Unlike the withdrawal syndrome seen with most other drugs of abuse, withdrawal from depressants can be life-threatening.

Bath Salts or Designer Cathinones (Synthetic Stimulants)

Synthetic stimulants that are marketed as bath salts are often found in a number of retail products. These synthetic stimulants are chemicals. The chemicals are synthetic derivatives of cathinone, a CNS stimulant, which is an active chemical found naturally in the khat plant. Mephedrone and MDPV (3-4 methylene-dioxypyrovalerone) are two of the designer cathinones most commonly found in these bath salt products. Many of these products are sold over the Internet, in convenience stores, and in "head shops." On the street, bath salts are referred to as bliss, blue silk, cloud nine, drone, energy-1, ivory wave, lunar wave, meow meow, ocean burst, pure ivory, purple wave, red dove, snow leopard, stardust, vanilla sky, white dove, white knight, and white lightning. Bath salt stimulant products are sold in powder form in small plastic or foil packages of 200 and 500 mg under various brand names. Mephedrone is a fine white, off-white, or slightly yellow-colored powder. It can also be found in tablet and capsule form. MDPV is a fine white or off-white powder.

Bath salts are usually ingested by sniffing or snorting. They can also be taken orally, smoked, or put into a solution and injected into veins. People who abuse these substances have reported agitation, insomnia, irritability, dizziness, depression, paranoia, delusions, suicidal thoughts, seizures, and panic attacks. Users have also reported effects including impaired perception of reality, reduced motor control, and decreased ability to think clearly.

Cathinone derivatives act as CNS stimulants causing rapid heart rate (which may lead to heart attacks and strokes), chest pains, nosebleeds, sweating, nausea, and vomiting. Drugs that have similar effects include amphetamines, cocaine, khat, LSD, and MDMA.

These substances are usually marketed with the warning "not intended for human consumption." Any time that users put uncontrolled or unregulated substances into their bodies, the effects are unknown and can be dangerous. On October 21, 2011, the U.S. Drug Enforcement Administration (DEA) published a final order in the *Federal Register* exercising its emergency scheduling authority to control three synthetic stimulants that are used to make bath salts: mephedrone, MDPV, and methylone. This action makes possessing and selling these chemicals, or the products that contain them, illegal in the United States except for uses that are authorized by law. As a result of this order, "bath salts" are designated as schedule I substances under the CSA. Schedule I status is reserved for those substances with a high potential for abuse, no currently accepted use for treatment in the United States, and a lack of accepted safety for use of the drug under medical supervision.

Alcohol

Alcohol, one of the oldest drugs known, has been used as far back as records exist. In fact, legal codes limiting its consumption date as far back as 1700 B.C.E. As has been noted, growing concern about alcoholism and related social problems prompted Prohibition in the United States during the 1920s and early 1930s. As the moral approach to alcohol abuse was gradually abandoned, a more scientific approach was adopted, referring to it as a disease. However, some experts have suggested that alcoholism is not as much a disease as a learned social behavior [36].

Although various types of alcohol exist, ethyl alcohol is the type consumed in drinking. In its pure form, it is a colorless, odorless substance. As a rule, people drink alcohol in three categories of beverages: beers, which are made from grain through brewing and fermentation and generally contain from 3 to 8 percent alcohol; wines, which are fermented from fruits such as grapes and generally contain from 8 to 12 percent alcohol naturally, and up to 21 percent when fortified by adding alcohol; and distilled beverages (spirits), such as whiskey, gin, and vodka, which typically contain from 40 to 50 percent alcohol. If not kept in check, drinkers may become physically addicted to any of these beverages [37].

The effects of alcohol vary considerably from one person to another. Mild sedation results from low doses; higher doses, insofar as they tend to reduce anxiety, may produce a temporary state of well-being leading to more serious effects such as depression and apathy. Intoxicating doses typically result in impaired judgment, slurred speech, and loss of motor skills. In addition to the dangers associated with drinking and driving and related accidents, chronic users incur risks from long-term involvement with depressants. Tolerance to the intoxicating effects of alcohol develops quickly, leading to a progressive narrowing of the margin of safety between a dose that is intoxicating and one that is lethal.

Alcohol's effects depend on the amount of alcohol in the blood, known as *blood alcohol concentration* (BAC), which varies with the rate of consumption, and the rate at which the drinker's physical system absorbs and metabolizes alcohol. The higher the alcohol content of the beverage consumed, the more alcohol will enter the bloodstream. The amount and type of food in the stomach also tend to affect the absorption rate. Some studies have shown that drinking when the stomach is filled with food is less intoxicating than when it is empty; the foods in the stomach, which contain fat and protein, delay alcohol absorption. Body weight is also a factor: the heavier the person, the slower the absorption of alcohol. After alcohol passes through the stomach, it is rapidly absorbed through the walls of the intestines into the bloodstream and carried to the various organ systems of the body, where it is metabolized.

Although small amounts of alcohol are processed by the kidneys and secreted in the urine, and other small amounts are processed through the lungs and exhaled in the breath, most of the alcohol is metabolized by the liver. As the alcohol is metabolized, it gives off heat. The body metabolizes alcohol at about the rate of three-fourths of an ounce to one ounce of whiskey an hour. Technically, it is possible to drink at the same rate as the alcohol is being oxidized out of the body. Most people, however, drink faster than this, and so the concentration of alcohol in the bloodstream keeps rising. Alcohol begins to impair the brain's ability to function when the BAC reaches 0.05 percent, or 0.05 grams of alcohol per 100 cubic centimeters of blood. Most state traffic laws in the United States are based on the assumption that a driver with a BAC of 0.08 percent to 0.10 percent is intoxicated. With a concentration of 0.20 percent (a level obtained from drinking about 10 ounces of whiskey), a person has difficulty controlling his or her emotions and may cry or laugh excessively. The intoxicated person will experience a great deal of difficulty in attempting to walk and will want to lie down.

When the BAC reaches about 0.30 percent, which can be attained when a person rapidly drinks about a pint of whiskey, the drinker will have trouble comprehending and may become unconscious. At levels from 0.35 percent to 0.50 percent, the areas of the brain that control breathing and heart action are affected; concentrations above 0.50 percent may result in death, although a person generally becomes unconscious before absorbing a lethal dose. Moderate or temperate use of alcohol is not harmful, but excessive or heavy drinking is associated with alcoholism and numerous other health problems. The effects of excessive drinking on major organ systems of the human body are cumulative and become evident after heavy, continuous drinking or after intermittent drinking over a period of time that may range from 5 to 30 years.

■ ■ Critical Thinking Task ■

Predict the effects on society if Americans, in an attempt to reduce body fat and strokes, greatly increase their consumption of wine. How would this activity affect social behavior, health, and the drug problem?

The parts of the body most affected by heavy drinking are the digestive and nervous systems. Digestive-system disorders that may be related to heavy drinking include cancers of the mouth, throat, and esophagus; gastritis; ulcers; cirrhosis of the liver; and inflammation of the pancreas. Disorders of the nervous system can include neuritis, lapses of memory (blackouts), hallucinations, and extreme tremors (as found in *delirium tremens*, also called "the DTs," which may occur when a person stops drinking after a period of heavy, continuous imbibing). Permanent damage to the CNS, including the brain, may also result from heavy drinking, including Korsakoff psychosis and Wernicke disease. Evidence also indicates that pregnant women who drink heavily may give birth to infants suffering from *fetal alcohol syndrome*, which is characterized by face and body abnormalities and, in some cases, impaired intellectual facilities. Additionally, the combination of alcohol and other drugs (e.g., commonly used sleeping pills, tranquilizers, antibiotics, and aspirin) can be fatal, even when both are taken in nonlethal doses.

Drinking habits vary considerably among different societies. Virtually every culture has its own general beliefs or sense of etiquette about the use and role of alcoholic beverages within its social structure. In some cultures, drinking is either forbidden or frowned upon. The Koran contains prohibitions against drinking, and Muslims are forbidden to sell or serve alcoholic beverages. Hindus also take a negative view of the use of alcohol; this is reflected in the Indian Constitution, which requires every state to work toward the prohibition of alcohol except for medicinal purposes. Abstinence from alcohol has also been the goal of large temperance movements in Europe and the United States. Some Christian religious groups, including Christian Scientists, Mormons, Seventh-Day Adventists, Pentecostals, and most Baptists and Methodists, strongly urge abstinence. In some ambivalent cultures, such as the United States and Ireland, the values of those who believe in abstinence clash with the values of mainstream society, which regards moderate drinking as a way of being hospitable and sociable. This accounts for an abundance of laws and regulations that restrict the buying of alcoholic beverages without prohibiting it outright. Some psychologists say that this indecision in society makes it harder for some people to develop a consistent attitude toward drinking.

Some cultures, including those of Spain, Portugal, Italy, Japan, and Israel, have a permissive attitude toward drinking. The proportion of Israelis and Italians who use alcohol is high, but the rates of alcoholism among them are lower than in Irish and Scandinavian groups. Some cultures may be said to look too favorably upon drinking, such as the French. In France, the heavy consumption of alcohol has been related to the high number of people engaged in viticulture and in the production and distribution of alcoholic beverages. Various surveys indicate that subgroups within a society or culture do not all have the same attitudes toward alcoholic beverages or the same drinking patterns. Drinking behavior also differs significantly among groups of differing age, sex, social class, racial status, ethnic background, occupational status, religious affiliation, and regional location.

Drugs and Driving

Persons driving automobiles while under the influence continue to cause problems for most communities. The extent of the problem is seen in recent statistics. For example, the U.S. Department of Transportation's most recent National Roadside Survey revealed that one in eight weekend nighttime drivers tested positive for illegal drug use [38].

Fatality Analysis Reporting System data show that one in three deceased drivers with a known drug test tested positive for an illegal drug. Younger drivers appear to be especially affected by the dangers of drugged driving. Roughly one in four fatally injured drivers who tested positive for drugs were between the ages of 15 and 24, and half were younger than 35 years old [39].

Research also shows that marijuana is frequently involved in fatal traffic crashes and drugged driving in general. In 2009, marijuana accounted for 25 percent of all positive drug tests for fatally injured drivers, and 43 percent of fatalities involving drivers 24 years of age and younger. Moreover, approximately one in eight high school seniors responding to the 2011 Monitoring the Future (MTF) study reported that in the 2 weeks prior to the survey interview, they had driven after smoking marijuana [40].

Teen Drinking
In spite of a nationwide campaign to overcome it, teen drinking remains a widespread problem in the United States. By 1988, the legal drinking age reached 21 in all 50 states, spurred by a 1984 federal law that tied federal highway funding to compliance by the states. After dropping significantly during the 1980s, when the legal drinking age was raised to 21, the amount of teen drinking leveled off but at alarmingly high rates; in 2005, there were 4767 teens aged 16–19 who died of injuries caused by motor vehicle crashes [41].

More recent statistics show that in 2010, 22 percent of drivers aged 15 to 20 involved in fatal motor vehicle crashes were drinking. In a national survey conducted in 2011, 24 percent of teens reported that, within the previous month, they had ridden with a driver who had been drinking alcohol, and 8 percent reported having driven after drinking alcohol within the same one-month period [42]. In 2010, 56 percent of drivers aged 15 to 20 who were killed in motor vehicle crashes after drinking and driving were not wearing a seat belt [43].

Binge Drinking
According to the CDC, *binge drinking* is a dangerous drinking pattern that is defined as the consumption of four or more alcoholic drinks for women (or five or more drinks for men) on an occasion. An occasion is generally considered to be about 2–3 hours. Binge drinking usually leads to acute impairment (intoxication), but most binge drinkers are not alcoholics or dependent on alcohol.

To a great extent, alcohol use in a community is affected by its price and availability. Accordingly, youth drinking behavior is affected by exposure to alcohol marketing. Youth drinking is also influenced by the drinking behavior of adults; youth often try to behave like young adults, and they often get alcohol from adults.

Binge drinking, especially by college students, is an ongoing concern. With each academic year comes a number of stories about young men and women who drank until they died, until they fell off a roof or out a window, or until they passed out and choked to death on their vomit.

Binge drinking appears to be even more serious for females than males. For example, according to a recent report, more than 14 million American women binge drink about three times a month, and they consume an average of six drinks per binge. Drinking too much, including binge drinking (defined for women as consuming four or more drinks on an occasion), results in about 23,000 deaths in women and girls each year and increases the chances of breast cancer, heart disease, sexually transmitted diseases, unintended pregnancy, and many other health problems [44].

Women's and girls' bodies respond to alcohol differently than men's. It takes less alcohol for them to get intoxicated because of their size and how they process alcohol. Binge drinking can lead to unintended pregnancies, and women and girls who are not expecting to get pregnant may not find out they are until later in their pregnancy. If women binge drink while pregnant, they risk exposing their fetus to high levels of alcohol during its early development, which can lead to miscarriage, low birth weight, sudden infant death syndrome, ADHD, and fetal alcohol spectrum disorders (FASDs).

Despite these risks, about one in eight adult women and one in five high school girls binge drink. Binge drinking is a problem for all women and girls, but it is most common in high school girls and young women, whites, and Hispanics, and among women with household incomes of $75,000 or more. Half of all high school girls who drink alcohol reported binge drinking [45].

Barbiturates

Barbiturates were introduced for medical use in the early 1900s. More than 2500 barbiturates have been synthesized, and at the height of their popularity, about 50 were marketed for human use. Today, about a dozen are in medical use. Barbiturates produce a wide spectrum of CNS depression, from mild sedation to coma, and have been used as sedatives, hypnotics, anesthetics, and anticonvulsants. The primary differences among many of these products are how fast they produce an effect and how long those effects last. Barbiturates are classified as ultrashort, short, intermediate, and long-acting.

The ultrashort-acting barbiturates produce anesthesia within about 1 minute after intravenous administration. Those in current medical use are the schedule IV drug methohexital (Brevital), and the schedule III drugs thiamylal (Surital) and thiopental (Pentothal). Barbiturate abusers generally prefer the schedule II short-acting and intermediate-acting barbiturates, which include amobarbital (Amytal), pentobarbital (Nembutal), secobarbital (Seconal), and Tuinal (an amobarbital–secobarbital combination product). Other short- and intermediate-acting barbiturates are in schedule III, and these include butalbital (Fiorinal), butabarbital (Butisol), talbutal (Lotusate), and aprobarbital (Alurate). After oral administration, the onset of action is from 15 to 40 minutes, and the effects last up to 6 hours. These drugs are primarily used for insomnia and preoperative sedation. Veterinarians use pentobarbital for anesthesia and euthanasia.

Long-acting barbiturates include phenobarbital (Luminal) and mephobarbital (Mebaral), both of which are in schedule IV. Effects of these drugs are realized in about 1 hour and last for about 12 hours; they are used primarily for daytime sedation and the treatment of seizure disorders.

Benzodiazepines

The *benzodiazepine* family of depressants is used therapeutically to produce sedation, induce sleep, relieve anxiety and muscle spasms, and prevent seizures. In general, benzodiazepines act as hypnotics in high doses, anxiolytics in moderate doses, and sedatives in low doses. Of the drugs marketed in the United States that affect CNS function, benzodiazepines are among the most widely prescribed medications. Fifteen members of this group are currently marketed in the United States, and about 20 additional benzodiazepines are marketed in other countries. Benzodiazepines are controlled in schedule IV of the CSA.

Short-acting benzodiazepines are generally used for patients with sleep-onset insomnia (difficulty falling asleep) without daytime anxiety. Shorter-acting benzodiazepines used to manage insomnia include estazolam (ProSom), flurazepam (Dalmane), temazepam (Restoril), and triazolam (Halcion). Midazolam (Versed), a short-acting benzodiazepine, is utilized for sedation or treating anxiety and amnesia in critical care settings and prior to anesthesia. It is available in the United States as an injectable preparation and as a syrup (primarily for pediatric patients).

Benzodiazepines with a longer duration of action are utilized to treat insomnia in patients with daytime anxiety. These benzodiazepines include alprazolam (Xanax), chlordiazepoxide (Librium), clorazepate (Tranxene), diazepam (Valium), halazepam (Paxipam), lorazepam (Ativan), oxazepam (Serax), prazepam (Centrax), and quazepam (Doral). Clonazepam (Klonopin), diazepam, and clorazepate are also used as anticonvulsants.

Benzodiazepines are classified in the CSA as depressants. Repeated use of large doses (or, in some cases, daily use of therapeutic doses) of benzodiazepines is associated with amnesia, hostility, irritability, and vivid or disturbing dreams, as well as tolerance and physical dependence. The withdrawal syndrome is similar to that for alcohol and may require hospitalization. Abrupt cessation of benzodiazepines is not recommended; tapering down the dose eliminates many of the unpleasant symptoms.

Given the millions of prescriptions written for benzodiazepines, relatively few individuals increase their dose on their own initiative or engage in drug-seeking behavior. Those individuals who do abuse benzodiazepines often maintain their drug supply by getting prescriptions from several doctors, forging prescriptions, or buying diverted pharmaceutical products on the illicit market. Abuse is frequently associated with adolescents and young adults who take benzodiazepines to obtain a "high." This intoxicated state results in reduced inhibition and impaired judgment. Concurrent use of alcohol or other depressants with benzodiazepines can be life-threatening. Abuse of benzodiazepines is particularly prevalent among heroin and cocaine abusers. A large percentage of people entering treatment for narcotic or cocaine addiction also report abusing benzodiazepines. Alprazolam and diazepam are the two most frequently encountered benzodiazepines on the illicit market.

Flunitrazepam

Flunitrazepam (Rohypnol) is a benzodiazepine that is not manufactured or legally marketed in the United States, but is smuggled in by traffickers. In the mid-1990s, flunitrazepam was extensively trafficked in Florida and Texas. Known as rophies, roofies, and roach, flunitrazepam gained popularity among younger individuals as a party drug. It has also been utilized as a "date rape" drug. In this context, flunitrazepam is placed in the alcoholic drink of an unsuspecting victim to incapacitate him or her and prevent resistance to sexual assault. The victim is frequently unaware of what has happened to him or her, and often does not report the incident to authorities. A number of actions by the manufacturer of this drug and by government agencies have resulted in reducing the availability and abuse of flunitrazepam in the United States.

Gamma Hydroxybutyric Acid

GHB is another name for the generic drug sodium oxybate; Xyrem (also sodium oxybate) is the trade name of the FDA-approved prescription medication. Analogs that are often substituted for GHB include GBL (gamma butyrolactone) and 1,4-butanediol (also called 1,4 BD or just BD). These analogs are available legally as industrial solvents used to produce polyurethane, pesticides, elastic fibers, pharmaceuticals, coatings on metal or plastic, and other products. They are also sold illicitly as supplements for bodybuilding, fat loss, reversal of baldness, and improved eyesight, and to combat aging, depression, drug addiction, and insomnia. GBL and BD are sold as "fish tank cleaner," ink stain remover, ink cartridge cleaner, and nail enamel remover for approximately $100 per bottle, which is much more expensive than comparable products. Attempts to identify the abuse of GHB analogs are hampered by the fact that routine toxicological screens do not detect the presence of these analogs.

Called easy lay, G, Georgia home boy, GHB, goop, grievous bodily harm, liquid ecstasy, liquid X, and scoop, GHB is usually sold as a liquid or as a white powder that is dissolved in a liquid (e.g., water, juice, or alcohol). GHB dissolved in liquid has been packaged in small vials or small water bottles. In liquid form, GHB is clear and colorless and slightly salty in taste.

GHB is abused for its euphoric and calming effects, and because some people believe it builds muscles and causes weight loss. GHB and its analogs are also misused for their ability to increase libido, suggestibility, and passivity, and to cause amnesia (no memory of events while under the influence of the substance), traits that make users vulnerable to sexual assault and other criminal acts.

GHB abuse became popular among teens and young adults at dance clubs and "raves" in the 1990s, and gained notoriety as a date rape drug. GHB is taken alone or in combination with other drugs, such as alcohol (primarily), other depressants, stimulants, hallucinogens, and marijuana. The average dose ranges from 1 to 5 grams (depending on the purity of the compound). However, the concentrations of these "homebrews" have varied so much that users are usually unaware of the actual dose they are drinking.

GHB occurs naturally in the CNS in very small amounts. Use of GHB produces CNS depressant effects, including euphoria, drowsiness, decreased anxiety, confusion, and memory impairment. GHB can also produce visual hallucinations and "paradoxically" excited and aggressive behavior. GHB greatly increases the CNS depressant effects of alcohol and other depressants.

Effects and Legal Status

GHB takes effect in 15–30 minutes, and the effects last 3–6 hours. Low doses of GHB produce nausea. At high doses, GHB overdose can result in unconsciousness, seizures, slowed heart rate, greatly slowed breathing, lower body temperature, vomiting, nausea, coma, and death. Regular use of GHB can lead to addiction and withdrawal, which includes insomnia, anxiety, tremors, increased heart rate and blood pressure, and occasional psychotic thoughts. Currently, there is no antidote available for GHB intoxication. GHB analogs are known to produce side effects such as topical irritation to the skin and eyes, nausea, vomiting, incontinence, loss of consciousness, seizures, liver damage, kidney failure, respiratory depression, and death.

GHB analogs are often abused in place of GHB. Both GBL and BD metabolize to GHB when taken and produce effects similar to those of GHB. CNS depressants such as barbiturates and methaqualone also produce effects similar to those of GHB. GHB overdose can cause death. GHB is a schedule I controlled substance, meaning that it has a high potential for abuse, no currently accepted medical use in treatment in the United States, and a lack of accepted safety for use under medical supervision. GHB products are schedule III substances under the CSA. In addition, GHB is a list I chemical. It was placed on schedule I of the CSA in March 2000. However, when sold as GHB products (such as Xyrem), it is considered schedule III, making it one of several drugs that are listed in multiple schedules. GHB is produced illegally in both domestic and foreign clandestine laboratories. The major source of GHB on the street is through clandestine synthesis by local operators. At bars or "rave" parties, GHB is typically sold in liquid form by the capful or "swig" for $5 to $25 per cap.

Paraldehyde

Paraldehyde (Paral) is a schedule IV depressant that is used most frequently in hospital settings to treat delirium tremens associated with alcohol withdrawal. Many individuals who become addicted to paraldehyde are initially exposed during treatment for alcoholism and, despite the disagreeable odor and taste, come to prefer it to alcohol. This drug is not used by injection due to resulting tissue damage; in addition, when taken orally, it can be irritating to the throat and stomach. One of the signs of paraldehyde use is a strong, characteristic smell to the breath.

Chloral Hydrate

The oldest of the hypnotic (sleep-inducing) depressants, *chloral hydrate* was first synthesized in 1832. Marketed as syrups or soft gelatin capsules, chloral hydrate takes effect in a relatively short time (30 minutes) and will induce sleep in about an hour. A solution of chloral hydrate and alcohol constituted the infamous "knockout drops" or "Mickey Finn" used by criminals to intoxicate unsuspecting victims. At therapeutic doses, chloral hydrate has little effect on respiration and blood pressure; however, a toxic dose produces severe respiratory depression and very low blood pressure. Chronic use is associated with liver damage and a severe withdrawal syndrome. Although some physicians consider chloral hydrate the drug of choice for sedation of children before diagnostic, dental, or medical procedures, its general use as a hypnotic has declined. Chloral hydrate, Noctec, and other compounds, preparations, or mixtures containing chloral hydrate are in schedule IV of the CSA.

Glutethimide and Methaqualone

Glutethimide (Doriden) was introduced in 1954, and methaqualone (Quaalude and Sopor) in 1965, as safe barbiturate substitutes. Experience demonstrated, however, that their addiction liability and the severity of withdrawal symptoms were similar to those of barbiturates. By 1972, "ludingout"—taking methaqualone with wine—was a popular college pastime. Excessive use leads to tolerance, dependence, and withdrawal symptoms similar to those of barbiturates. In the United States, the marketing of methaqualone pharmaceutical products stopped in 1984, and methaqualone was transferred to schedule I of the CSA. In 1991, glutethimide was transferred into schedule II in response to an upsurge in the prevalence of diversion, abuse, and overdose deaths. Today, there is little medical use of glutethimide in the United States.

Meprobamate

Meprobamate was introduced as an antianxiety agent in 1955 and is prescribed primarily to treat anxiety, tension, and associated muscle spasms. More than 50 tons are distributed annually in the United States under its generic name and brand names such as Miltown and Equanil. Its onset and duration of action are similar to those of the intermediate-acting barbiturates; however, therapeutic doses of meprobamate produce less sedation and toxicity than barbiturates. Excessive use can result in psychological and physical dependence. Carisoprodol (Soma), a skeletal muscle relaxant, is metabolized to meprobamate. This conversion may account for some of the properties associated with carisoprodol and likely contributes to its abuse.

More Recently Marketed Drugs

Zolpidem (Ambien) and *zaleplon* (Sonata) are two relatively new, benzodiazepine-like CNS depressants that have been approved for the short-term treatment of insomnia. Both of these drugs share many of the same properties as the benzodiazepines and are in schedule IV of the CSA.

Hallucinogens

Hallucinogens are among the oldest known group of drugs used for their ability to alter human perception and mood. For centuries, many of the naturally occurring hallucinogens found in plants and fungi have been used for a variety of shamanistic practices. In more recent years, a number of synthetic hallucinogens have been produced, some of which are much more potent than their naturally occurring counterparts.

The biochemical, pharmacological, and physiological basis for hallucinogenic activity is not well understood. Even the name for this class of drugs is not ideal, since hallucinogens do not always produce hallucinations.

However, when taken in nontoxic dosages, these substances produce changes in perception, thought, and mood. Physiological effects include elevated heart rate, increased blood pressure, and dilated pupils. Sensory effects include perceptual distortions that vary with dose, setting, and mood. Psychic effects include disorders of thought associated with time and space. Time may appear to stand still, and forms and colors seem to change and take on new significance. This experience may be either pleasurable or extremely frightening. It needs to be stressed that the effects of hallucinogens are unpredictable each time they are used.

Weeks or even months after some hallucinogens have been taken, the user may experience flashbacks—fragmentary recurrences of certain aspects of the drug experience in the absence of actually taking the drug. Flashbacks are unpredictable, but they are more likely to occur during times of stress and seem to occur more frequently in younger individuals. With time, these episodes diminish and become less intense.

The abuse of hallucinogens in the United States received much public attention in the 1960s and 1970s. A subsequent decline in their use in the 1980s may be attributed to real or perceived hazards associated with taking these drugs.

However, a recent resurgence in the use of hallucinogens is cause for concern. According to the 2003 MTF study, 10.6 percent of 12th graders reported hallucinogenic use in their lifetime. According to the 2003 National Survey on Drug Use and Health, approximately one million Americans were current hallucinogen users. Hallucinogenic mushrooms, LSD, and MDMA are popular among junior and senior high school students who use hallucinogens.

A considerable body of literature links the use of some of the hallucinogenic substances to neuronal damage in animals, and recent data support that some hallucinogens are neurotoxic to humans. However, the most common danger of hallucinogen use is impaired judgment that often leads to rash decisions and accidents.

Lysergic Acid Diethylamide

LSD is the most potent hallucinogen known to date. It was originally synthesized in 1938 by Dr Albert Hoffman, but its hallucinogenic effects were unknown until 1943, when Hoffman accidentally consumed some LSD. Because of its structural similarity to a chemical present in the brain and the similarity of its effects to certain aspects of psychosis, LSD was used as a research tool to study mental illness decades ago.

After a decline in its illicit use after its initial popularity in the 1960s, LSD made a comeback in the 1990s. However, the current average oral dose consumed by users is 30–50 micrograms, a decrease of nearly 90 percent from the 1960 average dose of 250–300 micrograms. Lower potency doses probably account for the relatively few LSD-related emergency incidents during the past several years and its present popularity among young people.

LSD is produced in crystalline form and then mixed with excipients or diluted as a liquid for production in ingestible forms. Often, LSD is sold in tablet form (usually small tablets known as *microdots*), on sugar cubes, in thin squares of gelatin (commonly referred to as *windowpanes*), and, most commonly, as blotter paper (sheets of paper soaked in or impregnated with LSD, covered with colorful designs or artwork, and perforated into

1/4-inch square, individual-dosage units). LSD is sold under more than 80 street names, including acid, blotter, cid, doses, and trips, as well as names that reflect the designs on the sheets of blotter paper.

Physical reactions to LSD may include dilated pupils, lowered body temperature, nausea, goose bumps, profuse perspiration, increased blood sugar, and rapid heart rate. During the first hour after ingestion, the user may experience visual changes with extreme variations in mood. The user may also suffer impaired depth and time perception, with distorted perception of the size and shape of objects, movements, color, sound, touch, and the user's own body image. Under the influence of LSD, the ability to make sensible judgments and see common dangers is impaired, making the user susceptible to personal injury. He or she may also injure others by attempting to drive a car or operate machinery. The effects of higher doses last 10–12 hours. After an LSD "trip," the user may suffer acute anxiety or depression for a variable period. Also, as mentioned in this chapter, users may also experience "flashbacks."

Much of the LSD manufactured in clandestine laboratories is believed to be located in northern California, and initial distribution sources for the drug are typically located in the San Francisco Bay area. A limited number of chemists, probably fewer than a dozen, are believed to be manufacturing nearly all of the LSD available in the United States. LSD is available in at least retail quantities in virtually every state, with supply increasing in some states. Retail-level distribution often takes place during concerts and all-night raves. Users usually obtain LSD from friends and acquaintances.

Peyote and Mescaline

Peyote is a small, spineless cactus, *Lophophora williamsii*, whose principal active ingredient is the hallucinogen mescaline (3,4,5-trimethoxy-phenethylamine). From earliest

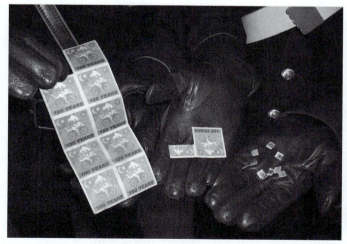

FIGURE 3.4 Law enforcement officials show part of 300 stamps soaked with LSD seized in February 2007. LSD is often sold soaked into sheets of paper covered with colorful designs or artwork. *Source: AP Photo/Carabinieri Press Office.*

A CLOSER LOOK: HOW DO HALLUCINOGENS AFFECT THE BRAIN?

LSD, peyote, psilocybin, and phencyclidine (PCP) are drugs that cause hallucinations, which are profound distortions in a person's perception of reality. Under the influence of hallucinogens, people see images, hear sounds, and feel sensations that seem real but are not. Some hallucinogens produce rapid, intense emotional swings.

LSD, peyote, and psilocybin cause their effects by initially disrupting the interaction of nerve cells and the neurotransmitter serotonin. Distributed throughout the brain and spinal cord, the serotonin system is involved in the control of behavioral, perceptual, and regulatory systems that include hunger, mood, body temperature, sexual behavior, muscle control, and sensory perception. In comparison, PCP acts mainly through a type of glutamate receptor in the brain that is important for the perception of pain, responses to the environment, and learning and memory.

There have been no properly controlled research studies on the specific effects of these drugs on the human brain, but smaller studies have shown some effects associated with the use of hallucinogens.

---

recorded time, peyote has been used by natives in northern Mexico and the southwestern United States as a part of their religious rites.

The top of the cactus above ground—also referred to as the *crown*—consists of disc-shaped buttons that are cut from the roots and dried. These buttons are generally chewed or soaked in water to produce an intoxicating liquid. The hallucinogenic dose of mescaline is about 0.3–0.5 grams and lasts about 12 hours. Although peyote produced rich visual hallucinations that were important to its Native American users, the full spectrum of effects served as a chemically induced model of mental illness. Mescaline can be extracted from peyote or produced synthetically. Both peyote and mescaline are listed in the CSA as schedule I hallucinogens.

Many chemical variations of mescaline and amphetamine have been synthesized for their "feel-good" effects. For example, 4-methyl-2,5-dimethoxyamphetamine (DOM) was introduced into the San Francisco drug scene in the late 1960s and was nicknamed STP, an acronym for "serenity, tranquility, and peace." Other illicitly produced analogs include 4-bromo-2,5-dimethoxyamphetamine (DOB) and 4-bromo-2,5-dimethoxyphenethyl-amine (2C-B or Nexus). In 2000, para-methoxyamphetamine (PMA) and para-methoxy-methamphetamine (PMMA) were identified in tablets sold as ecstasy. PMA, which first appeared on the illicit market briefly in the early 1970s, has been associated with a number of deaths in both the United States and Europe.

Newer Hallucinogens

A number of phenethylamine and tryptamine analogs have been encountered on the illicit market. Those recently placed under federal control include 2C-T-7 (dimethoxy-4-(n)-propylthiophenethylamine), which was permanently placed in schedule I in March 2004, and 5-MeO-DIPT (5-methoxy-diisopropyltryptamine) and AMT (alpha-methyltryptamine), which were placed in schedule I on an emergency basis in April 2003. In addition, a number of other analogs are being encountered. These include DIPT (*N,N*-diisopropyltryptamine), DPT (*N,N*-dipropyltryptamine), 5-MeO-AMT (5-methoxy-alpha-methyltryptamine), MIPT (*N,N*-methylisopropyltryptamine), and 5-MeO-MIPT (5-methoxy,*N,N*-methyliso-propyltryptamine), to name a few. Although these drugs are not specifically listed under the CSA, individuals trafficking in these substances can be prosecuted under the Federal Analog Act, which is the analog statute of the CSA. The ever-increasing number of these types of hallucinogens being encountered by law enforcement is a testament to the efforts of individuals to engage in profitable drug enterprises while trying to avoid criminal prosecution.

3,4-methylenedioxy-N-methylamphetamine (MDMA; "Ecstasy")

MDMA acts as both a stimulant and psychedelic, producing an energizing effect, distortions in time and perception, and enhanced enjoyment of tactile experiences. Adolescents and young adults use it to reduce inhibitions and to promote feelings of euphoria, closeness, empathy, and sexuality.

Although MDMA is known among users as ecstasy, researchers have determined that many ecstasy tablets contain not only MDMA but also a number of other drugs or drug combinations that can be harmful, such as methamphetamine, ketamine, cocaine, the over-the-counter cough suppressant dextromethorphan, the diet drug ephedrine, and caffeine. In addition, other drugs similar to MDMA, such as 3,4-methylenedioxyamphetamine (MDA) or PMA, are often sold as ecstasy, which can lead to overdose and death when the user takes additional doses to obtain the desired effect. Known on the street as Adam, beans, clarity, disco biscuit, E, ecstasy, Eve, go, hug drug, lover's speed, MDMA, peace, STP, X, or XTC, MDMA is primarily distributed in tablet form. Its tablets are sold with logos, creating brand names for users to seek out. The colorful pills are often hidden among colorful candies. MDMA is also distributed in capsule, powder, and liquid forms.

MDMA use mainly involves swallowing tablets (50–150 mg), which are sometimes crushed and snorted, occasionally smoked, but rarely injected. MDMA is also available as a powder. MDMA abusers usually take MDMA by "stacking" (taking three or more tablets at once) or by "piggybacking" (taking a series of tablets over a short period of time). One trend among young adults is "candy flipping," which is the co-abuse of MDMA and LSD. MDMA is considered a party drug. As with many other drugs of abuse, MDMA is rarely used alone. It is common for users to mix MDMA with other substances, such as alcohol and marijuana.

MDMA mainly affects brain cells that use the chemical serotonin to communicate with each other. Serotonin helps to regulate mood, aggression, sexual activity, sleep, and sensitivity to pain. Clinical studies suggest that MDMA may increase the risk of long-term, perhaps permanent, problems with memory and learning. MDMA causes changes in perception, including euphoria; an increased sensitivity to touch, energy, and sensual and sexual arousal; a need to be touched; and a need for stimulation. Some unwanted psychological effects include confusion, anxiety, depression, paranoia, sleep problems, and drug craving. All these effects usually occur within 30–45 minutes of swallowing the drug and usually last 4–6 hours, but they may occur or last weeks after ingestion.

Users of MDMA experience many of the same effects and face many of the same risks as users of other stimulants such as cocaine and amphetamines. These include increased motor activity, alertness, heart rate, and blood pressure. Some unwanted physical effects include muscle tension, tremors, involuntary teeth clenching, muscle cramps, nausea, faintness, chills, sweating, and blurred vision.

High doses of MDMA can interfere with the body's ability to regulate its temperature, resulting in a sharp increase in body temperature (hyperthermia), leading to liver, kidney, and cardiovascular failure. Severe dehydration can result from the combination of the drug's effects and the crowded and hot conditions in which the drug is often taken. Studies suggest that chronic use of MDMA can produce damage to the serotonin system. It is ironic that a drug that is taken to increase pleasure may cause damage that reduces a person's ability to feel pleasure.

No one other drug is quite like MDMA, but MDMA produces both amphetamine-like stimulation and mild mescaline-like hallucinations. In high doses, MDMA can interfere with the body's ability to regulate temperature. On occasions, this can lead to a sharp increase in body temperature (hyperthermia), resulting in liver, kidney, and cardiovascular system failure, and death. Because MDMA can interfere with its own metabolism (i.e., its breakdown within the body), potentially harmful levels can be reached by repeated drug use over short intervals.

MDMA is a schedule I drug under the CSA, meaning it has a high potential for abuse, no currently accepted medical use in treatment in the United States, and a lack of accepted safety for use under medical supervision. MDMA is a synthetic chemical made in laboratories. Seized MDMA in the United States is primarily manufactured in, and smuggled across our borders from, clandestine laboratories in Canada and, to a lesser extent, the Netherlands. A small number of MDMA clandestine laboratories have also been identified as operating in the United States.

Phencyclidine and Related Drugs

In the 1950s, PCP was investigated as an anesthetic, but due to its side effects of confusion and delirium, its development for human use was discontinued. It became commercially available for use as a veterinary anesthetic in the 1960s under the trade name of Sernylan and was placed in schedule III of the CSA. In 1978, due to considerable abuse, PCP was transferred to schedule II of the CSA, and manufacturing of Sernylan was discontinued. Today, virtually all the PCP encountered on the illicit market in the United States is produced in clandestine laboratories.

PCP is illicitly marketed under a number of other names, including angel dust, supergrass, killer weed, embalming fluid, and rocket fuel, reflecting the range of its bizarre and volatile effects. In its pure form, it is a white crystalline powder that readily dissolves in water. However, most PCP on the illicit market contains a number of contaminants resulting from makeshift manufacturing, causing the color to range from tan to brown and the consistency from powder to a gummy mass. Although sold in tablets and capsules as well as in powder and liquid form, it is commonly applied to a leafy material, such as parsley, mint, oregano, or marijuana, and smoked.

The drug's effects are as varied as its appearance. A moderate amount of PCP often causes the user to feel detached, distant, and estranged from his or her surroundings. Numbness, slurred speech, and loss of coordination may be accompanied by a sense of strength and invulnerability. A blank stare, rapid and involuntary eye movements, and an exaggerated gait are among the more observable effects. Auditory hallucinations, image distortion, severe mood disorders, and amnesia may also occur. In some users, PCP may cause acute anxiety and a feeling of impending doom; in others, paranoia and violent hostility; and in some, a psychosis indistinguishable from schizophrenia. PCP use is associated with a number of risks, and many believe it to be one of the most dangerous drugs of abuse.

Modification of the manufacturing process may yield chemically related analogs capable of producing psychic effects similar to those of PCP. Four of these substances—*N*-ethyl-1-phenylcyclohexylamine (PCE), 1-(phenylcyclohexyl) pyrrolidine (PCPy), 1-[1-(2-thienyl) cyclohexyl]piperdine (TCP), and 1-[1-(2-thienyl)cyclohexyl]pyrrolidine (TCPy)—have been encountered on the illicit market and have been placed in schedule I of the CSA. Telazol, a schedule III veterinary anesthetic containing tiletamine (a PCP analog), in combination with zolazepam (a benzodiazepine), is sporadically encountered as a drug of abuse.

Ketamine

Ketamine is a rapidly acting general anesthetic. Its pharmacological profile is essentially the same as that of phencyclidine. Like PCP, ketamine is referred to as a *dissociative* anesthetic because patients feel detached or disconnected from their pain and environment when anesthetized with this drug. Unlike most anesthetics, ketamine produces only mild respiratory depression and appears to stimulate, not depress, the cardiovascular system. In addition, ketamine has both analgesic and amnesiac properties, and is associated with less confusion, irrationality, and violent behavior than PCP. Use of ketamine as a general anesthetic for humans has been limited due to adverse effects, including delirium and hallucinations. Today, it is primarily used in veterinary medicine, but it has some utility for emergency surgery in humans.

Although ketamine has been marketed in the United States for many years, it was only relatively recently associated with significant diversion and abuse, and it was placed in schedule III of the CSA in 1999. Known in the drug culture as special K or super K, ketamine has become a staple at dance parties or raves. Ketamine is supplied to the illicit market by the diversion of legitimate pharmaceuticals (Ketaset and Ketalar). It is usually distributed as a powder, which is obtained by removing the liquid from the pharmaceutical products. As a drug of abuse, ketamine can be administered orally, snorted, or injected. It is also sprinkled on marijuana or tobacco and smoked. After oral or intranasal administration, effects are evident in about 10–15 minutes and are over in about an hour.

After intravenous use, effects begin almost immediately and peak within minutes. Ketamine can act as a depressant or a psychedelic. Low doses produce vertigo, ataxia, slurred speech, slow reaction time, and euphoria. Intermediate doses produce disorganized thinking, altered body image, and a feeling of unreality, with vivid visual hallucinations. High doses produce analgesia, amnesia, and coma.

Narcotics

Narcotics constitute a category of drugs that includes opium and opium derivatives or their synthetic substitutes. Generally speaking, these drugs are painkillers that are indispensable in medical treatment, but are also very potent and extremely addictive. The initial effects of the drugs may be unpleasant for the user and may include such side effects as nausea, vomiting, drowsiness, apathy, decreased physical activity, and constipation. Strong doses can lead to respiratory depression, loss of motor coordination, and slurred speech. Users who desire the brief euphoric effects of narcotic drugs may develop tolerance and increase their doses of the drug. Repeated use of narcotics will almost certainly manifest itself in both physical addiction and psychological dependence. Usually, narcotics are administered either orally or by injection. Intravenous drug users will commonly use one of two methods of injection:

- *Skin popping*. Injecting the drug just under the skin and into the muscle
- *Mainlining*. Injecting the drug directly into the veins

In the event that the physically addicted user is deprived of the drug, the first withdrawal signs are usually noticed shortly before the time of the next desired dose, which is anywhere from 36 to 72 hours after the last dose. Other symptoms (e.g., watery eyes, runny nose, yawning, and perspiration), however, will appear about 8–12 hours after the last dose. As the abstinence syndrome progresses, the user will experience loss of appetite, irritability, insomnia, goose bumps, and tremors, accompanied by severe sneezing. When the symptoms reach their peak, the user becomes weak and vomits while also experiencing stomach cramps, diarrhea, and an increase in heart rate. These symptoms linger for 5–7 days, and then disappear.

Narcotics are of both natural and synthetic origins. Of the natural-origin narcotics, the most common are opium, heroin, and morphine. All of these drugs are derived from the opium poppy plant. This plant grows only in certain parts of the world and is most commonly found today in South America, Southeast Asia, Southwest Asia, and Mexico.

The opium poppy produces a seed pod that when unripe was traditionally lanced with a knife by farmers to obtain a milky liquid that oozes out of the incision. A more modern method, however, is the industrial poppy straw process of extracting alkaloids from the mature dried plant (see Chapter 4).

Narcotics of Natural Origin

The poppy plant, *Papaver somniferum*, is the source for nonsynthetic narcotics. It was grown in the Mediterranean region as early as 5000 B.C.E. and has since been cultivated in a number of countries throughout the world. The milky fluid that seeps from incisions (lanced with a knife by farmers) in the unripe seed pod of this poppy has, since ancient times, been scraped by hand and air-dried to produce what is known as *opium*. A more modern method of harvesting is by the industrial poppy straw process of extracting alkaloids from the mature dried plant. The extract may be in liquid, solid, or powder form, although most poppy straw concentrate available commercially is a fine brownish powder. More than 500 tons of opium or equivalents in poppy straw concentrate are legally imported into the United States annually for legitimate medical use.

Opium

There were no legal restrictions on the importation or use of opium until the early 1900s. In the United States, the unrestricted availability of opium, the influx of opium-smoking immigrants from East Asia, and the invention of the hypodermic needle contributed to the more severe variety of compulsive drug abuse seen at the turn of the twentieth century. In those days, medicines often contained opium without any warning label. Today state, federal, and international laws govern the production and distribution of narcotic substances.

Although opium is used in the form of paregoric to treat diarrhea, most opium imported into the United States is broken down into its alkaloid constituents. These alkaloids are divided into two distinct chemical classes: phenanthrenes and isoquinolines. The principal phenanthrenes are morphine, codeine, and thebaine; the isoquinolines have no significant CNS effects and are not regulated under the CSA.

Morphine

Morphine is the principal constituent of opium and ranges in concentration from 4 to 21 percent. Commercial opium is standardized to contain 10 percent morphine. In the United States, a small percentage of the morphine obtained from opium is used directly (about 20 tons); the remaining is converted to codeine and other derivatives (about 110 tons). Morphine is one of the most effective drugs known for the relief of severe pain and remains the standard against which new analgesics are measured. Like most narcotics, the use of morphine has increased significantly in recent years. Since 1998, there has been about a twofold increase in the use of morphine products in the United States.

Morphine is marketed under generic and brand name products, including MS-Contin, Oramorph SR, MSIR, Roxanol, Kadian, and RMS. Morphine is used parenterally (by injection) for preoperative sedation, as a supplement to anesthesia, and for analgesia. It is the drug of choice for relieving the pain of myocardial infarction and for its cardiovascular effects in the treatment of acute pulmonary edema. Traditionally, morphine was almost exclusively used by injection. Today, morphine is marketed in a variety of forms, including oral solutions, immediate and sustained-release tablets and capsules, suppositories, and injectable preparations. In addition, the availability of high-concentration morphine preparations (e.g., 20 mg/ml oral solutions, 25 mg/ml injectable solutions, and 200 mg sustained-release tablets) partially reflects the use of this substance for chronic pain management in opiate-tolerant patients.

Codeine

Codeine is the most widely used naturally occurring narcotic in medical treatment in the world. This alkaloid is found in opium in concentrations ranging from 0.7 to 2.5 percent. However, most codeine used in the United States is produced from morphine. Codeine is also the starting material for the production of two other narcotics, dihydrocodeine and hydrocodone. Codeine is medically prescribed for the relief of moderate pain and cough suppression. Compared to morphine, codeine produces less analgesia, sedation, and respiratory depression, and is usually taken orally. It is made into tablets either alone (schedule II) or in combination with aspirin or acetaminophen (e.g., Tylenol with Codeine, which is schedule III). As a cough suppressant, codeine is found in a number of liquid preparations (these products are in schedule V). Codeine is also used to a lesser extent as an injectable solution for the treatment of pain. Codeine products are diverted from legitimate sources and are encountered on the illicit market.

Thebaine

Thebaine, a minor constituent of opium, is controlled in schedule II of the CSA as well as under international law. Although chemically similar to both morphine and codeine, thebaine produces stimulatory rather than depressant effects. Thebaine is not used therapeutically but is converted into a variety of substances, including oxycodone, oxymorphone, nalbuphine, naloxone, naltrexone, and buprenorphine. The United States ranks first in the world in thebaine utilization.

Semisynthetic Narcotics

The narcotics discussed in this subsection are among the more significant substances that have been derived from morphine, codeine, or thebaine.

Heroin

First synthesized from morphine in 1874, *heroin* was not extensively used in medicine until the early 1900s. Commercial production of the new pain remedy was first started in 1898. It initially received widespread acceptance from the medical profession, but physicians remained unaware of its addictive potential for years. The first comprehensive control of heroin occurred with the Harrison Narcotics Act of 1914. Today, heroin is an illicit substance having no medical utility in the United States. It is in schedule I of the CSA.

Four foreign source areas produce the heroin available in the United States: South America (Colombia), Mexico, Southeast Asia (principally Burma), and Southwest Asia (principally Afghanistan). However, South America and Mexico supply most of the illicit heroin that is marketed in the United States. South American heroin is a high-purity powder primarily distributed to metropolitan areas on the East Coast. Heroin powder may vary in color from white to dark brown because of impurities left from the manufacturing process or the presence of additives. Mexican heroin, known as *black tar*, is primarily available in the western United States. The color and consistency of black tar heroin result from the crude processing methods used to illicitly manufacture heroin in Mexico. Black tar heroin may be sticky like roofing tar or hard like coal, and its color may vary from dark brown to black.

Pure heroin is rarely sold on the street. A "bag" (slang for a small unit of heroin sold on the street) currently contains about 30–50 mg of powder, only a portion of which is heroin. The remainder could be sugar, starch, acetaminophen, procaine, benzocaine, quinine, or any of numerous cutting agents for heroin. Traditionally, the purity of heroin in a bag ranged from 1 to 10 percent. More recently, heroin purity has ranged from about 10 to 70 percent. Black tar heroin is often sold in chunks weighing about an ounce. Its purity is generally less than that of South American heroin, and it is most frequently smoked or dissolved, diluted, and injected.

In the past, heroin in the United States was almost always injected, because this is the most practical and efficient way to administer low-purity heroin. However, the recent availability of higher purity heroin at relatively low cost has meant that a larger percentage of today's users are either snorting or smoking heroin instead of injecting it. This trend was first captured in the 1999 National Household Survey on Drug Abuse, which revealed that 60 to 70 percent of people who used heroin for the first time from 1996 to 1998 never injected it. This trend has continued. Snorting or smoking heroin is more appealing to new users because it eliminates both the fear of acquiring syringe-borne diseases, such as HIV and hepatitis, as well as the social stigma attached to intravenous heroin use. Many new users of heroin mistakenly believe that smoking or snorting heroin is a safe technique for avoiding addiction. However, both smoking and snorting heroin are directly linked to high incidences of dependence and addiction.

According to the 2003 National Survey on Drug Use and Health, during the second half of the 1990s heroin initiation rates rose to a level not reached since the 1970s. In 1974, there were an estimated 246,000 heroin initiates. Between 1988 and 1994, the annual number of new users ranged from 28,000 to 80,000. Between 1995 and 2001, the number of new heroin users was consistently greater than 100,000. Overall, approximately 3.7 million Americans reported using heroin at least once in their lifetimes.

HYDROMORPHONE

Hydromorphone (Dilaudid) is marketed in tablets (2, 4, and 8 mg), suppositories, oral solutions, and injectable formulations. All products are in schedule II of the CSA. The drug's analgesic potency is 2–8 times that of morphine, but it is shorter acting and produces more sedation than morphine. Much sought after by narcotic addicts, hydromorphone is usually obtained by the abuser through fraudulent prescriptions or theft. The tablets are often dissolved and injected as a substitute for heroin. In September 2004, the FDA approved the use of Palladone (hydromorphone hydrochloride) for the management of persistent pain. This extended-release formulation could have the same risk of abuse as OxyContin, which is discussed in more detail in the "Oxycodone" section.

OXYCODONE

Oxycodone is synthesized from thebaine. Like morphine and hydromorphone, oxycodone is used as an analgesic. It is effective orally and is marketed alone in 10, 20, 40, 80, and 160 mg controlled-release tablets (OxyContin); in 5 mg immediate-release capsules (OxyIR); or in combination products with aspirin (Percodan) or acetaminophen (Percocet) for the relief of pain. All oxycodone products are in schedule II. Oxycodone either is abused orally or the tablets are crushed and sniffed or dissolved in water and injected. The use of oxycodone has increased significantly in recent years. In 1993, about 3.5 tons of oxycodone were manufactured for sale in the United States. In 2003, about 41 tons were manufactured.

Historically, oxycodone products have been popular drugs of abuse among the narcotic-abusing population. Recently, concern has grown among federal, state, and local officials regarding the dramatic increase in the illicit availability and abuse of OxyContin products. These products contain large amounts of oxycodone (10–160 mg) in a formulation intended for slow release over about a 12 hour period.

Abusers have learned that this slow-release mechanism can be easily circumvented by crushing the tablet and swallowing, snorting, or injecting the drug product for a more rapid and intense high. The criminal activity associated with illicitly obtaining and distributing this drug, as well as serious consequences of illicit use, including addiction and overdose deaths, is of an epidemic proportion in some areas of the United States.

HYDROCODONE

Hydrocodone is structurally related to codeine, but more closely related to morphine in its pharmacological profile. As a drug of abuse, it is equivalent to morphine with respect to subjective effects, opiate signs and symptoms, and "liking" scores. Hydrocodone is an effective cough suppressant and analgesic. It is most frequently prescribed in combination with acetaminophen (e.g., Vicodin and Lortab), but is also marketed in products with aspirin (Lortab ASA), ibuprofen (Vicoprofen), and antihistamines (Hycomine). All products currently marketed in the United States are either schedule III combination products primarily intended for pain management, or schedule V antitussive medications often marketed in liquid formulations. The schedule III products are currently under review at the federal level to determine whether an increase in regulatory control is warranted.

Hydrocodone is prescribed predominantly in the United States. International Narcotics Control Board reports that 99% of the worldwide supply in 2007 was consumed in the United States. Despite their obvious utility in medical practice, hydrocodone products are among the most popular pharmaceutical drugs associated with drug diversion, trafficking, abuse, and addiction. In every geographical area in the country, the DEA has listed this drug as one of the most commonly diverted. Hydrocodone is the most frequently encountered opiate pharmaceutical in submissions of drug evidence to federal, state, and local forensic laboratories. Law enforcement has documented the diversion of millions of dosage units of hydrocodone by theft, doctor shopping, fraudulent prescriptions, bogus "call-in" prescriptions, and diversion by registrants and Internet fraud.

Hydrocodone products are associated with significant drug abuse. Hydrocodone was ranked sixth among all controlled substances in the 2002 Drug Abuse Warning Network (DAWN) emergency department data. Poison control data, DAWN medical examiner (ME) data, and other ME data indicate that hydrocodone deaths are numerous, widespread, and increasing in number. In addition, hydrocodone–acetaminophen combinations (accounting for about 80 percent of all hydrocodone prescriptions) carry significant public health risk when taken in excess.

Synthetic Narcotics

In contrast to the pharmaceutical products derived from opium, synthetic narcotics are produced entirely within the laboratory. The continuing search for products that retain the analgesic properties of morphine without the consequent dangers of tolerance and dependence has yet to yield a product that is not susceptible to abuse. A number of clandestinely produced drugs, as well as drugs that have accepted medical uses fall within this category.

MEPERIDINE

Introduced as an analgesic in the 1930s, *meperidine* produces effects that are similar, but not identical, to morphine (shorter duration of action and reduced antitussive and antidiarrheal actions). Currently, it is used for pre-anesthesia and the relief of moderate to severe pain, particularly in obstetrics and postoperative situations. Meperidine is available in tablets, syrups, and injectable forms under generic and brand name (Demerol, Mepergan, etc.) schedule II preparations. Several analogs of meperidine have been clandestinely produced. During the clandestine synthesis of the analog Desmethylprodine (MPPP), a neurotoxic byproduct (MPTP) was produced. A number of individuals who consumed the MPPP–MPTP preparation developed an irreversible Parkinson's-like syndrome. It was later found that MPTP destroys the same neurons as those damaged in Parkinson's disease.

DEXTROPROPOXYPHENE

A close relative of methadone, *dextropropoxyphene* was first marketed in 1957 under the trade name of Darvon. Its oral analgesic potency is one-half to one-third that of codeine, with 65 mg approximately equivalent to about 600 mg of aspirin. Dextropropoxyphene is prescribed for relief of mild to moderate pain. Bulk dextropropoxyphene is in schedule II, whereas preparations containing it are in schedule IV. More than 150 tons of dextropropoxyphene are produced in the United States annually, and more than 25 million prescriptions are written for the products. This narcotic is associated with a number of toxic side effects and is among the top 10 drugs reported by medical examiners in drug abuse deaths.

FENTANYL

First synthesized in Belgium in the late 1950s, *fentanyl*, with an analgesic potency about 80 times that of morphine, was introduced into medical practice in the 1960s as an intravenous anesthetic under the trade name of Sublimaze. Thereafter, two other fentanyl analogs were introduced: alfentanil (Alfenta), an ultrashort-acting (5–10 minutes) analgesic, and sufentanil (Sufenta), an exceptionally potent analgesic (5–10 times more potent than fentanyl) for use in heart surgery. Today, fentanyls are extensively used for anesthesia and analgesia. Duragesic, for example, is a fentanyl transdermal patch used in chronic pain management, and Actiq is a solid formulation of fentanyl citrate on a stick that dissolves slowly in the mouth for transmucosal absorption. Actiq is intended for opiate-tolerant individuals, and is effective in treating breakthrough pain in cancer patients. Carfentanil (Wildnil) is an analog of fentanyl with an analgesic potency 10,000 times that of morphine and is used in veterinary practice to immobilize certain large animals.

Illicit use of pharmaceutical fentanyls first appeared in the mid-1970s in the medical community and continues to be a problem in the United States. To date, more than 12 different analogs of fentanyl have been produced clandestinely and identified in United States drug traffic. The biological effects of the fentanyls are indistinguishable from those of heroin, with the exception that the fentanyls may be hundreds of times more potent. Fentanyls are most commonly used by intravenous administration, but, like heroin, they may also be smoked or snorted.

PENTAZOCINE

The effort to find an effective analgesic with less dependence-producing consequences led to the development of pentazocine (Talwin). Introduced as an analgesic in 1967, it was frequently encountered in the illicit trade, usually in combination with tripelennamine, and was placed into schedule IV of the CSA in 1979. An attempt at reducing the abuse of this drug was made with the introduction of Talwin Nx. This product contains a quantity of antagonist (naloxone) sufficient to counteract the morphine-like effects of pentazocine if the tablets are dissolved and injected.

BUTORPHANOL

Although *butorphanol* can be made from thebaine, it is usually manufactured synthetically. It was initially available in injectable formulations for human (Stadol) and veterinary (Torbugesic and Torbutrol) use. More recently, a nasal spray (Stadol NS) became available, and significant diversion and abuse of this product led to the 1997 control of butorphanol in schedule IV of the CSA. Butorphanol is a clear example of a drug gaining favor as a drug of abuse only after it became available in a form that facilitated greater ease of administration (nasal spray versus injection).

Narcotics Treatment Drugs

When people have a mild headache or muscle ache, an over-the-counter pain reliever is usually enough to make them feel better. But if the pain is more severe, the person's physician might recommend something stronger—a prescription narcotic or "opioid." Opioids are a type of narcotic pain medication. They can have serious side effects if they are not used correctly. Opioid drugs work by binding to opioid receptors in the brain, spinal cord, and other areas of the body. They reduce the transmission of pain messages to the brain and reduce feelings of pain. Various narcotic and opioids are discussed in this subsection.

METHADONE

German scientists synthesized *methadone* during World War II because of a shortage of morphine. Although chemically unlike morphine or heroin, methadone produces many of the same effects. It was introduced into the United States in 1947 as an analgesic

(Dolophine). Today, methadone is primarily used for the treatment of narcotic addiction, although a growing number of prescriptions are being written for chronic pain management. It is available in oral solutions, tablets, and injectable schedule II formulations.

Methadone's effects can last up to 24 hours, thereby permitting once-a-day oral administration in heroin detoxification and maintenance programs. High-dose methadone can block the effects of heroin, thereby discouraging the continued use of heroin by addicts in treatment. Chronic administration of methadone results in the development of tolerance and dependence. The withdrawal syndrome develops more slowly, and is less severe but more prolonged than that associated with heroin withdrawal. Ironically, methadone used to control narcotic addiction is encountered on the illicit market. Recent increases in the use of methadone for pain management have been associated with increasing numbers of overdose deaths.

LEVO ALPHACETYLMETHADOL

Closely related to methadone, the synthetic compound *levo alphacetylmethadol*, or LAAM (Orlaam (trade name) or levo-α-acetylmethadol (LAAM) is a synthetic opiate), has an even longer duration of action (from 48 to 72 hours) than methadone, permitting a reduction in frequency of use. In 1994, it was approved as a schedule II treatment drug for narcotic addiction. Both methadone and LAAM have high abuse potential. Their acceptability as narcotic treatment drugs is predicated upon their ability to substitute for heroin, their long duration of action, and their mode of oral administration. Recent data regarding the cardiovascular toxicity of LAAM have limited the use of this drug as a first-line therapy for addiction treatment.

BUPRENORPHINE

Buprenorphine is a semisynthetic narcotic derived from thebaine. Buprenorphine was initially marketed in the United States as an analgesic (Buprenex). In 2002, two new products (Suboxone and Subutex) were approved for the treatment of narcotic addiction. Like methadone and LAAM, buprenorphine is potent (30–50 times the analgesic potency of morphine), has a long duration of action, and does not need to be injected. Unlike the other treatment drugs, buprenorphine produces far less respiratory depression, and is thought to be safer in overdose. All buprenorphine products are currently in schedule III of the CSA.

Cannabis

Cannabis sativa L., the cannabis plant, grows wild throughout most of the tropic and temperate regions of the world. Prior to the advent of synthetic fibers, the cannabis plant was cultivated for the tough fiber of its stem. Historically, in the United States, cannabis was legitimately grown only for scientific purposes. More recently, however, it has been grown for medicinal reasons in states authorizing its use.

Cannabis contains chemicals called *cannabinoids* that are unique to the cannabis plant. Among the cannabinoids synthesized by the plant are cannabinol, cannabidiol, cannabinolidic acids, cannabigerol, cannabichromene, and several isomers of tetrahydrocannabinol. One of these, delta-9-tetrahydrocannabinol (THC), is believed to be responsible for most of the characteristic psychoactive effects of cannabis. Research has resulted in the development and marketing of the dronabinol (synthetic THC) product, Marinol, for the control of nausea and vomiting caused by chemotherapeutic agents used in the treatment of cancer, and to stimulate appetite in AIDS patients. Marinol was rescheduled in 1999 and placed in schedule III of the CSA.

Cannabis products are usually smoked. Their effects are felt within minutes, reach their peak in 10–30 minutes, and may linger for 2 or 3 hours. The effects experienced often depend on the experience and expectations of the individual user, as well as the activity of the drug itself. Low doses tend to induce a sense of well-being and a dreamy state of relaxation, which may be accompanied by a more vivid sense of sight, smell, taste, and hearing, as well as by subtle alterations in thought formation and expression.

This state of intoxication may not be noticeable to an observer. However, driving, occupational, or household accidents may result from a distortion of time and space relationships and impaired motor coordination. Stronger doses intensify reactions. The individual may experience shifting sensory imagery, rapidly fluctuating emotions, fragmentary thoughts with disturbing associations, an altered sense of self-identity, impaired memory, and a dulling of attention despite an illusion of heightened insight. High doses may result in image distortion, a loss of personal identity, fantasies, and hallucinations.

Three drugs that come from cannabis—marijuana, hashish, and hash oil—are distributed in the United States illicit market. As mentioned, in a number of states, marijuana is authorized under state law to be sold as "medical marijuana." On the federal level, however, marijuana is listed as schedule I—having no accepted medical use. Today cannabis is illicitly cultivated, both indoors and out, to maximize its THC content, thereby producing the greatest possible psychoactive effect.

Marijuana

Marijuana is the most frequently encountered illicit drug worldwide. In the United States, according to the MTF study, 57 percent of adults aged 19 to 28 reported having used marijuana in their lifetime [46]. Among younger Americans, 17.5 percent of eighth graders and 46.1 percent of 12th graders had used marijuana in their lifetime [47]. The term *marijuana*, as commonly used, refers to the leaves and flowering tops of the cannabis plant that are dried to produce a tobacco-like substance. Marijuana varies significantly in its potency, depending on the source and selection of plant materials used.

The form of marijuana known as *sinsemilla* (Spanish *sin semilla*, "without seed"), derived from the unpollinated female cannabis plant, is preferred for its high THC content. Marijuana is usually smoked in the form of loosely rolled cigarettes called *joints*, in bongs or pipes, or in hollowed-out commercial cigars called *blunts*. Joints and blunts may be laced with a number of adulterants, including PCP, which substantially alter the effects and toxicity of these products. Street names for marijuana include pot, grass, weed, Mary Jane, and reefer.

Although marijuana grown in the United States was once considered inferior because of a low concentration of THC, advances in plant selection and cultivation have resulted in North American marijuana containing higher levels of THC. In 1974, the average THC content of illicit marijuana was less than 1 percent. In 2009, the ONDCP reported that marijuana potency reached a THC content of 8.5 percent, compared to an average 4 percent in 1983 [48].

Marijuana contains known toxins and cancer-causing chemicals. Marijuana users experience the same health problems as tobacco smokers, such as bronchitis, emphysema, and bronchial asthma. Some of the effects of marijuana use also include increased heart rate, dryness of the mouth, reddening of the eyes, impaired motor skills and concentration, and hunger with an increased desire for sweets. Extended use increases risk to the lungs and reproductive system, and suppresses the immune system. Occasionally, hallucinations, fantasies, and paranoia are reported. Long-term chronic marijuana use is associated with an *amotivational syndrome*, which is characterized by apathy; impairment of judgment, memory, and concentration; and loss of interest in personal appearance and pursuit of goals.

Hashish

Hashish consists of the THC-rich resinous material of the cannabis plant, which is collected, dried, and then compressed into a variety of forms such as balls, cakes, or cookie-like sheets. Pieces are then broken off, placed in pipes or under glass, and smoked. The Middle East, North Africa, Pakistan, and Afghanistan are the main sources of hashish. In the 1990s, the THC content of hashish that reached the United States, where demand is limited, averaged about 5 percent.

Hash Oil

The term *hash oil* is used by illicit drug users and dealers, but is a misnomer in suggesting any resemblance to hashish. Hash oil is produced by extracting the cannabinoids from plant material with a solvent. The color and odor of the resulting extract will vary, depending on the type of solvent used. Current samples of hash oil, a viscous liquid ranging from amber to dark brown in color, average about 15 percent THC. In terms of its psychoactive effect, a drop or two of this liquid on a cigarette is equal to a single "joint" of marijuana.

Steroids

The issue of performance-enhancing drugs, especially *anabolic steroids*, has once again gained international attention. These drugs are used by high school, college, professional, and elite amateur athletes in a variety of sports (e.g., weightlifting, track and field, swimming, cycling, and others) to obtain a competitive advantage. Bodybuilders and fitness buffs take anabolic steroids to improve their physical appearance, and individuals in occupations requiring enhanced physical strength (e.g., bodyguards, night club bouncers, and construction workers) are also known to use these drugs.

Concerns over a growing illicit market, abuse by teenagers, and the uncertainty of possible harmful long-term effects of steroid use led Congress in 1991 to place anabolic steroids as a class of drugs into schedule III of the CSA. The CSA defines anabolic steroids as any drug or hormonal substance chemically and pharmacologically related to testosterone (other than estrogens, progestins, and corticosteroids) that promotes muscle growth.

Once viewed as a problem associated only with professional and elite amateur athletes, various reports indicate that anabolic steroid abuse has increased significantly among adolescents. According to the 2003 MTF study, 2.5 percent of eighth graders, 3 percent of 10th graders, and 3.5 percent of 12th graders reported using steroids at least once in their lifetime.

Most illicit anabolic steroids are sold at gyms, at competitions, and through mail-order operations. For the most part, these substances are smuggled into the United States from many countries. The illicit market includes various preparations intended for human and veterinary use, as well as bogus and counterfeit products. The most commonly encountered anabolic steroids on the illicit market include testosterone, nandrolone, methenolone, stano-zolol, and methandrostenolone. Other steroids seen in the illicit market include boldenone, fluoxymesterone, methandriol, methyltestosterone, oxandrolone, oxymetholone, and trenbolone.

A limited number of anabolic steroids have been approved for medical and veterinary uses. The primary legitimate use of these drugs in humans is for the replacement of inadequate levels of testosterone resulting from a reduction or absence of testicular function. Other indications include anemia and breast cancer. Experimentally, anabolic steroids have been used to treat a number of disorders, including AIDS wasting (which is the involuntary loss of more than 10 percent of body weight, combined with more than 30 days of either diarrhea or weakness and fever), erectile dysfunction, and osteoporosis. In veterinary practice, anabolic steroids are used to promote feed efficiency and to improve weight gain, vigor, and hair coat. They are also used in veterinary practice to treat anemia, and to counteract tissue breakdown during illness and trauma.

Used in combination with exercise training and a high-protein diet, anabolic steroids can promote increased size and strength of muscles, improved endurance, and decreased recovery time between workouts. They are taken orally or by intramuscular injection. Users concerned about drug tolerance often take steroids on a schedule called a *cycle*. A cycle is a period of between 6 and 14 weeks of steroid use, followed by a period of abstinence or reduction in use. Additionally, users tend to "stack" the drugs, using multiple drugs concurrently. Although the benefits of these practices are unsubstantiated, most users feel that cycling and stacking enhance the efficiency of the drugs and limit their side effects.

Another mode of steroid use is called *pyramiding*. With this method, users slowly escalate steroid use (increasing the number of drugs used at one time and/or the dose and frequency of one or more steroids), reach a peak amount at midcycle, and gradually taper the dose toward the end of the cycle. The escalation of steroid use can vary with different types of training. Bodybuilders and weightlifters tend to escalate their doses to a much higher level than do long-distance runners or swimmers.

The long-term adverse health effects of anabolic steroid use are not definitely known. There is, however, increasing concern about possible serious health problems associated with the abuse of these agents, including cardiovascular damage, cerebrovascular toxicity, and liver damage. Physical side effects include elevated blood pressure and cholesterol levels, severe acne, premature balding, reduced sexual function, and testicular atrophy. In males, abnormal breast development (gynecomastia) can occur. In females, anabolic steroids have a masculinizing effect, resulting in more body hair, a deeper voice, smaller breasts, and fewer menstrual cycles. Several of these effects are irreversible. In adolescents, abuse of these agents may prematurely stop the lengthening of bones, resulting in stunted growth. For some individuals, the use of anabolic steroids may be associated with psychotic reactions, manic episodes, feelings of anger or hostility, aggression, and violent behavior.

A variety of nonsteroid drugs are commonly found in the illicit anabolic steroid market. These substances are primarily used for one or more of the following reasons: (1) to serve as an alternative to anabolic steroids, (2) to alleviate the short-term adverse effects associated with anabolic steroid use, or (3) to mask anabolic steroid use. Examples of drugs serving as alternatives to anabolic steroids include clenbuterol, human growth hormone, insulin, insulin-like growth factor, and GHB. Drugs used to prevent or treat the adverse effects of anabolic steroid use include tamoxifen, diuretics, and human chorionic gonadotropin. Diuretics, probenecid, and epitestosterone may be used to mask anabolic steroid use.

Over the last few years, a number of precursors to either testosterone or nandrolone have been marketed as dietary supplements in the United States. Some of these substances include androstenedione, androstenediol, norandrostenedione, norandrostenediol, and dehydroepiandrosterone. New legislation has been introduced in Congress to add several steroids to the CSA and to alter the CSA requirements needed to place new steroids under control in the CSA.

Inhalants

Inhalants are a diverse group of substances that include volatile solvents, gases, and nitrites that are sniffed, snorted, huffed, or bagged to produce intoxicating effects similar to those of alcohol. These substances are found in common household products such as glues, lighter fluid, cleaning fluids, and paint products. *Inhalant abuse* is the deliberate inhaling or sniffing of these substances to get high, and it is estimated that about 1000 substances are misused in this manner. The easy accessibility, low cost, legal status, and ease of transport and concealment make inhalants one of the first substances abused by children.

According to the National Survey on Drug Use and Health, there were more than 1 million new inhalant users in 2002. During 2003, almost 23 million (9.7 percent) people aged 12 and older reported using an inhalant at least once in their lifetimes. The MTF study from the University of Michigan reported that 8.7 percent of eighth graders, 5.4 percent of 10th graders, and 3.9 percent of 12th graders used inhalants in the past year [49]. The study also showed that 4.1 percent of eighth graders, 2.2 percent of 10th graders, and 1.6 percent of 12th graders used inhalants in the past month.

The highest incidence of use is among 10- to 12-year-old children, with rates of use declining with age. Parents worry about alcohol, tobacco, and other illicit drug use, but may be unaware of the hazards associated with products found throughout their homes. Knowing what these products are, understanding how they might be harmful, and recognizing the signs and symptoms of their use as inhalants can help a parent prevent inhalant abuse.

For example, volatile solvents are found in a number of everyday products. Some of these products include nail polish remover, lighter fluid, gasoline, paint and paint thinner, rubber glue, waxes, and varnishes. Chemicals found in these products include toluene, benzene, methanol, methylene chloride, acetone, methyl ethyl ketone, methyl butyl ketone, trichloroethylene, and trichlorethane. The gas used as a propellant in canned whipped cream and in small metallic containers called *whippets* (which are used to make whipped cream) is nitrous oxide or "laughing gas"—the same gas used by dentists for anesthesia. Tiny cloth-covered ampules, called *poppers* or *snappers* by abusers, contain amyl nitrite, a medication used to dilate blood vessels. Butyl nitrite, sold as tape head cleaner and referred to as rush, locker room, or climax, is often sniffed or huffed to get high.

Inhalants may be sniffed directly from an open container or huffed from a rag soaked in the substance and held to the face. Alternatively, the open container or soaked rag can be placed in a bag, where the vapors can concentrate before being inhaled. Some chemicals are painted on the hands or fingernails, or placed on shirt sleeves or wristbands to enable an abuser to continually inhale the fumes without being detected by a teacher or other adult. Although inhalant abusers may prefer one particular substance because of its taste or odor, a variety of substances may be used because of similar effects, availability, and cost. Once the substance is inhaled, the extensive capillary surface of the lungs allows rapid absorption of the substance, and blood levels peak rapidly. Entry into the brain is fast, and the intoxicating effects are short-lived but intense.

Inhalants depress the CNS, producing decreased respiration and blood pressure. Users report distortion in perceptions of time and space. Many users experience headaches, nausea, slurred speech, and loss of motor coordination. Mental effects may include fear, anxiety, or depression. A rash around the nose and mouth may be seen, and the abuser may start wheezing. An odor of paint or organic solvents on clothes, skin, and breath is sometimes a sign of inhalant abuse. Other indicators of inhalant abuse include slurred speech; staggering gait; red, glassy, watery eyes; and excitability or unpredictable behavior.

The chronic use of inhalants has been associated with a number of serious health problems. Sniffing glue and paint thinner causes kidney abnormalities; sniffing the solvents toluene and trichloroethylene causes liver damage. Memory impairment, attention deficits, and diminished nonverbal intelligence have been related to the abuse of inhalants. Deaths resulting from heart failure, asphyxiation, or aspiration have occurred.

K2 or "Spice"

K2 or "spice" is a mixture of herbs and spices that is typically sprayed with a synthetic compound chemically similar to THC, the psychoactive ingredient in marijuana. The chemical compounds typically include HU-210, HU-211, JWH-018, and JWH-073. K2 is commonly purchased in head shops, tobacco shops, and various retail outlets, and over the Internet. It is often marketed as incense or "fake weed." Purchasing over the Internet can be dangerous, because it is not usually known where the products come from or what amount of chemical is on the organic material. Also called bliss, black mamba, Bombay blue, fake weed, genie, spice, and Zohai, K2 is typically sold in small, silvery plastic bags of dried leaves and marketed as incense that can be smoked. It is said to resemble potpourri.

K2 products are usually smoked in joints or pipes, but some users make it into a tea. Psychological effects are similar to those of marijuana and include paranoia, panic attacks, and giddiness. Physiological effects of K2 include increased heart rate and blood pressure. It appears to be stored in the body for long periods of time, and therefore the long-term effects on humans are not fully known.

On March 1, 2011, the DEA published a final order in the *Federal Register* temporarily placing five synthetic cannabinoids into schedule I of the CSA.[1] The order became effective on March 1, 2011. Manufacturers of this product are not regulated and are often unknown since these products are purchased via the Internet whether wholesale or retail. Several websites that sell the product are based in China. Some products may contain an herb called *damiana*, which is native to Central America, Mexico, and the Caribbean.

Diet Drugs

In 1990, an appetite suppressant drug known as *fen-phen* (a combination of *fenfluramine* and *phentermine*) was hailed as the answer to many dieters' prayers. The drug was used widely and thought by many to be a valuable aid in weight control. But by the summer of 1997, a Mayo Clinic report surfaced on the potential dangers of fen-phen. The report identified 24 women who took a combination of fenfluramine and phentermine for an average of 1 year to lose weight and subsequently developed heart valve problems. Shortly after the release of the Mayo Clinic report, the FDA reported nine more women who developed the same problems while taking these medications.

In an urgent step, the FDA sent thousands of letters to doctors asking them to examine their fen-phen patients for possible heart valve damage and report any cases to the agency. The urgency was legitimate, for during 1996 alone, physicians wrote more than 20 million prescriptions for fenfluramine and phentermine, which are designed to curb appetite by affecting the serotonin levels in the brain and making patients feel full.

Although obesity is associated with more than 300,000 deaths a year, the majority of those deaths are linked to heart problems [50]. In September 1997, Florida was the first state to ban the sale of fen-phen and a similar drug, Redux, ordering physicians not to prescribe them. The drugs were later completely banned for medical use in the United States.

[1] The five substances are 1-pentyl-3-(1-naphthoyl)indole (JWH-018), 1-butyl-3-(1-naphthoyl)indole (JWH-073), 1-[2-(4-morpholinyl)ethyl]-3-(1-naphthoyl)indole (JWH-200), 5-(1,1-dimethylheptyl)-2-[(1R,3S)-3-hydroxycyclohexyl]-phenol (CP-47,497), and 5-(1,1-dimethyloctyl)-2-[(1R,3S)-3-hydroxycyclohexyl]-phenol (cannabicyclohexanol; CP-47,497 C8 homologue).

In the aftermath of the ban on fen-phen and Redux, new substitute products began to emerge. St. John's wort (*Hypericum perforatum*), an herb used for years by German doctors, emerged in late 1997 as a weight loss supplement. Also used for the treatment of clinical depression, it began appearing on the shelves of health food stores almost immediately after the other two diet drugs were removed. The herbs are consistent with herbal Phen Fuel, Diet Phen, and other St. John's wort blends designed to sound like the unavailable fen-phen. St. John's wort's negative effects are minimal and include dizziness, confusion, tiredness, and sedation. St. John's wort, which is native to Europe, North Africa, Asia, and the western United States, has a 2400-year history in folk medicine and is said to have been prescribed by Hippocrates (Table 3.1).

Summary

Perhaps one reason for drug abuse is a misunderstanding about the effects of drugs and their general pharmacology. Frequently, drug users listen to other drug users about the effects of a particular drug; such information is often incorrect. Drugs can be virtually anything that alters the user's physical or psychological makeup; they can be either legal or illegal to possess. Therefore, the word *drug* could rightfully refer to such compounds as heroin, LSD, and marijuana along with sugar, salt, and caffeine.

All drugs, whether or not they are controlled, fall into one of seven categories: stimulants, depressants, hallucinogens, narcotics, cannabis, steroids, and inhalants. Drugs in the stimulant category literally stimulate the CNS and make the user feel more alert. The most commonly abused illicit drugs in this category are cocaine (including crack), amphetamines, and methamphetamine. The depressant category represents drugs that have a different effect on the user. Although early stages of ingestion of depressants may create a feeling of exhilaration for the user, these drugs actually depress the CNS. Alcohol is a lawfully obtainable depressant, whereas depressants such as barbiturates and sedative hypnotics are usually physically addicting and pose great physical dangers to the drug abuser.

Hallucinogens are a unique category of drug; they are not physically addictive, and their use is not as common as other categories of drugs. Hallucinogens such as LSD, PCP, and MDMA are considered dangerous drugs for other reasons. For example, users of LSD encounter the possibility of "bad trips" or "flashbacks" resulting from the use of the drug. The most dangerous side-effect of ecstasy is overheating (hyperthermia) which can cause the body to reach extreme temperatures (41–42°C). This can result in a severe heatstroke which can cause unstoppable bleeding, liver and kidney failure, and ultimately death.

The narcotic category refers to drugs such as heroin, morphine, opium, and other derivatives and synthetic substitutes, which are physically addicting and emulate the effects of opium. All drugs within this category are controlled, and possession of lawfully manufactured narcotics is permitted only pursuant to a lawful prescription.

Cannabis is discussed as an individual category of drug, but the Drug Enforcement Administration considers it to be a mild hallucinogen. Although cannabis had a legitimate use during the early history of the United States, it is either outlawed or regulated

Table 3.1   NIDA's List of Commonly Abused Drugs

Substances: Category and Name	Examples of *Commercial* and Street Names	DEA Schedule*/How Administered**	*Acute Effects*/Health Risks
Tobacco			Increased blood pressure and heart rate/chronic lung disease; cardiovascular disease; stroke; cancers of the mouth, pharynx, larynx, esophagus, stomach, pancreas, cervix, kidney, bladder, and acute myeloid leukemia; adverse pregnancy outcomes; addiction
Nicotine	Found in cigarettes, cigars, bidis, and smokeless tobacco (snuff, spit tobacco, chew)	Not scheduled/ smoked, snorted, chewed	
Alcohol			In low doses, euphoria, mild stimulation, relaxation, lowered Inhibitions; in higher doses, drowsiness, slurred speech, nausea, emotional volatility, loss of coordination, visual distortions, impaired memory, sexual dysfunction, loss of consciousness/increased risk of injuries, violence, fetal damage (in pregnant women); depression; neurologic deficits; hypertension; liver and heart disease; addiction; fatal overdose
Alcohol (ethyl alcohol)	Found in liquor, beer, and wine	Not scheduled/ swallowed	
Cannabinoids			Euphoria; relaxation; slowed reaction time; distorted sensory perception; impaired balance and coordination; increased heart rate and appetite; impaired learning, memory; anxiety; panic attacks; psychosis/ cough; frequent respiratory infections; possible mental health decline; addiction
Marijuana	Blunt, dope, ganja, grass, herb, joint, bud, Mary Jane, pot, reefer, green, trees, smoke, sinsemilla, skunk, weed	I/smoked, swallowed	
Hashish	Boom, gangster, hash, hash oil, hemp	I/smoked, swallowed	
Opioids			Euphoria; drowsiness; impaired coordination; dizziness; confusion; nausea; sedation; feeling of heaviness in the body; slowed or arrested breathing/constipation; endocarditis; hepatitis; HIV; addiction; fatal overdose
Heroin	*Diacetylmorphine*: smack, horse, brown sugar, dope, H, junk, skag, skunk, white horse, China white; cheese (with OTC cold medicine and antihistamine)	I/injected, smoked, snorted	
Opium	*Laudanum, paregoric*: big O, black stuff, block, gum, hop	II, III, V/swallowed, smoked	

(Continued)

Table 3.1   NIDA's List of Commonly Abused Drugs—Cont'd

Substances: Category and Name	Examples of *Commercial* and Street Names	DEA Schedule*/How Administered**	*Acute Effects*/Health Risks
Stimulants			*Increased heart rate, blood pressure, body temperature, metabolism; feelings of exhilaration; increased energy, mental alertness; tremors; reduced appetite; irritability anxiety; panic; paranoia; violent behavior; psychosis/weight loss; insomnia; cardiac or cardiovascular complications; stroke; seizures; addiction*
Cocaine	*Cocaine hydrochloride:* blow, bump, C, candy, Charlie, coke, crack, flake, rock, snow, toot	II/snorted, smoked, injected	
Amphetamine	*Biphetamlne, Dexedine:* bennies, black beauties, crosses, hearts, LA turnaround, speed, truck drivers, uppers	II/swallowed, snorted, smoked, injected	*Also, for cocaine—nasal damage from snorting*
Methamphet-amine	*Desoxyn:* meth, ice, crank, chalk, crystal, fire, glass, go fast, speed	II/swallowed, snorted, smoked, injected	*Also, for methamphetamine—severe dental problems*
Club Drugs			*MDMA—mild hallucinogenic effects; increased tactile sensitivity, empathic feelings; lowered inhibition; anxiety; chills; sweating; teeth clenching; muscle cramping/sleep disturbances; depression; impaired memory; hyperthermia; addiction*
MDMA (methylene-dioxymetham-phetamine)	Ecstasy, Adam, clarity, Eve, lover's speed, peace, uppers	I/swallowed, snorted, injected	
Flunitraz-epam***	*Rohypnol:* forget-me pill, Mexican Valium, R2, roach, Roche, roofies, roofinol, rope, rophies	IV/swallowed, snorted	*Flunitrazepam—sedation; muscle relax-ation; confusion; memory loss; dizziness; impaired coordination/addiction*
GHB***	*Gamma-hydroxybutyrate:* G, Georgia home boy, grievous bodily harm, liquid ecstasy, soap, scoop, goop, liquid X	I/swallowed	*GHB—drowsiness; nausea; headache; dis-orientation; loss of coordination; memory loss/unconsciousness; seizures; coma*
Dissociative Drugs			*Feelings of being separate from one's body and environment; impaired motor function/anxiety; tremors; numbness; memory loss; nausea*
Ketamine	*Ketalar* Sl: cat Valium, K, Special K, vitamin K	III/injected, snorted, smoked	
PCP and analogs	*Phencyclldlne:* angel dust, boat, hog, love boat, peace pill	I, II/swallowed, smoked, injected	*Also, for ketamine—analgesia; impaired memory; delirium; respiratory depression and arrest; death*
Salvia divinorum	Salvia, Shepherdess's herb, Maria Pastora, magic mint, Sally-D	Not scheduled/ chewed, swallowed, smoked	*Also, for PCP and analogs—analgesia; psychosis; aggression; violence; slurred speech; loss of coordination; hallucinations*
Dextrometho-rphan (DXM)	Found in some cough and cold medications: Robotripping, Robo, Triple C	Not scheduled/ swallowed	*Also, for DXM—euphoria; slurred speech; confusion; dizziness; distorted visual perceptions*

Table 3.1   NIDA's List of Commonly Abused Drugs—Cont'd

Substances: Category and Name	Examples of *Commercial* and Street Names	DEA Schedule*/How Administered**	*Acute Effects*/Health Risks
	Hallucinogens		Altered states of perception and feeling; hallucinations; nausea
LSD	*Lysergic acid diethylamide:* acid, blotter, cubes, microdot, yellow sunshine, blue heaven	I/swallowed, absorbed through mouth tissues	**Also, for LSD and mescaline**—increased body temperature, heart rate, blood pressure; loss of appetite; sweating; sleeplessness; numbness; dizziness; weakness; tremors; impulsive behavior; rapid shifts in emotion
Mescaline	Buttons, cactus, mesc, peyote	I/swallowed, smoked	
Psilocybin	Magic mushrooms, purple passion, shrooms, little smoke	I/swallowed	**Also, for LSD**—Flashbacks, hallucinogen persisting perception disorder **Also, for psilocybin**—nervousness; paranoia; panic
	Other Compounds		*Steroids*—no intoxication effects/hypertension; blood clotting and cholesterol changes; liver cysts; hostility and aggression; acne; in adolescents—premature stoppage of growth; in males—prostate cancer, reduced sperm production, shrunken testicles, breast enlargement; in females—menstrual irregularities, development of beard and other masculine characteristics
Anabolic steroids	*Anadrol, Oxandrin, Durabolin, Depo-Testosterone, Equipoise: roids, juice, gym candy, pumpers*	III/injected, swallowed, applied to skin	
Inhalants	*Solvents (paint thinners, gasoline, glues); gases (butane, propane, aerosol propellants, nitrous oxide); nitrites (isoamyl, isobutyl, cyclohexyl): laughing gas, poppers, snappers, whippets*	Not scheduled/ inhaled through nose or mouth	*Inhalants (varies by chemical)*—stimulation; loss of inhibition; headache; nausea or vomiting; slurred speech; loss of motor coordination; wheezing/cramps; muscle weakness; depression; memory impairment; damage to cardiovascular and nervous systems; unconsciousness; sudden death

*Schedule I and II drugs have a high potential for abuse. They require greater storage security and have a quota on manufacturing, among other restrictions. Schedule I drugs are available for research only and have no approved medical use; Schedule II drugs are available only by prescription (unrefillable) and require a form for ordering. Schedule III and IV drugs are available by prescription, may have five refills in 6 months, and may be ordered orally. Some Schedule V drugs are available over the counter.

**Some of the health risks are directly related to the route of drug administration. For example, injection drug use can increase the risk of infection through needle contamination with staphylococci, HIV, hepatitis, and other organisms.

***Associated with sexual assaults.

Source: National Institute of Drug Abuse. Found at: http://www.drugabuse.gov, National Institutes of Health, U.S. Department of Health and Human Services.

to one extent or another in the United States. Its beneficial use in medicine is still under study, and 14 states have passed laws related to its medical use. Attitudes regarding marijuana regulation have also changed as some states as both Colorado and Washington have passed their own laws legalizing marijuana for recreational use.

The use of inhalants has become popular for many (especially adolescents) because inhalant substances are both readily available and legal to possess. Breathing the fumes of such household products as glue, paint, and gasoline, however, may pose more risk of physiological damage to the user's brain than other dangerous substances encountered on the street.

Do you recognize these terms?

- binge drinking
- blood alcohol concentration
- delirium tremens
- dopamine
- drug abuse
- fetal alcohol syndrome
- physical dependence
- psychological dependence
- tolerance
- withdrawal

Discussion Questions

1. Discuss the reasons why people use drugs.
2. Define the terms *psychological dependence* and *physiological dependence*.
3. Discuss the definition of the term *drug*.
4. List and discuss the different categories of drugs, and give examples of each.
5. List and discuss some widely used synthetic narcotic drugs.
6. What are designer drugs, and how do they affect the drug user?

References

[1] National Institute on Drug Abuse. (2010). *Drugs, Brains and Behavior: The Science of Addiction.* U.S. Department of Health and Human Services. August.

[2] Ibid.

[3] Nash, J. M. (1997). Addiction: Why do people get hooked? *Time*, 69–76. (May 5).

[4] Ibid.

[5] *Diagnostic and statistical manual of mental disorders (DSM-IV-TR).* (2000). Washington, DC: American Psychiatric Press.

[6] Ibid.

[7] Gilbert, R. (1984). Caffeine labeling. *Journal of the American Medical Association, 26,* 565. (August 10).

[8] Ibid.

[9] Brooke, J. (1994). Grim view from Brazil's coffee fields. *The New York Times*, D1–D3. (June 19).

[10] Hyman, T. (1986). The world of smoking and tobacco. *Journal of the American Medical Association.* (February 28).

[11] Lakatos, P. L., Szamosi, T., & Lakatos, L. (2007). Smoking in inflammatory bowel diseases: Good, bad or ugly? *World Journal of Gastroenterology, 13*(46), 6134–6139. 10.3748/wjg.13.6134. PMID 1806975.

[12] United Nations Office on Drugs and Crime. (2010). *World drug report 2009.* New York: United Nations Publications. Found at: www.unodc.org/unodc/en/data-and-analysis/WDR-2009.

[13] Centers for Disease Control and Prevention. (2006). *Web-based Injury Statistics Query and Reporting System (WISQARS).* Found at: www.cdc.gov/ncipc/wisqars.

[14] McGinnis, J. M., & Foege, W. H. (1993). Actual causes of death in the United States. *Journal of the American Medical Association, 170*(18), 2207–2212.

[15] Ibid.

[16] Ibid.

[17] Centers for Disease Control and Prevention. (2006). *Web-based Injury Statistics Query and Reporting System (WISQARS).* Found at: www.cdc.gov/ncipc/wisqars.

[18] Van Dyke, C., & Byck, R. (1982). Cocaine. *Scientific American, 236*(3), 108–119.

[19] Grinspoon, L., & Bakalar, J. (1985). *Cocaine: A drug and its social evolution.* New York: Basic Books.

[20] Ibid.

[21] Ibid.

[22] Van Dyke, C., & Byck, R. (1982). Cocaine. *Scientific American, 236*(3), 108–119.

[23] Grinspoon, L., & Bakalar, J. (1985). *Cocaine: A drug and its social evolution.* New York: Basic Books.

[24] Ibid.

[25] Van Dyke, C., & Byck, R. (1982). Cocaine. *Scientific American, 236*(3), 108–119.

[26] Lyman, M., & Potter, G. (1995). *Organized crime.* Englewood Cliffs, NJ: Prentice Hall.

[27] Scott, P. D., & Marshall, J. (1991). *Cocaine politics.* Berkeley, CA: University of California Press.

[28] National Institute of Drug Abuse Research: *Cocaine Abuse and Addiction;* Department of Health and Human Services, September 2009.

[29] Ibid.

[30] Ibid.

[31] Ibid.

[32] United Nations Office on Drugs and Crime (UNODC). (2010). *The globalization of crime: A transnational organized crime threat assessment.* New York: UNODC. 5–6.

[33] National Institute on Drug Abuse. (September 2006). *Special report: Methamphetamine abuse and addition.* U.S. Department of Health and Human Services.

[34] Ibid.

[35] Ibid.

[36] Bower, B. (1988). Intoxicating habits. *Science News,* 88–89. (August 6).

[37] Ibid.

[38] Lacey, J. H., Kelly-Baker, T., Furr-Holden, D., Voas, R. B., Romano, E., Ramirez, A., et al. (2009). *2007 National Roadside Survey of Alcohol and Drug Use by Drivers: Drug Results. DOT HS 811 249.* Washington, DC: National Highway Traffic Safety Administration.

[39] Office of National Drug Control Policy. (2011). *Drug testing and drug-involved driving of fatally injured drivers in the United States: 2005–2009.* Washington, D.C.: Executive Office of the President.

[40] Ibid.

[41] Centers for Disease Control and Prevention. (2007). *Quick stats: Binge drinking* Found at: www.cdc.gov/quickstats/binge_drinking.htm.

[42] Centers for Disease Control and Prevention. (2013). *Injury prevention & control: Teen driver's fact sheet.* Found at: http://www.cdc.gov/motorvehiclesafety/teen_drivers/teendrivers_factsheet.html. Accessed May 1, 2013.

[43] Ibid.

[44] Centers for Disease Control and Prevention. (2013). *Binge drinking: A serious under-recognized problem among women and girls.* Found at: http://www.cdc.gov/features/vitalsigns/bingedrinking-female/. Accessed May 1, 2013.

[45] Ibid.

[46] Johnston, L. D., O'Malley, P. M., & Bachman, J. G. (2001). *Monitoring the future: National results on adolescent drug use: Overview of key findings.* Washington, DC: U.S. Department of Health and Human Services.

[47] Ibid.

[48] Office of National Drug Control Policy. (2010). *National Drug Control Strategy 2010*. U.S. Department of Justice, Washington, DC: Executive Office of the President of the United States.

[49] Substance Abuse and Mental Health Services Administration. (2006). *Results from the 2006 national survey on drug use and health: National findings*. Rockville, MD: Office of Applied Studies, U.S. Department of Health and Human Services.

[50] Hellmich, N. (1997). Diet drug risks are a balancing act. *USA Today*. (July 10), 1A.

Further Reading

United Nations Office on Drugs and Crime (UNODC). (2011). *World drug report*. New York: UNODC. 8.

Herer, J. (2010). *The Emperor Wears No Clothes* (12th edition). AH HA Publishing. November. The Authoritative Historical Record of Cannabis and the Conspiracy Against Marijuana. Van Nuys, CA.

Schlosser, E. (2003). *Reefer Madness and Other Tales from the American Underground*. Allen Lane Publishing. The history of marijuana laws in the United States.

Centers for Disease Control. (2011). Vital Signs: Overdoses of Prescription Opioid Pain Relievers – United States, 1999–2008; 60:1–6.

4

The Illicit Drug Trade

This chapter will enable you to:

- Understand the various dynamics of the illegal drug business
- Comprehend the different facets of illicit drug marketing
- Understand the role of foreign drug source countries
- Discover the global magnitude of the world's drug problem

The criminal drug trade, by virtue of its illegal nature, is a covert enterprise in which people, business decisions, and transactions all occur outside the watchful eye of the public. Because of this secrecy, much misunderstanding exists about the inner workings of the illicit drug trade. For example, many questions exist regarding sellers, buyers, business decisions, business logistics, and organizational dynamics. Addressing these areas is the purpose of this chapter.

In 1927, bootlegger Al Capone told newspaper reporters that he was just a well-meaning businessman providing a public service that the government chose not to provide. Many of today's drug-trafficking entrepreneurs might also perceive themselves as businesspeople who are simply offering goods and services not legally available to the public. However, the realities of the drug trade are not as benevolent as this supposition suggests.

The truth is that the illicit drug business is a money-driven, calculated undertaking that gives little consideration to human anguish or social responsibility. Drug sellers and users alike demonstrate their disregard for law and order in their choice to participate in and become involved with illegal drugs. In addition, compared to legitimate businesses espousing a "customer is always right" philosophy, the drug trade is anything but user-friendly. Allegiances are weak (or nonexistent) at virtually all levels of production, manufacturing, transportation, and sales. Sellers typically lie about the quality and purity of drugs being sold, users distort information about the "benefits" of drugs to other potential users, arrested drug offenders regularly turn in long-time associates instead of going to prison, drug prices are inconsistent and unstable, and players in the drug trade are often suspicious about their associates' relationships with rival organizations, or are paranoid about the presence of undercover agents in their operations. Indeed, trust—or the lack of it—is the hallmark of the illegal drug trade. To understand public policy approaches to the illicit drug problem, these premises must be understood.

Despite the many negative aspects of the drug business, the organizational dynamics of the illicit drug trade parallel those of legitimate industry in many ways, which helps to explain why this business has endured in the United States, in one form or another, for more than a century. Considerations such as personnel management, manufacturing costs, market acquisition, wholesale and retail sales, corporate security, and overheads are included in today's illicit cocaine, heroin, and marijuana businesses. Furthermore, these commercial aspects are found in both international and domestic trafficking organizations. An understanding of how these dynamics operate and interface is crucial in the formation of national drug policy, as well as the development of criminal and constitutional law dealing with areas of drug control.

Illicit Drug Trafficking in the Twenty-First Century

In 2013, the most compelling questions facing scholars, public officials, and students of drug abuse are "What are the major trends that have characterized the evolution of illicit drug trafficking and organized crime (organized criminal networks) in the Americas over the last quarter of a century?" And "What have been the key transformations—economic, political, and organizational—that have taken place within the illegal drug economy during the first decade of the twenty-first century?" In 2012, researcher Bruce Bagley observed four key trends that characterize recent ongoing changes to the drug trade: (1) the increasing globalization of drug consumption; (2) the limited or "partial" victories and unintended consequences of the United States-led "war on drugs," especially in the Andes; (3) the spread of areas of drug cultivation and smuggling routes throughout the Western Hemisphere (so-called balloon effects); and (4) the fragmentation of organized criminal groups within countries and across regions ("cockroach effects") [1].

The Globalization of Drug Abuse

For years, Latin American political leaders have argued that if drug users in the United States did not consume such large quantities of illegal drugs, then Latin American and Caribbean countries would not produce such large quantities of illegal drugs like marijuana, cocaine, and heroin for export to meet that demand. Accordingly, the Americas would not be overwhelmed by the powerful and well-financed drug-trafficking organizations (cartels) that have sprung up throughout the Western Hemisphere since the late 1980s. Research continues to show that the United States has been for decades, and remains today, the largest single consumer market for illicit drugs in the world. Although there is no definitive estimate, the value of all illicit drugs sold annually in the United States may reach as high as $150 billion. Some $37 billion per year may be spent on cocaine alone [2].

Nonetheless, illegal drug use (and/or addiction) is not a uniquely "American" disease, despite the title of David Musto's pioneering book on the origins of drug control in the United States [3]. Since the turn of the twenty-first century, the number of cocaine users in the now 27 countries of the European Union (EU) has increased from 4.3 to 4.75 million, which represents 30 percent of the worldwide consumption of cocaine. Europeans are almost closing the gap with the approximately 5 million regular cocaine users found in the United States [4,5].

Undeniably, levels of cocaine use in the United States have dropped steadily since the early 1990s, while cocaine consumption in Europe soared exponentially during the first decade of the twenty-first century. In fact, the number of cocaine users in the four European Free Trade Area (EFTA) and 27 EU countries doubled from 1998 to 2006 [6]. What's more, Europeans pay more than twice as much per gram, ounce, kilo, or metric ton as do American drug buyers.

In 2011, the United Nations Office on Drugs and Crime (UNODC) reported that, combined, the Americas consumed 63 percent of the world's cocaine supply, 440 metric tons, while the European population consumed 29 percent. However, cocaine consumption in the United States has decreased by 40 percent from 1999 to 2009 [7].

The global heroin market represents its own business model and is considerably complicated in terms of its supply chain. For example, Afghanistan leads the world in heroin production, producing 380 metric tons, or 83 percent of the world supply. It has been estimated that Afghanistan produced 6,900 tons of opium in 2009 alone [8]. Other than Latin America, the heroin produced from Afghanistan is trafficked to every major region around the world.

Following Afghanistan, Mexico produces 9 percent of the world heroin supply, while Myanmar (formerly Burma) produces 5 percent. The supply produced in Mexico is trafficked to the United States. Colombia, on the other hand, accounts for only a single metric ton annually, which is less than 1 percent of the world supply of heroin. Over the last decade or more, the majority of the heroin consumed in Europe originated in Afghanistan, whereas most of the heroin consumed in the United States has come from either Mexico (roughly 9 percent of the world supply) or Colombia (as mentioned, less than 1 percent of the world supply). In comparison, cocaine is produced in only three countries in the Western Hemisphere: Colombia (45 percent), Peru (35–40 percent), and Bolivia (15–20 percent). It is trafficked from these three Andean countries to 174 countries around the world [9].

Cocaine consumption is not limited only to advanced markets such as those of the United States and Europe. In fact, its use in Latin America has also skyrocketed over the last decade. For example, Latin American consumers in 2010 were estimated to consume an estimated 200 metric tons of cocaine. In particular, because of the sheer size of its population, Brazil had the greatest number of users in South America.

As a consequence, a pronounced trend toward the proliferation of new global trafficking routes, and the increased involvement of criminal trafficking networks originating outside the Andean subregion, has become increasingly evident.

The Andean War on Drugs

Since the middle of the nineteenth century and through the mid-1980s, Peru and Bolivia were the two principal suppliers of both coca leaf and refined cocaine to the United States, European, and other world markets. For example, as of 1985, Peru produced roughly 65 percent of the world's supply of coca leaf, while Bolivia produced approximately 25 percent, and Colombia 10 percent or less. The limited victories achieved by the United States war on drugs in the southern Andes during the late 1980s and early 1990s moved coca cultivation in the region to Colombia by the mid- and late 1990s [10].

Funding by the United States resulted in two partial victories: (1) by crop eradication programs in Bolivia's Chapare region under President Victor Paz Estensoro after 1986 (Operation Blast Furnace) and under Presidents Hugo Banzer and Jorge Quiroga from 1998 to 2002 (*Plan Dignidad*); along with (2) Peruvian President Alberto Fujimori's interruption of the "air bridge" between the Alto Huallaga coca region in Peru and the clandestine cocaine laboratories located in Colombia in the mid-1990s [11]. Consequently, by 2000, Colombia cultivated an estimated 90 percent of the world's coca leaf, while production in Peru and Bolivia dwindled to historic lows [12].

The Early Cartels

In the early 1990s, Colombia's (United States-backed) war against drug lord Pablo Escobar and the Medellín cartel during the César Gaviria administration lead to Escobar's death on December 2, 1993, and the almost immediate demise of the Medellín cartel. Following that, plea bargaining in 1994–1995 during the Ernesto Samper administration with the major drug lords of the Cali cartel, specifically the Rodríguez Orejuela brothers, signaled the end of that cartel.

While some large criminal trafficking networks (e.g., the Cartel del Norte del Valle) continued to operate in Colombia in the late 1990s and early 2000s, some 300-plus smaller drug-trafficking organizations (known as *cartelitos*) surfaced to fill the vacuum left in Colombia's still highly profitable drug trade by the dismantling of the two major cartels. By the late 1990s, essentially as an unforeseen and unintended consequence of the destruction of the country's major cartels, Colombia's left-wing *Fuerzas Armadas Revolucionarias de Colombia* (Revolutionary Armed Forces of Colombia, or FARC) guerrillas and right-wing *Autodefensas Unidas de Colombia* (United Self-Defense Forces of Colombia, or AUC) paramilitary militias seized the opportunity to take control of coca cultivation and processing throughout rural Colombia. This resulted in an explosion of drug-related violence between these two heavily armed illegal actors, as each sought to eliminate the other and to consolidate its own territorial control over drug cultivation regions and the peasant growers across Colombia [13]. As of 2000, Colombia became one of the most dangerous and violent countries in the world.

As an unintended consequence of the United States-backed "war on drugs" in Colombia, criminal organizations trafficking cocaine gradually shifted northward from Colombia to Mexico. As a result, the major drug-trafficking networks in Mexico took advantage of the vacuum left in the drug trade to take control of cocaine-trafficking operations from Colombia to the United States. Expectedly, drug-related crime and violence shifted northward into Mexico as various Mexican trafficking organizations fought for control over the highly profitable smuggling trade from Colombia and the southern Andes to the large and profitable United States market [14].

Thus, Mexico's current drug-related bloodbath is, in part, directly attributable to the partial victory in the war on drugs achieved in Colombia in recent years via Plan Colombia. If the United States-backed Mérida Initiative, which is presently being implemented in

Mexico, achieves results similar to those of Plan Colombia, it will not halt drug trafficking or end organized crime in Mexico or in the region. The most likely outcome is that it will both drive it further underground in Mexico while also pushing many smuggling activities and trafficking operations into neighboring countries such as Guatemala and Honduras, and back to Colombia and the Andes. Currently, there is evidence that some Mexican drug-trafficking operations such as the Sinaloa and Zetas cartels, are moving from Mexico into Central America.

The Balloon Effect: The Spreading of Cultivation Areas and Smuggling Routes

In 2011, the UNODC World Drug Report indicated that Colombia successfully reduced the total number of hectares under coca cultivation within its national territory in the second half of the 2000s, and despite new increases in 2011, production has still not returned to pre-2000 levels. The true extent of reductions in Colombian coca cultivation since 2009 is a controversial topic for which no hard evidence exists. According to research, however, coca cultivation in both Peru and Bolivia, after almost two decades of decline, appears once again to have expanded [15].

Many believe that overall coca leaf production and cocaine availability in the Andean region remain roughly on par with 2000 levels and well above those of 1990 or 1995. Evidently, the *balloon effect* that allowed coca cultivation to shift north from Bolivia and Peru to Colombia in the 1990s continues to operate as cultivation moved back into Peru and Bolivia from Colombia at the end of the first decade of the 2000s.

Various observers have speculated about the possibility that the tropical variety of coca—known in Portuguese as *epadu*—may balloon coca cultivation from its traditional growing areas on the eastern slopes of the Andes into Brazil and elsewhere in the Amazon basin in coming years, if ongoing or renewed eradication efforts prove successful in Colombia, Peru, and Bolivia [16].

The main reason that Colombia appears to have experienced a significant decline in coca production in 2008 and 2009 is that the Uribe government moved away from its almost exclusive (United States-financed) reliance on aerial spraying to a more effective mixture of spraying and manual eradication linked to comprehensive alternative development programs in key coca-growing areas such as La Macarena. As a result of the weakening of FARC control in vast stretches of rural Colombia, and the partial demobilization of the paramilitary bands engaged in drug trafficking over the period 2002–2007, 2008–2009 marked the beginning of an important decline after at least 3 years of steady increases in total production [17].

Meanwhile, it appears that recent increases in coca cultivation in both Peru and Bolivia are because the United States has focused on Colombia and has neglected coca cultivation in those traditional coca-growing countries in the central Andes. As of the preparation of this text, in order to keep the *balloon effect* from pushing cultivation out of one country only to have it reappear in others, the current Obama administration will have to re-establish a working relationship with the government of President Evo Morales in Bolivia and find effective ways to combat the resurgence of *Sendero Luminoso* (Shining Path, an insurgent organization) and coca cultivation in Peru. Experts predict that a failure to achieve more effective drug control policies in both countries will likely result in a continuing shift of coca production back to Peru and Bolivia, thereby counteracting any progress made in reducing coca cultivation in Colombia [18].

The balloon effects produced by the temporary "victories" in the "war on drugs" in the Andes on both drug cultivation and drug-smuggling routes are clear. Over the past 25 years and more, drug control initiatives by the United States and its various Latin American and Caribbean allies succeeded repeatedly in shifting coca cultivation from one area to another in the Andes, and in forcing frequent changes in smuggling routes. However, they have proven unable to disrupt seriously, much less completely stop, either production or trafficking in the region. This is because the traffickers' ongoing ability to adapt to law enforcement efforts designed to end their activities have led to the progressive contamination of more and more countries in the region.

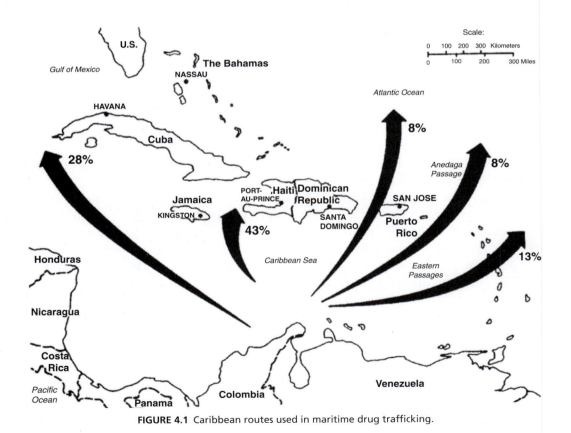

FIGURE 4.1 Caribbean routes used in maritime drug trafficking.

The Cockroach Effect: Dispersion and Fragmentation of Drug-Trafficking Groups

The differential insertion of individual countries into the political economy of drug trafficking in the Western Hemisphere has produced a variety of forms and types of intermediation between peasant growers of illicit crops and consumers. In Bolivia, the presence of peasant cooperatives in the countryside since the *Movimiento Nacional Revolucionario* (National Revolutionary Movement, or MNR) revolution of 1952 produced coca growers' associations and generally inhibited the rise of either criminal organizations or guerrilla movements as intermediaries, although the Bolivian military itself has on various occasions fulfilled this role [19]. In Peru, the absence of strong grassroots associations among peasant growers opened the way for both elements of the country's military apparatus (led by intelligence chief Vladimiro Montesinos) and guerrilla organizations (*Sendero Luminoso*) to perform the role of intermediaries or traffickers. In Colombia, the absence of both peasant organizations and military intermediaries paved the way for the rise of major criminal organizations such as the Medellín and Cali cartels to fill the role. The demise of the major cartels opened the way for illegal armed actors such as the FARC and the paramilitaries. In Mexico and Central America, elements of the military and/or police have sometimes performed the functions of intermediation in previous decades, but in the 1990s and 2000s, these countries followed the Colombian pattern of criminal intermediation owing to the absence of strong growers' associations [20].

Criminal organizations in Colombia and Mexico provide the two most important examples of the *cockroach effect* over the last 25 years. For example, in Colombia, the rise and fall of Medellín and Cali (and, subsequently, the Norte del Valle cartel) vividly illustrate the perils and vulnerabilities of large, hierarchical criminal trafficking organizations, especially when they attempt to confront the state openly. Both major cartels in Colombia were hierarchically structured and proved to be vulnerable targets for Colombian and international law enforcement agencies—including the U.S. Drug Enforcement Administration (DEA).

In the wake of Medellín and Cali, Colombia witnessed a rapid fragmentation and dispersion of criminal networks that have proven far more difficult for law enforcement authorities to track down and dismantle than their larger and more notorious predecessors [21].

Although there may be countertendencies leading to reconcentration among criminal trafficking organizations in Colombia today, the basic lesson to emerge from Colombia appears to be that smaller criminal networks are less vulnerable to law enforcement and state repression. For example, Colombia's emerging *Bandas Criminales* (BACRIM), the descendants of the now formally demobilized paramilitary groups that made up the AUC, represent a new generation of drug traffickers in Colombia.

The BACRIM differ from other groups in several important respects:

1. They are much more skillful and shrewd in seeking political alliances inside the Colombian economic and political establishment, often hiding their political linkages through indirect contacts and "clean" candidates without records of paramilitary affiliations or ties in the past.

2. They focus on establishing political influence at the municipal and departmental (provincial) levels rather than at the national level.
3. The focus of their activities includes not only Colombia's Caribbean coast, but also the Pacific southwest.
4. They have expanded their economic interests beyond drug trafficking to include other illegal activities (land piracy, gold mining, and timber) as well as legal enterprises. From the Colombian state's perspective so far, such organizations are far less threatening because they do not have the capacity to threaten state security directly [22].

In Mexico, as in Colombia in the 1980s and early 1990s, cocaine profits energized the country's major criminal organizations and unleashed a wave of violence among gangs seeking to strengthen and consolidate their control of key smuggling routes. In 2012, this struggle was still playing itself out in a brutal and bloody fashion.

Nonetheless, Mexico's criminal trafficking groups do appear to be gradually following the Colombian pattern of dispersion and fragmentation. For example, in 2000, the Tijuana cartel (Arellano-Félix family) and the Juárez cartel (Carrillo-Fuentes family) were the two largest and most dominant drug-trafficking organizations in Mexico. Since 2000, after the Vicente Fox administration first targeted Tijuana and Juárez, Mexico has seen the rise of at least five new major trafficking organizations—the Sinaloa, Gulf, Familia Michocana, Beltrán-Leyva, and Zetas cartels—and a host of smaller, lesser known groups.

This dispersion of criminal networks in Mexico may well represent the beginning of the kind of fragmentation seen in Colombia in the 1990s. Should this occur, the trend would be warmly welcomed by Mexican governing authorities because it would signal a considerable diminution in the capacity of organized criminal networks in Mexico to directly challenge its state authority and national security.

A key reason why some analysts do not accept the fragmentation of organized crime thesis in contemporary Mexico relates directly to the emergence of a new criminal network model as evidenced by the Sinaloa cartel. Unlike those who preceded it and current Mexican rivals, the Sinaloa cartel is less hierarchical and more akin to the "hub and spokes" model in its organizational structure.

Its principal leader, Joaquín "El Chapo" Guzmán Loera, has established a new type of "federation" that gives greater independence (and profits) to affiliated groups. To date, the Sinaloa cartel, also known as the Federation, seems to be winning the war against its rivals, although its fight against the Zetas (a paramilitary-style organization) is proving to be prolonged, costly, and bloody.

As in the Colombian case during the 1980s and 1990s, paramilitary groups have also surfaced in recent years in Juárez, Monterrey, and other parts of Mexico in response to the cartels and affiliated gang violence. The appearance of these paramilitary bands highlights the weak law enforcement capacities of the Mexican government, and its perceived inability to effectively confront and defeat the country's powerful drug-trafficking organizations.

Under pressure from Mexican and United States law enforcement, Mexican trafficking organizations have, since the mid-2000s if not earlier, sought to move at least part of their smuggling operations from Mexico into neighboring countries. Guatemala and Honduras are currently targets for both the Sinaloa cartel and the Zetas. This trend, observable throughout the Western Hemisphere, is sometimes labeled the *cockroach effect*, because it is reminiscent of the scurrying of cockroaches out of a dirty kitchen into other places to avoid detection after a light has been turned on them. Closely linked to the balloon effect, the cockroach effect refers specifically to the displacement of criminal networks from one city, state, and region to another within a given country, or from one country to another in search of safer havens and more pliable state authorities [23].

The Economics of Drug Trafficking

With few exceptions, the drug trade attracts entrepreneurs who are motivated by profit. As with any business, illicit or not, certain principles apply to the successful operation of the trafficking system. For example, drug traffickers in retail markets typically use a "just-in-time" business strategy. That is, in many cases only small amounts of drugs are supplied to street vendors, which minimizes their losses should the vendor be arrested by police or robbed by competitors. In many cities, the just-in-time strategy makes it possible for sellers to provide just enough drug product for street vendors to sell in one day's time, or for crack house operators to sell in about a week's time. Suppliers are aware that in addition to the type of drug seized, in some states the quantity of drugs seized plays a role in the severity of the criminal charge. So, if a vendor is in possession of small amounts when arrested, not only will he or she possibly be looking at a lesser charge, but also the supplier's credit standing with a wholesaler will not be jeopardized for future sales. Any such losses can easily be compensated for with future sales. With the drug trade being profit driven, both wholesale and retail pricing play important roles in realizing earnings.

Drug Prices

With profit being the mainstay of the drug business, a number of variables can be attributed to the establishment, rise, and decline of drug prices. In addition to other factors, the laws of supply and demand play a major role in determining whether a certain drug's price increases, falls, or remains stable. For example, drug dealers are keenly aware that police investigations result in the arrest and imprisonment of people associated with the drug trade. To insulate themselves from police detection, trafficking managers hire lower-level dealers to bear the risks of dealing on the street level. These sellers are often street-corner minions trading in small quantities of drugs, but they may also be couriers who have been entrusted with a greater amount of responsibility for transporting drug shipments.

Occasionally, dealers are arrested and their stashes of drugs seized by police. In addition to seizure by police, some drug shipments face other fates:

- Stolen by rival criminal organizations
- Thrown overboard vessels to avoid confiscation
- Not picked up because of fear of police surveillance
- Flushed down toilets for fear of seizure by police
- Abandoned after dealers are arrested by police

All these circumstances result in the drug supply not arriving at the designated point of delivery. Consequently, subsequent shipments of the same drug might be affected by an increase in the street price. This brings up another important business variable that parallels legitimate commerce: wholesale prices are much cheaper than retail prices. When cocaine, for example, is produced in South America, its wholesale price is often based on the amount that is purchased; the larger the purchase, the lower the price. After the drugs arrive in the United States for distribution, prices rise considerably. This occurs not only because of the cost of production and transportation of the drugs, but also because of the risks undertaken by dealers and distributors. Here is a hypothetical example: assume that 10 kg of opium from Mexico is valued at $40,000. Once this opium is transformed into heroin of 40–70 percent purity, it is sold for anywhere from $150,000 to $260,000 per kilogram in the United States at the wholesale level. Once the drugs reach the midlevel stage of distribution, heroin at 20–70 percent purity could be sold for roughly $500,000 per kilogram. According to DEA Heroin Signature Program (HSP) data, the wholesale purity of Mexican heroin was 40 percent in 2008 [24].

Black tar heroin of 20–60 percent purity can sell for $850,000 per kilogram. In sum, the street price of this heroin is between 153 and 183 times the price it was at the time it was cultivated. Further complicating the price structure is the fact that the prices of drugs also depend on the country of origin or other geographical factors. This is evident when we consider that in 1990, the price of a gram of cocaine varied from $35 in Miami to $125 in Los Angeles [25].

It is common for different grades of drugs to dictate the street price of that drug. For example, in the marijuana business, wholesale and retail prices of both commercial and sinsemilla grades were lowest in Houston. This is because the drugs were transported through Mexico to Houston, thus the distribution chain was shorter than if the drugs were transported to Omaha or Boston.

The price of a drug may also affect how drug buyers conduct business. For example, higher prices for a drug may result in the potential buyer choosing not to purchase the drug until prices come down, or until another dealer is located who is selling the drug for a cheaper price. Accordingly, the buyer may choose to cut back on the use of the drug because of the high price tag. Finally, buyers may opt to substitute a less expensive drug with similar effects for the expensive drug. In any case, it is clear that the more expensive a drug, the less likely it will sell as readily on the street. Knowledge of these business dynamics is the reason why drug control efforts by police often attempt to raise

---

WHY PRICES OF ILLICIT DRUGS VARY

- Distances the drugs travel
- Number of rungs on the distribution ladder before reaching retail levels
- Shortages of drug supplies due to wholesale and retail losses
- Changes in pricing at the export-import and subsequent levels
- Buyer preferences for drugs from a particular nation and of certain varieties or grades

---

the prices of drugs, thus making them too expensive for users to afford. In addition, high drug prices are also thought to deter would-be users from beginning the use of that particular drug.

Demand Elasticity

Demand elasticity refers to the relationship between the change in the use of an item and the price of that item. In legitimate business, if the price of a commodity rises, the total purchases of that commodity decrease. So too in the illicit drug trade: the amount that the total use of a drug decreases (due to high prices) depends on how sensitive the demand is to that rise in price. A close examination of retail drug prices tells us that demand elasticity hinges on the type of drug in question. For example, price elasticity is greater for heroin than it is for marijuana because heroin is a physically addictive drug, whereas marijuana is not. Therefore, drug users are more willing to pay more for a drug they "need" than for a drug they may simply desire.

Financing Drug Deals

In the world of legitimate commerce, businesses are much less concerned with hiding profits than are their illegal business counterparts. For this reason, it is not uncommon for businesses to borrow millions of dollars of capital from legitimate banking institutions. Once profits are realized, regular deposits can be made into banks or other financial institutions for disbursement or reinvestment. As one might guess, the rules of the game are quite different for business transactions in the illicit drug trade. Instead of borrowing money from a bank or other lending institution, drug dealers will often have a "revolving credit" arrangement with their suppliers, whereby payment for the drugs is not required until they have been sold. In such cases, payments are not made until the dealers take delivery of a subsequent drug shipment. In time, as the dealer's financial base grows, shell or front corporations are sometimes established that help disguise or "launder" drug profits.

The hiding of drug revenues is an essential component of the illicit drug trade, since profits are earned without paying taxes on those earnings. In legitimate business operations, businesses pay taxes on their profits in proportion to the amount of money changing hands. As a result, a large part of the profit realized by drug dealers is money that would otherwise be paid to the government. Chapter 6 addresses the issue of money laundering.

Merchandising and Distribution of Illegal Drugs

The *illicit drug-trafficking chain* refers to large shipments of drugs that are transported from their point of origin to their destination, where they are broken down into much smaller quantities for street-level distribution. With each stage in the distribution cycle, the price of the drug increases. Accordingly, as the shipment of drugs gets closer to the street, along with an increase in the price of the drug, the purity of the drug decreases. The *distribution chain* refers to the players along the trafficking route. For example, in a cocaine-trafficking operation, the first level of players consists of the coca farmers, who cultivate the coca plant and sell by the bushel to traffickers, who then hire people to process the leaves into coca paste. Once the coca paste has been produced, it is sold to midlevel producers, who dry the paste on drying tables, where it becomes cocaine hydrochloride or powder. Next, smugglers are hired to transport the cocaine to the United States to be delivered to wholesalers, who in turn sell quantities to retail salespeople. Finally, the retail salesperson sells small quantities to low-level street dealers, who bear a greater risk of arrest than any other player in the distribution chain.

At the retail level, the buying and selling of drugs often entails a complex exchange of schemes and roles. For instance, some people who are not necessarily involved in the actual sale of drugs may be used as *steerers*, who locate potential customers for dealers. Others may act as guards or lookouts, charged with locating police vehicles spotted in the area of drug sales. In other cases, one player is assigned to sell the drugs while a different person takes the money from the sale. This structure represents the classic division of labor in the drug trade, and illustrates how operatives can insulate themselves from detection because it may be more difficult for police investigators to observe transactions.

Marketing Illicit Drugs

It is common in the drug business for dealers to attempt to convince potential buyers of the purity or quality of their product. Typically, this is done by offering a specific drug with an identifiable label; for instance, Panama Red or Colombian Gold marijuana. In other cases, the seller asks the buyer to trust his or her reputation as an honest local drug dealer. In still other cases, drugs are sold based on the quantity offered. For instance, if a high price is being asked for a gram of cocaine, the seller may remind the buyer that there is actually a gram and a quarter available for the price of a single gram, giving the buyer the impression that he or she is getting more than his or her money's worth.

Marketing is also apparent in the packaging of certain drugs. In Columbia, Missouri, for example, *blotter acid* (lysergic acid diethylamide (LSD)) appeared on the street in the form of Grateful Dead album covers. Virtually every album cover image ever produced by this rock group was available to buyers in blotter acid form. For the potential buyer to purchase the entire album cover image, however, he or she had to purchase 12 individual dosage units of the drug, since the picture of the album was spread out over all 12 squares of paper, each of them containing LSD. Heroin dealers also use marketing techniques to persuade buyers to purchase their heroin over that of another dealer. Techniques include marking bags with colored tape, symbols, or pictures, or assigning a particular batch or

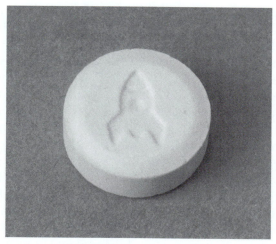

FIGURE 4.2 A rocket emblazoned on the designer drug ecstasy. Manufacturers and exporters of illegal drugs use identifiable labels and "brand names" to convince the buying public of the quality of their products. *Source: iStockPhoto.*

dealer's heroin a brand name like Red Lion heroin. Brand names help users identify the heroin thought to be of high quality. Interestingly, if an addict dies as a result of a drug overdose, other addicts will often seek out the specific drug used by the deceased, believing that the user failed to realize it was of such high quality.

As drug enforcement efforts become more successful and effective, and as different drugs become increasingly popular, drug dealers often shift their marketing strategies. These changes in drugs and drug use may result in the development of new drugs or analogs, or the reemergence of older drugs that have not been popular for a while. In any event, it is always the drug dealer's desire to increase the potency of the drug he or she sells. Once this can be accomplished, word will spread among drug buyers, who will seek out the new, more potent drug.

Distributing Illegal Drugs

Drug sales networks differ somewhat from one case to the next. For example, trafficking not only differs from rural to urban areas, but also depends on the type of drug and the techniques of the group distributing it. Most large urban areas have sections of town that are known as drug distribution areas. These areas, sometimes called *copping areas*, are typically well known to drug users. Often, these areas are nothing more than street corners or public parks where small amounts of drugs are sold. Here, it is common for many different drug sales to take place in a short period of time. Buyers go to the copping area, pay cash for the drugs, and leave—all in a matter of seconds. Investigations have shown that dealers operating in copping areas often sell to known customers and strangers alike. As a rule, dealers in copping areas will employ lookouts and steerers, who watch for both police and potential customers. Once dealers are tipped off about the presence of police in the area, they can dispose of their drugs before being caught in possession of them (Table 4.1).

Neighborhood bars, truck stops, or homes in affluent areas of town are sometimes fixed locations for drug dealing. Studies into the habits of dealers and users have revealed that middle-class buyers will often make their purchases away from the typical urban copping area to avoid getting arrested. In some cases, drug deals are arranged by telephone and a drop-off location is chosen. Crack houses are yet another example of a fixed location for drug dealing. Such locations emerged during the mid-1980s and are often abandoned buildings or apartments in public housing projects located near copping areas. In the crack house are the necessary paraphernalia for taking cocaine. This equipment includes needles and syringes for injecting, as well as pipes and heat sources for smoking crack. The Detroit Police Department identified two types of crack houses: (1) a "buy-and-get-high" party house, where drugs are consumed on the premises in conjunction with illicit sex acts; and (2) a "hole in the wall" house, where buyers would literally put cash into a hole in the wall at the front door of a house and receive crack cocaine from an unidentified seller on the other side.

Profit Margin

Although it is true that wholesale and midlevel drug dealers make hundreds of thousands of dollars and escape detection, people operating on the lower rung of the trafficking chain, especially those who are considered heavy drug users, accumulate few riches. The Bureau of Justice Statistics has cited several reasons for this:

- Their profits often support their own drug use.
- The drug business is a fragile enterprise subject to considerable disruption by police efforts, frequent absence of a reliable supply of drugs, and a high potential for loss by predatory competitors and disloyal employees.
- Their involvement in drug sales is often sporadic.
- Earnings tend to be spent ostentatiously on expensive cars, gold jewelry, and other consumer goods.
- Many dealers spend a substantial amount of their time in jail or prison [26].

The mystique of drug dealing is shadowed by an illusion that all drug dealers make a lot of money. Unquestionably, this is not always the case. Experts have also suggested that one reason for the small amount of money earned by low-level drug dealers is that they often deal drugs on a part-time basis. In fact, a study by the RAND Corporation concluded that the typical drug dealer netted between $25 and $2500 per month from sales. Interviews during the study showed that 75 percent of these dealers held jobs in addition to drug dealing, and that drug dealing only supplemented their income. The study also revealed that most small-time drug dealers were heavy drug users as well as sellers and spent an average of 25 percent of their earnings on drugs. In the case of marijuana

Table 4.1   How Do the Roles and Functions at Various Levels of the Drug Distribution Business Compare with Those in Legitimate Industry?

Approximate Role Equivalents in Legal Markets	Roles by Common Names at Various Stages of the Drug Distribution Business	Major Functions Accomplished at this Level
Grower/producer	Coca farmer, opium farmer, marijuana grower	Grow cocoa, opium, marijuana; the raw materials
Manufacturer	Collector, transporter, elaborator, chemist, drug lord	All stages for preparation of heroin, cocaine, marijuana as commonly sold
Traffickers		
Importer	Multikilo importer, mule, airplane pilot, smuggler, trafficker, money launderer	Smuggling of large quantities of substances into the United States
Wholesale distributor	Major distributor, investor, "kilo connection"	Transportation and redistribution of multikilograms and single kilograms
Dealers		
Regional distributor	"Pound-and-ounce man," weight dealer	Adulteration and sale of moderately expensive products
Retail store owner	House connections, suppliers, crack-house supplier	Adulteration and production of retail-level dosage units (bags, vials, grams) in very large numbers
Assistant manager, security chief, or accountant	"Lieutenant", "muscle man," transporter, crew boss, crack-house manager/proprietor	Supervises three or more sellers enforces informal contracts, collects money, distributes multiple dosage units to actual sellers
Sellers		
Store clerk, sales representative (door-to-door and phone)	Street drug seller, runner, juggler	Makes actual direct sales to consumer; private seller responsible for both money and drugs
Low-level distributors		
Advertiser, security guard, leaflet distributor	Steerer, tout, cop man, look-out holder, runner, help friend, guard, go-between	Assists in making sales, advertises, protects seller from police and criminals, solicits customers, handles drugs or money but not both
Servant, temporary employee	Runner of shooting gallery, injector (of drugs), freebaser, taster, apartment cleaner, drug bagger, fence, money launderer	Provides short-term services to drug users or sellers for money or drugs, not responsible for money or drugs

Source: Bureau of Justice Statistics. (1992). *Drugs, crime, and the justice system*. Washington, DC: U.S. Department of Justice.

dealers, profits were shown to be considerably smaller than for other types of drugs, and dealings were much more casual and sporadic than transactions involving other, "harder" drugs [27].

The enormous profits to be realized in the United States drug market have intrigued both domestic and foreign traffickers. Although many drugs, such as methamphetamine, LSD, and phencyclidine, are largely produced domestically, and a rapidly increasing proportion of the marijuana consumed in the United States is grown domestically, foreign traffickers supply an estimated 75 percent of illicit substances consumed in the United States [28]. Cocaine is a primary example of a drug imported by foreign drug networks. The United States' cocaine supply originates almost exclusively in South America; the coca plant is cultivated principally in Peru, Bolivia, Colombia, and Ecuador. Accordingly, processing laboratories have been seized in Colombia, Brazil, and Venezuela. Other South American and Caribbean countries have also served as transshipment centers for drugs.

Other drugs frequently smuggled into the United States from foreign countries are marijuana and hashish, both products of the hemp or cannabis plant. Mexico supplies an estimated 30 percent of cannabis to the United States; Colombia supplies an estimated 33 percent, although (as indicated previously) these percentages have been consistently declining due to increases in domestic marijuana production. Other foreign countries contributing to the United States marijuana market are Jamaica in the Caribbean and Belize in Central America.

Open-Air Drug Markets

It is difficult, if not impossible, to have a proper understanding of the illicit drug trade without a discussion of open-air drug markets. So-called open-air markets represent the lowest level of the drug distribution network. Open-air drug markets are typified by the corner drug dealer who sells drugs with little if any concern with whom he or she transacts business. In other words, in the mind of the drug dealer, the risk of arrest is overshadowed by the lure of quick and easy profits.

From a drug control perspective, these low-level markets need to be addressed by police effectively, not only because of the risks posed to market participants, but also to reduce the obvious harm that illicit drug use can inflict on the local community.

As with any other type of commodity, illicit drugs are traded in a market where buyer and seller have to locate one another in order to conduct a transaction [29]. There are two types of retail market systems: those that are "person specific," relying on social networks to communicate information about vendors, potential customers, and vendors' location and prices; and those that are "place specific" [30]. For the most part, open-air drug markets are place specific: they operate in geographically well-defined areas at identifiable times so buyers and sellers can locate one another with ease. A variety of drugs may be sold, most commonly including heroin, crack and powder cocaine, marijuana, and, to a lesser extent, methamphetamine.

Open-air markets are also likely to be *open markets*. This means that there will be few barriers to access, and anyone who looks like a plausible buyer will be able to purchase drugs. This makes transacting illicit drugs easy for the buyer and for the seller.

An open market has advantages for both buyers and sellers. Buyers know where to go in order to find the drugs that they want and can weigh quality against price, and sellers are able to maximize customer access. However, the nature of open markets means that market participants are vulnerable and exposed to both police enforcement and the dangers of buying from strangers—which may include rip-offs and robbery. Furthermore, if a buyer is dissatisfied with the transaction, there can rarely be any recourse as participants in illegal markets generally lack the means for resolving business conflicts. Especially in high-value markets, this can lead to widespread violence—whereby force is the normal means by which disagreements are resolved [31].

In response to the risks of law enforcement, open markets tend to transform into *closed markets*, where sellers will do business only with buyers they know or with buyers for whom another trusted person will vouch. The degree to which markets are closed—the barriers of access put in the way of new buyers—will depend largely on the level of threat posed by the police, undercover investigators, and their informants. Intensive policing can quickly transform open markets into closed ones [32]. Mobile communication technologies such as pagers and cell phones also aid this process. Although closed markets may exist alongside open markets, their method of operation is notably different and requires its own police response [33].

Open-air drug markets present a considerable and ongoing challenge for the police. Research has shown that those police operations that focus on simply arresting buyers and sellers have little impact in reducing the size of the market or the amount of drugs consumed [34]. This is especially true of low-level markets where if one dealer is arrested, there are, more than likely, several others to take their place. Moreover, drug markets are increasingly dynamic in that they can be highly responsive to enforcement efforts. But the form of that response is sometimes an adaptation that leads to unintended consequences for police, including displacement or increased revenue for dealers with fewer competitors [35].

Drug dealing in open-air markets generates or contributes to a wide range of social disorder and drug-related crime in the surrounding community that can have a marked effect on the local residents' quality of life [36]. For example, residents may feel a reduced sense of public safety as drug-related activity becomes more blatant, and there is evidence that public areas such as parks are often taken over by drug sellers and their customers, rendering them unsafe and off limits to local citizens [37]. Spin-off problems associated with drug dealing in open-air markets include the following:

- Traffic congestion
- Noise (from traffic and people)
- Disorderly conduct

- Begging
- Loitering
- Vandalism
- Drug use and littering (e.g., discarded drug paraphernalia)
- Criminal damage to property
- Prostitution
- Robbery
- Residential and commercial burglary
- Theft from motor vehicles
- Fencing stolen goods
- Weapons offenses
- Assaults and homicides [38]

When and Where Open-Air Drug Markets Operate

The characteristics of a drug market often depend on the type of drug being sold. In some areas, markets for different drugs exist alongside one another, although their methods of operation vary. It is likely that most illicit drug buying takes place in private or semipublic locations. Given the choice, most users would rather buy from sellers they know and trust, rather than run the risk of being ripped off by the drug dealers (e.g., through robbery or the sale of poor-quality drugs) or apprehended by the police. However, it may be that a need for regular supplies of drugs obtained in the shortest time possible forces drug users with chronic addictions to frequent street-based open markets. This may also be true for inexperienced or recreational users who have not yet established an alternative reliable source.

Typically, open-air drug markets are located in inner-city or other urban areas. There are four geographical features common to this type of drug market:

1. They are likely to be located in economically depressed neighborhoods;
2. Dealers will sell from static sites so customers know where to find them;
3. The market will probably be located around a transport hub, or along a main arterial route where there is a level of legitimate activity and proximity to through routes to allow buyers easy access to the market area; and
4. Markets that have a reputation for selling drugs can grow large in size, and the concentration of activity in a small area will be hard to hide [39].

The compulsive nature of drugs such as crack cocaine or the physical dependency that can occur from prolonged heroin use means that the market in which these drugs are sold could be open 24 hours a day, 7 days a week. The operational times of markets for other drugs, including cannabis and ecstasy, are probably more restricted.

The location of an open-air drug market can also be influenced by "situational factors." The local environment can facilitate drug dealing in a number of different ways. For example, thick or overgrown foliage offers a shield for exchanges of money or drugs.

Poor street lighting may also intensify residents' fear of crime and may increase incidences of robbery. Street layout can determine "ideal" places to stand so sellers can watch for the police, and it can provide easy escape routes in case of enforcement activity. Road systems and parking can also influence customers driving in from other areas, and vacant buildings have typically served as isolated locations for using drugs after purchase [40].

In support of drug dealers and drug trafficking are certain key figures, such as "place managers" such as landlords, housing authorities, and local business residents' and tenants' associations. Those who diligently control their apartment buildings or their business premises' forecourt will reduce the chance of an illicit market becoming established in their neighborhood; drug sellers will often operate from locations where place managers do not attempt to exert any control over illicit activity [41]. Open-air drug markets are therefore more likely to become established in areas where there is a high rate of rental properties and/or public housing, rather than in owner-occupied neighborhoods. Conversely, some place managers work with drug dealers by knowingly providing trafficking locations. These persons sometimes realize the financial benefits of providing a location for drug trafficking when they are the beneficiaries of the drug profits and can offer some degree of protection to traffickers.

The Structure of Open-Air Drug Markets

In order to understand the effect of police activities on open-air drug markets, it is important to consider the structure of their social organization. Criminal organizations often operate open-air drug markets with clear hierarchies and well-defined job functions [42]. Other drug distribution networks consist of fragmented systems represented by small groups of opportunistic newcomers from a range of backgrounds. At least four different types of organization for open-air drug markets exist:

1. Markets dominated by "freelance" sellers, characterized by a lack of formal hierarchy and alliances conducted on an ad hoc basis.
2. Markets dominated by family-based businesses that may have evolved out of freelance markets when groups of relatives begin to dominate their local area and drive out competition.
3. Markets dominated by culture-based organizations—family-based organizations may grow into businesses with a shared common culture.
4. Marketplaces dominated by corporations, which represent the highest level of organizational structure [43].

Dealers operating in open markets represent the lowest level of the distribution network and will typically be selling in order to finance their own use. Selling drugs provides those who are unemployed or otherwise socially disenfranchised with a means of earning money that can be highly profitable. Moreover, it does not require education or training, and it presents relatively low risk in terms of the likelihood of arrest [44].

That said, those operating in this type of market are unlikely to sell a substantial quantity of drugs to one customer because, first, they may not have a sufficient supply, and, second, they will be reluctant to carry a large quantity on them at one time for fear of arrest. However, in a busy market, the number of daily transactions can be notably high.

Within the community, sellers may attempt to buy the cooperation of local residents or employ them in various roles. For example, a mother with a baby could be a "look-out" or "holder." Other roles include the following:

- *Steerers*, who refer customers to a particular dealer
- "Touts," whose job is to locate customers
- "Middlemen," who transport money and drugs between the buyer and seller, who do not meet [45]

Supply and Demand

Popular debate about drugs tends to take for granted that illicit drug use is supply led, and that illicit drug use is best controlled by stopping drugs getting into the country and onto the streets. On the other hand, it has been suggested that supply follows demand and is a response to it. In reality, there is a dynamic and interactive relationship between the two: if there were no supply of illicit drugs, no demand would ever evolve; and, of course, unless drugs offered users some immediate attraction, there would be no demand.

A distinction is often made between supply reduction strategies and demand reduction strategies. However, this becomes hard to maintain because one will very likely affect the other. Reduction in the supply of drugs will eventually affect prices, which in turn should affect demand, especially of new and occasional users. Despite this, little is known about the impact that supply reduction has on prices, or the relationship between price and demand. Enforcement could lead to price increases in two ways. Firstly, removing drugs from the supply chain should result in limited availability and thus an increase in price. Secondly, the increased risks for market participants concomitant with enforcement should translate into higher prices.

It is difficult to untangle the effect that supply reduction strategies have on the price of drugs. In actuality, drug prices in several cities have declined in recent years, although, without enforcement, prices may have fallen even further [46]. However, it is also likely that supply reduction strategies have been insufficient in maintaining or increasing prices. In addition, drug markets are capable of adapting quickly to enforcement efforts, and effective enforcement can sometimes bring about perverse effects [47].

According to this argument, enforcement leads to sustained or increased risks of criminal sanctions; these risks are translated into maintained or increased prices, but the net result is to attract more people into the highly lucrative—if risky—drug business.

It is also important to consider how drug prices will affect levels of consumption. If most illicit drug use is controlled, an increase in price should lead to a decrease in demand.

However, problem drug users will be more inflexible in their ability to stop using than other users and are likely to simply spend more. In this case, it is important to find strategies that provide other, nonfinancial deterrents to discourage use.

Street-Level Enforcement

A factor contributing to the emergence of open-air drug markets was the low priority given to street-level drug enforcement. Until the mid-1980s, traditional narcotics enforcement in the United States concentrated resources on wholesale drug activity. This was partly due to the Knapp Commission Report (1972), which lambasted the New York City Police Department for widespread corruption related to local drug enforcement. The consequence of this report was that street-level enforcement across the country was effectively halted; neighborhood patrol officers were replaced by reactive units whose mission was to respond to (rather than prevent) crime, and open-air markets began to thrive [48].

The emergence of crack cocaine in the early 1980s fueled already buoyant drug markets and forced the police to reexamine street-level enforcement. Police authorities responded to the idea that enforcement tactics had been targeted at the wrong level of distribution and aimed to disrupt street-level markets, making them unpredictable for both buyer and seller. A principle of this method was "inconvenience policing," which aimed to increase the drug search time or to otherwise place obstacles in the way of the buying process. The idea was that although such measures would probably not deter serious and addicted users, casual and novice users would be discouraged from buying, and therefore the market would be constricted. Enforcement strategies aimed at this level included high-visibility policing, test purchase operations, and reverse stings. In addition, it became clear that police enforcement alone was ineffective at reducing drug-related activity, and lately there has been an increased focus on multiagency cooperation to implement innovative approaches such as civil enforcement procedures.

The International Perspective

Drug trafficking is a generic term referring to the commercial exchange of illegal drugs, including the equipment and substances involved in producing, manufacturing, and using illicit drugs. Prohibition has been established by governments to enforce, deter, and eradicate the exchange of such illegal goods.

Despite vigorous enforcement efforts, the United Nations estimates that only 10–15 percent of heroin and 30 percent of cocaine is intercepted worldwide. It is estimated that at least 70 percent of international drug shipments need to be intercepted to substantially reduce the industry [49]. The drug market continues to produce the same, or even higher, quantities of illicit drugs in spite of record seizures by law enforcement. Developed efforts of drug control authorities in some countries have merely moved drug-trafficking operations to weaker jurisdictions and forced greater organizational sophistication. Economists call this the *balloon effect* because these efforts are like squeezing a filled balloon: when the air is squeezed out of one part, it is simply transferred to another.

This balloon effect is commonly seen in South and Central Asia and in Latin America, where the majority of illicit drugs is produced and trafficked, and where international interdiction efforts are focused. Drug trafficking continues to expand, with networks including cross-border cooperation and international connections. This growth and increased organization result not only from an expanding consumer market, but also from poverty. The war against drugs increases the cost of drugs, making drug production and sales more profitable and therefore more attractive—particularly to those living in poverty. Drug trafficking across the world exists as a \$400 billion trade; drug traffickers earn gross profit margins of approximately 300 percent [50] (Table 4.2).

Table 4.2   Worldwide Illicit Drug Cultivation

	2005	2006	2007	2008	2009	2010
Afghanistan	107,400	172,600	202,000	157,000	131,000	119,000
Burma	40,000	21,000	21,700	22,500	17,000	In process
Colombia		2,300	1,000		1,100	In process
Guatemala	100					
Laos	5,600	1,700	1,100	1,900	1,000	In process
Mexico	3,300	5,000	6,900	15,000	19,500	In process
Pakistan	See note below					
Total poppy	**156,400**	**202,600**	**232,700**	**196,400**	**169,600**	
Bolivia	26,500	25,800	29,500	32,000	35,000	In process
Colombia	144,000	157,000	167,000	119,000	116,000	In process
Peru	34,000	42,000	36,000	41,000	40,000	In process
Total coca	**204,500**	**224,800**	**232,500**	**192,000**	**191,000**	
Mexico	5,600	8,600	8,900	12,000	17,500	In process
Total cannabis	**5,600**	**8,600**	**8,900**	**12,000**	**17,500**	

Notes on Colombia poppy cultivation: The 2008 and 2005 surveys could not be conducted due to cloud cover. Partial survey in 2007 due to cloud cover.
Note on Laos poppy cultivation: A partial survey of only the Phongsali growing area was conducted in 2009.
Notes on Pakistan poppy cultivation: There are no USG countrywide numbers for Pakistan. Please see the Pakistan Country Chapter for government of Pakistan estimates.
Notes on Colombia coca cultivation: Survey areas were expanded greatly in 2005 and to a lesser extent in 2006 and 2007.
Notes on Peru cultivation: In the 2006 survey, the Cusco growing area could not be completed; the value for that area is an average of the 2005 and 2007 estimates. The 2005 cultivation estimate was revised in 2007.

Mexico

Police in the United States have worked with Mexican authorities for decades to address the drug problem. In 2006, for example, Mexico extradited 63 criminals to the United States. Twenty-seven of these cases involved narcotics traffickers, including a member of the Tijuana-based Arellano-Félix organization. The eradication of illicit crops is still a priority for the Mexican Army, which eradicated nearly 30,000 ha of marijuana in 2006. Mexican authorities also seize significant amounts of drugs as they flow into Mexico and toward the United States. Mexican President Felipe Calderón has vowed to pursue the strong counterdrug commitment he inherited from his predecessor, Vicente Fox.

Although Mexican criminal syndicates have been involved in drug trafficking for decades, primarily dealing in marijuana and heroin, only relatively recently have they made an important appearance in the cocaine market—first as surrogates for, and then as partners of, Colombian drug syndicates. Mexico's 2,000 mile border shared with the United States, much of which is in isolated rural areas with rugged terrain, makes it an obvious transshipment site for drugs. Moreover, its extensive coastal and inland mountain systems create perfect havens for growing marijuana and opium poppies [51].

Early Mexican drug-trafficking groups were primarily transshipment agents for larger drug organizations. In the 1980s, the Mexican drug organizations provided cross-border smuggling services, charging between $1,000 and $2,000 a kilogram for cocaine. Once the cocaine was safely inside the United States, it would once again be turned over to Colombian traffickers for wholesale distribution.

By the end of the 1980s, Mexican drug traffickers were demanding increasingly greater remuneration for moving Colombian drugs. Now the Mexican drug syndicates wanted payment-in-kind, a share of the cocaine being transported (up to 50 percent of the load) for their smuggling services. This new arrangement offered Mexican drug syndicates an opportunity to get into the wholesale cocaine-trafficking business themselves, thereby vastly increasing their profits. Eventually, this arrangement with the Colombians resulted not only in dividing the cocaine shipments down the middle, but also in dividing much of the United States market down the middle. As the arrangement evolved over time, the Colombians retained the wholesale market in the eastern United States as their own, and Mexican drug cartels took over the wholesale market in the Midwestern and western states. By 1995, the Mexican syndicates had established themselves as major cocaine traffickers in their own right. Today, that arrangement continues to evolve. Dominican traffickers have challenged Colombian hegemony in the east, particularly in New York and New Jersey, and Mexican syndicates have begun establishing cocaine-trafficking operations in New York as well.

The structure and operations of Mexican drug syndicates are compartmentalized but exhibit a stronger chain of command from their Mexican bases than other drug syndicates. Mexican drug cartels have representatives or surrogates located throughout the United States who are responsible for managing the day-to-day activities of the syndicate.

However, unlike many other drug syndicates that have insulated their home country operations by granting greater autonomy to cells operating in foreign countries, the Mexican syndicates still retain a system whereby Mexican-based syndicate leaders provide specific instructions to their foreign-based syndicates on such issues as warehousing drugs, whom to use for transportation services, and how to launder drug money. Despite the use of encrypted faxes, computers, pagers, and cellular telephones, this arrangement still leaves a longer trail of communications evidence for law enforcement to follow and is considerably more risky than allowing foreign-based cells to operate with autonomy.

About two-thirds of the cocaine sold in the United States is transshipped over the Mexican border. Typically, large loads of cocaine come into Mexico from Colombia by air or boat. The cocaine is transported across land, usually in trucks, to a number of repository cities such as Juárez or Guadalajara. From these warehousing sites, cocaine loads are usually driven across the United States border to repository sites in the United States, most commonly in Los Angeles, Chicago, and Phoenix. Mexican trafficking syndicate representatives in those cities have contractual arrangements, usually with otherwise legitimate trucking companies, to move the cocaine across the country to smaller warehousing facilities closer to the point of sale. Individuals working in these "stash houses" guard the supplies and make arrangements for their distribution by cocaine wholesalers.

The size of Mexican cocaine operations is illustrated by a DEA investigation aimed at the American operations of the Amado Carrillo-Fuentes organization, which resulted in the seizure of 11.5 metric tons of cocaine, more than $18 million in American currency, almost 14,000 pounds of marijuana, and the arrest of 101 defendants. This particular investigation also illustrated the point made earlier that upper-echelon communications to local operatives in the drug market can be quite hazardous. It was through the interception and decoding of these communications that these arrests were made.

In addition to their expanded role in cocaine trafficking, Mexican drug syndicates continue to play a large role in the United States methamphetamine market. Mexican drug syndicates are now engaged in the large-scale production of methamphetamine. The meth market was revitalized as consumers shifted in the drug markets of the 1990s. The traditional control of the methamphetamine market by outlaw motorcycle gangs was broken by Mexican drug organizations operating in both Mexico and California.

Methamphetamine has a huge advantage over cocaine, heroin, and marijuana as a drug to be trafficked. Unlike the others, it is not dependent at all on agricultural production. Methamphetamine is manufactured directly from *precursor chemicals*, and those chemicals are easily available to Mexican syndicates from chemical companies in India, China, and the United States. Mexican drug syndicates operate clandestine laboratories in Mexico and California that are capable of producing hundreds of pounds of the drug. From the laboratories, the meth is moved to traffickers across the United States for sale.

From the 1930s onward—and certainly from the late 1940s and early 1950s, when gangster Mickey Cohen (showcased in the 2013 movie *Gangster Squad*) struck a deal with the Los Angeles Police Department (LAPD) to allow him to traffic in Mexican heroin—opium poppies cultivated and refined in Mexico have been an important source for the United States heroin market. Today, about 29 percent of the heroin on the United States market comes from Mexico. Mexican drug syndicates produce about 6 metric tons of heroin a year for resale in the United States. Because of crude refining methods used in manufacturing the heroin, Mexican heroin is frequently dark in color ("black") and sticky or gummy (like "tar"), resulting in its name of "black tar" heroin. Black tar heroin is widely distributed through the southwestern, northwestern, and Midwestern regions of the United States.

Mexico is the largest source of imported marijuana to the United States. At one time, from 1930 through the 1960s, Mexico supplied as much as 95 percent of the marijuana consumed in the United States. Domestic United States production cut that figure at least in half as of the 1990s, but Mexico retains its position as the largest foreign source for marijuana. That importing dominance was enhanced by the withdrawal of Colombian syndicates from the marijuana market in the 1970s. The Colombians simply decided that marijuana was too bulky a commodity to be safely transported. In addition, the profit margin for cocaine vastly exceeds that of marijuana. Mexican drug syndicates have begun to cultivate their marijuana in the United States. For example, in 1997, a group of people from Zacatecas, Mexico, were arrested in Idaho for cultivating 100,000 marijuana plants, weighing almost 20 tons.

Like most criminal organizations in the early stages of establishing their control of a market share in prohibited substances, Mexican syndicates cling to the excessive use of violence as a means of control. Like their centralized chain of command, this makes them particularly vulnerable, at least for the moment, to law enforcement intervention.

Mexican drug-trafficking organizations are still very much in the developmental stages. Their insistence on heavy use of violence and centralized control from headquarters in Mexico makes them more vulnerable than other drug organizations. But, as with the Colombian cartels, we can expect that these organizations will learn with time and restructure their operations accordingly. Today, a variety of Mexican organizations, operating from many major cities in Mexico, dominate the Mexican drug trade.

The Arellano-Félix organization (AFO) was one of the most aggressive of the Mexican trafficking groups. They moved multiton quantities of cocaine and marijuana and smaller, but still significant, amounts of heroin and methamphetamine. Benjamin Arellano-Félix was the head of this syndicate, which operated in Tijuana, Baja California, and parts of the Mexican states of Sinaloa, Sonora, Jalisco, and Tamaulipas. Syndicate activities were coordinated through his brothers. Benjamin Arellano-Félix was captured in 2002, just weeks after his brother, Ramón Arellano-Félix, was killed in a gunfight. The other brothers were captured subsequently. It has been said that the cartel is still operational under the leadership of the Félix brothers' nephew, Luis Fernando Sánchez Arellano, dubbed El Alineado (The Aligner).

The Caro-Quintero syndicate is based in Sonora, Mexico, and specializes in trafficking cocaine and marijuana. The syndicate was founded by Rafael Caro-Quintero, who has been incarcerated in Mexico since 1985 for his involvement in the murder of DEA Special Agent Enrique "Kiki" Camarena Salazar.

The Juárez cartel was headed by Amado Carrillo-Fuentes until his July 4, 1997, death during surgery in Mexico City. The Juárez cartel is still heavily involved in the trafficking of cocaine, heroin, and marijuana. Following Amado's death, a power struggle broke out that resulted in 60 murders in the Juárez area between August 1997 and September 1998. Apparently, that outbreak of violence was resolved when Vicente Carrillo-Fuentes, Amado's brother, took control of the organization. The Juárez cartel was featured battling a rival cartel in the 2000 motion picture *Traffic*. Since 2007, the Juárez cartel has been locked in a vicious battle with its former partner, the Sinaloa cartel, for control of Juárez. The fighting between them has left thousands dead in the Mexican state of Chihuahua.

The Amezcua-Contreras organization, also known as the Colima cartel, is based in Guadalajara and was directed by José de Jesús Amezcua-Contreras and supported by his brothers, Adán and Luis. It is a massive methamphetamine-trafficking syndicate and a major supplier of precursor chemicals to other methamphetamine syndicates. This syndicate controls much of the legitimate trade in chemicals in Mexico as well. In October 2008, the U.S. Department of the Treasury said that the organization has two leaders who are still at large: Patricia Amezcua (sister of Adán, Jesus, and Luis), who is responsible for the overall operations, and Telesforo Baltazar Tirado Escamilla [52].

Mexican Drug Smuggling

For years, marijuana and heroin were the mainstay of exported drugs from Mexico. Beginning in the early 1990s, law enforcement officials observed that Mexican traffickers were active in aiding Colombian traffickers in the transshipping of cocaine through Mexico to the United States. In fact, since 1995, several large-scale Mexican cocaine-trafficking organizations have been identified. One such organization, the Gulf cartel, was headed by 52-year-old Juan Garcia Abrego, a one-time Texas laborer who controlled one-third of the cocaine sold in the United States. In 1996, he was arrested and convicted by a federal jury in Houston on 22 trafficking counts. He was also forced to forfeit $350 million in illegal proceeds.

For the most part, Mexican traffickers utilize overland smuggling methods as the most prevalent mode of moving illicit drugs from the Mexican interior to the United States. States most directly affected by Mexican traffickers are Texas, California, Arizona, and New Mexico, which share the Mexican border with seven ports of entry. Observing the Mexican border, it is immediately evident that there is no wall, fence, or barricade separating most of Mexico from the United States. Moreover, United States Customs and Border Protection officers assigned to watch for illegal aliens and drug smugglers find themselves understaffed and lacking much of the necessary equipment and resources to do an effective job. The remoteness of much of the border area and the great distances to be covered make patrol an almost insurmountable responsibility. In fact, drug smugglers literally walk over the Mexican border to meet fellow traffickers on the United States side, often free of detection by border patrol agents. Ground smuggling techniques for marijuana and heroin have proved to be quite ingenuous over the years. Such methods include drugs concealed in false gas tanks as well as inside the backs of car seats, dashboards, and spare tires.

The movement of drugs through general aviation aircraft accounts for considerable drug-smuggling activity from Mexico. Illegal shipments of marijuana and heroin are flown from Mexico during the late hours of the night and are unloaded at predetermined locations by confederates in the United States. According to the DEA, more than 2,000 clandestine airstrips have been identified in Mexico; these are grouped into 10 different clusters. The number of these strips indicates the enormity of the air-smuggling problem, and illustrates Mexico's tenacious capacity for illicit drug production. It has been estimated that one-third of the airstrips are located around opium poppy–growing regions; the remainder are used for marijuana smuggling. Almost any type of plane can utilize these airstrips, ranging from small single-engine aircraft, such as the Cessna 172 and 182, to larger transport aircraft. The proximity of the Yucatán Peninsula to the United States also makes an ideal transit point for drug-smuggling flights, particularly those originating in the Guajira region of Colombia.

In a 1988 RAND Corporation study, project director Peter Reuter asserted that the Mexican government, unlike governments in Colombia, Bolivia, and Peru, does not incur any major political threats by cracking down on the drug trade. In fact, there is increasing willingness on the part of the Mexican government to do just that. This is due in part to the large numbers of Mexican police who have died in drug enforcement efforts. Indeed, it is likely that more Mexican than United States police have been killed while attempting to enforce United States drug policies [53].

Perhaps it is naïve to hope that Mexican officials could eliminate all transshipment efforts by Mexican traffickers, but a closer working relationship between the two countries is desirable. For example, as of the preparation of this text, there is no Mexican-United States provision for United States authorities to chase smugglers in "hot pursuit" across the border. Indeed, when United States chase planes approach the Mexican border, they are required under law to retreat.

■ ■ Critical Thinking Task ■

Support or refute this statement: Interdiction officers of both nations should be allowed to cross the Mexican-United States border in pursuit of drug smugglers. Predict outcomes if the current policy is changed.

The Emergence of Mexican Meth

Because of the rising popularity of methamphetamine in the United States, many Mexican cartels have started trafficking it, especially in the southwestern United States. They realize that they do not have to rely on their Colombian counterparts for raw material, as they do with cocaine, and their meth is of extremely high purity. The statistics are sobering; from mid-1993 to early 1995, Mexican traffickers were thought to have produced at least 50 tons of methamphetamine [54]. One of the most active Mexican methamphetamine-trafficking groups is the Amezcua organization (discussed in the "Mexico" section) [55]. It is thought to operate clandestine labs in Guadalajara and Tijuana, and to operate a series of cells in California.

Methamphetamine labs were traditionally the domain of outlaw motorcycle gangs, but the amount of meth being produced by Mexican groups is gaining considerable momentum. Within the United States, Mexican organizations are operating large-scale laboratories capable of producing 100 pounds at a time, many of them on remote ranches and farms throughout the inland valleys of California. Poorly paid Mexican immigrant farm workers often provide the labor that is needed to clean up the toxic residue remaining after a batch of meth is cooked.

One of the factors enabling the recent involvement of Mexican meth laboratories is the crucial ingredient *ephedrine*, a drug either extracted from the ephedra shrub or made synthetically for the treatment of asthma. In 1988, Congress imposed strict controls on ephedrine imports, which temporarily dried up the supply to American laboratories, but by 1991 Mexican methamphetamine was appearing on American streets. In one case in the mid-1990s, 3.4 metric tons of ephedrine traveling from Zurich to Mexico City was seized by customs agents at Dallas–Fort Worth Airport. It was then that the DEA learned that hundreds of tons of ephedrine were being shipped to Mexican front companies from India, China, and the Czech Republic. In the meantime, many traffickers have switched to *pseudoephedrine*, a similar drug that can be purchased as an over-the-counter decongestant.

The Mexican Heroin Trade

Mexico first emerged as a major heroin supplier during the early 1970s. This occurred just after the collapse of the *French Connection*, a massive heroin-trafficking operation between Marseilles, France, and New York. Mexico experiences an opium harvest season between September and April. This includes two harvests, which peak in November and March. After the opium harvest, raw opium gum is transported from the growing fields to nearby villages by pack mules, pedestrian couriers, or vehicles. Because of the vast number of back roads and footpaths in Mexico, interdiction at this stage is almost impossible. The opium reaches the heroin-processing laboratories by means of gatherers (called *acaparadors*). Their job is to purchase designated amounts of opium gum from the cultivators and deliver it, usually by general aviation aircraft, back to the processors who placed the order.

The process of converting raw opium to powdered heroin takes about 3 days and yields brown heroin with a wholesale purity of 65–85 percent. In contrast, white powdered heroin manufactured in the Middle East yields an average purity of 85–99 percent, which allows a much greater profit margin for traffickers. Most conversion laboratories are located in remote regions of the country, but some have been discovered in large cities such as Mexico City, Nuevo Laredo, and Tijuana.

Once the complicated laboratory processing is completed by experienced chemists, the traffickers transport the heroin to principal population areas and prepare it for clandestine shipment to the United States. Once in the United States, the principal market areas for Mexican heroin are in the western part of the country [56]. Although areas such as Chicago still account for a significant percentage of the market, Mexican heroin is virtually unavailable in the northeastern and southeastern United States.

A CLOSER LOOK: HOW TO SPOT FIREARMS TRAFFICKERS

TRAFFICKERS MAY:

- Want to buy a large number of the same model firearm, or similar firearms.
- Choose only military-style semiautomatic rifles and large-frame semiautomatic pistols.
- Structure their purchases to avoid Bureau of Alcohol, Tobacco, Firearms, and Explosives (ATF) reporting requirements.
- Attempt to conceal their conversations with each other.
- Do not haggle or question the price of firearms. Money is usually not an issue.
- Pay in cash with the same denominations.
- Have little or no knowledge of the firearms they are purchasing.
- Lack the physical stature to handle the firearm(s) being purchased.
- Avoid entering into conversation or become evasive when asked questions.

Source: *Project gunrunner: The Southwest border initiative*. Bureau of Alcohol, Tobacco, Firearms, and Explosives, (May 2008).

Drug Enforcement in Mexico

The primary authority for drug enforcement in Mexico is vested in the nation's chief law enforcement officer, the attorney general. It is the attorney general who dictates who will be prosecuted and for what drug offense. The responsibility for apprehension of drug offenders rests with the Mexican Federal Judicial Police (MFJP), which investigates all federal crimes, including drug offenses. Drug regulatory functions are the responsibility of the Department of Narcotics under the secretary of health and welfare and of the director of food, beverages, and drugs. The Department of Narcotics is responsible for enforcing drug violations in Mexico City and surrounding areas.

The 1985 murder of a DEA agent in Mexico has long illustrated the extremes to which Mexican traffickers will go to protect their trade. In her book *Desperados, Time* magazine correspondent Elaine Shannon exposed the circumstances surrounding the abduction and murder of DEA agent Enrique Camarena in Guadalajara (see Chapter 9). According to Shannon, certain Mexican officials not only helped plan the abduction and murder, but also created an elaborate cover-up, one that continues today. According to Shannon's account, the Mexican government's involvement in narcotics is second only to that of Panama's government [57].

■ ■ Critical Thinking Task ■

Considering the magnitude of the worldwide illicit drug trade and its impact on the United States, do you believe states should continue to criminalize drug use? Predict outcomes should current laws be either continued or abandoned.

Key Markets in the International Drug Trade

The global illicit markets represent the biggest transnational drugs and crime threats of our time. This is especially so regarding illicit drugs such as opiates, cocaine, stimulants (such as methamphetamine and amphetamine), and cannabis. Such drugs appear as persistent problems from a previous era of drug control.

Opiates are the most severe problem drugs worldwide, notably in Asia and Europe. Opiate use can lead to severe dependence, and is often associated with HIV/AIDS and hepatitis B and C, as well as high mortality rates. The mortality rate for dependent heroin users is between 6 and 20 times that expected for those in the general population of the same age and gender, as the difference between a "recreational dose" and a "fatal" one is small, and variations in street drug purity can result in overdoses [58]. Thus, in most countries, opiate consumption constitutes the main cause of drug-related deaths. In addition, the processing and trafficking of opiates constitute significant sources of income for insurgents in some opium-producing countries such as Afghanistan and Myanmar.

In Afghanistan, a conservative estimate suggests that Taliban insurgents generated some $125 million per year in profits from the local opiate trade alone in the past several years [59]. In Pakistan, Taliban allies such as al Qaeda and other like-minded groups have bases along the main heroin- and opium-trafficking routes and are well located to benefit from trafficking. Elsewhere in the world, other militant groups also seem to be financing themselves at least partly from the illicit opiate trade.

Accordingly, cocaine use constitutes a major health problem. Almost one-fifth (18 percent) of persons who used cocaine at least once in the previous year were found to be dependent on it in the United States—the world's largest cocaine market. This is a higher proportion than for any other drug, except heroin. Cocaine use also results in tens of thousands of deaths each year worldwide. While cocaine was involved in close to 40 percent of all drug deaths in the United States in 2008, the proportion is still far smaller in Europe (8 percent in the EU countries) [60].

After the opiates, cocaine is the most problematic drug worldwide, notably in North and South America. While the share has declined, almost half (46 percent) of all people entering drug treatment in the Americas do so due to cocaine.

There is also a clear link between cocaine use (in particular crack cocaine use) and crime. Statistics show that in 2005–2006, 11 percent of arrestees in the United Kingdom were found to have used crack cocaine in the month prior to their arrest, compared to between 29 and 35 percent of the male arrestees in the United States. With cocaine use falling strongly since the late 1980s (with past-month prevalence rates decreasing 56 percent between 1988 and 2008), overall crime has also declined in the United States, ranging from a 29 percent drop in property crime rates to a 43 percent decrease in murder rates over the 2000–2008 period [61].

Cocaine trafficking is also linked to corruption and has contributed to increasing corruption in transit countries, including those in West Africa. Furthermore, cocaine trafficking constitutes a major security threat, financing organized crime and insurgencies in a number of countries, including the FARC in Colombia and the Shining Path in Peru.

As for the other drugs, the impact of stimulant use is primarily on the health side. Data for the United States suggest that the use of methamphetamine may constitute similar threats to health as the abuse of crack cocaine, exceeding for the individuals concerned even the risks related to the consumption of cocaine hydrochloride.

Organized crime is involved in the diversion of precursor chemicals, and in the manufacture and distribution of stimulant drugs. Stimulant manufacture has a major negative impact on the environment, which is reflected in the difficulties in dismantling clandestine laboratories such as methamphetamine laboratories. Organized crime groups are clearly involved in illicit stimulant production, particularly in East and Southeast Asia, as well as in North America. Currently, less is known with regard to the financing of insurgencies (this seems to occur mainly in Myanmar) and violence related to its trafficking.

The International Cocaine Market

The global area under coca cultivation decreased by 5 percent from 167,600 ha in 2008 to 158,800 ha in 2009. This change is mainly due to a significant decrease in Colombia that was not offset by increases in Peru and Bolivia. The global area under coca cultivation declined by 28 percent over the 2000–2009 period. In 2009, Colombia represented about 43 percent of global cultivation, with Peru contributing 38 percent and Bolivia 19 percent [62].

The areas where cocaine is produced, trafficked, and consumed have varied substantially over time. While Colombian traffickers have produced most of the world's cocaine in recent years, between 2000 and 2009, the area under coca cultivation in Colombia decreased by 58 percent, mainly due to eradication. At the same time, coca cultivation increased by 38 percent in Peru and more than doubled in Bolivia (up 112 percent), while traffickers in both countries increased their own capacity to produce cocaine [63].

Demand for cocaine in the United States has been in long-term decline: in 1982, an estimated 10.5 million people had used cocaine in the previous year; in 2008, the figure was 5.3 million, about half as many. In the 2000s, however, the number of cocaine users in Europe doubled, from 2 million in 1998 to 4.1 million in the EU–EFTA countries in 2008. By 2008, the European market ($34 billion) was almost as valuable as the North American market ($37 billion). The value of the global cocaine market is estimated at around $88 billion (estimates range from $80 to $100 billion) [64].

These shifts, combined with interdiction efforts, have also affected trafficking patterns. As the Colombian government has taken greater control of its territory, traffickers are making more use of transit countries in the region, including Venezuela and Ecuador. Mexican drug cartels emerged over the last 10–15 years as the primary organizers for shipments of cocaine into the United States, largely replacing the previously dominant Colombian groups. In response to Mexican enforcement efforts, Central American countries are increasingly being used as transit countries. West Africa started to be used as a way station to Europe around 2004. The situation remains fluid, and the impact on transit countries can be devastating.

In 2008, the potential production of pure cocaine amounted to some 865 tons. This is considerably less than in 2004, when almost 1,050 tons were generated. Most of these drugs are destined for consumers in North America (6.2 million users in 2008) and Europe (4–5 million users in 2008). These two regions, with 70 percent of the global demand and 85 percent of the total value, play the main role in shaping the evolution of the global cocaine market. Another 2.7 million users are found in South America, Central America, and the Caribbean.

The Largest Cocaine Market: North America

North America is the largest regional cocaine market, with close to 40 percent of the global cocaine-using population. In 2008, it appears that 196 tons of pure cocaine were required to satisfy North American demand. To get this amount to the consumer, about 309 tons must have left the Andean region toward the north in 2008. This figure represents about half of the cocaine that left this region. According to forensic testing of the seized cocaine in the United States, most cocaine consumed in North America was produced in Colombia.

Currently, the cocaine market appears to be in decline. Household and school surveys along with reports from law enforcement all confirm that fewer people in North America are consuming cocaine than in the past. Cocaine use in the United States has been declining for some time, especially since 2006. This is most likely due to pressure on supply sources in Colombia and Mexico. Moreover, if there were a shortage in the supply of cocaine, the street prices for the drug would have gone up. This has not been the case. Rather, street prices for cocaine have fallen somewhat, but purity has been considerably reduced. According to research, cocaine dealers in the United States have appeared to opt for decreasing the purity of their product rather than increasing prices. This has resulted in a decline in the demand for the drug.

The Second Largest Cocaine Market: Europe

The world's second largest flow of cocaine is directed toward Europe, and this flow has been growing rapidly. The largest national cocaine market within Europe is the United Kingdom, followed by Spain, Italy, Germany, and France. Cocaine use prevalence levels are higher in the United Kingdom and Spain than in the United States.

Recent data suggest that the rapid growth of the European cocaine market is beginning to level off in some of the biggest national markets such as Italy, Spain, and Germany. Consumption is still growing in the United Kingdom and in some of the smaller European markets, however. In 2008, an estimated 124 tons of cocaine were consumed in Europe. To supply this demand, an estimated 212 tons departed South America toward Europe, about one-quarter of the total production. A greater share of this quantity comes from Peru and Bolivia than in the case of the United States.

The primary countries of entry to the European market are Spain and the Netherlands. Most of the trafficking is maritime. Significant transit routes flow from former colonies or overseas territories of the European nations to their counterparts on the continent. Flows through West Africa appear to have declined since 2007, but they could resume in the near future.

While the volumes are lower, as mentioned the value of the European cocaine market ($34 billion) is almost as high as in the case of the North American market ($37 billion), because purity-adjusted cocaine retail prices are higher in Europe. European street prices in 2008 are about half what they were in 1990, but purity has declined and the dollar has weakened against the euro. In dollar terms, the purity-adjusted price of cocaine in Europe has increased since 2002.

As in the North American market, only a fraction of the retail value goes to those who produce the drug. The intercontinental traffickers receive a larger share than in the North American case, but more than half of the retail value still accrues to wholesalers and retailers within Europe.

The International Heroin Market

Heroin is the most widely consumed illicit opiate in the world. It is derived from opium, which itself can have an illicit use. Of the opium that is not converted into heroin, two-thirds is consumed in just five countries: Iran (42 percent), Afghanistan (7 percent), Pakistan (7 percent), India (6 percent), and the Russian Federation (5 percent). Other opiates are also abused, including various poppy straw concoctions and prescription opioids, but heroin remains the most problematic opiate internationally.

With the exception of 2001, when there was hardly any opium poppy cultivation in Afghanistan, global opium production expanded remarkably in the first decade of the twenty-first century until 2007, apparently with no commensurate expansion in demand. Opium production subsequently declined over the 2007–2009 period (from 8,890 to 7,754 tons), though remaining significantly above estimated global demand (some 5,000 tons for consumption and seizures). The declining farm-gate price of opium in Afghanistan in recent years has been more pronounced than the decline in heroin prices. This may reflect a number of factors, including rising prices for heroin precursors (particularly acetic anhydride) in that country and a build-up of stocks of opium not processed into heroin.

Although Afghanistan is the source of most of the world's illicit opiates (6,900 tons of opium, or 89 percent of the world total in 2009), significant quantities are also produced in Myanmar (330 tons) and Latin America (notably in Mexico and Colombia). Since 2003, Mexico has been the world's third largest source of opium, and the quantities produced in 2008 (325 tons) came close to the quantities produced in Myanmar in 2009.

Both opium and heroin seizures continued to increase in 2008. Morphine seizures, however, continued a declining trend that started in 2007. Although heroin seizures have followed a generally increasing trend since 2002, they have been outpaced by the growth in global opium seizures, possibly reflecting difficulties faced by Afghan laboratory operators to obtain sufficient precursor chemicals to transform the large quantities of harvested opium into heroin. Most of the opium seizures continue to be made in Iran, which shares a border with Afghanistan. The global rise in opium seizures thus largely reflected the growing opium seizures made by the authorities in Iran.

The world's two largest markets for Afghan opiates are the Russian Federation and Western Europe, which together consume almost half the heroin produced in the world. About 340 metric tons of heroin are estimated to have been consumed globally in 2008. To meet this demand, accounting for seizures, some 430 tons would have had to be produced. UNODC estimates suggest that about 380 tons were produced from Afghan opium that year, supplying the bulk of global demand.

The Largest Heroin Market: Western Europe

The world's largest heroin market is Western Europe, and about half of this market is contained in just three countries: the United Kingdom, Italy, and France. Heroin use appears to be decreasing in most Western European countries, although the harms associated with heroin use seem to be increasing, as reflected in heroin-induced deaths.

Heroin sent from Afghanistan to Western Europe travels along the so-called Balkan Route, traveling through Pakistan, Turkey and the countries in Southeast Europe. It is estimated that 37 percent of all Afghan heroin travels along this route. Moreover, most of the heroin seized in the world is seized along the Balkan Route. Between them, Iran and Turkey are responsible for more than half of all heroin seized in 2008. The total quantity of heroin seized in Europe was around 7.6 tons in 2008—which is only one-fifth of the amount seized in Turkey and Iran in 2008. The prices of heroin on the wholesale level increase along the trafficking route from Southwest Asia to Europe. Recent figures show that wholesale prices ranged from less than $3000 per kg in Afghanistan to $10,300–$11,800 per kg in Turkey and an average of $44,300 per kg in Western and Central Europe.

The Second Largest Heroin Market: Russia

An estimated 25 percent (95 tons) of all Afghan heroin is trafficked each year from Afghanistan into Central Asia. Indeed, the demand for the drug in Russia is considerable, at an estimated 70 tons. The number of opiate users in Russia is estimated to be between 1.6 and 1.8 million people, equivalent to a prevalence rate of 1.6 percent of the population aged 15–64. There is also a very high prevalence of HIV among drug users (some 37 percent).

To exit Afghanistan on the way to Russia, traffickers can choose between three countries: Tajikistan, Uzbekistan, and Turkmenistan. Most of the flow appears to proceed through Tajikistan to Osh in Kyrgyzstan, before transiting Kazakhstan to the Russian Federation. Trafficking is conducted mostly in private and commercial vehicles, often in relatively small amounts. Of 45 heroin seizures above 500 g (a commercial quantity) made in Tajikistan between 2005 and 2007, 80 percent amounted to 10 kg or less, and of these, the average size was 2.6 kg. This is a rather small amount per seizure when compared to other regions, suggesting that small-scale trafficking operations are the rule rather than the exception.

While total seizures remained essentially stable in Tajikistan in 2008 (1.6 tons), seizures in Uzbekistan and Kazakhstan reached the highest levels on record, at 1.5 tons and 1.6 tons, respectively. In the Russian Federation, seizures have followed an upward trend, from 2.5 tons in 2006 to 2.9 tons in 2007, and 3.4 tons in 2008.

The International Stimulant Market

Stimulants are a group of tons synthetic substances composed of amphetamine-group (primarily amphetamine, methamphetamine, and methcathinone) and ecstasy-group substances (MDMA and its analogs, discussed in Chapter 3). These drugs can be made anywhere the precursors can be found, so manufacturing tends to happen close to the main consumer markets.

The number of stimulant-related clandestine laboratories increased recently by 20 percent, and for the first time revealed the existence of laboratories in Argentina, Brazil, Guatemala, Iran, and Sri Lanka. Information on the 8,432 detected laboratories came from 31 countries, with the largest numbers reported from the United States, the Czech Republic, Australia, China, Slovakia, New Zealand, the Netherlands, Canada, and Mexico. However, the number of laboratories is not representative of their output, as many countries with lower total counts report only laboratories with large-scale outputs.

Traditionally, different regions have had problems with different stimulants. For example, ecstasy has been associated with the dance club scene, initially located primarily in the Anglophone countries, but later expanding throughout Europe, the Americas, the Oceania region, and many parts of East and Southeast Asia. Methamphetamine has been problematic in East Asia and Southeast Asia since 1998, as well as in North America. Amphetamine was found primarily in Europe, though in recent years, the Middle East has emerged as a major new market, with demand for pills called *Captagon*. This was a brand name for a discontinued product that contained fenethylline, but these pills today mostly consist of amphetamine and caffeine. Pharmaceutical stimulants are widely misused in South America and in Africa. Research shows that trends and associations with stimulants are also changing:

- North America struggled with a rash of methamphetamine use, gradually moving from the west coast toward the east coast. Successes in precursor control, however, seem to have reduced this threat, though seizures increased.
- Ecstasy is becoming important in many parts of the developing world, including Asia, while its use seems to be leveling off or declining in Europe. The situation remains dynamic, with illicit ecstasy manufacturing emerging in new locations around the world, while European and other markets are increasingly discovering synthetic

substitution psychotropic substances in tablets that are sold as ecstasy. Piperazines, ketamine, and other substitutes, either marketed as "ecstasy" or under their own name, have grown in popularity as club drugs. With these changes in demand, the location of manufacturing operations has changed. In the past, most of the pills sold as ecstasy were manufactured in Europe, but this does not seem to be the case any longer. Manufacture of ecstasy has increased in North America (notably in Canada) and in several parts of Asia.

Stimulants are seized in a wider range of countries and in greater volumes than ever before. A key component of the volume increase is the growth in the seizures of pills branded as *Captagon*. In the more mature markets, however, stimulant use appears to have stabilized or declined, and seizures of tablets containing ecstasy-group substances in Europe have plummeted since 2006.

These broad trends mask a number of important regional developments. Manufacture of methamphetamine for the United States market, for example, underwent a dramatic transformation in response to domestic precursor controls implemented in 2005. Manufacturing was displaced over the border to Mexico.

The International Cannabis Market

Trends in cannabis production and trafficking are markedly different from those of the other drugs discussed in this chapter. This is because marijuana is grown locally and consumed widely. The most notable trend in cannabis production is the proliferation of indoor cannabis-growing operations—especially in North America, Australia, and Europe. Indoor cannabis growing is an extremely lucrative criminal enterprise for organized crime groups, and the seizures of the drug were at an all-time high in 2008.

Cannabis herb seizures appear to be growing most strongly in South America, in particular in Bolivia. For resin, the growth is strongest in Southwest Asia. In 2008, possibly the single largest drug seizure in history of 236.8 tons of cannabis resin occurred in Kandahar, Afghanistan.

Prices of cannabis herb vary greatly across different countries and regions. For example, extremely high retail prices are reported by Japan, Singapore, and two territories in East Asia (Hong Kong and Macao, China). The high price in Japan may be due to the fact that cannabis herb is mainly imported. Cannabis herb prices in Europe were also relatively high. In comparison, the lower end of the scale is seen in countries in Africa, South America, and East, Southeast, and South Asia.

Without question, cannabis remains the most widely used illicit substance in the world. Worldwide, the number of people who used cannabis at least once in a year's period of time is estimated between 129 and 191 million, or 2.9–4.3 percent of the world population aged 15–64. Cannabis use appears to be in long-term decline in some of its highest value markets, including North America and parts of West Europe. Comparatively, increasing cannabis use has been reported in South America.

Drug Trafficking and Instability in Transit Countries

There are two ways in which drug trafficking can pose a threat to political stability. The first involves countries where insurgents and illegal armed groups draw funds from taxing, or even managing, drug production and trafficking. The second concerns countries that do not face such a situation, but where the drug traffickers become powerful enough to take on the state through violent confrontation or high-level corruption. This section focuses on the second category, and it discusses the impact of cocaine trafficking on transit countries.

Between 2006 and 2008, more than half the maritime shipments of cocaine to Europe that were detected came from Venezuela. Ecuador has also been affected by an increase in transit trafficking, and both countries are experiencing increasing problems with violence.

The decline of the United States cocaine market and the rise of the European one have also contributed to increased violence in the Caribbean. In some cases, this is due to the establishment of new cocaine routes; in other cases, it is due to the loss of cocaine trafficking as a revenue source for local criminals.

The region currently most affected is the Northern Triangle of Central America: Guatemala, Honduras, and El Salvador. Here, intense drug-related violence has posed serious problems for local governments. While all these countries have had problems with violence in the past, the murder rate is highest not in the largest urban areas, but in those parts of the country particularly affected by the drug trade, including some ports and border areas.

As discussed in this chapter, there is considerable concern over drug-related violence in Mexico, but murder rates are considerably lower and the government is considerably stronger in Mexico. To a great extent, recent crackdowns on Mexican cartels have fueled violence, as it did in Colombia. Some argue that this may be a necessary experience to dismantle organized crime groups that have begun to challenge the state because it appears to have disrupted the cocaine supply to the United States. Also, it has uprooted widespread corruption and reasserted government control over the entire country. Since much of the drug violence in Central America is tied to these same cartels, many believe that progress in Mexico should aid the countries to the south.

On the other side of the Atlantic, large-scale cocaine trafficking has been a problem in West Africa since around 2004. While data on violence in West Africa are sparse, it is unlikely that the flow of drug money will cause the kind of drug wars that have been seen recently in Latin America, because the traffickers have been able to compromise top figures in some authoritarian societies.

The best known example is Guinea-Bissau, where the prime minister was recently detained and threatened by soldiers so that the chief of staff of the military could be removed. The man who engineered this "coup" has assumed the role of deputy chief. He has also been openly accused of involvement in drug trafficking. While the flow of cocaine through this region declined sharply after political turmoil in Guinea-Bissau and Guinea in 2008–2009, these recent developments suggest it may resume in the near future.

added a new criterion: the drug must be proven to be both safe and effective. Ironically, the thalidomide scare was one addressing safety, not efficacy. After the 1962 amendments, the FDA's role shifted from evaluating evidence to becoming an active participant in the research process. Between 1962 and 1967, the average review time for new drugs more than quadrupled, rising from 7 to 30 months. Although in recent years the FDA has attempted to streamline this process, NDA review time has not improved. By the end of the 1980s, the average NDA review time was 32 months [19]. In addition, the development time for new drugs, which averaged between 4 and 6 years in the 1960s, doubled to 10 years [20].

The obvious policy question stemming from the thalidomide experience is "How many lives are lost or damaged during the lengthy development and review process for new drugs?" Let's consider two examples. Misoprostol, approved in 1988, was the first medication used to prevent gastric ulcers that result from aspirin and other anti-inflammatory drugs. Such drugs are commonly taken by arthritis sufferers, who often develop ulcers, which are thought to cause 10,000–20,000 deaths each year through internal bleeding. Misoprostol is reported to produce a 15-fold reduction in such ulcers. By the time the drug was approved in the United States, it was already available in 43 foreign countries. Therefore, if the drug is 94 percent effective (as reported), and if the FDA's estimate of between 10,000 and 20,000 annual ulcer-related deaths is accurate, misoprostol could have saved between 8,000 and 15,000 lives during the FDA's 9.5-month review period.

Experts have debated the best way to deal with lengthy delays in the approval process for new drugs, but a consensus does not exist. Some have suggested that the FDA's veto power over new drugs be changed to a system of certification. Under this proposed system, new drugs that have not been approved could still be available by prescription, but would be clearly labeled as unapproved. This system would enable critically ill persons to go beyond the circle of official approval but remain under the supervision of a physician. Regardless of what happens with the approval process, it is clear that the pharmaceutical drug business faces two critical issues in the upcoming years: the development time for new drugs and the built-in expense of developing those drugs. Both are problems of such enormity that quick-fix solutions are unlikely.

Adverse Drug Reaction

Drugs can have wonderful benefits, but they also have risks. Consider the February 1997 case of 4-year-old Harry Donnelly, who died while having his adenoids removed during routine surgery at a Peekskill, New York, hospital. It was not the operation that killed him but rather a deadly combination of two common drugs—nonprescription Neo-Synephrine, an allergy medicine that also controls bleeding, and a beta-blocking drug that lowers high blood pressure. Both drugs are widely used by doctors and hospitals, but Harry's death was no fluke. Investigators discovered 12 other cases in which combining these two drugs during surgery caused adverse reactions, including two additional deaths. Such tragedies occur with shocking frequency.

A 1998 study published by *JAMA* estimated that of 30 million people hospitalized each year, an average of 100,000 die from bad reactions to legal prescription drugs. Another 2.2 million suffer side effects so severe that they are permanently disabled or require long-term hospital stays. The *JAMA* study ranked adverse drug reactions as the fourth leading cause of death [21]. Over the years, several observations have been made about drugs coming on the market:

- Heart medication can cause gum disease
- Diet medication may result in heart problems
- Hair growth medication may cause liver problems and high blood pressure
- New anti–breast cancer medicine may cause liver problems

The problem begs the obvious question: why are so many people being killed by our health care system? Some experts have argued that there is a system-wide breakdown in the manner in which powerful drugs are marketed, prescribed, and monitored, resulting in a lack of consumer protection. The protections that do exist depend on the voluntary efforts of pharmaceutical companies, which are interested in promoting their products, and of doctors and hospitals, which may have a greater incentive to hide mishaps than to be proactive in preventing them.

- *Haphazard monitoring.* Although the FDA has sped up the approval process for newly developed drugs, it is approving the sale of drugs with more serious side effects, especially for treatment of fatal diseases such as cancer and AIDS. Drug companies are required to report toxic side effects found in prescription medicines, but there are no mandatory requirements for hospitals and doctors to report deadly problems. Instead, the FDA maintains only a database of problems reported voluntarily through its MedWatch system. Some pharmacist groups have complained that the voluntary system misses all but a fraction of serious drug reactions, and that it increases the lag time before public notification about deadly side effects.
- *Hyping benefits over risks.* Drug companies spend more than $12 billion a year to promote the benefits of prescription drugs. It is safe to say that far fewer of their resources are directed at alerting hospitals and doctors to the dangers of drugs and educating them about the safest drug for any given medical condition. There is no legal requirement mandating that hospital patients receive information about the possible side effects of the medications they are given. Moreover, it was only after a 20-year fight that drug companies and pharmacists agreed in 1997 to begin providing warnings for prescriptions bought by consumers.
- *Medical ignorance.* Most medical schools provide doctors with little training in pharmacology. Moreover, the nurses who often administer drugs to patients frequently receive no formal education on drug therapy. In fact, both groups get most of their information from drug company representatives, who are interested in selling their particular product. As a result, health providers are often ill-informed about drug interactions and ways of spotting and counteracting deadly drug reactions.

- *Downplaying preventable mishaps.* Pharmacy associations estimate that only 40 percent of hospitals follow industry guidelines for monitoring and reporting adverse reactions. When mishaps occur, hospital officials admit that many hospitals discourage voluntarily alerting others to potential problems because of fear of malpractice suits. The *JAMA* report stated that 42 percent of the most serious drug reactions were preventable [22].

Speculation continues regarding what can be done to safeguard against adverse drug reactions, but one suggestion has been that diligent tracking of medical effects, along with increased communication among health care workers, is the key. It has been suggested that bedside computer terminals in hospitals could be one way to chart and track drugs. Another suggestion is federal regulations requiring hospitals to show that they regularly measure adverse drug events and medication error rates. Some feel that because hospitals, doctors, and pharmaceutical companies have little reason to move quickly, safeguarding requirements should be made law to protect unknowing and uninformed patients in future years.

Domestic Marijuana Cultivation

Over the decades, marijuana has consistently remained one of the economic staples in the illegal drug business. So far in this book, we have discussed several foreign cannabis sources that focus on smuggling their products into the United States. The majority of foreign marijuana operations consist of peasant farmers who grow the crop as their primary source of cash. Because marijuana grows in almost all 50 of the United States, domestic cultivation also contributes greatly to the nation's overall drug production. Whether foreign or domestic enterprises are concerned, marijuana cultivation and trafficking have proven to be a relatively easy-entry illicit market. All that is required for a simple growing operation is seeds, a water source, land, and a willingness to enter into a criminal enterprise that in some states can result in a prison term as long as 25 years.

In spite of potentially long prison sentences, marijuana growing appears to be on the increase. For example, in 2010, the National Drug Intelligence Center reported that domestic marijuana cultivation was occurring at high levels, and eradication was increasing across the United States [23]. Recent research shows that marijuana cultivation operations appear to be most prevalent in western states, but have been increasing in many eastern states as well. The most active states for cultivation operations are California, Hawaii, Kentucky, Oregon, Tennessee, Washington, and West Virginia. The average potency of marijuana has also steadily increased in recent years, reaching its highest recorded level in 2008 [24]. This continuous yearly increase can be partially attributed to improvements in outdoor and indoor cultivation methods, which are discussed in this chapter. No reliable estimates are available regarding the amount of domestically cultivated or processed marijuana.

Indoor marijuana cultivation has continued to be a preferred method for growers because this method helps them avoid detection and potential eradication, which is more difficult with outdoor growing sites. It also provides growers with higher profits, because they can sell higher grade marijuana. Statistics show that more than 8 million plants were eradicated in 2008.

In spite of continuing increases in the amount of domestically grown marijuana, much of the cannabis consumed in the United States is foreign produced. The two primary foreign source areas for marijuana distributed within the United States are Canada and Mexico. Mexican drug-trafficking organizations have relocated many of their outdoor cannabis cultivation operations in Mexico from traditional growing areas to more remote locations in central and northern Mexico, primarily to reduce the risk of eradication and gain easier access to United States drug markets. Asian criminal groups are the primary producers of high-potency marijuana in Canada.

The amount of marijuana available for distribution in the United States is unknown; an accurate estimate is not possible. Despite increasing eradication efforts in the United States, the availability of marijuana remains high, with stabilized prices.

Levels of marijuana use in the United States are higher than those for any other drug, particularly among adults; however, rates of marijuana use are decreasing among adolescents. Some law enforcement agencies identify marijuana as the greatest drug threat in their jurisdictions. Marijuana use can result in adverse health consequences to abusers, placing a burden on medical services.

No single criminal organization is thought to control domestic marijuana production and trafficking, probably due to the easy-entry nature of the business and the difficulty that criminal organizations would experience in attempting to monopolize it. Consequently, the domestic marijuana market has spawned the development of a rural criminal who lives and operates in a scarcely populated agrarian area. Law enforcement in these areas is often diffused, resulting in growers who can operate with impunity while their operations are cloaked by thick forests, lush vegetation, and inaccessible mountain slopes. These factors also help conceal marijuana-growing operations from rival growers or "pot poachers" in the area.

To help hide their plants, outdoor growers frequently disperse them among corn and tomato plants or along riverbeds and creeks. Over the years, police agents have discovered deadly booby traps in and around marijuana patches that are difficult to detect. Other deterrents used by growers include hidden steel-jaw traps, guard dogs, and armed guards. These devices are designed to serve not only as a deterrent for police and poachers, but also as a signal to nearby growers, who may be heavily armed and potentially violent. As mentioned in this chapter, growers have resorted to indoor growing operations not only to conceal their operations, but also to provide year-long harvesting opportunities.

■ ■ Critical Thinking Task ■

This section discusses the results of increased law enforcement efforts by rural police officers. In light of these results, do you agree or disagree that police should continue to vigorously enforce the law against marijuana cultivation in those areas?

Business Considerations

Marijuana growers are a somewhat fragmented group of traffickers who rely on kinship or local "good ole boy" networks. Operations are typically financed either by previous transactions or by "jobbers" furnishing special lighting, fertilizer, or other equipment in exchange for a percentage of the harvest. Police have documented cases, however, in which large-scale cultivation operations were financially backed by business executives looking for alternate ways to invest their money. The packaging of marijuana remains somewhat universal throughout the country. After harvest, it is usually placed in large trash bags for transportation to its destination. For smaller retail sales of one-quarter pound or less, smaller zipper-closing plastic bags are usually used.

Marijuana growers have learned that many police raids are a product of so-called search-and-destroy missions based on information from informants. Therefore, many growing operations are now automated, allowing the grower to be absent in case of a police raid. This explains why search-and-destroy operations are often unproductive and rarely are a top enforcement priority for police.

Types of Domestic Marijuana

As noted in Chapter 3, there are several types or grades of marijuana. It is becoming increasingly clear that the marijuana cultivation business is experiencing a horticultural revolution of sorts. That is, many growers, in search of higher profits, are continuously experimenting with techniques for producing more potent strains of marijuana. Each cultivated grade represents different types of growing technology, and results in differing degrees of potency (and prices) for the manicured retail marijuana plant. Although state and federal drug laws do not differentiate among the grades of marijuana (they only require a showing that the drug evidence is cannabis), the grower is very interested in producing the most potent plant for greater profit margins. The DEA has identified three basic types of marijuana that grow domestically:

- *Indian hemp* (commonly referred to as *ditchweed*) is the most prevalent type of marijuana that grows in the United States. This is wild-growing marijuana that has little market value and typically grows in uncultivated areas such as fields, ditch banks, and fence rows, and along railroad tracks. Indian hemp grows in many types of soil and reproduces itself each year by its own seeds from the previous year's crop. These seeds can lie dormant for up to 7 years. Because Indian hemp is not cultivated from potent seeds, its THC (tetrahydrocannabinol, also discussed in Chapter 3) content is quite low, averaging around 0.14 percent. Because of its low potency, it will sometimes be mixed with other, more potent marijuana as filler.
- *Commercial-grade marijuana* is the most common type of marijuana sold on the street. It is produced from cannabis plants that have been cultivated in a growing area where the male and female plants are permitted to grow in the same location, and the female plants have been fertilized. As a rule, the entire marijuana plant (usually the female)

is harvested, stripped of its leaves, and marketed. The growing season usually begins around mid-April, with harvest season beginning sometime during August. At maturity, plants may reach heights of 15 ft and can be harvested up until the first frost (usually some time in October). The THC content of the commercial marijuana plant ranges from 5 to 8 percent.

• *Sinsemilla*, a Spanish word meaning "without seed," is a cannabis plant that represents the most potent type of marijuana on the illicit market, and the type that will bring the highest profit return for the trafficker. Sinsemilla is produced from unfertilized female cannabis plants in a growing area where the male cannabis plants are removed before pollination. Marijuana plants allowed to grow in this fashion produce more flowers and resin in an attempt to attract male pollen. It is the resin and flowers that contain the highest amounts of THC, usually averaging between 8 and 12 percent potency. Frequently, only the female flower tops (buds) are harvested and marketed.

One high-grade strain of sinsemilla grown in the United States is *Cannabis indica*, which originally was imported from Afghanistan. This is popular because it grows into a short, squatty plant that produces 1–2 pounds of buds per plant. These buds are high in THC content and mature in 4–5 months.

Hashish is also produced from marijuana. This is accomplished by taking the drug-rich resinous secretions of the cannabis plant and drying and compressing them into a variety of forms such as balls or cookie-like sheets. Another form of cannabis, *hash oil*, is produced by repeated extraction of cannabis materials to yield a dark, tenacious liquid. The THC content of both hashish and hash oil is considerably higher than in the plant itself.

Many marijuana growers have perfected indoor growing techniques that enable them to harvest plants year-round. According to the DEA, Oregon pot growers have developed a technique called *cloning*. In this technique, growers cultivate hybrid marijuana and select the most superior plants. A "cut" is then taken from the mother plant and soaked in a root stimulant. After the cutting develops roots, it is planted in pots and aided by a halide lighting system. Another technique, called *hydroponics*, is also used to grow marijuana in a greenhouse. Hydroponics is the science of growing plants in a soil-free, mineral-rich solution, and is commonly used for indoor cultivation of tomatoes and cucumbers. Marijuana produced by the hydroponic method will typically have a THC content at least twice that of marijuana produced by traditional methods. The DEA estimates that it takes only one square foot of space to grow a mature plant. Therefore, a facility with only 400 sq ft of hydroponic growing area can, under optimal growing conditions, cultivate marijuana on a year-round basis and generate an estimated $5 million a year.

Marijuana cultivators and processors come from a wide range of backgrounds and operate in a variety of ways. For example, research by Ralph Weisheit found that many West Coast growers cultivate the plant for their own use and for sales to friends, but are

FIGURE 5.2 Law enforcement agents carry bundles of marijuana plants after clearing a patch of the plant from national forest land in Washington State. Illegal marijuana-growing operations are a problem in counties with huge tracts of open space and few resources to tackle them. *Source: AP Photo/Elaine Thompson.*

not necessarily large traffickers [25]. In fact, he suggested that a considerable number of domestic cultivators were still operating within the context of a counterculture frame of reference. Weisheit's research in other areas, such as the Midwest, has generally shown marijuana cultivating and processing to be a disorganized, ancillary business often engaged in by otherwise law-abiding farmers. Some research in Kentucky, however, has indicated that cultivation there is becoming more highly organized, with law enforcement officials warning of a "cartelization" of the trade [26].

In eastern Kentucky, in particular, where high-grade marijuana with a THC content as high as 18 percent is grown in small plots because of the rugged topography, there is increasing evidence of sophisticated organization in the marijuana market, and of the creation of incipient organized crime groups. Ironically, one factor that appears to have stimulated the change from small, ad hoc, disorganized growing to the creation of highly organized criminal groups is Kentucky's federally funded law enforcement campaign against the marijuana industry. Stepped-up enforcement seems to have resulted in the creation of a more efficient and more dangerous marijuana industry.

Clandestine Laboratories

As earlier pointed out in this book, of the many different drugs that have become popular over the years, some are organic in nature and some are synthesized by chemists in illicit drug laboratories. It should be noted here that even though some drugs may be of an organic origin, a degree of chemical synthesis is necessary for the completion of the finished product. This is true, for example, with heroin and cocaine. Many popular drugs that have emerged over the years are synthetic in nature and as portrayed in the popular AMC cable television series, *Breaking Bad.* These include the following:

- Hallucinogens (LSD, PCP, and ecstasy (MDMA))
- Stimulants (methamphetamine and amphetamines)
- Controlled substance analogs (designer drugs)

Drugs such as LSD seem to be available almost everywhere in the country, but their production appears to be regional. For example, for years LSD and PCP laboratories have been abundant in California, and much of the methamphetamine (meth) is produced in illegal laboratories in the West and Southwest. The size of most clandestine laboratories is relatively modest, since they generally produce one specific drug. Expertise to operate a laboratory is usually minimal, and much of the equipment and chemicals is readily available and inexpensive. This is true especially when the profits that can be realized are considered. Methamphetamine is one of the most commonly produced illicit drugs in the United States. One of its immediate precursors, phenyl-2-propanone, is easily synthesized into methamphetamine. Like many other drugs, the production of methamphetamine is fairly cheap and effortless. The actual setting up of a laboratory can cost as little as $2000 and can be enormously profitable, since one day's production can generate as much as $50,000 [27].

The spreading popularity of illicit laboratories is partly due to successes in federal drug interdiction efforts. Many traffickers feel safer making their own drugs domestically than they do risking detection and arrest as a result of dealing with foreign suppliers. As with the marijuana cultivator, the clandestine laboratory operator commonly seeks isolation in rural settings, where his or her activities will go unnoticed. For example, one of the largest illicit methamphetamine laboratories ever discovered in the United States was located in the mountains of rural McCreary County, Kentucky, and involved participants from Kentucky, Florida, Illinois, and Tennessee. Often, this desire for rural isolation is due to the distinctive odors emitted by meth and PCP laboratories. In an urban setting, these odors can reveal the existence of a laboratory (Table 5.2).

The Growing Meth Menace

In Salt Lake City, Utah, visitors are shown photographs of a woman in her late twenties who has been arrested several times for dealing in methamphetamine, a notoriously addictive and increasingly common street drug. She used the drug herself, and the photos show her appearance aging some 30 years over a 5-year period: cheeks sinking, eyes turning glassy, teeth rotting. Utah, a predominantly Mormon state, largely denounces coffee, tobacco, and alcohol. However, by the middle of the decade, it ranked third nationally in the percentage of arrested men who tested positive for meth, and meth-related crimes were said to account for perhaps 80 percent of the criminal activity in the state [28].

Meth—also known as ice, crank, crystal, or glass—is, in the eyes of many, America's leading drug problem. Limited to California and the Pacific Northwest in the 1990s, it has now spread across the country. In Missouri, 2,000 meth laboratories were discovered in

Table 5.2   Typical Chemicals Found in Clandestine Drug Laboratories

Acetic anhydride	Moderate	Moderate	Irritant, corrosive
Anhydrous ammonia	High	N/A	Rapid asphyxia
Benzene	Moderate-high	High	Blood disorders; carcinogen
Chloroform	Moderate	Low	Disorientation, unconsciousness; probable carcinogen
Cyclohexane	Low	High	Irritant
Ethyl ether	N/A	High	May form peroxides
Ethanol	Low	High	Disorientation
Hydrogen cyanide	Extreme	Low	Rapid asphyxia
Hydrochloric acid	High	Low	Irritant; corrosive
Hydriodic acid	High	Low	Irritant; corrosive
Hypophosphorus acid	N/A	Moderate	Corrosive
Iodine	N/A	Moderate	Oxidizer; corrosive
Lead acetate	High	Low	Blood disorders
Lithium aluminum hydride	Moderate	High	Water reactive, explosive
Mercury chloride	High	Low	Irritant; corrosive
Methylamine	High	Extreme	Corrosive
Petroleum ether	Low	Extreme	Disorientation, unconsciousness
Phenylacetic acid	Low	Low	Irritant
Piperdine	Moderate	High	Corrosive
Red phosphorus	Low	Low	Reactive & explosive
Safrole	High	Low	May cause cancer
Sodium (metal)	High	Low	Water reactive, corrosive
Sodium hydroxide	N/A	N/A	Corrosive
Thionyl chloride	High	Low	Water reactive; corrosive

Source: Based primarily on National Fire Protection Association Standards.

2004. Atlanta has become the gateway for meth distribution across much of the East Coast, with 174 pounds seized in one raid there in 2005.

The growing presence of methamphetamine is supported by recent trafficking patterns and national statistics. For example, according to the National Drug Intelligence Center, in 2008 the flow of methamphetamine into the United States from Mexico was generally on the increase, but during 2007 its availability decreased in the United States, causing instability in the methamphetamine supply chain. Before 2007, drug users in the United States relied on the strong flow of methamphetamine produced in Mexico, a supply system initially established in 2005 and strengthened in 2006. However, ephedrine and pseudoephedrine restrictions in Mexico resulted in a decrease in methamphetamine production there and reduced the flow of the drug from Mexico to the United States in 2007 and early 2008. By mid-2008, Mexican drug-trafficking organizations shifted their production operations from Mexico to the United States, particularly to California [29,30]. In addition, Mexican traffickers began adapting their operating procedures in several other ways, including smuggling restricted chemicals through new routes, importing nonrestricted chemical derivatives instead of precursor chemicals, using alternative production methods, and diverting precursor chemicals from sources in Southeast Asia and South America.

Methamphetamine can be made with a handful of ingredients—pseudoephedrine (a common ingredient in many cold remedies), red phosphorus, muriatic acid, fertilizer, and iodine. Recipes can be found widely on the Internet. One day's work in a kitchen can yield a dozen doses. Injected or smoked, methamphetamine works almost instantly on the brain, releasing far more dopamines (the brain's primary pleasure transmitters) than cocaine or heroin. Users feel intense pleasure followed by an energetic high that can last for days.

Meth's physical consequences are shocking. The rotten teeth of a "meth mouth" are common in heavy users, a byproduct of the drug's effects on the metabolic system plus the large quantities of sugary soft drinks consumed to alleviate the dry mouth caused by the drug. Methamphetamine drastically alters the brain, shrinking it 1 percent a year with heavy use.

In May 2005, federal and local police in Salem, Massachusetts, raided a nearby meth "superlab" run by Mexican nationals that was estimated to turn out 90 pounds of meth in 2–3 days, enough for 400,000 jolting doses. Big laboratories like this were common until recently, when restrictions on the sale of medicines containing pseudoephedrine slashed their numbers. Oklahoma, Illinois, Missouri, California, Ohio, and several other states limit the sale of cold cures; Oregon is discussing a complete ban.

Another recent development with newly imposed restrictions on precursors is a technique adopted by some methamphetamine traffickers known as ephedrine and pseudoephedrine smurfing. *Smurfing* is a method that enables traffickers to acquire large quantities of precursor chemicals. Meth producers purchase the chemicals at or below threshold levels from multiple retail locations. Traffickers often employ friends or associates to increase the speed with which chemicals can be acquired [31,32].

Categories of Illicit Laboratories

Despite the numerous types of drugs produced by illicit laboratories, the manufacturing process can be broken down into three distinct categories:

- The *extraction laboratory* produces illicit substances by removing elements from one substance and creating another. Both hashish and methamphetamine are often manufactured using the benzedrine inhaler method of extraction.

- The *conversion laboratory* converts existing illicit drugs to a different form of the same drug. Crack is an example; it is cocaine that is converted into a freebase form for street sale.
- The *synthesis laboratory* transforms one substance to another, resulting in a different and more powerful drug. For example, the precursor phenyl-2-propanone is a dangerous drug used to manufacture methamphetamine powder. This process is different from the methamphetamine extraction method.

Investigating a clandestine laboratory is especially dangerous for police because of the explosive, corrosive, and hazardous materials usually associated with the drug-manufacturing process, and because many laboratories are fortified with deadly booby traps. In many cases, even a slight spark can create a chain reaction resulting in a massive explosion of the laboratory. In some instances, agents have fainted from fumes emitted from the laboratories. For this reason, investigators who raid the laboratories now wear protective plastic jumpsuits, rubber gloves, respirators, and air tanks. Portable showers in vans are sometimes used to allow agents to wash off contaminants.

Criminal drug laboratory operators have been documented not only mixing deadly toxic chemicals, but also dumping toxic waste down bathroom drains or in holes dug outside in the ground. These actions make some laboratory locations akin to hazardous waste sites.

Clandestine laboratories are often operated by nonprofessional individuals with a limited knowledge of chemistry. Some laboratories are run by people who have learned various processing techniques through their peers in the criminal underworld. The methamphetamine market, for example, was dominated for many years by the Pagans motorcycle club. The skills utilized in drug processing and the safety procedures initiated by a group like the Pagans are highly suspect.

Controlling Precursor Chemicals

Legally obtained substances that are typically used by illicit laboratory operators to make their final product are known as *precursors*. Essential chemicals called *solvents* are also needed to produce the final drug product, but they do not actually become part of the drug itself. In 1988, the Chemical Diversion and Trafficking Act was passed, requiring detailed record keeping and reporting of transactions of all purchases over a designated quantity of each chemical, and reporting of all "suspicious" purchases to the DEA. In turn, the DEA is empowered to deny the sale of chemicals to any person or company they deem likely to use them for the making of an illegal drug.

By 2005, 42 state governments had passed their own legislation regulating the sale of precursor chemicals [33]. Several states require companies that manufacture these chemicals to obtain a license with a state agency and to maintain records that are regularly supplied to that agency. Essentially, the controlling of precursors is yet another way in which manufacturers of illicit drugs can be identified for arrest or possibly deterred from drug-trafficking activity.

Pharmaceutical Diversion

In August 2001, FBI agents arrested Kansas City, Missouri, pharmacist Robert Courtney for diluting expensive drugs used for chemotherapy cancer treatment. They charged that Courtney diluted the drugs Gemzar and Taxol to 39 percent of the prescribed dose, enabling him to skim hundreds of dollars per prescription. More alarming is that the diluted drugs were lifesaving prescriptions for cancer patients who were under the impression they were taking full-strength medications for their ailments. Although this case represents only one act of malfeasance on the part of pharmaceutical professionals, it illustrates the growing problem of drug diversion.

The Extent of the Problem

According to recent reports from law enforcement agencies, pharmaceutical diversion and abuse pose an increasing drug threat in their jurisdictions. Increases in prescription drug addiction are fueling increases in drug-related crimes, and, alarmingly, there is growing gang involvement in prescription drug trafficking. Among young people, diverted prescription drugs are now second only to marijuana as the most abused illegal drug [34]. Teens perceive prescription drugs as safer to abuse than illegal drugs, and parents are unaware of the problem. According to the 2009 *National Survey on Drug Use and Health* (NSDUH), there were 7.0 million (2.8 percent) persons aged 12 or older who used prescription-type psychotherapeutic drugs nonmedically within the past month, and these estimates were higher than in 2007 and 2008 [35].

The NSDUH study is conducted annually by the Substance Abuse and Mental Health Services Administration (SAMHSA). NSDUH defines "nonmedical use" as the use of prescription-type psychotherapeutic drugs *not prescribed* for the respondent by a physician or *used only for the experience or feeling they caused.* The specific illicit drugs that had the highest levels of past-year abuse were marijuana (4.3 million), pain relievers (1.9 million), and cocaine (1.1 million) [36]. The number of persons with marijuana dependence or abuse has not changed in a decade, but the number with pain reliever dependence or abuse has increased from 1.5 to 1.9 million Americans [37].

Crime, Emergency Room Visits, and Rising Public Welfare Costs

Prescription drug abuse is driving increased crime, a sharp rise in emergency room visits, and rising health care costs. Abuse and neglect of children comprise one of the most insidious ways that prescription drug addiction—oftentimes beginning with a legitimate prescription—affects our communities. Child welfare specialists are reporting fewer cases of parental abuse and neglect due to illegal drugs, but more cases of parental abuse due to prescription drugs like oxycodone, hydrocodone, and antianxiety drugs like Xanax. Sadly, most prescription drug crimes and overdose deaths are eminently preventable, with multiple missed intervention opportunities to get these users drug treatment before their behaviors become overly burdensome to society.

Prescription Pain Medications and Newborns

States plagued by prescription drug abuse have reported drastic increases in the number of newborns being treated for neonatal withdrawal syndrome. For example, treatment for neonatal withdrawal syndrome in Maine's largest hospitals jumped from 70 in 2005 to 276 in 2010. Florida and Ohio have experienced remarkably similar increases. For example, in 2010, 1,374 babies were born in Florida with withdrawal symptoms from drug abuse, a fourfold increase from 2003. The problem of expectant mothers abusing pain medication has become so prevalent that All Children's Hospital in Tampa estimates that, at any given time, there are at least 10 newborns being treated for prescription drug withdrawal. These numbers may, in fact, be much higher than reported because many pregnant women are neither tested for drug use nor admit to using prescription drugs during pregnancy.

Neonatal intensive care unit costs are the most significant contributor to total costs for treatment of drug-exposed women and their infants. Neonatal withdrawal syndrome is a collection of problems that will occur in a newborn who has been exposed to addictive illicit or prescription drugs while in the womb. Withdrawal symptoms include fever, seizures, blotchy skin, incessant shrill cries, respiratory problems, and extreme sensitivity to sound and light. Prescription drug abuse among pregnant women is so disturbing not just because of each precious life affected, but also because this tragedy is being repeated with ever more frequency as the numbers of addicted pregnant women have grown so dramatically in Florida over the past several years. Since pregnant women addicted to prescription medications cannot quit cold turkey because a full-blown drug withdrawal could endanger the fetus, serious discussions about how to alleviate both illicit and licit drug abuse problems must begin with how we can change the way society treats pregnant women who are more inclined to abuse such drugs.

Current research supports the policy of providing comprehensive drug treatment and obstetrical care services for drug-abusing pregnant women. This strategy is associated with substantial cost savings in the care and treatment of the infants born to this high-risk population of women. However, debate over how to properly treat pregnant women and newborn babies addicted to prescription medications continues without clear consensus.

More research must be conducted in order to determine the best way to help expectant mothers break their addiction to opiate painkillers, while preserving the health of the baby both in utero and after birth. For newborns, withdrawal symptoms take from 3 weeks to 2 months to pass. But because neonatal prescription drug addiction is so new, the ultimate health and developmental effects on these babies will not be discernible until years from now. To achieve a reduction in neonatal withdrawal syndrome, Florida's *Roadmap* advocates a strong two-pronged approach: first, create and expand drug prevention materials educating women about the impact of prescription medications on their pregnancy; and,

On August 6, 2008, the Miami-Dade (Florida) Police Department and the Miami-Dade County State Attorney General's Office announced arrest warrants for 62 individuals, 52 of whom were public employees, charging them with crimes related to alleged health insurance fraud to obtain large quantities of OxyContin. According to the Florida state attorney's office, beginning in January 2003, six recruiters enlisted local government employees and others to participate in an illegal operation in which those recruited would provide their health insurance identification information to a recruiter. The government employees and others who were recruited allegedly obtained prescriptions for OxyContin (for which they had no medical need) from the complicit physician. They then presented the fraudulent prescriptions at a local pharmacy in Miami-Dade County to obtain the OxyContin tablets and sold the pills for cash to another individual involved in the scam. The government employees and others recruited also submitted health insurance claims to their employer-issued health insurance company, fraudulently claiming reimbursement for the cost of the prescriptions. Officials estimate that approximately 130 medically unnecessary prescriptions for OxyContin were presented to the pharmacies, accounting for more than 12,000 tablets with an estimated street value of almost $400,000.

Source: National Drug Intelligence Center and Drug Enforcement Administration.

second, support new federal science research to determine the best ways to treat both pregnant women and those newborn babies addicted to prescription medications.

The passage of legislation during Florida's 2012 session creating a *Statewide Task Force on Prescription Drug Abuse and Newborns (SB 402/HB 227)* assisted in these efforts. The task force will be charged with examining the scope of neonatal withdrawal syndrome, the costs associated with caring for babies, and the long-term effects of (and strategies for preventing) prescription drug abuse by expectant mothers.

The 1970 Controlled Substances Act authorized the DEA to regulate all aspects of the drug-manufacturing and distribution process in the United States. For the more potent drugs, the DEA can even dictate the thickness of the warehouse walls where they are stored (e.g., 8 inches of concrete with steel rods). The DEA also controls the order form needed to purchase drugs (three copies, with one forwarded to DEA headquarters). Through these mechanisms, the DEA claims that much of the diversion from warehouses and factories has been controlled. The result has been increased diversion at the retail level, marked by a sharp rise in drugstore robberies and burglaries, along with increased pressure on some doctors and druggists to cross the line from "professional" to "pusher." Problems in drug diversion involve both medical professionals and people who attempt to acquire drugs through deceit and trickery. Persons in the latter category are often called *scammers*.

The Scammer

To aid in understanding the problem of drug diversion, investigators should look at the various scams used by street criminals to obtain pharmaceutical drugs. The word *scam* is defined by *Webster's Dictionary* as "to cheat or swindle, as in a confidence game." This is precisely what is happening within the medical care community. This criminal, known as the *scammer* or *professional patient*, acquires drugs through deceit and sells them on the street for profit.

Of all the scammer's targets, the most likely is the physician, because once a prescription has been successfully conned out of a physician, the scammer will experience little trouble having it filled by the pharmacist, since it appears to be legitimate. Pharmacists are the second most likely target of the scammer, especially in trying to pass forged or altered prescriptions. In addition to forgery and alterations of prescriptions, a pharmacist can be an unwitting partner to a scammer. Three methods are the most common: (1) filling prescriptions for the same drugs for the same patient from different physicians, (2) filling prescriptions for the same patient too frequently, and (3) accepting refills for prescriptions when the scammer calls in the prescription pretending to be the physician. Literally hundreds of diversion schemes have been uncovered throughout the years. The following examples, however, will give some insight into the practices of "professional patients."

The Fat Lady Scam
The "fat lady" scam is a common deception that is usually perpetrated by several women who are severely overweight. The plan involves the women moving into a new community and developing a schedule requiring each member to visit a maximum number of physicians each day for a week or so. The scam unfolds as each woman tells the physician that she is chronically unhappy with her life because of being overweight. Details may be added, such as that her husband is going to leave her and fight for custody of the children, she is considering having her stomach stapled, and so forth. At this point, the patient begins hinting about a particular drug, such as preludin, amphetamines, or another Schedule II drug. The physician will usually refuse to prescribe Schedule II drugs for this purpose, but might be willing to prescribe Didrex. After the patient is issued a prescription for this drug, the woman might request a prescription for Valium to keep her from getting too edgy. Instead of taking the prescribed drugs themselves, the women sell them for profit on the street.

The Breast Cancer Scam
This scam is a fairly common one in many states and involves individuals who are actually experiencing a legitimate medical problem. For example, the scam was first documented in the St. Louis area and involved a woman who truly suffered from breast cancer. The woman would simply appear at a physician's office and present her case for treatment. In the St. Louis case, Dilaudid was the only drug determined to give her relief, and physicians would usually agree to give her a prescription. The patient saw seven doctors on a regular basis in different surrounding towns. As with the previous scam, the prescription drugs she obtained were sold on the street for a substantial profit.

The Toothache Scam
The toothache scam is popular among narcotics addicts who are also experiencing a tooth-decay problem. These scammers will try to obtain Schedule II narcotics from dentists and

physicians at the same time. Sometimes, scammers have attempted to obtain telephone prescriptions for the desired drug without even seeing the dentist. If the scammers choose to see the dentist, they will appear with a concocted legitimate reason for having to be somewhere else, so the dentist will be pressured to issue a prescription for painkillers such as Demerol or Dilaudid. Once obtained, the drugs are sold on the illicit market.

The Altered "Scrip" Scam

Those prescribers who shortcut the proper prescription-writing practice, especially by using Arabic numerals for dose amounts (not reinforced by a written number), are easy targets for professional patients. By simply matching the ink color of the prescriber's pen, a prescription for "10" can be altered to "40", "5" can become "25," and so forth. A prudent prescription thus becomes excessive and proportionally more profitable to the professional patient.

Many other scams are facilitated by confidence artists who are elderly, handicapped, or simply clever or brazen enough to attempt such a fraud. All professionals within the medical community are obligated, however, to report any such attempts by criminals when they are first detected.

Doctors as Offenders

What is it that makes a professional registrant (legal handler of controlled substances: e.g., nurse, pharmacist, etc.) choose to become a law violator and a "white-collar" drug dealer? The following are some motivating factors.

- *Greed.* Pharmacists and physicians have easy access to drugs that command top dollar on the street. For example, they pay only about $50 for 500 tablets of Knoll Pharmaceutical Company's Dilaudid, a synthetic narcotic similar to morphine (see Chapter 2). On the street, Dilaudid will easily bring between $50 and $60 per tablet. Some corrupt professionals barter drugs or prescriptions for merchandise. Others make their living by operating "diet clinics," in which they freely dispense or prescribe amphetamine tablets, even though use of the drug for weight control is questionable.
- *Sexual favors.* Some investigations have revealed instances in which physicians and pharmacists give drugs or prescriptions in return for sexual favors. There have been cases of amphetamines being given to prostitutes to help them stay awake.
- *Salvaging a failing medical practice.* Drug diversion is a particular problem in cases of failing medical practices, which are caused by such circumstances as incompetence, impending retirement, or location problems. Illicit activity on the part of these physicians often results from being deep in debt or having been accustomed to high incomes that have been reduced. An unethical solution to the problem is to write illegal prescriptions or dispense pills for the easy income.
- *Self-addiction.* Addiction to drugs is an occupational disease for some members of the health care community. Long hours and the easy availability of drugs make the medical professional susceptible to drug abuse. Physicians who have become addicted may turn to diversion to finance their addiction.

- *Senility.* Some senile doctors and pharmacists have unwittingly yielded to the demands of drug abusers. In other cases, a nurse, medical receptionist, or family member has "taken over" the practice of a senile professional and allowed dangerous drugs to be diverted.
- *Rationalization.* Some professionals justify selling to abusers by rationalizing that they will get drugs anyway, perhaps through street crime or prostitution.

Some of the specific methods that physicians have commonly used to divert prescription drugs include the following:

- Physicians writing prescriptions in a patient's or family member's name, picking up the drugs themselves, and then telling the pharmacist they will deliver them to the patient.
- Physicians sending patients to pharmacies to have prescriptions filled but requiring the patient to bring the drugs back to the doctor's office, where only part of the drug is administered; the physician keeps the rest.
- Physicians writing prescriptions in their own name at various pharmacies at the same time.
- Physicians (and nurses) self-administering injectable drugs taken from nurses' stations, hospital emergency rooms, or hospital pharmacies.
- Physicians ordering drugs from a number of pharmacies at the same time using DEA official order forms, while ordering the same drugs from one of many mail-order drug companies.
- Physicians obtaining drug samples and self-administering them.

Although medical institutions have both a legal and a moral obligation to their employees, many shun the responsibility of reporting a suspected diversion problem, or they simply look the other way rather than address the situation. Responsible hospitals, through their boards of directors, regulate their personnel and establish formal policies regarding impairment with strict enforcement (or treatment) provisions. In the case of addicted registrants, many state hospital boards have adopted a policy whereby a physician or nurse can voluntarily submit to treatment under an employee assistance program and remedy the problem before it results in prosecution of the physician and embarrassment to the hospital. Similar problems are observed with nurses working within the medical field. A distinction should be made here between diversion of drugs for resale and diversion because of personal addiction. Studies have shown that many nurses who are diverting drugs do so because of personal physical addictions to those drugs, rather than a desire to profit from their sale.

Theft of Drugs

Most health care institutions experience some degree of diversion, and generally it is the employees who are the culprits. As indicated, employees who steal drugs are those who have access to drugs—for example, physicians, nurses, pharmacists, and others—and they

CASE IN POINT: CHARLES CULLEN: THE ANGEL OF DEATH

In addition to diversion of drugs for profit and to feed personal addictions, sometimes drugs are diverted for a more perverse motivation. One such case is Charles Cullen—the so-called Angel of Death.

No one will ever know how many patients Charles Cullen murdered over the course of his 16-year career as a night nurse. From 1987 until 2003, one of the United States' most prolific serial killers was the subject of dozens of complaints and disciplinary citations, a handful of police investigations, up to 20 suicide attempts, and several lockdowns in a psychiatric ward. Many of his supervisors and colleagues were aware of his dangerous and unethical practices, but his professional résumé remained untainted as hospitals sent him with glowing references to become someone else's problem. He worked at nine hospitals in total, murdering an unknown but large number of people—as many as 400 patients—with toxic intravenous injections. The media dubbed Cullen "the Angel of Death"—a nickname he relished—when he was finally arrested in 2003. He then was convicted and sentenced to 100 years in prison. Raised Catholic, Cullen had always viewed himself as a martyr, like the namesake apostle of Saint Barnabas Hospital in Newark, New Jersey, where he began killing patients with insulin overdoses in the early 1990s. He later injected patients with high levels of digoxin, a deadly drug used to treat congestive heart failure. Cullen was not the first serial killer in the medical profession. In 2000, a British doctor named Harold Shipman was convicted of murdering 15 patients (although an investigation revealed he killed hundreds more) and sentenced to life in prison. In 2013 a Brazilian doctor, Virginia Soares de Souza, was charged with murdering seven patients, although authorities warn that she also had hundreds of victims. What makes these crimes particularly chilling is that they were committed in the very institutions we entrust our lives to. A hospital letting a murderer work freely is perhaps even more chilling than other instances of institutions—like the Catholic Church or Penn State University—that protected themselves rather than the people they serve.

Many argue that while Cullen may have been brought to justice, the hospitals where he worked literally got away with murder. The unpopular graveyard shifts made it that much easier for Cullen to kill, and when hospital insiders suspected or accused him of malpractice, he reveled in their inability to stop him.

Sources: NPR Books. Found at: http://www.npr.org/2013/04/15/177029738/pretending-to-be-a-good-nurse-serial-killer-targeted-patients, Accessed April 28, 2013; *The Huffington Post article.* Found at: http://www.huffingtonpost.com/2013/04/19/charles-cullen-nurse-who-_n_3116750.html, Accessed April 28, 2013; *60 Minutes Overtime.* Found at: http://www.cbsnews.com/8334-504803_162-57580827-10391709/why-did-charles-cullen-murder-patients-in-his-care/, Accessed April 29, 2013.

will most commonly divert drugs such as Valium, morphine, Demerol, Tylenol III with Codeine, Percodan, Percocet, and Ritalin. The type of drug user and available opportunities will have a bearing on whether tablets, capsules, or injectable substances are preferred. Diversion may occur in many different areas of the health care facility, but is most commonly at one of the following locations: (1) the hospital pharmacy, (2) the nursing area, or (3) the recovery floor.

Substituting Drugs

In the event that the outright theft of drugs is not considered safe by the diversion-minded criminal, the substitution of a controlled drug for a noncontrolled substance might be considered. Substituting drugs may be accomplished, for instance, by appearing to inject a patient with the prescribed medication while, in fact, a worthless substance may be used in its place. This may cause the patient to suffer and could result in additional medical setbacks for the patient. Techniques for substitution vary but commonly include (1) theft through charting (a technique for backdating); and (2) forging the names of other nurses.

Addressing the Problem

Drug diversion persists, in part, because many facilities fail to discipline the people involved. Compounding the problem is the fact that, in many cases, violators themselves have ways of avoiding punishment. For example, suspected users might quit their positions and join other hospitals. This might happen if drug users on the job are suspected by one or more other employees; in an effort to avoid being confronted, the users simply change jobs. In such cases, when the diverter's new employer calls for an employee reference, incriminating information is frequently not shared, thereby allowing the user to carry on with unlawful activities.

■ ■ Critical Thinking Task ■

Assume that you are a member of the board of directors for a major hospital. Suggest a policy for the control of prescription drugs within your hospital. Include procedures for the prevention of diversion and for enforcement of the policy.

In other cases, employees who are caught diverting drugs are transferred rather than disciplined. Medical care professionals, like many other types of professionals, are somewhat clannish and reluctant to "snitch" on fellow workers. So, by transferring suspect employees, embarrassing publicity for the institution is avoided. Of course, these reactions offer no incentive for violators to discontinue their involvement in drug diversion activity.

Problems in Diversion Investigations

Even though pharmacists are required by law to account for every dose of dangerous drugs they order, suspicious fires, robberies, and break-ins can destroy prescription files and destroy evidence of shortages of pills. For these and many other reasons, evidence of diversion is difficult to acquire. For example, undercover agents investigating this type of criminal behavior may find that the suspect doctors claim that they were just "practicing medicine" and attempting to cure a patient by prescribing drugs for an illness. Other violations are more blatant, such as when physicians literally sell drugs to friends and associates or barter prescriptions for merchandise.

Other problems arise in the prosecution of diversion cases. For example, prosecutors are usually eager to file charges against drug dealers from the street, but when the drug dealer happens to be a physician in the community, charges are sometimes difficult to bring. Moreover, prosecutors are often reluctant to try "respectable" citizens who have the resources to mount an active defense against the charges. In addition, there are other pressures on prosecutors. They may have a social or political relationship with the registrant. If they are in a rural county where doctors' offices are few and far between, they know that any doctor forced out of business could leave some families without easy access to medical care. Furthermore, inconvenienced voters often have good memories when the prosecutor has to stand for reelection, creating a situation in which the prosecutor may actually be punished by the very public he or she serves for attempting to apply diversion laws to physicians. Even when charges are brought against physicians, prosecutors may have a difficult time convincing juries of the seriousness of the violation, or it may be difficult to explain the complexities of the diversion case to the jury. Because of these considerations, a conviction may not be forthcoming in the case.

The Drug Audit

One of the nine control mechanisms contained within the 1970 Controlled Substances Act is a record-keeping requirement for all registrants. This provision requires that full records of quantities of all controlled substances, regardless of which schedule they are under, be kept by registrants. This requirement applies to drugs when they are manufactured, purchased, sold, or inventoried. Limited exceptions to this requirement are available only to researchers and physicians. It is from these records that audits can be performed to trace the flow of any drug from the time it is first manufactured, to the wholesale level, to its final destination at a pharmacy, hospital, or physician's office, and on to the patient. The mere existence of this requirement is often enough to discourage many types of diversion. Under the record-keeping requirement, one distinction is made: the records for Schedule I and II drugs must be maintained separately from all other records of the registrant. The purpose of this requirement is to allow investigators the ability to audit the most abusable drugs more expeditiously.

Summary

Although foreign traffickers make significant contributions to the drug problem in the United States, many domestic criminals also play a significant role. Domestic drug production primarily centers on three types of illicit activities: marijuana cultivation; clandestine laboratories, which primarily manufacture methamphetamine and PCP; and pharmaceutical diversion.

The marijuana cultivator will produce one of two types of marijuana: commercial or sinsemilla. The commercial grade is the most common type of marijuana and is generally the easiest to grow. Sinsemilla, on the other hand, is a more potent type of marijuana and will bring twice the street price of the commercial strain. Explaining why fewer marijuana growers are involved with sinsemilla farming than with growing commercial marijuana is the fact that sinsemilla is much more difficult to grow and requires more personal attention and time on the part of the cultivator.

The clandestine laboratory problem is one of growing proportions in the United States. Laboratory operators are most active in the manufacturing of methamphetamine and PCP, both of which have achieved growing popularity throughout the nation.

Finally, we examined the problem of pharmaceutical diversion by both scammers (also known as *professional patients*) and registrants. The diversion of addictive and dangerous drugs happens for many reasons. Some reasons involve a profit motive; others are related to personal addictions developed by the registrants themselves. In either case, the problem results in the diversion of a significant amount of dangerous drugs that are eventually marketed on the street for exorbitant prices.

Do you recognize these terms?

- cloning
- commercial-grade marijuana
- conversion laboratory
- extraction laboratory
- hash oil
- hashish
- hydroponics
- Indian hemp
- precursors
- professional patient
- scammer
- sinsemilla
- smurfing
- synthesis laboratory

Discussion Questions

1. List the three most common types of marijuana grown in the United States.
2. How is sinsemilla grown, and why is its potency so much higher than that of commercial-grade marijuana?
3. What are the two most common methods of indoor growing of marijuana?
4. List the primary drugs manufactured by domestic clandestine laboratories, and explain why these laboratories are considered dangerous for police investigators.
5. Who are the most likely candidates for the diversion of pharmaceutical drugs?
6. What factors explain why a professional (e.g., a doctor or pharmacist) might become involved in the diversion of pharmaceutical drugs?
7. Discuss some ways in which controlled drugs can be diverted from legal channels of distribution.
8. Explain why a pharmaceutical drug case is usually so difficult to prosecute.

References

[1] National Institute on Drug Abuse. (2009). *Monitoring the future: National results for adolescent drug use – Overview of key findings 2008*. National Institutes of Health. U.S. Department of Health and Human Services.
[2] Goode, E. (1993). *Drugs in American society* (4th ed.). New York: McGraw-Hill.

[3] FiercePharmaManufacturing. (2013). Found at: http://www.fiercepharmamanufacturing.com/special-reports/top-12-gmp-violations.

[4] U.S. Department of Justice Office of Public Affairs. (2013). http://www.justice.gov/opa/pr/2009/April/09-ag-305.html. Accessed April 29, 2013.

[5] U.S. Department of Justice Office of Public Affairs. (2013). Found at: http://www.justice.gov/opa/pr/2012/July/12-civ-842.html. Accessed April 29, 2013.

[6] U.S. Department of Justice Office of Public Affairs. (2013). http://www.justice.gov/opa/pr/2009/April/09-at-313.html.

[7] U.S. Department of Justice. (2013). http://www.justice.gov/opa/pr/2009/January/09-civ-038.html.

[8] Ibid.

[9] Ibid.

[10] Kalb, C. (April 9, 2001). Playing with pain killers. *Newsweek*, 45–51.

[11] Office of National Drug Control Policy. (2012). *2012 National drug control strategy*. Washington, DC: U.S. Department of Justice. Executive Office of the President of the United States.

[12] Manning, P. K., & Redlinger, L. J. (2006). Invitational edges of corruption: Some consequences of narcotic law enforcement. In P. E. Rock (Ed.), *Drugs and politics* (pp. 279). New Brunswick, NJ: Transaction.

[13] Pryor, D. (March 1994). Prescription drug industry must be reformed. *USA Today*, 74–75.

[14] Ibid.

[15] Ibid.

[16] Ibid.

[17] Rovner, J. (July 1992). Prescription drug prices. *Congressional Quarterly*, 599.

[18] Friend, T. (1996). Prescription misuse costs nation billions. *USA Today*. (August 7), 2B.

[19] Kazman, S. (1991). The FDA's deadly approval process. *Consumer's Research*. (April), 31–36.

[20] Ibid.

[21] Sternberg, S. (April 15, 1998). Drug reactions kill 100,000 patients a year. *USA Today*, 1A.

[22] Ibid.

[23] National Drug Intelligence Center. (2010). *National drug threat assessment 2010*. February, Washington, DC: U.S. Department of Justice.

[24] Ibid.

[25] Weisheit, R. (1992). *Domestic marijuana: A neglected industry*. Westport, CT: Greenwood Press.

[26] Ibid.

[27] Braun, M. (2006). *Congressional testimony on "counternarcotics strategies in Latin America."* Washington, DC: Drug Enforcement Administration.

[28] The Economist. (June 16, 2005). Instant pleasure, instant ageing. *The Economist*, 30–31.

[29] United Nations Office on Drugs and Crime (UNODC). (2010). *The globalization of crime: A transnational organized crime threat assessment*. New York: UNODC, pp. 5–6.

[30] United Nations Office on Drugs and Crime (UNODC). (2011). *World drug report*. New York: UNODC, p. 8.

[31] United Nations Office on Drugs and Crime (UNODC). (2010). *The globalization of crime: A transnational organized crime threat assessment*. New York: UNODC, pp. 5–6.

[32] United Nations Office on Drugs and Crime (UNODC). (2011). *World drug report*. New York: UNODC, p. 8.

[33] Office of National Drug Control Policy. (2005). *The National Drug Control Strategy, Executive Summary*. Washington, DC: U.S. Government Printing Office.

[34] National Institute on Drug Abuse. (October 2011). *Research report series: Prescription drugs: Abuse and addiction*.

[35] *Found in Florida's prescription drug diversion and abuse roadmap 2012–2015*. (2012). Office of the Attorney General.

[36] National Institute on Drug Abuse. (October 2011). *Research report series: Prescription drugs: Abuse and addiction*.

[37] Ibid.

6

Drugs and Crime

This chapter will enable you to:

- Understand the relationship between various types of crime and drug abuse
- Comprehend the extent of the police corruption problem as it pertains to drug trafficking
- Understand the domestic and international problem of money laundering
- Realize who the money launderers are and how they operate
- Understand what legal tools are available to prosecutors to combat money laundering

In addition to the physiological effects and medical complications associated with drug abuse, one of the greatest public concerns is the rising spectrum of crime as it relates to the use of drugs. Clearly, a definitive but complex correlation exists between drug crimes and other types of crime, but the nature and extent of the link between drugs and crime are far from being understood. Therefore, the catch phrase *drug-related crime* remains somewhat general. Criminal justice researchers hope to clarify this category of crime in coming years, to predict both drug-trafficking patterns and non-drug-related criminal behavior.

The drugs and crime issue causes one to consider one fundamental question: to what extent does one perpetuate the other? For example, it is clear that abuse and trafficking and use of some substances are by their very nature illegal—users of heroin must possess the drug to use it, but possession of it is forbidden under law. Accordingly, stricter penalties exist on both the state and federal levels for heroin's transportation and sale. Moreover, some forms of drug abuse are more likely than not to spur particular types of antisocial behavior. For instance, amphetamine use has been linked to an increase in levels of aggression, which has been shown to lead to assaultive behavior in some cases. Frequency of drug use is another factor. One who uses drugs several times a day is at a greater risk of involvement in crime than one who is an occasional user. Finally, many crimes not normally associated with drug use or drug dealing result from drug-related behavior. For example, a user might steal to support his or her habit, or prostitution might finance one's drug use. In fact, studies have shown that criminal activity is almost two to three times higher among frequent users of heroin or cocaine than among irregular users or nonusers of drugs. This does not imply that if drugs were to be eliminated, so would crime, but it does suggest that a causal link may exist.

This chapter identifies and discusses three critical forms of drug-related crime: drug use and predatory crime, police corruption, and money laundering. Each of these plays a significant role in the overall drug problem and should be considered in seeking solutions to the nation's drug dilemma.

Drug Use and Predatory Crime

Some law enforcement officials and researchers have long suspected that a link exists between addictive drugs and the propensity of drug users to commit crime. The available empirical research indicates that drug addicts, particularly heroin addicts, commit crimes more frequently than other population groups. Drug addiction appears to escalate the rate of criminal participation, but that does not mean that drug use causes crime. The need for financial resources to ensure a steady supply of the drug appears to escalate the already manifest criminal involvement of drug users. Several important sources of information about drugs and crime are currently available for helping to determine the extent of drug use (e.g., urine testing of arrested persons; surveys of offender populations; criminal justice system records of arrests, convictions, and incarcerations; and surveys of drug users who have entered drug treatment programs).

Several highly regarded surveys of the United States population provide national estimates of varying aspects of drug (both illicit and prescription) and alcohol use in the general population. The National Survey on Drug Use and Health (NSDUH), sponsored by the Substance Abuse and Mental Health Administration (SAMHSA), is a large annual survey of United States households addressing alcohol, tobacco, and other drug use and health issues. Monitoring the Future, sponsored by the National Institute on Drug Abuse, is a survey of youths in the 8th, 10th, and 12th grades in a representative sample of schools across the nation, asking respondents about their drug, alcohol, and tobacco use, and related attitudes, beliefs, and behaviors. Finally, SAMHSA's Treatment Episode Data Set (TEDS) provides data on admission to publically funded drug and alcohol treatment programs.

The problem with these general population surveys is that they cannot provide information about those individuals who are not included in their samples—persons who are homeless, living in short-stay shelters, institutionalized, or in transient living arrangements (i.e., living in different residences or with different people at various times throughout the year), and people not seeking treatment.

One tool for measuring drug use and crime is the *Arrestee Drug Abuse Monitoring* (or ADAM II) survey conducted by the Office of National Drug Control Policy to gauge the prevalence of alcohol and illegal drug use among prior arrestees. For example, in their 2012 *Annual Report*, ADAM II reported that over 25 percent of arrestees were booked on a drug crime [1].

Jail inmate surveys also provide data regarding the link between drugs and crime. Twenty-nine percent of convicted offenders surveyed in 2002 reported that they had used illegal drugs at the time of their offense [2]. Prison inmate surveys tell a similar story. In the 2004 *Survey of Inmates in State and Federal Correctional Facilities*, 32 percent of state prisoners and 26 percent of federal prisoners said they had committed their offense under the influence of drugs [3].

Finally, two national studies have shown that most people in treatment for drugs had been arrested or had admitted to committing crimes for economic gain prior to entering treatment. The *Drug Abuse Reporting Program (DARP)* concluded that 71 percent had been in jail before entering treatment; the *Treatment Outcome Prospective Study (TOPS)* discovered that about 60 percent of people entering residential treatment programs reported they had committed one or more crimes for economic gain during the year before treatment.

It is also logical to assume that people who buy or sell drugs or who are under the influence of drugs may make likely targets for predatory attacks, because they are likely to possess some cash or drugs on their person. Because these people are involved in criminality themselves, other offenders may assume that they will be less likely to report robberies, assaults, or thefts to the police. In addition, a drug buyer or seller who chooses not to report being victimized to the police may choose to take the law into his or her own hands. This can lead to violent encounters such as murder, assault, drive-by shootings, and so forth.

Drugs and Violent Crime

Legal drugs such as alcohol, as well as illicit drugs such as cocaine, amphetamine, and phencyclidine, affect one's physiological functions, cognitive abilities, and mood. However, there is no existing evidence that shows a pharmacologically based drugs–violence relationship. It is the general impression of most experts in the field that the effects of alcohol and other drugs do not directly precipitate violence, but a combination of factors such as the type of drug, the user's personality, and other situational factors may influence one's propensity for aggressive behavior.

A study showing the relationship between certain drugs and violent criminality was conducted by Jeffery Roth for the National Institute of Justice [4]. In the study, several general observations were made. First, it was noted that violence is diverse, with acts as different as drive-by shootings and thoroughly planned serial killings. Second, the report noted that causes of violence are complex, involving a wide variety of factors that were broken down into four levels for study:

- *Macrosocial.* These are broad and economic forces that include cultural practices related to alcohol use, as well as the economic and social processes surrounding the sale of illicit drugs.
- *Microsocial.* These are encounters between people in particular settings that include group drinking in locations where violence is expected and even socially acceptable.
- *Psychosocial.* This relates to individual behavior development from childhood through adulthood. Examples include patterns of heavy drinking and aggression that develop during adolescence and continue into adulthood.
- *Neurobehavioral.* Neurobehavioral processes underlie all human behavior; they can include the effects of substance abuse on fetal development during pregnancy, and the effects of chronic drug abuse on brain functioning.

These factors may operate long before the occurrence of violent events, but it is evident that the causal events for violence are often linked to alcohol or other drugs [5]. Specific findings include the following:

- For the past several decades, alcohol drinking by the perpetrator of a crime, the victim, or both has immediately preceded at least one-half of all violent crimes.
- Chronic drinkers are more likely than others to have histories of violent behavior.
- Criminals who use illegal drugs commit robberies and assaults more frequently than do nonuser criminals, and they commit them especially frequently during periods of heavy drug usage.
- About 60 percent of arrestees booked for violent crimes were confirmed by laboratory tests to have used at least one illegal drug in the hours before arrest.

Interestingly, alcohol and other drugs modify encounters between people in ways that make such substances a particular risk for violence. Specifically in the case of alcohol, the risk of violence tends to be associated with the substance's effects on the user, compared to illegal drugs, for which most violence is associated with the business of drug purchases and sales. This is illustrated by the fact that many therapists who treat violent sex offenders have reported that their patients have both histories of alcohol abuse and high levels of testosterone. This is further validated by animal studies showing that although alcohol tends to reduce levels of testosterone in some animals, in those with high testosterone levels it promotes aggression at greater levels [6].

As indicated in Chapter 4, the business of drug trafficking is also linked to violent crime. Drug markets, which operate outside the world of contract law that is used by legal businesses as a means for arbitrating disputes, substitute illegal mechanisms that have been developed for handling "business-related" problems. Violence is often used to protect or expand markets, intimidate competitors, and retaliate against sellers and buyers who are thought to be cheating. In addition, violence is focused against the police, witnesses, and informers who threaten to identify and convict the trafficker. It has even been suggested that the illicit drug trade attracts people who are prone to violence [7].

Problematic situations abound in the drug trade and can include the following:

- Protection of drug-producing crops during harvest season
- Territorial disputes between rival drug organizations
- Robberies of drug dealers and their subsequent retaliation
- Interpersonal violence between buyers and sellers of drugs
- Elimination of drug informers and witnesses
- Punishment for selling poor-quality or adulterated drugs
- Failure to pay debts
- Violence involving people other than buyers and sellers, such as victims of robberies

Finally, it is important to mention that a great deal of violence is related indirectly to the illicit drug trade. Examples include the robbery of a business by a person who has spent his rent money on drugs, or spousal assaults arising out of disputes over money.

The Relationship between Drugs and Drug-Related Violence

Drugs and drug-related violence do not overlap in either time or space: "Even without the protection of the state and courts, illegal drug markets are generally peaceable. However, occasionally specific markets exhibit high levels of violence" [8]. Mexico, for example, has had drug trafficking for a century, and while there were individual cases of murder associated with drugs, the illegal drug industry was relatively peaceful. Only in the last decade has it become extremely violent. Until the late 1990s, the share of the illegal drug sector in the Gross National Product (GNP) was significantly higher in Bolivia and Peru than in Colombia, but drug-associated violence was very high in the latter and very low in the former two [9]. During the 2000s, illegal drug income accounted for about one-third of Afghanistan's GNP, but drug-associated violence has been remarkably low. The empirical evidence shows clearly that there is no direct "cause-and-effect" relationship between drugs and violence. In other words, when there are very large, easy-to-obtain illegal drug profits, it is not "natural" that people kill each other for them.

In both Colombia and Mexico, one frequently hears claims such as "Drug legalization is the only solution, because when there is demand, there will always be a supply." There is no doubt that if there were no demand, there would be no supply, but if demand would be the determining factor for production, then every country where coca and poppy could grow would be growing them, and every country where cocaine and heroin could be refined and trafficked would be doing so. The map of illegal drugs shows a very high concentration in production. All coca and cocaine are produced in only three countries: Colombia, Peru, and Bolivia. Three countries produce 95 percent of the opium poppy and heroin—Afghanistan, Myanmar, and Laos—and if Mexico and Colombia are thrown in, it becomes 99 percent [10].

There is no market theory that can explain this extreme concentration. Why does Colombia face much more competition in the international coffee markets than in cocaine, and why does Mexico have more competition in clothing manufacture than in heroin? In Mexico, many argue that the country's location halfway between Colombia and the United States is the reason for its involvement in drug trafficking. This is reminiscent of similar explanations in Colombia in the 1980s: the country was halfway between Bolivia and Peru to the south and the United States to the north. Location matters, of course, but being a transit country does not imply that the nationals of that country should dominate the trafficking networks.

The concentration shown by the maps of drugs and violence forces the observer to seek domestic explanations: for example, what do Colombia and Mexico have that has resulted in their dominance of some international drug markets, and why in those markets is there or has there been so much violence?

Factors Promoting Crime and Illegal Drugs

When looking at domestic factors that encourage the development of criminal organizations and illegal drugs, people normally attribute causality to poverty, income and wealth inequality, economic crises, frustrated expectations, corruption, and the like. These factors may play important roles, but they are not causes in the sense that once they occur, crime and drugs also occur. Indeed, most poor people in very unequal societies or facing economic crises do not become criminals. On the other hand, some members of the upper classes have been involved in illegal drugs and crime. Corruption may encourage crime, but crime itself is a principal supporter of corruption. These are contributing factors to crime and illegal drugs, but none of them is either necessary or sufficient for criminality and drugs to appear [11].

In order to have illegal drugs, it is necessary to have an illegal demand and an illegal supply. This is why "legalization" is so appealing: it eliminates a necessary factor. For many reasons (not discussed here), the world will not legalize the cocaine and heroin markets. So, for the sake of countries like Colombia and Mexico, it is imperative to ask: what are the necessary conditions for supply to develop? Illicit drug industries require the performance of several industry-specific tasks that are not required by legal activities: the growing of illegal crops, the development of illegal distribution networks, and so on. "Successful performance of these tasks requires special 'illegal skills' used to develop illegal business organizations, social support networks to protect the industry from law enforcement efforts, and contract enforcement and conflict resolution systems within the criminal organizations, to have the will to break economic laws and regulations and to use violence if necessary" [12]. To achieve this, there have to be people willing to break some laws, and a support network of people who consider such illegal activities appropriate.

When the rule of law prevails, crime is limited to that committed by a few "bad apples," and common law enforcement efforts can keep crime levels low. When a significant group does not accept the formal rules as legitimate, and if breaking laws is justified to them because they are or appear to be enacted by particular groups that benefit from them, then the society becomes vulnerable to the development of organized crime. There are other necessary factors related to cocaine and heroin production, such as knowing how to refine cocaine or heroin and having the appropriate environmental conditions to grow coca or poppy. The labor skills needed are abundant in almost every country today and can easily be bought.

The existence of strong criminal organizations does not necessarily indicate high levels of violence. Criminal organizations control the use of violence to avoid government focus on them. Needless to say, a very wealthy drug trafficker cannot enjoy his money in the cemetery. It is only when those controls weaken because the structure of the organization changes or when the organization itself decides to fight the state that violence erupts. These eruptions are particularly bloody and savage if the perpetrators are willing to use violence without regard to the consequences for society, or when they simply want to "hit where it hurts the most", that is, family members, children, and so on.

Other Factors

Cities both large and small across the United States are now targeted by an array of drug gangs claiming turf for drug sales. According to a report by the Department of Justice, an estimated 80 percent of these individuals have already been in jail or prison, with one of every five having six or more convictions on his or her record [13]. Based on these figures, it seems apparent that a more specifically defined public policy is needed in the many areas of drug abuse, and a closer interaction between antidrug programs and the criminal justice system is necessary.

Police Corruption

It's not hard to understand how the illicit drug trade breeds police corruption. The consensual nature of the drug trade makes it very hard to produce evidence against willing buyers and sellers. Fabricating evidence, lying on the stand, and conducting illegal searches have become routine police practices. Law enforcement officers also have to deal with the fact that their efforts, no matter how diligent, are in many ways fruitless. After spending billions of taxpayer dollars on law enforcement efforts and arresting millions of drug offenders, drugs are cheaper, purer, and more available than ever. Day in and day out, police officers see one arrested drug seller replaced by another [14]. No matter how many illegal drugs are seized and confiscated, more pour in. Drug law enforcement is a Sisyphean task that rarely pays off. Exposed to suitcase after suitcase of illegal cash and drugs, many officers cannot resist helping themselves—and from there, it's a slippery slope to more corruption and abuse. Corruption, regardless of who perpetuates it, erodes communities and the governments that oversee them. Where official corruption exists, an overall lack of public trust and credibility can result. The tentacles of the drug trade sometimes extend to those sworn to protect us from it.

Similar to the alcohol prohibition of the 1920s, current drug prohibition legislation breeds police corruption and abuse. A report by the General Accounting Office noted that on-duty police officers involved in drug-related corruption engage in serious criminal activities such as (1) conducting unconstitutional searches and seizures, (2) stealing money and/or drugs from drug dealers, (3) selling stolen drugs, (4) protecting drug operations, (5) providing false testimony, and (6) submitting false crime reports. Approximately half of all police officers convicted as a result of FBI-led corruption cases between 1993 and 1997 were convicted for drug-related offenses, and nationwide more than 100 cases of drug-related corruption are prosecuted each year. Every one of the federal law enforcement agencies with significant drug enforcement responsibilities has seen an agent implicated in a corruption case [15].

Explaining the growth of corruption is not a difficult task. Relative to other opportunities, legitimate or illegitimate, the financial temptations are enormous. Many police officers are demoralized by the scope of drug trafficking. No matter how diligent an officer may be, eradication programs and millions of arrests have done little to stop the illicit supply of drugs, which are now cheaper, purer, and more available than ever. Given the dangers of the law enforcement job, the indifference of many citizens and the frequent lack of appreciation are no doubt disheartening. Some police also recognize that their real function is not so much to protect victims from predators but to regulate an illicit market that cannot be suppressed and that much of society prefers to keep underground.

One of the United States' worst cases of drug-related police corruption occurred in 2000–2001 in California after an officer caught stealing eight pounds of cocaine from a police department's evidence locker turned on his fellow officers to get a reduced sentence. In what was known as the *Rampart scandal*, more than 100 convictions were overturned as police misconduct—ranging from the planting of evidence to "confessions" obtained through beatings—were uncovered. Officers were indicted on corruption charges, including torture, murder, drug dealing, and framing innocent people. The unit's criminal behavior became known as the "Rampart way." *Rampart* refers to a predominately poor, immigrant neighborhood in East Los Angeles that was patrolled—and during that time controlled—by the police officers [16]).

Some other examples of police corruption include the following:

- In Detroit, federal agents arrested three city police officers who were planning a home invasion in the suburb of Southfield, Michigan, with the intent to steal $1 million in cash.
- Starr County (Texas) Sheriff Eugenio Falcon resigned from office after pleading guilty to conspiracy to commit burglary. The investigation revealed that Falcon and other officers referred prisoners to a local bail bond business in exchange for kickback payments. On some occasions, payments were made directly at the sheriff's department.
- In a 69-count federal indictment in New Jersey, nine current or former West New York police officers were charged with taking part in a $600,000 bribery and kickback scheme.

Cases such as these differ somewhat from those of earlier generations of police officers, when officers were simply paid to look the other way while prostitution or gambling rings prospered. It is becoming increasingly clear that many police officers are choosing to cross the line and become active participants in crime.

It is impossible to gauge exactly how much corruption there is in United States policing today. However, despite the fact that many police officers are reluctant to openly discuss the problem of corruption, a substantial body of literature is available to help provide a general understanding of the magnitude of the problem.

As far back as 1930, the *Wickersham Commission* declared that in nearly all large cities there existed an alliance between criminals and politicians. Since then, it has generally been the case that efforts to control corruption have proved ineffective at best. Even in cases in which corruption was identified and successfully dealt with by police administrators, it was not uncommon to see its return.

James Inciardi (1992) wrote that one of the more pervasive problems in the political arena is the wholesale corruption of both individuals and institutions. With regard to institutional corruption, money laundering has long tainted the banking industry. Official corruption also affects law enforcement and public safety. For example, it permits criminals to continue in their activities, erodes the reputation of the department and the morale of officers, and hampers the general effectiveness of community crime control efforts [17].

Corruption on the official level may take many forms. Specifically, one who has been compromised by criminal elements may take either a passive or an active role in corruption. A good example of this situation occurred in 1988, when more than 75 Miami police officers were under investigation at one time for possible involvement in criminal activities. Allegations included drug dealing, robbery, theft, and even murder. One investigation in particular revealed several officers who had ambushed drug dealers bringing cocaine into Miami. This investigation revealed that officers stole $13 million in cocaine from a boat anchored in the Miami River and loaded it into marked police vehicles. Duffel bags full of cocaine were reportedly stacked to the ceilings of the patrol cars. Three of the suspects, in an effort to escape, jumped into the river and drowned.

Preconditions for Corruption

The problem of corruption has been exacerbated by the problem of drugs and drug abuse. Millions of dollars in seized currency create temptations for officers predisposed toward wrongdoing. Some argue that undercover police officers, who are involved in proactive investigative enforcement efforts regarding drugs, gambling, and prostitution, are more vulnerable to corruption than uniformed officers. This is primarily because crimes discovered by the undercover officer have not yet come to the official attention of the department. Therefore, the vice officer can "easily agree to overlook offenses known only to him or to even participate in illegal transactions (e.g., buying and selling drugs) for his own gain rather than the organization's advantage" [18].

A management dilemma relating to the drug abuse problem is the number of police officer applicants who have drug abuse in their past. Many police departments are now receiving applications from individuals who are former or even current drug users. In fact, a study by Peter Kraska and Victor Kappeler found that more than 20 percent of the police officers in a local police department used marijuana and nonprescription drugs while on duty [19]. Corruption opportunities are not limited to vice or narcotics officers, however; they are also readily available to officers working in the patrol capacity. Money and drug seizures made by patrol officers may actually take place with much less supervision than those made by the drug enforcement division; this creates a greater opportunity for corruption.

The *police socialization* process also contributes to the corruption problem in that rookie officers are often advised to forget all they have learned in the police academy and learn the "rules of the street" in order to survive. The implication is that some rules need to be bent or even broken in order to survive on the streets and to climb the career ladder in police work. Sherman suggests that the socialization process also creates a situation in which officers learn to "map out the environment." This means that as officers gain experience on the job and encounter various circumstances, they develop attitudes that rationalize their own deviant behavior. Sherman identified some common rationalizations:

- The public is the enemy and doesn't want the law enforced
- Politicians are crooked and shouldn't be trusted

- Minorities are amoral, a drain on society's resources, and cop haters who are not to be believed or shown respect
- Everybody's on a hustle
- Judges are too lenient
- Police administrators are the enemy [20])

When such attitudes become a part of a police officer's view of police work, they likely will become part of that officer's attitude toward society as well.

Types of Police Corruption

As definitions of the term suggest, corruption is not limited to its most conspicuous form—the acceptance of cash in exchange for an official favor. Several experts have identified different varieties of police corruption. For example, Michael Johnston cited four major corruption categories:

1. *Internal corruption.* This includes acts among police officers themselves and involves behaviors ranging from bending rules to outright commission of illegal acts.
2. *Selective enforcement.* Police officers exploit their discretion. For example, a detective who arrests and releases a drug trafficker in exchange for valuable information about the trafficker's organizations is not abusing his or her authority, but one who releases the same trafficker for money is in clear abuse of his or her discretion and authority.
3. *Active criminality.* Police officers participate in serious criminal activity using their positions of power and influence to commit the criminal acts they are entrusted to enforce.
4. *Bribery and extortion.* This occurs when police officers use their vested authority to generate a personal source of money. Bribery is initiated by the citizen, whereas extortion is initiated by the officer [21].

Another researcher, Ellwin Stoddard, constructed a list of several specific forms of behavior that he considers corrupt in nature:

- *Bribery.* The receipt of cash or a "gift" in exchange for past or future assistance in avoidance of prosecution, as by an officer claiming to be unable to make a positive identification of a criminal, being in the wrong place at a time when a crime is to occur, or taking (or avoiding) any other action that may be excused as carelessness but not offered as proof of deliberate miscarriage of justice. It is distinguished from "mooching" (also discussed here) by the higher value of the gift and by the mutual understanding in regard to services to be performed upon the acceptance of the gift.
- *Chiseling.* The demand for price discounts or free admission to places of entertainment regardless of any connection with official police work. This differs from "mooching" (also discussed here), because it is initiated by the officer, not the business proprietor. In this case, business owners and workers comply out of fear that the police officer will be less than responsive when and if a crime is ever committed on the premises, or from

fear that the officer will look closer for some kind of violations committed by the business or its employees if the favor is not granted.

- *Shakedown.* The common practice of holding "street court" by which minor traffic tickets can be avoided with a cash payment to the officer and no receipt given. Using the shakedown, police have also been known to extort money from tavern owners and other businesses by threatening to enforce city health and zoning codes.
- *Favoritism.* The practice of issuing license tabs, window stickers, or courtesy cards that exempt users from arrest or citation from traffic offenses (frequently extended to family members of officers).
- *Mooching.* The acceptance of free coffee, cigarettes, meals, liquor, groceries, and the like, which is justified by the police as being necessary in an underpaid profession, or is accepted in exchange for future acts of favoritism performed for the donor. Many restaurant chains as well as doughnut and coffee shops have adopted policies of providing discount meals on a regular basis. This ensures that there will be a continued police presence at the establishment at virtually all times, and is justified as being cheaper than hiring a full-time security guard for protection.
- *Perjury.* A willingness to lie under oath to provide an alibi for fellow officers apprehended in unlawful activity.
- *Prejudice.* Treatment of minority groups in a manner less than impartial, neutral, or objective, especially members of such groups who are unlikely to have "influence" in city hall that might cause trouble for the arresting officer.
- *Premeditated theft.* Predatory criminal activity that includes planned burglary involving the use of tools, keys, or other devices to gain entry, or any prearranged plan to acquire property unlawfully. This form of corruption, unlike some others, is rarely tolerated by police departments.
- *Shopping.* Opportunistic theft, such as picking up small items such as cigarettes, candy bars, jewelry, money, and so on, at a store that has accidentally been left unlocked at the close of business hours or at the scene of a fire or burglary [22].

Even seemingly benign actions such as accepting a free cup of coffee or free admittance to the local movie theater may constitute corruption, or at least a predisposition for such behavior. H.W. More suggested that although on the surface the acceptance of a free meal or cup of coffee may seem insignificant, there is every reason to believe it creates an atmosphere conducive to corruption [23]. So, to ensure a police force that can function within the community while being free of compromises, all such behavior should be closely scrutinized. This will protect the citizenry from a police force that gives preferential treatment to businesses that offer gratuities.

Police corruption is nothing new in the United States. A good deal of official corruption in the areas of liquor and gambling was documented during the early part of the twentieth century, when Prohibition was in effect. In many such cases, a link was established between police and politicians: favored clients would be protected while competitors would be harassed.

Drug Corruption in New York City

Of the many examples of United States police corruption, perhaps the most highly publicized investigation in twentieth-century history stemmed from charges made in the 1970s by two New York Police Department (NYPD) police officers, Frank Serpico and David Durk. The corruption problem surfaced when the officers began to protest to fellow officers about corrupt practices in their precinct. They were told to shut up and mind their own business, or to go along with the others and their corrupt practices. Out of frustration, Serpico and Durk then complained about corruption to the "top brass," those high up in the police department hierarchy. Although they were assured that their charges were being fully investigated, nothing was ever done. Finally, Serpico and Durk took their story to the *New York Times*, and the paper ran a series of stories about the corruption problem in the NYPD. As a result of widespread public concern, the *Knapp Commission* was appointed to investigate the allegations.

Serpico's testimony before the Knapp Commission provided revealing information about corruption within the NYPD. Although the commission's findings revealed that minor offenses were much more commonplace than serious ones, it still concluded that overall corruption was widespread in the department. The majority of officers who received outright bribes usually did not vigorously seek cash payments but rather took advantage of offers that came their way from contractors, trucking operators, and criminals. Specific findings of the commission included that (1) plainclothes officers received regular payoffs on a semiweekly or weekly basis, (2) detectives in some divisions were involved in shakedowns, (3) undercover officers in the narcotics division were receiving payoffs, (4) midlevel managers such as sergeants and lieutenants had been taking bribes, and (5) uniformed officers were receiving payoffs from local business owners and gamblers.

In addition, the commission found that in five of the 17 plainclothes divisions, corruption followed the same basic pattern. That is, officers assigned to the vice divisions were receiving payoffs from criminals. Detectives collected payoffs ranging up to $3500 per month from each gambling location. This amount represented a "nut" (the officer's share) that ranged anywhere from $300 to $1500 of the "pad" (list of payoff money). As might be expected, those officers who were higher in rank would receive a higher payoff. Specifically, supervisors would receive a share-and-a-half, which ranged from $450 to $2250. Plainclothes officers who were newly assigned were required to wait 2 months before they were eligible for payoff "benefits" [24].

■ ■ Critical Thinking Task ■

Suppose that large-scale corruption is discovered within the police department in your community. You are a member of a citizens' group who has been asked by the city council to study the corruption problem and suggest means of correcting it and preventing future incidents. What suggestions will you make to the city council?

The commission also reported that uniformed officers were receiving much smaller payoffs than their plainclothes counterparts—typically less than $20. Such payoffs included shakedowns from small-time gamblers, payoffs for "fixing" traffic tickets, and bribes and payoffs from bars, grocery stores, and other places of business. Although these payoffs were small, they were plentiful enough to significantly enhance an officer's income.

Another form of corruption identified by the commission was the incidence of payoffs between officers on the force. These consisted of bribes to receive more desirable assignments, or to speed up certain police procedures. Other types of corruption included special "pads" for sergeants only, excluding participation by subordinate officers. However, the Knapp Commission was unable to identify evidence of corruption on the part of officers above the rank of lieutenant, although much circumstantial evidence supported this assertion. The lack of evidence was partly due to the fact that superiors would commonly use lower-ranking officers to collect payoffs or serve as "bagmen" (participants who collect payoffs), and as a result it was extremely difficult to implicate supervisory personnel.

Arising out of the Knapp Commission's findings were two unique descriptive terms used to characterize corrupt officers: *grass eaters* and *meat eaters*. The grass eater is an officer who accepts payoffs as they are presented to him or her while performing normal police duties. In comparison, the meat eater is considerably more aggressive and contentious in his or her pursuit of illegal uses of police power for personal gain. However, the commission reported, "Although meat eaters get huge payoffs, getting all of the headlines, they represent a small percentage of corrupt officers. The truth is the vast majority on the take don't deal in large amounts of graft" [25]. In fact, the commission felt that grass eaters were at the center of the problem, and that other officers looked at those who were involved as respectable.

The specter of police corruption in New York City came into the public spotlight once again in September 1993, when a special commission was appointed by Mayor David Dinkins to investigate police corruption in the 30,000-member police force. The *Mollen Commission*, headed by former appeals judge Milton Mollen, made new inquiries into the problem. The Mollen Commission's star witness was 32-year-old police officer Michael Dowd, who described his indoctrination by superiors into petty crime and brutality and an evolution of behavior that resulted in his own drug dealing. Ultimately, more than 25 police officers were implicated in organized corruption activities.

Dowd shocked listeners in describing how he would do lines of cocaine off the dashboard of his patrol car while his partner watched. His testimony revealed that his weekly "take" rose from $200 per week to an $8000 payoff from a drug dealer. In his statement, he said that he became a "hero" to rookie cops who wanted to know how he acquired his red Corvette, expensive wardrobe, and many vacations. Probably the most troubling testimony Dowd provided was regarding his education into corruption, which began at the police academy. He claimed that officers at the academy promoted an "us-against-them" mentality—"Us is the police officers and them is the public." Dowd's testimony also revealed how drinking on the job sealed a social pact of illegal activity by officers.

In doing so, officers comprising literally the entire patrol force in Brooklyn's 75th Precinct would "regularly rendezvous at a hidden location for drinks, laughs, shooting off guns and other 'immature stuff'" [26]. In addition to Dowd's testimony, the commission focused on issues of brutality by officers. One such officer was Bernie Cawley. Also known as "the Mechanic", Cawley gave statements about how he would "tune [beat] people up with night sticks and lead-lined gloves." According to his testimony, "it was nothing to kick 'johns' out of bed and force prostitutes to have sex with him ... and nothing to lie before grand juries as well as steal drugs and money from drug dealers" [27].

Perhaps one of the more disturbing aspects of the Mollen Commission's findings was the involvement of upper-echelon police managers and administrators in corrupt activities. In fact, one of the common denominators in the inquiry was the specter of widespread corruption coupled with a total disregard for the police department's system of internal scrutiny. During the inquiry, internal affairs detective Sergeant Joseph Trimboli testified how the 5-year investigation was systematically stymied by top police supervisors working within the internal affairs division itself. In fact, after presenting a Brooklyn police commander with the identities of corrupt officers in the 75th Precinct, the commander advised his officers to cover it up.

Drug Corruption in Texas

In July 1999 in the small town of Tulia, Texas, 43 residents were arrested in early-morning drug raids. Forty of those arrested were black—making up more than 10 percent of the town's African-American population. The only evidence against them was the testimony

FIGURE 6.1 In this June 16, 2003, photo, attorney Jeff Blackburn (standing), whose clients were among those serving time in a now-discredited series of drug busts in Tulia, Texas, makes a statement in the Swisher County courtroom of Judge Ron Chapman. A decade later, the only physical evidence that remains of one of the most controversial drug investigations in state history is whited-out lines in a Swisher County docket book. *Source: AP Photo/LM Otero, Pool.*

of one white undercover officer, who worked alone and had no audiotapes, video surveillance, or eyewitnesses. It was later discovered that the undercover officer had quit his last law enforcement job and fled town to avoid theft charges. Former coworkers described him as hot-tempered and "a compulsive liar" [28–33]. Despite the fact that the only evidence was the word of one man, many of the accused ended up with very harsh sentences (some first-time offenders were sentenced to more than 20 years in prison). In response to this scandal, the Texas legislature passed legislation preventing a drug conviction based solely on the testimony of an informant. The U.S. Justice Department has launched a federal civil rights investigation.

In April 2001, a state prosecutor dismissed charges against 17 residents of the small town of Hearne in central Texas who were arrested by a drug task force accused of focusing on African Americans. The prosecutor dismissed the cases after the informant who was responsible for most of the arrests failed polygraph tests when questioned about tampering with the evidence in some of the cases [28–33].

In the late 1990s, a massive scandal erupted in Dallas. After an auto mechanic was arrested in August for allegedly possessing hundreds of thousands of dollars' worth of cocaine with intent to sell, his family convinced a defense attorney that he was innocent. When the man passed a polygraph test, his attorney, noting the similarity of his case to other recent drug cases, had the prosecutor order a test of the alleged cocaine. It turned out to be chalk-like material used in Sheetrock and other brands of wallboard. It had been ground into powder and packaged to resemble cocaine. When other defense lawyers heard of the case, they demanded similar laboratory tests of evidence against their clients. In at least 18 cases involving alleged cocaine seizures by the Dallas Police Department's narcotics units in the past year, seized evidence was all, or nearly all, ground-up wallboard material and not illegal drugs.

In each case, after allegedly seizing the powder, officers wrote in arrest reports that field tests showed it was cocaine, a result considered by experts to be statistically improbable. In each of the cases, those arrested were blue-collar Mexican immigrants who spoke little or no English and had few, if any, arrest records. The revelations have led to the dismissal of over 40 cases (although some of those arrested have already been deported). Two narcotics officers central to the cases have been suspended, pending an investigation. So far, the investigation has focused on a longtime informant who worked with the two officers. The unidentified informant has worked with narcotics officers in more than 70 investigations, for which he was paid about $200,000 over 2 years. The U.S. Justice Department has launched a federal civil rights investigation.

Drug Corruption in California

As mentioned in this chapter, over the course of 2000 and 2001, the State of California was rocked by what became known as the "Rampart" scandal, as officer after officer in a Los Angeles antidrug unit was indicted on corruption charges, including torture, murder, drug dealing, and framing innocent people.

The scandal erupted after an officer caught stealing eight pounds of cocaine from a police department's evidence locker turned on his fellow officers to get a reduced sentence. In the end, over 100 convictions were overturned due to police misconduct, ranging from the planting of evidence to "confessions" obtained through beatings. In one case, an unarmed man was shot by police and paralyzed. Officers planted a rifle on him and then charged him with shooting first. He served 13 months of a 23-year sentence before being released. In another case, a suspect bled to death as officers worked with supervisors to concoct a plausible reason for shooting him, before calling an ambulance [34–37]. As noted in this chapter, the unit's criminal behavior became known as the "Rampart way." A report by the Los Angeles Police Department's Board of Inquiry found that the unit "routinely made up its own rules and, for all intents and purposes, was left to function with little or no oversight" [34–37].

Later that year, a major police scandal erupted in Oakland. Four narcotics officers were arrested on misconduct charges. In all, they were indicted on more than 60 charges, including conspiracy to obstruct justice, kidnapping, assault, filing false police reports, filing false documents, and making false arrests. The officers, who called themselves "The Riders," committed their offenses over a span of at least 5 years. Dozens of convictions were overturned as a result of the scandal.

Drug Corruption in Florida

In February 2001, three South Florida police officers were indicted for drug trafficking, including using their patrol cars to transport drugs for drug dealers. Their actions came

FIGURE 6.2 In May 2013, Los Angeles Police Chief Charlie Beck stands next to a poster with an enlarged view of the dismissal of the 2001 LAPD consent decree, ending federal oversight of the department prompted by the Rampart corruption scandal. *Source: AP Photo/Reed Saxon.*

to light when one of the officers attempted to shake down an undercover officer posing as a drug dealer. Acting on a tip from an informant, the officer pulled over the undercover officer's car, seized the $200,000 he was carrying, and split the money with his informant.

In September 2001, nearly a dozen current and former Miami SWAT (Special Weapons and Tactics), narcotics, or special crime suppression officers were charged with stealing evidence, planting guns at crime scenes, and covering up their actions in a string of police shootings that killed three people, including the shooting death of an unarmed 73-year-old man in 1996. In that case, officers raided the man's apartment to serve a drug warrant, sprayed his bedroom with 123 bullets, and then lied and said he had a gun [38–42]. No drugs were found. The corruption and abuse were reminiscent of the "Miami River Cops" scandal in the 1980s in which more than 100 Miami police officers were arrested, suspended, or punished in a series of drug-related cases [38–42].

In October 2001, two current and former Hialeah police officers were charged with protecting and assisting drug dealers, setting up three robberies (including the robbery of a 7–11 store), serving as lookouts, and providing police badges, handcuffs, and pepper spray to robbers.

In November 2001, a Sarasota woman brought a $3 million lawsuit against five Manatee County sheriff's deputies who planted drugs in her home. All five deputies were sentenced to prison for various offenses, including planting drugs on suspects, stealing money from people under arrest, and lying. The men were part of an elite drug-fighting group called the Delta Task Force, and prosecutors said their offenses occurred from 1995 to 1999. The woman lost custody of her baby for 18 months after she was convicted in 1997 on drug charges during a trial in which the deputies lied to jurors.

It should be noted that although there appear to be areas of widespread corruption within some police departments, other forms of corruption exist in other parts of the criminal justice system as well. For example, prosecutors enjoy considerable discretion in filing cases, dismissing cases, and plea bargaining, and judges are vested with powers that can mold the trial process and make determinations regarding the sentencing of offenders.

Institutional Corruption

In his pioneering research, Lawrence Sherman suggests that *institutional corruption* can also exist in police departments themselves. Such organizations can be categorized on the basis of the level and type of corruption existing within them. He identifies three types:

- *Type I: Rotten pockets and rotten apples.* A Type I police department consists of a few scattered corrupt police officers using their position for personal gain ("rotten apples"). When these officers get together, they form a "rotten pocket." Rotten pockets help institutionalize corruption because they expect newcomers to conform to their corrupt practices and to a code of secrecy.

- *Type II: Pervasive unorganized corruption.* A Type II police department employs a majority of officers who are corrupt, but who have little relationship to one another. Although each officer may be involved in a variety of styles of corruption, most are not working in collusion with others on the police force for personal gain.
- *Type III: Pervasive organized corruption.* A Type III police department is a police force in which almost all the officers are involved in organized and systematic corruption for personal gain. Such a situation was identified in New York by the Knapp Commission when a group of corrupt officers working out of the vice division would regularly extort money from local criminals and businesses. Such behavior was accepted by the officers as part of the job [43].

In addition to the blatant acceptance of currency for official services rendered, corruption may also include subtle arrangements in which an agreement is implied. Sometimes referred to as conflicts of interest, such agreements (such as those discussed in this chapter) often encompass situations in which the officer becomes the beneficiary of favors or gifts from people with whom the officer conducts his or her duties.

Fighting Police Corruption

It is difficult to offer a simple and comprehensive explanation for some of the abuses of police power and authority. Clearly, however, better formal training and socialization may be the key to reducing deviant behavior among police officers. Policy changes are necessary to address those officers who are borderline or who have already become tainted by corruption.

Why, then, do some police officers become corrupt while others do not? Several explanations can be considered. For example, some argue that the type of individual who becomes a police officer is at the root of the problem. Studies show that most police personnel have been recruited from lower-class neighborhoods, and many lack the financial wherewithal to adopt a middle-class lifestyle. As the cynical, authoritarian police personality develops, the acceptance of graft seems to be a logical method for attaining financial security [44].

Corruption can also be viewed as a function of police institutions and practices, for example in terms of the degree of discretion that police officers enjoy. The police officer's ability to intervene or not, coupled with low visibility and lack of supervision in communities and within agencies, may create an atmosphere conducive to corruption. Institutionalization of corruption is also evident when corrupt officers are protected by the code of secrecy within their ranks, as well as by their own supervisors, who have risen through the ranks and may be less than willing to report any wrongdoing.

A third explanation holds that corruption is a product of society's reservations toward the enforcement of many types of vice-related crimes. Because vice crime is so difficult to control, and because a large segment of society wants it to persist, officers who are charged with enforcing vice laws might feel they are justified in accepting money from criminals involved in these types of crimes.

Corruption in Foreign Countries

When we consider the problem of official corruption in the drug trade, it is often difficult to determine whether complicity in criminal actions is on an individual basis by officials seeking their own financial enhancement, or whether it is systematic and under the sanction of an entire government or official unit of that government. The corrupt official is the *sine qua non* (essential element) of drug trafficking, and it is his or her participation through the corruption of an official office that protects and aids sophisticated criminals in manufacturing, smuggling, and distributing illicit drugs. We have briefly discussed how corruption affects law enforcement domestically; let's now examine how corruption affects drug control in illicit drug source countries.

The International Opiate Trade

Worldwide, more than 15 million people consume illicit opiates (opium, morphine, and heroin). The large majority use heroin, the most lethal form. More users die each year from problems related to heroin use, and more are forced to seek treatment for addiction, than for any other illicit drug. Among illicit narcotics, opiates are also the most costly in terms of treatment, medical care, and, arguably, drug-related violence. In addition, heroin is the drug most associated with injection, which brings about a host of acute and chronic health problems, including the transmission of blood-borne diseases such as HIV/AIDS and hepatitis C. In Central Asia, Ukraine, and the Russian Federation, injecting opiates is linked to nearly 60–70 percent of all HIV infections.

Getting opiates from producers to consumers worldwide is a well-organized and, most importantly, profitable activity. The most lucrative of illicit opiates, heroin, presently commands an estimated annual market value of $55 billion. When all opiates are considered, the value may reach up to $65 billion. Traffickers, essential to the transportation of drugs from production areas to lucrative end-user markets, pocket most of the profits of this trade. A rough estimate of the number of traffickers involved in moving this illegal commodity across countries and regions would likely stand at well above 1 million people.

The supply source for this huge underground economy is now concentrated in three areas: Afghanistan, Southeast Asia (mostly Myanmar), and Latin America (Mexico and Colombia). Together, they supply nearly all the world's illicit opium and heroin, but Afghanistan stands out among this group, accounting for around 90 percent of global illicit opium production in recent years.

Afghanistan is the world's largest opium producer and exporter, but it is also an important consumer. The country accounted for 7 percent of total world demand, or 80 tons a year, for an estimated 150,000 users in 2008 (rising to 200,000–250,000 in 2009). A large volume of opium is consumed in the Islamic Republic of Iran, approximately 450 tons, according to official estimates. But all of Afghanistan's neighbors report concern about opium use. Excluding China, consumption in the countries bordering Afghanistan (the Islamic Republic of Iran, Pakistan, Tajikistan, Uzbekistan, and Turkmenistan) is estimated at 650 tons per year, 60 percent of global consumption. Although small-scale cultivation occurs in these countries, such as in Pakistan and Central Asia, the main supply source for the region's opium consumers is Afghanistan.

Afghan Opium Production

Production of opium in Afghanistan increased from around 200 tons in 1980 to 3,300 tons in 2000, reaching a peak of 8,200 tons in 2007, before dropping slightly to 7,700 tons in 2008 and again to 6,900 in 2009. Expressed as a proportion of the global illicit opium production, Afghanistan's share rose from around 20 percent in 1980, to 70 percent in 2000, and to more than 90 percent since 2006. This is directly related to decreased output in the "Golden Triangle," which encompasses Thailand, Laos, and Myanmar. Myanmar was the world's leading opium producer in the 1970s and 1980s, although between 2003 and 2008 opium production in Myanmar fell by 59 percent, from 810 to 410 tons.

Turning to the Americas, the average amount of opium estimated to be produced in Latin America and Mexico was around 130 tons per year until 2006. In 2008, a reported 120 percent increase in opium production in Mexico made it the third biggest opium-producing country after Myanmar, with 325 tons potentially produced in 2008.

Some data suggest that limited illicit opium cultivation also takes place in other countries, such as Egypt and India. At the time of writing, no information was available on the quantities cultivated and produced, which, in the case of Egypt, may be negligible. Algeria reports the eradication of approximately 80,000 opium poppy plants every year, but this production appears to be limited to supplying the local market.

In 2008, approximately 2,700 tons of Afghanistan's opium were refined into an estimated 380 tons of heroin to supply the global market. Placed a distant second are Myanmar and Laos, whose production yielded some 40 tons of heroin in 2008, all of it processed in Myanmar. The remainder, some 30–40 tons in 2008, is shared among mostly Latin American countries (including Colombia and Mexico). Processing Mexico's opium output alone would potentially yield some 38 tons of pure heroin in 2008. Lastly, lower levels of heroin production continue to exist in places like India.

The International Cocaine Trade

Cocaine has been a popular recreational drug for decades, and while demand appears to be on the wane in its largest markets, it has gained popularity in an ever-widening range of countries. "Cocaine" comprises at least two distinct drug products: powder cocaine, on one hand, and a range of cocaine-based products, mostly falling under the heading of "crack," on the other. Powder cocaine produces a more subtle effect, is more expensive to use, and has become emblematic of economic success in some circles. Demand for it has emerged in many developing countries, particularly among elites. Crack is cheaper, more intense, and associated with prostitution and street crime. Traditionally, crack use was rare outside the United States and United Kingdom, but this also appears to be changing, especially in Latin America and parts of Africa [45].

Starting in the 1960s and 1970s, global production, trafficking, and consumption of cocaine rose strongly. Until the mid-1960s, global cocaine seizures were measured in the tens of kilograms annually. In recent years, they have been in the hundreds of tons. Based on seizure figures, it appears that cocaine markets grew most dramatically during the 1980s, when the amounts seized increased by more than 40 percent per year. The number of countries reporting cocaine seizures has also grown during this period, from 44 in 1980 to 87 in 1990 and 123 in 2008 [46].

The extent, as well as the pattern, of global cocaine production has changed significantly over the last four decades. From the end of World War II until the late 1990s, almost all of the world's coca bush (the raw material for the manufacture of cocaine) was grown in Peru and Bolivia, and since the 1970s, most of this output was refined into cocaine in Colombia. This increased over time, and, in 1997, coca cultivation in Colombia exceeded that of the traditional growers for the first time.

In the twenty-first century, the pendulum has swung back again. Coca cultivation in Colombia decreased by 58 percent between 2000 and 2009, mainly due to large-scale eradication. At the same time, it increased by 38 percent in Peru and more than doubled in Bolivia (+112 percent), and both of these countries have acquired the ability to refine their own cocaine. Despite the increases in Peru and Bolivia, the net decline in the global area under coca cultivation over the 2000–2009 period was significant, amounting to 28 percent. A far smaller area is now under coca cultivation than in any year of the 1990s [47].

In 2008, an estimated 865 metric tons of pure cocaine were produced. This was the lowest level in 5 years and considerably less than the level a year earlier, when over 1,000 tons were produced. In 2008, Colombia appears to have been responsible for about half of global production, with Peru contributing over one-third and Bolivia making up the balance.

North America is the largest regional cocaine market, with some 6.2 million annual users, close to 40 percent of the global cocaine-using population. The United States still remains the single largest national cocaine market in the world, but this market has declined since the early 1980s. In 1982, an estimated 10.5 million people in the United States had used cocaine in the previous year. In 2008, the figure was 5.3 million, about half as many. This long-term decline occurred despite falling prices and can be attributed to a number of causes, including increased prevention, treatment (complemented by the establishment of "drug courts"), and "social learning." Crack cocaine became a stigmatized drug in the second half of the 1980s, and powder cocaine also became less fashionable.

This long-term demand-driven decline appears to have been complemented by a recent, more dramatic, supply-driven one. The annual prevalence rate of cocaine use in the United States fell from 3 percent of the adult population in 2006 to 2.6 percent in 2008 [48]. Recent declines have also been reported in Canada, with adult annual use rates falling from 2.3 percent in 2004 to 1.9 percent in 2008 [49]. Household surveys in Mexico showed an increase after 2002.

Cocaine is typically transported from Colombia to Mexico or Central America by sea (usually by Colombian traffickers), and then onward by land to the United States and Canada (usually by Mexican traffickers). The United States authorities estimate that close to 90 percent of the cocaine entering the country crosses the United States–Mexico land border, most of it entering the state of Texas and, to a lesser extent, California and Arizona, although the relative importance of Arizona seems to be increasing. According to United States estimates, some 70 percent of the cocaine leaves Colombia via the Pacific, 20 percent via the Atlantic, and 10 percent via Venezuela and the Caribbean [50]). The routes have changed over the years.

Trafficking of cocaine to Europe is, to a significant extent, organized by Colombian organized crime groups that forge alliances with various criminal groups operating in Europe, notably with groups in Spain, Italy, and the Netherlands. In most European countries, the majority of those arrested for drug trafficking are local citizens, but the Colombian groups act as importers and, to a lesser extent, as wholesalers. Their involvement in retail markets is limited to Spain. Between 21 and 26 percent of all foreigners arrested for cocaine trafficking in Spain over the 2004–2007 period were Colombian nationals. The proportion rose to 29 percent, or nearly 1,000 individuals, in 2008 [51].

In addition, groups from the Caribbean region play a role, including Dominicans in Spain, Jamaicans in the United Kingdom, and Antilleans in the Netherlands. Other South Americans are also prominent, especially on the Iberian Peninsula. In a number of countries in continental Europe, West Africans are active as retailers (as well as small-scale importers), including in France, Switzerland, Austria, Italy, Germany, and Portugal.

Money Laundering

Money laundering is the process that drug traffickers use to introduce the monetary proceeds gained through the sale or distribution of controlled substances into the legitimate financial market. The International Monetary Fund (IMF) estimated in 2000 that money laundering amounts to between 2 and 5 percent of the world's gross domestic product (GDP), about $600 billion annually [52]. Money laundering allows concealment of the true source of the funds gained through the sale and distribution of drugs, and converts the funds into assets that appear to have a legitimate, legal source. The need to launder conspicuously large amounts of small-denomination bills renders the traffickers vulnerable to law enforcement interdiction. Tracking and intercepting this illegal flow of drug money are important tools used to identify and dismantle international drug-trafficking organizations.

Current Money-Laundering Trends

Drug traffickers use various methods to launder their profits both inside and outside the United States. Currently, some of the more common laundering methods include the Black Market Peso Exchange (BMPE), cash smuggling (couriers or bulk cash shipments), gold purchases, structured deposits to or withdrawals from bank accounts, purchase of monetary instruments (cashier's checks, money orders, travelers checks, and the like), wire transfers, and forms of underground banking, particularly the Hawala system (a system whereby money is transferred via brokers). The BMPE is a complex system used by drug-trafficking organizations to launder billions of dollars of drug money each year by utilizing the advantages of Panama's Colon Free Zone (CFZ), which serves as an integral link in the Colombian money-laundering chain. It is discussed further in the "Mexican Money-Laundering Techniques" subsection of this chapter.

Today's organized crime leaders are strong, sophisticated, and destructive, and they have the capability to operate on a global scale. Organizational leaders have at their disposal airplanes, boats, vehicles, radar, communications equipment, and weapons in quantities that rival the capabilities of some legitimate governments.

Whereas previous organized crime leaders were millionaires, the Colombian drug traffickers and their counterparts from Mexico are billionaires. They have learned to exploit a variety of weaknesses to protect their drug profits, which are the lifeblood of these organizations. Their ultimate purpose is to amass large sums of money to maintain their lavish lifestyles, free from the boundaries or confines of the law.

Today, money laundering remains an ongoing problem in the fight against drugs and drug trafficking. Recent statistics bear this out. For example, in 2007, the National Money Laundering Strategy identified some significant trends:

- Banks and other depository institutions remain the primary gateway to the United States financial system
- Internet and remote banking present ongoing challenges in identifying people involved in electronic financial transactions
- Money service businesses offer an alternative to banks for money laundering
- Smuggling cash out of the country is a well-established money-laundering method and is on the rise
- The most complex money-laundering methods involve international business transactions to disguise cash transfers
- Casinos are cash-intensive businesses that provide money-laundering opportunities [53].

Overview

Illegal narcotic sales in the United States generate billions of dollars annually, most in cash. Efforts to legitimize or "launder" this cash by the Colombian drug cartels are subject to detection because of the intense scrutiny that United States banks place on large financial transactions. To avoid detection, the cartels have developed a number of money-laundering systems in an attempt to avoid financial transaction reporting requirements and manipulate facets of the economy unrelated to the traditional financial services industry.

The various money-laundering methods utilized in today's financial world can be reduced to four categories: bulk movement, the use of financial institutions, the use of commercial businesses, and movement through the underground banking system.

However, an organization may use several of these methods in a chain to arrive at its goal: the integration of drug money into the economy as licit profits.

Colombia

Despite the rise to power by the Mexican crime syndicates and their increasing influence on the drug trade in the United States, Colombian traffickers still control the manufacture of the vast majority of cocaine in South America, and a majority of the wholesale cocaine market in the eastern United States. They move cocaine from their clandestine laboratories in the jungles from southeast Colombia to Mexico and through the Caribbean, using commercial maritime vessels, go-fast boats, containerized cargo, and private aircraft. The methods are varied, and to thwart interdiction efforts traffickers frequently alter both their routes and their modus operandi.

The Colombian trafficking organizations' influence in the Caribbean remains overwhelming. Several major organizations based in the north coast of Colombia have established command-and-control functions in Puerto Rico and the Dominican Republic. These drug traffickers use the Caribbean Basin to funnel tons of cocaine to the United States each year, and they direct networks of transporters that oversee the importation, storage, exportation, and wholesale distribution of cocaine destined for the continental United States. Seizures of 500–2,000 kilos of cocaine are common in and around Puerto Rico, the Dominican Republic, and the Bahamian island chain [54].

The Dominican trafficking groups, already firmly entrenched as low-level cocaine and heroin wholesalers in the larger northeastern cities, were uniquely placed to assume a far more significant role in the multibillion-dollar cocaine and heroin trade. From Boston to Charlotte, North Carolina, well-organized Dominican trafficking groups are controlling and directing the sale of multi-hundred-kilogram shipments of cocaine and multikilogram quantities of heroin. This change in operations somewhat reduces profits for the syndicate leaders; however, it succeeds in reducing their exposure to United States law enforcement.

Due to geographical considerations, Colombian traffickers face many difficulties during the initial placement phase of the money-laundering process that Mexican syndicates do not encounter. Colombian drug organizations have in the past relied on a multifaceted collection process. They have amassed currency in strategic locations; used a variety of methods—including smuggling and bribery—to introduce the cash into the United States banking system; and subsequently transferred the cash to Colombia. In an effort to avoid the high risks associated with direct deposits in United States or European banks, many Colombian drug traffickers have returned to the simplest of money-laundering methods, the bulk movement of cash. Currently, the vast majority of United States currency bound for the bank accounts of the Colombian drug lords leaves the United States either through air cargo or commercial cargo freighters. Due to the enormous amount of commercial trade that the United States has with Colombia, this method makes the traffickers' operations not only less complicated, but also less vulnerable to discovery by law enforcement. In addition, Colombian drug trafficking will exploit any means possible to safely launder their drug proceeds.

CASE IN POINT: CARTEL VIOLENCE SOMETIMES SPILLS ACROSS THE BORDER

When an ambulance from Ciudad Juárez screams into El Paso, Texas, with a shooting victim, SWAT team officers from the sheriff's office rush to Thomason Hospital to tighten up security. "They're afraid the cartel is going to come in and finish the job," says former city Police Chief Richard Wiles, who took over as county sheriff in January 2013. "Because that's what they do in Juárez—they'll go in there and kill them."

In 2012, 43 high-risk Mexican gunshot victims were whisked from Mexico to the El Paso hospital, including Fernando Lozano Sandoval, a commander in the Chihuahua State Investigation Agency, who was hit five times. During his hospital stay, police installed metal detectors at Thomason.

Their caution was well founded. In 2005, gunmen killed Mexican federal agent Victor Estrada Gutiérrez, who was recovering from gunshot wounds in a Chihuahua City hospital south of Juárez. And a year ago, popular singer Zayda Peña, also wounded by gunfire, was shot to death in a hospital in Matamoros, near Brownsville, Texas. For some reason, artists in her "grupera" musical genre have been targeted for hits on several occasions.

Mexican drug gangs boast extensive contacts and business interests all along the United States side of the border, but so far they have not sent killers into American hospitals. The cartel bosses generally steer clear of the states, too, because many have United States indictments hanging over them. "You're not going to have the main leader of the Juárez or Sinaloa cartels traveling here," says Ralph Reyes, United States Drug Enforcement Administration section chief for Mexico and Central America. While United States law enforcement agents at the border have had confrontations with drug smugglers, the streets of border towns and cities are generally free of cartel violence—at least as far as innocent citizens are concerned. "We have had a few instances where the violence has spilled across the border in the sense that there have been shootings on this side involving persons who were participants or associated with a group south of the border," FBI Director Robert Mueller told the House Judiciary Committee in September, "but they, thankfully, have been relatively few."

Indeed, the United States side is safe enough that Mexican officials hole up north of the border when they're under threat. After Agua Prieta Police Chief Ramón Tacho Verdugo was gunned down in February 2007, Mayor Antonio Cuadras stayed in nearby Douglas, Arizona, says former Mayor Ray Borane, border affairs and immigration adviser to then–Arizona Governor Janet Napolitano, who currently heads the United States Department of Homeland Security.

To be sure, murders may be uncommon on the American side because the cartels prefer to do their killing in Mexico. "We have had kidnappings where people are taken over the border to Juárez and murdered," says Wiles. "Several years ago, they were trying to kidnap a guy on the east side of town to take him to Juárez. He fought them, so they shot him and left him on the street."

The Justice Department's National Drug Information Center (NDIC) reported that in the San Diego area, kidnappings increased 25 percent in 2006–2007; the NDIC called it "a widely underreported problem. Many of the victims' families are unwilling or afraid to report the crime to law enforcement for fear that the victim will be killed."

A Las Vegas kidnapping this year drew national attention because the victim was a 6 year old. In October, three men disguised as police officers snatched Cole Puffinberger from his mother's home. Law enforcement authorities said they were working for Mexican traffickers trying to recoup money they thought the boy's grandfather had stolen. Cole was found unharmed, and the grandfather was charged with racketeering after allegedly mailing $60,000 in suspected drug proceeds from Mississippi to Nevada.

(Continued)

Aside from their occasional violent incursions into the United States, trafficking organizations have storage sites in and around border cities where newly smuggled drugs are repackaged for sale to United States distributors, including prison-based gangs and outlaw motorcycle organizations, the NDIC reports.

United States gangs also supply weapons to cartels, and play a major part in smuggling drug profits back to Mexico. "In January 2008, the El Paso County Sheriff's Office seized approximately $1 million from a tractor-trailer during a routine traffic stop," the NDIC reported. "The Texas Department of Public Safety seized over $2 million concealed behind a flat-screen television in a van on United States Highway 54 in El Paso in May 2007."

Currency smuggling is a vital part of the drug trade. Once the cash reaches Mexico, it's often deposited in Mexican banks or money-changing businesses, then sent back to the United States through legal channels. "In the United States, the illicit funds appear as proceeds from a Mexican financial institution ... giving the funds the appearance of legitimacy," the NDIC reports. From there, the money can be used to buy legal and illegal goods in Latin America.

The extraordinary profitability of the drug trade also complicates routine law enforcement. "We used to deal real closely with federal, state and local agencies in Juárez because we're right there, it's really one community," Wiles says. But the days of cooperating on drug issues are over. "You're trying to share intelligence and work on projects, but you don't know if the person you're talking to is being paid off by the cartels," he says.

Sources: Corchado, A. (Feb 28, 2008). *In Juárez, drug war gets bloodier*. Dallas Morning News, p. A1; *Intentan ejecutar a comandante*. El Mexicano, (Jan 22, 2008). www.oem.com.mx/elmexicano/notas/n567329.htm; Campo-Flores, A., & Campbell, M. (Dec 8, 2008). Bloodshed on the border. *Newsweek*. www.newsweek.com/id/171251; *Atrae PGR Investigación de AFI Asesinado en Hospital de Chihuahua*. Press Release, (June 8, 2005). www.pgr.gob.mx/cmsocial/bol05/jun/b58805.htm; Tobar, H. (Dec 4, 2007). 2 more grupera singers slain in Mexico. *Los Angeles Times*, A8; See House Judiciary Committee holds hearing on oversight of FBI. *Congressional Transcripts*. (Sept 16, 2008); On Verdugo killing, see "Restaurant owner is latest victim of *N. Sonora violence*." Arizona Daily Star, (Nov 9, 2007). www.azstarnet.com/sn/metro/210783.php; National Drug Intelligence Center. (May 2008). *Drug market analysis 2008, California Border Alliance Group*, p. 8. www.usdoj.gov/ndic/pubs27/27487/27487p.pdf; Serrano, R. A., & Quinones, S. (Nov 16, 2008). Mexico drug war spills across border. *Los Angeles Times*. www.latimes.com/news/printedition/front/la-na-cartels16-2008nov16,0,1843318,full.story; National Drug Information Center. (May 2008). *Drug market analysis, 2008, West Texas high-intensity drug trafficking area*, p. 11. www.usdoj.gov/ndic/pubs27/27514/27514p.pdf; *Drug market analysis ... California*. op. cit., p. 10.

Mexico

Mexico is not only a major drug transshipment and producer nation, but also a conduit and repository for the laundering of drug proceeds generated in the United States. The 2,000-mile United States–Mexico border, close working relationships between Colombian and Mexican drug-trafficking organizations, widespread corruption, and the relative ease with which large amounts of United States currency can be absorbed into Mexican financial systems make Mexico an ideal target for money-laundering organizations.

Laundering drug proceeds for Mexican crime syndicates is commonly accomplished by relatively simple and direct means: the bulk shipment of currency back to Mexico. Tractor trailers and cars with hidden compartments are frequently used to smuggle drugs out of Mexico into the United States, and then these same vehicles are packed with the proceeds from the street sale of the drugs and returned to Mexico. Drug traffickers based in Colombia also move the proceeds from their operations in the United States to Los Angeles, New York, and Miami for bulk shipment out of the United States. Both the Colombians and the Mexicans frequently use vehicles with hidden compartments to carry large quantities of United States currency. The bulk movement of United States cash to Mexico has resulted in significant increases of financial seizures along United States roadways. It is estimated that most of the seized currency was destined for drug-trafficking organizations operating out of Mexico.

Mexican Money-Laundering Techniques: The Black Peso System

One critical step in the illegal drug business is the process of laundering huge amounts of cash—profits from the street sales of drugs—into usable assets. In the early 1980s, when Carlos Lehder, Pablo Escobar, and the Ochoa brothers began massive distribution of cocaine and formed the Medellín Cartel, they could not imagine the sheer quantity of United States dollars they would end up making.

In the early days of the cocaine business, some of the cash was flown back down to Colombia in the same airplanes that were flying in cocaine. This cash was converted into pesos at willing Colombian banks, or kept on hand for operating costs. One famous Colombian trafficker died with so many United States dollars buried on his property that the locals claimed the rivers downstream would occasionally become clogged with dollars that rain or floods had unleashed from their hiding places.

But traffickers generally preferred bank accounts to burial sites. So in the early 1980s, United States cocaine distributors began carting huge amounts of cash into United States banks. During the day, traffickers could deposit boxes of money inside a bank. Banks would have rooms set up with counting machines, and even employees from the bank to assist traffickers in setting up accounts.

Another method that became popular in the mid-1980s was to simply fly the cash to offshore banking havens like the Bahamas, Aruba, the Caymans, and the British Virgin Islands, and deposit it there. While this method is still used today, it became more difficult for traffickers as enforcement was strengthened at airports and seaports. The United States government passed the first money-laundering laws and suspicious transaction reporting requirements in the early 1970s, but these laws were widely ignored by banks. The law states that United States banks must report any transaction involving more than $10,000 in cash [55].

Most Colombian drug kingpins live in Colombia and rarely leave their safe havens of Medellin, Cali, or other Colombian cities. They need pesos in Colombia to live their lives, purchase homes, buy political protection, and pay the Colombian coca producers, the laboratories, and smuggling costs. When they sell the drugs on the streets of the United States, they collect huge quantities of United States dollars, and these dollars need to somehow be converted into pesos.

Because of restrictive Colombian currency controls and tax laws, a black market to exchange currency has existed for decades for Colombian businesspeople. Even a rich Colombian doctor who is sending his daughter to college in the United States will use the black market to buy dollars with which to pay the United States tuition in order to save money. So as banks around the world became stricter about money-laundering laws, Colombian traffickers began avoiding using the legitimate bank system, and started infiltrating the black market to launder their drug money. This sophisticated method would eventually become known as the *BMPE*, and it is still one of the most successful money-laundering methods ever devised.

The BMPE has been called the largest, most insidious money-laundering system in the Western Hemisphere. Traffickers have transformed the black market into their own illegitimate international banking system. The system is fairly simple. A phone call is made to a BMPE broker from a Colombian trafficker or an American counterpart. They negotiate an exchange rate of Colombian pesos for United States dollars, usually 40 percent below the official exchange rate. Once they agree on a price, the drug trafficker arranges to have drug dollars dropped off at the broker's office, or at some less conspicuous location. The money could be in boxes, shopping bags, suitcases, or a car. In some cases, the money is in the trunk of a car and the traffickers just provide the keys to the car. At that point, the traffickers' side of the deal is complete and they simply wait for pesos to be delivered into their Colombian bank accounts several days or weeks later. The broker now has to process the cash. The broker maintains a large staff of runners who take the cash and deposit it into hundreds of United States bank accounts in amounts of less than $10,000 per transaction. Once the money is in a bank, it can be moved and manipulated [56].

The broker can wire transfer or deposit money directly into the United States bank accounts of legitimate companies in exchange for goods. Customs and Drug Enforcement Administration cases reveal that legitimate companies, such as General Electric, Whirlpool, Phillip Morris, and Intel Computers, have all become involved in this system in the past. The dollars received from the traffickers go to the legitimate businesspeople, and the pesos received from them go to the drug traffickers in Colombia. The peso broker makes commissions and the difference in exchange rate, making this a very profitable business. Even though the process is illegal, some United States companies and Colombian businesspeople have been happy with the arrangement because it is good for business.

Once the United States currency arrives in Mexico, a variety of alternatives for laundering it are available. The United States currency transported to Mexico is generally in small-denomination bills, such as $10s and $20s. Money service businesses (MSBs), which include wire remittance services, cashier check companies, and *casas de cambio* (money exchange house) systems, are readily available for the transfer and exchange of these small-denomination dollars into pesos. The MSBs function as a parallel banking system in Mexico. In addition to the ability to exchange currency, they can transfer funds into any banking system worldwide. They provide currency conversion, exchanges, and money movement services for a fee. Legitimate businesses, as well as drug-trafficking organizations, seek the services that MSBs provide. For example, Mexican immigrants have traditionally used wire remittance services to send dollars they've earned in the United States back to Mexico to support their families.

The Laundering Specialists

Technology and the modern conveniences of the twenty-first century make it possible for modern-day money launderers to ply their craft. However, because most criminals fear detection by police agents, many have chosen to employ specialists to aid them. For a fee, laundering specialists sell their services to criminals, often in the form of multiservice packages but sometimes in a simple one- or two-step laundering process. Three types of laundering specialists can be identified for this purpose.

- *Couriers* arrange for the movement of currency to a site designated for laundering, where the cash is converted to another method of payment, such as money orders. In the event that the courier is employed by a foreign trafficker, cash may be smuggled out of the country to a safe foreign jurisdiction with strict bank secrecy laws. The value of the courier rests in its apparent legitimacy and lack of any obvious connection with the criminal who actually owns the money. In many cases, couriers do not even know the identity of the true owner of the currency.
- *Currency exchange specialists* operate both formal and informal businesses that can be either a front for laundering operations or dedicated to illegal clientele. One of the most common formal exchanges is the *casa de cambio*, which exchanges dollars for pesos. As a rule, the exchanges are legitimate foreign currency exchange houses used by criminals seeking quasibanking services.
- *Business professionals* include attorneys, accountants, and even bankers who provide investment counseling, create nominee trust accounts, handle international funds transfers, and take advantage of tax avoidance schemes in foreign countries. The goal is to conceal the true origin of the assets under their control.

Specialists who launder cash for large criminal organizations may create informal organizations to facilitate their services. Many laundering organizations are loose confederations united by a common criminal objective: profit. On only very rare occasions does a laundering organization operate as part of a larger organization. Instead, specialists operate as part of a loose-knit network of entrepreneurs who sell their services on a piecemeal basis. Such organizations might work for more than one criminal organization at a time, in addition to working for individuals who manage large criminal organizations at high levels.

Concealment

The first and foremost objective of the money-laundering process is to conceal cash, the source of its ownership, and the future destination of the illegal funds. If money launderers are not successful in hiding their cash and the ownership of it, they run the risk of exposure to police, subsequent forfeiture of those assets, and possible imprisonment. To this end, launderers must consider a second objective—anonymity. This option becomes more practical with the threat of detection by police. So, the backup strategy becomes obvious: even if the illegal cash is discovered, its connection to the owner becomes obscure. One of the most typical ways of deterring investigation is through layers of false ownership and sales documents.

Money-Laundering Techniques

Illegal drug transactions are usually cash transactions that use large amounts of currency to pay off the different actors in each drug deal and to purchase sophisticated equipment. It is important for the trafficker to legitimize cash proceeds in a fashion that permits the trafficker to spend it wherever and whenever he or she desires without attracting suspicion. Obviously, the trafficker could choose to store the cash in a strongbox or wall safe, but such methods would not be plausible for one who generates hundreds of thousands or even millions of dollars in illegal cash each year.

The techniques for laundering illicit proceeds are limited only by a trafficker's imagination and cunning. An entire "wash cycle" to transform small denominations of currency to legitimate business accounts, money market deposits, or real estate may take as little as 48 hours. The chosen method used by any given trafficker will reflect his or her own situation and any unique circumstances involved.

Money laundering consists of a three-stage process [57]. The first stage involves the *placement* of proceeds derived from the illegal activities—the movement of proceeds, frequently currency, from the scene of the crime to a place or into a form that is less suspicious and more convenient for the criminal. For example, a government official may take a bribe in the form of cash and place it in a safe-deposit box or bank account opened under the name of another person, to hide its existence or conceal ownership.

Layering constitutes the second stage of the laundering process. It involves the separation of proceeds from the illegal source through the use of complex transactions designed to obscure the audit trail and hide the proceeds. This phase of the laundering process can include the transfer of money from one bank account to another, from one bank to another, from one country to another, or any combination thereof. Criminals layer transactions to increase the difficulty of tracing the proceeds back to their illegal source. They frequently use shell corporations and offshore banks at this stage because of the difficulty in obtaining information to identify ownership interests and acquiring necessary account information from them.

Integration, the third stage of money laundering, represents the conversion of illegal proceeds into apparently legitimate business earnings through normal financial or commercial operations. Integration creates the illusion of a legitimate source for criminally derived funds and involves techniques as numerous and creative as those used by legitimate businesses to increase profit and reduce tax liability. Common techniques include producing false invoices for goods purportedly sold by a firm in one country to a firm in another country, using funds held in a foreign bank as security for a domestic loan, commingling money in the bank accounts of companies earning legitimate income, and purchasing property to create the illusion of legal proceeds upon disposal.

■ ■ Critical Thinking Task ■

Write a letter to one of your United States senators or representatives asking that stricter laws be enacted to combat money laundering by drug traffickers. Be specific in your suggestions.

The successful money-laundering operation closely approximates legal transactions routinely employed by legitimate businesses. In the hands of a skillful launderer, the following strategies may be used: (1) the payment for goods that appeared to have been delivered by one company based on an invoice of sale prepared by another company covers the laundering of the purchase price when the goods never existed and the companies are owned by the same party; (2) the sale of real estate for an amount far below market value, with an exchange of one-half the difference in an under-the-table cash transaction, launders what on the surface appears to be capital gain when the property is sold again; and (3) a variety of lateral transfer schemes among three or more parties or companies covers the trail of monetary transactions between any two of them.

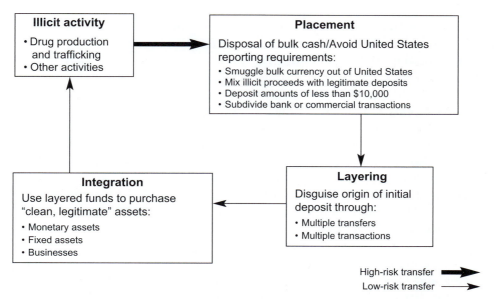

FIGURE 6.3 Money laundering. *Source: Office of National Drug Control Policy (1994) [58].*

Fighting Money Laundering

One principal tool utilized to detect, measure, and punish money laundering is the Bank Secrecy Act (BSA), originally passed into law in 1970. The BSA can help authorities flag the movement of illegally acquired cash moving through banking institutions and across international borders. However, the very inclusion of a minimum dollar amount has given traffickers a way to skirt around the law. Criminals can simply deposit less than the $10,000 amount that triggers banking records of a deposit. In any case, the current regulations under this act, issued by the secretary of the treasury, provide law enforcement with several basic tools to investigate money laundering:

- A paper trail of bank records must be maintained for up to 5 years.
- A *Currency Transaction Report* (*CTR*) must be filed with the Internal Revenue Service within 15 days when a currency transaction is more than $10,000. Notably omitted from the reporting requirements, however, are wire transfers, bank checks, bank drafts, or other written orders of transfer. In 1989, the United States government processed an estimated 7 million CTRs, compared to an estimated 100,000 just 10 years earlier. Traffickers quickly circumvented this requirement by bribing bank employees.
- A *Currency or Monetary Instrument Report* (*CMIR*) must be filed whenever currency or monetary instruments of more than $10,000 are taken into or out of the United States. CMIRs are filed with the U.S. Customs Service. Cashier's checks and bearer bonds made out to "Cash" (rather than to an individual) are not covered by the reporting requirements.

Another powerful tool to combat money laundering is the Currency and Foreign Transactions Reporting Act, which empowers the United States government to compel other countries to maintain certain records similar to those used under the BSA. Finally, one of the greatest prosecutorial and investigative aids in years was the enactment of the Money Laundering Control Act. Prior to its passage by Congress in 1986, money laundering per se was not a crime, although various federal statutes were used to prosecute different stages of the money-laundering process. Under the new act, money laundering was made a separate violation of federal law punishable by a fine of $500,000 or twice the value of the property involved, whichever is greater, and 20 years' imprisonment. Powerful forfeiture clauses were also added to federal law in 1988, which provide for the seizure of any property associated with a money-laundering scheme.

The Money Laundering Prosecution Improvement Act of 1988 included a provision authorizing the U.S. Department of Treasury to require financial institutions to verify the identity of people who purchase bank checks or money orders in amounts of $3000 or more. The law also authorized the secretary of the treasury to target certain types of institutions or geographic areas for special reporting requirements. More recently, the Money Laundering and Financial Crime Strategy Act of 1998 called for the development of a national strategy to combat money laundering and related financial crimes. In response,

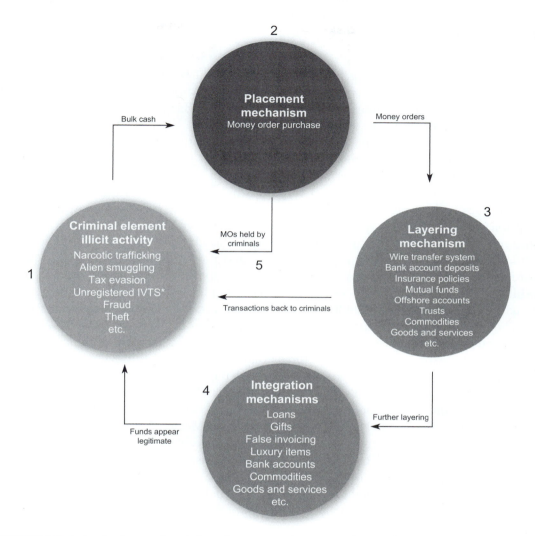

FIGURE 6.4 Typical cycle of money laundering using money orders. *IVTS refers to Informal Value Transfer Systems.

the Departments of Justice and the Treasury developed a strategy designating high-risk money-laundering zones to direct coordinated efforts by police, providing for greater scrutiny of suspicious transactions, creating new legislation, and intensifying pressure on nations that lack adequate money-laundering controls.

These techniques represent only a few of the ways that traffickers hide their illicit revenues from drug sales. It is generally thought that traffickers, regardless of their national origin, make regular use of these techniques. The fact that so many different mechanisms exist for money laundering makes investigation of these crimes difficult, and presents many unique challenges to the investigator.

Summary

When the so-called drug problem is discussed, the subject of drug-related crime is also deliberated. The very term *drug-related crime* means different things to different people because it represents many types of criminal activity. Although many people consider drug crimes to be street crimes (e.g., robbery, assault, burglary, and murder), other crimes also accompany drug abuse.

Studies of the behavior of drug users have revealed that the crime rate (street-type crimes) for users may be anywhere from four to six times as high as for people who do not use drugs. In addition to street crimes associated with drug use, ancillary crimes such as corruption and money laundering accompany drug use. Official corruption in the United States poses a major problem for drug control strategists and enforcement officials. Corruption is pervasive and may take any of several forms, from bribery, extortion, favoritism, and mooching to more serious types of corruption such as perjury, premeditated theft, and shakedowns of suspects. Both the Knapp and the Mollen Commissions' inquiries into police corruption in New York shed light on corruption within police departments. In addition, many cases of police and official corruption have surfaced around the country, making it clear that the drug trade can penetrate even the most reputable of professions.

The problem of foreign corruption parallels that experienced in the United States, but with even greater repercussions. Many drug source countries, such as Colombia, Peru, and Myanmar, are experiencing criminal forces that threaten to rival the legitimate government because of political influence gained through payoffs. Unscrupulous links have been documented between Panama's former dictator Manuel Noriega and Fidel Castro, between Colombian traffickers and Honduran officials, and between high-ranking Mexican Federal Judicial Police officials and known heroin traffickers in Mexico. For decades, the laundering of illegally obtained currency has been a logistical problem for many organized crime operations. The trafficker's basic concern is how to transform illegally obtained money to currency that appears to be legitimate.

The 1970 BSA has provided investigators with much-needed legal tools with which to combat this type of crime. These tools consist of specific reporting requirements for banking institutions and individuals alike. These reporting requirements enable investigators to follow the path of illicitly gained currency to its source.

Do you recognize these terms?

- Currency Transaction Report (CTR)
- Drug Abuse Reporting Program
- grass eaters
- institutional corruption
- integration
- Knapp Commission
- layering
- meat eaters
- Mollen Commission
- money laundering
- placement
- police socialization
- Treatment Outcome Prospective Study
- Wickersham Commission

Discussion Questions

1. List three reasons why corruption is considered a threat to public safety.
2. Discuss the different types of corruption that are commonly practiced by corrupt police officers.
3. Discuss the use of currency exchanges in money-laundering operations.

References

[1] ADAM II 2011 Annual Report. (2012). *Executive summary.* Washington DC: Executive Office of the President, p. xiii.
[2] Bureau of Justice Statistics. (2005). *Substance dependence, abuse, and treatment of jail inmates, 2002.* Washington, DC: U.S. Government Printing Office.
[3] Ibid.
[4] Roth, J. (1994). *Understanding and preventing violence.* National Institute of Justice, Research in Brief. (February).
[5] Ibid.
[6] Ibid.
[7] Haller, M. H. (1989). Bootlegging: The business and politics of violence. In T. R. Garr (Ed.), *Violence in America* (pp. 146–152). Newbury Park, CA: Sage.
[8] Reuter, P. (2009). Systemic violence in drug markets. *Crime Law and Social Change, 52,* 275–284.
[9] Ibid.
[10] Astorga, L. (2005). *El siglo de las drogas: El narcotráfico, del Porfiriato al nuevo milenio.* Mexico City: Random House Mondadori.
[11] Astorga, L. (2009). Necessary, sufficient and contributory factors generating illegal economic activity, and specifically drug-related activity in Colombia. *Iberoamericana, 35.*
[12] Thoumi, F. (2003). *Illegal drugs, economy, and society in the Andes.* Baltimore: Johns Hopkins University Press.
[13] Brantley, A. C., & DiRosa, A. (1994). *Gangs: A National Perspective.* Washington, DC: U.S. Department of Justice.
[14] General Accounting Office. (May 1998). *Report to the Honorable Charles B. Rangel, House of Representatives, law enforcement: Information on drug-related police corruption.* Washington, DC: USGPO.
[15] Drug Policy Alliance. (2007). *Drugs, police & the law: Police corruption.* Found at: www.drugpolicy. org/law/police/.
[16] Ibid.
[17] Inciardi, J. A. (1992). *The War on Drugs II.* Mountain View, CA: Mayfield.
[18] Abadinsky, H. (2007). *Organized crime* (8th ed.). Belmont, CA: Thomson/Wadsworth.
[19] Kraska, P., & Kappeler, V. (1988). Police on-duty drug use: A theoretical and descriptive examination. *American Journal of Police, 7*(1), 1–28.
[20] Sherman, L. (1982). Learning police ethics. *Criminal Justice Ethics, 1*(1), 10–19.
[21] Johnston, M. (1982). *Political corruption and public policy in America.* Monterey, CA: Brooks/Cole.
[22] Stoddard, E. L. (1968). The informal code of police deviancy: A group approach to blue-coat crime. *Journal of Criminal Law, Criminology, and Police Science, 12,* 37–39.
[23] More, H. W. (1998). *Special topics in policing* (2nd ed.). Cincinnati: Anderson.
[24] Knapp, W. (1972). *Commission report: New York Commission to investigate allegations of police corruption and the city's anti-corruption procedures.* (September 15).
[25] Ibid.
[26] Frankel, B. (September 28, 1993). Ex-NYC officer tells stark tale of cops gone bad. *USA Today,* 3A.
[27] Ibid.
[28] Arrests by a drug task force in Texas comes under fire. (April 4, 2001). New York Times.

[29] Dallas sniffs police scandal. (January 20, 2002). Seattle Times.

[30] Massive drug sweep divides Texas town. (January 22, 2001). Washington Post.

[31] Police officer admits role in drug trafficking. (August 30, 2001). Austin American-Statesman.

[32] Sheetrock scandal hits Dallas police. (January 18, 2002). Washington Post.

[33] The heat is on a Texas town after the arrests of 40 blacks. (October 7, 2000). New York Times.

[34] Four cops face felony charges. (November 2, 2000). Oakland Tribune.

[35] LA police made up own rules, report says. (March 2, 2000). Baltimore Sun.

[36] LA police mired in misconduct scandal. (March 13, 2000). Baltimore Sun.

[37] Police corruption charges reopen wounds in Oakland. (November 30, 2000). New York Times.

[38] Current and ex-officers charged in robbery spree. (October 20, 2001). Tallahassee Democrat.

[39] 11 Miami officers facing U.S. Charges in string of shootings. (September 8, 2001). New York Times.

[40] Officers accused of drug crimes. (February 7, 2001). Miami Herald.

[41] Sarasota woman framed by corrupt deputies files federal lawsuit. (November 17, 2001). Naples Daily News.

[42] 13 Miami cops charged. (September 8, 2001). Register-Guard.

[43] Sherman, L. (1974). *Police corruption: A sociological perspective*. Garden City, NY: Doubleday.

[44] Johnston, M. (1982). *Political Corruption and Public Policy in America*. Monterey, CA: Brooks/Cole.

[45] World Drug Report. (2010). *United Nations Office on Drugs and Crime*. New York: United Nations.

[46] Ibid.

[47] Ibid.

[48] SAMHSA. *Results from the 2008 National Survey on Drug Use and Health*. The data were re-adjusted to the internationally comparable age group 15–64.

[49] Health Canada. (2009). *Canadian Alcohol and Drug Use Monitoring Survey 2008*. Ottawa. The decline from 1.9% of the population age 15 and above in 2004 to 1.6% in 2008 is equivalent to a decline from 2.3% to 2.0% if the numbers are re-adjusted to the internationally comparable age group of those aged 15–64.

[50] National Drug Intelligence Center. (December 2008). *National drug threat assessment 2009*.

[51] World Drug Report. (2010). *United Nations Office on Drugs and Crime*. United Nations: New York.

[52] Crime Prevention. (2000). *Global Illicit Drug Trends, 1999*. New York: UNODCCP.

[53] Karchmer, C. L. (1989). *Illegal money laundering: A strategy and resource guide for law enforcement agencies*. Washington, DC: Police Executive Research Forum.

[54] Guillen, E. M. (June 23, 2000). *Statement by Edward M. Guillen, Chief of Financial Operations, Drug Enforcement Administration, before the House Subcommittee on Criminal Justice, Drug Policy, and Human Resources. Congressional Testimony*.

[55] Zill, O., & Bergman, L. (2012). *The black peso money laundering system*. PBS. Found at: http://www.pbs.org/wgbh/pages/frontline/shows/drugs/special/blackpeso.html.

[56] Ibid.

[57] Schroeder, W. R. (2001). Money Laundering: A Global Threat and the International Community's Response. *FBI Law Enforcement Bulletin, (May)*, 1–8.

[58] Office of National Drug Control Policy. (1994). *The National Drug Control Strategy, Executive Summary*. Washington, DC: U.S. Government Printing Office.

Gangs and Drugs

Organized crime has historically played an important role in United States society. The drug problem specifically has afforded many organized criminals increased sources of revenue with which to expand their operations and influence throughout the nation's communities. Accordingly, conflicts between these organizations have also escalated, resulting in gangs warring with each other over territory as well as recruiting new members from schools. Furthermore, larger crime organizations have developed the resources and capabilities to insulate themselves from detection by infiltrating legitimate businesses and corrupting public officials. This section examines the concept of organized crime, its origins and growth, and its increasing alliance with the illicit drug trade.

Organized Crime
and the Drug Trade

This chapter will enable you to:

- Understand the term *organized crime*
- Differentiate between traditional and nontraditional organized crime
- Understand the alien conspiracy theory
- Understand the factors that contribute to the growth of nontraditional organized crime

The Nature of Drug Trafficking

As noted in Chapter 1, there is no single drug problem in the United States, but rather myriad separate drug problems that interact with one another. Likewise, there is no single, predictable pattern for drug-trafficking organizations. They vary widely in size, sophistication, area of operation, clientele, and product. They also have varying degrees of vertical and horizontal integration, different proclivities for the use of violence, and distinct patterns of interaction with one another.

Drug-trafficking organizations share the distinct characteristic of being engaged in the same illegal business. For that reason, however, they do not have access to and are not subject to the normal channels of production, distribution, sales, finance, taxation, regulation, and contract enforcement that shape the legitimate business arena. Ironically, a dichotomy presents itself, since this illicit business is still subject to many of the same dynamics as the laws of supply and demand, the need for efficiency in operation, and the necessity for a set of rules by which to operate. Traffickers must operate outside the normal financial and legal structures of commerce, while at the same time remaining subject to all the market pressures normally accommodated by that structure. Recognizing this dichotomy is one of the keys to understanding the nature of drug-trafficking organizations.

To best understand this nature, we must realize that such organizations recreate the structures of legitimate commerce. Experience shows us that many of these organizations do so with astonishing precision, yet they are skewed by the limitations of the illicit nature of their activities. Some of the more well-established organizations may have a board of directors, a chief executive officer (CEO), and a bureaucracy that is disciplined and whose functions and benefits mirror those of the management in modern corporations. To that extent, many participants enjoy amenities such as expense accounts, bonuses, and even company cars. On the other hand, the normal commercial concepts of contracts (in which disputes are adjudicated by an impartial judiciary) and restitution (which is almost always of a financial nature) are skewed in the world of drug trafficking. Here, a system exists in which the rule of law has been replaced by the threat of violence and retribution.

Although there is no single type of organizational structure that describes major drug-trafficking organizations, a few well-defined patterns have been identified. First, there are major, international, vertically integrated trafficking organizations that are best exemplified by the Mexican drug cartels (see Chapter 6). In addition, other groups (e.g., outlaw motorcycle gangs (OMGs)) operate domestically and tend to have smaller, less sophisticated operations. For example, their lines of supply are shorter, their bank accounts are fewer, and the quantities of drugs transported are not as great. Next, there are city-based groups (e.g., youth gangs) that operate in many large inner-city areas. These groups tend to have minimal organization at the management end of their operations, but they still have extensive distribution networks run by low-level operatives, many of whom work directly on the street and concentrate primarily on the local distribution and retail aspects of drug distribution (see Chapter 4).

Two features common to many of the larger trafficking organizations are their abilities to (1) tap into alternate sources of supply, and (2) adapt to readily changing conditions. For example, the Cali cartel was able to buy its coca leaves or paste in Peru, Bolivia, Ecuador, or Colombia itself. This flexibility enables major traffickers to regroup and redirect a segment of their operations without disrupting the entire organization. In many respects, Colombian trafficking organizations are on the cutting edge of international technology. They operate across international borders, and the flexibility of their organizational structure enables them to form partnerships with other groups.

Like large legitimate corporations, major traffickers are immense because they are good at what they do. Careless errors are few, as are unnecessary risks. Leaders of these organizations are keenly aware of the importance of being insulated from street-level drug sales. One of the characteristics that prevails in the world of drug trafficking is the predilection for dealing in cash and the incentive to transfer that cash into the legitimate economy so that it can be converted into goods and services from the legitimate business community. This alone represents one of the biggest problems for trafficking organizations. In fact, so much cash is involved in the drug trade that it is often more advantageous for police to track cash proceeds than the drugs themselves. Indeed, it is money from which even the most cautious drug manager cannot be totally isolated. Accordingly, tracking this money remains one of the most challenging investigative endeavors for drug control agents.

Reminiscent of Prohibition-era gangs, today's drug-trafficking organizations are varied and have become increasingly organized and powerful. With an array of ethnically and geographically based groups, today's illicit drug-trafficking organizations have surpassed the sophistication and influence of many of their early twentieth-century counterparts.

Crime in the United States has undergone many significant changes since the 1920s. It has become more pernicious due to two interrelated developments: drug abuse and organized crime. For decades, the Mafia was thought to have monopolized the drug trade, but today many different criminal groups compete for the tax-free profits offered by illicit drugs, and for territory on which to sell them. For many years, the term *organized crime* was synonymous with La Cosa Nostra, or the Mafia. This term generally refers to the popular public view of Italian and Sicilian criminal groups. Although both Sicilian and Italian-American criminal organizations are involved in the lucrative drug trade, so are many other criminal groups. All of these groups have their sights set on the immense profits to be earned in drugs. Today, groups whose criminal enterprises focus on the illegal drug trade include OMGs, Jamaican posses, African-American organized crime groups, and California-based youth gangs, to name a few.

Organized crime has demonstrated not only an alarming degree of violence, but also an ability to corrupt public officials at the highest levels. The pervasiveness of such activity threatens legitimate businesses and neighborhoods. To operate both efficiently and effectively, large-scale drug-trafficking operations require superb organization. This is essential to avoid police detection while maintaining the ability to compete with other criminal groups. To this end, these organizations can be characterized by a number of common activities:

- Obtaining the illicit substances (or the raw materials with which to manufacture them)
- Making "connections" to acquire the illicit substances
- Arranging for the processing of drugs (either through overseas or domestic sources)
- Developing smuggling networks with which to transport illicit materials
- Arranging for protection of the operation through corrupting public officials or hiring enforcers
- Locating distributors on both the wholesale and retail levels
- Developing a process whereby illegal money can be laundered or otherwise concealed from detection by law enforcement authorities
- Utilizing the Internet to recruit new members

Chapters 7, 8, and 9 examine some of the significant actors on the criminal side of the "war on drugs." The following segment, however, is intended to acquaint the reader with various gang characteristics so that rational conclusions can be drawn regarding the role of organized crime in the United States drug scene.

Gangs

Gangs represent a serious public threat in many communities throughout the United States. Recent investigations show that gang members are increasingly migrating from urban to suburban areas, and are responsible for a growing percentage of crime and violence. To a great extent, gang-related criminal activity involves drug trafficking, but recently gang members are increasingly engaging in alien and weapons trafficking [1]. Additionally, a rising number of United States-based gangs are seemingly intent on developing working relationships with United States- and foreign-based drug-trafficking organizations and other criminal organizations to gain direct access to foreign sources of illicit drugs.

Recent statistics show the prevalence of gangs in the United States and the extent they are involved in criminal activity. For example, the National Gang Intelligence Center (NGIC) reported that in the United States in 2008, there were approximately 20,000 gangs with an estimated 1 million members. These gangs have been reported as operating in 58 percent of state and local law enforcement agency jurisdictions. Furthermore, law enforcement groups report that criminal gangs are thought to commit as much as 80 percent of the crime in many communities. These crimes include alien smuggling, armed robbery, assault, auto theft, drug trafficking, extortion, fraud, home invasions, identity theft, murder, and weapons trafficking. Gang members are also the primary retail-level distributors of most illicit drugs [2].

The gang migration from urban areas to suburban and rural locations, which began more than two decades ago, is a significant and growing problem in most areas of the country. Gangs are now fully well-established in many communities across the nation. Most gangs were formed in major cities and then expanded into neighboring communities in the 1970s. By the 1990s, full-scale migration was taking place. Many notable gangs (e.g., the Gangster Disciples and Latin Kings) were originally formed as organizations of political and social reform during the 1960s, but soon thereafter the focus of many of these gangs changed from reform to criminal activity in the pursuit of profit.

The movement of gang members to suburban areas often resulted in territorial conflicts between rival urban gang members competing for the new territory, in addition to conflicts with the few existing suburban gang members. Gang members who migrated from urban areas often formed new, neighborhood-based local gangs, and generally these gangs controlled their territories through violence and intimidation. Moreover, they sought to increase their size by recruiting new members, who were typically from single-parent, low-income households, and who possessed limited education. Local gangs engaged in a wide range of criminal activity, including retail-level drug distribution.

During the 1980s, some gangs began to expand their drug distribution networks into suburban communities influenced by local gangs. The larger gangs, who already controlled drug distribution in city drug markets, were motivated to move into adjoining communities to generate additional income by capitalizing on the growing cocaine (both powder and crack) markets. Billions of dollars were generated from trafficking illegal drugs, and this money enabled the gangs to recruit new members and forced smaller local gangs to either disband or join forces with the larger groups. As large urban gangs increasingly dominated and expanded into drug markets in suburban and rural communities, they often were met with initial resistance by local gangs. This resistance resulted in an increased number of homicides and drive-by shootings.

Gang-related violence and drug trafficking became fully ingrained in suburban areas throughout the 1990s. Because of violent gang activity, law enforcement devoted significant resources to fighting gun crime and disrupting the most violent gangs. The crackdown on violent gang activity targeted key gang leaders in an effort to dismantle highly structured gangs. In conjunction with this practice, federal law enforcement officers began to target violent gang members from Mexico and Central America, most of whom were in the United States illegally. Moreover, a large number of gang members in prison formed associations along ethnic lines in an attempt to protect their organizations and operations, giving rise to large, influential prison gangs.

Gang migration has led to the recruitment of new, younger gang members in many suburban and rural communities. According to recent statistics, the percentage of suburban students age 12–18 who reported that gangs were present at school during the previous 6 months increased by 17 percent from 2003 to 2005, after remaining stable from 2001 to 2003 [3]. Gang activity at schools is rising, in part because gangs are using middle schools and high schools as venues for drug distribution. Law enforcement agencies in numerous jurisdictions report that gangs are directing teenage members who had dropped out of school to reenroll, primarily to recruit new members and sell drugs.

Recent Research Findings

Gangs are currently expanding, evolving, and posing an increasing threat to United States communities nationwide. Many gangs are sophisticated criminal networks with members who are violent, distribute wholesale quantities of drugs, and develop and maintain close working relationships with members and associates of transnational criminal drug-trafficking organizations. Gangs are becoming more violent while engaging in lower-risk crime that is also less typical for them, such as prostitution and white-collar crime. Gangs are more adaptable, organized, sophisticated, and opportunistic, exploiting new and advanced technology as a means to recruit, communicate discreetly, target their rivals, and perpetuate their criminal activity. Based on state, local, and federal law enforcement reporting, the NGIC concluded the following:

- There are approximately 1.4 million active street, prison, and OMG members comprising more than 33,000 gangs within all 50 American states, the District of Columbia, and Puerto Rico. Gang membership increased most significantly in the Northeast and Southeast regions, although the West and Great Lakes regions boast the highest number of gang members. Neighborhood-based gangs, hybrid gang members, and national-level gangs such as the Sureños are rapidly expanding in many jurisdictions. Many communities are also experiencing an increase in ethnic-based gangs such as African, Asian, Caribbean, and Eurasian gangs [4].
- Gangs are responsible for an average of 48 percent of violent crime in most jurisdictions, and up to 90 percent in several others, according to NGIC analysis. Major cities and suburban areas experience the most gang-related violence. Local neighborhood-based gangs and drug crews continue to pose the most significant criminal threat in most communities. Aggressive recruitment of juveniles and immigrants, alliances and conflict between gangs, the release of incarcerated gang members from prison, advancements in technology and communication, and Mexican drug-trafficking

organization involvement in drug distribution have resulted in gang expansion and violence in a number of jurisdictions.

- Gangs are increasingly engaging in nontraditional gang-related crime, such as alien smuggling, human trafficking, and prostitution. Gangs are also engaging in white-collar crime such as counterfeiting, identity theft, and mortgage fraud, primarily due to the high profitability, as well as the much lower visibility, risk of detection, and punishment compared to drug and weapons trafficking.

Gang membership continues to expand throughout communities nationwide, as gangs evolve, adapt to new threats, and form new associations. Consequently, gang-related crime and violence are increasing as gangs employ violence and intimidation to control their territory and illicit operations. Many gangs have advanced beyond their traditional role as local retail drug distributors in large cities to become more organized, adaptable, and influential in large-scale drug trafficking. Gang members are migrating from urban areas to suburban and rural communities to recruit new members, expand their drug distribution territories, form new alliances, and collaborate with rival gangs and criminal organizations for profit and influence. Local neighborhood, hybrid, and female gang membership is on the rise in many communities. Prison gang members, who exert control over many street gang members, often engage in crime and violence upon their return to the community. Gang members returning to the community from prison have an adverse and lasting impact on neighborhoods, which may experience notable increases in crime, violence, and drug trafficking.

As mentioned in this section, approximately 1.4 million active street, OMG, and prison gang members, comprising more than 33,000 gangs, are criminally active in the United States [5]. The NGIC attributes this increase in gang membership primarily to improved reporting, more aggressive recruitment efforts by gangs, the formation of new gangs, new opportunities for drug trafficking, and collaboration with rival gangs and drug-trafficking organizations. Law enforcement in several jurisdictions also attribute the increase in gang membership in their region to the gangster rap culture, the facilitation of communication and recruitment through the Internet and social media, the proliferation of generational gang members, and a shortage of resources to combat gangs.

- More than half of NGIC law enforcement partners report an increase in gang-related criminal activity in their jurisdictions over the past 2 years. Neighborhood-based gangs continue to pose the greatest threat in most jurisdictions nationwide.
- Recent data indicate that, since 2009, gang membership increased most significantly in the Northeast and Southeast regions, although the west and north central regions—particularly Arizona, California, and Illinois—boast the highest number of gang members.
- Sureño gangs, including Mara Salvatrucha (MS-13), 18th Street, and Florencia 13, are expanding faster than other national-level gangs, both in membership and geographically. Twenty states and the District of Columbia report an increase of Sureño migration into their region over the past 3 years. California has experienced a substantial

migration of Sureño gangs into northern California and neighboring states, such as Arizona, Nevada, and Oregon.

- Law enforcement reporting indicates a significant increase in OMGs in a number of jurisdictions, with approximately 44,000 members nationwide comprising approximately 3000 gangs [6]. Jurisdictions in Alaska, Arizona, Colorado, Connecticut, Delaware, Florida, Georgia, Iowa, Missouri, Montana, Oregon, Pennsylvania, South Carolina, Tennessee, Utah, and Virginia are experiencing the most significant increase in OMGs, increasing the potential for gang-related turf wars with other local OMGs. The Wheels of Soul (WOS), Mongols, Outlaws, Pagans, and Vagos have expanded in several states.

Gang Membership

Gang membership in the United States was conservatively estimated at 1 million members as of September 2008. However, current estimates include approximately 900,000 gang members residing within local communities across the country, and more than 147,000 documented gang members incarcerated in federal, state, and local correctional facilities. Increased gang membership is most likely the result of gang recruitment efforts and the release of incarcerated gang members [7].

Gang Sophistication

Gang members are becoming more sophisticated in their structure and operations, and are modifying their activity to avoid scrutiny by police and elude gang laws focusing on

FIGURE 7.1 A few months prior to his resignation in 2009, Los Angeles Police Chief William Bratton speaks at a news conference to announce an indictment naming 24 leaders, members, and associates of MS-13, part of the Mara Salvatrucha gang affiliated with the Mexican Mafia prison gang. *Source: AP Photo/Nick Ut.*

gangs. Gangs in several jurisdictions have modified or ceased traditional or stereotypical gang indicia and no longer display their colors, tattoos, or hand signs. Others are forming hybrid gangs to avoid police attention, and to make it more difficult for law enforcement to identify and monitor them, according to NGIC reporting. Many gangs are engaging in more sophisticated criminal schemes, including white-collar crime and cybercrime; targeting and infiltrating sensitive systems to gain access to sensitive areas or information; and targeting and monitoring law enforcement.

Gang Types

Gangs vary extensively regarding membership, structure, age, and ethnicity. However, three basic types of gangs have been identified over the years: street gangs, prison gangs, and OMGs.

Street Gangs

Street gangs operating throughout most of the United States control a large geographical area, and therefore criminal activities such as violence and drug trafficking perpetrated by street gangs pose a great threat. The threat becomes magnified as national- and regional-level street gangs migrate from urban areas to suburban and rural communities, expanding their influence in most regions and broadening their presence outside the United States to develop associations with drug-trafficking organizations and other criminal organizations in Mexico, Central America, and Canada.

Today, 11 national-level street gangs have been identified in the United States, and associates or members have been identified in foreign countries, according to analysis of federal, state, and local law enforcement [8]. National gangs typically have several hundred to several thousand members nationwide who operate in multiple regions. Established cells in foreign countries assist gangs operating in the United States in further developing associations with drug-trafficking organizations, as well as other organizations in those countries.

Regional-level street gangs increasingly distribute drugs at the wholesale level. According to recent statistics, at least five street gangs—specifically, Florencia 13, the Fresno Bulldogs, the Latin Disciples, Tango Blast, and United Blood Nation— have been identified as operating at a regional level. Regional-level gangs are usually organized with several hundred to several thousand members. They may have some members in foreign countries, and maintain contacts with drug-trafficking organizations operating in the United States [9].

Local street gangs, which are sometimes referred to as *neighborhood-based gangs* or *drug crews*, also present an ongoing problem for local law enforcement agencies. Currently, most street gangs are local-level gangs that operate in single locations. Membership generally ranges from three to several hundred members. Most of these gangs engage in violence in conjunction with a variety of crimes, including retail-level drug distribution; however, they usually have no direct ties to larger criminal organizations.

But recent reports by police agencies claim that a few local gangs have established ties to wholesale-level drug-trafficking organizations operating along the United States–Mexico border [10].

Prison Gangs

Over the past three decades, *prison gangs* have gained prominence in society. This is especially the case with national-level prison gangs who affiliate with Mexican drug-trafficking organizations and maintain a considerable amount of influence over street gangs in the communities in which they operate. Prison gangs are highly structured criminal networks that operate within the federal and state prison systems. They also operate in local communities through members who have been released from prison. Released members typically return to their home communities and resume their former street gang affiliations, acting as representatives of their prison gang to recruit street gang members who perform criminal acts on behalf of the prison gang.

Prison gangs often control drug distribution within correctional facilities, and heavily influence street-level distribution in some communities. These gangs exert considerable control over mid- and retail-level drug distribution in the southwestern United States and southern California. Their trafficking activities are facilitated through their connections with Mexican drug-trafficking organizations, which ensure access to a continuous supply of illicit drugs that are distributed through their networks in prison or are supplied to affiliated street gangs. Three different levels of prison gangs have been identified:

- *National-level prison gangs.* Prison gangs at this level maintain ongoing relationships with drug-trafficking organizations. Of the five identified national-level prison gangs, two have members or associates in at least two foreign countries. Prison gangs at this level are well organized and governed by established sets of rules and codes of conduct that are rigorously enforced by gang leaders. For example, the California-based Mexican Mafia (La Eme) uses fear and intimidation to control Latino street gangs whose members are in prison and on the street in California, giving them command over an estimated 50,000–75,000 gang members and associates [11].
- *Regional-level prison gangs.* Gangs at the regional level are increasingly developing associations with known drug-trafficking organizations. Regional-level prison gangs have organizational structures similar to those of national-level gangs, but typically are limited to operating in one or two state prison systems. The most significant regional-level prison gangs operate in Texas, and most have ties to at least one Mexican drug-trafficking organization [12].
- *Local or state-level prison gangs.* Gangs at the local or state level, particularly those operating along the United States–Mexico border, are an ongoing concern for law enforcement. Local prison gangs typically operate within the department of corrections of a single state. As members are released from prison, they settle in local communities, where they recruit and associate with local street gang members and conduct criminal activities on behalf of the prison gang [13].

Outlaw Motorcycle Gangs

OMGs pose a threat to communities because of their wide-ranging criminal activity, propensity to use violence, and ability to counter law enforcement efforts. OMGs are highly structured criminal organizations, and their members engage in violent crime, weapons trafficking, and drug trafficking. These groups maintain a strong centralized leadership that implements rules regulating membership, conduct, and criminal activity.

Membership in OMGs is considerable. As of June 2008, state and local law enforcement agencies estimated that between 280 and 520 OMGs were operating in United States. These organizations range in size from a single chapter to hundreds of chapters worldwide. Current law enforcement intelligence estimates indicate that more than 20,000 validated OMG members, divided among the hundreds of OMGs, reside in the United States [14]. As with other organized crime groups, OMGs can be identified on three different levels:

- *National-level OMGs.* With memberships ranging into the thousands, these groups maintain strong associations with transnational drug-trafficking organizations and other criminal organizations. In addition, national-level OMGs maintain criminal networks of regional and local motorcycle clubs, commonly referred to as *support clubs* (also called *puppet* or *duck clubs*), whose members conduct criminal activities in support of the larger group and which serve as a source for new members. Moreover, some members of support clubs have acquired employment with private businesses or government agencies, which enables them to provide national-level OMGs with business, government, and financial information that can be used to protect their criminal enterprises.
- *Regional-level OMGs.* OMGs on the regional level range in size from 50 to several hundred members. In the United States, 109 regional-level OMGs have been identified by law enforcement; most support one of the national-level groups. A number of regional-level OMGs maintain independent contact with transnational drug-trafficking organizations [15].
- *Local-level OMGs.* The local-level OMG typically operates in a single state or in a few neighboring states and has fewer than 50 members. They are often support clubs for regional- and national-level OMGs. In general, OMGs on this level have no ties to international drug-trafficking organizations.

Criminal Activities

Gangs are responsible for much of the crime in many urban and suburban communities across the United States, and much of it is associated with drug-trafficking activities. Recent statistics show that gang members are responsible for as much as 80 percent of the crime in some locations. Violence resulting from disputes over control of drug territory and enforcement of drug debts frequently occurs among street gangs. Gang members also engage in a host of other criminal activities such as auto theft, assault, alien smuggling, burglary, drive-by shootings, extortion, firearms offenses, home invasion robberies, homicide, identity theft, insurance fraud, mortgage fraud, operation of prostitution rings, and weapons trafficking.

Drug distribution by gang members on the retail level is on the increase, as is their participation in wholesale-level drug distribution in urban and suburban communities. For example, in 2004 it was estimated that 45 percent of gangs were involved in drug distribution; in 2008, that figure rose to 58 percent. The primary drug distributed by gangs is marijuana, followed by powder and crack cocaine, MDMA (ecstasy), methamphetamine, diverted pharmaceuticals, and heroin.

Gang-related violent crime is also increasing in many areas around the country. In San Diego, for example, fatal gang-related homicides increased 56 percent, from 18 in 2006 to 28 in 2007 [16]. Accordingly, recent research shows that gang members are increasingly using firearms in conjunction with their criminal activities. Gang members typically buy, sell, and trade firearms among their associates. Gang members often obtain these firearms through thefts and straw purchases. These firearms are for personal use, or for use by fellow gang members in committing homicides and armed robberies. For example, members and associates of the Los Angeles–based Black P. Stone Bloods and Rolling 20s Crips were arrested in July 2008 for illegally selling more than 119 firearms. Furthermore, members of the California-based Mara Salvatrucha gang obtain weapons for their personal use, and sell weapons and ammunition to members of other gangs in California for profit [17].

Financing Illicit Operations

Gangs earn the profits that are essential to maintaining their criminal operations and the lifestyles of their members primarily through drug distribution. Most gang members are retail-level dealers who use drug proceeds to make typical consumer purchases, pay their living costs, or purchase luxury goods such as vehicles and jewelry.

Recent statistics show that gang members typically launder profits from criminal activities through front companies and real estate investments. Gang members use front companies such as clothing stores, hair salons, and music recording and production companies to commingle illicit proceeds earned from drug sales with licit income from these businesses. Some gang members also use mortgage fraud schemes, or purchase real estate as investments or as a means to commingle illicit funds with rental payments. For example, members of the Chicago-based Latin Kings, Black Disciples, Vice Lords, and Gangster Disciples use mortgage fraud schemes that employ straw purchases and unscrupulous mortgage brokers and appraisers to purchase property at a minimal cost and sell it at a higher value to a third party. The gang members receiving the profits from the sales seemingly legitimatize the income, whereas their associates typically default on loans, often defrauding banks or mortgage companies.

Gang Communications

Gang members use cell phones and the Internet to communicate and promote their illegal activities. Street gangs often use voicemail and text messaging to conduct drug transactions and prearranged meetings with customers. Members of street gangs use multiple cell phones that frequently are discarded while conducting their traffic operations. For example, the leader of an African-American street gang operating in Milwaukee was found to use more than 20 cell phones to coordinate drug-related activities. Most were prepaid telephones that the leader routinely discarded and replaced. Internet-based methods such as social networking sites, encrypted e-mail, Internet telephones, and instant messaging are also used by gang members to communicate with one another and with drug customers.

For example, members of the Crips gang in Hampton, Virginia, used the Internet to intimidate rival gang members and maintain websites to recruit new members. On October 23, 2007, a 15-year-old Crips gang member was arrested for shooting a rival gang member in the leg. Additionally, he was charged with the recruitment of persons for a criminal street gang through the use of the gang's social networking site.

Alien Smuggling and Human Trafficking

Alien smuggling involves facilitating the illegal entry of aliens for financial or other tangible benefits. It can involve an individual or a criminal organization. Business relationships typically cease once the individual has reached his or her destination. Alien smuggling, or *human trafficking*, involves the recruitment, transportation, and harboring of persons through force, fraud, or coercion for labor or services that result in slavery, involuntary prostitution or servitude, or debt bondage. The business relationship does not end and often becomes exploitative and violent.

Many street gangs are becoming involved in alien smuggling as a source of revenue. According to United States law enforcement officials, tremendous incentive exists for gangs to diversify their criminal enterprises to include alien smuggling, which can be more lucrative and less risky than the illicit drug trade. In recent years, numerous federal, state, and local law enforcement agencies nationwide have reported gang involvement in incidents of alien smuggling. In some instances, gang members were among those being smuggled across the border into the United States following deportation. In other cases, gang members facilitated the movement of migrants across the United States –Mexico border. According to the United Nations, more than 90 percent of Mexican migrants illegally entering the United States are assisted by professional smugglers. Although most of the migrants are smuggled in trucks, many have been smuggled by rail, on foot, and via tunnels [18].

Prostitution

Prostitution is also a major source of income for many gangs. Gang members often operate as pimps, luring or forcing at-risk, young females into prostitution and controlling them through violence and psychological abuse. Asian gangs, Bloods, Crips, Gangster Disciples, MS-13, Sureños, Vice Lords, and members of OMGs are involved in prostitution operations, according to the FBI, the NGIC, and reports of multiple law enforcement agencies.

Prostitution is reportedly the second largest source of income for San Diego, California, gangs. According to November 2010 open source reporting, African-American street gangs in San Diego are pimping young females to solicit males.

Defining Organized Crime

Organized crime is a complex criminal phenomenon that conjures up an image of gangsters with broad-brimmed hats, dark pinstriped suits, and Thompson submachine guns. Over the years, this popular image has been perpetuated by movies, television, and novels, and tends to leave the average person with a limited concept of the term. Contributing to the enigma of organized crime is the absence of a codified, legal definition of the term. Ironically, despite the lack of an official definition, many federal statutes address the types of criminal activity typically involving organized crime. For example, statutes exist dealing with criminal conspiracies, continuing criminal enterprises (CCEs), and racketeer-influenced and corrupt organizations (RICOs), but all of these are separate from and more specific than the general term *organized crime*.

The very words *organized crime* imply criminal involvement by a group of individuals operating in an organized fashion. However, it is not clear whether this broad definition includes a group of three youths involved in a shoplifting scheme, or should be applied only to larger, more sophisticated criminal organizations. The general term itself fails to give adequate guidelines to criminal justice professionals, who are in need of a more precise distinction between a high-level organized drug-trafficking organization and a group of two or three low-level "street-corner" drug dealers. In 1968, Congress passed into law the first major organized crime bill, the Omnibus Crime Control and Safe Streets Act, which is the only federal statute that uses the term *organized crime*. In the act, the term is loosely described as follows:

> *[Organized crime includes] the unlawful activities of members of a highly organized, disciplined association engaged in supplying illegal goods or services, including but not limited to gambling, prostitution, loansharking, narcotics, labor racketeering, and other unlawful activities. …*

Clarity was given to the term when the President's Commission on Organized Crime concluded in 1986 that several variables that make up an organized crime unit can be identified [19]. These include (1) the criminal group, which is made up of core people who share certain bonds; (2) the protectors, who protect the group's interests; and (3) specialized support, which consists of people who knowingly render services on an ad hoc basis [20] (Table 7.1).

The Criminal Group

The *criminal group* is composed of individuals who are usually bound by ethnic, racial, geographic, or lingual ties. The individuals display a willingness to engage in criminal activity for profit while using violence and intimidation to protect their criminal interests and to avoid detection. Organized crime groups are characterized by the longevity of the groups themselves, which outlasts the lives of individual members. Such a group

Table 7.1   Gang Definitions

Gang	Definition
Street gangs	Street gangs are criminal organizations that are formed on the street and operate throughout the United States.
Prison gangs	Prison gangs are criminal organizations that originated within the penal system and operate within correctional facilities throughout the United States, although released members may be operating on the street. Prison gangs are also self-perpetuating criminal entities that can continue their criminal operations outside the confines of the penal system.
Outlaw motorcycle gangs (OMGs)	OMGs are organizations whose members use their motorcycle clubs as conduits for criminal enterprises. Although some law enforcement agencies regard only One Percenters as OMGs, the NGIC, for the purpose of this assessment, covers all OMG criminal organizations, including OMG support and puppet clubs.
"One Percenter" OMGs	The Bureau of Alcohol, Tobacco, Firearms, and Explosives (ATF) defines *One Percenters* as any group of motorcyclists who have voluntarily made a commitment to band together, to abide by their organization's rules (which are enforced by violence), and to engage in activities that bring them and their club into repeated and serious conflict with society and the law. The group must be an ongoing organization that is an association of three or more persons who have a common interest and/or activity characterized by the commission of, or involvement in, a pattern of criminal conduct. ATF estimates that there are approximately 300 One Percenter OMGs in the United States.
Neighborhood and local gangs	Neighborhood and local street gangs are confined to specific neighborhoods and jurisdictions and often imitate larger, more powerful national gangs. The primary purpose for many neighborhood gangs is drug distribution and sales.

maintains rules and a code of conduct while its management is structured in a hierarchical or pyramid-style chain of command. Membership in the organized crime group is restricted and is usually based on a common trait, talent, or need of the group. Acceptance into the criminal group is closely scrutinized by the existing members, and typically an initiation is required for all recruits. Motivation for individual membership is based on the premise that the successful recruit will enjoy economic gain, protection by the group, and a certain prestige within the organization.

The Protectors

The *protectors* are usually associates of the criminal group who appear (at least on the surface) to be law-abiding members of the community. In fact, this group may include prominent members of the community such as corrupt politicians, bankers, attorneys, or accountants. They work to insulate the criminal group from government interference and to protect the assets of the organization.

Specialized Support

The larger the criminal group, the more it is in need of *specialized support.* Those individuals offering specialized support for an organized crime unit possess talent that enables the group to attain its goals and objectives. Unlike the seemingly lawful existence of the protectors, specialists include laboratory chemists, smuggling pilots, and enforcers (professional killers) for organized crime units. Most organized crime specialists are overtly involved in criminality.

In addition to these specialists, the organized crime group relies on outside individuals (members of the general public) for financial and other support:

- *User support* includes those individuals who purchase the organized crime group's illegal goods and services. These individuals include drug users, patrons of prostitutes, bookmakers, and those who willfully purchase stolen goods.
- *Social support* includes individuals and organizations who grant power and an air of legitimacy to organized crime generally, and to certain groups and their members specifically. Social support includes public officials who solicit the support of organized crime figures, business leaders who do business with organized crime figures, and others who portray the criminal group or organized crime in a favorable or glamorous light [21].

In considering organized crime organizations in both the United States and foreign countries, several operative characteristics can be recognized. One such characteristic is the group's attempt to compete with the functions of legitimate government. Historic examples include the following:

- *In Colombia.* During the 1980s, cocaine cartels such as the Medellín and Cali cartels were competing with the legitimate government by attempting to control segments of the society, offering to pay off the country's national debt, and generally acting like an alternative government.
- *In Italy.* During the 1970s and 1980s, the Sicilian Mafia was responsible for the assassinations of many investigators and federal police who were assigned to anti-Mafia investigations. In addition, judges, mayors, union leaders, and government representatives have been killed by organized crime members because those individuals opposed the political or criminal activities of the Mafia.

In the United States, such displays of violence against the government are not quite as blatant, but many of the same principles are still at work. In one case, for example, organized crime members in Chicago attempted to levy a "street tax" on bookmakers and pornographers. Although these activities are illicit, the function of taxing can be viewed as one rightfully belonging to legitimate government. Additionally, many cities that have experienced an influx of youth gangs recognize that these groups have attempted to take control of neighborhoods for crack distribution. In many cases, witnesses who have offered to testify against criminal organizations have been intimidated because of the organization's reputation, and have been encouraged (through threats of violence) not to cooperate with the government. Clearly, this characteristic of organized crime units threatens many of the fundamentals of a free, civilized society.

According to the U.S. Department of Justice, for a criminal group to be considered an organized crime group, several variables must be present. It must have an organizational structure, it has to engage in a continuing criminal conspiracy, its underlying goal must be the generation of profits, and it must have sufficient continuity to carry out its purpose over a long period of time [22]. Groups that fit into this category include both foreign and domestic organizations.

Numerous similarities are evident between the groups discussed in Chapters 6, 7, and 8. They all have taken advantage of the burgeoning market for illegal drugs and the numerous international sources for those drugs. Other similarities include a common disrespect for the law, a willingness to use violence to further their individual group goals, and the use of corruption to aid them in achieving their criminal intentions. Individually, each organized crime group poses an individual threat to society and public order, but collectively they make up what is generally considered the true scope of organized crime in the twenty-first century.

■ ■ Critical Thinking Task ■

Hollywood occasionally produces films and programs about organized crime (e.g., *Bugsy, Casino, Donnie Brasco, The Godfather* trilogy, *Goodfellas, Scarface*, and HBO's *The Sopranos*). Evaluate the role that the entertainment industry plays in supporting organized crime.

The Alien Conspiracy Theory

The term *organized crime* tends to invoke images of men of foreign descent, steeped in feudal traditions and sharing a blind allegiance to the organization to which they belong. These images are what some criminologists have dubbed the *alien conspiracy theory* of organized crime. This theory holds that organized crime is a direct spin-off of a secret society: the Mafia, a criminal organization dating back to Sicily during the mid-1800s. The basic premise of the theory is that the Mafia is a single organization that is centrally coordinated through a national commission that arbitrates disputes and mandates policy [23].

There is considerable debate among scholars as to whether such a multinational organization actually exists, although some local, state, and federal law enforcement agencies are convinced of its existence, and base the formation of public organized crime policy on that premise. Disbelievers in the alien conspiracy theory argue that the Mafia is a figment of both the media's and law enforcement's imagination. They insist that organized crime consists of numerous ethnically diverse groups who compete for profits in the provision of illegal goods and services. Furthermore, they claim that these groups are not bound by a single, national organizational leadership, but act independently.

Supporters of the alien conspiracy theory conceive two organized crime contingencies: traditional organized crime (the Mafia) and nontraditional organized crime. The latter is organized crime groups that have emerged during the past two decades and have focused on the illegal drug trade as their major source of illegal revenue. They are largely made up of ethnic groups, including blacks, Hispanics, and Asians. The "The Mafia" section briefly discusses the alleged role of the Mafia as traditional organized crime participants in the drug trade, followed by a discussion of some emerging nontraditional drug-trafficking groups.

■ ■ Critical Thinking Task ■

Do you believe the Mafia exists, or is it merely a myth or an exaggerated stereotype? Support or refute your belief in the alien conspiracy theory.

The Mafia

At the core of the alien conspiracy theory is the traditional crime group known as *La Cosa Nostra* (Italian, meaning "this thing of ours") or, more commonly, the *Mafia*. Operating in different factions in both Sicily and the United States, the Mafia is thought to be composed of "crime families" in 24 or so major United States cities. It is estimated that although total membership is around 1,700 "made men" or "wise guys," the influence of the organization is much greater due to a vast network of associates who are not actual members. In 1986 the President's Commission on Organized Crime estimated that as many as 17,000 associates are criminally involved in the businesses of the "mob" [24].

Mafia crime families are believed to operate in geographically assigned areas around the United States. In New York City, for example, five families—Gambino, Colombo, Lucchese, Bonnano, and Genovese—operate, each named after their founding godfathers and each heavily involved in both illicit and legitimate businesses.

Most traditional crime families got their start during Prohibition (1920–1933) in the illegal liquor business. The Prohibition era created a multimillion-dollar bootlegging business following violent wars over territory and the control of illegal rackets. Today, believers of the alien conspiracy theory argue that the Mafia represents a highly sophisticated criminal network with a complex structure and chain of command emulated by many other new and emerging crime groups. Although not every Mafia family participates in the illicit drug trade, many do. For decades, the primary illicit drug sold by alleged Mafia members was heroin. Today, heroin is still worth an estimated $40 million per year to the organization, but trafficking in cocaine and marijuana has also been documented. In addition to drugs, Mafia families deal in loan sharking, illegal gambling operations, public corruption, money-laundering operations, and an array of legal business enterprises designed to cloak their criminal rackets [25].

In many cities, the nontraditional crime organizations, such as the Colombian cartels and the youth gangs, have rivaled the Mafia for territory. In some cases, drug territory has even been surrendered to the newer gangs, with drugs being viewed as too risky or competitive. In recent years, advocates of the alien conspiracy theory argue that the Mafia is still a strong criminal organization with criminal interests all over the world. However, they assert that a new breed of Mafioso is beginning to emerge. The new Mafiosi are more willing to inform on fellow Mafiosi, and seem to be more oriented toward individual gain than family organization. For example, in 1992, New York mob boss John Gotti was convicted after his underboss became a federal witness and offered damaging testimony regarding Gotti's role in the murder of former mob boss Paul Castellano.

Drug Gangs as Organized Crime

Criminal organizations concerned solely with drug trafficking share many of the same characteristics as more established organized crime. In the 1970s, a new kind of drug-trafficking organization began to emerge. Four fundamental factors can be seen as contributing to the genesis of organized crime organizations that differ structurally from their predecessors of the 1920s:

- Profound social, political, and economic changes in the drug-producing and drug-consuming nations combined to accelerate and intensify the spread of drugs.
- There was vastly increased mobility within and among consuming and producing nations, aided by cheap, readily available, international transportation. Immigration also greatly increased from South America and Asia to the United States.

FIGURE 7.2 Convicted crime boss John Gotti depicted by courtroom artist Marilyn Church as his life sentence is read in 1992. He died in prison in June 2002 of complications from head and neck cancer. *Source: AP Photo/ Marilyn Church.*

- In the opium-producing countries, many peasants and urban workers had surplus time for the kinds of work needed to sustain the drug traffic.
- In the consuming nations, old restrictions against many types of behavior, including drug taking, declined sharply.

All of these factors made possible a new kind of trafficking [26].

In attempting to understand these organizations as a whole, one should first recognize that no one drug-trafficking organization is "typical." Rather, many trafficking organizations follow a few well-defined patterns. Thus, several conditions exist that seem to lend cohesiveness to the modern-day drug-trafficking organization:

- *Vertical integration.* Vertical integration is illustrated by the major international trafficking groups, such as the Colombian cartels, and some domestic criminal groups, such as OMGs, that control both the manufacturing and wholesale distribution of drugs. Also, city-based operations such as the California street gangs, which concentrate on domestic distribution and retail sales, represent organizations with operations that are more directly linked to the end user than are the Colombian cartels or the motorcycle gangs.
- *Alternate sources of supply.* Among the various types of organizational structures and operational types, most have common distribution channels and operating methods. Many cocaine- and heroin-trafficking groups acquire illicit drugs outside the United States and from any of a number of sources. This principle was illustrated when the Turkish government clamped down on the illicit cultivation of opium poppies; drug organizations shifted their production to regions in the Golden Triangle in Southeast Asia and the Golden Crescent in Southwest Asia. Exceptions are marijuana and certain drugs made in domestic clandestine laboratories. Consequently, distribution channels are long and complicated. For instance, there are numerous links between the coca leaves grown and harvested in the Huallaga Valley of Peru and the destination of the finished product—often, a United States city.
- *Exploitation of social and political conditions.* Drug-trafficking organizations today demonstrate a willingness to capitalize on vulnerable social and national milieus. This occurs, for instance, in inner-city areas and even countries where labor markets are willing to take risks to partake in the huge profit potential offered by drug-trafficking operations. Generally, most players drawn into drug trafficking are expendable, provided that the leaders remain untouched. The leaders can then choose individuals from a large pool of unskilled labor. These individuals must be willing to take personal risks, and be able to learn one or two menial duties in the trafficking system. Traffickers have demonstrated that they can manipulate market conditions to make trafficking more profitable. In particular, the introduction of black tar heroin in the mid-1980s was a response to heroin shortages, whereas the change from cocaine hydrochloride to crack in the mid-1980s was also an effort to offer affordable cocaine to the nonaffluent drug user.

- *Insulation of leaders.* The organizational structure of a drug-trafficking group can be described as a solar system, with the leaders at the center. It is only these leaders (or *kingpins*) who see the organization as a whole. Trafficking leaders minimize any contact with drug buyers, or the drugs themselves, as a strategic effort to insulate themselves from governmental detection [27].

Although the four preceding operational variables help explain how drug-trafficking organizations function, they fail to explain adequately the tremendous growth of such groups. The growth of a particular organization can be partially attributed to the highly addictive qualities of some drugs such as heroin. This accounts, at least in part, for a certain degree of return business for many trafficking organizations. Here the drug users themselves effectively become sales representatives, or *ambassadors*, who work on behalf of the drug-trafficking organization by introducing drugs to new users. Additionally, drugs in powder form, such as heroin, can be much more easily transported (smuggled) than a bulkier commodity such as marijuana.

The political climate in foreign source countries also contributes to the growth of trafficking organizations. In many countries, the cultivation of raw materials for drugs is actually encouraged. Five of the most significant source countries—Mexico, Colombia, Ecuador, Peru, and Myanmar—are currently experiencing serious economic and political problems reflective of their move from conventional crops to coca, opium poppies, and marijuana crops; legitimate crops simply fail to provide incomes parallel to those realized by the illicit harvests.

■ ■ Critical Thinking Task ■

Applying your personal code of ethics, do you believe that the benefits of participating in organized crime outweigh the risks, or is the reverse true? Do you think you would ever be tempted to participate in organized crime?

The structure of today's drug-trafficking organizations poses serious tactical and investigative challenges to law enforcement officials. Additionally, significant public policy issues with regard to the law, personal freedoms, and priorities addressing the social order arise from investigations of drug-trafficking organizations. The volume of drugs entering the United States, the great number of trafficking organizations in existence, and the fact that methods of operation used by these groups can change so quickly dictate that unconventional approaches to detecting and prosecuting drug-related organized crime be considered by public officials.

Summary

To understand the many problems associated with the illicit drug trade, one must first comprehend what constitutes organized crime. Defining organized crime is no easy task, and there is no official definition of the term. According to researchers, certain characteristics are unique to the "criminal group" or members of the organized crime unit. Such characteristics include the provision of illicit goods or services; the arbitrary use of violence; the establishment of a code of conduct for members; the ability to corrupt public officials; and a recruitment strategy based on ethnic, racial, geographical, or kinship factors.

Those who belong to the criminal group are usually supported by individuals belonging to two other categories of criminals: the protectors and specialized support. The protectors are not full-fledged members of the group, but still work on behalf of the organization while appearing to be legitimate members of society. Protectors include accountants, attorneys, and government officials. The specialized support group also consists of individuals who are not official members of the organization, but who possess certain talents necessary for its success. They can be professionals such as pilots or chemists, or they can be enforcers (professional killers).

Modern-day gangs are in part distinguished from traditional organized crime organizations by their recent vintage. For instance, the genesis of groups such as the Jamaican posses, the California youth gangs, and the Colombian cocaine cartels occurred around 1970, when drug abuse began to flourish in the United States. Four characteristics unique to the emerging groups are vertical integration, the use of alternate sources of supply, a propensity to exploit social conditions to further the organization, and the insulation of leaders from street-level dealers.

Do you recognize these terms?

- alien conspiracy theory
- criminal group
- La Cosa Nostra
- Mafia
- organized crime
- outlaw motorcycle gangs

- prison gangs
- protectors
- specialized support
- support clubs
- street gangs
- vertical integration

Discussion Questions

1. Define the term *traditional organized crime*, and discuss how it pertains to the illicit drug trade.
2. Compare and contrast the differences and similarities between legitimate and illegal business enterprises.
3. Discuss the three kinds of gangs active in the United States, and differentiate their influence on the drug market.
4. Having examined organized crime's criminal and protector groups, discuss them, then compare them to the players in an organized crime support group.
5. What factors created the spawning of the new drug-trafficking groups during the early 1970s?
6. Discuss some of the more successful drug-trafficking organizations and how they have been able to manipulate the drug user market to improve profits.

7. List and discuss the four conditions that lend cohesiveness to the modern-day drug-trafficking organization.

8. Give examples of criminal drug-trafficking groups that may be considered vertically integrated.

Class Project

1. Research the historical roots of traditional organized crime groups in the United States. Compare their emergence to the emergence of today's drug-trafficking organizations.

References

[1] National Drug Intelligence Center (NDIC). (January 2009). *National gang threat assessment 2009.* Washington, DC: U.S. Department of Justice.
[2] Ibid.
[3] Bureau of Justice Statistics. (2009). *Indicators of school crime and safety.* Washington, DC: U.S. Department of Justice. Found at: http://bjs.ojp.usdoj.gov/content/pub/pdf/iscs09.pdf.
[4] National Gang Intelligence Center. (2012). *National Gang Assessment Center – 2011.* Washington, DC: Emerging Trends.
[5] Ibid.
[6] Ibid.
[7] National Drug Intelligence Center. (2008). *National-level gang-drug trafficking organization connections.* April, Washington, DC: U.S. Department of Justice.
[8] Ibid.
[9] National Drug Intelligence Center. (December 2008). *National drug threat assessment 2009.* Washington, DC: U.S. Department of Justice.
[10] Ibid.
[11] Ibid.
[12] Ibid.
[13] Ibid.
[14] Ibid.
[15] National Drug Intelligence Center. (January 2009). *National gang threat assessment 2009.* Washington, DC: U.S. Department of Justice.
[16] Ibid.
[17] Ibid.
[18] Ibid.
[19] President's Commission on Organized Crime. (1986). *The edge: Organized crime, business and labor unions.* Washington, DC: U.S. Government Printing Office.
[20] Ibid.
[21] Ibid.
[22] President's Commission on Organized Crime. (1986). *America's habit: Drug abuse, drug trafficking and organized crime.* Washington, DC: U.S. Government Printing Office.
[23] Cressey, D. (1969). *Theft of the nation.* New York: Harper and Row.
[24] President's Commission on Organized Crime. (1986). *The impact: Organized crime today.* Washington, DC: U.S. Government Printing Office.
[25] Ibid.
[26] President's Commission on Organized Crime. (1986). *The edge: Organized crime, business and labor unions.* Washington, DC: U.S. Government Printing Office.
[27] President's Commission on Organized Crime. (1985). *Organized crime and heroin trafficking.* Washington, DC: U.S. Government Printing Office.

8

Domestic Drug-Trafficking Organizations

This chapter will enable you to:

- Distinguish between traditional and nontraditional organized crime
- Learn about the origins of the criminal group known as the Mafia
- Understand the role of outlaw motorcycle gangs (OMGs) in the illegal drug trade
- Understand the role of youth gangs in the drug trade
- Learn the origins of prison gangs and their involvement in the illicit drug trade

The problem of organized crime in the United States is nothing new. In fact, it has been an American phenomenon for close to 100 years. The drug trade, however, has reshaped organized crime by creating new, violent, and more sophisticated criminal groups. Although these groups frequently clash with one another, increasingly more of them are learning to work together, as they did during Prohibition, to maximize profits and minimize their risk of detection. This chapter examines some of the largest and most active organized crime groups in the domestic illicit drug trade.

Traditional Organized Crime: The Mafia

As discussed in Chapter 7, the Mafia, or La Cosa Nostra (LCN), has been a source of controversy in criminology and law enforcement in the United States for more than 80 years. Because its roots are in Italy and Sicily, where they were founded in the mid-1800s, this group could very well be discussed in Chapter 9, which deals with foreign trafficking organizations; however, because some argue that the Mafia plays such a significant role in criminality in the United States and because a great number of its alleged members are American citizens, the Mafia is commonly referred to as a *domestic* criminal organization. Today, two factions of traditional organized crime operate in the United States: the alleged American Mafia (also called the Italian Mafia or Italian-American Syndicate) and the Sicilian Mafia.

The Mafia's History

The Sicilian Mafia has established itself as Italy's premier criminal group through corruption, assassination, extortion, and manipulation. Its criminal influence reaches around the globe, with particular strength in Western Europe, North America, and South America. Sicily is an island located off the southwestern coast of Italy, and it is the main region of influence of the Sicilian Mafia. This area, known as the *mezzogiorno*, is a territory claimed by another powerful Italian organized crime group, the Camorra.

The Camorra has a lengthy history as a prison gang originating in Italy. Spanish kings ruled Naples and Sicily between the years 1504 and 1707, and again between 1738 and 1860. The Camorra was organized during the first Spanish reign. The Sicilian Mafia, which was considered the most powerful criminal organization during the eighteenth and nineteenth centuries, was formed during the second reign. The Camorra and the Sicilian Mafia shared similar traits:

- Each existed by selling criminal services to either individuals or corrupt members of the government.
- Each had a formal organizational structure: the Camorra was organized into brigades, or *brigata*, while the Sicilian Mafia was organized into *families*.
- Each (1) had a strict code of silence, or *omerta*, that dictated that family members never cooperate with government officials; and (2) instituted the *vendetta*, a code of retribution against anyone that in any way attacked or insulted a member of the family.

The word *Mafia* appeared for the first time in a newspaper in November 1860, when it was acknowledged that a Camorra group had established itself in the general area of Palermo, Sicily. In 1878, Giuseppe Esposito, a Sicilian Mafioso, was credited as being the first Sicilian Mafia member to relocate, along with six others, to the United States. Upon arrival in New York, Esposito and his men not only found the United States hostile to non-English-speaking immigrants, but also they witnessed a criminal underworld dominated by Irish and Jewish groups. Consequently, Esposito moved to New Orleans with his Sicilian entourage, where he organized and headed the flourishing Sicilian Mafia. After being arrested in 1881 by New Orleans Police Chief David Hennessey on an outstanding Italian fugitive warrant, Esposito was transported to New York and then extradited back to Italy.

Joseph Macheca, an American-born member of the organization, succeeded Esposito as crime boss of New Orleans. He soon began reinforcing the numbers of the New Orleans Mafia with new immigrants from Sicily, a practice commonly used by the American Mafia over the years. In 1890, David Hennessey was assassinated; 10 members of the Macheca crime family were charged with the murder. After a lengthy trial, all were acquitted amidst claims of jury tampering. The acquittals created public outrage, and an angry crowd stormed Parish Prison, where 19 Sicilian prisoners were housed. The ensuing carnage resulted in the largest lynching in history—16 prisoners were murdered. Some were shot, and many were hanged from the city's lampposts. However, this violence failed to prevent the rise of the Mafia in New Orleans. Indeed, as the turn of the twentieth century approached, other Sicilian Mafia families formed around the United States in cities such as San Francisco, St. Louis, Chicago, New York, and Boston.

The Prohibition era, which lasted from 1920 to 1933, was probably the single most influential factor in providing up-and-coming Mafia families with what they needed most: enough money to infiltrate legitimate business. Such capital would make their illicit enterprises more difficult to detect, and would give the Mafiosi an aura of public respectability. During this time, some of the more notorious Mafiosi were arriving in the United States. Carlo Gambino, Joe Profaci, Joe Magliocco, Mike Coppola, and Salvatore Maranzano joined the likes of Joe (Joe Bananas) Bonanno and Charles (Lucky) Luciano. During the 1930s, Luciano and other Italian organized crime bosses solidified their base of operation, which some believe grew into a national organization that now occupies 24 American cities with close to 2,000 members. One of the most important developments during the 1930s was the formation of a national Mafia alliance, or *commission*, whereby heads of some of the most influential Mafia families would meet to divide territory, choose rackets, approve new members, and arbitrate disputes between families.

The Mafia and the Drug Trade

During the late 1960s and early 1970s, France became well known as a distribution point for an estimated 80 percent of the world's heroin. Marseilles became the center of heroin laboratories that processed raw opium brought in from Turkey. Heroin was then smuggled into the United States by French Corsicans as well as Sicilian Mafia members (the "French Connection"). In the early 1970s, the French Connection was broken up as a result of a joint investigative effort by American and French authorities. Today, France is no longer considered a major producer of heroin sold on the United States market.

In 1986, the President's Commission on Organized Crime stated that "heroin is the biggest moneymaker for the Mafia." It is thought that since the collapse of the French Connection, Italy and Sicily became distribution points for heroin. Intelligence sources also indicated that French chemists assumed their traditional role of converting raw opium into heroin. The opium is transported from sources in the eastern Mediterranean countries of Syria, Lebanon, Pakistan, and Jordan. The Sicilian Mafia controls the transshipment of heroin through Italy to the United States from both Southwest Asia and Southeast Asia (see Chapter 4). Methods of smuggling by the Sicilian Mafia have included members or associates traveling by air and wearing body packs of 2–3 kg of heroin, as well as hiding heroin in toys, statues, wheels of provolone cheese, film canisters, coffee machines, dry cell batteries, cans of baby powder, electronic appliances, mail, and clothing.

The Pizza Connection

The investigation that revealed the extent to which the Sicilian Mafia operated in the United States is popularly known as the *Pizza Connection*. The Pizza Connection was a massive operation involving heroin smuggling and money laundering by Sicilian Mafia members operating in the United States, and it was headed by Sicilian crime boss Gaetano Badalamente. Through the aid of crime-boss-turned-witness Tommaso Buscetta, arrests stemming from the Pizza Connection were made possible.

The operation ultimately led to the 1984 indictments in New York of 35 alleged members of the Sicilian Mafia. The investigation revealed that between 1982 and 1983, the Sicilian

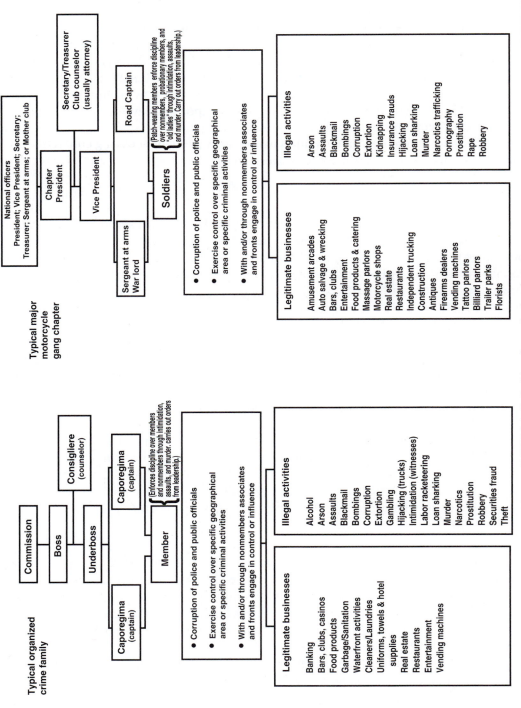

Typical organized crime family

Commission

Boss

Underboss

Consigliere
(counselor)

Caporegima
(captain)

Caporegima
(captain)

Member

{Enforces discipline over members
and nonmembers through intimidation,
assaults, and murder; carries out orders
from leadership.}

• Corruption of police and public officials
• Exercise control over specific geographical
  area or specific criminal activities
• With and/or through nonmembers associates
  and fronts engage in control or influence

Legitimate businesses

Banking
Bars, clubs, casinos
Food products
Garbage/Sanitation
Waterfront activities
Cleaners/Laundries
Uniforms, towels & hotel
  supplies
Real estate
Restaurants
Entertainment
Vending machines

Illegal activities

Alcohol
Arson
Assaults
Blackmail
Bombings
Corruption
Extortion
Gambling
Hijacking (trucks)
Intimidation (witnesses)
Labor racketeering
Loan sharking
Murder
Narcotics
Prostitution
Robbery
Securities fraud
Theft

Typical major motorcycle gang chapter

National officers
President; Vice President; Secretary;
Treasurer; Sergeant at arms; or Mother club

Secretary/Treasurer
Club counselor
(usually attorney)

Chapter
President

Vice President

Road Captain

Sergeant at arms
War lord

Soldiers

(Patch-wearing members enforce discipline
over nonmembers, probationary members, and
"old ladies" through intimidation, assaults,
and murder. Carry out orders from leadership.)

• Corruption of police and public officials
• Exercise control over specific geographical
  area or specific criminal activities
• With and/or through nonmembers associates
  and fronts engage in control or influence

Legitimate businesses

Amusement arcades
Auto salvage & wrecking
Bars, clubs
Entertainment
Food products & catering
Massage parlors
Motorcycle shops
Real estate
Restaurants
Independent trucking
Construction
Antiques
Firearms dealers
Vending machines
Tattoo parlors
Billiard parlors
Trailer parks
Florists

Illegal activities

Arson
Assaults
Blackmail
Bombings
Corruption
Extortion
Kidnapping
Insurance frauds
Hijacking
Loan sharking
Murder
Narcotics trafficking
Pornography
Prostitution
Rape
Robbery

FIGURE 8.1 Similarities of organizational structure.

Mafia had scheduled 1.5 tons of heroin with an estimated wholesale value of $333 million for importation to New York. In addition, between 1980 and 1983, the New York Sicilian Mafia was reported to have shipped in excess of $40 million in cash from New York to Sicily via Switzerland.

The breadth of the investigation expanded worldwide, with Mafia members identified in such countries as Brazil, Canada, Spain, Switzerland, Italy, and the United States. So vast was the investigation that it took federal prosecutors one full year to try the case. Ultimately, the trial turned out to be the most costly and lengthy criminal proceeding in United States history, but it proved rewarding by securing convictions for all but two of the defendants. Those convicted received lengthy sentences. As a result of the information produced at this trial, some argued that not enough was being done to fight drug trafficking. Columnist Shana Alexander stated, "[The case] did not make the slightest dent in the nation's desperate drug problem. More heroin and cocaine are on the streets today than before 'Pizza' began. The trial severely overtaxed every branch of the Italian legal system law enforcement, bench, and bar and taxed unfortunate jurors worst of all" [1].

Testimony revealed that one member of the Sicilian Mafia operating in the United States, Salvatore Salamone, was entrusted with the job of changing small-denomination bills to large-denomination bills and transporting the money in suitcases overseas. Once the money arrived in Switzerland, several other individuals converted the bills into Swiss francs and then to Italian lira for delivery to Sicily. The Pizza Connection illustrates a working relationship between Sicilian and United States-based Mafia operatives and their "common interests" in drug trafficking and money laundering. Each organization needed the other, and the relationship was established on a basis of mutual trust and respect. In 1987, the FBI observed the following:

- The Sicilian Mafia operates in the United States as a separate criminal organization specializing in heroin smuggling. The first allegiance of its members is to the "family" in Sicily.
- Before initiating a major heroin-smuggling operation, the Sicilian Mafia obtains the sanction of certain American Mafia families.
- As payment to the American Mafia family that grants its sanction for the operation, the Sicilian Mafia pays the American Mafia family up to $5,000 per kilogram of heroin brought into the United States.

The number of Sicilian Mafiosi operating in the United States is hard to predict. They are, however, thought to concentrate in the northeastern United States, principally in New York City and New Jersey, and are thought to operate without geographical jurisdictions.

The Mafia Wars

Over the decades, Italy's Mafia has undergone several periods of severe repression by police authorities. For example, in the 1920s, Mussolini attempted to purge LCN from the island of Sicily, which resulted in many members migrating to the United States seeking safe havens in United States-based families. Many of these refugees later became formidable bosses of the most influential crime families in the nation.

During the early 1980s, Italy experienced an increase in violence among members of the estimated 20 Mafia families operating in and around Palermo. The violence resulted in the murders of mobsters, police officers, judges, and politicians in what was dubbed the "heroin wars." The central government of Italy has since taken initiatives toward controlling Mafia-related criminal activity. These initiatives include anti-Mafia legislation enacted on September 11, 1982, which features these measures:

- "Association" with known Mafia types is illegal, whether a crime is committed or not.
- "Association" also applies to the Camorra and other "Mafia-type" groups.
- "Exile" locations for convicted Mafiosi have been established in towns with populations of fewer than 10,000, and an unauthorized exit of the location shall result in imprisonment.
- Property and other assets are subject to confiscation.
- Telephone wiretaps are authorized on persons suspected of belonging to "Mafia-type" organizations.
- The term *omerta* is defined in its most negative connotation as a "conduct of noncooperation with public safety officials due to fear" [2].

The implementation of this law resulted in the 1984 arrests of more than 450 suspected Mafiosi and the subsequent trial that has become known as the Maxi-Processo (maxitrial). The arrests, which are considered the greatest Mafia crackdown since Mussolini's 1920s Mafia purge, resulted from a 40-volume, 8,632-page indictment that outlined more than 90 murders, countless kidnappings, and even the use of torture chambers. Additionally, the indictment included charges of heroin smuggling and money laundering for Mafia members. In spite of all the media fanfare over the Mafia trials, it now appears they were little more than just show trials, for the Mafia continues to operate with virtual impunity in Italy and Sicily.

The Mafia Controversy

While there is a substantial body of opinion arguing that LCN, or the Mafia, is the dominant organized crime group in the United States and plays a major role in drug trafficking, considerable controversy surrounds what this organization actually is and what it actually does. Many scholars and law enforcement officials have come to doubt the view presented by the FBI and other federal agencies that it is a hegemonic Italian organized crime syndicate. They argue that the evidence to support the existence of such a group is weak and open to other interpretations, and that empirical research has failed to confirm the existence of such a dominant, complex, hierarchically organized criminal group.

Criticisms of the Mafia model fall into two distinct categories: (1) the historical evidence is sometimes weak and contradictory; and (2) empirical research conducted on organized crime fails to demonstrate the existence of the Mafia as a single criminal conspiracy, and there are alternative models of organized crime that explain the reality of criminal entrepreneurship. To this list, we will add a third criticism: the evidence of LCN or Mafia "domination" of the drug trade is fragmentary and debatable.

Historical Controversies

Anthropological, historical, and social studies of the Sicilian Mafia, such as those conducted by Henner Hess and Anton Blok, have failed to turn up evidence of a single criminal organization [3,4]. Rather, the studies point strongly to a series of localized village-based organizations, which were primarily created to protect the interests of absentee landlords and foreign invaders. These organizations formed a kind of "shadow government" in Sicily, meting out justice, controlling jobs, and providing for social control in an unstable society. Although the Mafia may have had its origins in such a rural ruling class, it is not the same Mafia proposed by conspiracy theorists.

In addition, evidence relating to Italians' importation of organized crime to the United States is open to similar questions. For example, proponents of the Mafia theory cannot tell us how it is that Italian immigration brought this criminal organization to the United States while similar waves of Italian immigration did not bring the same organization to England, Australia, and other nations.

Supporters of the Mafia model have failed to account for organized crime's existence in the United States long before the inception of Italian immigration. Further, proponents of the Mafia model must engage in considerable factual acrobatics to account for non-Italian figures who appear to have been dominant forces in the history of American organized crime—men like Arnold Rothstein, Meyer Lansky, Abner "Longie" Zwillman, Benjamin "Bugsy" Siegel, George "Bugs" Moran, Dutch Schultz (Arthur Flegenheimer), Owen "Owney" Madden, and dozens of others. Finally, specific historical "facts" presented by proponents of the Mafia model appear weak under close scrutiny. The Mafia's 1890 assassination of Police Chief David Hennessey is a prime example. Was Hennessey killed by the Mafia? Or was the Mafia concept created, as Dwight Smith Jr. suggested, to justify the "lynching" of innocent immigrants [5]? The fact is that the New Orleans grand jury failed to turn up any evidence of an Italian conspiracy, and the courts failed to convict any of the defendants. Similarly, questions have been raised about other proofs offered for the Mafia model.

Research on Organized Crime

Far more significant to this discussion, however, is the failure of empirical research on alleged LCN families to substantiate the model proposed by the federal government. For example, Francis A.J. Ianni's study of an LCN family in New York suggested that the only organizational arrangement was one of an extended family [6]. For Ianni, kinship became the prime variable in explaining how and why Italian Americans worked together in both legal and illegal businesses. He found no evidence of an interconnected, national Italian-American crime syndicate [7]. Joseph Albini's study of organized crime in Detroit also failed to confirm the existence of a monolithic crime structure [8]. Albini reviewed historical documents and journalistic accounts, interviewed both law enforcement officials and participants in organized crime operations, and concluded that organized crime was based on a series of loosely constructed "patron–client relations," not on a massive criminal conspiracy [9].

Other studies, such as the one conducted by William Chambliss, focused on organized crime in Seattle and found a syndicate composed of local political and business leaders, leading Chambliss to argue that "organized crime" was a misnomer and that the study of official corruption would be more revealing in describing criminal syndicates [10]. In addition, Mark Haller's study of organized crime operations in Chicago, New York, and Florida concluded that rather than being dominated by a tightly organized criminal conspiracy, organized crime was a series of complex and often overlapping business partnerships in illicit enterprise [11].

Peter Reuter's exhaustive study of the gambling and loan-sharking industries in New York City failed to turn up either LCN domination or even widespread participation in those industries [12]. Reuter argued that if the Mafia existed at all, it was a "paper tiger" living off its popular reputation, which was fueled by journalistic and law enforcement speculation [13]. Finally, a study of organized crime in Philadelphia revealed that not only did the Mafia not dominate organized crime in the past (at best, its alleged members were functionaries of other, very large criminal syndicates), but also the alleged LCN in that city. Additional studies by Alan Block, John Gardiner, Virgil Peterson, Jay Albanese, and many others have served to dispute the theory of any dominant role of LCN [14,15].

Although some law enforcement officials tenaciously cling to the view of LCN as a single, massive criminal conspiracy, others have moved away from that position. The Pennsylvania Crime Commission, for example, has been quite active in exploring the role of other organized crime groups, particularly black crime groups and motorcycle gangs, in drug trafficking and other illicit business ventures. Potter and Jenkins (1985), in their study of organized crime in Philadelphia, identified black gangs, Greek-American gangs, the Irish K & A gang, and motorcycle gangs as more important in drug trafficking than traditional Italian-American groups [16].

There is little doubt that some individuals linked with Italian-dominated criminal organizations in both the United States and Sicily have been involved in large-scale drug trafficking, as we have seen in the case of the Pizza Connection. However, one should be cautious in attributing any degree of hegemony to these groups in the drug market. Drug trafficking is conducted by thousands of different criminal organizations, many of which are complex and quite large compared to LCN groups. Despite many successful Mafia-related drug investigations, the focus on the Mafia or LCN has tended to distort the perception of organized crime's role in drugs. For example, it ignores the vital role played by organizations headed by Frank Matthews, Nicky Barnes, Jeff Fort, and other crime figures. It also ignores the role of non-Italians, such as Meyer Lansky and Nig Rosen, who played the major coordinating role in the infamous French Connection. Finally, it ignores the major role in the organization of drug trafficking played by some truly pioneering organized crime figures, such as Arnold Rothstein, Happy Meltzer, "Dopey" Bennie Fein, and others. The role of the Mafia must be kept in perspective, and the roles of other major drug-trafficking groups must be given attention.

Outlaw Motorcycle Gangs

OMGs are organizations whose members use their motorcycle clubs as conduits for criminal enterprises. OMGs are highly structured criminal organizations whose members engage in criminal activities such as violent crime, weapons trafficking, and drug trafficking. There are more than 300 active OMGs within the United States, ranging in size from single chapters with five or six members to hundreds of chapters with thousands of members worldwide. The Hells Angels, Mongols, Bandidos, Outlaws, and Sons of Silence pose a serious national domestic threat and conduct the majority of criminal activity linked to OMGs, especially activity relating to drug trafficking and, more specifically, cross-border drug smuggling. Because of their transnational scope, these OMGs are able to coordinate drug-smuggling operations in partnership with major international drug-trafficking organizations.

Bandidos Motorcycle Club

The Bandidos Motorcycle Club (Bandidos) is an OMG with a membership of 2000–2500 persons in the United States and 13 other countries; in the United States, approximately 900 members belong to 93 chapters. The Bandidos constitute a growing criminal threat to the United States, and law enforcement authorities estimate that the Bandidos are one of the two largest OMGs operating in the United States. The Bandidos are involved in transporting and distributing cocaine and marijuana, and are involved in the production, transportation, and distribution of methamphetamine. The Bandidos are most active in the Pacific, southeastern, southwestern, and west central regions of the United States. The Bandidos are expanding in each of these regions by forming additional chapters and allowing members of supporting clubs—known as "puppet" or "duck" club members, who have sworn allegiance to another club but who support and do the "dirty work" of a mother club—to form new or join existing Bandidos chapters.

Black Pistons Motorcycle Club

The Black Pistons Motorcycle Club (Black Pistons) is the official support club for the Outlaws Motorcycle Club (Outlaws). Established in 2002 with the backing of the Outlaws, the Black Pistons have expanded rapidly throughout the United States, Canada, and Europe. The Black Pistons have an estimated 70 domestic chapters in 20 states, and an unknown number of foreign chapters in Belgium, Canada, Germany, Great Britain, Norway, and

Poland. The exact number of Black Pistons members is unknown, but the figure is estimated to be more than 200 in the United States. The Outlaws use the Black Pistons chapters as a recruitment source for prospective Outlaws members. The Outlaws also use the Black Pistons chapters to conduct criminal activity, especially for the transportation and distribution of drugs. Members of the Black Pistons are also known to engage in assault, extortion, fraud, intimidation, and theft.

Hells Angels Motorcycle Club

The Hells Angels Motorcycle Club (Hells Angels) is an OMG with between 2000 and 2500 members who belong to more than 230 chapters in the United States and 26 foreign countries. The Hells Angels pose a criminal threat on six continents. United States law enforcement authorities estimate that, domestically, the Hells Angels have more than 92 chapters in 27 states, with a membership in excess of 800 persons. The group is involved in the production, transportation, and distribution of marijuana and methamphetamine, as well as the transportation and distribution of cocaine, hashish, heroin, LSD (lysergic acid diethylamide), ecstasy, PCP (phencyclidine), and diverted pharmaceuticals. The Hells Angels are also involved in other criminal activity, including assault, extortion, homicide, money laundering, and motorcycle theft.

Mongols Motorcycle Club

The Mongols Motorcycle Club (Mongols) is an extremely violent OMG that poses a serious criminal threat to the Pacific and Southwestern regions of the United States. The Mongols are engaged in the transportation and distribution of cocaine, marijuana, and methamphetamine. The Mongols are also known to commit violent crime, frequently including assault, intimidation, and murder, in defense of their territory and to uphold the reputation of the club. A majority of the Mongols membership consists of Latino males who live in the Los Angeles area, and many are former street gang members with a long history of using violence to settle grievances. Agents with the Bureau of Alcohol, Tobacco, Firearms, and Explosives (ATF) have called the Mongols the most violent and dangerous OMG in the nation. In the 1980s, the Mongols seized control of southern California from the Hells Angels; today, the Mongols are allied with the Bandidos, the Outlaws, the Sons of Silence, and the Pagans against the Hells Angels. The Mongols have also maintained their ties with Latino street gangs in Los Angeles.

Outlaws Motorcycle Club

The Outlaws Motorcycle Club (Outlaws) has more than 1700 members who belong to 176 chapters in the United States and 12 foreign countries. United States law enforcement authorities estimate that, domestically, the Outlaws have more than 86 chapters in 20 states with more than 700 members. The Outlaws also identify themselves as the

FIGURE 8.2 U.S. Attorney Thomas P. O'Brien speaks during a news conference in Los Angeles in 2008. Dozens of Mongol motorcycle gang members were arrested by federal agents in six states, including Washington, on warrants ranging from drug sales to murder after a 3-year undercover investigation in which four agents successfully infiltrated the group. *Source: AP Photo/Ric Francis.*

A.O.A. (American Outlaws Association) and the Outlaws Nation. The Outlaws are the dominant OMG in the Great Lakes region. They are involved in the production, transportation, and distribution of methamphetamine, and the transportation and distribution of cocaine, marijuana, and, to a lesser extent, ecstasy. The Outlaws engage in various criminal activities, including arson, assault, explosives, extortion, fraud, homicide, intimidation, kidnapping, money laundering, prostitution, robbery, theft, and weapons violations. The Outlaws compete with the Hells Angels for both members and territory.

Pagans Motorcycle Club

The Pagans Motorcycle Club (Pagans) is a violent OMG whose membership distributes cocaine, methamphetamine, marijuana, and PCP. The Pagans are one of the most prominent OMGs in the Mid-Atlantic region. The Pagans have an estimated 200–250 members among 41 chapters in 11 states. The Pagans have been tied to traditional organized crime groups in Philadelphia, Pittsburgh, and New York, and have engaged in criminal activities such as arson, assault, bombing, extortion, and murder.

Sons of Silence

The Sons of Silence Motorcycle Club (SOSMC) is one of the largest OMGs in the United States, with 250–275 members among 30 chapters in 12 states. The club also has five chapters in Germany. SOSMC members have been implicated in numerous criminal activities, including murder, assault, drug trafficking, intimidation, extortion, prostitution operations, money laundering, weapons trafficking, and motorcycle and motorcycle parts theft.

Vagos Motorcycle Club

The Vagos Motorcycle Club (Vagos) has hundreds of members in the United States and Mexico and poses a serious criminal threat to those areas in which its chapters are located. United States law enforcement authorities report that the Vagos have approximately 300 members among 24 chapters located in the states of California, Hawaii, Nevada, and Oregon, and three chapters located in Mexico. The Vagos produce, transport, and distribute methamphetamine, and are also involved in the distribution of marijuana. The Vagos have also been implicated in other criminal activities, including assault, extortion, insurance fraud, money laundering, murder, vehicle theft, witness intimidation, and weapons violations. In the United States, the Vagos are mainly active in the Southwest and Pacific regions.

■ ■ Critical Thinking Task ■

Suggest creative methods by which society can protect itself from organized crime, both traditional and nontraditional.

Special Youth Gang Problems

Police experience great difficulty in monitoring and controlling youth gangs. Undercover agents are more effective in targeting adult gangs than youth gangs, because most youth gang recruiters know their recruits from the neighborhood. Additionally, a youthful gang member is dealt with in a considerably more lenient fashion by the juvenile justice system than is his or her adult counterpart in the adult justice system. One factor making it hard for police to estimate the number of gang members is difficulty in determining the status of a possible member. For example, a hardcore leader is commonly called an *original gangster*, while a part-timer and would-be member is called a *wannabe*. Confusing the matter is the varied ethnic composition of youth gangs. In 1989, a U.S. Justice Department survey estimated that about 50 percent of the nation's youth gang members are black, 35 percent are Latino, and the rest are white or Asian [17]. Another problem with most youth gangs is difficulty in determining whether a particular assault, robbery, or murder was committed by an individual who happened to belong to a gang, or by a gang member furthering the gang's objectives.

Asian gangs, one of the fastest-growing segments of ethnic gangs, are posing special problems for authorities. Language and cultural barriers in particular make investigation of these gangs difficult. In addition, Chinese, Vietnamese, Laotian, and Cambodian gangs have a fluid membership and are highly mobile. A new trend of the Asian gangs over the past 20 years is the *home invasion*. Home invasions against Asian nationals have resulted in many rapes, robberies, beatings, and shootings of innocent people. Most of the violence occurs when valuables are not readily surrendered. Victims of home invasions are often distrustful of the criminal justice system, and many times are reluctant to report the crimes for fear of retaliation.

Police departments respond in different ways to the gang problem and have adopted various approaches. In Chicago, special gang units exist with as many as 400 officers, compared to other large cities such as New York and Philadelphia that designate fewer than 10 officers as gang specialists. The creation of such units can cause controversy within the community. For example, some critics argue that a police department that recognizes a gang problem in the community may do so to justify a greater operational budget. Accordingly, members of the community may become unrealistically fearful of the gang problem. On the other hand, police departments that fail to recognize a gang problem in light of mounting evidence may not be adequately serving the needs and best interests of the community.

■ ■ Critical Thinking Task ■

Place yourself in the position of a youth gang member. Describe what would have to happen to induce you to leave the gang.

In the 1950s and 1960s, the typical police approach to gangs was intervention. That is, officers encouraged youths not to join gangs or employed social service agencies to work with gang members themselves. During the 1970s and 1980s, most police departments used a suppression policy that focused on identifying gangs and arresting their members. It is unclear which, if either, method worked. Today, debate still exists about which approach is more effective.

Defining the Youth Gang

A major problem in the study of youth gangs is the lack of consensus as to what defines a youth gang. Is it correct to refer to any congregation of youths as a gang? Many law enforcement agencies use the term narrowly to refer to a group of delinquents who hold and defend self-claimed territory, or *turf*. Sociologist Frederick Thrasher, in his pioneering study, attempted to define the term *youth gang*:

> *A gang is an interstitial group originally formed spontaneously and then integrated through conflict. It is characterized by the following types of behavior: meeting face-to-face, milling, movement through space as a unit, conflict, and planning. The result of this collective behavior is the development of tradition, unreflective internal structure, esprit de corps, solidarity, morale, group awareness, and attachment to local territory* [18].

This definition, first appearing in 1927, still captures the essence of group cohesiveness that remains the prevailing characteristic of many gangs. Yet another behavioral scientist, Malcolm Klein, offered a more recent description of a youth gang, which includes the element of danger:

> *Any denotable group of youngsters who (1) are generally perceived as a distinct aggregation by others in their neighborhood; (2) recognize themselves as a denotable group (almost invariably with a group name); and (3) have been involved in a sufficient number of delinquent incidents to call forth a consistent negative response from neighborhood residents and/or law enforcement agencies* [19].

Another prominent sociologist, Lewis Yablonsky, made an important contribution to the understanding of the youth gang with his definition of a *near group*. According to Yablonsky, human collectives tend to range from highly cohesive, tight-knit organizations to mobs with anonymous members who are motivated by their emotions and led by disturbed membership [20]. Teenage gangs fall somewhere in between, and are therefore categorized as near groups. Near groups have the following traits:

- Diffuse role definition
- Limited cohesion
- Impermanence
- Minimal consensus norms
- Shifting membership
- Disturbed leadership
- Limited definition of membership expectations [21]

Gang Formation

Unlike legitimate businesses, organized crime groups such as youth gangs do not have employment recruiting drives. In many inner-city areas, programs such as Little League baseball are nonexistent, leaving gangs as the only membership option for many. Typically, social scientists have suggested that gangs appeal to kids in areas marked by poverty, racial strife, broken families, and limited job and educational opportunities. In fact, that premise is widely supported by media accounts and scholars alike. Experts have suggested that when minority youths do not have jobs or an education, they attempt to demonstrate their power in other ways. The gang represents a means whereby members can feel they are a part of something. This is not to suggest, however, that gangs do not exist among the American middle class—they do.

Historically, gang formation has been closely linked with surges in immigration. With many such groups, especially those with strong language and cultural barriers, well-paying jobs were nonexistent. In other cases, social prejudice made it difficult for immigrants to secure jobs and earn a respectable living. Essentially, ethnic groups who found themselves at the bottom of the social ladder were more likely to end up involved in gang activity.

Youth gangs of various ethnic origins have been a nuisance throughout United States history. In fact, Benjamin Franklin lamented the trouble caused by youth gangs in pre–Revolutionary War Philadelphia. However, only since the early to mid-1980s have youth gangs become violent and well established in most major United States cities.

Prison Gangs

Prison gangs are criminal organizations that originated within the penal system, and they have continued to operate within correctional facilities throughout the United States. Prison gangs are also self-perpetuating criminal entities that can continue their operations outside the confines of the penal system. Typically, a prison gang consists of a select group of inmates who have an organized hierarchy and are governed by an established code of conduct. Prison gangs vary in both organization and composition, from highly structured gangs such as the Aryan Brotherhood (AB) and Nuestra Familia, to gangs with a less formalized structure such as the California-based Latino prison gang the Mexican Mafia (La Eme). Prison gangs generally have fewer members than street gangs and OMGs, and are structured along racial or ethnic lines. Nationally, prison gangs pose a threat because of their role in the transportation and distribution of narcotics. Prison gangs are also an important link between drug-trafficking organizations, street gangs, and OMGs, often brokering the transfer of drugs from drug traffickers to gangs in many regions. Prison gangs typically are more powerful within state correctional facilities than they are within the federal penal system.

Aryan Brotherhood

The AB was originally ruled by consensus, but is now a highly structured entity with two factions, one located within the California Department of Corrections (CDC) and the other within the Federal Bureau of Prisons (BOP). The majority of the members of the AB are Caucasian males, and the gang is primarily active in the Southwestern and Pacific regions of the United States. The main source of income for the AB is derived from the distribution of cocaine, heroin, marijuana, and methamphetamine within the prison systems as well as on the street. Some AB members have established business relationships with Mexican traffickers that smuggle illegal drugs into California for distribution by the AB. The AB is notoriously violent and is frequently involved in murder for hire. Although the AB is historically linked to the Mexican Mafia, tension between the AB and La Eme is becoming increasingly evident, as demonstrated by recent fights between Caucasians and Latinos within the CDC.

Barrio Azteca

The Barrio Azteca is one of the most violent prison gangs operating within the United States. Barrio Azteca is a highly structured criminal entity and has an estimated membership of 2,000 persons. Most members of the Barrio Azteca are either Mexican nationals or Mexican-American males. Barrio Azteca is most active in the southwestern region of the United States, primarily in federal, state, and local correctional facilities in Texas, as well as outside prison in communities located in southwestern Texas and southeastern New Mexico. Barrio Azteca's main source of income is derived from the smuggling of heroin, powdered cocaine, and marijuana from Mexico into the United States for distribution both inside and outside the prison systems. Members of the Barrio Azteca often transport illicit drugs across the United States–Mexico border on behalf of drug traffickers [22]. Barrio Azteca members are also involved in crimes such as alien smuggling, arson, assault, auto theft, burglary, extortion, intimidation, kidnapping, robbery, and weapons violations.

Black Guerrilla Family

The Black Guerrilla Family (BGF), originally called the Black Family or the Black Vanguard, is a prison gang founded in 1966 at the San Quentin State Prison in California. The BGF is highly organized along paramilitary lines with a supreme leader and a central committee. BGF has an established national charter, a code of ethics, and an oath of allegiance. BGF members operate primarily in the states of California and Maryland. BGF has approximately 100–300 members, a majority of whom are African-American males. A primary source of income for the BGF is derived from the distribution of cocaine and marijuana. BGF members obtain drugs primarily from Nuestra Familia and Norteño members, or from local Mexican drug traffickers. BGF members are also involved in other criminal activities, including auto theft, burglary, drive-by shooting, and homicide [23].

Dead Man Incorporated

Dead Man Incorporated (DMI) is a violent prison gang that originated in the 1980s with three prison inmates. DMI operates primarily in the Maryland Division of Corrections (MDOC), where gang membership is estimated to be more than 370 members, consisting of predominantly white males. In 2006, leadership within the MDOC gave the go-ahead to a DMI member to begin recruiting in Virginia. The DMI member then assaulted a law enforcement official to ensure his incarceration and ability to begin recruiting DMI membership in the Virginia prison system. The main source of income for DMI gang members is committing murder for hire, acts of intimidation and violence, and drug distribution.

The Four Horsemen, Tangos, and Tango Blast

Texas prison officials first noted the presence of a gang known as the Four Horsemen in 1998. Some Latino gang members entering the Texas Department of Criminal Justice (TDCJ) from the cities of Austin, Dallas, Fort Worth, and Houston were not interested in joining an established prison gang and established the Four Horsemen to protect one another and to engage in illegal activities, particularly drug trafficking, to make money. The Four Horsemen became known as the Tangos, because its members wore tattoos that reflected the town (or tango) in which they resided prior to their incarceration. As interest in the Tangos grew among Latino gang members entering the TDCJ from other areas of Texas, only inmates from west Texas, the Rio Grande Valley, San Antonio, and El Paso were allowed into the gang. Of the eight groups now recognized as Tangos, six are part of what is now known as Tango Blast or Puro Tango Blast. Tango Blast includes Tangos from these four cities as well as the west Texas and Rio Grande Valley areas. Tango Blast differs from the Tangos in that separate Tango Blast members sometimes band together to help one another. The rapid growth of Tango Blast poses a significant new security threat within the TDCJ, and elements of the Tango Blast appear to be challenging the Texas Syndicate (TS) for control of illegal prison activities. Upon release from prison, Tango members appear to return to their local street gangs rather than continue their prison-based gang affiliations.

Hermanos de Pistoleros Latinos

The Hermanos de Pistoleros Latinos (HPL) is a Latino prison gang formed in the TDCJ in the late 1980s. HPL operates in most prisons and on the streets in many communities in Texas, particularly Laredo. HPL is also active in several cities in Mexico, and its largest contingent in that country is located in Nuevo Laredo. HPL is structured and estimated to have 1000 members [24]. HPL members maintain close ties with Mexican traffickers, and are involved in the trafficking of large quantities of cocaine and marijuana from Mexico into the United States for distribution.

Mexican Mafia (La Eme)

The Mexican Mafia prison gang, also known as La Eme (Spanish for the letter *M*), was formed in the late 1950s within the CDC. La Eme is a loosely structured criminal organization with strict rules that must be followed by its estimated 350–400 members. Most members of La Eme are Mexican-American males who previously belonged to a southern California street gang. La Eme is primarily active in the southwestern and Pacific regions of the United States; however, its power base remains in California. The Mexican Mafia's main source of income is extorting drug distributors outside prison and distributing methamphetamine, cocaine, heroin, and marijuana within the prison systems and on the outside streets. Some members of La Eme have direct links to Mexican criminal organizations and broker deals for both themselves and their associates. La Eme is also involved in other criminal activities, including controlling gambling and prostitution within the prison systems.

Mexikanemi

The Mexikanemi prison gang, also known as the Texas Mexican Mafia (La Eme) or Emi, was formed in the early 1980s within the TDCJ. The Mexikanemi is highly structured and is estimated to have 2,000 members, most of whom are Mexican nationals or Mexican-American males who were living in Texas at the time of their incarceration. Mexikanemi poses a significant drug-trafficking threat to communities in the southwestern United States, particularly in Texas. Mexikanemi gang members reportedly traffic multikilogram quantities of powdered cocaine, heroin, and methamphetamine; multiton quantities of marijuana; and thousand-tablet quantities of ecstasy from Mexico into the United States for distribution both inside and outside prison. Mexikanemi gang members obtain narcotics from associates or members of the Jaime Herrera-Herrera, Osiel Cardenas-Guillen, and/or Vicente Carrillo-Fuentes Mexican crime organizations. In addition, Mexikanemi members maintain a relationship with Los Zetas, a Mexican paramilitary-criminal organization employed by the Cardenas-Guillen trafficking organization as its personal security force.

Nazi Low Riders

The Nazi Low Riders (NLR) are a violent California-based prison gang that subscribes to a white supremacist philosophy. The NLR has approximately 800–1000 members, most of whom are Caucasian males with a history of street gang activity and drug abuse. The NLR operates in correctional facilities and communities, primarily in the Pacific and southwestern regions of the United States. The primary sources of income for the NLR are derived from the distribution of multiounce to multipound quantities of methamphetamine, the retail-level distribution of heroin and marijuana, and the extortion of independent Caucasian drug dealers and members of other white power gangs. The NLR also engages in violent criminal activity such as armed robbery, assault, assault with deadly weapons, murder, and attempted murder; in addition, they commit identity fraud, money laundering, witness intimidation, and witness retaliation.

Ñeta

Ñeta is a prison gang that began in Puerto Rico and spread to the United States. Ñeta is one of the largest and most violent prison gangs, with approximately 7,000 members in Puerto Rico and about 5,000 in the United States [25]. Ñeta chapters in Puerto Rico exist exclusively inside prisons; once members are released from prison, they no longer are considered to be part of the gang. In the United States, Ñeta chapters exist both inside and outside prisons in 36 cities and within nine states, primarily in the northeastern region. Ñeta's main source of income is derived from retail distribution of powdered and crack cocaine, heroin, marijuana, and, to a lesser extent, LSD, ecstasy, methamphetamine, and PCP. Ñeta members also commit crimes, including assault, auto theft, burglary, drive-by shooting, extortion, home invasion, money laundering, robbery, weapons and explosives trafficking, and witness intimidation.

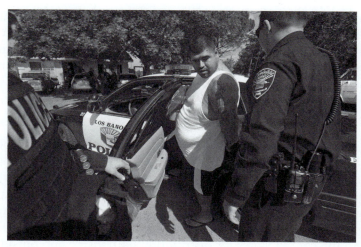

FIGURE 8.3 Nuestra Familia gang leader Gonzalo Esquivel is placed in a police car after his arrest in June 2011. Esquivel was charged with conspiring to distribute methamphetamine. The arrest warrant was among nearly 100 served in San Joaquin Valley, California, as part of a sweep by law enforcement to cripple the gang that has ties with Mexican drug operations. *Source: AP Photo/Rich Pedroncelli, File.*

Nuestra Familia

Nuestra Familia and its subordinate organization, Norteños, are highly structured and extremely violent prison gangs. Originating within the California penal system, Nuestra Familia has an estimated 250 members, while Norteños membership is estimated to be more than 1,000 persons, consisting primarily of Mexican-American males who formerly belonged to street gangs in central and northern California [26]. Nuestra Familia and Norteños are active primarily in state and federal prisons and in communities of the United States Pacific region. The main sources of income for Nuestra Familia and Norteños are derived from distributing cocaine, heroin, marijuana, and methamphetamine within prison systems as well as in outside communities, and by extorting drug distributors on the streets. Nuestra Familia is also involved in other criminal activities, including homicide and robbery.

Public Enemy Number One

Public Enemy Number One (PEN1) is the fastest-growing Caucasian prison gang in the United States, with an estimated membership of between 400 and 500 persons [27]. PEN1 operates in the prison systems and communities of California, and, to a lesser extent, in locations throughout the northeastern, Pacific, southwestern, southeastern, and west central regions of the United States. PEN1 members espouse a white supremacist philosophy and pose a criminal threat both inside and outside prison due to their alliance with the AB and the NLR. PEN1 members derive their income from distributing midlevel and retail-level quantities of methamphetamine. In addition, PEN1 members engage in violent criminal activities such as assault, attempted murder, homicide, auto theft, burglary, identity theft, and property crimes.

Texas Syndicate

The TS is one of the largest and most violent prison gangs active on both sides of the United States–Mexico border, and it poses a significant drug-trafficking threat to communities located in the southwestern United States. The TS is highly structured and is estimated to have about 1,300 members, most of whom are Mexican-American males between the ages of 20 and 40. Members of the TS smuggle multikilogram quantities of powdered cocaine, heroin, and methamphetamine, and multiton quantities of marijuana, from Mexico into the United States for distribution both inside and outside of prison. TS gang members have a direct working relationship with associates and/or members of the Osiel Cardenas-Guillen organization of Mexican traffickers. In addition, TS gang members maintain a relationship with Los Zetas, the paramilitary-criminal organization employed by the Cardenas-Guillen organization.

■ ■ Critical Thinking Task ■

If prison gangs in fact operate within the walls of prisons, do they pose a threat to public safety? Defend your answer.

Ancillary Trafficking Organizations

In addition to those organizations already discussed in this chapter, many other smaller organizations operate throughout the United States. These organizations do business in both urban and rural settings and account for a significant segment of the domestic drug-trafficking picture.

The urban trafficking organizations make up a significant category of drug dealers. These organizations are frequently well organized and highly structured, and are usually composed of extremely violent career criminals. In many cases, the groups consist of younger criminals who assume a leadership role as they age. Many are later convicted and sent to prison, or they are killed. This places the urban trafficking organizations in a constant state of metamorphosis.

Urban drug gangs exist throughout the country, but have been particularly active in such cities as Chicago, Detroit, St. Louis, and East St. Louis, Illinois. It is common for members to be heavily armed with fully automatic weapons and to be especially violence prone. Violence by these organizations frequently occurs because of rivalries between trafficking groups over "turf," but the violence may also manifest itself as aggression toward police, prosecutors, and witnesses in drug prosecutions.

As discussed earlier in this volume, most drug sources are either Mexican or Latin American nationals. Women are commonly used as couriers from the source city to the ultimate destination. Profits acquired for drugs are usually considerably high. For example, a kilogram of cocaine purchased in a source city may cost $12,000–$15,000 but can be resold for much more. Because of this enormous profit margin, control of the industry is a primary goal of the urban trafficking organization [28].

There are also other small-time trafficking organizations operating in the rural United States. In some cases, drug trafficking may be a variation of another type of criminal activity that has been going on for some time. For example, in some parts of the southeastern United States, rural dwellers whose families once produced moonshine have discovered that marijuana is more profitable. The isolation of many rural areas enables traffickers to conduct operations such as marijuana farming and clandestine laboratories. In doing so, traffickers remain relatively free of detection from law enforcement authorities. In many cases, such locations are also good areas for use as "drop zones," or secluded landing strips for smuggling pilots.

Summary

Because of the profit potential for drug trafficking, criminal organizations with both foreign and domestic origins compete for market share. This chapter deals with domestic drug-trafficking organizations; many of these have their roots in foreign countries or are relatively new to the illegal drug trade.

The term *traditional organized crime* is most commonly associated with Italian criminal groups or La Cosa Nostra (LCN, also known as the Mafia). The LCN originated in Italy and Sicily during the 1800s and is now considered the premier criminal group in Italy and a major criminal phenomenon in the United States. The origins of Italian organized crime in prisons parallel those of many domestic prison gangs in the United States.

The first Mafioso arrived in the United States in the late 1800s and gained a foothold in New York and New Orleans. Prohibition (1920–1933) was conducive to Mafiosi criminal activities, which spread to other large cities throughout the United States. The FBI website estimates that the LCN has approximately 25,000 members in total, with 250,000 affiliates worldwide. There are more than 3,000 members and affiliates in the United States, scattered mostly throughout the major cities in the Northeast, the Midwest, California, and the South. Their largest presence is in New York, southern New Jersey, and Philadelphia.

OMGs represent yet another type of domestic criminal group actively involved in the drug trade. Originating in the late 1940s, gangs such as the Hells Angels, the Pagans, the Bandidos, and the Outlaws have considerable criminal influence in the methamphetamine market and frequently dwell in cities outside the continental United States. These gangs have also gained a reputation for violence, and on many occasions have worked in collusion with other criminal groups such as LCN. The U.S. Drug Enforcement Administration has estimated that there are several hundred OMGs currently operating in the United States. Some of these organizations have demonstrated considerable sophistication and pose a very real threat to many major United States cities.

Do you recognize these terms?

- home invasion
- near group
- original gangster
- Pizza Connection
- wannabe

Discussion Questions

1. Discuss the hierarchical structure of La Cosa Nostra.
2. Review some of the reasons that some researchers perceive La Cosa Nostra as a fragmented group of semiorganized criminals.
3. List the domestic criminal organizations most actively involved in cocaine trafficking.
4. What is the relationship between the American Mafia and the Sicilian Mafia in the illicit drug trade?
5. Name and discuss the structure and other similarities of the four major OMGs discussed in this chapter.
6. To what extent does the Mexican Mafia (EME) play a role in drug trafficking?

References

[1] Alexander, S. (1988). *The Pizza Connection: Lawyers, money, drugs and Mafia.* New York: Weidenfeld and Nicolson.
[2] President's Commission on Organized Crime. (1986). *The edge: Organized crime, business and labor unions.* Washington, DC: U.S. Government Printing Office.
[3] Blok, A. (1974). *The Mafia of a Sicilian village, 1860–1960.* New York: Harper and Row.
[4] Hess, H. (1973). *Mafia and Mafioso: The structure of power.* Lexington, MA: D.C. Heath.
[5] Smith, D. C., Jr. (1975). *The Mafia mystique.* New York: Basic Books.
[6] Ianni, E. (1972). *A family business: Kinship and social control in organized crime.* New York: Russell Sage Foundation.
[7] Ianni, E. (1974). *Black Mafia: Ethnic succession in organized crime.* New York: Simon and Schuster.
[8] Albini, J. L. (1971). *The American Mafia: Genesis of a legend.* New York: Appleton-Century-Crofts.
[9] Ibid.
[10] Chambliss, W. J. (1971). Vice, corruption, bureaucracy, and power. *Wisconsin Law Review.* (Spring), 4.
[11] Haller, M. H. (1989). Bootlegging: The business and politics of violence. In T. R. Garr (Ed.), *Violence in America* (pp. 146–152). Newbury Park, CA: Sage.
[12] Reuter, P. (1983). *Disorganized crime: The economics of the visible hand.* Cambridge, MA: MIT Press.
[13] Ibid.
[14] Albanese, J. (2011). *Organized Crime in Our Times* (6th ed.). Boston: Elsevier (Anderson Publishing).
[15] Gardiner, J. A. (1970). *The politics of corruption: Organized crime in an American city.* New York: Russell Sage Foundation.

[16] Potter, G., & Jenkins, P. (1985). *The City and the Syndicate: Organizing Crime in Philadelphia.* Lexington, MA: Ginn Press.

[17] National Institute of Justice. (August 3, 1989). *Drug trafficking: A report to the president of the United States.*

[18] Thrasher, F. M. (1927). *The gang.* Chicago: University of Chicago Press.

[19] Klein, M. (1971). Violence in American juvenile gangs. In D. Mulvihill, M. Tumin & L. Curtis (Eds.), *Crimes of violence. National Commission on the Causes and Prevention of Violence:* (Vol. 13)). Washington, DC: U.S. Government Printing Office.

[20] Yablonsky, L. (1966). *The violent gang.* Baltimore: Penguin Books.

[21] Ibid.

[22] United States Department of Justice. (2013). Found at: http://www.justice.gov/criminal/ocgs/gangs/prison.html.

[23] Ibid.

[24] Ibid.

[25] Ibid.

[26] Ibid.

[27] Ibid.

[28] Ibid.

9

Transnational Drug-Trafficking Organizations

This chapter will enable you to:

- Understand the role of Colombian drug criminals in global drug trafficking
- Understand the development of Mexican domination of the illicit drug market
- Understand the link between drug trafficking and terrorism
- Differentiate between various organizations of Asian drug traffickers
- Learn about the role of foreign drug-trafficking organizations as it relates to the United States market

In Chapter 4, some general dynamics of foreign drug source countries were discussed. This chapter takes a closer look at the criminal trafficking groups originating in those countries. Today, it is clear that drug abuse in the United States has created a growing incentive for escalating foreign involvement in the drug trade; the allure of profits for traffickers is considerable. The degree to which various criminal organizations are involved depends greatly on factors such as the type of drug trafficked, the source country's proximity to the United States and established trafficking routes, and the ability to move money and personnel in and out of the country.

In 2013, the operational landscape of drug trafficking has changed dramatically since the last edition of this book. No longer are the Colombian *cartels* the most significant manufacturers and importers of illicit drugs to the United States. Rather, Mexican trafficking organizations have gained international prominence, and have become considerably more able than ever to control all aspects of the trafficking of many drugs from their production to transportation to both wholesale and retail distribution. Thus, the focus of this chapter is on the rise in prominence of Mexican criminal organizations in the trafficking of marijuana, heroin, methamphetamine, and MDMA (also known as ecstasy, discussed in Chapter 3). Although cocaine is still a problem, its availability and use have decreased dramatically in recent years. We also examine other drug-trafficking groups that still fill a niche in the overall transnational drug-trafficking scheme.

Drug Trafficking on the Southwest Border

The southwest border of the United States is the main delivery zone for most of the illegal drugs smuggled into the country. Specifically, most of the cocaine, marijuana, methamphetamine, and Mexican heroin available in the United States are smuggled into the country across the southwestern border. This area of the United States is particularly vulnerable to drug smuggling because of the enormous volume of people and goods legitimately crossing the border between the two countries every day. Furthermore, large sections of the nearly 2,000-mile land border between Mexico and the United States are both expansive and remote, providing considerable drug-smuggling opportunities for Mexican traffickers. Once at the border, Mexican traffickers use every method imaginable to smuggle drugs into this country, including aircraft, backpackers, couriers, horses and mules, maritime vessels, rail, tunnels, and vehicles.

Today, no other country in the world has a greater impact on the drug situation in the United States than does Mexico. Because of the shared border, the influence of Mexico on the United States drug trade is unmatched. Moreover, Mexico's success in the illicit drug trade is complemented by (1) its strategic location between drug-producing and drug-consuming countries; (2) a long history of cross-border smuggling; and (3) the existence of diversified, polydrug, profit-minded drug-trafficking organizations.

Each of the four major drugs of abuse—marijuana, cocaine, heroin, and methamphetamine—are either produced in or transshipped through Mexico before reaching the United States. The great majority of bulk currency intercepted within the United States originates from drug-trafficking activities. It is estimated that approximately $18–$39 billion annually is moved from the interior of the United States to the southwest border on behalf of Mexican and Colombian drug-trafficking organizations. As such, billions of dollars in United States currency are sent back to Mexico annually. From the Mexican perspective, the flow of large sums of money creates corruption that hinders drug enforcement. As discussed in this book, it is instructive to briefly consider Mexico's illicit drug products:

- *Heroin.* Mexico is an opium poppy-cultivating and heroin-producing country. Though the country accounts for only about 6 percent of the world's opium poppy cultivation and heroin production, it is a major supplier of heroin to abusers in the United States [1]. Mexican black tar and brown heroin have appeared increasingly in the eastern United States. Mexico was identified as the source country for 39 percent of the samples classified under the Drug Enforcement Administration's (DEA) Heroin Signature Program (HSP) during 2008, the largest representation of Mexican-source heroin in the United States in the past 20 years [2].
- *Marijuana.* Mexico is also the number-one foreign supplier of marijuana abused in the United States. In fact, according to 2008 statistics, marijuana is the top revenue generator for Mexican drug-trafficking groups. The profits derived from marijuana trafficking—an industry with minimal overhead costs, controlled entirely by the traffickers—are used not only to finance other drug enterprises by Mexico's multidrug-producing cartels, but also to pay ongoing "business" expenses, purchase weapons, and bribe corrupt officials.
- *Methamphetamine.* In addition to Mexico's involvement in heroin and marijuana production, it is also the number-one foreign supplier of methamphetamine to the United States. Although the Mexican government has seen some success in controlling— even banning—the importation of methamphetamine precursor chemicals such as

ephedrine, pseudoephedrine, and phenyl acetic acid, Mexican trafficking organizations have proven to be extremely resourceful in circumventing regulatory measures put in place by Mexico's Felipe Calderón administration (2006–2012). As with heroin, there is considerable financial incentive for the Mexican traffickers to maintain a trade they control from manufacture to distribution. In fact, Mexican authorities seized more methamphetamine laboratories in 2009–2010 than in the five previous years combined [3].

- *Cocaine.* Mexican traffickers also maintain an important role in the cocaine trade. Since the 1980s, Mexico has served as a primary transportation corridor—transshipment point—for cocaine destined for the United States. Though Mexico is not a coca-producing country, and therefore cannot control the trade from beginning to end, traffickers in Mexico have managed nonetheless to exert increasing control over the trade in exchange for shouldering the greater risk inherent in transporting the cocaine and ensuring its distribution in the United States.

Since 2007, Mexican trafficking organizations have established cooperation with Colombian sources of supply and developed relationships with alternate sources of supply in other cocaine-producing countries—particularly Peru. Consequently, Mexican drug traffickers have developed into intermediate sources of supply for cocaine in Europe, Australia, Asia, and the Middle East. Moreover, Mexican traffickers control the wholesale distribution of cocaine and other drugs of abuse throughout the United States. As of the preparation of this book, estimates suggest that approximately 93 percent of the cocaine leaving South America for the United States moves through Mexico.

During 2009, however, the majority of cocaine stopped first in a Central American country before moving onward to shipment into Mexico [4]. This suggests that drug control efforts by the Calderón administration had a positive impact on how the cartels do business—requiring them to take the extra (and more costly and risky) step of arranging multistage transportation systems.

Changes in cocaine movement patterns are not the only measurable trend. Beginning in January 2007—immediately after the Calderón government was installed—the price per gram of cocaine in the United States began to rise, with a correlative drop in cocaine purity. During this period, prices increased by almost 72 percent, and purity fell by nearly 33 percent [5].

Mexican Domination of the Illicit Drug Market

Much activity has occurred in the realm of Mexican drug trafficking since the last edition of this text. Many trafficking groups have expanded operations and spread their influence in intimidating and corrupting Mexican authorities, rival traffickers, and innocent citizens in both Mexico and the United States. In 2009, the National Drug Threat Assessment stated, "Mexican drug trafficking organizations represent the greatest organized crime threat to the United States and control most of the U.S. drug market" [6,7]. They have proven to pose even a greater United States threat than Asian, Colombian, or Dominican organized

CASE IN POINT: TRAFFICKERS USE SUBTERRANEAN TUNNELS ALONG THE SOUTHWEST BORDER

The number of tunnels extending from Mexico into the United States has increased, suggesting that drug traffickers consider these tunnels useful investments to smuggle drugs into the United States. For example, in 2008, U.S. Border Protection officials discovered 16 subterranean tunnels, the majority of which were in the Tucson sector, which encompasses a border area of 262 miles from the New Mexico state line to Yuma County, Arizona. In 2009, 26 subterranean tunnels were discovered; 20 of those were in the Tucson area, primarily in the area of Nogales. During this same period, five tunnels were discovered in California. In February 2009, U.S. Customs and Border Protection initiated a program designed to hamper the construction of tunnels in Nogales's extensive drainage system. The initiative involved the construction of a 12-foot-deep steel and concrete underground wall that extends 100 yards along the border near the DeConcini point of entry in Nogales.

Source: U.S. Customs and Border Protection. (2009). *National Southwest Border Counternarcotics Strategy.*

crime groups. Between 2008 and 2009, more than 7000 people have been murdered in connection with Mexico's drug cartel wars [8].

Mexican cartels allegedly have used their vast financial resources to corrupt Mexican public officials, who either turn a blind eye to cartel activities or work directly for them. Beginning in 2005, the Mexican government began to make continued efforts to purge corrupt police. In December 2006, President Felipe Calderón launched operations against the cartels in nine of Mexico's 32 states. He has pledged to use extradition as a tool against drug traffickers and sent 64 criminals to the United States as of August 2007, including the alleged head of the Gulf cartel [9].

Calderón's efforts had some notable results. For example, from January 2000 through September 2006, the Mexican government arrested more than 79,000 people on charges related to drug trafficking. Of these arrests, some 78,831 are low-level drug dealers. Mexico also arrested 15 cartel leaders, 74 lieutenants, 53 financial officers, and 428 hitmen (*sicarios*). Mexican authorities arrested nearly 10,000 people on drug-related charges from December 2006 to August 2007. On August 16, 2006, the U.S. DEA and Coast Guard arrested Tijuana cartel leader Francisco Javier Arellano Félix, along with other Tijuana cartel leaders, on a boat off the Mexican coast. His brother, Francisco Rafael Arellano Félix, was extradited to the United States in September 2006. In January 2007, Mexico extradited 15 people wanted for prosecution in the United States, including four senior drug traffickers [10].

Police agencies in the United States have reported Mexican drug-trafficking operations in an estimated 230 United States cities. These operations have been found to employ maritime, air, and overland transportation methods. Furthermore, Mexican traffickers have taken advantage of high-technology communication methods to avoid detection. For example, "cross-communication" centers have been discovered on both sides of the

United States–Mexico border, using methods such as voice-over-Internet protocol (VoIP), satellite technology (broadband satellite instant messaging), encrypted messaging with rolling codes, cell phone technology, two-way radios, scanner devices, and text messaging to communicate with members [11].

The Mexican Takeover of the Cocaine Trade

Recent history has shown extreme changes in the dynamics of transnational drug trafficking. As of 2010, Mexican drug traffickers were slowly assuming control of Colombia's multibillion-dollar cocaine industry, which was previously controlled by well-known cartels from cities such as Medellín and Cali. With the dismantlement of the former Colombia cartels and the retraction of these cartels from key geographic locations outside Colombia, the Mexican cartels have filled the void by assuming supremacy of the cocaine distribution market first in the United States, and in recent years in a much broader global context.

That was illustrated in a case that unfolded in 2009 in which a conglomerate of Mexican drug cartels were arrested while attempting to smuggle 1,200 tons of cocaine into the United States from Colombia. That case demonstrated how Mexicans, including the Beltrán-Leyva and Sinaloa cartels, were in charge of major drug shipments from Colombia to the United States, with Colombians assuming a diminished role.

The Mexican cartels have representatives in Colombia who coordinate with Colombian drug-trafficking organizations on the acquisition of cocaine and transportation to Central America and Mexico. As recently as 2000, the exact opposite could be said, in that the Colombian cartels were embedded in Mexico and coordinating with the Mexican drug-trafficking organizations.

Despite efforts by President Calderón to quash the cartels, the drug organizations have become more aggressive in expanding their global operations. In doing so, law enforcement officials say they have strangled the communities in the regions they control. The situation has led to the deaths of hundreds of people along the United States–Mexico border. By not stopping the cartels when they were first organizing more than 10 years ago, narcotraffickers like Chapo "Shorty" Guzman's Sinaloa cartel, the Gulf cartel, and others have grown in size to numbers exceeding 100,000 [12].

Key Mexican Trafficking Organizations

Like most criminal organizations in the early stages of establishing their control of a market share in prohibited substances, Mexican syndicates still cling to the excessive use of violence as a means of control. As of late 2009, Mexican drug traffickers had been documented forging alliances with United States drug gangs such as prison gangs and outlaw motorcycle gangs to expand their operations in the United States [13]. The use of such United States gangs has made it difficult for police to identify the managers of Mexican drug operations. Of the many drug cartels operating in Mexico, the most prominent are the Gulf, Sinaloa, Juárez, and Tijuana cartels.

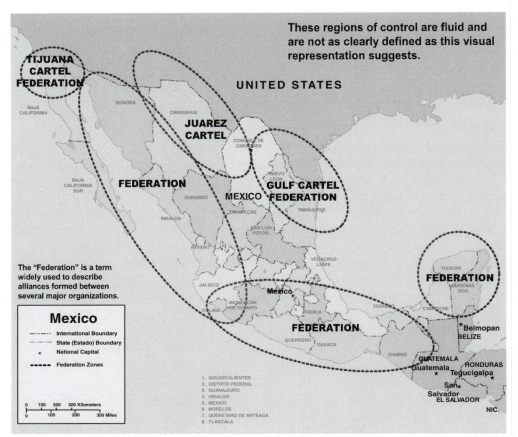

FIGURE 9.1 Mexican cartel areas of influence. *Source: U.S. Drug Enforcement Administration, adapted by CRS (P. McGrath 3/2/2007).*

The Gulf Cartel

The *Gulf cartel* is a Mexican drug cartel based in Matamoros. The Zetas, a criminal group in Mexico, have created their own niche among drug enforcer gangs, in that they operate "as a private army under the orders of Cárdenas's Gulf cartel, the first time a drug lord has had his own paramilitary." Most reports indicate that the Zetas were created by a group of 30 lieutenants and sublieutenants who deserted from the Mexican military's Special Air Mobile Force Group (Grupo Aeromovil de Fuerzas Especiales, or GAFES) to the Gulf cartel in the late 1990s. As such, the Zetas were able to carry out more complex operations and use more sophisticated weaponry [14].

The Zetas were instrumental in the Gulf cartel's domination of the drug trade in Nuevo Laredo, and have fought to maintain the cartel's influence in that city following the 2003 arrest of its leader, Osiel Cárdenas. Press reports have charged that these soldiers-turned-cartel-enforcers were trained in the United States; however, the Washington Office on Latin

> **CASE IN POINT: INCREASING COORDINATION BETWEEN MEXICAN DRUG CARTELS, ALIEN SMUGGLING NETWORKS, AND UNITED STATES-BASED GANGS**
>
> Federal, state, and local law enforcement officials are observing a growing nexus between the Mexican drug cartels, illegal alien smuggling rings, and United States-based gangs. The alien smuggling networks that operate along the Southwest border are unable to move human cargo through drug cartel-controlled corridors without paying a fee. The typical Mexican illegal alien now pays approximately $1,200–$2,500 for entry into the United States. The fee is considerably higher for aliens smuggled from countries other than Mexico, which may even be more alluring for the cartels. It is estimated that criminals earn billions of dollars each year by smuggling aliens through Mexico into the United States.
>
> _Source_: U.S. Congress. (2011). *House Committee on Homeland Security.*

America was unable to confirm this claim. Estimates on the number of Zetas range from 31 up to 200. Reports indicate that although the Zetas initially comprised members of special forces, they now include federal, state, and local law enforcement personnel, as well as civilians. In September 2005, testimony to the Mexican Congress by then Defense Secretary Clemente Vega indicated that the Zetas had also hired at least 30 former Guatemalan special forces (*Kaibiles*) to train new recruits because "the number of former Mexican special forces men in their ranks had shrunk from 50 to no more than a dozen, and they were finding it hard to entice more members of the Mexican military to join" [15].

The Zetas act as assassins for the Gulf cartel. They also traffic arms, kidnap, and collect payments for the cartel on its drug routes. Mexican law enforcement officials report that the Zetas have become an increasingly sophisticated, three-tiered organization with leaders and middlemen who coordinate contracts with petty criminals to carry out street work. The Zetas have maintained the territory of the Gulf cartel in the northern cities of Matamoros and Nuevo Laredo, and in addition they are believed to control trafficking routes along the eastern half of the United States–Mexico border. Thus, the Zetas now have a presence in southern Mexico, where the Gulf cartel is disputing territory previously controlled by the Juárez and Sinaloa cartels. A recent federal investigation found that the Zetas also engage in kidnapping, drug dealing, and money laundering. In July 2006, local police in the southern state of Tabasco unknowingly arrested Mateo Díaz López, believed to be a leader of the Zetas. The arrest prompted an assault on the police station, killing four people, including two police officers. However, the assault did not succeed in liberating Díaz López, who was subsequently transferred to a prison in Guadalajara. The Zetas also trained the Michoacán-based La Familia enforcer gang, which has carried out numerous executions in that state. La Familia maintains close ties to the Zetas but is a smaller entity.

The Sinaloa Cartel

The *Sinaloa cartel* is another powerful cartel in Mexican drug trafficking. It claims the territory of Baja California, Sinaloa, Durango, Sonora, and Chihuahua. The cartel also goes by the names of the Guzmán-Loera Organization and the Pacific cartel, the latter due to the coast of Mexico from which it originated.

The Sinaloa cartel is known to have smuggled many tons of cocaine and large amounts of heroin into the United States between 1990 and 2008 [16].

Pedro Avilés Pérez was a pioneer drug lord in the Mexican state of Sinaloa in the late 1960s. He is considered the first generation of major Mexican drug smugglers of marijuana who marked the birth of large-scale Mexican drug trafficking. He also pioneered the use of aircraft to smuggle drugs to the United States. Second-generation Sinaloan traffickers such as Rafael Caro Quintero, Ernesto Fonseca Carrillo, Miguel Ángel Félix Gallardo, and Avilés Pérez's nephew Joaquín "El Chapo" Guzmán would claim they learned all they knew about narcotrafficking while serving in the Avilés organization. Miguel Ángel Félix Gallardo, who eventually founded the Guadalajara cartel, was arrested in 1989. While incarcerated, he remained one of Mexico's major traffickers, maintaining his organization via mobile phone until he was transferred to a maximum-security prison in the 1990s. At that point, his old organization broke up into two factions: the Tijuana cartel, led by his nephews, the Arellano Félix brothers; and the Sinaloa cartel, run by former lieutenants Héctor Luis Palma Salazar, Adrián Gómez González, and Joaquín Guzmán Loera El Chapo [17].

The Sinaloa cartel used to be known as *La Alianza de Sangre* (Blood Partnership). When Héctor Luis Palma Salazar (aka El Güero) was arrested by the Mexican Army, his partner Joaquín Guzmán Loera took leadership of the cartel. Guzmán was captured in Guatemala in 1993 and extradited to Mexico, where he was jailed in a maximum-security prison, but in January 2001 he escaped and resumed his command of the cartel. Guzmán has two top lieutenants, Ismael Zambada García and Ignacio Coronel Villareal. Guzmán and Zambada became Mexico's top drug kingpins in 2003, after the arrest of their rival Osiel Cárdenas of the Gulf cartel. Another close associate, Javier Torres Félix, was arrested and extradited to the United States in December 2006. According to the Mexican embassy, as of mid-2007, Guzmán and Zambada have evaded operations to capture them [18].

The Sinaloa cartel has a presence in 17 states, with important centers in Mexico City, Tepic, Toluca, Cuautitlán, and most of the state of Sinaloa. The cartel is primarily involved in the smuggling and distribution of Colombian cocaine, Mexican marijuana, methamphetamine, and Mexican and Southeast Asian heroin into the United States [19]. It is believed that a group known as the Herrera organization would transport multiton quantities of cocaine from South America to Guatemala on behalf of the Sinaloa cartel. From there, it is smuggled north to Mexico and later into the United States. Other shipments of cocaine are believed to originate in Colombia from Cali and Medellín drug-trafficking groups. The Sinaloa cartel handles transportation across the United States border to distribution cells in Arizona, California, Texas, Chicago, and New York [20].

By the mid-1990s, according to one court opinion, the Sinaloa cartel was believed to be the size of the Medellín cartel during its prime. The Sinaloa cartel was believed to be linked to the Juárez cartel in a strategic alliance following the partnership of their rivals, the Gulf cartel and Tijuana cartel. Following the discovery of a tunnel system used to smuggle drugs across the United States–Mexico border, the group has been associated with such means of trafficking [21].

By 2005, the Beltrán-Leyva brothers, who were formerly aligned with the Sinaloa cartel, had come to dominate drug trafficking across the border with Arizona. By 2006, the cartel had eliminated all competition across the 330 miles of Arizona border; it was suspected they had accomplished this by bribing state government officials. The Beltrán-Leyva cartel are now allies of the Zetas of the Gulf cartel [22].

In January 2008, the cartel allegedly split into a number of warring factions, and this is a major contributor to Mexico's current drug violence epidemic. On February 25, 2009, the United States government announced the arrest of 750 members of the Sinaloa cartel across the United States in *Operation Xcellerator*. They also announced the seizure of more than $59 million in cash and numerous vehicles, planes, and boats [23].

In March 2009, the Mexican government announced the deployment of 1,000 federal police officers and 5,000 Mexican Army soldiers to restore order in Ciudad Juárez, where the Sinaloa cartel had been battling the Zetas of the Gulf cartel. The city has suffered more than 1,600 deaths related to drug trafficking, the highest in the country [24].

The Sinaloa cartel's loss of partners in Mexico does not appear to have affected its ability to smuggle drugs from South America to the United States. On the contrary, based on seizure reports, the cartel appears to be the most active smuggler of cocaine. It has also demonstrated the ability to establish operations in previously unknown areas, such as Central America and South America, and even as far south as Peru, Paraguay, and Argentina. It also appears to be active in diversifying its export markets; rather than relying solely on United States consumers, it has made an effort to also supply distributors of drugs in Latin American and European countries [25].

The Sinaloa cartel has been waging a war against the Tijuana cartel (the Arellano Félix Organization) over the Tijuana smuggling route to the border city of San Diego, California. The rivalry between the two cartels dates back to the Miguel Ángel Félix Gallardo setup of Palma's family. Félix Gallardo, following his imprisonment, bestowed the Guadalajara cartel to his nephews in the Tijuana cartel [26]. In 1992, Palma struck out against the Tijuana cartel at a disco in Puerto Vallarta, Jalisco, where eight Tijuana cartel members were killed in the shootout, the Arellano Félix brothers having successfully escaped from the location.

In retaliation, the Tijuana cartel attempted to set up Guzmán at Guadalajara Airport on May 24, 1993. In the shootout that followed, six civilians were killed by the hired gunmen from the Logan Heights, San Diego-based 30th Street gang. Among the dead was Roman Catholic Cardinal Juan Jesús Posadas Ocampo [27].

The Juárez Cartel

The *Juárez cartel* is another influential drug-trafficking organization. It is based in Ciudad Juárez, Chihuahua, Mexico, across the border from El Paso, Texas. The Juárez cartel is an important player in modern-day drug trafficking because it controls one of the main transportation arteries for illegal drug shipments entering the United States from Mexico. The Juárez cartel has a reputation for being a brutal and dangerous drug-trafficking organization. For example, its members have been known to decapitate their rivals, mutilate their corpses, and dump them in public to intimidate the public, the police, and their rivals [28].

Rafael Aguilar Guajardo founded the cartel in the 1970s, and in 1993 handed it down to Amado Carrillo Fuentes. Amado's brothers and his son were later brought into the business. In 1997, after Amado died following complications from plastic surgery, a brief turf war began over the control of the cartel, and Amado's brother Vicente Carrillo Fuentes surfaced as leader [29].

As recently as 2005, the Juárez cartel was the leading player in the center of Mexico, controlling a large percentage of the cocaine traffic from Mexico into the United States [30]. The death of Amado Carrillo Fuentes in 1997, however, was the beginning of the decline in the cartel's prominence. This has resulted in some elements of the group being absorbed by the Sinaloa cartel, a relatively new but aggressive organization that has taken over much of the Juárez cartel's former territory [31–33]. Since 2007, the Juárez cartel has been at war with its former partner, the Sinaloa cartel, for control of Juárez. The fighting between them has left thousands dead in Chihuahua state.

The Juárez cartel relies on two enforcement gangs to exercise control over both sides of the border: La Linea, a group of current and former Chihuahua police officers, is prevalent on the Mexican side; and the large street gang Barrio Azteca operates on the United States side of the border in Texas cities such as El Paso, Dallas, and Austin, as well as in New Mexico and Arizona [34].

The Tijuana Cartel

The *Tijuana cartel*, based in Tijuana, Baja California, is another powerful Mexican trafficking organization. Covering the northwestern part of Mexico, the Tijuana cartel competes with the Juárez cartel (central), the Gulf cartel (east), and the Sinaloa cartel. The Tijuana cartel has been called "one of the biggest and most violent criminal groups in Mexico" [35].

For the most part, the majority of Mexico's smuggling routes are controlled by three key cartels—Gulf, Sinaloa, and Tijuana—and the latter is the least powerful. The Tijuana cartel was weakened in August 2006 when its leader, Javier Arellano Félix, was arrested by the U.S. Coast Guard on a boat off the coast of southern California. In January 2007, Mexican army troops were sent to Tijuana in an operation to restore order to the border city and expel corrupt police officers who were cooperating with the Tijuana cartel. As a result, the Tijuana cartel has been unable to project much power outside its base in Tijuana.

The Arellano Félix family was initially composed of seven brothers and four sisters, who inherited the organization from Miguel Ángel Félix Gallardo upon his incarceration in Mexico in 1989 for his complicity in the murder of DEA Special Agent Enrique Camarena.

Although the brothers' arrest was a blow to the Arellano Félix cartel, it did not dismantle the organization, which currently is led by Eduardo's nephew, Luis Fernando Sánchez Arellano [36].

The Tijuana cartel has infiltrated the Mexican law enforcement and judicial systems and is directly involved in street-level trafficking within the United States. This criminal organization is responsible for the transportation, importation, and distribution of multiton quantities of cocaine and marijuana, as well as large quantities of heroin and methamphetamine. The organization has a reputation for extreme violence. Ramón Arellano Félix ordered a hit that resulted in the mass murder of 18 people in Ensenada, Baja California, on September 17, 1998. Ramón was eventually killed in a gun battle with police at Mazatlán, Sinaloa, in 2002 [37].

The Tijuana cartel is present in at least 15 Mexican states, with important areas of operation in Tijuana, Mexicali, Tecate, and Ensenada in Baja California and in parts of Sinaloa. Fourteen Mexican drug gang members were killed and eight others were injured in a gun battle in Tijuana near the United States border on April 26, 2008, one of the bloodiest shootouts in the narcowar between the Tijuana cartel and the Sinaloa cartel.

The Sonora Cartel

The *Sonora cartel* was formerly a Mexico-based criminal cartel. When the cartel collapsed, its leaders were brought into the Tijuana and Sinaloa cartels. The DEA considered the Sonora cartel one of the oldest and best-established cartels. Its roots were in the Guadalajara cartel, which dissolved after the 1989 arrest of its cofounder, Miguel Ángel Félix Gallardo [38]. The Sonora cartel had direct links to Colombian drug cartels and operated routes into California, Arizona, Texas, and Nevada.

The Sonora cartel is believed to be one of the earliest cartels to begin shipping cocaine from Colombia, particularly from the Cali cartel. The cartel was primarily involved in the cultivation and distribution of marijuana; however, secondary functions included the transportation and distribution of methamphetamine. Operating out of north-central Mexico, the cartel was believed to smuggle drugs into Arizona, Texas, and California from a network of ranches along the northern border region, where the drugs were stored prior to shipment. The Sonora cartel has been specifically linked to the Mexican cities of Hermosillo, Agua Prieta, Guadalajara, Culiacán, San Luis Potosi, Durango, Sinaloa, and Sonora.

The La Familia (the Family) Michoacana Cartel

La Familia Michoacana is yet another powerful drug-trafficking cartel based in the Mexican state of Michoacán. Formerly allied to the Gulf cartel—as part of the Zetas—in 2006, La Familia Michoacana split off as its own organization. Its leader, Nazario Moreno González, known as El Más Loco (The Craziest One), advocates the cartel's right to eliminate enemies. He carries a "bible" of his own sayings and insists that his army of traffickers and enforcers avoid using the drugs they sell. Nazario Moreno's partners are José de Jesús

Méndez Vargas, Servando Gómez Martínez, and Dionicio Loya Plancarte, each of whom has a bounty of $2 million for his capture.

La Familia was first established in the 1980s with the stated purpose of bringing order to Michoacán and helping to protect the poor. Initially, La Familia formed as a group of vigilantes, spurred to power to counter interloping kidnappers and drug dealers, who were their stated enemies. Since then, it has capitalized on its reputation, building its myth, power, and reach to transition into a criminal gang itself [39].

La Familia emerged in the foreground in the 1990s as the Gulf cartel's paramilitary group, designed to seize control of the illegal drug trade in the Mexican state of Michoacán from rival drug cartels. Trained with Los Zetas, in 2006 the group splintered off into an independent drug-trafficking operation. La Familia has a strong rivalry with both Los Zetas and the Beltrán-Leyva cartel, but strong ties with the Sinaloa cartel and the Tijuana Arellano Félix cartel, making them one of the strongest cartels in Mexico [40].

The La Familia cartel is sometimes described as quasi-religious because its current leaders, Moreno González and Méndez Vargas, refer to their assassinations and beheadings as "divine justice." They may have direct or indirect ties with devotees of the New Jerusalem religious movement, which is noted for its concern for justice issues.

The "bible" of La Familia's boss Nazario Moreno González was seized by Mexican federal agents and was shown to reveal an ideology that mixes evangelical-style self-help practices with insurgent peasant slogans. Moreno González seems to have based much of his doctrine on the work of Christian writer John Eldredge. The Mexican justice department stated in a report that Gonzalez Moreno has made Eldredge's book, *Salvaje de Corazón* (*Wild at Heart*), required reading for La Familia gang members, and has paid rural teachers and the National Council of Educational Development (CONAFE) to circulate Eldredge's writings throughout the Michoacán countryside. An idea central to Eldredge's message is that every man must have "a battle to fight, a beauty to rescue and an adventure to live." Eldredge quotes from Isaiah 63, which describes God wearing blood-stained clothes, spattered as though he had been treading a wine press.

The La Familia cartel emphasizes religion and family values during recruitment and has placed banners in areas of operations, claiming that it does not tolerate substance abuse or exploitation of women and children. According to Mexico Public Safety Secretary Genaro Garcia Luna, it recruits members from drug rehabilitation clinics by helping addicts recover, and then forces them into service for the drug cartel (those who refuse are killed). Advancement within the organization depends as much on regular attendance at prayer meetings as on target practice. The cartel gives loans to farmers, businesses, schools, and churches, and it advertises its benevolence in local newspapers to gain social support [41].

In April 2009, about 400 federal police agents raided a christening party for a baby born to a cartel member. Among the 44 detained was Rafael Cedeño Hernández (El Cede), the gang's second in command and the person in charge of indoctrinating the new recruits into the cartel's religious values, morals, and ethics [42,43]. In July 2009,

Servando Gómez Martínez (La Tuta) identified himself as the "chief of operations" of the cartel. In his televised message, Gómez stated, "La Familia was created to look after the interests of our people and our family. We are a necessary evil." And when asked what La Familia really wanted, Gómez replied, "The only thing we want is peace and tranquility." Former President Felipe Calderón's government refused to strike a deal with the cartel and rejected their calls for dialogue.

Even by Mexican standards, La Familia has been known to be unusually violent. Its members use murder and torture to quash rivals while building a social base in the Mexican state of Michoacán. It is the fastest-growing cartel in the country's drug war. In one incident in Uruapan in 2006, the cartel members tossed five decapitated heads onto the dance floor of the Sol y Sombra night club along with a message that read "The Family doesn't kill for money. It doesn't kill women. It doesn't kill innocent people, only those who deserve to die. Know that this is divine justice" [44].

The cartel has moved from smuggling and selling drugs to become a much more ambitious criminal organization that acts as a parallel state in much of Michoacán. It extorts "taxes" from businesses, pays for community projects, controls petty crime, and settles some local disputes. Despite its short history, it has emerged as Mexico's largest supplier of methamphetamine to the United States, with supply channels running deep into middle America, and has increasingly become involved in the distribution of cocaine, marijuana, and other narcotics [45].

Michael Braun, former DEA chief of operations, states that the cartel operates *super-labs* in Mexico that are capable of producing up to 100 pounds of meth in 8 hours. However, according to DEA officials, the cartel claims to oppose the sale of drugs to Mexicans. It also sells pirated DVDs, smuggles people to the United States, and runs a debt-collecting service by kidnapping defaulters. Because cartel members often use fake (and sometimes original) uniforms of several police agencies, most of their kidnap victims are stopped under false pretenses of routine inspections or report of stolen vehicles and then taken hostage [46].

As of 2009, twenty municipal officials had been murdered by La Familia in Michoacán, including two mayors. Having established its authority, the cartel then names local police chiefs. In May 2009, the Mexican Federal Police detained 10 mayors of Michoacán and 20 other local officials suspected of being associated with the cartel. On July 11, 2009, a cartel lieutenant—Arnoldo Rueda Medina—was arrested; La Familia members attacked the federal police station in Morelia to try to free Rueda shortly after his arrest. During the attacks, two soldiers and three federal policemen were killed. When that failed, cartel members attacked federal police installations in at least a half-dozen Michoacán cities in retribution [47]. Three days later, on July 14, 2009, the cartel tortured and murdered 12 Mexican federal police agents who were investigating crime in Michoacán and dumped their bodies along the side of a mountain highway, along with a written message: "So that you come for another. We will be waiting for you here." President Calderón responded to the violence by dispatching an additional 1,000 federal police officers to the area.

Table 9.1   Proliferation of Mexican Cartels 2006–2010

Pacífico cartel	Pacífico cartel	Pacífico cartel
	Beltrán Leyva cartel	Pacífico Sur cartel
		Acapulco independent cartel
		"La Barbie" cartel
Juárez cartel	Juárez cartel	Juárez cartel
Tijuana cartel	Tijuana cartel	Tijuana cartel
	"El Teo" Faction	"El Teo" Faction
Golfo cartel	Golfo-Zetas cartel	Golfo cartel
		Zetas cartel
La Familia Michoacana	La Familia Michoacana	La Familia Michoacana
Milenio cartel	Milenio cartel	La Resistencia
		Jalisco cartel-Nueva Generación

Source: Bagley, B. (2012). *Drug Trafficking and Organized Crime in the Americas*. Woodrow Wilson International Center for Scholars. Smithsonian Institution, Washington D.C., August.

The infusion of police, which more than tripled the number of officers patrolling the area, angered Michoacán Governor Leonel Godoy Rangel, who called it "an occupation" and said he had not been consulted. The governor's half-brother, Julio César Godoy Toscano, who was elected in July 2009 to the lower house of Congress, was discovered to be a top-ranking member of the La Familia Michoacana drug cartel, and was accused of being in charge of protection for the cartel. Days later, 10 municipal police officers were arrested in connection with the slayings of the 12 federal agents [48].

President Calderón stated that the country's drug cartels had grown so powerful that they now posed a threat to the future of Mexican democracy. His strategy of direct confrontation and law enforcement was not popular with some segments of Mexican society, where battling violent drug gangs has led to several human rights charges against the Mexican military (Table 9.1).

Official Corruption in Mexico

The role of corruption in organized crime was discussed in Chapter 1. The influence of corruption has profoundly impacted the Mexican drug-trafficking industry and hampered enforcement efforts in that country. Like many organized crime groups, Mexican cartels advance their operations in part by corrupting or intimidating law enforcement officials. One example is the Nuevo Laredo Police. Nuevo Laredo municipal police have reportedly been involved in the kidnapping of Gulf cartel competitors to hand them over to the Zetas. The Zetas then hold them for ransom or torture them for information about their drug operations [49].

Research has shown that some agents of Mexico's Federal Investigative Agency (AFI) work as enforcers for the Sinaloa cartel. The Attorney General's Office (PGR) reported in December 2005 that one-fifth of its officers were under investigation for criminal activity. Specifically, nearly 1,500 of AFI's 7,000 agents were under investigation for suspected criminal activity, and 457 were facing charges [50]. In November 2005, a video depicting the interrogation of four Zetas who revealed their methods of torture, ties to Mexican law enforcement agencies, and recruitment techniques was given to *The Dallas Morning News*. The video ends with the murder of one of the Zetas. The Mexican government sent "mixed signals" about the involvement of AFI agents in the kidnapping of the Zetas, first announcing that eight agents were under investigation, and then announcing that AFI agents had no connection to the kidnapping and murder of the Zeta member. However, a report from a nongovernmental organization concluded that AFI agents probably kidnapped the Zetas in the resort city of Acapulco, then handed them over to members of the Sinaloa cartel to be interrogated and executed.

Since 2005, the Mexican federal government has conducted purges and prosecutions of police forces in Nuevo Laredo, Apatzingan, Michoacán, and Tijuana, Baja California. The presidential administration of Vicente Fox (2000–2006) launched *Operation Secure Mexico* in 2005 to combat drug violence and police corruption in cities with high incidences of drug violence. Federal officers arriving in Nuevo Laredo were fired on by municipal police, leading to the arrest of 41 municipal police and the suspension of the entire 700-member police force in order to investigate corruption. Less than one-half were later cleared to return to duty. Later in that same year, federal police rescued 44 people, most of whom claimed they had been kidnapped by municipal police before being transferred to Gulf cartel safe houses. In spite of these efforts, reports indicate that the Zetas continue to have influence over Nuevo Laredo's municipal police and that warring cartels are gaining influence in all law enforcement present in the city.

In 2006 Mexico launched the Northern Border (*Frontera Norte*) initiative, which included the deployment of 800 Federal Protective Police (PFP) officers to Nuevo Laredo. These officers are in addition to the 300 federal officers already deployed in Nuevo Laredo under Operation Secure Mexico. In March 2006, four PFP officers were killed after locating a cartel safe house. Federal officials announced that initial evidence indicated that municipal police officers were responsible for the killings [51].

The anticartel operations begun by President Calderón in 2006 included ballistic checks of police weapons in places such as Tijuana, where there is concern that police are also working for the cartels. In 2007 more than 100 state police officers in the northern state of Nuevo León were suspended due to corruption concerns, and 284 federal police commanders were ousted, including federal commanders of all 31 states and the federal district [52]. These commanders were suspended and subjected to drug and polygraph tests. The Mexican government immediately named replacements for the dismissed commanders, who were able to pass an array of examinations designed to weed out corrupt officers, including financial checks, drug testing, and psychological and medical screening.

Drug Violence in Mexico

Since 2008, Mexico has experienced an extraordinarily high incidence of violence. To some extent, the high levels of violence are an indicator of the successful crime crackdown campaigns by military and law enforcement officials there. Three types of violence have been identified in Mexico:

- Intracartel violence (among and between members of the same criminal syndicate)
- Intercartel violence (between rival groups)
- Cartel-versus-government violence

Intra- and intercartel violence have long been associated with the Mexican drug trade, but the current levels of violence are unprecedented. It is instructive to consider the background of the "culture of violence" associated with Mexican drug-trafficking organizations, along with the cyclical nature of the "violence epidemics" seen in Mexico. A recent historical example is the cross-border killing spree engaged in by Zetas operatives in the Laredo–Nuevo Laredo area during 2004–2005. Since 2007, there have been more than 22,000 drug-related murders in Mexico, as reported by the Mexican Attorney General's Office. Stories abound about the arrest of a *pozolero* (stew maker), a killer who disposes of his victims' body parts in barrels of acid, or the discovery of a mass grave containing the remains of countless victims decomposing under layers of lime. These and other grisly tactics are not new; however, what is new are the sustained efforts of Mexican trafficking organizations to use violence as a tool to weaken public support for the government's antidrug efforts.

Traffickers have made a determined effort to send a public message through their reign of violence. Particularly worrisome are tactics intended to intimidate police, public officials, and law-abiding citizens. The cartels are known today to resort to leaving the beheaded and mutilated bodies of their tortured victims out for public display with the intent of intimidating government officials and the public alike. Moreover, the intimidation of public and police officials through violence or the threat of violence has a more insidious side. Not all corruption is a clear-cut, money-for-cooperation negotiation. Rather, the intimidation of officials, which includes threats against their lives or their families' lives, is a much more widespread and effective tactic, and probably accounts for the extent to which law enforcement officials have been corrupted in Mexico.

Pressure on the Traffickers

To a great extent, successes by the military and law enforcement have provided the basis for much of the violence. Tens of thousands of military troops have been deployed specifically to confront traffickers in "hot spots" throughout the country. Moreover, specialized law enforcement operations targeting specific cartel members or import–export locations have interrupted supply routes both in and out of Mexico. Additionally, since 2008, entry ports for large maritime shipments of cocaine from South America, previously controlled by the cartels, are patrolled and inspected by members of Mexico's armed forces. The lucrative transportation corridors within Mexico and into the United States, which were once completely controlled by cartel "gatekeepers" and "plaza bosses," are now populated with military checkpoints and monitored by Mexican law enforcement. As a result, closed supply routes translate to extreme competition between the drug-trafficking organizations that control routes that are still viable. Making things worse are drifting alliances, longstanding feuds, and record-breaking seizures by the Mexican national government.

The Problem of Spillover Violence

Extreme violence by Mexican traffickers presents problems for both Mexico and the United States. For example, in 2009, United States intelligence and law enforcement agencies worked to reach a consensus view on what has been termed "spillover" violence and the violent tactics used by Mexican trafficking groups. *Spillover violence* involves deliberate, planned attacks by drug cartels on United States assets, including civilian, military, or law enforcement officials; innocent American citizens; or physical institutions such as government buildings, consulates, or businesses. This definition does not include trafficker-on-trafficker violence.

Spillover violence presents a complicated issue. It is important to understand the difference between the intentional targeting of innocent civilians in the United States (or official United States government interests in Mexico or the United States) and actions that are characteristic of violent drug culture, such as the killing of someone who owes a drug debt to the organization. Certain isolated incidents in the United States, such as the torture by a Mexican trafficker of a Dominican drug customer in Atlanta, are frightening but do not represent a dramatic departure from the violence that has always been associated with the drug trade.

Younger generation traffickers pose much of the risk of spillover violence, since their approach to the drug trade is less rational and profit-minded than that of their "elders," or multinational street and prison gangs working in concert with Mexican cartels as enforcers and street-level drug distributors. As the Mexican government has successfully disrupted the trafficker's organizational structure, less experienced "junior" cartel members have been assuming roles formerly held by traffickers of long standing who, though violent, tended to be more thoughtful and cautious in their actions.

One of the most significant ramifications of the unrest along the border has been a string of kidnappings involving United States citizens. Between May 2004 and May 2005, there were 35 reported abductions of United States citizens in this region [53]. Thirty-four of these abductions occurred in Nuevo Laredo and involved people who had crossed the border.

It is reported that these numbers probably represent only a fraction of the actual occurrences, because many kidnappings of United States citizens go unreported. There are two reasons for the underreporting of abductions along the border: first, victims and their families fear reprisal from kidnappers. Second, because many victims are alleged to be involved in drug trafficking, they and their families are reluctant to cooperate with law enforcement.

Nuevo Laredo

The city of Nuevo Laredo, directly across the border from Laredo, Texas, has been particularly hard hit by drug violence since the Sinaloa cartel began to contest the Gulf cartel's

FIGURE 9.2 Police forensic experts examine the scene where three men were found dead along a highway on the edge of Nuevo Laredo, Mexico, on May 11, 2007. The men were tortured and shot in the head and were found near a sign bearing a threat to the Sinaloa drug cartel from a rival gang. Another body was later found nearby. *Source: AP Photo/Str.*

domination of Nuevo Laredo following the arrest of Osiel Cárdenas. The warring cartels are thought to compete for influence over law enforcement and the media, and they use intimidation and murder to further their cause. This is the most publicized of Mexico's turf wars due to the intensity of the violence and its proximity to the United States. More than 60 United States citizens have been kidnapped in Nuevo Laredo since the beginning of the turf war, and as of 2007, at least 20 were still missing. Reports indicate that hundreds of Mexicans have been kidnapped in Nuevo Laredo, and murders continue to increase. Nuevo Laredo has not had a police chief in nearly a year due to the violence. The most recent chief resigned, and his predecessor was murdered.

United States Ambassador Tony Garza closed the United States consulate in Nuevo Laredo from July 29 to August 8, 2005, due to safety concerns, and submitted a diplomatic note to the Mexican government in January 2006 expressing concern over violence in this border city. Journalistic enterprises have been affected as well. In 2006, gunmen suspected of ties with drug traffickers critically injured a reporter in an attack on offices of the daily *El Mañana* after it published a picture of a federal police officer, linking him to the Sinaloa cartel. The paper subsequently announced that it would scale back coverage of drug violence. In July 2007, drug cartels reportedly threatened to kill an unnamed American journalist in Laredo for writing reports on the cartels. Around this time, the Committee to Protect Journalists noted a high level of self-censorship among media in Nuevo Laredo and other parts of northern Mexico, and both the *Dallas Morning News* and *San Antonio Express-News* took measures to protect their journalists working in the area [54].

On February 19, 2007, the day after President Calderón announced the expansion of his counternarcotics operation into Nuevo Laredo, gunmen believed to be working for the

A CLOSER LOOK: US-BASED GANGS WITH TIES TO MEXICAN DRUG-TRAFFICKING ORGANIZATIONS

- Arizona New Mexican Mafia
- Aryan Brotherhood
- Avenues
- Bandidos
- Barrio Azteca
- Barrio Westside
- Black Guerilla Family
- Bloods
- California Mexican Mafia (Eme)
- Crips
- Hardtimes 13
- Happytown Pomona
- Hells Angels
- Hermanos de Pistoleros Latinos (HPL)
- La Nuestra Familia
- Latin Kings Lennox 13
- Mara Salvatrucha (MS-13)
- Mexican Mafia
- Mongols Norteños
- Satans Disciples
- Sureños
- Tango Blast
- Texas Mexican Mafia (Mexikanemi)
- Texas Syndicate
- Tri-City Bombers
- Vagos Vatos
- Locos Westside Nogalitas
- Wetback Power
- Wonder Boys
- 18th Street Gang

Source: National Drug Intelligence Center. (2011). *National Gang Threat Assessment 2011: Emerging Trends.* Washington, DC: U.S. Department of Justice.

Gulf cartel wounded Mexican Congressman Horacio Garza and killed his driver in Nuevo Laredo. In April 2007, the State Department began advising Americans to use caution when traveling in Mexico due to drug violence.

Narcoterrorism

A distinction exists between the motives of organized crime groups and the motives of terrorist groups. Organized crime is generally associated with a profit motive, as opposed to terrorist groups, who share more political motives. On the other hand, *narcoterrorism* is characterized as "a subset of terrorism in which terrorist groups or associated individuals participate directly or indirectly in the cultivation, manufacture, transportation, or distribution of controlled substances and the monies derived from these activities" [55].

The term *narcoterrorism* originated in 1983 with former President Fernando Belaúnde Terry of Peru, when he described terrorist-type attacks against his nation's antinarcotics police. Narcoterrorism is generally understood to mean the attempts of narcotics traffickers to influence the policies of a government or a society through violence and intimidation, and to hamper the enforcement of the law by the threat or use of such violence. As a case in point, Colombian Pablo Escobar's ruthless violence in his dealings with the Colombian and Peruvian governments is probably one of the best-known examples of narcoterrorism.

The term has become a subject of controversy, largely due to its use in discussing violent opposition to the United States government's "war on drugs." The term has also been used increasingly for known terrorist organizations that engage in drug-trafficking activity to fund their operations and gain recruits and expertise. These organizations include FARC (Revolutionary Armed Forced of Colombia), ELN (National Liberation Army), and AUC (United Self-Defense Forces of Colombia or *Autodefensas Unidas de Colombia*) in Colombia, and Peru's PCP-SL (Communist Party of Peru).

The links between narcoterrorism groups and drug trafficking include the following:

- Some groups raise funds through extortion or by protecting laboratory operations. In return for cash payments or possibly in exchange for weapons, the groups protect cocaine laboratories in southern Colombia. They also encourage coca planting and discourage licit alternative development.
- In 2001, three members of the Irish Republican Army (IRA) were arrested in Colombia for collaborating with the FARC. The three men were charged with traveling on false passports and providing the FARC with weapons instruction.
- Some terrorist groups apparently have assisted drug-trafficking groups in transporting and storing cocaine and marijuana within Colombia. In particular, some groups protect clandestine airstrips in southern Colombia.
- Elements of some FARC units in southern Colombia are directly involved in drug-trafficking activities, such as controlling local cocaine base markets. At least one FARC front has served as a cocaine source of supply for one international drug-trafficking organization.
- Although there is no evidence that the FARC or ELN have elements established in the United States, their drug-trafficking activity impacts the United States and Europe.
- Several self-defense groups also raise funds through extortion or by protecting laboratory operations in northern and central Colombia [56].

The FARC has been characterized as the most dangerous international terrorist group based in the Western hemisphere. It occupies large swaths of territory in Colombia and is a hierarchical organization that in 2010 comprised 12,000–18,000 members [57]. At the lowest level, the FARC is made up of 77 distinct military units, called *fronts*, organized by geographical location. These in turn are grouped into seven *blocs*. The FARC is led by a seven-member Secretariat and a 27-member Central General Staff, or Estado Mayor, responsible for setting the cocaine policies of the FARC. The FARC is responsible for the production of more than half of the world's supply of cocaine and nearly two-thirds of the cocaine imported into the United States, and it is the world's leading cocaine manufacturer [58]. The FARC initially involved itself in the cocaine and cocaine paste trade by imposing a "tax" on individuals involved in every stage of cocaine production.

Later, FARC leadership ordered that the FARC become the exclusive buyer of the raw cocaine paste used to make cocaine in all areas under FARC occupation. In the late 1990s, the FARC leadership met and voted unanimously in favor of a number of resolutions, including resolutions to expand coca production in areas of Colombia under FARC control, expand the FARC's international distribution routes, increase the number of crystallization laboratories in which cocaine paste would be converted into cocaine, appoint members within each Front to be in charge of coca production, raise prices that the FARC would pay to *campesinos* (peasant farmers) from whom they purchased cocaine paste, and mandate that better chemicals be used to increase the quality of cocaine paste [59].

In April 2010, the U.S. Department of Justice indicted two top members of the 16th Front of the FARC, including Juan Jose Martinez-Vega, known as Chiguiro, and Erminso Cuevas Cabrera, known as Mincho. Martinez-Vega worked as the FARC's chief associate in its 16th Front, exchanging large quantities of cocaine for tons of weapons, explosives, ammunition, and other logistical supplies. In that capacity, Martinez-Vega coordinated a network of arms suppliers and cocaine traffickers throughout Colombia and neighboring countries. Cuevas Cabrera, the brother of FARC Southern Bloc commander Fabian Ramirez, worked as the chief of cocaine manufacturing for the FARC's 14th Front. In that capacity, Cuevas Cabrera directed the weekly production of thousands of pounds of cocaine at hidden jungle laboratories controlled by the FARC, and coordinated the sale and transportation of this cocaine [60].

The 16th Front has been known for operating out of a remote village in eastern Colombia, where they operate an airstrip, engage in trafficking activities, and control all the operations in that particular arena. The cocaine that the 16th Front transports out of that area is paid for with currency, weapons, and equipment [61].

In March 2002, the Colombian Army and the Colombian National Police reclaimed the demilitarized zone from the FARC and uncovered significant evidence of the FARC's involvement in drug trafficking. The police went into the demilitarized zone and found two major cocaine laboratories. In all, the police seized 5 tons of processed cocaine from that particular site, demonstrating the enormity of this one processing site alone. Also present at the site was a 200-foot communications tower that the FARC operated. This seizure was significant in that it was the first time evidence was uncovered that the FARC was involved in the cocaine trade from start to finish, from cultivation to processing and distribution.

The violent activities of the FARC and other groups have not been limited to Colombia. They have also become a destabilizing force along the northern border of Ecuador, where violence and coca-processing activities have increased. Similarly, the FARC's violence and coca-processing activities have also spread to Panama. Venezuela, too, is experiencing increased violence.

In response to insurgent violence, right-wing "self-defense groups" emerged in Colombia during the 1980s. Hundreds of illegal self-defense groups—financed by wealthy cattle ranchers, emerald miners, coffee plantation owners, drug traffickers, and so on—conduct paramilitary operations throughout Colombia. The loose coalition known as the AUC is the best known of these self-defense groups. Carlos Castano is the best recognized leader of the AUC.

In 2000, the United States began funding Plan Colombia, intending to eradicate drug crops and to take action against drug lords accused of engaging in narcoterrorism (e.g., the leaders of the FARC and the AUC). The United States government is funding large-scale drug eradication campaigns and supporting Colombian military operations seeking the extradition of notorious commanders such as Manuel Marulanda Velez, among others.

Although al-Qa'ida is often said to finance its activities through drug trafficking, the *9/11 Commission Report* notes that "while the drug trade was a source of income for the Taliban, it did not serve the same purpose for al-Qa'ida, and there is no reliable evidence that bin Laden was involved in or made his money through drug trafficking." The organization gains most of its finances through donations, particularly those from "wealthy Saudi individuals."

■ ■ Critical Thinking Task ■

Terrorists sometimes use drug trafficking as a means of raising funds. How can law enforcement differentiate between terrorists and drug runners when these crimes overlap? Should penalties differ depending on the motive behind the trafficking operation?

East African Gangs

Somali Gangs

Somali gang presence has increased in several cities throughout the United States. Somali gangs are most prevalent in the Minneapolis–St. Paul, Minnesota; San Diego, California; and Seattle, Washington areas, primarily as a result of proximity to the Mexican and Canadian borders, according to ICE, National Gang Intelligence Center (NGIC), and law enforcement reporting. Somali gang activity has also been reported in other cities throughout the United States such as Nashville, Tennessee; Clarkston, Georgia; Columbus, Ohio; East Brunswick, New Jersey; and Tucson, Arizona. Unlike most traditional street gangs, Somali gangs tend to align and adopt gang names based on clan or tribe, although a few have joined national gangs such as the Crips and Bloods.

Recent research suggests that East African gangs are present in at least 30 jurisdictions, including ones in California, Georgia, Minnesota, Ohio, Texas, Virginia, and Washington. Somali gangs are involved in drug and weapons trafficking, human trafficking, credit card fraud, prostitution, and violent crime. Homicides involving Somali victims are often the result of clan feuds between gang members. Sex trafficking of females across jurisdictional and state borders for the purpose of prostitution is also a growing trend among Somali gangs.

In November 2010, 29 suspected Somali gang members were indicted for a prostitution trafficking operation, according to open-source reporting. Over a 10-year period, Somali gang members transported underage females from Minnesota to Ohio and Tennessee for prostitution.

In February 2009, five Somali gang members were arrested for murdering drug dealers in Dexter and Athens, Ohio, during home invasion robberies, according to law enforcement reporting [62]. Although some Somali gangs adopt Bloods or Crips gang monikers, they typically do not associate with other African-American gangs. Somali nationals— mostly refugees displaced by the war(s) in Somalia and surrounding countries—tend to migrate to specific low-income communities, which are often heavily controlled by local Bloods and Crips street gangs. The Somali youth may emulate the local gangs, which frequently leads to friction with other gangs, such as Bloods, Crips, and Ethiopian gangs [63].

Sudanese Gangs

Sudanese gangs in the United States have been expanding since 2003, and have been reported in Iowa, Minnesota, Nebraska, North Dakota, South Dakota, and Tennessee. Some Sudanese gang members have weapons and tactical knowledge from their involvement in conflicts in their native country. The *African Pride* gang is thought to be one of the most aggressive and dangerous of the Sudanese street gangs in Iowa, Minnesota, Nebraska, and North and South Dakota.

Nigerian Drug Traffickers

Nigerian-based organized crime groups have been heavily involved in the smuggling of large quantities of Southeast Asian heroin to the United States since the mid-1980s. Early Nigerian drug trafficking revolved around groups of Nigerian naval officers who were being trained in India and gained access to Southwest Asian heroin, which they subsequently moved on to the United States. Subsequently, Nigerian criminal organizations shifted their sourcing from Southwest to Southeast Asian heroin, primarily from Thailand. Nigerian traffickers obtain their heroin in Thailand and then pay couriers (usually fellow Nigerians) to smuggle small amounts of heroin to the United States on commercial aircraft. The fee paid to drug couriers is far in excess of what a Nigerian citizen could legitimately earn in a year [64,65].

Nigerian drug couriers tend to use rudimentary and rather crude techniques to move drugs. Devices such as hollowed-out shoes and false-bottom suitcases are common modalities of smuggling. In addition, some couriers engage in a practice known as *swallowing*, which involves the ingestion of up to 150 condoms full of heroin that will be expelled upon the couriers' arrival in the United States. This is a dangerous practice because the breakage of just one condom will result in a fatal overdose of high-purity heroin.

Because of law enforcement targeting of Nigerian citizens, Nigerian drug traffickers are increasingly turning to couriers of other nationalities, in particular young women of European or United States citizenry who they believe are less likely to be selected for search. Members of the United States military traveling in uniform are also frequently recruited by Nigerian traffickers. Some Nigerian criminal organizations have actually set up courier training schools to instruct couriers in methods to avoid or divert the attention of customs officials, and to instruct them in how to avoid drug courier profiling.

The usual pattern followed by Nigerian-employed couriers begins with the acquisition of the heroin in Bangkok. The courier then flies to a transit country (often Indonesia or Egypt), where the drugs are handed off to a second courier, who flies to another transit country where they are less likely to raise suspicions of United States customs officials. There the drugs are transferred to a third and last courier. The point of these complicated arrangements is to conceal the point of origin for the drug (Bangkok) from United States officials.

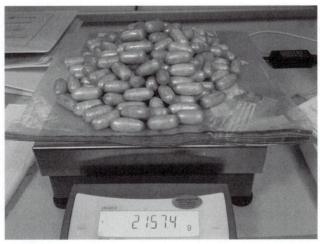

FIGURE 9.3 This photo provided by the U.S. Customs and Border Protection shows nearly 5 pounds of ingested heroin pellets. Customs officials at Dulles International Airport say a Nigerian woman set a record when she allegedly tried to smuggle nearly 5 pounds of swallowed heroin into the country. She was charged with drug smuggling in federal court in Alexandria, Virginia. *Source: AP Photo/US Customs and Border Protection.*

Nigerian traffickers also frequently employ an additional smuggling technique known as *shotgunning*, which is the practice of placing many couriers on the same flight to the United States. The hope is to overwhelm customs officials upon arrival. If some couriers on the flight are detained, the others will inevitably get through. The profit margin for heroin is so high that the loss of even a significant portion of a shipment still leaves the traffickers with immense profits. In addition to human couriers, some Nigerian trafficking syndicates have begun to use express mail as means of getting the drugs to the United States.

Once in the United States, the heroin is sold by Nigerian wholesalers. Nigerian syndicates are especially active in cities with large Nigerian émigré populations, such as Chicago, which is home to 200,000 Nigerian nationals. In the city, the Nigerian wholesalers sell the heroin to street-level retailing organizations, particularly street gangs such as the Blackstone Rangers and the Vice Lords.

By the end of the twentieth century, Nigerian traffickers controlled 57–90 percent of the market for Southeast Asian heroin in the United States. During the 1980s, high-purity Southeast Asian heroin was the most common substance on the United States market. However, the entry of Colombian drug syndicates into the heroin market in the late 1990s seriously undercut the Nigerian share of the market. Importing heroin from Southeast Asia is very expensive; importing from Colombia is far cheaper. High-grade Colombian heroin is now available at a much lower price than Nigerian-imported Southeast Asian heroin. This competition from the Colombians has caused the Nigerians to begin to seek markets for their heroin in Europe.

Dominican Drug-Trafficking Organizations

The Dominican Republic is one of the poorest countries in the world. Dominican drug-trafficking organizations started out as retail cocaine dealers in emigrant communities in the United States. Perhaps the most famous of these communities was the Washington Heights area of Manhattan, in New York City. Starting in the mid-1970s, Dominican immigrants moved into this community and began handling Colombian-supplied cocaine. Soon thereafter, their trafficking activities had spread into New Jersey, Connecticut, and some of the affluent suburbs of New York [66,67].

Dominican drug traffickers were for the most part retail operators until the 1990s. It was at that point that many Colombian drug syndicates began to divest themselves of wholesale operations, passing them on to Mexican drug syndicates. The Mexicans were charging a transport fee of 50 percent of the drug shipment. Traffickers from the Dominican Republic saw this as an opportunity to get into the wholesale cocaine business. The Dominican Republic is closer to New York City than is Mexico, emigrant Dominican communities had already been established in New York, and drug distribution systems had already been established in those communities. The Dominican trafficking syndicates made the Colombians an offer they couldn't refuse. For transportation of wholesale cocaine shipments to the New York City area, they would charge only 25 percent of the shipment as a fee, thereby undercutting the Mexican syndicates.

As a result of this business arrangement with Colombian cocaine traffickers, two major Dominican drug syndicates emerged. One syndicate, operating out of the Dominican Republic itself, provides stash sites for cocaine shipments from Colombia. This cocaine is transported into the Dominican Republic in small boats or by air drops. Traffickers from the Dominican Republic take it from there, smuggling the drugs into Puerto Rico in boats, repackaging the drugs, and shipping them to the continental United States by way of containerized maritime cargo ships or routine commercial air flights.

Once in New York City, the drugs are distributed by ethnic Colombian wholesalers or, increasingly, by a second syndicate of ethnic Dominicans, which now operates up and down the East Coast. Dominican drug syndicates also operate in smaller cities on the East Coast, including Fall River, Massachusetts, and Lewiston, Maine. Many of these smaller cities have brought in Dominican immigrants to work in low-wage, labor-intensive industries, such as garment manufacturing. Operations in these smaller cities have several advantages for Dominican syndicates. First, they expand their customer base. Second, they face virtually no competition from other established drug-trafficking organizations.

A CLOSER LOOK: DRUG PROFITS AND TERRORISM

Drug trafficking's vast financial profits have long been associated with funding numerous criminal enterprises, not the least of which is terrorism. In 2008, federal authorities identified evidence for the first time that an illegal drug operation in the United States was funneling proceeds to Middle East terrorist groups like Hezbollah. The investigation, a DEA initiative called Operation Mountain Express, smashed several major methamphetamine operations between 2006 and 2008. Arrests were made in Detroit, Cleveland, Chicago, Phoenix, and several California cities. The raids resulted in criminal charges against 136 people and the seizure of nearly 36 tons of pseudoephedrine, 179 pounds of methamphetamine, $4.5 million in cash, eight real estate properties, and 160 cars used by the drug gangs.

Evidence gathered by the DEA indicates that a methamphetamine drug operation in the Midwest involving men of Middle Eastern descent had been shipping money back to terrorist groups, officials said. A majority of the men were smuggling large quantities of the chemical pseudoephedrine from Canada into the Midwest. The smuggling went through two primary Midwest locations, Chicago and Detroit, and involved several men with ties to Jordan, Yemen, Lebanon, and other Middle East countries.

Pseudoephedrine is used in some popular cold and allergy medications. It is an essential ingredient in the creation of methamphetamine, a powerful and increasingly popular drug known on the streets as "ice," "poor man's cocaine" or "crystal meth." Users generally inject or smoke meth. The powdery substance is produced by heating about a dozen chemicals.

The Middle Eastern suspects then were diverting some of the proceeds from the pseudoephedrine sales back to the Middle East to accounts that authorities had begun to connect to terrorist groups. Some of the connections involved the Iranian-backed terror group Hezbollah, and some of the money has been traced to accounts in Lebanon and Yemen.

Dominican syndicates rotate members in the United States. Typically, they move operatives in for a 2-year stay and then retire them to the island. Once back on Dominican soil, drug traffickers are protected by restrictive extradition laws to the United States.

Like many newer trafficking syndicates, the Dominicans still make heavy use of violence as a means of establishing their reputation and protecting their turf. One Dominican syndicate in New York City was directly linked to seven murders, including the shooting of a police officer who had been ambushed after responding to a false 911 call. In the early 1990s, incidents in Massachusetts indicated the violent nature of these traffickers. In Lowell, six people were found hogtied and choked to death as a result of a dispute with Dominican traffickers; in Lawrence, 146 houses were subjected to arson in a turf battle between several emerging Dominican gangs.

The *Trinitarios*, the most rapidly expanding Caribbean gang and the largest Dominican gang, are a violent prison gang with members operating on American streets. They are involved in homicide, violent assaults, robbery, theft, home invasions, and street-level drug distribution. Although predominantly in New York and New Jersey, the Trinitarios have expanded to communities throughout the eastern United States, including Georgia, Massachusetts, Pennsylvania, and Rhode Island. *Dominicans Don't Play* (DDP), the second largest Dominican gang, is based in Bronx, New York; DDP is known for its violent machete attacks and drug-trafficking activities in Florida, Michigan, New Jersey, New York, and Pennsylvania [68,69].

Haitian Gangs

Haitian gangs, such as the Florida-based *Zoe Pound*, have proliferated in many states (primarily along the east coast) in recent years, according to NGIC reporting. According to NGIC reporting, Haitian gangs are present in Connecticut, Florida, Georgia, Indiana, Maryland, Massachusetts, New Jersey, New York, North Carolina, South Carolina, and Texas.

The Zoe Pound gang, a street gang founded in Miami, Florida, by Haitian immigrants in the United States, is involved in drug trafficking, robbery, and related violent crime. In February 2010, 22 suspected members in Chicago, Illinois, were charged with possession of and conspiracy to traffic powder and crack cocaine from Illinois to Florida, according to FBI reporting.

Albanian Drug-Smuggling Networks

The break-up of Yugoslavia in the early 1990s and the subsequent local conflicts between ethnic Serbs, Croats, Bosnians, and Albanians have focused attention on small, highly localized, but increasingly important organized crime groups of Albanian decent, operating primarily from Kosovo or from Albania itself. Albanian organized crime groups tend to be tightly organized groups of individuals related to one another in an ethnic clan system. Though these groups are primarily located in the Balkans and are frequently associated with the Kosovo Liberation Front, their drug-trafficking activities have resulted in a proliferation of small criminal organizations throughout Europe and now in the United States [70,71].

Albanian organized crime groups typically started out in partnership with larger Italian or Russian organized crime syndicates. Their criminal enterprises are varied but usually include smuggling drugs, arms, and cigarettes; alien smuggling; and trafficking women for the purpose of prostitution. Partly as a result of regional conflicts in the Balkans, Albanian émigré and refugee communities have sprung up in many large Western European cities. Using these communities as an organizing base, Albanian organized crime groups have followed.

Initially drug smuggling was just an activity ancillary to arms trafficking, but in the mid-1990s Albanian organized crime groups began purchasing large amounts of heroin from Turkish wholesalers. In the years that followed, Albanian drug syndicates developed their own sources for Southwest Asian (Golden Crescent) heroin, moving the drug to central and northern Europe and becoming major competitors to their former Turkish partners. In addition, by 1999, Albanian crime syndicates were challenging the hegemony of Italian syndicates in heroin trafficking and alien smuggling in Italy. Indeed, Italian law enforcement sources believe the Albanians had taken over most of the prostitution enterprises in Italy by 1999 and were trafficking heroin, hashish, weapons, and cigarettes through Italy for shipment to other European destinations. According to Italian law enforcement, by 2000 the Albanians had literally taken the illicit trade in women and children away from traditional Italian syndicates in Italy itself.

Although Albanian prostitution and heroin operations in the United States are still small-scale, it is clear that Albanian syndicates have been moving into the cities of the northeastern United States for the last several years.

Asian Organized Crime

Asian criminal enterprises have been operating in the United States since the early 1900s. The first of these groups evolved from Chinese *tongs*—social organizations formed by early Chinese-American immigrants. A century later, the criminalized tongs are thriving and have been joined by similar organizations with ties to East and Southeast Asia. Members of the most dominant Asian criminal enterprises affecting the United States have ties—either directly or culturally—to China, Korea, Japan, Thailand, the Philippines, Cambodia, Laos, and Vietnam. Other enterprises are emerging as threats, however, including groups from the South Pacific island nations.

Asian criminal enterprises rely on widespread networks of national and international criminal associates that are extremely mobile. They also adapt easily to the changes around them, have multilingual abilities, can be highly sophisticated in their criminal operations, and have extensive financial capabilities. Some enterprises have commercialized their criminal activities and can be considered business firms of various sizes, from small family-run operations to large corporations.

Asian criminal enterprises have prospered thanks largely to the globalization of the world economies, and to communications technology and international travel. Generous immigration policies have provided many members of Asian criminal enterprises the ability to enter and live on every populated continent in the world today undetected.

There are two categories of Asian criminal enterprises. Traditional criminal enterprises include the Chinese triads (or underground societies) based in Hong Kong, Taiwan, and Macau, as well as the Japanese *yakuza* or *boryokudan*. Nontraditional criminal enterprises include groups such as Chinese criminally influenced tongs, triad affiliates, and other ethnic Asian street gangs found in several countries with sizeable Asian communities.

Asian criminal enterprises conduct traditional racketeering activities normally associated with organized crime: extortion, murder, kidnapping, illegal gambling, prostitution, and loansharking. They also smuggle aliens, traffic heroin and methamphetamine, commit financial fraud, steal autos and computer chips, counterfeit computer and clothing products, and launder money.

There are several trends among Asian criminal enterprises. First, it is more common to see criminal groups cooperate across ethnic and racial heritage lines. Also, some gangs and criminal enterprises have begun to structure their groups in a hierarchical fashion to be more competitive, and the criminal activities they engage in have become globalized. Finally, more of these criminal enterprises are engaging in white-collar crimes, and are commingling their illegal activities with legitimate business ventures.

In 2010, the National Drug Threat Assessment concluded that Asian trafficking organizations have filled a niche by trafficking high-potency marijuana and MDMA—a drug not typically trafficked by Mexican, Colombian, or Dominican trafficking organizations [72]. Asian criminal enterprises have been identified in more than 50 metropolitan areas in the United States. They appear to be more prevalent in Boston, Chicago, Honolulu, Las Vegas, Los Angeles, New Orleans, New York, Newark, Philadelphia, Portland, San Francisco, Seattle, and Washington, DC.

Chinese Organized Crime

Chinese organized crime groups have always posed a particular difficulty for United States law enforcement. Culturally and ethnically organized groups are among the most difficult to infiltrate and accumulate intelligence about. Chinese syndicates, operating primarily in the ethnically defined, tightly organized Chinese communities of many major cities, have been virtually impossible to penetrate. The triads, tongs, and Chinese street gangs operating in the United States have traditionally been able to deflect most law enforcement efforts to control their activities. That problem has become even more difficult at the turn of the twenty-first century because a fourth Chinese organized crime entity—syndicates from mainland China—has now also established a presence in the United States [73].

The large, traditionally organized *triads*, headquartered in Hong Kong, Macau, and Taiwan, continue to be the largest Chinese organized crime groups operating worldwide. Triads, most of which trace their origins to seventeenth-century China, continue to control traditional illicit enterprises such as extortion, illegal gambling, gunrunning, and drug trafficking. However, these newer mainland criminal organizations may be more aggressive and more difficult to control. First, they are not encumbered by the traditional organizational structure of the triads, which is more ceremonial than functional in the world of organized crime. The newer groups tend to be more loosely organized and more flexible. They are therefore much more responsive to law enforcement pressure and to economic fluctuations and opportunities. Second, they have moved more aggressively than the triads into newer enterprises such as software piracy, product counterfeiting, credit card fraud, and computer chip theft, allowing them to quickly build vast reserves to finance their forays into drug trafficking.

Traditionally, the triads established close working relationships with ethnic Chinese groups in major cities on the Pacific Rim of the United States and in Europe. Working with *tongs* and street gangs, they easily established local criminal structures to facilitate their enterprises and to purchase their drugs. The newer criminal syndicates from the mainland have apparently broken this monopoly and now deal directly with the tongs and the street gangs themselves. This means that, like the more traditional triads, they now have a broad range of criminal contacts in many countries that can broker deals and provide logistical support.

Chinese organized crime groups have for decades had a strong presence in the many ethnic Chinese neighborhoods and urban enclaves around the world. Gambling operations, prostitution, loan sharking, and narcotics trafficking were the mainstay of these criminal organizations operating through the triads, tongs, and street gangs. What has changed is that another, newer type of criminal syndicate has been added to the milieu.

Chinese criminal organizations, no matter their origin, have always derived great strength from their ability to overlook ethnic differences and cooperate freely and openly with other groups around the world. In the United States and Europe, for example, Chinese organized crime groups have worked closely with Italian, Dominican, and occasionally Mexican and Colombian drug traffickers in trafficking heroin.

The well-established ethnic Chinese communities of Europe and North America have created established and relatively safe footholds for Chinese organized crime, thus making the United States and Europe major markets for illegal goods and services. In addition to the United States, Chinese organized crime activity is particularly prominent in the Netherlands, the United Kingdom, and Germany. Since the late 1980s and early 1990s, Chinese criminal organizations have also established strong footholds in central Europe, a major conduit for moving illegal Chinese immigrants to Western Europe.

Triads and Tongs

Although traditional triad societies are based in Hong Kong, Macau, or Taiwan, they have also exercised great power in every country that has a sizeable émigré Chinese community. Estimates are that the triads, collectively, have a worldwide membership that exceeds 100,000. The triads are traditionally organized associations of Chinese businessmen and Chinese organized criminals who are involved in a panoply of criminal enterprises. Most Hong Kong-based triads have evolved over the years from traditional cultural groups into loose-knit associations of both illicit and licit businessmen, cooperating with each other and sharing mutual business interests. Contrary to some perceptions, triad leaders neither dictate what criminal enterprises their members should pursue nor receive any direct monetary remuneration from those enterprises. They simply provide introductions and facilitate mutual association.

There are 60 different triad societies operating in Hong Kong alone. Hong Kong's largest triad is the Sun Yee On, which is also the only remaining triad with the traditional hierarchical structure. The 14K triad, probably the second most influential in Hong Kong, has abandoned traditional hierarchies and is now a loose confederation of more than 15 separate groups. In addition to their drug-trafficking activities, the Hong Kong triads have been expanding their criminal enterprises into new ventures, including high-tech computer crime and the manipulation of the stock and futures markets. By the 1990s, the Hong Kong triads were engaged in an expansion that would have been unthinkable just a few years earlier, extending their criminal activities from Hong Kong into the Guangdong region of south China.

The largest triads, such as Hong Kong's 14K and Sun Yee On, and Taiwan's United Bamboo, have autonomous branches extending worldwide. It is important to understand that these are affiliated organizations—not extensions of one massive criminal organization into other countries. In addition, in response to the booming economy of the United States during the Clinton administration, the triads began investing heavily in legitimate businesses in the United States and Europe.

Triad groups frequently share resources and cooperate on specific projects, but it is important to understand that there is no international triad organization and no centralized control of triad groups. Enterprises such as alien smuggling tend to center on small-scale triad-affiliated organizations, whereas drug trafficking seems to involve more ad hoc collusion. The key distinction, though, is that it is ad hoc collusion based on mutual interests in a specific project or at a particular point in time, not an overarching criminal conspiracy.

The Chinese Tongs

Chinese criminal enterprises are those ethnic Chinese organized crime groups engaged in racketeering activities. Chinese criminal enterprises can be categorized into two types: traditional criminal enterprises (e.g., the Wo Hop To Triad and 14K Triad) and nontraditional Chinese criminal enterprises (e.g., the Fuk Ching Gang and Tai Huen Chai, aka Big Circle Boys). Traditional Chinese criminal enterprises are based in Hong Kong, Macau, and Taiwan. Many nontraditional Chinese criminal enterprises are based in various countries that have sizeable Asian communities.

Traditional Chinese criminal enterprises are triad groups that share the following similarities: (1) a historical origin that can be traced back several hundred years, and (2) a rigid hierarchical organizational structure and a ritual that binds their members together.

For example, San Yee On of the Chiu Chow group was formed exclusively by the Chiu Chow minority people in Hong Kong, has a rigid hierarchical organizational structure, and uses the triad rituals, such as an initiation ceremony for new members and a promotion ceremony for members promoted to the Office Bearer rank. Leaders of triad societies do not direct the activities of their members in other countries, but their influence is international due to their financial strength and global business and personal connections.

Most of the senior members of these well-established triad societies are quasilegitimate businessmen. Many of them have obtained foreign passports for themselves and their family members, and have diversified their businesses and invested their criminal proceeds in other countries. They cooperate with overseas triad members to undertake international crimes, such as drug trafficking, alien smuggling, credit card fraud, theft of computer equipment and automobiles, piracy of intellectual property, and money laundering.

With some exceptions, the organizational structure of modern-day Chinese triads is flatter and simpler. Most triad societies have been decentralized to the extent that there is no ultimate central committee to unify different factions of the society that fight against one another for turf control. Modern triad members who only look out for their personal benefits are individualistic entrepreneurs. They switch triad societies almost at will and are rarely loyal to the organization to which they belong. They weigh the benefits they can get out of their Dai Lo (Big Brother). If they are not satisfied with the relationship, they can approach a new Dai Lo from another triad group and request to come "under his wings." They use their triad organization as a power base that provides them with a network through which they can assemble resources to organize criminal activities for fast money.

Nontraditional Chinese criminal enterprises are organized crime groups operating outside of Hong Kong, Macau, Taiwan, and the People's Republic of China (PRC) that may or may not share the name of a Hong Kong or Taiwan triad, but are not otherwise related. Although many nontraditional Chinese criminal enterprises in the United States have ties to Chinese criminal groups in other countries, they are independent entities. For example, the Tung On Gang was a major criminal organization in New York City that had expanded its activities in the northeastern and mid-Atlantic United States. The former leader of this gang was a Red Pole (high-level Office Bearer) of the San Yee On Triad in Hong Kong. In addition to its usual street gang activities, such as debt collection, protection, and enforcement, the Tung On Gang also conducted organized crime activities such as extortion, murder, illegal gambling, alien smuggling, drug trafficking, and money laundering. The Tung On Gang's activities were directed locally. The San Yee On Triad in Hong Kong was its connection only for importing and distributing Southeast Asian heroin at the wholesale and retail levels.

After the 1989 Tiananmen Square incident, the United States adopted a liberal policy in granting PRC citizens "political asylum," which attracted a large number of Chinese immigrants to this country. Fueled by the dramatic increase of Chinese immigrants and the large amount of money that has continuously flowed into North America from Hong Kong, Taiwan, and recently China, the Chinese communities in North America have grown rapidly and prosperously. This has provided a huge market for local gang members to expand their influence.

To maintain their competitiveness, some strong gang leaders have attempted to solidify their power bases in various Asian communities by forming alliances with gangs in other regions. The dominant position of members of old triad societies from Hong Kong, Taiwan, and Macau and criminally influenced tongs is challenged by newer criminal groups, such as the Big Circle Boys and Fuk Ching Gang, which originated in mainland China. It is reported that the freedom with which these newer Chinese organized crime groups can operate in China is unmatched by that of any other crime groups. They also have contacts worldwide that enable them to carry out various sophisticated crimes that require extensive coordinated efforts of members in other regions or countries. Chinese criminals represent the entire spectrum of Asian criminal enterprises in their criminal activities and their levels of criminality (from the simple street gang members to the quasi-legitimate businessmen with international connections).

Chinese Syndicates from the Mainland

Criminal syndicates based in mainland China (PRC) are typified by the Big Circle Boys and the Fuk Ching Gang. Both of these gangs have smaller cells operating in Chinese communities around the world. These cells cooperate with each other and with the mainland organizations on an ad hoc basis, but the cells themselves operate autonomously, without centralized authority or direction. Local cell leaders use their connections in Chinese ethnic communities and with the mainland groups to mount what appear to be some very complex criminal operations that are well planned and highly organized. Once again, though, that planning and organization are integral to the cell—not to the overall criminal organization. Because cells have contact with other cells worldwide, they are able to carry out large-scale drug-trafficking, arms-trafficking, and human-trafficking enterprises with surprising ease and success.

Canadian and United States law enforcement intelligence analysts report that the Big Circle Boys, the largest of the mainland groups, has become the most active Asian criminal organization in the world, and has achieved that status in less than a decade. By the end of the 1990s, the Big Circle Boys had established cells in Canada, the United States, and Europe and was extensively engaged in drug trafficking, human trafficking, vehicle theft and trafficking, financial fraud, product counterfeiting, and high-tech crimes. Big Circle Boys cells are also highly sophisticated in their use of technology, which has made them virtually immune from electronic eavesdropping and surveillance. The Big Circle Boys first surfaced in the United States in the early 1990s, and by the end of the decade had major criminal organizations operating in New York, Boston, Seattle, San Francisco, and Los Angeles. The Fuk Ching Gang is best known for its human-trafficking activities, but is also heavily involved in drug trafficking, particularly heroin and methamphetamines.

Yakuza

When all of the many criminal organizations composing the *yakuza* are considered, the *yakuza* would have to rank among the largest and most powerful of the world's organized crime confederations. *Yakuza* organizations are extremely diverse in their criminal enterprises. They also tend to be highly structured and well organized. *Yakuza* organizations not only dominate the Japanese underworld, but also are powerful actors in the legitimate economy. In fact, using their extortionate practice of *sokaiya*, they have successfully penetrated all aspects of social, economic, and political life in Japan [74–76].

There are at least 3,000 separate *yakuza*-affiliated criminal organizations in Japan, with about 90,000 members. Approximately 60 percent of them are housed under the aegis of three large *yakuza* organizations: the Yamaguchi-Gumi, the Sumiyoshi-Kai, and the Inagawa-Kai. These three associations of *yakuza* groups control most gun trafficking, drug trafficking, human trafficking, prostitution, illegal gambling, extortion, and white-collar criminal activity in Japan. Scholars estimate that the scope of *yakuza* activity in Japan amounts to an annual revenue of about $13 billion [77–79].

Most *yakuza* criminal enterprises are based in Japan, although *yakuza* groups have a well-established presence (often in legitimate business activities) in Australia, the United States, and most of Asia. Transnational criminal activity engaged in by *yakuza* groups primarily involves drugs, guns, and trafficking in women for prostitution in the Japanese market.

Most *yakuza* organizations purchase their heroin and methamphetamine supplies from Chinese organized crime groups based in Taiwan and Hong Kong. In recent years, *yakuza* organizations have also established working relationships with South American drug traffickers as a means of obtaining cocaine to be sold in Japan. Chinese and Russian organized crime groups are primary *yakuza* sources for firearms. The arms-trafficking business is one of the most profitable for *yakuza* groups because of extremely restrictive Japanese laws regulating firearms. About 90 percent of the firearms in Japan originate from international sources.

Yakuza organizations also are heavily involved in the international trafficking of human beings, particular foreign workers for the Japanese construction industry, and foreign women for *yakuza*-owned entertainment and prostitution businesses. Yamaguchi-Gumi-affiliated groups are particularly active in the prostitution business and rely heavily on women imported from Russia, Southeast Asia, and Latin America. There is little or no evidence that *yakuza* groups traffic women to the United States.

Most *yakuza* transnational crime activities are used to supply or support criminal enterprises internal to Japan. In the 1990s, *yakuza* organizations apparently began developing more permanent working relationships with Russian organized crime groups. In 1992 the Yamaguchi-Gumi established a more permanent working relationship with Russian organized groups as suppliers of firearms and prostitutes. The establishment of more open trade arrangements between Japan and Russia, and the scheduling of regular flights between major cities in Russia and Japan, have facilitated this relationship.

Yakuza groups traffic drugs in Japan, but there is little evidence that they are involved in drug trafficking in the United States. The real threat posed by *yakuza* in the United States is in the area of legitimate business investment and money laundering. *Yakuza* groups are heavy investors in United States and Canadian real estate, with particularly heavy investments in golf courses and hotels. *Yakuza* groups also launder their criminal profits in the United States by playing the United States stock market and making substantial and potentially destabilizing investments. The Inagawa-Kai *yakuza* confederation, which is involved in drug and arms trafficking, extortion, investment frauds, and money laundering, has invested heavily in Hawaii and the states on the west coast of the United States.

Vietnamese Gangs

A growing threat to Vietnamese communities throughout the United States is the expansion of Vietnamese youth gangs. Preying mostly on members of their own communities, their crimes include extortion, rape, assault, auto theft, murder, and a relatively new brand of robbery: the home invasion. The ages of the members typically range from 14 to 23. Gambling houses are often operated in the homes of Vietnamese gang members and their associates, making it difficult for police to conduct surprise raids.

Southwest Asia

Afghanistan, the Taliban, and Osama bin Laden

The Islamic State of Afghanistan has been a major source country for the cultivation, processing, and trafficking of opiate and cannabis products. In 2000, Afghanistan produced more than 70 percent of the world's supply of illicit opium. Morphine base, heroin, and hashish produced in Afghanistan are trafficked worldwide. Due to the warfare-induced decimation of the country's economic infrastructure, narcotics are a major source of income in Afghanistan.

United States intelligence confirmed a connection between Afghanistan's former ruling Taliban and international terrorist Osama bin Laden and the al-Qa'ida organization. Al-Qa'ida leader Osama bin Laden has been documented as being involved in the financing and facilitation of heroin-trafficking activities [80]. On May 2, 2011, bin Laden was shot and killed inside a private residential compound in Abbottabad, Pakistan, by members of the U.S. Naval Special Warfare Development Group and Central Intelligence Agency operatives in a covert operation.

For decades, Afghanistan has been a formidable producer of opium. According to the official United States government estimates for 2001, Afghanistan produced an estimated 74 metric tons of opium from 1,685 ha of land under opium poppy cultivation. This is a significant decrease from the 3,656 metric tons of opium produced from 64,510 ha of land under opium poppy cultivation in 2000 [81].

In 2002, opium prices in Afghanistan ranged 9–11 times higher than in 2000 (February 2000: $30–43/kg; March 2002: $333/kg). The war on terrorism during 2001 markedly affected the production of opium in Afghanistan. During that year, the United States government estimated that 74 tons of opium were produced, down from more than 3,600 metric tons (75 percent of world production) one year earlier [82]. By October 2009, the Taliban were back in the opium production business, supporting the opium trade and deriving funding from it [83].

The United Wa State Army

Methamphetamine and heroin trafficking finances the efforts of the United Wa State Army (UWSA), which, at 20,000 members, is said to be the largest ethnic army in Myanmar (formerly known as Burma) [84]. The UWSA exists primarily as a separatist organization, seeking autonomy from Myanmar's central government. There is no recognized Wa State in Myanmar, which is divided into divisions, states, and special regions. UWSA funds its separatist activities by being the major international drug-trafficking organization in the region.

Summary

Illicit drugs in the United States finance drug-trafficking organizations with both domestic and foreign origins. The Mexican cartels, which have dominated the news in recent years, were preceded by Colombian cartels, which at one time were one of the more visible types of modern-day drug-trafficking organizations.

Drugs have also attracted the participation of terrorist and insurgent groups in the cocaine trade, such as Colombia's FARC, ELN, and AUC and Peru's PCP-SL. Such groups have been documented as operating in Latin American countries and exerting influence over significant portions of the drug trade. The existence of these groups is fueled by the unstable governments and economies of many source countries. The influence of these types of terrorist organizations reaches other Latin American countries as well.

Asian criminal organizations, such as the Chinese triads and tongs and the Japanese *yakuza*, operate in both the United States and Hong Kong. They also are active in the illicit drug trade. With the increase in Asian nationals in the United States, the ranks of the Chinese tongs are growing in Los Angeles, New York, and other cities.

Do you recognize these terms?

- cartels
- narcoterrorism
- Operation Secure Mexico
- Operation Xcellerator
- spillover violence
- superlabs
- tong
- triad
- yakuza

Discussion Questions

1. List the various foreign organized crime groups that are considered the greatest contributors to the United States' drug abuse problem. Specify the drugs with which each organization is most likely to be involved.

2. What role do the Mexican cartels play in the illicit global drug trade?
3. Identify and discuss the link between FARC (and other insurgent groups in Colombia and Peru) and drug traffickers.
4. Discuss the interplay between drug trafficking and insurgent terrorists.
5. Historically, what events have played the most significant roles in Cuban immigration into the United States?
6. Explain the role of Asian organized crime groups in the illicit drug trade.

References

[1] Perkins, K., & Placido, A. (May 5, 2010). "Drug trafficking violence in Mexico: Implications for U.S." Statement before the U.S. Senate Caucus on International Narcotics Control. *Eurasia Review*. Found at: www.eurasiareview.com/drug-trafficking-violence-in-mexico-implications-for-us.html.
[2] Ibid.
[3] Ibid.
[4] Ibid.
[5] Ibid.
[6] United Nations Office on Drugs and Crime (UNODC). (2010). *The globalization of crime: A transnational organized crime threat assessment*. New York: UNODC, pp. 5–6 .
[7] United Nations Office on Drugs and Crime (UNODC). (2011). *World drug report*. New York: UNODC, p. 8.
[8] Johnson, K. (2010). Violent surge doesn't cross border: Patrols push down rate of drug killings. *USA Today, Mexican-Caribbean Edition.* (January 2–3), 3A.
[9] Congressional Research Service. (2007). *Mexican drug cartels.* October 16, Washington, DC: U.S. Government Printing Office.
[10] Ibid.
[11] National Drug Intelligence Center. (2010). *National drug threat assessment 2010.* February, Washington, DC: U.S. Department of Justice.
[12] Ibid.
[13] Ibid.
[14] Ibid.
[15] Congressional Research Service. (2007). *Mexican drug cartels.* Washington, DC: U.S. Government Printing Office October 16.
[16] Drug Enforcement Administration. (July 23, 2009). *DEA announces Gulf cartel/Los Zetas most-wanted list.* Found at: www.justice.gov/dea/pubs/states/newsrel/2009/dallas072309.html. Accessed January 8, 2010.
[17] Congressional Research Service. (2007). *Mexican drug cartels.* Washington, DC: U.S. Government Printing Office October 16.
[18] Embassy of the United States, Mexico. (May 17, 2007). *Major Mexican drug trafficker's assets in U.S. frozen.* Press Release. Found at: http://mexico.usembassy.gov/eng/releases/ep070517Zambada.html.
[19] Ibid.
[20] Congressional Research Service. (2007). *Mexican drug cartels.* Washington, DC: U.S. Government Printing Office October 16.
[21] Ibid.
[22] Ibid.
[23] Drug Enforcement Administration. (October 2009). *La Familia Michoacana Fact Sheet.* Found at: www.justice.gov/dea/pubs/pressrel/pr102209a1.pdf.
[24] Ibid.
[25] Congressional Research Service. (2007). *Mexican drug cartels.* Washington, DC: U.S. Government Printing Office October 16.
[26] Drug Enforcement Administration. (April 27, 2007). *Two Tijuana cartel figures plead guilty.* Found at: www.justice.gov/dea/pubs/states/newsrel/sd042707.html. Accessed January 4, 2010.

[27] National Drug Intelligence Center. (December 2008). *National drug threat assessment 2009.* Washington, DC: U.S. Department of Justice.

[28] Trahan, J., Londono, E., & Corchado, A. (December 13, 2005). Drug wars' long shadow. *The Dallas Morning News.* Retrieved August 17, 2009.

[29] Ibid.

[30] Burton, F. (May 2, 2007). Mexico: The price of peace in the cartel wars. *Stratfor Global Intelligence.* Found at: www.stratfor.com/mexico_price_peace_cartel_wars. Retrieved August 16, 2009.

[31] Drug Enforcement Administration. (2009). *Hundreds of Alleged Sinaloa Cartel Members and Associates Arrested in Nationwide Takedown of Mexican Drug Traffickers.* February 25. Found in: www.justice. gov/dea/pubs/states/newsrel/2009/la022509.html. Accessed January 10, 2010.

[32] Drug Enforcement Administration. (2009). *La Familia Michoacana Fact Sheet* October. Found at: www.justice.gov/dea/pubs/pressrel/pr102209a1.pdf.

[33] National Drug Intelligence Center. (December 2008). *National drug threat assessment 2009.* Washington, DC: U.S. Department of Justice.

[34] Trahan, J., Londono, E., & Corchado, A. (December 13, 2005). Drug wars' long shadow. *The Dallas Morning News.* Retrieved 17.08.09.

[35] Steller, T. (April 15, 1998). Mexican drug runners may have used C-130 from Arizona. *The Arizona Daily Star.* Archived at California State University Northridge. Found at: www.csun.edu/Communi- cationStudies/ben/news/cia/980415.steller.html. Retrieved September 26, 2007.

[36] Burton, F. (May 2, 2007). *Mexico: The price of peace in the cartel wars. The stratfor global intelligence.* Found at: www.stratfor.com/mexico_price_peace_cartel_wars. Retrieved 16.08.09.

[37] Ibid.

[38] Congressional Research Service. (2007). *Mexican drug cartels.* Washington, DC: U.S. Government Printing Office. October 16.

[39] Drug Enforcement Administration. (July 23, 2009). *DEA announces Gulf cartel/Los Zetas most- wanted list.* Found at: www.justice.gov/dea/pubs/states/newsrel/2009/dallas072309.html. Accessed 08.01.10.

[40] Grayson, G. W. (February 2009). *La Familia: Another deadly Mexican syndicate.* Foreign Policy Research Institute. Archived from the original on 15.09.09. Found at: www.webcitation.org/5joR97DuX.

[41] Ibid.

[42] Associated Press. (2010). *La Familia Cartel Targeted, Police Arrest More Than 300 Across U.S.* October 22, 2009. Found at: www.streetgangs.com/news/102209_lafamiliacartel.

[43] Drug Enforcement Administration. (October 2009). *La Familia Michoacana Fact Sheet.* Found at: www.justice.gov/dea/pubs/pressrel/pr102209a1.pdf.

[44] Drug Enforcement Administration. (July 23, 2009). *DEA announces Gulf cartel/Los Zetas most-wanted list.* Found at: www.justice.gov/dea/pubs/states/newsrel/2009/dallas072309.html. Accessed 08.01.10.

[45] Richey, W. (2009). "U.S. Strikes at Mexican Cartel's Drug-and-Gun Trade." *The Christian Science Monitor.* October 22.

[46] Drug Enforcement Administration. (2009). *175 Alleged Gulf cartel members arrested in massive inter- national law enforcement operation* September 17. Found at: www.justice.gov/dea/pubs/pressrel/ pr091708.html. Accessed January 8, 2010.

[47] Richey, W. (October 22, 2009). U.S. strikes at Mexican cartel's drug-and-gun trade. *The Christian Science Monitor.*

[48] Ibid.

[49] Congressional Research Service. (2007). *Mexican drug cartels.* Washington, DC: U.S. Government Printing Office. October 16.

[50] Ibid.

[51] Pinkerton, J. (June 29, 2005). Freed captives in Mexico say police abducted them. *Houston Chronicle.*

[52] Ibid.

[53] Ibid.

[54] Congressional Research Service. (2007). *Mexican drug cartels.* Washington, DC: U.S. Government Printing Office. October 16.

[55] Hutchinson, A. (2002). *Congressional testimony before the Senate Judiciary Committee, Subcommittee on Technology, Terrorism, and Government Information.* Washington, DC: Drug Enforcement Administration.

[56] Office of National Drug Control Policy. (2010). *National drug control strategy 2010.* Washington, DC: U.S. Department of Justice. Executive Office of the President of the United States.

[57] Drug Enforcement Administration. (July 23, 2009). *DEA announces Gulf cartel/Los Zetas most-wanted list.* Found at: www.justice.gov/dea/pubs/states/newsrel/2009/dallas072309.html. Accessed 08.01.10.

[58] Ibid.

[59] Ibid.

[60] Ibid.

[61] Office of National Drug Control Policy. (2010). *National drug control strategy 2010.* Washington, DC: U.S. Department of Justice Executive Office of the President of the United States.

[62] Congressional Research Service. (2007). *Mexican drug cartels.* Washington, DC: U.S. Government Printing Office. October 16.

[63] Ibid.

[64] Rake, A. (June 1995). Drugged to the eyeballs. *New African,* 16–19.

[65] Smith, R., Holmes, M., & Kaufmann, P. (1999). *Nigerian advance fee fraud.* Canberra, Australia: Australian Institute of Criminology.

[66] Jackall, R. (1997). *Wild cowboys: Urban marauders and the forces of order.* Cambridge, MA: Harvard University Press.

[67] Pellerano, R., & Jorge, E. (1997). Money-laundering rules in the Dominican Republic. *Banking Law Journal, 114*(2), 136–141.

[68] United Nations Office on Drugs and Crime (UNODC). (2010). *The globalization of crime: A transnational organized crime threat assessment.* New York: UNODC, pp. 5–6.

[69] United Nations Office on Drugs and Crime (UNODC). (2011). *World drug report.* New York: UNODC, p. 8.

[70] DeStefano, A. (September 9, 1985). Balkan connection: Brazen as the Mafia, ethnic Albanian thugs specialize in mayhem; active in the heroin trade, the faction is so violent, prosecutors need guards. *The Wall Street Journal,* 1.

[71] Galeotti, M. (1998). Turkish organized crime: Where state, crime and rebellion conspire. *Transnational Organized Crime, 4*(1), 25–41.

[72] National Drug Intelligence Center. (January 2009). *National gang threat assessment 2009.* Washington, DC: U.S. Department of Justice.

[73] Robinson, J. (1999). *The merger: How organized crime is taking over Canada and the world.* Toronto: McClelland and Stewart.

[74] Huang, F., & Vaughn, M. (1992). A descriptive analysis of Japanese organized crime: the boryokudan from 1945 to 1988. *International Criminal Justice Review, 2,* 19–57.

[75] Shibata, Y. (1996). Quaking Lenders: How Gangsters Complicate Japan's Banking Crisis. *Global Finance,* (10 January), pp. 40–41.

[76] Song, J., & Dombrink, J. (1994). Asian emerging crime groups: Examining the definition of organized crime. *Criminal Justice Review, 19*(2), 228–243.

[77] Huang, F., & Vaughn, M. (1992). A descriptive analysis of Japanese organized crime: The boryokudan from 1945 to 1988. *International Criminal Justice Review, 2,* 19–57.

[78] Smith, R., Holmes, M., & Kaufmann, P. (1999). *Nigerian advance fee fraud.* Canberra, Australia: Australian Institute of Criminology.

[79] Song, J., & Dombrink, J. (1994). Asian emerging crime groups: Examining the definition of organized crime. *Criminal Justice Review, 19*(2), 228–243.

[80] Hutchinson, A. (2002). *Congressional testimony before the Senate Judiciary Committee, Subcommittee on Technology, Terrorism, and Government Information.* Washington, DC: Drug Enforcement Administration.

[81] Ibid.

[82] Ibid.

[83] Schmitt, E. (October 18, 2009). Many sources feed Taliban's war chest. *New York Times.* Found in: http://www.nytimes.com/2009/10/19/world/asia/19taliban.html?_r=1&hp=&adxnnl=1&adxnnlx=1281434453-R/H5H6liJIBpB/OuLEm2Iw. Accessed August 10, 2010.

[84] Johnson, T. (August 29, 2009). China urges Burma to bridle ethnic militia uprising at border. *The Washington Post.* Found at: www.washingtonpost.com/wp-dyn/content/article/2009/08/28/AR2009082803764.html.

Fighting Back

Because drug abuse is so diverse and because it touches so many different lives, many concerned people throughout our communities have strong commitments to combating the problem. These people include police officers, social workers, educators, church officials, and concerned parents, to name only a few. Each of these people seeks new and innovative ways to control drug abuse and crime in their neighborhoods. To this end, some important questions can be asked: in addition to relying on the police, what other community resources can be used to confront drug abuse? Should drug control policy focus on controlling the supply side or the demand side of the drug abuse problem? What role should churches and schools play in ensuring a drug-free community? To what extent can the average person make a difference in society's fight against drugs? The remaining five chapters of this book deal with these questions and more by addressing both the government's and the public's responses to the nation's drug abuse dilemma.

10
The Drug Control Initiative

This chapter will enable you to:

- Understand the various goals of drug control
- Learn the different categories of drug laws
- Learn the strategies of drug enforcement agencies
- Understand the role of federal interdiction efforts
- Gain insight regarding the assorted efforts involved in drug control

Many controversial and vital issues must be considered in designing drug control strategies. A paradox of sorts becomes evident when we see, for instance, one interest group demand that law enforcement officers be given more police authority with which to perform their drug control duties, while others protest that expanding the roles of government authority decreases the constitutional and personal freedoms of individuals.

Controlling dangerous drugs involves a profusion of tasks that are sometimes contradictory; these include reducing the overall demand for drugs, reducing both the international and the domestic supplies of drugs, controlling organized crime, minimizing the spreading of dangerous diseases (such as AIDS) through intravenous drug use, using nontraditional drug enforcement tactics, such as reverse stings and criminal profiling, and minimizing the use of dangerous drugs in professional and amateur sports.

The government's response to the nation's drug problem on both state and federal levels has been shaped by a number of important variables. For example, both levels of government must consider their statutory and constitutional authority to intervene. In addition, the jurisdiction of each law enforcement agency must be considered along with the realization that the extent of drug use across the country varies according to cities and communities. For instance, crack cocaine and heroin are predominantly big-city problems, with marijuana and methamphetamine primarily plaguing rural areas.

Strategies to combat the drug problem also vary widely depending on community public opinion, the resources and jurisdiction of the law enforcement agencies in those communities, and the type of drugs most commonly abused and sold on the streets. Common community strategies include drug education, drug testing of workers, and police intervention on both the supply and demand sides of abuse and trafficking.

The Goals of Drug Control

In addition to controlling drug use and crime associated with drug use, it is the goal of law enforcement agencies to disrupt criminal organizations that infiltrate neighborhoods and communities. As discussed in Chapter 4, many business-related facets exist in the drug trade, including the production, manufacturing, transportation, and sale of drugs. It is these various components of the drug trade that drug law enforcement attempts to upset. Therefore, each level of the drug business remains a viable enforcement target. These levels are (1) the source of the drugs, which is the location of the cultivation and production of opium poppies, coca leaves, and marijuana; (2) smuggling operations, which transport drugs into the country and across state lines; (3) wholesale distribution of drugs; and (4) retail sales.

It could be argued that the enforcement of drug laws makes selling drugs all that much more enticing and exciting for criminals. In addition, it increases the cost of the drugs, while making the drug business more dangerous for those involved in it. Risks incurred by law enforcement officials at each stage of the drug trade increase from one level to another. The philosophy behind enforcement efforts is that if police seize drugs and other assets belonging to traffickers, and then they arrest and imprison the traffickers and their associates, it will deter others who are considering entering the trade. For those not deterred, incarceration prevents their continued participation in the drug trade.

Drug Laws

An illegal sale of drugs violates both state and federal laws. Depending on which law enforcement agency is able to document the violation, either state or federal charges are brought against the offender. In any case, those laws provide the essence of reducing the supply of and demand for drugs. Drug laws are specific about what constitutes a criminal violation, and although specific features of those laws vary across jurisdictions and levels of government, three categories of law can be identified:

- *Possession or use.* This category of law prohibits people from possessing controlled drugs on their person, in their car, or in their home. The only notable exception is possession of drugs pursuant to a lawful prescription. Some states even go so far as to prohibit persons from being under the influence of drugs or using them. The specific levels of proof, such as the amount of the drug that differentiates simple possession from possession with intent to sell, vary from one state to another.
- *Manufacturing.* These laws generally include any activity related to the production of controlled drugs. The term *manufacturing* is broadly used in some legal language and can include cultivation, conversion of certain chemicals to other forms, and preparation and packaging of drugs for retail sale.
- *Distribution.* This category of laws generally refers to the sale and delivery of drugs on both the wholesale and retail levels. Also included are provisions for transportation, importation, and storage of drugs. Generally, the type of drug involved will dictate the specific charge to be filed against the offender.
- *Other prohibited activity.* In addition to the three categories of laws discussed here, many other types of laws are available for the prosecution of drug offenses, including:
  - Drug paraphernalia laws
  - Drug precursor laws

- Money-laundering laws
- Conspiracy laws
- Forfeiture laws
- Racketeering laws (i.e., the Racketeer-Influenced and Corrupt Organizations (RICO) Act)
- Drug diversion laws

A virtual alphabet soup of federal law enforcement agencies are charged in one fashion or another with the task of domestic and/or international drug enforcement. These agencies include the Drug Enforcement Administration (DEA), the Federal Bureau of Investigation (FBI), the U.S. Customs and Border Protection (CBP), the Coast Guard, and U.S. Immigration and Customs Enforcement (ICE). In addition, a wide variety of other federal agencies have been organized to coordinate certain aspects of drug enforcement activities. Because of the bureaucratic fragmentation of federal law enforcement agencies charged with drug enforcement, the exchange of information, as well as coordination and cooperation between agencies, are often problematic and difficult to achieve.

The History of Federal Drug Enforcement

Alcohol prohibition marked the first legal recognition of problems emanating from social consumption of alcohol. The enforcement mechanism for the National Prohibition Act was placed under the commissioner of internal revenue. In addition, a narcotics unit was created, originally employing 170 agents and with an appropriation of $250,000. The narcotics unit operated between 1919 and 1927. By 1927, all powers of drug enforcement were transferred to the secretary of the treasury.

During the years of the narcotics unit's operation, the general public associated narcotics enforcement with the unpopular liquor enforcement efforts of the era. Additionally, scandals tarnished the image of narcotics agents when some agents were found to be falsifying arrest records and accepting payoffs from drug dealers. In response, Congress moved the responsibility of narcotics enforcement to the newly created Federal Bureau of Narcotics (FBN) in 1930. It was after the creation of the FBN that the term *narcotics agent* was generally adopted to refer to FBN drug enforcement personnel.

For the next 35 years, the mission of federal drug enforcement remained somewhat consistent. Through the mid-1960s, the federal government's drug suppression efforts were primarily directed toward the illegal importation of drugs into the country. The authority of the FBN was expanded in 1956 with the passing of the Narcotics Control Act, which, among other things, authorized narcotics agents to carry firearms, and granted them authority to serve both search and arrest warrants.

In 1965, the Drug Abuse Control Amendments (to the 1956 Narcotics Control Act) were passed. These amendments addressed the problem of drugs in the depressant and stimulant category being diverted from legal channels. In 1966, another agency was created to enforce the amendments: the Bureau of Drug Abuse Control (BDAC), within the Department of Health, Education, and Welfare's Food and Drug Administration (FDA). Another advance in drug enforcement occurred in the late 1960s as a result of a study conducted by the Katzenbach Commission. The study concluded with the following recommendations to reduce both the supply of and demand for drugs:

1. Substantially increase the enforcement staffs of the FBN and the Bureau of Customs.
2. Permit courts and correctional authorities to deal flexibly with violators of the drug laws.
3. Undertake research to develop a sound and effective framework of regulatory and criminal laws relating to dangerous drugs.
4. Develop within the National Institute of Mental Health a core of educational and informational materials relating to drugs.

In 1968, for the first time in history, the U.S. Department of Justice was given authority for the enforcement of federal drug laws. With this authority, the FBN and the BDAC were abolished and enforcement responsibility was passed to the newly created Bureau of Narcotics and Dangerous Drugs (BNDD). This was done to eliminate friction between enforcement agencies, and to minimize bureaucratic fragmentation within the federal government's drug enforcement effort.

To assist state and local drug enforcement agencies, the Office for Drug Abuse and Law Enforcement (ODALE) was established in 1972. Several months after the creation of ODALE, the Office of National Narcotic Intelligence (ONNI) was created to serve as a clearinghouse for any information considered useful in the administration's antidrug initiative. ONNI was also charged with disseminating information to state and local law enforcement agencies for which there was a demonstrated "legitimate official need."

In 1973, President Richard Nixon implemented a drug enforcement reorganization plan that addressed the supply side of drug abuse, as well as the demand component of the problem. One of the most important directives of the plan was the creation of the DEA within the Department of Justice. Under the plan, the administrator of the DEA would report directly to the attorney general, and would assume all personnel and budgets of the BNDD, ODALE, and ONNI. The drug enforcement agencies discussed in this chapter are currently the agencies responsible for drug control on the national level.

The Drug Enforcement Administration

As mentioned, the DEA, established in 1973, was declared the lead agency in the federal government's efforts to suppress the illicit drug trade. Acting under the U.S. Department of Justice, the DEA is the only federal law enforcement agency for which drug enforcement is the only responsibility. The DEA has primary responsibility for investigating drug-related events, as well as collecting and disseminating drug-related intelligence information. In addition, the agency tries to coordinate efforts among federal, state, and local law enforcement agencies also involved in drug suppression.

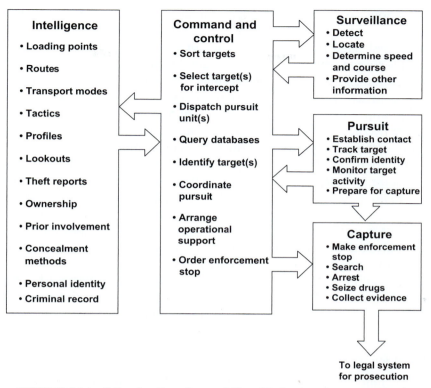

FIGURE 10.1 Interdiction functions. *Source: Office of Technology Assessment (1987).*

The dominant philosophy of the DEA is to eliminate drugs as close to their sources as possible and to disrupt the drug-trafficking system by identifying, arresting, and prosecuting traffickers. In furtherance of this philosophy, drug shipments are sometimes permitted to enter the United States while under close surveillance by agents. Once a shipment is delivered, agents can arrest traffickers and, hopefully, leaders of the drug-smuggling organizations. The DEA philosophy, which focuses on investigation and conviction, conflicts with the mission of other agencies, such as the CBP, which are charged with interdiction of drugs as soon as they enter the United States. Interagency rivalries are therefore created that tend to hamper the overall effectiveness of the federal drug enforcement initiative.

The DEA's mission is both domestic and foreign, with a total of more than 5,000 special agents and intelligence analysts located throughout the United States and in 42 other countries [1]. Agents stationed in foreign countries possess no arrest powers and act primarily as liaisons with the host law enforcement agencies. DEA agents and analysts provide information about general trends in drug trafficking, as well as specific information regarding the actions of drug criminals. The information collection process begins in drug source countries and includes analysis of drug production (illicit farming operations, and laboratories) and transportation methods (smuggling) used by traffickers.

Intelligence collected by the DEA is a major source of information about drugs in transit, and it is shared with other law enforcement agencies. Through the DEA's El Paso Intelligence Center (EPIC), intelligence is collected, analyzed, and disseminated from all enforcement agencies. During recent decades, the DEA's budget and workforce have burgeoned. For example, in 1980, the DEA employed a total of 4,149 employees, with 1,941 special agents; by 2006, the DEA workforce included 10,891 employees, including 5,320 special agents. Although supporters of the federal drug enforcement initiative claim that the greater numbers of agent personnel account for the rising number of arrests and seizures, detractors of federal drug policy claim that hiring more enforcement agents is not the best way to approach the drug problem. In 1990, John Lawn expressed his frustration with drug enforcement initiatives by resigning his post as DEA administrator and conceding that the DEA is unable to keep pace with many of today's drug-trafficking organizations. Many analysts agree and suggest that the best way to confront the drug problem is to make a systematic analysis of every aspect of the way that major drug-trafficking organizations operate, and then attack the *choke points* of distribution, as opposed to mounting an all-out effort on "every front." In short, the suggestion is to make better use of raw intelligence information by drug enforcement personnel who are already in place.

The Federal Bureau of Investigation

The FBI is the chief law enforcement arm of the federal government and is a division of the Justice Department. In 1982, Attorney General William French Smith delegated to the FBI concurrent jurisdiction with the DEA for the overall drug law enforcement effort. This was a major change in the FBI's normal jurisdiction, which had traditionally included all federal laws not specifically assigned to other enforcement agencies.

Since assuming these new drug enforcement responsibilities, the FBI has assigned more than 1,000 special agents to drug investigations. The primary impetus of the FBI's role in drug enforcement is the investigation of organized crime activity in the drug trade. These activities include probing into specific trafficking organizations, as well as scrutinizing illegal financial transactions pertaining to drug trafficking.

Both the DEA and FBI are responsible for enforcement of the Controlled Substances Act of 1970 (CSA). The FBI, however, is more concerned with drug-related violations of such laws as the Continuing Criminal Enterprise (CCE) Statute and the RICO Act. Although the participation of the FBI in domestic drug enforcement benefits the overall goals and objectives of the federal effort, some degree of conflict, overlapping responsibilities, and confusion about jurisdiction between the DEA and the FBI still exists. As an offshoot of the FBI's involvement in drug enforcement, the Organized Crime Drug Enforcement Task Force (OCDETF) concept was adopted in 1983. Through this joint law enforcement initiative, many high-level cases have culminated (see the "The Organized Crime Drug Enforcement Task Force" section).

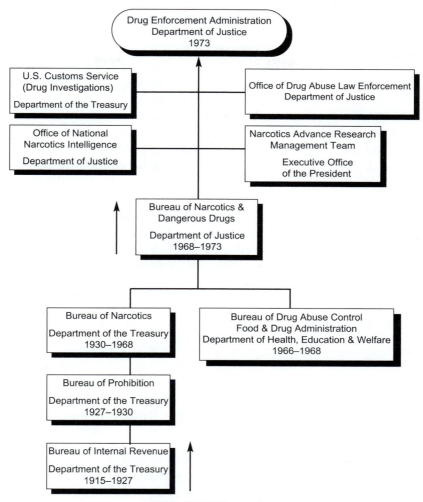

FIGURE 10.2 DEA genealogy.

Drug Interdiction

In September 2004, the U.S. Navy and Coast Guard intercepted a fishing vessel, the *Lina Maria*, 300 miles off the coast of the Galápagos Islands. Agents discovered more than 15 tons of cocaine secreted in compartments. As a result, 10 suspects were arrested [2].

The *Lina Maria* seizure was one of the largest single seizures in an ongoing investigation to stop the pipeline of drugs from the eastern Pacific Ocean to the shoreline of the United States. But it also demonstrates the success of combined efforts by the U.S. Navy, the U.S. Coast Guard, and federal law enforcement.

The process of interdicting drug smugglers is one of the primary focuses of United States drug control policy. Through intercepting and seizing contraband, *interdiction* prevents the entry into the United States of illegal drugs from foreign sources. As we have learned, drugs enter the country in a variety of ways, and drug smugglers regularly vary their methods to counter enforcement actions. Basically, interdiction consists of five rather broad categories of activity: (1) intelligence, (2) command and control, (3) surveillance, (4) pursuit, and (5) capture. The interdiction process addresses areas offshore and within the 12-mile "customs search" radius surrounding the United States as well as all ports of entry.

In 1990, the U.S. Air Force introduced a new long-range radar system that was originally designed to provide early warning of a Soviet attack. Its newer application is to detect airborne drug smugglers. The system, located in Maine, consists of two gigantic antennas, each spreading more than two-thirds of a mile and forming the first "over-the-horizon" radar capable of seeing 10 times farther than conventional systems—up to 1,800 miles.

The system is operated by bouncing signals off the ionosphere, and a series of computer screens maps every plane flying over a 4-million-square-mile area of the Atlantic, from Iceland to South America. In theory, the system will match the aircraft against known flight plans and air traffic control information, identifying suspected drug flights and scrambling CBP or Coast Guard pursuit planes.

The U.S. Coast Guard

The Coast Guard focuses on identification and interdiction of maritime smuggling, principally by private, seagoing vessels. The Coast Guard concentrates on larger cases in the open ocean, although it also conducts patrols and makes seizures in near-shore areas, where it has concurrent jurisdiction with the CBP. Primarily, the Coast Guard concentrates on the areas in and around the Gulf of Mexico, the Caribbean, and south Florida. U.S. Coast Guard seizures are of three distinct types:

- *Incidental seizures.* These occur while officers are carrying out other, more standard missions. Many incidental seizures occur during search-and-rescue missions in which the vessel in trouble turns out to be involved in smuggling activity.
- *Intelligence-based seizures.* The second most common type of Coast Guard seizure is one that results from hard criminal intelligence. Such intelligence pinpoints the specific location and time of the smuggling operation. This type accounts for a large percentage of Coast Guard seizures.
- *Interdiction patrol operations.* The third and predominant type of seizure results from drug interdiction patrol operations. U.S. Coast Guard cutters, usually accompanied by Coast Guard interdiction aircraft, search for, identify, visually inspect, and board suspect target vessels.

Designated choke points are heavily patrolled by Coast Guard cutters in four Caribbean and Gulf of Mexico areas. The primary goal of this operation is to identify, through a system of profiling, "mother ships," which meet contact boats near the coast that deliver drugs into the United States. The Coast Guard's ability to intercept illicit drug shipments is restricted in several ways. Although the Coast Guard will focus on choke points, these areas frequently are expanses of ocean that are up to 100 miles wide and patrolled by a single cutter. The number of vessels traveling through the choke points is large, and only a small number of the vessels can be searched. Furthermore, the Coast Guard can conduct choke point coverage only part of the time. Not only does it have limited equipment and personnel resources, but also its cutters must escort seized vessels to a port, which could tie up a cutter for several days at a time and leave the choke point unpatrolled. Finally, the mission of the Coast Guard interdiction and search and rescue will always take precedence over investigating a suspected smuggling operation.

U.S. Customs and Border Protection

The CBP, under the auspices of the Department of Homeland Security, has primary interdiction responsibilities for border smuggling through official ports of entry on land, as well as concurrent jurisdiction with Coast Guard vessels in coastal waters of the United States up to 12 miles offshore, also known as the *customs zone*.

Prior to 2003, the Border Patrol was part of the Immigration and Naturalization Service (INS), an agency within the U.S. Department of Justice. The INS was disbanded as of March 2003. With the establishment of the Department of Homeland Security, the functions and jurisdictions of several border and revenue enforcement agencies were combined and reconstituted into ICE. The agencies that were either moved entirely or merged in part, based on their law enforcement functions, included the investigative and intelligence resources of the U.S. Customs Service, the law enforcement resources of the INS, and the U.S. Federal Protective Service.

The priority mission of the CBP, as a result of the 9/11 attacks and the organization's merging into the Department of Homeland Security, is to prevent terrorists and terrorist weapons from entering the United States. However, the Patrol's traditional mission remains the deterrence, detection, and apprehension of illegal immigrants and individuals involved in the illegal drug trade, who generally enter the United States other than through designated ports of entry.

Currently, the CBP employs more than 45,600 sworn federal agents and officers, and it is responsible for patrolling 19,000 miles of land and sea borders [3]. CBP personnel are deployed primarily at the United States–Mexico border, where they are assigned to control drug smuggling. The CBP has the authority to search outbound and inbound shipments, and it uses targeting to carry out its mission in this area. Under Section 596 of the Tariff Act (passed in 1930), the CBP is required to seize and forfeit all merchandise that is stolen, smuggled, or clandestinely imported or introduced. The CBP is also required to seize and forfeit controlled substances, certain contraband articles, and plastic explosives that do not contain a detection agent.

Cargo, vessels, and passengers from foreign locations are regularly inspected by customs officials to ensure the payment of required duty, as well as to stop the flow of contraband. Each of these is a formidable task.

Dogs trained to smell illicit drugs are used at ports of entry and are an important tool in interdiction. In 2005, CBP Canine Enforcement Program teams at ports of entry seized more than 407,447 pounds of narcotics and more than 20 million illegal drug units (including various pills, capsules, or vials). At checkpoints and between the official ports of entry, canine teams made 3809 seizures totaling more than 504,290 pounds of narcotics [4].

It is also the responsibility of the customs inspectors to inspect all international cargo; all vessels entering seaports from foreign countries; all aircraft entering the United States from foreign countries (including general and commercial aircraft); all land vehicles such as trucks, automobiles, trains, and buses; and all international mail. The service's interdiction strategy at ports of entry has several components:

- It operates most effectively when it has prior reliable intelligence. Intelligence sources include informants, private citizens, transportation companies, and intelligence agencies.
- Profiles of people, vehicles, and cargo are used to initiate searches. Profiles include data such as the origin of the individual or cargo, and the sex, age, or citizenship of the individual (see Chapter 11).
- Inspectors conduct periodic blitz-type inspections of passengers and cargo.
- Officials use dogs, along with metal detection devices and a variety of support and detection technologies, to track suspect aircraft, to sniff out hidden drugs.

One responsibility of the CBP is to interdict drugs in the nation's near-shore waters. This initiative utilizes the marine branch of the service, which uses a system of stopping and searching incoming vessels that behave suspiciously (especially small boats, referred to as "go-fast" boats).

The best-developed marine interdiction capabilities appear to be in the Miami area, where the Blue Lightning Operations Center (BLOC) operates. This initiative was implemented in February 1986 and is a joint operation between the CBP and the Coast Guard that is designed to collect and coordinate information from air and marine centers. The BLOC tracks suspicious vessels, plots the course and speed of the suspect target, and directs interceptors toward it.

The CBP air branch is responsible for interdicting airborne drug smuggling. Drug smugglers prefer light, twin-engine, general aviation aircraft, and will usually fly at a low altitude, placing them under the line-of-sight coverage of coastal scanners. These smugglers will typically operate at night to minimize their chance of detection by law enforcement. Once suspicious aircraft have been sighted, they are normally tracked both by cutters and/or by high-speed chase planes. The interdiction process usually involves customs strike teams that are transported to the landing site by helicopters.

As will be discussed further in Chapter 13, a 1988 study by the RAND Corporation revealed some disturbing conclusions regarding the military's ability to affect drug demand successfully through interdiction. The study, commissioned by the U.S. Department of Defense (DOD) and directed by Peter Reuter, concluded that it was more costly for the government to attempt to interdict drugs than it was for traffickers to replace seized shipments. In the study, Reuter found that the drug traffickers' assets are so vast that the losses caused by interdiction go unnoticed. Dealers have to spend more on transporting shipments than police can on stopping them. He claims this is because raw materials and highly skilled labor are surprisingly cheap in the markets utilized by drug traffickers.

To facilitate the study, Reuter developed a computer model called SOAR to estimate more exactly how smugglers would adapt if interdiction efforts were increased. In an all-out drug war, assuming that the interdiction rate on 10 of 11 routes could be more than doubled, SOAR estimated that the cost of smuggling would increase 70 percent, but the retail price of drugs would increase only 10 percent. The increase would therefore affect the street crack user by $2 per purchase.

Interdiction Support Agencies

In addition to the interdiction efforts by the U.S. Coast Guard and the CBP, other support agencies share certain responsibilities. Such support services share intelligence, equipment, and other resources. The primary support groups used in the interdiction effort are the DOD, the Federal Aviation Administration (FAA), and various state and local law enforcement agencies.

- *The Department of Defense.* The historical separation of powers between the police and the military is defined under a law known as the Posse Comitatus Act. It was refined in 1981, resulting in a relaxation of the provisions for using military equipment and personnel for domestic law enforcement. Though DOD personnel cannot make arrests, the new provisions of the law allow sharing of intelligence equipment and assisting in certain operations that lead to arrests.
- *The Federal Aviation Administration.* The FAA supports the drug interdiction effort with its flight information systems. The FAA requires all pilots of private aircraft flights originating in foreign countries to file flight plans 24 hours in advance and to land at the airport nearest to their point of entry that has a customs officer. Those aircraft crossing the border without having filed a flight plan are automatically considered suspicious and are subsequently investigated.

Other agencies sharing certain drug enforcement responsibilities include the Internal Revenue Service (IRS), the U.S. Marshals Service (USMS), and the Bureau of Alcohol, Tobacco, Firearms, and Explosives (ATF). Most of this cooperation is carried out on a case-by-case basis.

Coordination Organizations

Drug traffickers are mobile and respect neither political boundaries nor the division of jurisdictions between law enforcement agencies. Therefore, police have responded to the drug problem by joining their efforts. Coordination efforts can be either horizontal, involving efforts between agencies operating in a particular region, or vertical, involving agencies at various levels of government. Several agencies offer services to the primary drug enforcement agencies in the federal and state governments.

Operation Alliance

Operation Alliance was developed as a multiagency effort to prevent drug smuggling across the Mexican border. Essentially serving as a task force under the direction of the INS's Border Patrol, the alliance includes officers from the DEA and INS, people from the U.S. Attorney's Office, and officers from state and local law enforcement agencies. The philosophy of Operation Alliance is to share resources while seeking to interdict the flow of drugs coming from Mexico.

The National Drug Enforcement Policy Board

The National Drug Enforcement Policy Board (NDEPB) was created by the 1984 National Narcotics Act. The board originated as a cabinet-level agency consisting of the attorney general as chair and the secretaries of state, treasury, defense, transportation, and health and human services, as well as the directors of the Central Intelligence Agency and the Office of Management and Budget, as members. Despite the diversity of federal agencies involved, it was the board's objective to coordinate and focus strategies in the fight against drug abuse. Specifically, the statutory language outlining the mission of the NDEPB was as follows:

1. Maintain a national and international effort against illegal drugs.
2. Coordinate fully the activities of the federal agencies involved.
3. Charge a single, competent, and responsible high-level board of the United States government, chaired by the attorney general, with responsibility for coordinating United States policy with respect to national and international drug law enforcement.

In 1988, the NDEPB was dissolved to make way for the Office of National Drug Control Policy (ONDCP).

Office of National Drug Control Policy

In 1988, the ONDCP was created to assume control of the federal drug policy effort and was to be directed by a high-level *drug czar*. Director William Bennett, the former United States secretary of education, was the first person to assume this office (in 1989) and was charged with formulating a workable plan for drug control on a nationwide basis. Each year, the ONDCP releases a number of reports detailing the national drug control strategy. Each of these reports specifies the goals and objectives of both domestic and foreign drug control initiatives.

In 1990, the ONDCP designated five areas as *high-intensity drug-trafficking areas*: New York, Miami, Los Angeles, Houston, and along the southwestern United States border. The program's goals are to identify and disrupt drug-trafficking organizations operating in these areas that are thought to be major contributors to the United States drug problem. Funding for this program is provided to federal and state local law enforcement projects that cannot be funded on individual agency budgets.

The Regional Information Sharing System

The Regional Information Sharing System (RISS) program is an innovative, federally funded program that was created to support law enforcement efforts and to combat organized crime activity, drug trafficking, and white-collar crime. The RISS project began with funding by the Law Enforcement Assistance Administration (LEAA) discretionary grant program. Since 1980, the U.S. Congress has made a yearly appropriation of funds to the RISS project as a line item in the Department of Justice budget.

The primary impetus of the project is to augment existing law enforcement agencies with intelligence information on criminal activities in their jurisdictions. Additionally, the RISS project provides services to member agencies regarding assistance in asset seizures, funds for covert operations, analysis of investigative data on organized criminals, loans of investigative equipment, and training in the use of such equipment in criminal investigations. The RISS program operates within seven Regional Information Sharing Projects:

- *Mid-State Organized Crime Information Center (MOCIC)*: Missouri, Kansas, Illinois, Iowa, Nebraska, South Dakota, North Dakota, Minnesota, and Wisconsin.
- *Western States Information Network (WSIN)*: California, Oregon, Washington, Hawaii, and Alaska.
- *Rocky Mountain Information Network (RMIN)*: Colorado, New Mexico, Arizona, Nevada, Wyoming, Idaho, and Montana.
- *Regional Organized Crime Information Center (ROCIC)*: Texas, Oklahoma, Arkansas, Louisiana, Tennessee, Mississippi, Alabama, Georgia, Florida, Kentucky, South Carolina, North Carolina, Virginia, and West Virginia.
- *Middle Atlantic Great Lakes Organized Crime Law Enforcement Network (MAGLOCLEN)*: Indiana, Ohio, Pennsylvania, New York, Michigan, Rhode Island, New Jersey, Maryland, and Delaware.
- *New England State Police Information Network (NESPIN)*: Massachusetts, Maine, Vermont, Connecticut, New Hampshire, and Rhode Island.
- *LEVITICUS.* Alabama, Georgia, Indiana, Kentucky, New York, Pennsylvania, and Virginia. The LEVITICUS Project also provides coordination to agencies investigating crimes related to the coal, oil, and natural gas industries.

The National Narcotics Border Interdiction System

The National Narcotics Border Interdiction System (NNBIS) was created to provide guidance for interdiction systems and is under the direction of the vice president. Regional NNBIS units are established at six locations throughout the country. These regional components are chaired by the heads of various regional enforcement agencies that have responsibility for that particular geographical area. For example, three of these regional directors are admirals in the U.S. Coast Guard.

The Organized Crime Drug Enforcement Task Force

The Organized Crime Drug Enforcement Task Force (OCDETF) Program was established in 1982 to mount a comprehensive attack against organized drug traffickers. The program requires its participants to identify major Regional Priority Organization Targets as part of the annual Regional Strategic Plan process.

OCDETF was originally formed as a part of a true "task force" approach against sophisticated criminal organizations, with prosecutors and law enforcement personnel working side by side in the same location. "OCDETF Strike Forces" in key cities around the country aggressively target the highest level trafficking organizations and function as a central point of contact for OCDETF agents and prosecutors nationwide, gathering intelligence and disseminating leads throughout the neighboring areas.

The OCDETF Fusion Center (OFC) is the cornerstone of OCDETF's intelligence efforts and was created to enhance OCDETF's overall capacity to engage in intelligence-driven law enforcement, an essential component to the OCDETF Program. The OFC is essentially a data center that collects and analyzes drug and related financial investigative information and intelligence from a variety of sources to support OCDETF's coordinated, comprehensive, multijurisdictional investigations of the most significant drug-trafficking and money-laundering networks.

The Task of Agency Coordination

A formidable task in the nation's drug war is the coordination of enforcement efforts between agencies located within both the state and federal governments. As mentioned, both NNBIS and OCDETF were designed to pool resources in the enforcement effort, but many organizational problems still prevail. On the federal level, "turf wars" and interagency bickering often result in a reluctance to share information or coordinate enforcement efforts. Confusion often results when many different departments play some role in the drug suppression effort. For example, the CBP is responsible for interdiction, yet the armed services also monitor the military's role in interdiction. The FBI and DEA have similar roles in investigating federal violations of the CSA.

■ ■ Critical Thinking Task ■

Refute or defend a need for additional drug enforcement agencies in the United States. What, if any, changes would you support in the jurisdiction of existing agencies?

Cannabis Eradication

Each year during the summer months, marijuana cultivation becomes big business. To counter the growers who cultivate marijuana, an alliance between the DEA and state and local law enforcement agencies has been formed. Initiated in 1979 by the DEA, the Domestic Cannabis Eradication/Suppression Program (DCE/SP) gives state and local police such resources as technical assistance, training, and special equipment for this task. By 1985, all 50 states were participating in the program, which operates in conjunction with other

FIGURE 10.3 The San Bernardino County Sheriff Department's Marijuana Eradication Team seized more than 1,700 marijuana plants from a residential home in Oak Hills, California, on May 16, 2013. Shown in the photo is only one of the rooms used for marijuana cultivation. *Source: AP Photo/Daily Press, David Pardo.*

federal agencies. Included are the U.S. Forest Service, the Bureau of Land Management, the Bureau of Indian Affairs, and the DOD. In many states, the National Guard has also provided a workforce and equipment for this undertaking. According to the DEA, in 2009 the DCE/SP was responsible for the eradication of almost 10 million cultivated outdoor cannabis plants and more than 400,000 indoor plants. In addition, the DCE/SP has documented 10,073 arrests and the seizure of in excess of $37.3 million of cultivator assets. The program also removed 5,569 weapons from cannabis cultivators [5].

As discussed in Chapter 5, indoor growing operations pose special problems to police. By the late 1980s, these operations had emerged in great numbers throughout the nation, and government statistics indicate that the number of indoor operations is increasing. One initiative designed to identify such operations was the DEA's Operation Green Merchant, organized in the late 1980s to target suppliers of cannabis seeds, growing equipment, and cultivation information, as well as the growers themselves [6].

Investigating Illicit Laboratories
As with marijuana cultivation, illegal drug laboratories also pose serious problems for drug control officials. During the 1980s, the number of such laboratories soared, and in addition to their being illegal in nature, they pose specific dangers for investigators. The federal government estimated that one in five discovered illicit laboratories are uncovered as a result of fire or explosion. As discussed in Chapter 5, drug laboratories are volatile and unstable, posing dangers to both laboratory operators and police alike. Adding to the dangers of investigating drug laboratories are countersurveillance measures such as cameras, automatic weapons, and booby traps, which are all commonly associated with these operations.

Because of the nature of illicit drug laboratories, many pose an environmental hazard when dangerous chemicals are indiscriminately disposed of by laboratory operators. In one case, a California drug laboratory operator dumped chemicals into the sewer system in a remote rural area. Consequently, the laboratory's chemicals killed the bacteria that were used to treat sewage, resulting in the raw sewage being returned to the environment.

Another problem associated with investigating drug laboratories is disposal of the chemicals used in the drug-making process once they are seized. Most of the chemicals used in lysergic acid diethylamide, methamphetamine, and phencyclidine labs are corrosive, explosive, and unstable, and when they are seized by police, they must be disposed of properly. One of the challenges that police face is the identification and tracking of precursor chemicals used in the laboratory process. Aiding police was the passing of the 1988 Chemical Diversion and Trafficking Act, which is designed to prevent the use of legal chemicals to process illicit drugs. According to the provisions of the law, domestic distributors of precursor and essential chemicals must meet specific reporting and records requirements. The law requires distributors to do the following:

- Identify their regular customers
- Maintain records of sales for a specified period of time
- Declare the import of such chemicals
- Report questionable orders to the DEA

Under the law, it is the seller who makes the decision as to whether a specific purchase is shady. A classic example is an order for a large quantity of chemicals that is under the minimum amount of chemicals required for reporting purposes from a buyer who is not involved in the type of business in which that chemical is normally used.

Strategies for Street-Level Enforcement

Although the problem of foreign drug traffickers smuggling dangerous drugs into the country is one of the federal government's highest priorities, the coexisting problem of controlling local street-level dealers prevails. Adopting a policy that effectively deals with the street-level dealer is a major priority.

Discreet and Nondiscreet Markets

Primary responsibility for this task has typically rested with the local law enforcement agency and has been associated with two distinct illegal street markets: *discreet markets* and *nondiscreet markets*. Discreet drug markets are those in which the drug seller and the drug buyer are well acquainted. Drug transactions taking place under these circumstances typically involve exchanges of drugs for money in the workplace, or within a social environment such as a bar or nightclub. It is often difficult for police to discover these operations because of the private nature of the transactions, and therefore, they may go undetected for long periods of time.

In comparison, nondiscreet drug markets differ from the discreet drug trade in that the drug seller is rarely acquainted with the drug buyer. The nondiscreet market accounts for the so-called open-air trade that flourishes in public places. This type of drug market is attractive for the drug dealer because it will generate more profits due to the greater number of available customers. The nondiscreet market is also an easy target for police intervention and control, since its whereabouts are easily learned through police surveillance operations and informants.

The Kingpin Strategy

Enforcement strategies differ from one jurisdiction to another. Some are aimed at the heads, or *kingpins*, of the organizations. Under this strategy, police believe that once the top manager of a drug-trafficking organization has been eliminated from the organization, the rest of the organization will shut down. Thus, the quantity of drugs on the streets will be reduced and the price of drugs available to buyers will rise, making them less attractive to consumers. Some research, however, has shown no documented cases in which these drug reduction strategies have actually resulted in a reduction in drug consumption [7]. Some experts also disagreed with the assumption that no new management figures would assume control of the organization once the "kingpin" was removed.

However, one expert in the field, Mark Moore, suggested that strategies such as undercover operations targeting drug kingpins tend to make the organizations more cautious, which results in some transactions being restricted out of fear of discovery by police. In addition, Moore argues that enforcement successes against organizations result in a loss of inventory and the future capacity to supply drugs [8].

Marijuana Citations

One original approach by many municipalities in dealing with offenders caught with small amounts of marijuana is the issuing of citations by uniformed patrol officers. For example, when a small amount of marijuana is seized as a result of a vehicle stop, instead of the officer taking the violator into custody, a citation is written and signed by the violator. This process basically works like a traffic citation, since it requires the offender to appear in court on a later date.

This procedure has generally been considered a successful street-level enforcement tactic because it reduces the commitments of time and money by the police, the prosecutor, and the courts through streamlining the adjudicatory process. At the same time, the practice enables law enforcement agents to identify and convict drug users in the community who might otherwise escape detection by the criminal justice system.

Undercover Operations

Due to the secret nature of drug-trafficking organizations, information on their activities is difficult to obtain. In Chapter 4, we discussed the fact that the number of people involved in drug-trafficking organizations is limited to ensure control by managers. Therefore, one method of learning the inner workings of such operations is through the use of *undercover* operatives. The typical undercover operation involves an undercover officer buying drugs and then arresting the seller; this is called a *buy-and-bust*.

Both police officers and informants are used in the undercover capacity, which typically focuses on street-level dealers who are easily persuaded to exchange information for leniency. Undercover operations also depend heavily on surveillance, which sometimes includes wiretaps, examination of financial records, and the use of other electronic monitoring devices.

Other Concerns

It is clear that law enforcement initiatives alone are not successful in adequately containing the existing problem of street drug trafficking. Modern-day strategies must include tactics such as enlisting the support of community groups, seizing assets of both sellers and users, and cracking down on all street-sales operations.

Drug dealing, a fragmented and broadly generalized term, addresses all levels of illicit drug distribution and many different types of drugs. Although different types of drugs, such as marijuana, methamphetamine, and heroin, are prevalent in different geographical areas of the country, many law enforcement departments have identified the problem of crack cocaine sales as an enforcement priority. The popularity of crack cocaine among dealers is closely related to its popularity among the drug-using public; that is, crack is a highly addictive drug that consequently creates much repeat business for the seller and generates a correspondingly high profit margin. Street sales of crack cocaine and powdered cocaine seem to follow two distinct patterns: the use of the crack house and the nondiscreet market.

The crack house is the most common means of dealers' street distribution of crack cocaine. Frequently, the crack house is an abandoned residence that has been commandeered by street dealers for use as a base of operation. These houses are often structurally fortified with steel bars on windows and metal doorjambs to prevent easy access by police. The crack house sometimes operates in an "open" fashion, which enables the drug buyer or user to enter the house, purchase the crack, and ingest it on the premises.

Street-corner sales have also contributed greatly to the proliferation of the crack cocaine problem. Although primarily an inner-city phenomenon, this nondiscreet method for retail crack sales has, in some cases, created vehicular traffic congestion because of dealers who literally approach any passing automobile and ask the driver if he or she is interested in purchasing crack. This system of illicit drug trafficking illustrates the arrogant and lackadaisical attitude that many street dealers share with regard to the criminal justice system.

■ ■ Critical Thinking Task ■

Suggest guidelines by which law enforcement agencies may better monitor the activities of undercover drug agents and thus reduce police corruption.

Specific tactics used to reduce street sales largely depend on the scope of the problem in each community. The task force concept (as discussed in this chapter) is one such tactic that has proven to be one of the more effective enforcement tools in the fight against street trafficking and for use in interdiction.

Newer nontraditional strategies of street enforcement are being considered by many law enforcement agencies. One such tactic is the use of the reverse sting. This innovative approach to controlling street drug sales involves undercover police officers posing as drug dealers rather than buyers (as in the "buy-and-bust" technique). The focus of this strategy is to arrest people who purchase crack or attempt to engage in an illicit drug transaction. The reverse sting concept has three primary advantages: (1) the ability to identify and seize personal assets of the drug dealer (discussed in this chapter), (2) the ability to arrest large numbers of street dealers and thus deter criminal activity, and (3) the ability to generate positive media coverage of police department activities.

A common problem for police crackdowns on street-level drug operations is displacement. For decades, traditional vice units have dealt with the problem of the displacement of offenders in attempting to control operations such as prostitution. Typically, once a strong police presence is detected by potential violators, alternative markets for criminal activity are identified and pursued. If law enforcement efforts are not as concentrated in outlying areas as in the area of the crackdown, drug dealers will almost assuredly set up their operations in these outlying areas.

Police–Community Drug Control Efforts

In neighborhoods infested with drugs and drug traffickers, law-abiding people are sometimes aware of who the drug dealers and users are. Granted, the specific names and addresses of those involved with illicit drugs may not be known, but drug transactions are routinely witnessed as dealers come and go from crack houses, and as acts of violence are committed. As discussed in this chapter the practice of community and problem-oriented policing is designed to tap into this crucial source of information by cultivating community–police partnerships. The premise of this philosophy rests on two realities: first, the police need public assistance in pinpointing locations of drug production and sales, as well as learning the identities of those responsible. Second, the community relies on the police to eradicate drugs and drug dealers from neighborhoods within the community. Many studies have been conducted in areas where such partnerships have been tried, and it is clear that closer ties between the police and the community result in safer neighborhoods. For

FIGURE 10.4 A police car patrols near a popular hangout for drug pushers in Philadelphia, as part of an antidrug campaign designed to shut down this and 300 other notorious drug corners throughout the city with a 24-hour police presence. *Source: AP Photo/Mark Stehle.*

example, experience has shown that the implementation of foot patrol programs in some cities has raised citizen satisfaction with the police, as well as the quality of life for residents.

Community Policing

Apprehending and incarcerating retail drug dealers are not the only way to intercept street-level drug sales. Maintaining a high police profile in the community often can deter street dealers from initially entering a neighborhood. The *community policing* concept integrates the police into the community so that its citizens will be more receptive and willing to exchange information with the police. Patrols on foot are thought to be one of the most important aspects of community policing, because citizens in that setting are apt to feel that the police are greater contributors to the overall safety of the community.

Some communities have even found that the presence of police officers who stand in the vicinity of open-air drug markets (blatant street drug dealing) or conspicuously take pictures of dealers and prospective drug buyers tended to deter potential customers and forced drug dealers to leave the area. In one case, patrol officers in Charleston, South Carolina, kept drug dealers moving from block to block, preventing them from establishing a foothold in a neighborhood. Officers also knock on the doors of suspected crack houses, which often frightens the dealers into flushing their illegal drug inventory down the drain. In other cases, officers in both Yakima, Washington, and Fort Lauderdale, Florida, deterred drug dealers by sending owners of cars seen cruising near drug markets written notice that their vehicles were observed in an area known to be filled with drug dealers.

Asset Forfeiture

Many criminals are motivated by greed and the acquisition of material goods. Therefore, the ability of the government to seize property connected with criminal activity can be an effective law enforcement tool by reducing the incentive for illegal behavior. Asset forfeiture "takes the profit out of crime" by helping to eliminate the ability of the offender to command the resources necessary to continue illegal activities.

The goal of asset forfeiture is to destroy the financial infrastructure of the criminal enterprise. As discussed in Chapter 4, criminal enterprises in many ways emulate legitimate businesses. In doing so, they require employees, equipment, and cash flow to operate. Criminal enterprises, like lawfully operated businesses, also generate a profit from the sale of their "product" or "services." The obvious difference is that the profit generated from criminal enterprises is derived from criminal activity. Asset forfeiture can remove tools, equipment, cash flow, profit, and sometimes the product itself from the criminals and the criminal organization, rendering the criminal organization powerless to operate.

The seizure of criminal assets is a practice long used by governments. For example, in English common law, the value of an inanimate object could be forfeited to the English Crown if that object caused the death of a person. Therefore, the forfeiture of property was generally justified as a penalty for carelessness. This tradition and justification have, over time, merged with a belief that the right to own property could be denied an individual who engaged in criminal conduct.

The forfeiture sanction is a legal concept that involves the application of procedures resulting in the transfer of the ownership of property to the government. Many of the criminal laws enforced by law enforcement contain forfeiture provisions. Some of these forfeiture provisions are excellent deterrents, such as forfeiture under federal drug laws and under money-laundering laws. Other provisions may be used infrequently, including the forfeiture of prison-made goods illegally transported in interstate commerce.

The seizure of property by law enforcement authorities generally is authorized when the property is evidence of a crime or is subject to forfeiture.

Types of Asset Forfeiture Actions

There are two types of asset forfeiture actions: criminal and civil. The criminal forfeiture action is referred to as an *in personam action*, meaning that the action is against the person and that, upon conviction, the punitive effect of forfeiture can be used against the convicted offender. The civil forfeiture action is referred to as an *in rem action*, meaning that the action is against the property. The two actions differ in many ways, including (1) the point at which they occur in the proceeding, generally at which the property may be seized; (2) the burden of proof necessary to forfeit the property; and (3) in some cases, the type of property interests that can be forfeited.

Criminal Forfeiture Actions

A criminal forfeiture action must be a court action. The property subject to forfeiture is named in the same indictment that charges the defendant with a criminal violation. The jurisdiction of the court over the defendant provides the court with jurisdiction over the defendant's property interests. While there is some disagreement among the appellate courts, generally the government must meet the legal standard of proof, beyond a reasonable doubt, necessary to convict the defendant in order to forfeit the property. The property may be forfeited in this manner only if the defendant is convicted of the underlying offense charged, and the trier of fact finds that the property named in the indictment was illegally tainted.

As a general rule, the seizure of the property through criminal forfeiture may not occur until after the property has been forfeited. Under federal law, the district court then issues an order to seize the property, and the seizure is made by the USMS. There are some exceptions to this rule. For example, a seizure warrant may be used in certain circumstances in a criminal forfeiture matter under the CSA and under the Money Laundering Control Act (MCLA). Criminal forfeiture laws provide for a postforfeiture hearing by the court, called an ancillary hearing, to consider the claims of third parties to the forfeited property.

Criminal forfeiture provisions such as those found in the RICO Act and the CSA identify property that can be forfeited upon conviction of a defendant in broader terms than the provisions of law concerning most civil forfeitures. Criminal forfeiture laws name interests subject to forfeiture that are more complex, including property acquired or maintained in violation of RICO, and various types of legal interests in property that have afforded a source of influence over the illegal enterprise. The civil forfeiture laws generally name specific property that is integrally connected with prohibited activity, including conveyances used, money furnished, and real property used.

Civil forfeiture actions: A civil forfeiture action is effected through a summary, administrative, or judicial procedure. A summary forfeiture procedure is limited to the CSA and then only to a narrow category of property.

Administrative forfeiture: An administrative forfeiture procedure can be commenced by a seizing agency against most property if it is valued at $500,000 or less, unless the property is a monetary instrument, in which case there is no maximum monetary limit. If the administrative action is not contested in a timely manner, any legal claim to the property is thereafter barred, and the agency may declare the property forfeited.

An administrative action can be contested by the filing of a claim of ownership. A timely claim to the property forces the government to terminate the administrative forfeiture action and to commence a civil judicial action.

Burden of Proof

The burden of proof on the FBI to seize property for civil, administrative, and judicial forfeiture is probable cause. This burden must be met to satisfy both statutory and constitutional requirements. A civil forfeiture action commences upon notification by mail and publication of the government's intent to forfeit the property.

Probable cause for an administrative forfeiture is defined as a reasonable ground for belief of guilt, supported by less than *prima facie* proof, but more than mere suspicion. The initial burden of proof in a judicial action is also probable cause. After seizure, the U.S. Attorney's Office must make an independent determination of whether the property can be forfeited. After finding the forfeiture action has merit, a verified complaint must be filed, in effect charging the property with violating the law. The government then has to prove that the property is subject to forfeiture by a different burden of proof, preponderance of the evidence. Preponderance of the evidence is defined as "superior evidentiary weight that, though sufficient to free the mind wholly from all reasonable doubt, is still sufficient to incline a fair and impartial mind to one side of the issue rather than the other."

One must remember that a civil judicial forfeiture action is a civil proceeding, rather than a criminal proceeding. Discovery processes under these rules are different than those found in criminal procedures.

Asset forfeiture is beneficial for at least three reasons. First, it is intended to reduce criminal activity by denying offenders the profits from their crimes. Second, a byproduct of asset forfeiture is more drug arrests. Third, yet perhaps most controversially, forfeiture helps cash-strapped law enforcement agencies augment their discretionary budgets to further target criminal activity.

More Drug Arrests

As is clear by now, there are financial incentives for police agencies to pursue asset forfeiture. This raises a proverbial "chicken or the egg" question: do forfeiture laws increase enforcement activity, or does enforcement activity increase the prospects for asset forfeiture? One study found that state forfeiture laws are closely connected to drug arrests and, secondarily, to forfeiture. In other words, states with the most generous forfeiture laws, those that return the greatest percentage of forfeiture proceeds to police, saw the greatest arrest activity: "police focus relatively more effort on drug control when they can enhance their budgets by retaining seized assets" [9].

Controversially, this takes the focus from finding solutions to specific crime problems to revenue generation. Yet it is difficult to fault police departments for seeking revenue to support continued crime fighting.

Whether more drug arrests are desirable depends, of course, on the particular drug-related problem. Careful analysis of a local drug problem should be conducted before making this judgment. If, for example, high-volume drug arrests overwhelm the courts and/or compromise public support for law enforcement efforts, then more drug arrests (and, by extension, forfeiture) may be undesirable.

The obvious advantage of asset forfeiture is its potential to boost an agency's bottom line. Although forfeiture can yield a profit, it can be sufficient for forfeiture to simply yield enough proceeds to offset the costs of drug enforcement, such as the operation of a multijurisdictional drug task force. Researchers have found, indeed, that forfeiture can assist agencies by augmenting their discretionary budgets [10].

Possible Criticisms and Negative Consequences

Forfeiture also has been fairly heavily criticized. Critics point to the "drug war's hidden economic agenda" and refer to the means by which forfeiture compromises due process protections and encourages law enforcement blunders [11]. Critics further claim that forfeiture circumvents proper appropriation channel, threatens due process protections, and guarantees a conflict of interest between effective crime control and creative financial management.

The Civil Asset Forfeiture Reform Act of 2000 (CAFRA) made several changes to federal forfeiture law. Key provisions of the law include the creation of an innocent owner defense (for cases in which an innocent individual's property is targeted for forfeiture), and a shift in the burden of proof from the property owner to the government. Concerning the latter, property owners were previously required to prove their property was not subject to forfeiture. Now the government must prove by a preponderance of the evidence that property is subject to forfeiture. Although CAFRA minimized much of the controversy associated with asset forfeiture, several criticisms of the practice still stand out.

Profit Motive

In a rather creative study, Miller and Selva used covert participant observation to document asset forfeiture activities [12]. One of the authors acted as a confidential informant for a city's undercover narcotics operation after he established a relationship with drug enforcement officials in the area. The results of the study were startling: agents were selective in their enforcement efforts, and the goal of seizing assets took precedence over the goal of taking narcotics out of circulation.

The Miller and Selva study was published in 1994, well before federal forfeiture reforms were put in place. Even so, some more recent studies have raised similar concerns. For example, the author of one study surveyed 1400 law enforcement administrators from around the nation and found that more than 60 percent of them either agreed or strongly agreed with the statement "Forfeiture is a necessary budgetary supplement for my agency" [13]. The authors of another study found that law enforcement agencies in restrictive forfeiture states receive considerably more equitable-sharing payments than their counterparts in generous forfeiture states [14].

The logic is that the agencies in restrictive forfeiture states teamed up with federal officials to participate in adoptive forfeitures in an effort to enhance the prospects of receiving forfeiture proceeds. In fairness, at least one published study showed that forfeiture activities have no apparent connection with state legal arrangements [15]. In particular, "asset forfeiture does not have a substantial impact on the policing priorities of local agencies" [16]. The study, which was limited to jurisdictions in Ohio, also found that agencies pursued criminal forfeiture more often than civil forfeiture. The reason for this is that Ohio civil forfeiture laws require that a criminal prosecution accompany a civil forfeiture action.

Neglecting Other Crimes

Forfeiture laws tend mostly to target "consensual" crimes and those with the greatest potential for profit. To the extent that law enforcement agencies are drawn to forfeiture due to the potential to receive proceeds, this could discourage them from channeling resources into areas where the potential to receive forfeiture proceeds is nil. At the least, generous forfeiture laws appear to increase agencies' enforcement activities in areas where the chances of receiving proceeds are greatest. As one study concluded, since the Comprehensive Crime Control Act of 1984, "The relative allocation of state and local law enforcement resources has shifted dramatically towards drug enforcement, the major source of asset confiscations" [17]. In fairness, though, it can be argued that much of the nation was focused on waging a war on drugs during that time, irrespective of forfeiture laws.

Appearance of Impropriety

Forfeiture windfalls can also reek of impropriety. For example, some small-town agencies have received an excess of forfeiture proceeds and used the money to purchase items that some considered unnecessary [18].

Some jurisdictions have also received negative publicity for controversial plea agreements with known drug offenders. In one case, a dealer faced 15 years in prison under one state's tough antidrug laws. The dealer surrendered his interest in $31,300 in cash seized from his apartment and received only a 5-year prison term. Plea agreements such as these raise several questions and, to some, seem like a version of sanctioned extortion. Researchers have uncovered many other examples of forfeiture-related plea agreements that look at least somewhat questionable [19].

■ ■ Critical Thinking Task ■

Create a scenario in which you are a prosecutor attempting to bring several organized crime racketeers to trial. Describe and illustrate the type of conspiracy involved and your methods of proving the racketeer's complicity.

Drug Courts

Over the past decade, many communities have addressed drug abuse concerns through judicial initiatives by establishing drug courts. A drug court is a specialized or problem-solving court-based program that targets criminal offenders and parents with pending child welfare cases who have alcohol and other drug addiction and dependency problems. As of December 31, 2011, there were over 2,600 drug courts operating throughout the United States. More than one-half of these target adult offenders; others address juvenile, child welfare, and different court case types [20]. Although adult drug courts vary with regard to whom they serve and resources, they are generally based on a comprehensive model involving:

- Offender assessment
- Judicial interaction
- Monitoring (e.g., drug testing) and supervision
- Graduated sanctions and incentives
- Treatment services

Recent research has shown that the stability of a drug court program and its judge play key roles in successful case management and reducing offenders [21].

Although drug courts vary with regard to those whom they serve and their resources, most programs are managed by a multidisciplinary team including judges, prosecutors, defense attorneys, community corrections, social workers, and treatment service professionals [22]. Adult drug courts are designed to reduce drug use relapse and criminal recidivism among defendants through risk and needs assessment, judicial interaction, monitoring and supervision, graduated sanctions and incentives, treatment, and various rehabilitation services.

A related initiative, juvenile drug courts, applies a program model that is similar to those designed for adults, but tailored to the needs of juvenile offenders. Juvenile drug courts provide youth and their families with counseling, education, and other services to accomplish the following:

- Promote immediate intervention
- Treatment
- Improve level of functioning
- Address problems that may contribute to drug use
- Build skills that increase their ability to lead drug- and crime-free lives
- Strengthen the family's capacity to offer structure and guidance
- Promote accountability for all involved [23].

Family drug courts emphasize treatment for parents with substance use disorders to aid in the reunification and stabilization of families affected by parental drug use. These programs apply the adult drug court model to cases entering the child welfare system that include allegations of child abuse or neglect in which substance abuse is identified as a contributing factor. Program goals include helping the parent to become emotionally, financially, and personally self-sufficient; promoting the development of parenting and coping skills adequate for serving as an effective parent on a day-to-day basis; and providing services to their children (Table 10.1).

Other types of drug courts have emerged to address issues specific to unique populations, including tribal, driving under the influence (DUI) or driving while intoxicated (DWI), campus, reentry, veterans, and mental health courts.

Table 10.1 Number and Types of Drug Courts in the United States (as of December 31, 2011)

Type of Drug Court	Number
Adult drug courts	1,435
Juvenile drug courts	458
Family drug courts	329
Tribal drug courts	79
Designated driving under the influence (DUI) courts	192
Campus drug courts	5
Reentry drug courts	31
Federal reentry drug courts	46
Veterans drug courts	95
Co-occurring disorder courts	20

Source: National Institute of Justice Research.

Summary

When we study the extensive history of the United States federal drug control policy, we can observe many interesting occurrences in drug abuse trends, and in the formation of public policy relating to drug abuse. Prohibition created the need for enforcement of the federal antiliquor laws. From the first narcotics unit operating under the Department of Internal Revenue in 1919 to the current DEA, formed in 1973, many policies and agencies have been implemented. Some of these have been more successful than others.

To date, the primary thrust of drug enforcement is carried out by the DEA, the FBI, and the CBP. Many other federal agencies share different degrees of enforcement responsibility with regard to drug control. A priority of the federal drug enforcement initiative is interdiction, which is the interception of drugs coming into the country. The CBP and the U.S. Coast Guard play major roles in this effort.

Other organizations exist that act as task forces for drug trafficking in the United States. The ONDCP serves as the coordinating agency for the federal drug control effort. The ONDCP is charged with coordinating efforts with all federal agencies to reduce drug abuse and trafficking. The federal OCDETF also plays a major role in detecting and prosecuting domestic drug traffickers. The OCDETF is made up of agents representing the DEA; the FBI; ICE; the ATF; the USMS; the IRS; and the U.S. Coast Guard, in cooperation with the Department of Justice Criminal Division, the Tax Division, the 93 United States attorney's offices, and state and local law enforcement.

On the local level, many different drug enforcement and suppression organizations and strategies exist. Strategies include ways to reduce or eliminate both discreet and nondiscreet drug markets operating in communities. This is accomplished by the use of community policing and problem-oriented policing by the patrol function of local police departments. These initiatives are designed to unite the police more closely with the general public, as well as to empower police to make certain managerial enforcement decisions within their own jurisdictions.

Do you recognize these terms?
- choke points
- community policing
- customs zone
- discreet markets
- drug czar
- high-intensity
- drug-trafficking areas
- interdiction
- nondiscreet markets
- undercover

Discussion Questions

1. Explain the evolution of the DEA and its current role in federal drug control policy.
2. Under what circumstances was OCDETF developed, and what purpose does it serve in the overall federal drug suppression effort?
3. Explain why there was so much bureaucracy in the development of the various drug enforcement agencies during and after Prohibition.
4. Explain the role of the RISS project in drug enforcement.
5. Describe the concepts of community policing and how they relate to drug control in communities.
6. Discuss some drug enforcement strategies that deal with reducing the supply of illicit drugs.
7. Characterize and discuss the differences between discreet and nondiscreet illicit drug markets.

References

[1] Braun, M. (2006). *Congressional Testimony on Counternarcotics Strategies in Latin America*. Washington, DC: Drug Enforcement Administration.
[2] Kakesako, G. K. (September 28, 2004). Pearl ship makes huge drug bust. *Honolulu Star-Bulletin*. Found at: www.starbulletin.com/2004/09/28/news/story7.html.
[3] U.S. Customs and Border Protection. Found at: http://www.cbp.gov/xp/cgov/newsroom/publications/frontline_magazine/.
[4] U.S. Customs and Border Protection. (2006). *U.S. Customs and Border Protection Canine Enforcement Program*. Washington, DC: U.S. Department of Homeland Security. Found at: www.cbp.gov/xp/cgov/newsroom/fact_sheets/k9_enforce/fact_sheet_canines.xml.
[5] Drug Enforcement Administration. (2013). At: http://www.justice.gov/dea/index.shtml. Accessed March 1, 2013.
[6] Bureau of Justice Statistics. (1992). *Drugs, crime and the justice system*. Washington, DC: U.S. Department of Justice.

[7] Kleiman, M. A. R., & Smith, K. D. (1990). State and Local Drug Enforcement: In Search of a Strategy. In M. Tonry & J. Q. Wilson (Eds.), *Drugs and Crime, Volume 13: Crime and Justice*. Chicago: The University of Chicago Press.

[8] Moore, M. H. (1990). Supply reduction and drug law enforcement. In M. Tonry & J. Q. Wilson (Eds.), *Drugs and Crime*, Volume 13: *Crime and Justice*, (pp. 109–157). Chicago: The University of Chicago Press.

[9] Mast, B., Benson, B., & Rasmussen, D. (2000). Entrepreneurial Police and Drug Enforcement Policy. *Public Choice, 104*, 285–308.

[10] Benson, B., Rasmussen, D., & Sollars, D. (1995). Police bureaucracies, their incentives and the war on drugs. *Public Choice, 83(1–2)*, 21–45.

[11] Jensen, E., & Gerber, J. (1996). The Civil Forfeiture of Assets and the War on Drugs: Expanding Criminal Sanctions while Reducing Due Process Protections. *Crime and Delinquency, 42*, 421–434.

[12] Miller, J., & Selva, L. (1994). Drug Enforcement's Double Edged Sword: An Assessment of Asset Forfeiture Programs. *Justice Quarterly, 11*, 313–335.

[13] Worrall, J. (2001). Addicted to the Drug War: The Role of Civil Asset Forfeiture as Budgetary Necessity in Contemporary Law Enforcement. *Journal of Criminal Justice, 29*, 171–187.

[14] Worrall, J., & Kovandzic, T. (2008). Is Policing For Profit? Answers from Asset Forfeiture. *Criminology and Public Policy (forthcoming)*.

[15] Clingermayer, J., Hecker, J., & Madsen, S. (2005). Asset Forfeiture and Police Priorities: The Impact of Program Design on Law Enforcement Activities. *Criminal Justice Policy Review, 16*, 319–335.

[16] Ibid.

[17] Benson, B., Rasmussen, D., & Sollars, D. (1995). Police bureaucracies, their incentives and the war on drugs. *Public Choice, 83(1–2)*, 21–45.

[18] Hyde, H. (1995). *Forfeiting Our Property Rights: Is Your Property Safe from Seizure?* Washington, D.C.: Cato Institute.

[19] Colquitt, J. (2001). Ad Hoc Plea Bargaining. *Tulane Law Review, 75*, 695–776. Congressional Research Service. (2007).

[20] National Institute of Justice Research to Practice Initiative. Found at: http://www.nij.gov/nij/topics/courts/drug-courts/welcome.htm. Located 14.04.13.

[21] Ibid.

[22] United Institute of Justice Office of Justice Programs. (May 2012). *Drug courts*. Reference # NCJ 238527.

[23] Ibid.

11

Critical Issues in Drug Control

This chapter will enable you to:

- Discover contemporary policy options in drug control
- Understand how the reverse sting tactic is used by police
- Understand the utility of electronic surveillance and its legal implications
- Learn the issues surrounding drug-testing policies
- See how officials attempt to control drug use in sports
- Understand the developments in medical marijuana and "cannabusiness"

Accepting responsibility is often a first step in problem solving on any scale. Just as an alcoholic must first acknowledge his or her condition to be able to overcome it, the United States must acknowledge the extent to which it provides a market for drugs in order to combat the drug menace. This leads to several critical issues facing actors in the war on drugs: are United States strategies properly balanced? Are United States strategies aimed at both domestic and international criminals? Are United States strategies tackling both ends of the supply–demand cycle? Are United States strategies sufficiently flexible to protect civil liberties for the general public while giving adequate authority to drug enforcement officials? These are just a few of the issues facing drug enforcement policy makers.

Many strategies for drug control are controversial. Conventional methods often seem to offer little hope for controlling the problem. Unconventional methods frequently create controversy because they tend to rely on expanded police powers, leading some citizens to fear an erosion of personal freedom. On the other hand, many unconventional methods of drug enforcement have proven more effective and innovative than the traditional approaches.

Drug Lord Abductions

In recent years, the United States government triggered considerable controversy by using the power to seize drug traffickers, terrorists, and other fugitives abroad for the purpose of prosecuting them under the United States justice system. As a long-standing practice, United States law enforcement agents occasionally engaged in state-sponsored abductions in lieu of extradition as a more expedient means of arresting fugitive offenders in foreign jurisdictions.

Over a century ago, the U.S. Supreme Court established that state-sponsored abductions of foreign criminal defendants did not deprive federal courts of jurisdiction to prosecute and convict these individuals.

Extradition is a formal process through which a state diplomatically surrenders criminal suspects to foreign governments requesting transfer of such persons. Extradition is premised upon fundamental principles of international law. States typically cooperate in establishing specific procedures for extradition under a treaty agreement. Where no treaty exists, the principles of reciprocity and comity govern extradition. Irregular rendition is another method of overseas arrest.

One example of an unconventional drug control tactic is the controversial police practice of kidnapping or abducting drug lords in foreign countries. Such a practice is favored by some, partly due to the degree of official corruption observed in many foreign countries that commonly protect drug lords from prosecution or extradition. One such case was the abduction of multimillionaire drug baron Juan Ramon Matta Ballesteros, who was taken from his home in Honduras by United States marshals in 1988 to face trial in Los Angeles. He was convicted of drug trafficking and conspiracy in the kidnapping-murder of Drug Enforcement Administration (DEA) agent Enrique "Kiki" Camarena in 1985. Though the 50-year-old Matta argued that he was illegally kidnapped by United States authorities, judges found no gross misconduct by the federal agents that would warrant overturning of the verdicts. Matta was given a life term in prison.

In a related case, Humberto Alvarez-Machain, a Mexican citizen, was abducted in 1990 from his medical office in Guadalajara, Mexico, by a group of Mexican mercenaries working for the DEA. Alvarez was one of 19 people also wanted by the federal government in connection with the 1985 kidnapping-murder of Camarena (see Chapter 6).

Although this practice usually occurs on foreign soil, many detractors claim it is an erosion of police authority. The issue was resolved in 1992 when the U.S. Supreme Court reviewed the Alvarez-Machain abduction case [1]. In court, Alvarez-Machain moved to dismiss the indictment against him, claiming that the federal court system had no jurisdiction to try him because he had been abducted in violation of an extradition treaty between the United States and Mexico. After reviewing the case, the Supreme Court decided that Alvarez-Machain's abduction was not in violation of the extradition treaty; therefore, such abductions did not deprive the United States district court of jurisdiction in a criminal trial.

The practice of abducting criminal suspects in foreign countries and bringing them to United States soil for trial is nothing new. In fact, it is more than a century old, and in numerous cases, United States courts have found it perfectly legal. Other official abductions include the following:

- Mexican trafficker Rene Verdugo-Urquidez, who was accused of involvement in the Camarena murder along with Juan Ramon Matta Ballesteros, was shoved through a border fence by Mexican authorities in 1986. He was ultimately convicted in United States courts.
- Roberto Suarez Levy, the son of Bolivian trafficker Roberto Suarez Gomez, was arrested in Switzerland in 1980 on drug charges. After 9 months of waiting, federal agents arranged with local police to have Suarez smuggled out of the country to Miami to face charges.

The precedents addressing abductions clearly show that judges need not consider how a defendant got into their courtroom. Such morality judgments have generally been left to law enforcement agencies. In deciding the Alvarez-Machain case, the courts cited the case of Frederick Ker, recognizing that the practice of abducting criminals from foreign countries began more than a century ago. Ker was an embezzler who absconded to Peru (*Ker v. Illinois*, 1886) but was hunted down and brought within the court's jurisdiction by reason of a "forcible abduction." Although Ker's lawyer argued that he was kidnapped, the Supreme Court ruled in 1886 that Ker had no right to due process while abroad, and that how he was brought to the courtroom in Chicago had nothing to do with the charges he was facing there.

In another abduction case, however, an exception was delineated by the courts. In 1974, Francisco Toscanino was abducted in Uruguay and transported to the United States. Toscanino's attorney claimed that his client had been tortured en route to the United States. In that case, the court held that it is appropriate for judges to consider the apprehension of defendants if there is a suggestion that the behavior of apprehending officers might "shock the conscience of the court." The *Toscanino* case also recognized that a United States judge may throw out an arrest if another country objects to the manner in which an arrest was made within its borders.

We will now examine several enforcement alternatives currently in effect or under consideration by drug enforcement authorities in the United States.

Drug Courier Profiling

The practice of law enforcement officers profiling suspected drug couriers is another innovative method of apprehending drug traffickers. The technique, originally developed in the 1970s by the DEA for use in detecting drug smugglers in airports, has been extended to the highways for identifying automobiles driven by drug couriers.

Drug courier profiling involves trained officers watching vehicles on highways and looking for certain characteristics common to drug traffickers. The practice gained national attention after a segment on the television show *60 Minutes* featured an interview with a Florida state trooper who had achieved a certain reputation for his ability to spot or profile such vehicles. To make the stop, the officer must watch cars on those traveled routes most likely to be used by smugglers. If the officer identifies any traffic violation, such as speeding, the car can be stopped. The officer then looks for other telltale signs of a typical "drug runner." These include "inappropriate dress," a large roll of cash, nervousness around police, the use of a rental car with no car rental papers available for inspection, and the lack of any travel gear such as luggage. Finally, the officer asks the driver for consent to search the vehicle.

Although drug courier profiling has resulted in numerous drug seizures and arrests, it has been criticized by the American Civil Liberties Union (ACLU), which views it as a violation of one's personal freedoms and an unfair infringement of one's Fourth Amendment rights regarding search and seizure. Critics of the technique argue that a vague profile is not enough to create "reasonable suspicion" in the officers' minds.

The decision in *United States v. Sokolow* (1989) [2] addressed the issue of whether drug courier profiling is valid under the Fourth Amendment. The Supreme Court said that there is nothing wrong with such use in this case because the facts, taken in totality, amounted to a reasonable suspicion that criminal conduct was taking place. The Court suggested that whether the facts in the case fit a "profile" was less significant than the fact that, taken together, they establish a reasonable suspicion. So, in essence, the Court was saying that although a drug courier profile might be helpful, the totality of the circumstances is more important in establishing the legality of the stop and the subsequent search [3].

Lawyers for the DEA's criminal law division claimed in 1989 that agents did not make stops on the basis of profiles. Defense attorneys, on the other hand, maintain that suspicion triggered by a profile will often lead to an arrest on the pretext of a traffic violation. They also assert that "voluntary" questioning and searches by police can in fact be highly coercive. Yet another unanswered question is "By what standard should one's behavior be analyzed to determine whether it is suspicious?" Standards for what is "suspicious" can be very subjective. For example, to some officers, the first person getting off a plane may be suspicious, whereas to other officers, the last person getting off a plane may seem suspicious.

Some previous high-court decisions have upheld the informal questioning of suspects fitting a suspect profile, but have prohibited coercive searches and formal arrests unless the police have additional evidence on which to base a decision. Until terms such as *coercive*, *profile*, and *voluntary* have been further defined, the U.S. Supreme Court may have to continue to fine-tune its conclusion regarding the constitutionality of this drug enforcement technique.

The Reverse Drug Sting

The most common technique for sting operations directed at drug dealing in various environments is the *reverse sting*, also called a "buy-and-bust" (an officer pretends to be a drug dealer and sells to an unsuspecting customer). However, in contrast to storefront stings, police more often use drug stings in conjunction with other responses such as sweeps, crackdowns, and beefed-up patrols in known dealing locations. Those operations that combine stings with other responses are most often rated as successful. While it is probably a good idea to combine stings with other operations targeted at reducing drug dealing, this practice makes it difficult for researchers to assess whether an operation's success was a result of the sting itself or of the other responses used. Many studies deem a sting operation "successful" if it results in massive arrests. In general, the conviction rates range up to 50 percent of arrestees, considerably lower than the rates for arrestees from storefront operations.

Some drug stings, especially those lasting a longer period, result in short-term reductions not only of the targeted crime, but also of other crimes such as robbery. On the other hand, one study found that while significant reductions in drug trafficking were achieved, there was some evidence that it was displaced to other locations that were not part of the sting. In fact, drug dealers were forced underground, which made it more difficult to maintain a buy-and-bust operation. In sum, while stings clearly have short-term effects on drug dealing, no scientific studies have demonstrated a long-term effect. Finally, because sting operations are expensive, it is necessary to assess whether the overall cost of these operations is worth it. One study found that it took 802 officer hours per violent crime deterred, another that it took 6.6 officer hours per arrest [4].

■ ■ Critical Thinking Task ■

Profile the "typical" drug dealer in your community; that is, how would you recognize this individual?

Critiques of Sting Operations

Sting operations create problems and concerns. As with many covert operations, these concerns relate to cost, privacy, and the effectiveness of such operations [5]. Here are a few concerns:

They do not reduce or prevent recurring crime problems: Few scientific studies of stings have shown that particular crimes were prevented in the long term. Where the relevant data were collected, it is commonly shown that the targeted crime was reduced as a result of the sting, but for only a limited period—at best, from 3 months to a year. In fact, since most studies showing any extended crime reduction benefits of sting operations have also reviewed other police responses used with the operations, it cannot be concluded that stings, on their own, solve a recurring crime problem.

They may increase crime: A number of well-conducted studies have shown that, contrary to expectations, sting operations may actually increase the targeted crime because they provide new opportunities for offenders to commit the crime when they use decoys, baits, and the actual selling or receipt of stolen goods. Furthermore, when police assume undercover roles, such as that of a drug dealer, they may themselves be victimized, thus making possible new crimes that were not the sting's target. This raises a serious ethical issue concerning the role of police (and government generally). The police role is to reduce crime, not increase it. If sting operations are found to increase crime, they are surely very difficult to justify, regardless of the benefits described in this chapter. However, at least one careful study found that sting operations did not increase crime in the two projects studied. This suggests that there is no hard-and-fast rule concerning the facilitating effects of stings on crime rates, and that the possible effects of each sting operation may be specific to the crime type and location.

They may be deemed unethical: Detractors frequently point out that sting operations are unethical because their use of deception is simply another form of lying, and lying is morally wrong, period. And is it ethically even worse if the deceiver holds a government office? Police defend their actions on two main grounds: (1) the moral and social benefits of a successful sting operation far exceed the ethical cost of using deception; and (2) citizens have given the police the right to use a degree of coercion to protect the community, and deception is "soft" coercion compared with other types that police may use, such as tough interrogation techniques (which themselves may include lying and deceiving the offender).

The government may overreach: Is it the government's role to construct enticements and situations that encourage all citizens to commit a crime? Studies of selling stolen goods—for example, in bars and other places—have found a remarkably high proportion of ordinary people prepared to buy stolen articles, people who, had they not been provided the opportunity to do so, would not have committed the crime. Thus, there is a very strong potential for the government to overreach. Indeed, there is a strong incentive to do so, given the positive publicity that is likely to follow the sting operation, even if no offenders were convicted.

Privacy issues: The invasion of privacy is much greater in sting operations because police surreptitiously collect far more information about nonoffenders as well as offenders, and in many instances, there are no offenders at all until the sting operation reaches a critical point. Do citizens have a right not to be spied on? This is an old ethical problem in policing that is intensified by sting operations that rely almost entirely on these tactics.

Entrapment concerns: Of all the negative features of sting operations, *entrapment* is by far the most widely cited. This is because many of the ethical issues described here come together to form the "entrapment defense," used by offenders to argue that the police tricked them into committing the crime. There are many legal tests for entrapment, and every United States state's law recognizes the defense. While we need not go into the legal technicalities, there are two legal tests of entrapment: the "subjective" and "objective" tests, both of which take as their starting point that the government encouraged or induced the offense in question. The subjective test asks whether the offender had a predisposition to commit the act, that is, it focuses on the offender's psychological state. The objective test asks whether the government's encouragement exceeded reasonable levels; thus, it focuses on the government's actions in constructing enticements—and whether it went "too far." How each of these is assessed, of course, is the subject of legal wrangling, and it may in the long run depend on a jury decision.

They are expensive: The popular—and more elaborate—stings require expensive props (storefronts, money upfront to make illegal purchases or pay informers, decoy cars, video cameras, eavesdropping equipment, etc.). Often, police can obtain these by approaching businesses affected by the crime to help out. But there is also the greater financial cost of staff time—undercover work required in complex stings is very time-demanding and may take months or even years. Finally, there is considerable cost in the time required to train officers in how to carry out a successful sting operation. Not included in the police budget, except for officer time in court, is the cost of the very lengthy trials that occur to gain sting convictions, since the entrapment defense is commonly used and has become extremely complex. In summary, sting operations can be expensive, are demanding on personnel, and generally offer limited relief from recurring crime and disorder problems. This is not to say that they should never be used. They may be beneficial when used in concert with other police responses known to provide long-term solutions to the problem, such as a tool to collect information that will help in mounting other preventative operations. Clearly, they do provide some attractive benefits to police departments, particularly by facilitating investigation, increasing arrests, and fostering a cooperative spirit between prosecutors and police, all of which result in favorable publicity. However, you need to assess these benefits against the negative ethical and legal problems associated with sting operations, especially the finding that in some cases they increase crime, and in the long term, with some exceptions, they generally do not reduce it.

The War on Drugs as a War on Women

One of the most devastating aspects of the United States' drug war has been its impact on women in general, and minority women in particular. According to the 2008 *National Survey on Drug Use and Health* (NSDUH), approximately 42.9 percent of female respondents age 12 or older reported using an illicit drug at some point in their lives. Approximately 12.2 percent of females age 12 and older reported past-year use of an illicit drug, and 6.3 percent reported past-month use of an illicit drug [6].

A study by the Correctional Association of New York, focusing on the arrests and prosecutions of "drug mules" in Queens, illustrates the impact of the drug war on women. The study found a drastic increase in the number of women arrested and subsequently charged with felony narcotics offenses. Many of these women were first-time offenders arrested for attempting to smuggle drugs through JFK International Airport, a major entry point for international travelers. As a result of the combined effect of New York's "Rockefeller Drug Laws" and the accessorial liability statute, women suspected of being drug couriers in the employ of smuggling syndicates faced mandatory prison sentences of 15 years to life on their first felony arrests. If they were also charged under federal laws, they faced the additional risk of a 50-years-to-life federal sentence [7].

Investigations determined that many of these women were either unwitting agents of drug smugglers, or only marginally involved in drug-smuggling operations. Because of the severe sentences they faced, most of these women did not go to trial. Instead, they accepted plea bargains carrying sentences of 3 years to life, a sentence that is out of proportion to other first-time felony sentences. Many of these women were mothers who were either unable or unwilling to be separated from their children for potentially very long periods if they were convicted of the original charges. In fact, it has been found that 80 percent of all women prisoners in the United States are the sole caretakers of children under the age of 18 [8]. Moreover, according to the study, many female drug couriers who were charged pleaded guilty, even if they had valid defenses or were innocent of the charges being proffered [9].

In many drug courier cases, women are disproportionately impacted by restrictions on judicial discretion in mandatory-sentencing drug statutes. The defendant's inability to present evidence of mitigating circumstances in such cases is particularly crippling [10]. As a result, the rate of incarceration for women grew dramatically in the 1980s, increasing by 275 percent from 1980 to 1992 in the United States as a whole, and increasing by 433 percent (from 2,370 to 12,633) between 1986 and 1991 for drug defendants incarcerated in state prisons. By 1991, one out of every three women incarcerated in a state prison was there as the result of a drug conviction, up from one in eight in 1986 [11].

The impact of the drug war on women does not end with women as drug defendants. With drug policy emphasizing enforcement and punishment rather than education and rehabilitation, the impact on families is profound. When fathers are incarcerated on drug-trafficking or, more likely, drug possession charges, it is usually women who are left as single heads of households to raise the children. When male children are arrested for drug sales, it is their mothers who bear the brunt of the civil forfeiture laws, losing possessions as well as what meager funds they may have accumulated in bank accounts, and facing almost certain eviction from their domiciles. When male addicts share needles because of a policy that makes the provision of clean needles a criminal offense, the women with whom they have sex also face the risk of HIV infection.

For women who are not drug couriers or traffickers but merely users with addictions, legal discrimination is the most intense. These women face not only the threat of arrests for possession, but also mandatory reporting requirements and child abuse and neglect laws that can deprive them of access to medical care, prenatal care, and even drug counseling and treatment. Pregnant and new mothers face the danger of criminal prosecution on charges ranging from drug distribution to assault and murder. This discourages any effort to seek drug treatment, prenatal care, or even postnatal care for their babies. These kinds of criminal charges are the most discriminatory of all, excluding men from any participation and possibly endangering the health of mothers and children far more egregiously than any pattern of drug use ever could.

FIGURE 11.1 A guard keeps a close watch in the doorway of an inmate's cell in Buen Pastor women's prison in Bogota, Colombia. Drug traffickers are increasingly recruiting non-Colombians like this woman to ferry drugs to the United States and Europe via commercial flights. *Source: AP Photo/William Fernando Martinez.*

Mandatory Minimum Sentencing

As suggested in the "The War on Drugs as a War on Women" section, one of the more controversial issues in drug control today is the mandatory minimum sentencing policy of the federal court system. At the core of the issue is the realization by police and prosecutors that drug dealers are innovative and cunning, and will employ many measures to avoid detection. Because one of the drug dealer's greatest fears may be a prison sentence, experts have suggested that the best deterrent to drug crime is the threat of mandatory incarceration. So, under mandatory minimum sentencing laws, an arrested offender has two choices: to go to prison if convicted or to become a government witness against his or her supplier. This is the basis and hallmark of mandatory minimum sentencing, one that police argue is an effective tool for legal leverage against drug dealers. It gives prosecutors the option to not file a drug charge provided the offender agrees to work with police in collecting evidence against others in the drug-trafficking operation. As experience has shown, the informant who is cooperating with authorities in exchange for prosecutorial leniency ("working a beef") has proved to be one of the most powerfully motivated players in the criminal investigation process, and clearly it is the codefendant who is most knowledgeable about a drug-trafficking enterprise.

In 1986, Congress enacted mandatory minimum sentencing laws, which force judges to deliver fixed sentences to individuals convicted of a crime, regardless of culpability or other mitigating factors. Federal mandatory drug sentences are determined based on three factors: (1) the type of drug, (2) the weight of the drug mixture (or alleged weight, in conspiracy cases), and (3) the number of prior convictions. Judges are unable to consider other important factors such as the offender's role and motivation, and the likelihood of recidivism. Only by providing the prosecutor with "substantial assistance" (information that aids the government in prosecuting other offenders) may defendants reduce their mandatory sentences. This creates huge incentives for people charged with drug offenses to provide false information in order to receive a shorter sentence.

Although Congress intended mandatory sentences to target "kingpins" and managers in drug distribution networks, the U.S. Sentencing Commission reports that only 5.5 percent of all federal crack cocaine defendants and 11 percent of federal drug defendants are high-level drug dealers. This is because the most culpable defendants are also the defendants who are in the best position to provide prosecutors with enough information to obtain sentence reductions—the only way to reduce a mandatory sentence. Low-level offenders, such as drug mules or street dealers, often end up serving longer sentences because they have little or no information to provide the government.

■ ■ Critical Thinking Task ■

Support or refute the federal court system's policy of mandatory minimum sentencing for the possession of crack cocaine.

The U.S. Sentencing Commission and the Department of Justice have both concluded that mandatory sentencing fails to deter crime. Furthermore, mandatory minimums have worsened racial and gender disparities, and have contributed greatly toward prison over-crowding. Mandatory minimum sentencing is costly and unjust. Mandatory sentencing does not eliminate sentencing disparities; instead, it shifts decision-making authority from judges to prosecutors, who operate without accountability. Mandatory minimums fail to punish high-level dealers. Finally, mandatory sentences are responsible for sending record numbers of women and people of color to prison. For example:

- *Prison overcrowding.* More than 80 percent of the increase in the federal prison population from 1985 to 1995 is due to drug convictions.
- *Racial injustice.* In 1986, the year Congress enacted federal mandatory drug sentences, the average federal drug sentence for African Americans was 11 percent higher than for whites. Four years later, the average federal drug sentence for African Americans was 49 percent higher.
- *Women.* Between 1986 and 1996, the number of women in prison for drug law viola-tions increased by 421 percent. This led U.S. Bureau of Prisons Director Kathleen Hawk-Sawyer to testify before Congress, "The reality is, some 70-some percent of our female population are low-level, nonviolent offenders. The fact that they have to come into prison is a question mark for me. I think it has been an unintended consequence of the sentencing guidelines and the mandatory minimums" [12].

Electronic Surveillance

The past 40 years have seen a virtual revolution in technology relevant to electronic sur-veillance. Advances in electronics, semiconductors, computers, imaging, databases, and related technologies have greatly increased technological options for police surveillance activities. Although the use of electronic surveillance in drug control is nothing new, tech-niques such as the wiretap have raised renewed concerns over the protection of privacy.

Title III of the Omnibus Crime Control and Safe Streets Act of 1968, the major law addressing electronic surveillance, was designed to protect the privacy of wire and oral communications. At the time this act was passed, electronic surveillance was primarily limited to telephone taps and hidden microphones (bugs). Since then, however, basic communications have undergone rapid technological changes with the advent of such technologies as personal pagers, personal computers, cellular telephones, e-mail, elec-tronic bulletin boards, social networking sites, and more. Many of these devices are now commonly used by drug traffickers to assist them in communicating with drug suppliers and customers.

Because new and increasingly mobile drug gangs are evident throughout the country, law enforcement agencies at both the state and federal levels are making more frequent use of electronic surveillance technology to combat drug trafficking. Public concerns arise with regard to the circumstances under which these technologies are applied and how they might infringe on First, Fourth, and Fifth Amendment rights. At the same time, however, the public is also concerned about crime (especially violent crime) and generally supports the use of electronic technology in criminal investigations. As a result, balancing these concerns remains a critical issue in drug control.

The primary purpose of electronic surveillance is to monitor the behavior of individuals, including individual movements, actions, communications, emotions, and/or various combinations of these. From a law enforcement and investigative standpoint, the potential benefits offered through new technologies may be substantial—for example, the development of more accurate and complete information on suspects, the possible reduction in time and human resources required for case investigation, and the expansion of options for preventing and deterring crimes. From a societal perspective, the possible benefits are also important, including the potential for increasing one's physical security in the home and on the streets, strengthening efforts to prevent drug trafficking, and enhancing the protection of citizens and government officials from terrorist actions.

Electronic surveillance is used primarily in gambling and narcotics cases. For years, gambling was the most common object of electronic surveillance, and narcotics was the second most common; more recently, the order was reversed. The difficulty in using intrusion as a principle by which to evaluate both a "reasonable expectation of privacy" and the appropriateness of using a particular surveillance device is that no criteria have yet been explicitly formulated to determine intrusiveness. Instead, the facts of individual cases seem to determine individual courses of action.

Still, based on court rulings, congressional statutes, and executive orders, it is possible to isolate five important dimensions in determining whether the situation warrants violation or protection of ordinary civil liberties. The five dimensions are (1) the nature of the information, (2) the nature of the area or communication to be placed under surveillance, (3) the scope of the surveillance, (4) the surreptitiousness of the surveillance, and (5) pre-electronic analysis. In evaluating the legitimacy of the government's use of surveillance devices, three dimensions are considered: (1) the purpose of the investigation, (2) the degree of individualized suspicion, and (3) the relative effectiveness of the surveillance.

It appears that the use of higher technology in surveillance activities by law enforcement agencies will prevail. With the more frequent use of detection devices and electronic equipment by drug traffickers, surveillance equipment will become more sophisticated. Implementing such technology will no doubt continue to fall under close scrutiny by courts and public groups in the coming years. Its use, however, is clearly an important factor in the detection and documentation of covert criminal activity in the drug trade.

Needle Exchange Programs

Needle sharing is a major problem in inner cities in which heroin addiction prevails. The heroin addict typically injects himself or herself with the drug several times a day. Because sterile needles are not always available, the sharing of needles between one person and another sometimes occurs.

The AIDS problem dominates much of the medical profession's public health and policy concerns. Although transmission of the disease is often accomplished through sexual activity, an estimated 20 percent of AIDS cases were reported to have been transmitted through intravenous (IV) drug users sharing needles. According to testimony before the U.S. House of Representatives in April 1989, one HIV-infected drug user can conceivably expose up to 100 other users over the course of a few months [13]. (Other communicable diseases such as hepatitis are also transmitted in this fashion.) In an effort to curb the spread of the disease, both researchers and medical professionals have considered the controversial idea of exchanging clean needles for the dirty needles belonging to drug addicts.

Most needle exchange programs consist of three basic functions:

1. To dispense sterile needles to current IV users
2. To promote and accept returns of used needles to control how needles are discarded
3. To change the behavior of IV drug users through health education and counseling

A debate continues to rage about needle exchange programs across the country. Needle exchange programs offer clean needles to drug users in exchange for dirty ones in an effort to cut down on the number of blood-borne diseases among IV drug users, but many feel that such programs encourage drug use, that the needles will not be used, and that the programs will only create more drug addicts and, accordingly, more AIDS carriers. The assertion that the needles will not be used is based on the view that needle sharing is a ritualistic practice, deeply embedded into the subculture of IV drug users. Another argument against the exchange programs is that giving away needles is illegal. The question of legality may be a valid one, at least in certain jurisdictions, and is constantly being addressed at the state and local government levels.

Proponents of needle exchange programs argue that they help not only the drug users at risk, but their sex partners and children as well. Opponents of needle exchange programs suggest that the programs may cost lives. At the political crux of the issue is this question: should the federal government, which spends billions on the drug war, do anything that may encourage drug use? Supporters claim that the scientific case for such programs is overwhelming, since needle exchange programs have been shown to cut HIV infection rates without increasing drug use. Opponents claim that the studies showing this finding are flawed. However, scientific reviews sponsored by the federal Centers for Disease Control and Prevention, Institute of Medicine, National Institutes of Health, and General Accounting Office all have agreed on the usefulness of needle exchange programs [14].

■ ■ Critical Thinking Task ■

Assume you are on the New York City Council. Explain your "yea" or "nay" vote to continue the City Health Department's $230,000-per-year program to exchange addicts' used needles for sterile ones.

When considering the appropriateness of such a program, perhaps one should consider the success or failure of similar programs in England, the Netherlands, Sweden, and Australia, where needle-sharing programs have been operational since 1984. The results are extremely consistent. In Amsterdam, for example, researchers noted that 80 percent of needle exchange users in the program stopped sharing equipment since the program began, compared to 50 percent of nonexchangers.

Forfeiture of Attorney's Fees

Considering the enormous cash flow of many drug traffickers, it is logical to assume that much of the money earned through illicit drug transactions ends up in the bank accounts of lawyers who represent drug traffickers. Through the use of carefully sculpted laws such as the 1984 Federal Comprehensive Forfeiture Act (CFA), the instances of lawyers knowingly accepting "dirty" money or assets for legal fees have greatly decreased. The most conspicuous legal precedents addressing the issue were handed down by the Supreme Court in 1989 in *United States v. Monsanto* and *Caplin & Drysdale, Chartered v. United States*. These decisions basically held that the government's ability to enforce forfeiture extends to drug assets needed to pay attorney's fees.

In reviewing these cases, the *Monsanto* decision involved a defendant who was facing charges under the federal Continuing Criminal Enterprise (CCE) statute of creating a continuing criminal enterprise. The indictment asserted that the defendant had acquired an apartment, a home, and a sum of $35,000 in cash as a result of drug-trafficking activities. The government subsequently sought to freeze all of the defendant's assets until the trial was over. In response, the defendant claimed that those assets were necessary to retain a competent lawyer for his defense. His claim was rejected by the district court.

As the trial progressed, an appellate court reviewed the district court's ruling and found that the frozen assets should indeed be used to pay attorney's fees. The defendant, however, declined because of the advanced stage of the trial. He was ultimately convicted of the trafficking charges and was required to forfeit his assets. At a later stage in the appeals process, the Supreme Court agreed to hear the case involving forfeiture of attorney's fees. The Court ruled that the sale or transfer of potentially forfeitable assets is forbidden.

The issue of lawyers accepting drug assets in lieu of payment for services rendered raises several legal and ethical questions. Such legal questions include whether the defendant's Fifth or Sixth Amendment rights are violated through the use of such a tactic. Those opposed to the forfeiture practice point out that the Sixth Amendment provides the accused the right to counsel, and the Fifth Amendment protects the right to due process under law. On both issues, however, the Supreme Court has upheld forfeiture sanctions against attorney's fees.

The ethical concerns of forfeiture have centered on three issues. First, in the two preceding cases, opponents to forfeiture argued that the CFA actually encouraged attorneys to be less than thorough in investigating a client's case, so that any fees they might have received would be protected from forfeiture. Additionally, some argue that when faced with losing legal fees under the CFA, an attorney may compromise his or her client's position during plea bargaining if a longer prison sentence were suggested in lieu of forfeiture of legal fees. In a third scenario, an attorney may be tempted to manipulate the justice system by representing a client on a contingency basis. Although the practice is considered unethical by the American Bar Association, the attorney could conceivably make an agreement with his or her client that only after the client's acquittal would the attorney be paid the designated fee. Thus, the unscrupulous attorney could avoid losing his or her fee under the CFA.

On the same day the government argued its case in *Monsanto*, the Supreme Court heard oral arguments in the *Caplin* case. In this case, illicit-drug importer Christopher Reckmeyer paid the law firm of Caplin and Drysdale $25,000 for preindictment legal services. Before the case could go to trial, Reckmeyer pleaded guilty to the charges, and virtually all his assets were declared forfeitable by the court, including fees paid to the law firm. After an extended legal process whereby the firm's lawyers attempted to secure a release of the fees already paid to them, the Supreme Court ultimately ruled that the forfeiture was lawful and that there are no statutory, ethical, or constitutional impediments to the forfeiture of attorney's fees under the Federal CFA.

Drug Control and Sports

Athletes have always tried to improve their performance with various naturally occurring or chemically modified agents. Medical and pharmacological advances in the nineteenth and twentieth centuries produced new performance-enhancing substances, and more sophisticated understanding of their potential benefits—as well as their risks. By the 1960s, some sports organizations and medical associations were recognizing the widening use of performance-enhancing drugs in Olympic and professional sports, and calling for steps to combat the practices.

In ancient times, Greek athletes took mushrooms to improve their performance and trained on special diets that included dried figs. Egyptians believed that ingesting the ground rear hooves of the Abyssinian ass could boost performance. Roman gladiators took stimulants to overcome fatigue and injury. The sixteenth-century Spanish conquerors of Peru found widespread use among the native Incas of the coca leaf as a stimulant.

By the nineteenth century, athletes were experimenting with a variety of stimulants. Scientists in Europe first isolated cocaine around 1860; there were reports in 1869 of cyclists using heroin–cocaine mixtures to increase endurance. Through the late nineteenth and early twentieth centuries, cyclists in various countries were reported to have used ether-soaked tablets (Belgium), caffeine tablets (France), or mixtures with some combinations of strychnine, heroin, brandy, and cocaine (England). In 1904, a United States marathoner, Tom Hicks, collapsed and died at the St. Louis Olympics after ingesting a strychnine–brandy cocktail.

The modern era of performance-enhancing drugs can be dated from various scientific developments in the 1930s, including the isolation of the male hormones *androsterone* (1931) and testosterone (1935), and the discovery of medical applications of the stimulant amphetamine (late 1930s). The German military used testosterone in the 1930s and in World War II to increase the strength and aggressiveness of soldiers, and similarly found that amphetamines helped overcome fatigue during combat. Scientific studies in the early 1940s showed improved strength and endurance from using anabolic steroids.

Steroid use by Olympic participants and athletes in strength sports like football increased largely unchecked through the 1960s. An American Medical Association committee had warned that athletes were abusing amphetamines as early as 1957, and amphetamines were linked to the deaths of at least three world-class cyclists in the 1960s. But steroids were legal, their use somewhat openly acknowledged, their benefits touted, and their side effects either unknown or ignored.

The International Olympic Committee (IOC) finally established a medical commission to control drug use in 1967, and a year later it instituted the first drug-testing program during the Mexico City Olympics. The Olympics' first antidoping enforcement action came in 1972. In an action that remains controversial today, Richard James DeMont was stripped of his gold medal for the 400 m freestyle at the Munich Games after testing positive for ephedrine. The swimmer, who was also barred from participating in other events at the games, had informed United States team physicians beforehand that he was taking an antiasthma drug, but the information apparently did not reach IOC medical authorities.

By the late 1980s and early 1990s, suspicion was also falling on baseball, as players bulked up and home run output increased. But Mark McGwire's use of the then-legal steroid precursor *andro* fell short of a scandal when acknowledged in 1998. Four years later, though, former San Diego Padre third baseman Ken Caminiti admitted that he had heavily used steroids for years—including in 1996, when he won the National League's Most Valuable Player award. When Caminiti's admission was published in the *Sports Illustrated* story "Totally Juiced," the article described the use of steroids and other performance-enhancing drugs as "rampant."

Why Athletes Use Drugs

Athletes face enormous pressure to excel in competition. They also know that winning can reap them more than a gold medal. A star athlete can earn a lot of money and fame, and athletes have only a short timeframe in which to do their best work. Athletes know that training is the best path to victory, but they also get the message that some drugs and other practices can boost their efforts and give them a shortcut, even as they risk their health and their athletic careers.

For as long as there have been competitive sports, athletes have taken performance-enhancing substances, going back to the stimulating potions taken by ancient Greek sportsmen. In the nineteenth century, cyclists and other endurance athletes kept themselves going with caffeine, alcohol, and even (as mentioned in this chapter) strychnine and cocaine. In 1928, the precursor of the International Association of Athletics Federations (IAAF) became the first world sporting body to forbid stimulants. The ban was ineffective, though, because there was no way of testing for many of them. The invention of artificial hormones in the 1930s made the problem more severe.

In the 1960s, the world bodies for cycling and soccer became the first to introduce doping tests. However, there was no reliable test for steroids until the 1970s. Once a test was introduced, there was a big rise in the number of athletes being disqualified, culminating in the scandal of Ben Johnson, who broke the world 100 m sprint record at the 1988 Olympics, only to be stripped of his gold medal afterward when his urine sample showed the presence of steroids. Johnson insisted that he was far from alone in using banned substances, and he seems to have been right: in the 1990s, as improved doping tests made it harder to cheat, the results achieved by top-level athletes in some sports showed a notable decline.

To date, it is unclear how long athletes have been taking tetrahydrogestrinone (THG), or how widespread its abuse is. The THG doping threat raises the prospect of national heroes being stripped of their medals. In 2003, the USA Track and Field (USATF) Foundation announced a *zero-tolerance* policy on doping that included plans to impose lifetime bans on athletes caught using illegal substances, rather than the former 2-year ban.

The side effects of steroid abuse range from liver and kidney cancer to infertility, baldness, and even transmission of HIV (if the syringes used to inject the drug are shared). However, there seems no limit to the lengths to which some athletes are driven by their will to win. In the 1970s, some tried "blood boosting"—reinfusing themselves with their own blood to boost the level of oxygen, a practice that was banned by the IOC in 1986. Some then turned to erythropoietin (EPO), a blood-enhancing drug. Although this was banned in 1990, a reliable test for the drug was not available until the 2000 Olympics. Now, although a test for THG has been developed, there are concerns that some athletes are taking human growth hormone.

Reports of athletes possessing, using, and distributing illicit drugs have become commonplace in newspapers, in magazines, and on television. One popular illicit drug, cocaine, is used by many athletes for both recreation and performance enhancement. In addition, the nonmedical use of steroids is becoming more commonplace among athletes and nonathletes alike.

The high visibility of athletes, especially the successful ones, makes their drug problems more newsworthy than those of the average citizen. Most of the media accounts of drug abuse involving athletes report the use of illicit recreational drugs. Such activities have created a public outcry for control, and have prompted athletic organizations to initiate antidrug programs. What is it that attracts athletes to drug abuse? Three different reasons can be identified to help explain their involvement with illicit drugs:

1. Drugs taken at the time of competition immediately enhance performance.
2. Drugs taken during training or well before competition enhance performance.
3. Athletes use recreational drugs for the same reasons that nonathletes do.

World Antidoping Code

As stated in this chapter, the use of performance-enhancing drugs (doping) is prohibited within the field of professional (and amateur) sports. Athletes who are found to have used

---

A CLOSER LOOK: PERFORMANCE-ENHANCING DRUGS

The classification of substances as performance-enhancing drugs is not entirely clear-cut. Although the phrase *performance-enhancing drugs* is popularly used in reference to anabolic steroids or their precursors, world antidoping organizations apply the term broadly. The phrase has been used to refer to several distinct classes of drugs:

- *Lean mass builders* drive or amplify the growth of muscle and lean body mass; sometimes, they are used to reduce body fat. This class of drugs includes anabolic steroids, xenoandrogens, beta-2 agonists, selective androgen receptor modulators (SARMs), and various human hormones, most notably human growth hormone, as well as some of their precursors. Performance-enhancing drugs are also found in animals as synthetic growth hormone.
- *Stimulants*: These stimulate the body and mind to perform optimally by enhancing focus, energy, and aggression. Some examples are caffeine, amphetamine, and methamphetamine.
- *Painkillers*: These mask athletes' pain so they can continue to compete and perform beyond their usual pain thresholds. Blood pressure is increased, causing the cells in the muscles to be better supplied with vital oxygen. Painkillers used by athletes range from common over-the-counter medicines (e.g., nonsteroidal anti-inflammatory drugs (NSAIDs) such as ibuprofen) to powerful prescription narcotics.
- *Sedatives*: These are sometimes used by athletes in sports like archery that require steady hands and accurate aim, and also by athletes attempting to overcome excessive nervousness or discomfort. Alcohol, diazepam, propranolol, and marijuana are examples.
- *Diuretics*: These expel water from athletes' bodies. They are often used by athletes such as wrestlers who need to meet weight restrictions. Many stimulants also have a secondary diuretic effect. (Diuretics are also used as masking drugs, which are also discussed in this list.)
- *Blood boosters* increase the oxygen-carrying capacity of blood beyond the individual's natural capacity. Their misuse is centered on endurance sports like cycling and Nordic skiing. EPO is the most publicly known drug in this class.
- *Masking drugs* are used to prevent the detection of other classes of drugs. These evolve as quickly as do testing methods, although a time-tested classic example is the use of epitestosterone, a drug with no performance-enhancing effects, to restore the testosterone–epitestosterone ratio (a common criterion in steroid testing) to normal levels after anabolic steroid supplementation.

---

such banned substances, through either a positive drug test or public admission, receive a competition ban for a length of time that reflects the severity of the infraction. Athletes who are found to have banned substances in their possession, or who tamper with (or refuse to submit to) drug testing, can also receive bans from the sport. Short competitive bans are also given to athletes who test positive for prohibited recreational drugs or minor stimulants that serve little performance-enhancing effects for competitors in athletics. Essentially, any athlete who tests positive for banned substances after having served a previous ban receives a lifetime ban from his or her sport. The sports authority responsible for determining which substances are banned in athletics is the World Anti-Doping Agency (WADA).

In 2004, the *World Anti-Doping Code* was created by sports organizations prior to the Olympic Games in Athens, Greece, coordinating the rules and regulations governing anti-doping across all sports and all countries for the first time in history. As of this writing, more than 600 sports organizations have adopted the Code.

Following an extensive consultation period, revisions to the World Anti-Doping Code were unanimously adopted at the Third World Conference on Doping in Sport in November 2007 to integrate the experience gained from the enforcement of the initial Code. These revisions took effect on January 1, 2009. They include numerous measures that strengthen the global fight against doping in sport.

Given that many governments cannot be legally bound by a nongovernmental document such as the World Anti-Doping Code, they are implementing it by individually ratifying the UNESCO International Convention against Doping in Sport, the first global international treaty against doping in sport, which was unanimously adopted by 191 governments at the UNESCO General Conference in October 2005, and came into force in February 2007. More than 145 governments (including the United States) have ratified the Convention to date, setting a UNESCO record.

The UNESCO Convention is a practical and legally binding tool enabling governments to align domestic policy with the World Anti-Doping Code, thus harmonizing the rules governing antidoping in sport. It formalizes governments' commitment to the fight against doping in sports, including by facilitating doping controls and supporting national testing programs; encouraging the establishment of "best practice" in the labeling, marketing, and distribution of products that might contain prohibited substances; withholding financial support from those who engage in or support doping; taking measures against manufacturing and trafficking; encouraging the establishment of codes of conduct for professions relating to sport and antidoping; and funding education and research.

Doping Allegations and Lance Armstrong

Cyclist Lance Armstrong, for much of the second phase of his career, encountered ongoing allegations of doping. Until 2010, no official investigation was undertaken. During most of his career, Armstrong denied allegations of doping until an interview with Oprah Winfrey on January 14, 2013, wherein he confessed that he has used banned performance-enhancing drugs throughout much of his cycling career, most recently in 2005. He admitted that he used EPO and human growth hormone, and that he had blood-doped. He said that doping helped him for each of his seven Tour de France wins.

Throughout his career, Armstrong continually denied using illegal performance-enhancing drugs and has described himself as the most tested athlete in the world. A 1999 urine sample showed traces of *corticosteroid*. A medical certificate showed he used an approved cream for saddle sores that contained the substance. From the fall of 2008 through March 2009, Armstrong submitted to 24 unannounced drug tests by various antidoping authorities. All of the tests were negative for performance-enhancing drugs. United States federal prosecutors pursued allegations of doping by Armstrong from 2010 to 2012. The effort convened a grand jury to investigate doping charges; this included taking statements under oath from Armstrong's former team members and other associates; meeting with officials from France, Belgium, Spain, and Italy; and requesting samples from the French antidoping agency.

In May 2011, former Armstrong teammate Tyler Hamilton told *CBS News* that he and Armstrong had together taken EPO before and during the 1999, 2000, and 2001 Tours de France. Armstrong's attorney, Mark Fabiani, responded that Hamilton was lying. In a subsequent investigation by *60 Minutes*, two other former Armstrong teammates, Frankie Andreu and George Hincapie, were alleged to have told federal investigators that they witnessed Armstrong taking banned substances, including EPO, or supplied Armstrong with such substances. The federal investigation was led by Agent Jeff Novitzky, who also investigated suspicions of steroid use by baseball players Barry Bonds and Roger Clemens. The probe was terminated on February 3, 2012, with no charges filed.

When interviewed for the BBC News Channel's *Hardtalk*, Hamilton continued to insist that he and Armstrong had doped together. Rejecting the fact that Armstrong had passed numerous drug tests, Hamilton said that he himself had also passed hundreds of drug tests while doping.

In the 2012 documentary *The World According to Lance Armstrong*, attorney Jeffrey Tillotson stated that he thought the evidence that he and his team developed showed that Armstrong had been using performance-enhancing drugs dating back to the start of his career. Tillotson was engaged by an insurer that unsuccessfully tried to refuse to pay Armstrong $5 million in bonuses for Armstrong's performance in the Tour de France in 2006, based on their collection of evidence on Armstrong using performance-enhancing drugs.

In June 2012, the United States Anti-Doping Agency (USADA) accused Armstrong of doping and trafficking of drugs, based on blood samples from 2009 to 2010 and testimony from witnesses, including former teammates. Armstrong, denying all doping use in a statement, was suspended from competition in cycling and the triathlon. Armstrong was charged in a letter from USADA, along with five others, including former team manager Johan Bruyneel. USADA said Armstrong used banned substances, including the blood booster EPO and steroids, as well as blood transfusions dating back to 1996. On October 10, 2012, USADA said Armstrong was part of "the most sophisticated, professionalized, and successful doping program that sport has ever seen," in advance of issuing its long-awaited report detailing the evidence it acquired.

Armstrong resigned as director of the Lance Armstrong Foundation and was dropped by sponsors RadioShack and Nike on October 17, 2012. On the same day, Anheuser-Busch said it would not renew its relationship with Armstrong at the end of 2012, but would continue to support the racer's cancer charity. Other sponsors who cut ties with Armstrong were Trek Bicycle Corporation, Giro, FRS Healthy Performance, Honey Stinger, 24-Hour Fitness, bicycle parts manufacturer SRAM, and Oakley. It was announced on October 30 that Armstrong was stripped of the key to Adelaide, which he had received as an honor for his three participations in the Tour Down Under. At the end of November 2012, he was elected as the top "Anti-Sportsman of the Year" by *Sports Illustrated*.

Medical Marijuana

In the United States federal government, cannabis has been made criminal by implementation of the Controlled Substances Act, which classifies cannabis as a Schedule I drug; this is the strictest classification, and it is also applied to heroin, lysergic acid diethylamide, and ecstasy. The Supreme Court ruled in 2005 that the Commerce Clause of the U.S. Constitution allowed the government to ban the use of cannabis, including medical use. The U.S. Food and Drug Administration (FDA) states that "marijuana has a high potential for abuse, has no currently accepted medical use in treatment in the United States, and has a lack of accepted safety for use under medical supervision."

Two American for-profit companies, Cannabis Science and Medical Marijuana, are working toward getting FDA approval for cannabis-based medicines (including smoked

HOW DOPING CASES PROCEED

The U.S. Anti-Doping Agency is breaking ground in its attempt to sanction athletes for drug violations based on evidence other than a positive test. Though the process is unprecedented, the protocol will be the same as for a positive test. The process includes the following:

- Notification of a potential violation: The sending of notice letters is the first step toward determining whether sport antidoping rules have been violated.
- An independent review board, consisting of experts with legal, technical, and medical knowledge of antidoping matters, will consider the alleged violations and make a recommendation as to whether USADA should proceed with a formal charge.
- Under the USADA protocol, those who are notified of potential violations are innocent unless and until a formal charge has been brought and they accept the sanction, or a panel of arbitrators, after a full hearing, determines that a doping violation has occurred. The review panel's recommendation will be forwarded to the athlete, the sport's national governing body, the U.S. Olympic Committee, the international federation, and WADA.
- Within 10 days after being notified of a sanction, the athlete must notify USADA in writing if he or she desires a hearing to contest the sanction.
- If an athlete accepts the sanction proposed by USADA, it then will be publicly announced.
- Or an athlete can choose arbitration. Athletes have two choices for the hearing, which is held in the United States:
  - Selecting the American Arbitration Association (AAA). A single arbitrator will rule, unless either party wants a three-arbitrator panel. Arbitrators come from a pool of the North American Court of Arbitration for Sport (CAS) arbitrators. If an athlete chooses an AAA hearing, either party can appeal the decision to CAS.
  - Or an athlete can choose to go straight to CAS for a single, final hearing. The CAS decision shall be final and binding on all parties, and shall not be subject to further review or appeal.

cannabis). Cannabis Science wants to have medical cannabis approved by the FDA so that anyone, regardless of the state in which they live, will have access to the medicine. In addition, the nonprofit Multidisciplinary Association for Psychedelic Studies (MAPS) is working toward getting cannabis approved by the FDA for posttraumatic stress disorder (PTSD).

Medical marijuana refers to the use of cannabis as a form of medicine or herbal therapy approved by a physician. While the extent of the medicinal value of marijuana has been disputed, it does have a number of documented beneficial effects that many researchers have applauded Aggarwal [15]. Among these are suppression of nausea and vomiting, stimulation of hunger in chemotherapy and AIDS patients, lowered eye pressure (for treating glaucoma), as well as general benefits of pain relief.

Synthetic marijuana is available as a prescription drug in some countries, including the United States. There are numerous methods for administering cannabis, including vaporizing or smoking dried buds, drinking or eating extracts, and taking capsules. The comparable efficacy of these methods was the subject of an investigative study conducted by the National Institutes of Health.

Marijuana as a recreational drug is illegal in most parts of the world. However, its use as a medicine is legal in a number of countries, including Canada, Austria, Germany, the Netherlands, Spain, Israel, Italy, Finland, and Portugal. In the United States, under federal law, marijuana is illegal for any type of use, while permission for medical marijuana varies among states. Distribution is usually accomplished within a system identified by local laws.

Medical marijuana remains a controversial issue worldwide. In a 2002 review of medical literature, medical cannabis was shown to have established effects in the treatment of nausea, vomiting, premenstrual syndrome, unintentional weight loss, insomnia, and lack of appetite. Medical marijuana has also been found to relieve certain symptoms of multiple sclerosis and spinal cord injuries [16].

As of the preparation of this text, 18 states and the District of Columbia have legalized medical marijuana or effectively decriminalized it, starting with California. These states are Alaska, Arizona, California, Colorado, Connecticut, Delaware, Hawaii, Maine, Massachusetts, Michigan, Montana, Nevada, New Jersey, New Mexico, Oregon, Rhode Island, Vermont, Virginia, and Washington.

In 2008, California's medical marijuana industry took in about $2 billion a year and generated $100 million in state sales taxes. With an estimated 2100 dispensaries, cooperatives, wellness clinics, and taxi delivery services in the sector, it is colloquially known as "cannabusiness" [17].

At the federal level, cannabis has been made criminal by implementation of the Controlled Substances Act, but in 2009, new federal guidelines were enacted. U.S. Attorney General Eric Holder announced that the federal government will not make it a priority to use federal resources to prosecute patients with serious illnesses or their caregivers who are complying with state laws on medical marijuana, but drug traffickers who hide behind claims of compliance with state law will not be tolerated. Cannabis remains illegal throughout the United States and is not approved for prescription as medicine, although

18 states – Alaska, Arizona, California, Colorado, Connecticut, Delaware, Hawaii, Maine, Massachusetts, Michigan, Montana, Nevada, New Jersey, New Mexico, Oregon, Rhode Island, Vermont, and Washington – as well as the District of Columbia approve and regulate its medical use.

Criticisms of Medical Marijuana

One of the biggest criticisms of marijuana as medicine is opposition to smoking as a method of consumption. The FDA issued an advisory against smoked medical marijuana, stating that marijuana has a high potential for abuse, has no currently accepted medical use in treatment in the United States, and has a lack of accepted safety for use under medical supervision. Furthermore, current evidence states that smoked marijuana is harmful [18].

The Institute of Medicine, run by the U.S. National Academy of Sciences, conducted a comprehensive study in 1999 to assess the potential health benefits of cannabis and its constituent cannabinoids. The study concluded that smoking cannabis is not recommended for the treatment of any disease condition, but it did conclude that nausea, appetite loss, pain, and anxiety can all be mitigated by marijuana use.

While the study expressed reservations about smoked marijuana due to the health risks associated with smoking, it concluded that until another mode of ingestion was perfected that could provide the same relief as smoked marijuana, there was no alternative. However, modern vaporizers and the ingestion of cannabis in a decarboxylated state have laid most of these concerns to rest [19].

In addition, the study pointed out the inherent difficulty in marketing a nonpatentable herb. The fact is that pharmaceutical companies will not substantially profit unless there is

FIGURE 11.2 In Seattle a woman uses a vaporizer to get one of her daily doses of medical marijuana. The State of Washington adopted a law in 1998 legalizing the use, possession, and cultivation of cannabis for patients with a medical certificate. In 2012, Washington joined Colorado to become the first two states to legalize the drug for nonmedical purposes.

a patent (see Chapter 5). For that reason, experts argue that there is little future in smoked cannabis as a medically approved medication.

Summary

Controversy is nothing new in considering the fate of the drug abuse problem in the United States. Much of the controversy in drug control stems from the tactics adopted by law enforcement officials. On one hand, many traditional police tactics have proven less than effective, but on the other hand, the use of more unconventional enforcement techniques, such as needle exchange programs or the forfeiture of ill-gotten attorneys' fees, raises concerns for civil liberties and expanded police authority.

One controversial technique that has proved effective in identifying drug traffickers is the criminal profile. Although police tend to shy away from the word *profile*, the use of this tactic has resulted in many major seizures. The profiling procedure focuses on drug couriers in transit. The 1989 *Sokolow* decision gave legitimacy to this procedure, which enables agents to stop and question individuals who look or act like "typical" drug dealers. In this decision, the court recognized that certain traits are common to drug dealers and typically are not evidenced in the general population.

The reverse sting is another enforcement technique that has proved effective in identifying drug buyers (or users) rather than sellers. This technique requires the undercover officer to pose as a drug seller. The officer is authorized to sell a quantity of drugs to a prospective buyer, but the buyer is immediately arrested and the drugs are seized as evidence. People who criticize this technique claim that an atmosphere of entrapment prevails and that police are enticing people to commit crimes. The proper use of this technique, however, requires police to show a defendant's "criminal intent" and his or her predisposition to purchase the drugs.

The practice of surveillance is common. Because covert observation by the police has always generated a certain degree of skepticism by the public, the police must take great care in initiating certain surveillance operations. Officers must be careful that the activities for which the suspect is under investigation are authorized (for investigation) under federal guidelines. In addition, the concerns of both the government and civil libertarians must be observed throughout the operation.

Drug testing is not a new concern for drug control strategists, but the issue is far from being resolved. Most of the concern revolves around the questions of who should be tested, where, and under what sets of circumstances. Drug testing of federal transportation and law enforcement employees has been authorized, but what about drug testing in the general workplace? Some claim that the examination of a blood or urine sample violates one's Fourth and Fifth Amendment rights.

The subject of drug testing leads to the discussion of the problem of drugs and sports. This issue deals with several aspects, including nonaddictive and recreational drug use and the use of drugs such as steroids, which are designed to aid athletes in their particular sports. Regulatory agencies governing drug use in sports have created punitive provisions for those who use dangerous drugs. Such provisions may include fines, suspension, or expulsion from professional athletics and even criminal prosecution.

Medical marijuana refers to the use of cannabis as a form of medicine or herbal therapy approved by a physician. While the extent of the medicinal value of marijuana has been disputed, it does have beneficial effects, such as the suppression of nausea and vomiting, stimulation of hunger in chemotherapy and AIDS patients, lowered eye pressure (for treating glaucoma), and pain relief. Currently, 18 states and the District of Columbia have legalized medical marijuana or effectively decriminalized it. At the federal level, cannabis use is still illegal.

Do you recognize these terms?

- drug courier profiling
- entrapment
- World Anti-Doping Code
- medical marijuana
- reverse sting
- zero tolerance

Discussion Questions

1. Discuss some of the more valid concerns regarding the practice of "officially" abducting drug traffickers wanted in the United States.
2. List some possible options that the United States government could consider for the elimination of international drug trafficking.
3. What fears do civil libertarians have regarding the practice of drug courier profiling by police?
4. What is meant by the term *zero tolerance*, and why has the term become so controversial?
5. Discuss some of the legal and moral ramifications of the practice of seizing attorney fees.
6. Discuss why needle exchange programs are controversial throughout the world.
7. Discuss the different circumstances under which one may be tested for drugs in the workplace. What are the pros and cons of drug testing in such a manner?
8. Discuss the physiological effects of steroids on the human body.

Class Project

1. Study the controversies surrounding drug control in your community. Discuss them in terms of both their strong and weak attributes.

References

[1] *United States v. Alvarez-Machain.* 504 U.S. 655 (1992).
[2] *United States v. Sokolow.* 490 U.S. 1 (1989).
[3] del Carmen, R. V., & Walker, J. T. (2012). *Briefs of Leading Cases in Law Enforcement.* (8th ed.). Boston: Elsevier (Anderson Publishing).

[4] Center for Problem Oriented Policing. (2013). *Sting operations according to crime targeted.* Found at: http://www.popcenter.org/responses/sting_operations/3.

[5] Ibid.

[6] Johnston, L. D., O'Malley, P. M., & Bachman, J. G. (2001). *Monitoring the Future: National results on adolescent drug use: Overview of key findings.* Washington, DC: U.S. Department of Health and Human Services.

[7] Correctional Association of New York. (1992). *Injustice will be done: Women drug couriers and the Rockefeller Drug Laws.* New York: Correctional Association of New York.

[8] Greenfield, L., & Harper, S. (1991). *Women in Prison.* Washington, DC: U.S. Bureau of Justice Statistics.

[9] Ibid.

[10] Letwin, M. (April 18, 1994). Sentencing Angela Thompson. *New York Law Journal,* 2.

[11] Mauer, M., & Huling, T. (1995). *Young black Americans and the criminal justice system: Five years later.* Washington, DC: The Sentencing Project.

[12] Drug Policy Alliance. (2007). *Drugs, police and the law: Police corruption.* Found at: www.drugpolicy. org/law/police/.

[13] Office of National Drug Control Policy. (2010). *National drug control strategy 2010.* Washington, DC: U.S. Department of Justice. Executive Office of the President of the United States.

[14] Painter, K. (1997). Needle exchanges in the eye of AIDS debate. *USA Today.* (September 18), 1D.

[15] Aggarwal, S. K., Carter, G. T., Sullivan, M. D., ZumBrunnen, C., Morrill, R., & Mayer, J. D. (2009). Medicinal use of cannabis in the United States: Historical perspectives, current trends, and future directions. *J Opioid Manag 5*(3), 153–168. Lay summary – SF Weekly (15 September 2009). http://students. washington.edu/sunila/JOM_5-3-03.pdf.

[16] Grotenhermen, F. (2002). *"Review of therapeutic effects." Cannabis and cannabinoids: Pharmacology, toxicology and therapeutic potential.* New York City: Haworth Press. ISBN 978-0-7890-1508-2. http:// books.google.com/books?id=JvIyVk2IL_sC&pg=PA123.

[17] Harvey, M. (2009). California dreaming of full marijuana legislation. *The San Francisco Sunday Times,* September 28, p. 1.

[18] Food and Drug Administration. (April 20, 2006). Inter-agency advisory regarding claims that smoked marijuana is a medicine. *News Release.* Found in: http://www.fda.gov/NewsEvents/Newsroom/ PressAnnouncements/2006/ucm108643.htm.

[19] Division of Neuroscience and Behavioral Health, Institute of Medicine. (1999). In J. E. Joy, S. J. Watson Jr. & J. A. Benson Jr. (Eds.), *Marijuana and medicine: Assessing the science base.* Washington, DC: National Academy Press.

12

The Issue of Legalizing Drugs

This chapter will enable you to:

- Understand the basis for the drug legalization argument
- Understand the distinctions between decriminalization and legalization
- Appreciate public policy concerns with regard to the legalization issue
- Compare pros and cons of the drug legalization debate
- Learn why legalization has not worked in other countries
- Discover alternative solutions for the reduction of drug abuse

As an alternative to the growing problem of drug abuse in the United States, some politicians and social scientists have suggested that the laws governing drug control be repealed or at least modified ("decriminalized"). Glaring questions about the social responsibility of such a policy surface when a radical shift is considered. We have learned thus far that because attitudes about drugs are complicated and contradictory, resolution of the drug issue is enigmatic at best. For example, both cigarettes and alcohol are thought to be harmful, yet both are legal and readily available. On the other hand, cocaine and heroin are generally considered to be dangerous drugs, and both are controlled under federal and state laws. When we add in the factor of addiction, which is present in both controlled and legal drugs, the stage is set for combat between political conservatives and liberals.

Most people agree that the problem of drug abuse cannot be ignored. Crimes in which the suppliers of drugs and some addicts regularly engage (the latter to finance their habits) exact their price both financially and in terms of victims' lives. Illegal drugs are the financial cornerstone for organized crime around the world. Drug abuse can draw users into a world of syringes, dirty needles, poisoned doses, disease, deceit, and drug dealers bent on selling increasingly more addictive and potent drugs. However, the manner in which government might undermine such effects has basically focused on tough law enforcement. We know that cigarettes are considered to be one of the most affordable causes of death in the world, second only to alcohol, which not only deprives drinkers of their health but causes many deaths along the highways as well. Yet, here the notion of dissuasion within the law is broadly accepted. To address the problem, some have suggested that drug *legalization*—or its lesser form, *decriminalization*—be considered. Concurrent with this proposition is the fear that changing the laws would increase drug consumption and addiction. An important question in the legalization issue is "How will legalization affect the crime rate and public health?"

Opinions about the drug legalization–decriminalization issue span the spectrum. Some reformers argue that drug use is a personal moral decision, and that it is not the responsibility of government to police social morality. Additionally, many people who want to legalize drugs claim that crime rates soar as high as they do because drugs are treated as a criminal problem rather than a medical problem. Opponents of legalization argue that although regulation of public morality may conflict with some personal freedoms, the government has a legitimate responsibility to ensure order and public safety in our society.

Public Opinion

Compared with the peak years of the late 1970s, government statistics showed that drug use was down in the United States by 2007. In prior years, use of illicit drugs among adults was stable, and over the past decade the use of illegal drugs by workers declined by more than half. Teen drug use had held steady for the past 4 years after rising sharply in the early 1990s. Teen use of some drugs, such as lysergic acid diethylamide, methamphetamine, and cocaine, has been down somewhat, but use of some other drugs (e.g., ecstasy) has increased, according to the University of Michigan's annual *Monitoring the Future* survey.

Despite the overall decline, most Americans still regard illegal drugs as one of the nation's most serious problems. More than half of the public worries that a family member might become addicted, and seven in 10 people say that the government is not doing enough to address the problem [1].

Getting Tougher with Dealers

Historically, federal and state governments have used two strategies to combat drug use: reducing the supply of illegal drugs, and curbing the demand. When most people talk about the "war on drugs," they are thinking about efforts to reduce supply: more aggressive police investigations, tougher sentences for drug users and dealers, greater efforts to intercept drugs before they cross United States borders, and greater support of antidrug efforts by drug-producing nations. The number of drug offenders in United States prisons has risen dramatically over the past two decades, and drug arrests have doubled since 1985 [2].

Reducing demand has often meant drug education programs in schools, public service messages in the media, treatment programs, and drug testing. Despite civil liberties concerns, the courts have generally upheld drug-testing programs for employees, and even for students involved in extracurricular activities. In addition, over the years, the federal government has spent millions in antidrug advertising campaigns.

Critics of the "war on drugs," including an increasing number of law enforcement officials and even a few public officials (such as former New Mexico Governor Gary Johnson), say the campaign has not worked and have called for drug legalization. They argue that legalization, like the ending of the prohibition on alcohol, would undercut drug gangs and allow the nation to focus on drug abuse as a medical problem. Those critics, however, are still a distinct minority.

Is Marijuana Medicine?

One area in which advocates of legalization have made progress is in the medical use of marijuana. Although the federal government does maintain an extremely limited medical marijuana program, federal policy for decades has held marijuana to be a dangerous and addictive drug.

As noted in Chapter 11, in 1996 Californians approved a ballot proposition allowing physicians to prescribe marijuana for specific illnesses such as glaucoma, even though federal laws ban marijuana's sale and distribution. Several states followed suit, and marijuana is now legalized in several states and the District of Columbia. In March 1999, a panel of experts convened by the federal Institute of Medicine found that marijuana does have legitimate medical uses for treating symptoms of cancer and AIDS. Although the panel found no evidence that marijuana leads to harder drugs like cocaine, the scientists did warn that marijuana smoke was even more toxic in the long term than tobacco smoke.

Polls vary, but nationwide at least two-thirds of the public supports the use of marijuana to ease severe pain. Although most people regard marijuana as a much less dangerous drug than cocaine or heroin, a solid majority opposes general legalization of marijuana. In a 2004 poll commissioned by the American Association of Retired Persons (AARP), 72 percent of respondents ages 45 and older thought marijuana should be legal for medicinal purposes if recommended by a doctor [3–5].

Mixed Attitudes

Opinion polls show that the public tends to favor a variety of approaches to the drug problem, mixing liberal and conservative attitudes. There is strong public support for doing everything possible to intercept drug supplies and punish dealers. At a time when the nation's prisons are filled with criminals serving sentences for drug-related crimes, most Americans want even stricter penalties for dealers. A substantial majority of Americans opposes the overall legalization of drugs.

Many people also think permissive messages from parents and the media are one of the main causes of the drug problem. They favor expanded antidrug efforts to discourage use. Expanded drug treatment is favored as well, although this tactic is not as widely supported as stepped-up enforcement.

The Basis for the Debate: Three Approaches

Based on surveys and opinion polls, three general approaches have been consistently identified over the years. Each point of view comes with arguments for and against, along with some potential costs and trade-offs.

- One perspective emphasizes strict enforcement of the drug laws, intercepting drug supplies, and doing whatever is necessary to catch and punish drug dealers.
- A second perspective emphasizes cutting demand by preventing drug use, and doing everything possible to change tolerant attitudes toward it.
- A third perspective regards drug abuse primarily as a health problem, and favors stepped-up treatment to help users rather than punish them. Advocates generally favor legalization of some drugs.

Approach #1: Stopping Drugs at the Source by Cutting off the Supply
This approach takes a get-tough stance. Proponents hold that certain drugs are illegal for a reason—they are so dangerous that there is no safe way to have them in our society. We have to do everything possible to keep illegal drugs out of the country and off the streets. We need to cut off the supply of drugs by targeting traffickers and dealers, both wholesalers and street-corner drug dealers. Tougher enforcement and stricter sentencing of dealers and users helped to deal with the crack cocaine epidemic of the 1990s and kept overall drug use at stable levels. To win the war on drugs, we need to pursue this strategy aggressively, making every effort to identify, prosecute, and imprison drug dealers, thus cutting off the drug supply both at home and abroad.

Advocates for this approach suggest that the government take more aggressive measures to prevent drugs from crossing our borders while helping drug-producing nations with eradication efforts and other enforcement activities, including the destruction of clandestine laboratories and airfields. They argue that the United States should demand international cooperation in cutting off the drug supply while rewarding countries that crack down on drug growers. Rewards would be in the form of aid and support, and economic sanctions would be imposed on countries that refuse.

This approach holds that the United States should impose swift and certain punishment on drug dealers, including consistent mandatory minimum sentences, while expanding sanctions against convicted dealers. This would include confiscating automobiles and other personal property, and taking away driver's licenses. Those who make the case for this approach typically argue that illegal drug use is morally wrong and terribly destructive and that there can be no compromises, no unenforced laws, and no distinctions between hard and soft drugs or between dealers and casual users. They further argue that drug dealers and users are also likely to commit other crimes, either to support their habits or to protect their businesses. Consequently, they believe that cracking down on drug offenses will help cut crime in general.

Opponents argue that this approach is a losing battle and that as long as drugs are illegal and very profitable, there will be dealers willing to sell them. They complain that the "war on drugs" comes at a huge cost in money and jail space, and, thanks to rigid mandatory sentences, the country imprisons drug users who might be able to change if we gave them treatment. Furthermore, opponents contend that the get-tough policy has taken an unfair toll on poor, minority communities, where drugs are common and too many people have too few alternatives in life. This no-holds-barred approach to drug enforcement infringes on civil liberties.

The trade-off under this alternative is that it may be necessary to spend even more to imprison drug sellers, dealers, and users. Drug searches mean that the houses of innocent people may, on occasion, be searched by mistake, but proponents believe that is a small price to pay for a more effective war on drugs.

Approach #2: Reducing Demand by Holding Users Accountable
According to this perspective, the drug problem has persisted because millions of drug users continue to buy them. Despite abundant evidence of their corrosive effect on users

and society as a whole, drug use is still widely tolerated and even glamorized in the media. Sports stars use steroids, and many people abuse even over-the-counter inhalants and prescription drugs. The war on drugs will be won only when millions of users are persuaded to stop and young people are persuaded not to start. We have to make zero tolerance for drugs a top national priority—starting at home, in the schools, and in the workplace.

This approach holds that society must do everything possible—in the schools, in the workplace, in homes, and in the media—to convey the message that drug use is dangerous, unacceptable, and not chic. In addition, drug users should be punished by fines, arrest, and forfeiture of driver's licenses. This would even apply to those who only occasionally use drugs. This is one of the strongest ways of sending an antidrug message.

Advocates for this approach argue that because it is impossible to stop the supply of illegal drugs, the only way to win the war against drugs is to reduce the appetite for them. They claim that because drug use is not always apparent, testing is the only way to ensure that people remain drug free, and it is an effective deterrent. Finally, another position is that drug users may be victims, but they do not hurt only themselves. Rather, the use of illegal drugs is linked to domestic violence, school failure, crime, AIDS, and workplace injuries. For everyone's sake, we need to force drug users to take responsibility for the consequences of their actions.

People who oppose this approach complain that although no one opposes antidrug educational programs, there is not much evidence that this approach actually reduces drug use. They suggest that addiction is a medical problem and that society should not punish people for getting sick. Besides, addicts need treatment to get clean—so how does it help to leave them unemployed and without health insurance?

A harder line argument is that as long as illegal drugs are available, some people will be tempted to use them. The only way to win the war is to cut them off at the source by targeting growers and drug dealers, not drug users. Furthermore, alcohol and tobacco are both addictive substances that cause a great deal of social damage, yet both are legal. Millions more are addicted to drugs legally prescribed by their own doctors. So, why should we treat other drugs differently? Under this perspective, people must be ready to accept the notion that it may take a long time before expanded drug education efforts turn around the drug problem.

Approach #3: Redefining Drug Use as Addiction, Not Criminal Behavior
Those in support of this argument contend that the drug problem has persisted (and, in some respects, worsened) because we have gone about it the wrong way. The "war on drugs" is not working, and, even if it was, the price is too high. The prohibition on drugs leads to black-market prices. It generates crime and violence as dealers fight over turf and sales, and as drug users steal to buy illicit substances at inflated prices. The drug laws turn users—who need treatment—into criminals. We would be far better off if drug use were regarded as a health problem. We should legalize at least some drugs, and reduce the harm they cause by regulating their sale and treating their victims.

To accomplish this goal, it is argued that society should treat drug abuse as a public health problem rather than a law enforcement issue and eliminate criminal penalties for personal drug use. The government should regulate drug sales and permit the use of some drugs (such as marijuana) under a doctor's care, while expanding drug treatment programs, including those in prison. Furthermore, insurance companies should be required to cover substance abuse in the same way as they would any physical illness. The goal should be to provide treatment to anyone who needs it.

Those in favor of this approach argue that the harm done by drugs is predominantly caused by the fact that they are illegal. A more sensible policy would control their distribution and discourage their use. Prohibition of alcohol did not work in the 1920s, and drug prohibition does not work now.

Decriminalizing drug use would destroy the illicit drug trade. Advocates of this view also suggest that the war on drugs has done tremendous harm by sending thousands of drug users to prison instead of salvaging their lives and communities through treatment. Drug treatment should be widely available and stigma-free.

Those who oppose this approach argue that making it easier to get drugs would inevitably make them more widely available. For example, legal prescription drugs are tightly regulated but are still the second most common drugs of abuse. They are also concerned that too many people believe that making something legal also makes it moral. If one considers drug abuse to be morally wrong, blurring this fact by calling it a health problem will only compound the problem.

They further argue that treatment programs, although important, are not the whole answer to the illegal drug problem. This is because many treatment programs have low success rates (i.e., many people relapse). Additionally, opponents to this approach are concerned that organized gangs will not simply go away if we legalize drugs. Rather, they'll move into other forms of crime, just as the bootleggers did after Prohibition ended. The bottom line is that some people believe that a result of decriminalizing drug use is that more people may experiment with drugs. Legalizing drugs may lead to more drug abuse in inner cities, where addicts are more numerous and there are few treatment programs.

The Pros: Arguments for Legalization

Many people who advocate the legalization of drugs base their arguments on assertions regarding the historical practice of policing "victimless" crimes. The experience of Prohibition is particularly singled out. Reformers allege that the passage of the 1920 Volstead Act outlawing the production, possession, and use of alcohol created more problems than it resolved, and that the end of Prohibition in 1933 saw bootlegging gangsters, along with their violence and corruption, fade away. This argument is now put forth to support legalization as a means of disbanding modern-day drug gangs in the same fashion.

Many scholars who support legalization assert that Prohibition was responsible for the transformation of organized crime from small, isolated vice peddlers serving urban political machines to major crime syndicates. This occurred as a result of the profits realized from Prohibition, the political and law enforcement contacts that gangsters made, the respectability that came from serving the drinking public, and the logistical and structural reorganization of organized crime that bootlegging required (see Chapter 13 for a more comprehensive look at Prohibition and public policy).

Proponents of drug legalization base their argument on a number of points. One such point is the traditionally liberal argument stating that a free society allows its people to do as they wish as long as they harm no one. The state, therefore, should be reluctant to use criminal law to constrict personal freedoms. In addition, drug reformers argue that drug laws fail to impact the availability of illicit drugs, and may even make the situation worse. For example, a study of the national Marijuana Interdiction Program by Mark A.R. Kleiman of Harvard's Kennedy School of Government concluded that the interdiction campaign stimulated domestic production, increased the supply of marijuana in the United States, and raised the potency of available marijuana from 1 to 18 percent [6]. A similar study of marijuana eradication campaigns in Kentucky also concluded that the result of the campaigns was increased supply, increased potency, the introduction of new dangerous drugs to the market, and the creation of marijuana syndicates in place of the usually small, disorganized growers who had dominated the market before the eradication effort.

Skeptics question the specific correlations between the eradication program and advances in the marijuana production trade. For example, trends toward the rising potency of marijuana and toward indoor hydroponic-growing methods had been well documented since the late 1960s, prior to implementation of the eradication program. Additionally, research has concluded that one fundamental reason why traditional organized crime (La Cosa Nostra) has been unable to dominate the domestic marijuana trade is because it represents an easy-entry market for entrepreneurs. According to a 1984 *DEA*

FIGURE 12.1 A supporter of California's Proposition 19, the legalization of marijuana initiative, shows his support for the control and taxation of cannabis during a rally sponsored by the Students for Sensible Drug Policy, UC Berkeley Chapter. *Source: AP Photo/Paul Sakuma.*

Special Intelligence Report on Domestic Marijuana Trafficking, "efforts to organize certain dispersed [marijuana-trafficking] elements of society would prove futile and too costly." This illustrates how difficult and impractical (if not impossible) it would be for the government to attempt to control and tax the marijuana market after legalization.

Reformers also point to the connection between illegal drugs and crime, arguing that addicts are lured to other crimes such as prostitution, burglary, and robbery as ways to help finance their expensive habits. In addition, it is argued that the illegality of drugs forces consumers to enter a criminal underworld to purchase them, thereby having contact with criminal actors with whom they would not ordinarily interact, creating conditions for both victimization and subsequent criminality.

Proponents of drug legalization argue that those crimes traditionally associated with drug dealing would be greatly reduced if the context of drug control were changed from a law enforcement model to a *medical model*. The organized crime groups formed around the drug trade would find the illicit market constricted under a medical model, and would leave the black market in drugs for other criminal opportunities. In addition, legalization proponents argue that law enforcement and political corruption associated with drug trafficking, the abuses of due process and procedural rights sometimes associated with drug enforcement, and the problem of selective drug enforcement would also be mitigated under a medical model.

The Futility of Enforcement

As discussed, drug law enforcement has come under considerable critical scrutiny. Some researchers claim there has been no reduction in supply from enforcement efforts, and they point to an alarming fall in the retail price of drugs and an increase in their potency. Adding support to this claim are findings from a federally funded study of intensive street-level drug enforcement in Lynn, Massachusetts, which pointed to "temporary" and "transitory" successes. This finding is considered by some to indicate not much more than a marginal success.

In addition, it is argued that fully suppressing the demand for drugs would require the jailing of a large proportion of the nation's population. At least 70 million Americans have admitted to having used drugs. Federal studies estimate that despite constantly escalating numbers of drug arrests, we are still reaching less than 1 percent of users with law enforcement efforts.

The Restriction of the Drug Market

Reformers also argue that legalization of some drugs, particularly the so-called *recreational drugs*, would serve to restrict the drug market. Because most drug experts agree that marijuana, cocaine, and heroin are the preferred substances for most drug users, their legal availability might reduce demand for more dangerous illegal substances such as methamphetamine (meth) and angel dust (PCP). This would reduce the economic incentive for the production and distribution of these more dangerous substances.

The Hypocrisy of Drug Laws

It is also argued that it is hypocritical to ban drugs when our society has already legalized two exceedingly dangerous drugs: tobacco and alcohol. The argument is that a much larger percentage of the population is threatened through health risks, automobile collisions, assaults, and associated family problems attributed to these drugs than it is by the drugs currently proscribed by law. One should recognize, however, that in 2013 Colorado and Washington legalized recreational use of marijuana, but it remains controlled under federal statutes. Some argue that problems with drug laws are also apparent when different state laws and punishments for drug offenses are compared. For example, charges for possession of some drugs are based on the amount of the drug in the defendant's control. Not only do these charges vary from one state to another, but also sentences for those convicted differ greatly from one jurisdiction to another.

International Relations

Some drug reformers have also pointed to problems created by drug enforcement efforts—specifically, our strained relationships with some foreign countries. These reformers argue that foreign relations with countries such as Mexico, Peru, and Colombia are being hampered by the intensity of enforcement efforts and the political rhetoric attached to the drug war. More compellingly, some critics argue that foreign policy considerations have resulted in a double standard in drug enforcement in the United States. These critics point to the lack of intense criticism directed to countries such as the Bahamas (a major transshipment site for cocaine made safe by massive political corruption), Chile (where the DINA, Chile's secret police, has been actively engaged in cocaine trafficking for more than two decades), Thailand (a major heroin-refining center), and Taiwan (source of much of the financial backing and logistical support for the Southeast Asian heroin trade). Critics are also disturbed by the relations between United States intelligence agencies and drug traffickers; the Central Intelligence Agency's role in Australia's drug money-laundering Nugan-Hand Bank and in Caribbean drug money-laundering enterprises; and support for fundamentalist Muslim Afghan groups actively engaged in heroin trafficking.

Personal Freedoms

To some critics of present drug enforcement policies, the possibility of severe threats to personal freedoms posed by tougher drug laws creates concern. New and expanded search-and-seizure powers granted to law enforcement officers, random drug testing by employers, and the use of the military in domestic law enforcement raise major concerns about potential due process abuses, further erosion of constitutional protections, and the potential for serious systematic corruption.

The Crime Rate

As mentioned in this chapter, reformers also claim that legalization would cut down on street crimes because addicts could acquire their drugs inexpensively rather than by committing burglary, robbery, and murder for drug money. Drug reformers also argue that legalization would reduce the drug turf wars that have driven urban homicide rates to record levels in recent years.

Public Health

Proponents of drug legalization argue that the drug laws themselves create many of the severe health problems normally associated with drug use. The spread of AIDS, closely associated with the sharing of needles by intravenous drug users, is one such concern. Reformers also point to the problem of pregnant drug addicts, who, out of fear of legal repercussions, may not seek prenatal care.

Finally, some have argued, at least in the case of heroin, that illegality of heroin means there is no control over the quality of the drug being purchased. Heroin and other drugs are commonly adulterated with dangerous substances by retail dealers, and users are unsure of the potency or quality of the drugs they have purchased. From a pharmacological point of view, unadulterated heroin causes little physical damage to the human body (this, of course, excludes such health threats as AIDS and brutal physical addiction). It is the uncontrolled nature of street heroin that causes poisoning and overdose.

Despite recent shifts in Colorado and Washington State toward marijuana legalization, such a radical shift in public policy has not yet been embraced by all states. Some reformers have complained that they have not had equal access to federal research monies with which to formulate their approach. Those monies have been exclusively reserved for research on drug abuse pathologies and drug repression strategies.

■ ■ Critical Thinking Task ■

Explain your own view of marijuana use—both "medical" and recreational use. Defend or refute arguments in favor of decriminalizing the possession, consumption, and sale of marijuana.

Issues to Consider

In 1988, Democratic Congressman Charles Rangel, who represents the traditionally drug-infested Harlem district in New York City and who has come out in strong opposition to legalization, posed questions that drug policy reformers will have to answer in coming years:

1. Which drugs should be legalized—marijuana, or the harder drugs such as heroin and cocaine?
2. How would the legalized drugs be sold: by prescription or over the counter, by hospitals or pharmacies?
3. Would there be an age limit, and, if so, how would it be enforced?
4. As addictions and dependencies developed, would any limit be placed on the amount of drugs that users could purchase?

5. Who would manufacture the drugs—private companies or the federal government?
6. Would the drugs be provided to the public at cost? If not, how much profit margin would be allowed?
7. Would they be taxed?
8. Who would assume the responsibility of allowing a drug user to take so much of a particular drug: the government or a physician?
9. Should recreational use of drugs be authorized or just drug use for treatment?

In response to these questions, some reformers have offered the argument that drugs could be sold in the same fashion as alcohol—that is, sold only to licensed dealers, who would be taxed and held under close government scrutiny. Regulations would include prohibiting the sale of drugs to anyone younger than 21 years of age. Another proposal is a lesser form of legalization, called *decriminalization*. This concept generally calls for reducing criminal penalties for drug use or possession, while retaining a degree of social disapproval. Regardless of which approach is most popular, it seems increasingly clear, at least to some, that a serious fault does exist in the current public policy addressing drug control. The fault is that current policy has failed to cut drastically the supply of drugs through the use of police action alone.

The Cons: Arguments against Legalization

The prevailing opposition against drug legalization is voiced by many politicians, law enforcement officials, and concerned citizens. Opponents of legalization contend that the problems created by Prohibition were minuscule compared to today's situation. Specifically, children of the 1920s were not the victims of alcohol consumption, at least not in an addictive sense.

Additionally, according to opponents, users would possibly face a greater risk of debilitating dependencies from cocaine and narcotics if those drugs were legalized. Today, almost 80 years after the repeal of Prohibition, alcoholism is considered—more so now than ever—one of the United States' most lethal killers. The legalization of drugs would very likely provide drug lords, both foreign and domestic, the vehicle to success for which they have been waiting: the conversion of the black market to an open market.

A primary concern about the reform of drug laws is the erosion of public morals. Specifically, many feel that the simple act of legalizing drugs would send a message about society's lack of social responsibility and its unwillingness to deal with a major health and public safety issue, which would be tantamount to surrendering to the drug dealers of the world. Opponents, therefore, predict that adoption of such a public policy would increase drug abuse, and would multiply the ancillary problems of poor health, violence, and broken families.

Certainly, legalization could serve as a "quick fix." How responsible is it, some might argue, to take a crime against society and legalize it for the sole purpose of eliminating it as a criminal problem and as a threat to public safety? This is a complex question that has been raised with regard to the legalization of prostitution, gambling, abortion, and pornography, as well as drugs.

According to some treatment officials, the rate of addiction to alcohol is only 10 percent of those who use it. The addiction rates for crack cocaine and methamphetamine, however, would soar; these are statistics that reformers strategically avoid [7].

The Alcohol Argument

Opponents to drug reform acknowledge alcohol as a dangerous and addictive drug, but they believe that the fact that alcohol is so harmful to society is the very reason that other dangerous substances of abuse should not be added to the list of legal drugs. The toll of alcohol consumption is well documented in terms of broken homes, violence, ruined careers, accidents, and lost productivity on the job and in school. The question is whether legalized alcohol and other drugs would create a worse situation than has been realized by legalized alcohol alone.

The Crime Rate

Although proponents of reform argue that legalized drugs would cause a decrease in the crime rate, opponents claim just the opposite—that although some drug-related crimes would be reduced (e.g., smuggling), a black market would always exist. This idea is particularly significant, considering that many addicts would be unable to hold down jobs because of their addictions to even the cheapest of "government-issued" drugs.

Many people involved in drug enforcement have suggested that numerous drug-related felonies are committed by people who were involved in crime before they started taking drugs. The drugs, which are routinely available in criminal circles, make the criminals more violent and unpredictable. Certainly there are some kill-for-a-fix crimes, but how logical is it to assume that a cut-rate price for drugs at a government outlet will stop such behavior? It is a simple fact that under the influence of drugs, normal people do not behave normally, and abnormal people may function in chilling and horrible ways. This argument extends to children, who are among the most frequent victims of violent, drug-related crimes that have nothing to do with the cost of acquiring the drugs [8].

New Revenues

In response to those who claim that legalizing drugs would bring in billions of tax dollars, opponents are convinced that the black market would actually be broadened because of the lack of taxes on illicit drugs. After all, cigarette bootlegging is still one of organized crime's varied enterprises because of high tax-rate differentials. Additionally, it can be argued that stepped-up enforcement, in conjunction with powerful forfeiture laws providing for government seizure of drug money, property, and assets, would substantially reduce the costs of drug enforcement. Furthermore, it is maintained that what the government might save in law enforcement costs would be spent many times over as a result of traffic deaths, lost productivity, and medical costs.

FIGURE 12.2 This photo, released by the Bureau of Alcohol, Tobacco, Firearms, and Explosives, shows a vehicle that agents stopped on Interstate 95 in 2005, from which they recovered 1,600 cartons of black market cigarettes. Opponents to drug legalization point out that black markets do not disappear just because a substance is legalized and regulated. *Source: AP Photo/ATF.*

The Addicts

Another viewpoint opposing reform is the argument that money would still be required to purchase drugs even if drugs were legalized. Specifically, it is believed that many addicts would not hold regular jobs, and therefore would continue to commit ancillary crimes such as robbery, prostitution, and theft in order to acquire money. Even though some studies have indicated that heroin addicts are able to lead fairly normal lives if their drug needs are met, there is no evidence that all addicts would choose to leave the drug crime subculture. Additionally, the number of drug-related crimes committed by intoxicated drug users, including assault, spouse and child abuse, and drug-related traffic accidents, would no doubt rise.

Additionally, perhaps we should remember that when pornography was legalized de facto by the Supreme Court, it did not just go away, as some had anticipated. In fact, it gradually became more extreme because of public boredom with the product. For example, *Playboy* magazine was superseded by *Penthouse*, which was then outdone by *Hustler*. Then came the sadistic "snuff" films that depicted gang rapes, sadism, and, ultimately, murder.

Organized Crime

The legalization of drugs would likely have three profound effects with regard to the black market: (1) it would give drugs a social sanction, creating a broader use of drugs (as was the case with legalized gambling, which created more gamblers rather than reducing the influence of organized crime in the market); (2) it would make drugs available without risk of arrest and prosecution; and (3) if the legal price of drugs did not undercut the price on the illicit market, users would continue to purchase drugs from drug dealers on the street, and organized crime would continue to reap its drug-related profits.

After all, legal lotteries have not dismantled the illegal numbers racket. In addition, the end of Prohibition did not devastate organized crime—it merely led to diversification and new areas of criminal enterprise. Many supporters of legalization are willing to admit that drugs such as crack and PCP are simply too dangerous to allow the shelter of the law. Thus, former drug czar William Bennett argues that criminals will provide what the government will not. "As long as drugs that people very much want remain illegal, a black market will exist," says legalization advocate David Boaz of the Liberation Cato Institute (Bennett, 1990). Crack is a good example. In powdered form, cocaine was an expensive indulgence. Then, however, street chemists found that a better, far less expensive (and more dangerous) high could be achieved by mixing cocaine with baking soda and heating it. So, crack was born, and "cheap" cocaine invaded low-income communities with furious speed. It could be argued that if government drugstores do not stock crack, addicts will find it in the clandestine market or simply bake it themselves from their legally purchased cocaine.

Finally, there exists the issue of children and teenagers. Certainly, under the legalization model they would be barred from drug purchases, just as they are now prohibited from buying beer, wine, and liquor. Drug dealers, though, will no doubt continue to cater to these young customers with the time-honored come-on—a couple of free fixes to get them hooked. What good is antidrug education if these children observe their older brothers and sisters, parents, and friends smoking, snorting, or shooting up with government permission? According to Bennett, legalization will give us the worst of both worlds: millions of new drug users, and a thriving criminal black market [9].

Personal Freedoms

Proponents of legalization contend that drug laws increasingly deprive people of their personal freedoms, and that drug users should be permitted to consume drugs in their own homes if they desire. Although this argument entails a rather lofty debate over political philosophy, it should be pointed out that a counterargument can be made that whenever one person's personal freedoms are safeguarded, someone else's may be restricted. In a nation with more than 300 million people, carte blanche cannot be given to everyone who desires to live his or her own way without regard to the rights and needs of others.

The Cost of Legalization

Although legalization proponents argue that taxes from legal drugs and reduced expenditures related to drug enforcement would result in reductions in government spending, that argument fails to provide for the exorbitant social costs of such a program. For instance, a study prepared by the Lewin Group for the National Institute on Drug Abuse and the National Institute on Alcohol Abuse and Alcoholism estimated the total economic cost of alcohol and other drug abuse to be $245.7 billion. Of this cost, $97.7 billion was due to abuse of drugs other than alcohol. This estimate includes substance abuse treatment and prevention costs, other health care costs, costs associated with reduced job productivity or lost earnings, and other costs to society such as crime and social welfare. The study also determined that these costs are borne primarily by governments (46 percent), followed by those who abuse drugs and members of their households (44 percent) [10].

Given that more than one-half of this enormous figure was attributed to work-related accidents and lost productivity, is it not logical to assume that legalized drugs, which probably would sell for a fraction of the price of illicit drugs and therefore be more widely used, might increase that cost figure by many times? Many experts in the field believe so.

Even those who oppose legalization recognize that drug enforcement places a critical financial burden on the nation's resources, but they argue that the price of not doing so would be too costly for society. After all, all civilized societies have seen fit to exert some form of control over mind-altering substances. Even the few experiments in legalization have shown that when drugs are more widely available, addiction increases. For example, in 1975, Italy liberalized its drug laws and now has one of the highest heroin-related death rates in Western Europe. As discussed in this chapter, in Alaska, where marijuana was decriminalized in 1975, the relaxed atmosphere increased use of the drug, particularly among children. Since 1998 medical marijuana has been legal in Alaska.

Drugs in Amsterdam: The "Dutch Way"

Some countries, such as the Netherlands, have legalized drugs as a remedy for their drug problems. Although drugs are not totally legal in Amsterdam, they are, for the most part, tolerated. In fact, the law in the Netherlands allows marijuana to be bought, sold, and used openly by anyone over 18 years of age.

The country's policy on marijuana evolved from the Opium Law, passed in 1976, after a heroin epidemic in the Netherlands. The law allows coffee shops to sell amounts of marijuana to patrons over the age of 18, but does not allow for wholesale trade. The "open policy" was meant to distinguish between low-risk drugs such as marijuana, and high-risk drugs such as cocaine and heroin. However, the open policy has resulted in Amsterdam becoming a center of the drug culture in Europe, spawning a whole new travel category dubbed "drug tourism" [11].

There are more than 1,000 coffee shops around the country. Most of them also sell beer and other alcoholic drinks along with marijuana. At a small counter, customers can purchase marijuana in "joints," or loose in small plastic bags. Rather than listing food, the menu lists different grades of marijuana and hashish, with varying tastes and strengths. Coffee shop owners, like many Dutch officials, believe that allowing soft drugs to be used openly actually reduces the attraction by taking away the adventure [12]. Indeed, over the years Amsterdam, a city of 700,000, has earned the reputation of being a drug mecca in

Western Europe. Only a few blocks from Amsterdam's business district, cocaine and heroin dealers operate without fear of being arrested, because the government has adopted a strategy by which these dealers are quarantined to the area of town designated as the *red-light district*, a location known for drug dealing and other "vice" activities. This selling is tolerated because Dutch police authorities feel that drug trafficking can be more closely monitored if it is confined to a small area, thereby providing controls over not only drug dealing, but also all ancillary criminal behaviors. Throughout the rest of the city, marijuana and hashish are treated much like alcohol and tobacco are treated in the United States.

The Dutch policy separates marijuana and hashish from harder drugs. It is generally felt that if young people can purchase marijuana in coffee shops rather than from criminal drug dealers who also sell harder drugs, it is less likely the customer will be tempted by the seller to try other more potent and addictive substances.

In addition, the Dutch have adopted a policy that they believe makes drug use "boring" and less glamorous. The ease with which cannabis products can be obtained removes the mystique often attached to acts of rebellion and nonconformity that many young people engage in as part of the maturing process. Marijuana reformers claim that available data indicate strikingly low patterns of drug use in Amsterdam. For example, in 1986, drug users under the age of 26 accounted for 28 percent of Holland's drug users, but by 1995, that number had fallen to just 4 percent [13].

The Dutch government takes the stance that young people will experiment with drugs no matter what laws the government tries to enforce. Because they also believe there is danger in using drugs, the government has adopted a policy called *harm reduction*. Rather than punish young people for experimenting, the government tries to supervise their drug use. For example, at a local all-night club where marijuana was being used, the Drug Advice Bureau set up a booth to test the drug ecstasy (MDMA), a popular but illegal stimulant, before people took it—with no threat of arrest. In this fashion, the government attempts to guard young people against drugs that are unusually strong or toxic, rather than enforce the law. The government claims that this is why the number of young people addicted to hard drugs is so low.

Ancillary to the liberal law enforcement approach in Amsterdam is a concomitant medical model used to treat addiction and abuse. In Amsterdam, a widespread methadone maintenance program, targeting heroin addicts, makes use of mobile units that travel around the city bringing methadone treatment to addicts. The methadone program in Amsterdam is beset by many of the same problems as United States experiments with the heroin substitute. In particular, methadone, which is also an addicting drug, has failed to divert users from heroin, so that some addicts have adopted a style of use combining both heroin and methadone.

In 1988, the Amsterdam health department estimated that there were 7,000 addicts in the city, 20 percent of whom were foreigners. Additionally, police estimate that 60 percent of petty crimes are committed by members of the addict population in Amsterdam. It should also be noted, however, that drug-related homicides in Amsterdam are very rare events. Washington, D.C., has 15 times as many drug-related murders annually compared to Amsterdam. On the other hand, it is likely that the Netherlands has considerably more control over street crime than does the United States.

Unlike many United States cities, Amsterdam has a large and well-funded police department. Amsterdam's police strength is about 3,500, of which 2,900 are uniformed officers assigned to street beats. An estimated 400 of these officers are assigned to the diminutive four-block area of the red-light district in order to contain the high rate of crime there.

Some Dutch police officials are concerned with the overall rise in the crime rate that has occurred since the tolerance policy toward drugs went into effect. This increase in crime cannot be blamed entirely on Dutch drug users. As with many countries that experience a flourishing drug abuse problem, blame is conveniently placed on other countries whose stringent drug control policies have succeeded in ridding the country of many drug abusers and related criminals. It makes sense to assume that someone who steals to support a drug habit in Germany would not pass up an opportunity to steal just because he or she is in Amsterdam, where there is greater availability and affordability of drugs. One side effect of the Amsterdam project is the emergence of droves of pornography shops and houses of prostitution in the drug district. Dutch officials are quick to admit that the crime rate has dramatically risen since the so-called Dutch way was adopted.

Those who lend support for the Amsterdam experiment, however, claim that the relationship between sexual trafficking and drugs is difficult to establish because of several perceived factors. For example, some of the prostitution and pornography enterprises in Amsterdam preceded the legalization of drugs in that country. In addition, such red-light districts exist in European cities where drug retailing is not tolerated, although history has shown that the sex and drug industries are very closely correlated. In the United States, one need only travel through Boston's Combat Zone, San Francisco's Tenderloin, or Philadelphia's Arch Street districts to find evidence of close links between the sex and drug industries.

The British Experiment

Great Britain passed legal controls regarding dangerous substances at about the same time the United States passed similar laws; the first such measure was passed in 1916. The early drug control efforts in both countries were aimed at controlling drug addiction and abuse by outlawing cocaine, opium, and their derivatives. Much confusion surrounded the application of drug control laws in both Great Britain and the United States.

A second piece of antidrug legislation, known as the Dangerous Drug Act, was passed by Parliament in 1920. Basically, the law prohibited possession of opiates or cocaine except with a lawful prescription. Paralleling problems with the Harrison Act in the United States, confusion over the specifics of the new British legislation led to difficulty in its interpretation and enforcement. In 1924, a committee of British physicians was formed to determine whether drug abuse should be approached as a criminal justice problem or a medical problem. The committee was inclined toward the latter and instituted the so-called *British system*, which prevailed well into the late 1960s.

POLICIES, STRATEGIES, AND TACTICS FOR DRUG CONTROL

A wide variety of policies, strategies, and tactics have been used to control the illegal drug problem

Policies

Prohibition is the ban on the distribution, possession, and use of specified substances made illegal by legislative or administrative order, and the application of criminal penalties to violators.

Regulation is control over the distribution, possession, and use of specified substances. Regulations specify the circumstances under which substances can be legally distributed and used. Prescription medications and alcohol are the substances most commonly regulated in the United States.

Strategies

Demand reduction strategies attempt to decrease individuals' tendency to use drugs. Efforts provide information and education to potential and casual users about the risks and adverse consequences of drug use, and treatment to drug users who have developed problems from using drugs.

Supply reduction focuses diplomatic, law enforcement, military, and other resources on eliminating or reducing the supply of drugs. Efforts focus on foreign countries, smuggling routes outside the country, border interdiction, and distribution within the United States.

User accountability emphasizes that all users of illegal substances, regardless of the type of drug they use or the frequency of that use, are violating criminal laws and should be subject to penalties. It is closely associated with zero tolerance.

Zero tolerance holds that drug distributors, buyers, and users should be held fully accountable for their offenses under the law. This is an alternative to policies that focus on only some violators, such as sellers of drugs or users of harder drugs such as cocaine and heroin, while ignoring other violators.

Tactics

Criminal justice activities include enforcement, prosecution, and sentencing activities to apprehend, convict, and punish drug offenders. Although thought of primarily as having supply reduction goals, criminal sanctions also have demand reduction effects by discouraging drug use.

Prevention activities are educational efforts to inform potential drug users about the health, legal, and other risks associated with drug use. Their goal is to limit the number of new drug users and dissuade casual users from continuing drug use as part of a demand reduction strategy.

Taxation requires those who produce, distribute, or possess drugs to pay a fee based on the volume or value of the drugs. Failure to pay subjects violators to penalties for this violation, not for the drug activities themselves.

Testing individuals for the presence of drugs is a tool in drug control that is used for safety and monitoring purposes, and as an adjunct to therapeutic interventions. It is in widespread use for employees in certain jobs such as those in the transportation industry and criminal justice agencies. New arrestees and convicted offenders may be tested.

> **POLICIES, STRATEGIES, AND TACTICS FOR DRUG CONTROL—Cont'd**
>
> Individuals in treatment are often tested to monitor their progress and provide them an incentive to remain drug free.
>
> *Treatment* (therapeutic interventions) focuses on individuals whose drug use has caused medical, psychological, economic, and social problems for them. The interventions may include medication, counseling, and other support services delivered in an inpatient setting or on an outpatient basis. These are demand reduction activities to eliminate or reduce individuals' drug use.
>
> *Source*: Bureau of Justice Statistics (1992) [4].

drug control efforts were restricted to tactics within federal authority—in particular, the ability to tax the people and develop international treaties. During the late 1800s, state laws (specifically those aimed at cocaine and morphine) required that drugs be obtainable only by a doctor's prescription. These laws were generally ineffective because controlled drugs could be transported from other states that did not have such restrictions. At the turn of the twentieth century, the federal government became active in drug control efforts through the State Department's participation in international initiatives. The majority of these were in the form of international conferences such as the 1909 Shanghai Opium Convention, the 1911 International Conference on Opium, and the 1913 International Opium Convention. The result was the 1914 congressional approval of the Harrison Narcotics Act, which used the federal government's authority to raise taxes and regulate the manufacture and sale of certain drugs. The broad enforcement powers of the Harrison Narcotics Act were upheld in two crucial U.S. Supreme Court decisions: *United States v. Doremus* and *Webb et al. v. United States*. For the following 50 years, the Harrison Narcotics Act remained the basis for federal narcotics regulation.

In 1970, the myriad regulations and amendments to the Harrison Narcotics Act were consolidated into a new piece of federal legislation that became known as the Controlled Substances Act (officially titled the Comprehensive Drug Abuse Prevention and Control Act). Under the new legislation, courts interpreted powers of commerce as the new basis for drug control, supplanting the need for government to portray the police function of drug control as a tax measure.

Policy-Related Factors

Although the federal government has adopted its own drug control policy and enforcement initiatives, for the most part such efforts are a local option. This means that drug laws, policing policies, and prosecution philosophies are all driven by local governmental initiatives. For example, in the case of drug enforcement options, a drug dealer facing state criminal charges may be given the choice to cooperate with police, testify against other drug dealers, or risk going to jail. Local authorities have full authority to make such an offer, and they do so every day. Police can also choose any number of enforcement methods and techniques, including gang sweeps, undercover operations, wiretaps, and reverse stings.

Regardless of the enforcement options chosen, these tactics have a significant impact on the criminal justice system in the community, especially on the adjudicatory process, which includes the courts, prosecution, and public defense. For example, operations such as street sweeps result in a high number of people being arrested and ultimately being convicted and receiving prison sentences. On the other hand, so-called kingpin strategies, by which police target upper-level traffickers, often result in lengthy trials and related criminal proceedings that also place financial and logistical burdens on the justice system. Even the investigation phase of drug kingpins poses special concerns to police in that these investigations are costly and lengthy, and the only outcome may be the arrest of a handful of people. Although those arrested may be primary managers in crime organizations, members of the public are sometimes slow in realizing the importance of such investigations as opposed to street sweeps of low-level dealers whose arrests make attractive media headlines, but in actuality are easily replaced by the kingpins whom they serve.

A factor complicating drug control policy is the problem of variances in drug use from one area to another. Crack cocaine seems to be the predominant problem in many major cities, whereas in rural areas drugs such as methamphetamine and marijuana are more widely abused. In addition to the different drugs of abuse, consequences of the drug trade also differ from one area to another.

Private Sector Responses

Organizations and agencies not affiliated with government have also risen to combat the nation's drug abuse problem. Many companies have developed extensive drug prevention programs for their communities. As discussed in Chapter 14, the Drug Abuse Resistance Education (DARE) program frequently has corporate sponsorship. Furthermore, the media provide free airtime for public service drug abuse prevention announcements, and many companies require prospective employees to undergo drug testing. In recent years, private companies whose employees have developed drug problems offer employee assistance programs whereby referral services offer treatment options. In addition, many treatment facilities are privately owned, and benefits are usually covered by private insurance companies.

The Role of the Military

We learned how thousands of military veterans during the Civil War became hopelessly addicted to morphine. With the exception of that war, the military has had little experience with controlling drug abuse and trafficking. It was in 1967, during the Vietnam War, that a special Department of Defense (DOD) task force was established to study the extent of drug abuse by American troops assigned to Vietnam and areas in Europe. In 1972, a key policy directive, born out of the "drug scare" of the 1960s, recommended preventive alcohol and other drug abuse education, along with strict enforcement procedures and the establishment of treatment policies.

In 1980, a new DOD directive was established to replace the 1972 initiative. The new policy reflected a less tolerant attitude toward drug abuse and was a drastic departure from the military's previous treatment-oriented attitude. Nineteen-eighty was also an important year due to the investigation of a major incident—the crash of a jet airplane on the aircraft carrier *U.S.S. Nimitz* that killed 14 U.S. Navy personnel and seriously injured 44 others. This incident uncovered widespread drug use on the ship, illustrating the extent of the military's drug problem and, by 1981, resulting in the establishment of urine testing for drugs. The DOD's drug-testing policy is still firmly in place today.

Development of United States Drug Policy

The United States drug control policy has evolved over time and has undergone a number of distinctive phases. As discussed in Chapter 1, the earliest drug control efforts focused on regulation (the 1906 Food and Drug Act), taxation (the 1914 Harrison Narcotics Act), and prohibition (the 1970 Controlled Substances Act). *Regulation* of drugs specifies the circumstances under which they can be lawfully distributed and used. Prescription medications and alcohol are the most commonly regulated drugs. *Taxation* requires those who legally produce, distribute, or possess drugs to pay a fee based on the quantity or value of the drugs. Criminal penalties result from failure to pay taxes, rather than from specific drug violations themselves.

Next, international efforts attempted to establish cooperation between the United States and foreign countries that share similar drug abuse problems. Afterward, policies moved toward prohibition efforts, with a focus on enforcement of criminal sanctions and, more recently, civil penalties. The essence of *prohibition* is the ban on manufacturing, distribution, and use of drugs that are designated as illegal under state and federal laws. Violators face prosecution and an array of penalties from fines to imprisonment.

Today, criminal penalties for drug violations have become firmly embedded in drug control public policy. Although it is unlikely that there will be much support for the abandonment of criminal sanctions, a few scholars and legal practitioners have suggested that the *crime control* model of drug control be abandoned, and that drug legalization be considered under a new *medical model* of drug control. Suggestions have ranged from totally removing criminal penalties to imposing a system of regulation similar to that used in the manufacture and distribution of cigarettes and alcohol. Instead of total legalization, some have even suggested a system of decriminalization whereby penalties for possession or distribution of certain drugs would be reduced. During the 1970s, several states attempted to do just that.

Complicating the drug policy question is the fact that drug abuse trends change over time. For example, at the turn of the twentieth century, heroin and opium products were the main drugs of concern. Through the years, other drugs such as marijuana, barbiturates, lysergic acid diethylamide, phencyclidine, and, more recently, crack cocaine rose in popularity.

Because of the complexity of today's drug problem, control initiatives are varied and widely utilized. Each policy incorporates its own tactics and strategies to further its successful implementation. For example, drug prohibition is the predominant control policy in today's local and national arena. Strategies for accomplishing drug prohibition include the reduction of both demand and supply, and each of these is supported by law enforcement and drug treatment programs.

Let's now consider some particulars of demand and supply, since these strategies are the cornerstone of our national drug control policy.

Demand Reduction

People who believe that the market for illicit drugs is the reason for the country's drug problem generally think that police should target drug users. In theory, once users are sufficiently afraid to purchase drugs for fear of being arrested, fewer customers mean higher prices for drugs. If prices can be raised high enough, the profit margin for dealers will be too low to make it worth their while. Another demand reduction philosophy focuses on changing the behavior of drug users or potential users. This is to be accomplished by programs such as DARE, which are aimed at teaching children to resist peer pressure, and informing people about the dangers of drug abuse. The power of such programs is supposed to be in their ability to thwart the onset of drug use by potential first-time users. Zero tolerance was discussed in Chapter 11 as a demand reduction policy option. This policy holds drug users, sellers, and buyers fully accountable for their offenses under law. The philosophy behind zero tolerance is that violators of drug laws, even for the smallest amounts of drugs, should be held criminally responsible for their actions.

The Supply Reduction Paradigm

The drug war is based on a supply reduction strategy that seeks to (1) eradicate or control drugs at their source, (2) interdict or seize drugs as they enter the country, and (3) engage in intense domestic drug enforcement efforts primarily aimed at users and drug consumers. All three components of the supply reduction paradigm are so seriously flawed and ineffective that they have made the problem of illicit drug sales and consumption much worse than a strategy of simply doing nothing.

The major problem with the supply reduction paradigm is that it assumes a stable and static supply of illegal drugs. The fact is that such an assumption is wrong. The supply of drugs is infinitely elastic, and trying to seize enough illicit produce to impact the market is the rough equivalent of trying to empty the Mississippi River with a teaspoon. The river is always going to win. The fact is that "suppliers simply produce for the market what they would have produced anyway, plus enough extra to cover anticipated government seizures" [5].

The supply reduction paradigm is doomed to failure by basic facts of geography and horticulture. Drugs such as heroin, cocaine, and marijuana can be grown and processed in a wide variety of locations, making crop eradication programs impossible to implement. Even if a particular locale is targeted and eradication programs are successfully carried out there, growers in other locations will merely make up for the deficit in supply. If heroin supplies in the Golden Crescent (Afghanistan, Iran, and Pakistan) are targeted, opium growers in the Golden Triangle (Thailand, Myanmar, and Laos), Mexico, or Colombia will simply grow more and supply the demand. These regions have had no problem with supplying the demand for heroin for the last century, although the relative importance of each fluctuates with local growing conditions, enforcement efforts, and the vagaries of geopolitics.

The case of cocaine is even more instructive. In theory, cocaine should be the easiest of the illicit crops to subject to an eradication strategy. It grows only in South America, principally in Peru and Bolivia (with Colombia, Ecuador, and Brazil making small, but increasing, contributions as growers). The world's entire cocaine supply is grown on 700 square miles of arable land. Even so, it would still be prohibitively costly to eradicate the crop. But the fact is that cocaine, even though it can be grown only in certain areas of South America, can be grown on 2,500,000 square miles of arable land [6]. Eradication as a control strategy is doomed to failure by Mother Nature herself.

Even assuming no expansion in coca leaf production, efforts to destroy the drug at its source have been miserable failures. For example, in 1998 the Colombian government seized a record amount of cocaine and related coca products—about 57 metric tons. In addition, it also destroyed 185 cocaine laboratories. The net effect was a zero decrease in the processing or exporting of cocaine hydrochloride from Colombia, and greater availability of cocaine within the United States [7]. In fact, the GAO (Government Accounting Office) reported that after a 2-year program of extensive herbicide spraying of Andean coca fields (in Peru, Bolivia, and Colombia), net coca cultivation increased by 50 percent [8]. Despite the expenditure of $625 million on narcotics control operations in Colombia between 1990 and 1998, cocaine availability in the United States increased, cocaine production increased, and Colombia surpassed Bolivia and Peru as the major source country for cocaine [9]. According to the World Drug Report, in 2009 Colombia remained the world's largest cultivator of coca bush, followed by Peru and then Bolivia [10].

The cost of crop eradication is enormous, especially considering its failure to reduce drug supplies. To achieve a 1 percent diminution in cocaine consumption in the United States (assuming eradication programs were successful), the cost would be $783 million. To achieve the 1 percent reduction in cocaine consumption, the cost of a strategy emphasizing drug treatment programs would be $34 million (Rydell & Everingham, 1994). The lack of impact on the United States market is obvious. From 1982 to 1999, federal expenditures on the drug war increased from $1.65 to $17.7 billion. From 1982 to 1999, the percentage of high school seniors who said they could obtain their illegal drug of choice "fairly easily" or "very easily" increased from 82 to 89 percent [11].

One additional concern with regard to crop eradication programs is that in attempting to comply with United States demands for domestic control of drugs, source countries often engage in programs that are environmentally disastrous. Colombia is a case in point. To meet United States demands to control coca production, the Colombian government initiated a program of aerial spraying that drops herbicides on more than 100,000 acres of land each year. As a result, Colombian peasants who are dependent on the coca crop as their only source of income have moved into the Amazon rainforests. The movement of coca growers to the rainforest has resulted in the clearing of at least 1.75 million acres of rainforest [12]. This is important because Colombia's forests account for about 10 percent of the world's biodiversity. In fact, Colombia is the second most biodiverse country in the world [13]. Moreover, despite these obvious problems, the aerial coca fumigation program in Colombia has been a failure.

In addition to the aerial-spraying program, the illegality of cocaine manufacture in Colombia is also a source of severe environmental damage. Cocaine manufacturers hide their laboratories deep in the Colombian forests. This obviously makes it impossible for them to safely dispose of the hazardous wastes associated with the refining of cocaine. As a result, some 10 million liters of sulfuric acid, 16 million liters of ethyl ether, 8 million liters of acetone, and 40–770 million liters of kerosene are poured directly into the ground and into streams annually [14].

A word needs to said about domestic crop eradication programs as well. Efforts to eradicate the marijuana crop in the United States have not only failed, but have also made the marijuana industry stronger and more dangerous than ever [15]. In Kentucky, where the state participates in a federally funded program to find and burn the marijuana crop, the net effect of the eradication program has been to spread marijuana cultivation throughout the state, and to increase both the quantity and the quality of the marijuana being produced. In addition, the eradication program has taken what was essentially a "mom and pop" industry and turned it into a highly organized criminal cartel that not only is dangerous, but also enjoys a high degree of community support in the marijuana belt counties.

The second prong of the supply reduction paradigm, interdiction, is no more successful. Interdiction assumes that with sufficient resources, drugs can be stopped from entering the United States by controlling the borders. Using the most optimistic claims of interdiction success, about 8–15 percent of the heroin and about 30 percent of the cocaine in international drug shipments is seized [16]. The difficulty with interdiction strategies can be illustrated by taking a quick look at the cocaine market. The entire demand for cocaine in the United States, the largest market in the world, can be satisfied by 13 pickup truckloads of cocaine a year. Considering that the United States has 88,633 miles of shoreline, 7,500 miles of international borders with Canada and Mexico, and 300 ports of entry, finding 13 truckloads of anything would be virtually impossible [17].

As these numbers indicate, interdiction has failed with regard to both heroin and cocaine. The only minor success that the interdiction campaign can claim is with marijuana, a bulky commodity that is difficult to transport. But the net effect of that success has been an even bigger problem. Marijuana smugglers and growers in other countries have simply moved to cocaine and heroin as substitutes for marijuana, resulting in even more of those drugs being imported to the United States, and domestic marijuana production has increased dramatically in the past 10 years. A RAND Corporation evaluation study of interdiction determined that "even massively stepped-up drug interdiction efforts are not likely to greatly affect the availability of cocaine and heroin in the United States" [18]. Consider this simple fact: the criminal justice system cannot keep drugs out of maximum-security prisons, much less seal the nation's borders to drug trafficking.

One other point needs to be made with regard to interdiction and eradication as supply control strategies. In addition to the false assumption that the world's supply of illicit drugs is stable, there is a similar assumption that drug traffickers do not adjust to the exigencies of new enforcement strategies—an assumption that is similarly incorrect. For example, United States enforcement efforts in Colombia in the 1980s and 1990s resulted in the creation of hundreds of small, decentralized drug-trafficking organizations that are virtually impossible to find, let alone control. And, as mentioned in Chapter, these new traffickers have altered their product significantly by using a chemical process to produce "black cocaine," which evades detection by drug-sniffing dogs and chemical tests. The chemical process is simple and inexpensive; it primarily requires adding charcoal and a couple of chemicals to their cocaine shipments [19]. Interdicting cocaine was a hit-and-miss operation before; now, it is primarily a miss.

The final component of the supply control paradigm is intensive street-level drug enforcement in the United States directed at consumers and users. These efforts have also shown little hope of success in the drug war. Intensive street-level law enforcement efforts are very expensive. Although they result in the arrests of thousands of low-level drug dealers and users, they have little impact on the other elements involved in illicit drug supply. Although some of these enforcement efforts have been able to claim "temporary and transitory success," they have not had any impact at all on the availability of illegal drugs. In fact, all illegal drug prices have fallen, purity has increased, the supply has increased, and use levels have increased in jurisdictions where intensive street-level enforcement has been tried. In addition, crimes ancillary to drug trafficking have increased in almost every case in which saturation enforcement strategies have been utilized.

Drug Use

The supply reduction paradigm promises an enormous expenditure of resources, vast expansion of law enforcement authority, and large numbers of citizens being arrested and imprisoned. It is supposed to have a deterrent effect on drug use as well. Statistics, however, show that more Americans are using illegal drugs with greater regularity than ever before. Just a few statistics exemplify this trend:

- By 2008, more than 117 million Americans over the age of 12 (47 percent of the population) had used illicit drugs.
- More than 102 million Americans (41 percent of the adult population) have used marijuana, and almost 26 million used marijuana in 2008.
- Almost 37 million Americans (almost 15 percent of the adult population) have used powder or crack cocaine, and a little more than 5 million of them used cocaine or cocaine derivatives in 2008 [20].

Despite the arrests, the media campaigns, and the adoption of draconian penalties for drug use violations, one out of every eight adult citizens of the United States chose to violate the drug laws in 2001. But the numbers are even more compelling when we look at the youngest of drug users, the population group that will drive these numbers even higher in the future. Surveys of high school seniors show that more than half of them had used an illegal drug while in high school [21]. Despite the enormous law enforcement emphasis of the drug war, 89 percent of high school seniors reported that marijuana is "very easy" or "fairly easy" to obtain, and 49 percent of those high school seniors have actually used marijuana [22]. The United States, with its get-tough-on-drugs policy, has a higher rate of illegal drug use by young people than any European nation. In 1999, 41 percent of American tenth graders had used marijuana, compared to 17 percent of similar students in Europe, where drug restrictions are much weaker [23].

Researchers note that the legal threats accompanying drug use have little or no impact on use levels, describing the legal threat as "very weak;" they have argued persuasively that market forces, not law enforcement efforts, have the most impact on patterns of drug use [24,25]. They argue that legal institutions have almost no impact on the drug market. In fact, there is a credible argument to be made that the existence of drug laws and the intensive enforcement campaign accompanying them may stimulate drug use, and may be responsible for the production of larger numbers of addicts than we might otherwise have had. Mishan, for example, suggested that the crucial factor in spreading addiction is the enormous profits in the drug trade made possible by the illegality of drugs [26]. As long as drugs are illegal, virtually every addict becomes a drug salesperson in order to raise sufficient funds to pay for his or her habit [27]. In addition to the profits that can be realized from the sale of illegal drugs, illegality also stimulates experimentation, particularly among adolescents, by raising the specter of the "forbidden fruit" that simply must be tasted in order to fully experience life [28].

Despite the failure of intensive street-level drug enforcement, the law enforcement campaign to arrest as many drug users as possible and put them in prison continues unabated. As a result, the United States has the largest prison population in the world, with an incarceration rate of 756 per 100,000 adults [29]. Not only are more drug offenders in prison, but also they serve far longer sentences that most other offenders, and have sentences almost as severe as those of the most violent offenders. By any measure, the drug war has not only failed to deter illegal drug use—it also has done nothing to make drugs harder to find or obtain.

As we have learned with regard to the reduction of illicit drug use, the drug war has been a dismal failure. The extent of that failure is easily gauged when drug use in the United States is compared to drug use in the Netherlands, where marijuana is available for legal sale and a harm reduction policy has replaced a law enforcement emphasis as the keystone of efforts to control harder drug use.

Other Variables

Other factors that have an impact on supply and demand should also be considered. For example, intense police initiatives such as gang sweeps, undercover operations, and reverse stings also tend to (at least temporarily) disrupt supplies in local drug markets and make drug buyers themselves fearful of being arrested. In other cases, courts have imposed mandatory drug treatment of addicts, resulting in many of them reducing their drug usage and consequently reducing their frequency of drug purchases.

Strategies in National Drug Control

Since the early 1970s, the United States government has devised a series of strategies designed to combat the nation's drug problem. Strategies are the means through which drug policy can be set in motion; they typically include an array of programs and tactics. During 1973, 1974, and 1975, *Federal Strategy for Drug Abuse and Drug Traffic Prevention* documents were published. Each was designed to identify problems and possible solutions to drug abuse trends in the nation. Similar publications were produced in 1976, in 1979, and again in 1982, all focusing on similar drug-related issues. In 1984, the first federal effort referring to itself as a "national strategy" was published by the White House Drug Abuse Policy Office, followed in 1987 and 1988 by publications from the White House Conference for a Drug-Free America.

The 1973 strategy focused on the reduction of drug abuse and the identification of the drugs that cause the greatest harm to society. The focus shifted somewhat by 1976, when the federal strategy initiated the lead agency concept by making the Justice Department responsible for enforcement of federal drug laws. In 1988, the Office of National Drug Control Policy (ONDCP) was developed. As part of its charge, comprehensive plans are required to be published each year on federal drug control policy issues. Statistics are also offered regarding issues such as the following:

- Current overall drug use
- Cocaine use
- Adolescent drug use
- Drug availability

- Marijuana production
- Student attitudes toward drugs

In addition, each National Drug Control Strategy identifies national priorities in the areas of drug enforcement, prevention, treatment, international initiatives, and drug education.

Politics and the ONDCP

One of the perennial hindrances to a workable drug control policy is the political arena. This is apparent in virtually all political campaigns, but can be best illustrated by the role and function of the ONDCP. The ONDCP was created in 1988 at the behest of a Democratic Congress that forced reluctant Republican bureaucrats to make the concept a reality. As originally envisioned, the "drug czar" was to study the fragmented drug war effort and better organize, coordinate, and consolidate the "troops" [30]. In actuality, during its early phases the office had no real power and soon gained the reputation of being little more than a ministry of propaganda.

The first drug czar was former Education Secretary William Bennett, who brought respectability to the office by his zeal for media coverage and his willingness to take on difficult policy questions in many different public forums. Next, defeated Florida Governor Bob Martinez was appointed drug czar by President George H.W. Bush. Interestingly, none of Martinez's top 11 aides had ever worked for any of the nation's lead drug enforcement agencies; in addition, another 40 percent of the office's jobs went to political appointees, a figure that dwarfed the numbers of political appointees in other federal departments [31]. Finally, with the election of President Bill Clinton, the staff of the ONDCP was cut from 146 people

FIGURE 13.1 U.S. Senator Jay Rockefeller, center back, is joined by Congressman Nick Rahall, second from left, and White House Drug Czar Gil Kerlikowske, center right, during a roundtable discussion on prescription drug abuse and trafficking in February 2013. *Source: AP Photo*/The Charleston Daily Mail, *Tom Hindman.*

to 25, which forced many policy experts to question the sincerity of Clinton's drug policy intentions. Clinton's budget cuts also jeopardized many meaningful drug control programs, including the Counter-Drug Technology Assessment Center, which drug experts had touted as being an effective program. R. Gil Kerlikowske currently holds the "drug czar" (Director of the Office of National Drug Control Policy) position under the Obama administration.

Prohibition Then and Now

As discussed in Chapter 1, many social scientists have characterized Prohibition as a dismal failure to control human behavior. Although this premise is supported by many elements of the era, let us pose the question: could any aspects of the experiment be termed a success? Surprisingly, the answer is yes. For decades, many experts have suggested that alcohol abuse actually increased during the Prohibition years. In actuality, and contrary to popular myth, alcohol consumption was fairly well controlled during the Prohibition era; records reveal that levels of alcohol consumption declined significantly during the era and rose again sharply after its repeal [32]. However, because alcohol consumption was a clandestine practice during Prohibition, no reliable data are available that can be scrutinized. In a thought-provoking discussion on the matter, Goode has suggested that rates of cirrhosis of the liver (which are closely related to alcoholism) be considered before, during, and subsequent to Prohibition to determine the extent of alcohol abstinence. He points out that the rate of death from cirrhosis of the liver remained between 12 and 17 per 100,000 people each year between 1900 and 1919, but it dropped to between seven and nine per 100,000 in the 1920s and early 1930s, a reduction of almost one-half. After 1933 (the end of Prohibition), however, it began to escalate again [33].

So, why is it generally believed that excessive alcoholism during the period was common? One explanation could be the popular belief that speakeasies, jazz clubs, and the like existed around every street corner, and that opportunistic gangsters such as Al Capone had bootleg beer and whiskey all but flowing in the streets. Movies, books, and other popular literature tend to foster the notion that everyone was drinking, partying, and living the high life. The truth about Prohibition, however, is that it was an unexciting period in which most Americans did not drink, and those who did drink alcohol drank considerably less than they did before or after the passing of the Eighteenth Amendment.

Despite the "successes" of Prohibition, several important lessons were also learned about the era and the notion of prohibition as a public policy option. First, the illegal alcohol made available by criminal entrepreneurs during the era was considerably stronger than that which was obtainable before the Prohibition period. Before Prohibition, low-alcohol beer made up almost one-half of the alcohol consumed, compared to the rise in availability of distilled spirits during the era. Second, much of the available alcohol was adulterated with toxins, which were used as substitutes for ethyl alcohol [34]. In fact, in one case, a medicinal tonic known as "Jake," a Jamaican ginger extract containing 75 percent alcohol, resulted in more than 50,000 people becoming permanently paralyzed. Finally, as we have learned, bootleg alcohol products provided organized crime groups with the financial boost they needed to become more integrated into society. This resulted in their increased power on the street and in the ranks of politics. It has been said that Prohibition actually increased the number and types of people involved in the production and distribution of alcohol [35].

Comparative Lessons from Prohibition

So, what have we learned from all this? First, the Prohibition era of the 1920s and 1930s did what it was intended to do—make people stop or reduce their alcohol intake. We have also learned that along with the medical successes of this policy, other unforeseen social problems resulted, which probably overshadowed the original social concern of alcohol. Comparing Prohibition of alcohol during the 1920s to the prohibition of drugs today is tricky, because many of today's social and political variables are considerably different.

For example, the prohibition of alcohol gave rise to loose-knit gangs and transformed them into powerful crime organizations. Today, however, these organizations are already in place—well funded, highly organized, and interlaced throughout both the criminal and legitimate business worlds. If drug legalization is being considered as a policy option, its intent must be carefully considered, especially if it is designed for doing away with these immense criminal empires. Would this be a realistic outcome today? Second, at the time of its imposition, Prohibition had the general support of the American people. Today's drug prohibition, according to national polls, also enjoys considerable support by the American people. Assuming that a democracy represents a government by and for the people, then, if for no other reason, how socially responsible is it for our elected officials to pursue a public policy (e.g., legalization) that lacks public support? Next, we should consider how decriminalization or legalization has worked in other states. The discussion in Chapter 12 about Alaska's 15-year experiment (between 1975 and 1990) with marijuana decriminalization shows how on the surface such policies appear to be a workable solution, but in practice can create problems of their own.

A fourth point is that there is evidence that alcohol prohibition did work in reducing alcohol consumption. Accordingly, we see trends of reduced drug abuse in recent years under our current prohibition policy. We also see the positive effects of innovative drug laws such as Racketeer-Influenced and Corrupt Organizations (RICO), Continuing Criminal Enterprise (CCE), and forfeiture statutes, which in many cases have resulted in the successful arrest, prosecution, and conviction of dangerous drug lords and organized crime figures.

Finally, although many experts have suggested the abolition of drug prohibition in place of a policy of regulation, we must remember that we have already been there. Our current policy of drug prohibition originated from a time when drugs were perfectly legal in this nation and readily available over the counter. Slowly, as the dangers of drug abuse were realized, taxation and regulation were imposed to "reduce and control" drug abuse without arbitrarily outlawing drugs. So, after 75 years of legally obtainable drugs (before 1878) and regulation (e.g., the 1906 Federal Food and Drug Act, the 1914 Harrison Narcotics Act, and the 1937 Marijuana Tax Act), the United States willfully adopted the current system of prohibition as its chosen public policy regarding drug control. Even inexpensive, highly regulated pharmaceutical drugs such as cocaine have not deterred Colombian criminals from producing large amounts of it on the black market at exorbitant prices.

Alcoholics still abound in today's United States. Erich Goode claims that alcohol consumption was fairly well controlled during Prohibition. He points to the decline in death rates from cirrhosis of the liver that occurred during the era, and the rise of those death rates after Prohibition's end in 1933.

This discussion illustrates how the solution to formulating a successful drug control policy is unclear. Contradictions in facts, opinions, and impressions of prohibition—both then and now—have only served to muddy the waters. Although it is difficult to recommend one policy option without condemning another, responsible social policy must consider not just what the people need, but also what they want.

Legal Tools in Drug Control

As discussed, the use of innovative antidrug laws has proved to be one of the most powerful weapons against drug trafficking and a strong ally in the development of drug control policy. Although some of the most effective laws have been in place for some time, many new laws have been written to address the many unique aspects of the drug trade and the constantly changing structure of drug organizations. We now know that most drug prosecutions occur at the state and local levels; those laws are discussed in previous chapters of this book. However, due to the influence and mobility of organized crime groups in the drug trade, several significant federal laws have become widely used over the past two decades.

Our current system of justice is predicated on crimes that for the most part affect individual behavior and specific, unrelated incidents. For example, the burglar, the armed robber, the rapist, and the drug dealer are all persons whose behavior violates specific criminal codes. Organized crime represents group criminal behavior, which presents a more complicated way of viewing drug-related crime. In the past, prosecutors have been forced to approach organized crime with a narrow and shortsighted focus, convicting criminals either one at a time or in a single conspiracy. For example, over the past 60 years, federal prosecutors have attempted to prosecute the heads of the Genovese crime family, beginning with Charles "Lucky" Luciano, who was convicted of operating a prostitution ring in Manhattan. His successor, Frank Costello, was convicted of federal tax evasion. This was followed by the conviction of Vito Genovese, who was found guilty of running a drug conspiracy, and so on. For years, federal prosecutors were able to incapacitate (temporarily) the heads of a crime organization for various crimes, but were never able to sufficiently weaken the organization's power. When finally removed, the head of an organization was easily and quickly replaced, and the organization continued to flourish. As a result, in 1970 Congress passed legislation that incorporated antiracketeering elements that targeted the criminal organization instead of the individual. Such laws are today's primary weapon against criminal organizations and the people who control them. This section looks at some of the most effective federal drug control tools.

The Racketeer-Influenced and Corrupt Organizations Act

The 1970 RICO Act is an invaluable tool in the fight against organized crime in the drug trade. RICO's purpose is to broaden the prosecutor's power by allowing one prosecution of a multidefendant criminal organization for all the criminal enterprises in which it is involved. In addition to imprisonment of members of the crime group, RICO allows for the seizure of assets and proceeds from illegal enterprises. Successful application of the RICO statute in recent years has resulted in the conviction of top-level La Cosa Nostra members in Kansas City, St. Louis, Philadelphia, and Cleveland. Cases such as these help illustrate to the general public the magnitude of organized crime organizations and the extent of their operations.

Under RICO, a person who is a member of an enterprise that has committed any two of 35 crimes—27 federal crimes and eight state crimes—within a 10-year period can be charged with racketeering. Those found guilty of racketeering can be fined up to $25,000 and sentenced to 20 years in prison per racketeering count. In addition, the racketeer must forfeit all ill-gotten gains and interest in any business gained through a pattern of "racketeering activity." RICO also permits a private individual harmed by the actions of such an enterprise to file a civil suit; if successful, the individual can collect treble damages (damages in triple the amount of actual and compensatory damages).

When a United States attorney decides to indict someone under RICO, he or she has the option of seeking a pretrial restraining order or injunction to temporarily seize a defendant's assets and prevent the transfer of potentially forfeitable property, as well as require the defendant to put up a performance bond. This provision was placed in the law because the owners of Mafia-related shell corporations often absconded with the assets. An injunction and/or performance bond ensures that there is something to seize in the event of a guilty verdict.

In many cases, the threat of a RICO indictment can force defendants to plead guilty to lesser charges, in part because the seizure of assets would make it difficult to pay a defense attorney. Despite its harsh provisions, a RICO-related charge is considered easy to prove in court, as it focuses on patterns of behavior as opposed to criminal acts.

There is also a provision for private parties to sue. A "person damaged in his business or property" can sue one or more "racketeers." The plaintiff must prove the existence of an "enterprise." The defendant(s) are not the enterprise; in other words, the defendant(s) and the enterprise are not one and the same. There must be one of four specified relationships between the defendant(s) and the enterprise: the defendant(s) invested the proceeds of the pattern of racketeering activity into the enterprise; the defendant(s) acquired or maintained an interest in, or control over, the enterprise through the pattern of racketeering activity; the defendant(s) conducted or participated in the affairs of the enterprise "through" the pattern of racketeering activity; or the defendant(s) conspired to do one of the above. In essence, the enterprise is the illegal device of the racketeers. A civil RICO action, like many lawsuits based on federal law, can be filed in state or federal court. Both the federal criminal and civil components allow the recovery of treble damages.

Although RICO has been law since 1970, it was not widely used until the early 1980s. Before that time, prosecutors tended to apply the statute to criminals who were not members of large crime organizations or who were not management-level organized crime players. RICO is a statute that criminalizes a pattern of conduct characteristic of organized crime. Specifically outlined in the RICO statute are the criminal acts that constitute a *pattern of racketeering*, which means that at least two so-called predicate criminal acts must have occurred during the previous two of which must have occurred during the previous 10 years. Under RICO, racketeering is defined as "any act or threat involving murder, kidnapping, gambling, arson, robbery, bribery, extortion, or trafficking in narcotics or dangerous drugs."

The Continuing Criminal Enterprise Statute

The federal CCE Statute (U.S. Code Section 848, Title 21), enacted as part of the Comprehensive Drug Abuse Prevention and Control Act of 1970, is one of the strongest statutory weapons against drug trafficking. Like RICO, this statute gives prosecutors the means to reach the organizers, managers, and supervisors of major drug-trafficking organizations. Prosecution under this statute requires proof of five elements to sustain prosecution:

1. The defendant's conduct must constitute a felony violation of federal narcotics laws.
2. The conduct must take place as part of a continuing series of violations.
3. The defendant must undertake this activity in concert with at least five other individuals.
4. The defendant must act as the organizer, manager, or supervisor of this criminal enterprise.
5. The defendant must obtain income or resources from this enterprise.

CCE provides for some of the most severe criminal penalties for illicit drug trafficking. These include imprisonment for a minimum of 10 years with no possibility of parole. In addition, the court may impose a life sentence with no provision for parole and fines totaling $100,000. Moreover, under CCE, all profits and assets that have afforded the defendant a source of influence over the illegal enterprise are subject to forfeiture.

Conspiracy Laws

The use of conspiracy laws in drug enforcement has proven to be one of the most beneficial tactics of the last decade. Although conspiracy laws have existed for quite some time, their use is now common among federal, state, and local authorities alike. Although state law in this area may differ from one jurisdiction to another, the basic principles of conspiracy are the same. *Conspiracy* is defined as an agreement between two or more persons who have the specific intent either to commit a crime or to engage in dishonest, fraudulent, or immoral conduct injurious to public health or morals. In studying this definition, one can easily see the benefits of such a law in the area of drug control.

Drug trafficking is a criminal endeavor that usually requires more than one player: for example, a grower sells drugs to a manufacturer, who contracts with a smuggler for transportation. The smuggler then transports the drugs to a wholesale buyer, who in turn sells them to a retail distributor. The retail distributor then sells the drugs to numerous dealers and users on the street. Given the documentation that investigators require, conspiracy charges can be brought against all such players in a drug operation. Because most conspiracy cases involve numerous defendants, a degree of confusion may result. Generally, three types of conspiracy cases are most commonly used in prosecutions of drug traffickers. These are the chain, the wheel, and the enterprise conspiracy:

- *The chain.* A *chain conspiracy* occurs when a criminal endeavor is dependent on the participation of each member of the criminal organization. Each member represents a link in the chain, and the success of the criminal goal requires all participants. If one link in the chain is broken (i.e., a member fails to accomplish his or her particular task), the criminal act will be incomplete. To successfully prosecute a chain conspiracy, each member must be shown to be aware of the operation's intended goal.
- *The wheel.* A *wheel conspiracy* comprises one member of a criminal organization who is the "hub," or organizer, of the criminal plan, and members who make up the "spokes." Wheel conspiracies must show that all members who serve as spokes are aware of each other and agree with each other to achieve a common illegal goal. For this reason, the wheel conspiracy is a difficult one to prosecute, since it is difficult to show a common agreement between the spokes.
- *The enterprise.* As discussed under the RICO section of this chapter, a person who has been shown to participate in two or more patterns of racketeering may be prosecuted. The definition of *enterprise conspiracy* makes it a separate crime to conspire to commit any of the substantive offenses under RICO. Basically, RICO defines the term as an agreement to enter into an enterprise by engaging in a pattern of racketeering. The enterprise conspiracy recognizes that in some criminal organizations, not all members have one common goal. Therefore, all that must be shown is a member's willingness to join a criminal organization (an "enterprise") by committing two or more acts of racketeering.

Criminal Forfeiture

When criminal forfeiture is used, it accompanies a criminal conviction. For example, if a high-profile drug trafficker is convicted of controlled substance law violations, the convicted person's property that was connected with such activity may be forfeited. Criminal forfeiture is, by some accounts, less common than civil forfeiture, mainly because of the burden of proof in criminal cases (i.e., proof beyond a reasonable doubt). Criminal forfeiture is a sentencing option only if the statute used to convict the offender also provides for forfeiture. Also, when a third party has an interest in the property subject to forfeiture, ancillary hearings are often held to ascertain the nature of that interest and make adjustments as deemed necessary.

Drug Tax Laws

One innovative approach to drug enforcement is the implementation of drug tax laws. During the 1980s, such laws were enacted in 21 states, with provisions similar to the 80-year-old Harrison Narcotics Act. Most drug tax laws are covered under state tax codes, and failure to pay the required taxes on illicit drugs results in both civil and criminal penalties—in addition to any penalties the offender faces regarding the drug violation itself. State drug tax codes include stamp, sales, and excise taxes on specified criminal activities, which include the manufacture, sale, acquisition, and possession of drugs in the state—virtually all types of drug-related activities. Typically, the tax is $3.50 for each gram of marijuana and $200 for each gram of other illegal substances. In addition, there is a specified amount for drugs sold in a manufactured form of dosage units.

Drug taxes work as follows: when someone comes into possession of drugs, he or she is required to buy a state drug stamp—a procedure that is usually performed anonymously. Law enforcement officials are aware that, in most cases, drug traffickers will be hesitant to do so because they do not want to inform the police about being in possession of illicit drugs (this would warrant an investigation). If a person is found to be in illegal possession of dangerous drugs for which tax has not been paid, he or she is subject to a financial penalty and a prison sentence for tax evasion (not drug possession). Prosecution for possession of drugs is a separate criminal matter carrying additional penalties.

The primary reason for the drug tax is to give investigators a powerful tool for investigating large-scale drug traffickers, as opposed to small-time dealers. Such offenders can be found guilty of a civil violation of the state tax code, providing that the state can show they have not paid the tax. As a result, violators can be required to pay back taxes and fines that can be substantial. For example, a trafficker caught with 1 kg (2.2 pounds) of cocaine might be subject to taxes of $200,000, as well as a civil fine of $200,000. He or she might also be required to pay a criminal fine of up to $10,000, as well as serve a prison term. Revenues resulting from drug taxes are often used for drug enforcement efforts, treatment, and prevention programs such as DARE.

Grand Juries and Immunity

The use of the grand jury has proven effective in drug suppression efforts because of the broad range of power that it enjoys. The roots of the grand jury go back to the twelfth century, when it served as a safeguard against governmental abuse. The grand jury sought citizen approval for prosecutorial actions. Some of the more powerful rights granted to the grand jury are represented by its authority to subpoena persons and documents, to punish, to grant immunity, to issue indictments, and to maintain secrecy of its proceedings.

The grand jury has been used successfully on both the federal and state levels, and in the case of the latter, the authority to call a grand jury may rest with the governor, the state attorney general, or the local prosecutor. As indicated, the grand jury's ability to grant immunity broadens the powers of this investigative body. This ability is particularly useful because many witnesses are criminals who have intimate knowledge of criminal operations.

Most criminals are aware that under the Fifth Amendment, they cannot be compelled to give testimony against themselves. When a criminal "takes the Fifth," prosecutors may pursue one of several options:

1. The prosecutor can compel testimony by seeking a contempt citation if prosecutors can prove that the testimony would not incriminate the witness.
2. The prosecutor can release the witness and continue the proceedings without the benefit of the witness's testimony.
3. A plea bargaining agreement can be sought, whereby the witness's testimony would be given with the understanding that a lesser charge could be levied against the witness than if he or she did not give the testimony.
4. Total immunity from prosecution can be given by the prosecutor in exchange for the witness's testimony. In this case, once the witness is given total immunity, he or she can then be compelled to testify. Refusal under these circumstances can result in punishment of the witness.

Two kinds of immunity may be granted to witnesses in organized crime prosecutions:

1. *Transactional immunity.* A witness given *transactional immunity* for testimony about a specific criminal act is literally immune from ever being prosecuted for that particular crime in the future. Some witnesses in the past have attempted to blurt out additional crimes connected with the primary offense in an attempt to take an "immunity bath" and be free from all responsibility for those crimes. In fact, immunity is not attached when the witness purposely mentions additional crimes. It is extended to other crimes, however, when the prosecutor chooses to mention them during the examination of the witness in court.
2. *Derivative use immunity.* When *derivative use immunity* is granted to a witness, the witness is immune only from having his or her own testimony later used against him or her. If evidence of an independent nature is uncovered, however, the witness may be prosecuted on the basis of that evidence.

Derivative use immunity has considerable advantages for the prosecutor over transactional immunity. When using transactional immunity, a witness may give broad-sweeping and vague testimony referring to specific criminal acts, thus bringing him or her under the "umbrella" of the immunity grant, but being ambiguous enough so that specifics essential to prosecution are not provided [36]. A grant of derivative use immunity will not bar prosecution.

The Witness Security Program

The U.S. Marshals Service provides for the security of government witnesses, and their immediate dependents, whose lives are in danger as a result of their testimony against drug traffickers, terrorists, organized crime members, and other major criminals. The *Witness Security Program (WITSEC)* was authorized by the Organized Crime Control Act of 1970 and

FIGURE 13.2 This 2005 photo shows Henry Hill, who was a part of the federal witness protection program in the 1980s. Due to his numerous crimes while in witness protection, he was expelled from the program in the early 1990s. His life as a mobster and FBI informant was the basis for the Martin Scorsese film *Goodfellas*. He died in June 2012. *Source: AP Photo/Nati Harnik.*

amended by the Comprehensive Crime Control Act of 1984. United States marshals have protected, relocated, and given new identities to more than 8,500 witnesses and 9,900 of their family members since the program began in 1971 [37].

The successful operation of this program is widely recognized as providing a unique and valuable tool in the government's battle against major criminal conspirators and organized crime. Witnesses and their families typically get new identities with authentic documentation. Housing, subsistence for basic living expenses, and medical care are provided to the witnesses. Job training and employment assistance may also be provided.

The U.S. Marshals Service provides 24-hour protection to all witnesses while they are in a high-threat environment, including pretrial conferences, trial testimonials, and other court appearances.

The Marshals Service boasts that as of 2013, no WITSEC participant who followed security guidelines has been harmed while under the active protection of the United States marshals. In both criminal and civil matters involving protected witnesses, the United States marshals cooperate fully with local law enforcement and court authorities to bring witnesses to justice or to have them fulfill their legal responsibilities [38].

▪ ▪ Critical Thinking Task ▪

Evaluate the federal WITSEC program in terms of its success or failure to contribute to a reduction in drug-related crime in the United States. Do you believe that tax dollars are well spent in allowing drug criminals to evade prosecution and to begin new lives?

Summary

Modern drug control policy is earmarked by a number of policy strategies, each designed to address a specific aspect of the nation's drug problem. These strategies include demand reduction, supply reduction, eradication, education, and treatment. However, despite many notable successes, none of these policies has proven successful in reducing drug abuse to what could be termed an acceptable level. The implementation of control strategies involves a concerted effort by many organizations and agencies. Those in both the public and private sectors share responsibility for fighting the drug abuse problem in our communities and schools. These include law enforcement agencies on the federal, state, and local levels as well as local schools, the military, and private businesses that offer support for prevention and treatment programs.

Today's drug control policy originated with a series of federal laws designed to regulate the manufacture, sale, and use of dangerous drugs. Drug control efforts in the United States, however, date back to the late 1800s, when opium and its extracts were first recognized as dangerous. Momentum on the federal level began in 1906 with the passing of the Pure Food and Drug Act, which required medications containing opium or coca derivatives to say so on their label. In 1914, the Harrison Narcotics Act further controlled opiates by restricting their dispensing to medical purposes that required a written authorization. Ambiguities in the law, however, prevented this act from being fairly enforced.

In 1937, marijuana was controlled under the Marijuana Tax Act in much the same way as opiates were under the Harrison Narcotics Act. Taxes were imposed for people who grew marijuana in an effort to deter growers from involvement with this plant. Finally, in 1970, the Controlled Substances Act was passed as an effort to update all preexisting federal drug laws. This comprehensive act placed all supposedly dangerous drugs in one of five schedules. Each drug was categorized according to its level of danger. The law also set forth new criminal and civil penalties for the possession and distribution of drugs.

Nineteen-seventy also marked the enactment of several new and innovative drug control laws that are still being used today. One such law, the RICO Act, enables law enforcement to prosecute leaders of large criminal organizations, and to seize assets associated with the organizations. A similar law, the CCE Act, also affords authorities special powers in arrest and forfeiture of assets of drug kingpins. To provide further aid in the drug enforcement initiative, conspiracy and forfeiture legislation has greatly enhanced law enforcement officers' ability to arrest dealers and their associates. These laws also provide the legal basis to seize assets acquired by drug offenders.

Drug control, by virtue of its economic, political, and social implications, is extremely complicated. Not everyone agrees on the most effective and efficient manner in which to contain the nation's drug abuse problem, but the strategies and policies discussed in this chapter demonstrate the breadth and complexity of control efforts, regardless of how successful they are or have been.

Do you recognize these terms?

- chain conspiracy
- derivative use immunity
- enterprise conspiracy
- eradication
- pattern of racketeering
- prohibition
- regulation
- taxation
- transactional immunity
- wheel conspiracy
- WITSEC

Discussion Questions

1. What major drug control legislation was passed during the Reagan administration?
2. The RICO statute requires that a pattern of racketeering be established. What are the predicate offenses that constitute a pattern of racketeering?
3. Discuss the elements of a conspiracy.
4. How do the forfeiture sanctions under federal law help in the national drug control effort?
5. Discuss why the grand jury is considered a valuable asset in the prosecution of drug offenders.
6. List and discuss the two types of immunity most commonly used in federal drug prosecutions.
7. Discuss how the federal WITSEC aids in the prosecution of high-level organized crime figures.

References

[1] Wilkinson, E. (May 5, 1994). A separate peace. *Rolling Stone*, 26–29.
[2] Office of National Drug Control Policy. *National drug control strategy 2013*. Budget and Performance Strategy.
[3] President's Commission on Organized Crime. (1986). *America's habit: Drug abuse, drug trafficking and organized crime*. Washington, DC: U.S. Government Printing Office.
[4] Bureau of Justice Statistics. (1992). *Drugs, Crime and the Justice System*. Washington, DC: U.S. Department of Justice.
[5] Rydell, C. P., & Everingham, S. E. (1994). *Controlling Cocaine: Supply Versus Demand Programs*. Santa Monica, CA: RAND.
[6] Nadelmann, E. A. (1988). U.S. drug policy: A bad export. *Foreign Policy, 70*(Spring), 83–108.
[7] U.S. General Accounting Office. (1999). *Drug control: Narcotics threat from Colombia continues to grow*. Washington, DC: U.S. Government Printing Office.
[8] Ibid.
[9] Ibid.
[10] Office of National Drug Control Policy. (2010). *National drug control strategy 2010*. Washington, DC: U.S. Department of Justice. Executive Office of the President of the United States.
[11] Johnston, L. D., O'Malley, P. M., & Bachman, J. G. (2000). *Results of monitoring the future study*. Ann Arbor: University of Michigan.
[12] Trade and Environment Database (TED). (1997). *TED case studies: Colombia coca trade*. Washington, DC: American University.
[13] Ibid.
[14] Ibid.

[15] Potter, G., Gaines, L., & Holbrook, B. (1990). Blowing smoke: An evaluation of marijuana eradication in Kentucky. *American Journal of Police, IX*(1), 97–116.
[16] United Nations Office for Drug Control and Crime Prevention. (1999). *Global illicit drug trends, 1999.* New York: UNODCCP.
[17] Frankel, G. (June 8, 1997). Federal agencies duplicate efforts, wage costly turf battles. *The Washington Post*, A1.
[18] Reuter, P., Crawford, G., & Cace, J. (1988). *Sealing the borders: The effects of increased military participation in drug interdiction, R-3594-USDP.* Santa Monica, CA: RAND.
[19] U.S. General Accounting Office. (1999). *Drug control: Narcotics threat from Colombia continues to grow.* Washington, DC: U.S. Government Printing Office.
[20] *National Survey on Drug Use and Health: National findings.* Rockville, MD: Office of Applied Studies, U.S. Department of Health and Human Service. Found at www.oas.samhsa.gov/nsduh/2k8nsduh/2k8Results.cfm#1.1. Accessed March 15, 2010.
[21] Johnston, L. D., O'Malley, P. M., & Bachman, J. G. (2000). *Results of monitoring the future study.* Ann Arbor: University of Michigan.
[22] Ibid.
[23] Ibid.
[24] Erickson, P., & Cheung, Y. (1992). Drug crime and legal control: Lessons from the Canadian experience. *Contemporary Drug Problems, 19*, 247–260.
[25] Fagan, J., & Spelman, W. (1994). Market forces at work. *The New York Times.* (February 11), A34.
[26] Mishan, E. (1990). Narcotics: The problem and the solution. *Political Quarterly, 61*, 441–458.
[27] Zion, S. (1993). *Battle Lines in the War on Drugs: Make Them Legal.* (December 15), A27. The New York Times.
[28] Ostrowski, J. (1989). *Thinking about drugs legalization. Policy analysis* (Vol. 121). Washington, DC: Cato Institute.
[29] Walmsley, R. (2008). *World prison population list* (8th ed.). London: International Center for Prison Studies.
[30] Witkin, G. (February 22, 1993). How politics ruined drug-war planning. *U.S. News & World Report*, 29.
[31] Ibid.
[32] Goode, E. (1993). *Drugs in American society* (4th ed.). New York: McGraw-Hill.
[33] Ibid.
[34] Morgan, J. P. (1991). Prohibition is perverse policy: What was true in 1933 is true now. In K. Melvin & E. Lazear (Eds.), *Searching for alternatives: Drug control policy in the United States* (pp. 405–423). Stanford, CA: Hoover Institution Press.
[35] Levine, H. G., & Reinarman, C. (1992). From Prohibition to regulation: Lessons from alcohol policy for drug policy. *The Milbank Quarterly, 69*(3), 1–34.
[36] Kenney, D., & Finckenauer, J. (1995). *Organized crime in America.* Belmont, CA: Wadsworth.
[37] United States Marshal's Service web site. Found at: http://www.usmarshals.gov/witsec/. Accessed May 5, 2013.
[38] Ibid.

14

Control through Treatment and Prevention

This chapter will enable you to:

- Understand public opinion as it relates to drug treatment
- Understand the drug user
- Appreciate the plight of the drug addict
- Compare and contrast drug treatment programs
- Learn differences in treatment philosophies
- Discover what works in drug treatment and what does not

Although many drug enforcement and community efforts are designed to deter drug abuse, there will always be people who develop dependencies on addictive substances, or who seek escape through the use of alcohol and other drugs. Drug addiction is a complex but treatable brain disease. It is characterized by compulsive drug craving, seeking, and use that persist even in the face of severe adverse consequences. For many people, drug addiction becomes chronic, with relapses possible even after long periods of abstinence. In fact, relapse of drug abuse occurs at rates similar to those for other well-characterized, chronic medical illnesses such as diabetes, hypertension, and asthma. As a chronic, recurring illness, addiction may require repeated treatments to increase the intervals between relapses and diminish their intensity until abstinence is achieved. Through treatment tailored to individual needs, people with drug addiction can recover and lead productive lives.

The ultimate goal of drug addiction treatment is to enable an individual to achieve lasting abstinence, but the immediate goals are to reduce drug abuse, improve the patient's ability to function, and minimize the medical and social complications of drug abuse and addiction. Like people with diabetes or heart disease, people in treatment for drug addiction will need to change their behavior to adopt a more healthful lifestyle.

In 2004, approximately 22.5 million Americans age 12 or older needed treatment for substance (alcohol or illicit drug) abuse and addiction. Of these, only 3.8 million people received it. Untreated substance abuse and addiction burden families and communities with significant costs, including those related to violence and property crimes, prison expenses, court and criminal costs, emergency room visits, health care utilization, child abuse and neglect, lost child support, foster care and welfare costs, reduced productivity, and unemployment.

In 2002, it was estimated that the costs to society of illicit drug abuse alone amounted to $181 billion. Combined with alcohol and tobacco costs, costs exceeded $500 billion, including costs for health care, criminal justice, and lost productivity. Successful drug abuse treatment can help reduce this cost and related crime, as well as the spread of HIV/AIDS, hepatitis, and other infectious diseases. It is estimated that for every dollar spent on addiction treatment programs, there is a $4–$7 reduction in the cost of drug-related crimes. With some outpatient programs, total savings can exceed costs by a ratio of 12:1 [1].

In 2013, the National Institute on Drug Abuse (NIDA) reported that substance abuse currently costs our nation more than $600 billion annually [2]. Drug addiction treatment has been shown to reduce associated health and social costs by far more than the cost of the treatment itself. Treatment is also much less expensive than its alternatives, such as incarcerating addicted persons. According to NIDA, the average cost for one full year of methadone maintenance treatment is approximately $4,700 per patient, whereas one full year of imprisonment costs approximately $24,000 per person [3].

Understanding the Drug User

Drug-dependent people present a danger not only to themselves, but also to those around them. Users may lie to friends and family. They may take advantage of those who attempt to help them. They may steal from loved ones to support their habit, and may be involved in a lifestyle that includes predatory criminal acts such as robbery, assault, and murder. This is why society's response to the drug problem involves not only the medical and health care industries, but also the criminal justice system.

Today, society bears most of the burden for offering treatment to those who have fallen victim to drug abuse. Failure to provide a means for addicts to "get well" not only endangers the lives of the addicts, but also threatens the well-being of those who become victims of drug crimes, communicable diseases such as AIDS, and other related problems. The belief that drug treatment is a supple, nurturing, and easy way out of drug dependency is quite far from the truth. Indeed, to the drug addict, the successful drug treatment program is one that imposes stringent physical and emotional demands, and is therefore an unappealing experience.

It is also a misconception that all drug users develop a dependency and require drug treatment. Indeed, most people who use drugs do not become addicted the first time they use them. For example, the casual drug user (one who uses drugs no more than once a month) does not usually need drug treatment in order to stop using drugs. However, a social and governmental climate of intolerance of drug use is an important ingredient in building a drug-free community.

The heroin or cocaine user who uses the drug once a week is a different story. This person may be able to ward off dependency on his or her own, but is more likely to require a treatment program than those users who fall into the once-a-month category. Still, there are others who are persuaded only by arrest and adjudication through the criminal justice system. Finally, there are those addicts who are physically and psychologically addicted to drugs, and who genuinely require a formalized treatment program such as Narcotics Anonymous (NA).

Studies have been conducted over the past several decades in hopes of identifying biological or personality factors to connect drug use to potential drug users. To date, no empirical evidence exists to show what type of person is the most likely candidate for drug use or addiction, nor is there evidence as to which user can control drug use and which cannot. In reality, many drug users make poor assessments about their ability to tolerate the effects of drugs. In fact, they are often the last to realize that they are addicted.

The use-to-abuse cycle is one that slowly engulfs the drug user. For example, many addicts experience what could be termed a "honeymoon" of drug use early in their abuse cycle. Typically, this begins with the use of alcohol, cigarettes, and sometimes marijuana at a young age. The use-to-abuse cycle then expands over time to the use of harder, more effective drugs. The honeymoon stage may last several years and is usually a manageable period for the drug user. Once the potency of drugs and the instances of use increase, the honeymoon is over and the user is well on his or her way to physical dependency.

Addressing the problem of treatment of drug abusers, former drug czar William Bennett stated in his 1989 National Drug Control Strategy:

> *If our treatment system is to do the job required of it, the system must be expanded and improved. We need more treatment "slots," located where the needs are, in programs designed to meet those needs. We must improve the effectiveness and the efficiency of treatment programs by holding them accountable for their performance. We must find ways to get more drug dependent people into treatment programs, through voluntary and, when necessary, involuntary means. And we need much better information about who is seeking treatment, who is not, and why [4].*

Adding to the list of drug abuse misconceptions is the premise that addicts will eventually come to their senses and seek treatment. Several reasons can be identified to explain why addicts avoid treatment. First, addicts have chosen to seek out the euphoric effects of drugs; they can logically be expected to prefer such effects to the demands of a formal treatment setting. Second, treatment by its very nature denies addicts a form of pleasure: drugs. Finally, because abuse usually involves ingesting illicit drugs, many addicts fear that confidentiality will not be maintained, and that local police may learn their identities.

Many addicts who begin treatment programs eventually drop out and return to their drug-abusing lifestyle. Sometimes this is because addicts are lured back into drug abuse circles by associates. Additionally, they may hope to "stay clean" for a period of time so that their drug tolerance goes down; smaller and cheaper amounts of drugs will then produce better "highs." As mentioned, the drug addiction cycle is compounded by the common use of addictive drugs such as caffeine, alcohol, and nicotine. Regardless of the type of drug on which one becomes dependent, a treatment program must be identified. The immediate objectives of most treatment and rehabilitation programs can be generally characterized in three ways:

1. To control or eliminate drug abuse
2. To give drug users alternatives to their (drug-using) lifestyle
3. To treat medical complications (both physical and psychological) associated with drug use

Problems of drug abuse and addiction also prevail, in part, because such activity is covert in nature. Accordingly, drug use usually comes to the attention of the family and the community only when it has developed into either a personal or a public problem. At this juncture, the drug-dependent person must pursue any of a number of treatment options, which we discuss in this chapter.

The Rise in Addiction

Chapter 2 discussed our nation's gradual acceptance of drug use over many decades, but the problem of addiction has not always been clearly understood. Historically, Americans have alternated between viewing addiction as a medical problem and viewing it as a social ill. Accordingly, the public's response to addiction has vacillated between treatment of offenders and aggressive police crackdowns. During the nineteenth century, medications such as opiates were essential for use by medical practitioners. By the late 1800s, thousands of middle-class women whose doctors had prescribed powdered morphine had become hopelessly addicted. Even then, physicians established asylums to treat those who had become addicted. By the early 1900s, however, synthetic, injectable forms of morphine had been developed, and public concern grew about so-called pleasure users of the drug.

In 1914, the Harrison Narcotics Act was passed as a measure to control the distribution of narcotics. This was followed by Prohibition in 1920, which was designed to curb alcohol consumption. During this period, the government also cracked down on drugs by closing the remaining municipal clinics that had provided low-cost morphine, heroin, and cocaine to registered addicts. As a result, virtually no treatment facilities remained in existence throughout the country. Soon the jails filled with addicts. To ease the overcrowding problem, Congress authorized the building of two massive prisons for narcotic addicts—one in Lexington, Kentucky, which opened in 1935, and the other in Fort Worth, Texas, which opened in 1938. Both institutions offered a mixture of penal and psychotherapeutic environments.

As the 1940s approached, heroin use was growing in major United States cities, followed by what was later called a heroin epidemic in the 1950s. In 1964, Vincent Dole, a physician, and Marie Nyswander, a psychiatrist, published an article about methadone in the *Journal of the American Medical Association*. They reported that addicts who took methadone orally experienced neither withdrawal symptoms nor euphoria from the drug. As a result, they were able to return to reasonably productive lives. Hence, the medical model of addiction was born. As a result, the Nixon-era war on crime helped finance the expansion of methadone maintenance clinics with the hope that addicts would no longer have to commit crimes to finance their drug habits.

Philosophies of addiction were reconsidered during the 1980s with the rise in cocaine use and the arrival of crack on the United States drug scene. Until then, cocaine was so expensive that it was affordable only by the rich and affluent. Almost overnight, crack was available in most major cities at a price almost anyone—especially adolescents—could afford: $5–$10 per rock. Soon crack had replaced heroin as the inner-city drug of choice. This phenomenon forced drug treatment professionals to refocus their efforts from heroin and opiate addiction to cocaine dependency. Accordingly, special problems arose because cocaine use altered the brain's dopamine receptors, which govern the user's sense of pleasure, making users not want to stop. This factor alone presented new and special treatment concerns for clinicians in the 1980s and 1990s.

Treatment Programs

We have thus far learned that there exist many different types of drugs of abuse, drug users, and explanations for involvement in drug-abusing behavior. Just as there is no single typology of drug abuser, programs for drug treatment are diverse, since there is no single treatment for what we know as drug abuse. It might be tempting to try to understand drug abuse under a simple medical model of acute illness, but it is far more complex than that. Symptoms of this chronic disorder and those interventions employed to treat the symptoms range well beyond the physiological and psychological, and may even include explanations that are social, legal, and economic. A treatment program that works well for one user may not work for another due to the dynamics of what motivates drug abuse in the first place.

Treatment programs incorporate psychological and pharmacological components, but also rely on efforts to teach communication skills, interpersonal skills, and the ability to deal with one's involvement in criminal behavior. As noted in Chapter 6, many types of criminal activity are associated with the drug user. Included are drug crimes, such as dealing and possessing controlled drugs; property crimes, such as burglary and larceny; and acts of interpersonal violence. These actions depend on the type of drug being used and the extent of one's dependency. Experts believe a small number of drug users are responsible for the majority of drug-related crime. In general, treatment programs serve both alcohol- and drug-dependent clients, and most of the nation's 5000 treatment programs take place in one of two settings: (1) nonresidential, where the client receives treatment at a specific location but lives elsewhere; and (2) residential, where clients receive treatment and reside at the treatment facility. Typically, residential facilities include hospitals or halfway houses.

In addition to the two types of settings, treatment programs can be divided into one of five categories: (1) detoxification programs, usually inpatient, which have the short-range goal of ending a user's physical addiction to substances; (2) chemical dependency units, primarily private inpatient or residential 3- to 4-week programs; (3) outpatient clinics, offering counseling and support for those who want to stop using drugs while they continue to work in the community; (4) methadone maintenance programs, which treat addicts by coupling counseling with the administration of methadone, a prescription medicine that blocks the craving for heroin while eliminating the usual pain of withdrawal; and (5) residential therapeutic communities, where users may spend up to 18 months in a highly structured program.

Detoxification

When treatment alternatives are considered, the term *detoxification* (often abbreviated to *detox*) is frequently used. Detoxification is usually the first step of the treatment process, and is designed to withdraw patients slowly from their dependence on a particular drug. Its aim is to stabilize heavy drug users until their bodies are relatively free of drugs. This process generally takes from 21 to 45 days and is best performed on an inpatient basis. Detox, in and of itself, is not considered a form of treatment. The distinction is that detoxification helps users get off drugs, whereas treatment helps them stay off. Therefore, experts generally agree that the detoxification process does little good unless it is followed up by a sound treatment program.

Subsequent to the detoxification process, the patient is no longer physically addicted to the drug and, theoretically, is able to abstain from future use of the drug. Research suggests that there is no single method of detoxification that is considered effective in the treatment of all drug abusers. Detoxification procedures are, therefore, individualized to meet the needs of each patient.

A patient's susceptibility to this form of treatment depends on several variables. These include the type of drug to which the patient is addicted, the degree of tolerance that has developed, and how long the patient has been dependent on the particular drug. Let's now look at some typical detoxification scenarios:

- *Heroin detoxification.* The detoxification process for heroin addicts is often futile due to the high incidence of relapse among addicts. Opiate drug addicts tend to have a high relapse rate because they return to peer and social groups that are still involved in drug abuse. Methadone maintenance, which is also discussed in this chapter, is considered one of the more successful ways to accomplish the goal of detoxification.
- *Self-treatment*, or the "cold turkey" approach, is fairly common among heroin addicts and is usually attempted at the addict's home. In some cases, this approach is undertaken in therapeutic communities or with the support of friends. In almost all cases, this type of detoxification is not successful.
- *Alcohol and barbiturate detoxification.* Detoxification or withdrawal from either alcohol or barbiturates is considered extremely dangerous and should be performed only under medical supervision. In this situation, withdrawal may not occur until several days after the last dose. With these two drugs, detoxification is usually accomplished by a physician administering increasingly smaller doses of the drug to the patient to ward off withdrawal symptoms.

- *Marijuana and other hallucinogens.* Because these two categories of drugs are not physically addicting and there are no withdrawal symptoms, detoxification can usually be accomplished with little or no hospitalization.
- *Cocaine and amphetamine detoxification.* Of the two, cocaine poses the greatest challenge in treatment, primarily due to the addict's craving for the drug. So far, there are no proven successful treatment strategies comparable to those that have been developed for heroin addiction. Depression is common in patients experiencing withdrawal from these drugs, and suicide attempts are prevalent. Treatment for cocaine and amphetamines is not usually life-threatening, but can cause great discomfort for the patient.

Maintenance (Substitute Therapy)

Maintenance refers literally to maintaining a drug abuser on a particular type of drug for the purpose of helping him or her avoid the withdrawal syndrome. Opiate drug addiction, for example, is a common problem for many treatment programs because it is so widespread. Because cross-tolerance and cross-dependence exist between all opiates, any of them can be used to eliminate withdrawal symptoms and to detoxify the addicted patient.

Methadone maintenance is the most common type of maintenance program. Methadone, a synthetic narcotic analgesic, was introduced during World War II because of a shortage of morphine. It is an odorless, white crystalline powder that shares many of the same effects as morphine, but the two are structurally dissimilar. Methadone is best known for its use in the controversial methadone maintenance program that was introduced in 1964.

The use of methadone in treatment of people addicted to opiates has always been a controversial practice, but the drug does have one distinct advantage over heroin: methadone is a longer acting drug, requiring less frequent administering. Additionally, the effects of methadone differ from those of heroin. In particular, methadone has a longer duration of action, lasting up to 24 hours and thereby permitting the administration of the drug once a day as treatment for heroin addiction. Time-tested results of methadone maintenance reveal that addicts who went through the program had much less criminal involvement, and were better able to function within their communities.

As mentioned, the effects of methadone closely resemble the effects of morphine and heroin, but fail to provide the user with the euphoric effects caused by those two drugs. Methadone is also an extremely physically addicting drug—a fact that has created much of the controversy surrounding its use. The program is structured so that the patient leaves a urine sample at the clinic, where the urine is tested for signs of morphine (heroin is excreted as morphine) and other drugs. Once patients have demonstrated that they are responsible and committed to rehabilitation, they are permitted to take a one-day supply of methadone. Later, the take-home dosage is increased to a three-day supply.

Detoxification is achieved through slowly reducing the amount of methadone mixture administered to the patient. Frequently, however, addicts find that their psychological dependence is more difficult to overcome than their physical dependence, and therefore many addicts remain in the program for most of their lives.

FIGURE 14.1 Protesters hold signs supporting MAD (Middlesboro Against Drugs) in their opposition to a methadone clinic in Middlesboro, Kentucky. *Source: AP Photo/Middlesboro Daily News.*

Narcotic Antagonists

The term *narcotic antagonists* refers to a category of drugs that are developed as a treatment for heroin addiction, but that do not produce physical dependence. These drugs, as the name implies, block or reverse the effects of drugs in the narcotic category. Naloxone (Narcan), which has no morphine-like effects, was introduced in 1971 as a specific antidote for narcotic poisoning. Nalorphine (Nalline), introduced into clinical medicine in 1951 and now under Schedule III, is termed a narcotic agonist-antagonist. In a drug-free individual, nalorphine produces morphine-like effects, whereas in an individual under the influence of narcotics, it counteracts these effects. Another agonist-antagonist is pentazocine (Talwin). Introduced as an analgesic in 1967, it was determined to be an abusable drug and was placed under Schedule IV in 1979.

■ ■ Critical Thinking Task ■

Assume that your community has committed local funds to building and maintaining a drug treatment center and you have been asked to serve on the center's board of directors. After studying various kinds of treatment centers, you decide which one would best fit the needs of the city. Defend your choice to the rest of the board.

Naltrexone

Naltrexone is a long-acting synthetic opiate antagonist with few side effects that is taken orally either daily or three times a week for a sustained period of time. For opiate addicts, treatment using naltrexone usually is conducted in outpatient settings, although initiation of the medication often begins after medical detoxification in a residential setting.

To prevent precipitating an opiate abstinence syndrome, individuals must be medically detoxified and opiate-free for several days before naltrexone can be taken. When the substance is used this way, all the effects of self-administered opiates, including euphoria, are completely blocked. The theory behind this treatment is that the repeated lack of the desired opiate effects, as well as the perceived futility of using the opiate, will gradually over time result in breaking the habit of opiate addiction. Naltrexone itself has no subjective effects or potential for abuse, and it is not addicting. Patient noncompliance is a common problem. Therefore, a favorable treatment outcome requires that there also be a positive therapeutic relationship, effective counseling or therapy, and careful monitoring of medication compliance.

Many experienced clinicians have found naltrexone most useful for highly motivated, recently detoxified patients who desire total abstinence because of external circumstances, including impaired professionals, parolees, probationers, and prisoners in work-release status. Patients stabilized on naltrexone can function normally. They can hold jobs, avoid the crime and violence of the street culture, and reduce their exposure to HIV by stopping injection drug use and drug-related high-risk sexual behavior [5].

The Therapeutic Approach

As with most psychotherapeutic types of treatment, a lengthy commitment is generally required on the patient's part. The role of the psychoanalyst in drug treatment is to identify repressed feelings in the patient that were experienced early in life and may contribute to drug abuse. Once the feelings or thoughts are uncovered, they can be dealt with through traditional psychoanalytic methods. Studies have shown that the length of treatment ranges from a few weeks to several years, and that the success rate for recovery is marginal at best.

Group Treatment

Group therapy in drug treatment has demonstrated one of the highest success rates of any type of drug treatment program. Group treatment programs use an approach that creates an environment of personal interaction between peers. In theory, group interaction is more successful than the one-on-one interaction between the psychoanalyst and the patient. This is because the analyst often lacks a basic understanding of the drug abuse process and other variables that contribute to addiction. The analyst, therefore, often acts as a facilitator for the group. The treatment group may be formed during different phases of addiction and treatment, and may involve not just the patients but their families and friends as well.

Long-Term Residential Treatment

Long-term residential treatment provides care 24 hours per day, generally in a nonhospital setting. The best-known residential treatment model is the *therapeutic community* (TC), but residential treatment may also employ other models, such as cognitive-behavioral therapy. TCs are residential programs with planned lengths of stay of 6–12 months. TCs focus on the "resocialization" of the individual and use the program's entire "community," including other residents, staff, and the social context, as active components of treatment. Addiction is viewed in the context of an individual's social and psychological deficits, and treatment focuses on developing personal accountability and responsibility, and socially productive lives. Treatment is highly structured and can at times be confrontational, with activities designed to help residents examine damaging beliefs, self-concepts, and patterns of behavior and to adopt new, more harmonious, and more constructive ways to interact with others. Many TCs are quite comprehensive and can include employment training and other support services on site.

Compared with patients in other forms of drug treatment, the typical TC resident has more severe problems, with more co-occurring mental health problems and more criminal involvement. Research shows that TCs can be modified to treat individuals with special needs, including adolescents, women, those with severe mental disorders, and individuals in the criminal justice system.

Short-Term Residential Programs

Short-term residential programs provide intensive but relatively brief residential treatment based on a modified 12-step approach. These programs were originally designed to treat alcohol problems, but during the cocaine epidemic of the mid-1980s, many began to treat illicit drug abuse and addiction as well. The original residential treatment model consisted of a 3- to 6-week hospital-based inpatient treatment phase followed by extended outpatient therapy and participation in a self-help group, such as Alcoholics Anonymous (AA). Reduced health care coverage for substance abuse treatment has resulted in a diminished number of these programs, and the average length of stay under managed care review is much shorter than in early programs.

Outpatient Drug-Free Treatment

Outpatient drug-free treatment is yet another alternative that costs less than residential or inpatient treatment, and often is more suitable for individuals who are employed or who have extensive social supports. Low-intensity programs may offer little more than drug education and admonition. Other outpatient models, such as intensive day treatment, can be comparable to residential programs in services and effectiveness, depending on the individual patient's characteristics and needs. In many outpatient programs, group counseling is emphasized. Some outpatient programs are designed to treat patients who have medical or mental health problems in addition to their drug disorder.

Narcotics Anonymous

Narcotics Anonymous (NA) is an organization devoted to helping addicts recover from drug addiction. It began in California in 1953. Since then, NA has spread to all parts of the

United States (and some foreign countries) and supports a World Service Office that unifies its global efforts. The NA program was adapted from AA, from which NA borrowed its 12-step program for recovering addicts. The philosophy of NA basically says: if you want what we have to offer and are willing to make the effort to get it, then you are ready to take certain steps. The NA group operates in a relatively structured manner; that is, it has regular meetings at specified places and times. It is suggested that group members follow the Twelve Steps of Narcotics Anonymous. NA groups are registered with the World Service Office in Los Angeles.

The goal of the organization is to carry the wellness message to the addict, as well as to provide group members a chance to express themselves and hear the experiences of others. NA offers two types of meetings: open (to the general public) and closed (for addicts only). The meetings vary in format from group to group; some are participation meetings, some are question-and-answer sessions, some are meetings for the discussion of special problems, and some are a combination of some or all of these formats.

THE TWELVE STEPS OF NARCOTICS ANONYMOUS

1. We admitted that we were powerless over our addiction, that our lives had become unmanageable.
2. We came to believe that a Power greater than ourselves could restore us to sanity.
3. We made a decision to turn our will and our lives over to the care of God as we understood Him.
4. We made a searching and fearless moral inventory of ourselves.
5. We admitted to God, to ourselves, and to another human being the exact nature of our wrongs.
6. We were entirely ready to have God remove all these defects of character.
7. We humbly asked Him to remove our shortcomings.
8. We made a list of all persons we had harmed, and became willing to make amends to them all.
9. We made direct amends to such people wherever possible, except when to do so would injure them or others.
10. We continued to take personal inventory and when we were wrong promptly admitted it.
11. We sought through prayer and meditation to improve our conscious contact with God as we understood Him, praying only for knowledge of His will for us and the power to carry that out.
12. Having had a spiritual awakening as a result of these steps, we tried to carry this message to addicts, and to practice these principles in all our affairs.

Source: Reprinted by permission of NA World Services, Inc. All rights reserved. Twelve Steps of NA reprinted for adaptation by permission of AA World Services.

Does Drug Treatment Work?

Occasionally, newspaper articles about recovered addicts surface, giving the impression that another addicted life has been spared through successful treatment. However, one of the hard truths about drug treatment is that experts know very little about the effectiveness of such programs. The assumption that drug treatment works is based on reports from clinicians and recovered drug addicts. Most research is so poorly conducted that it is difficult to know whether treatment cures any more people than would have stopped using drugs on their own [6]. For example, studies have shown that between 45 and 70 percent of alcoholics are known to recover, but little empirical information is available for the rate of recovery for illegal drug users [7].

To assess the effectiveness of drug treatment programs, we should first consider the goals of treatment. Although total abstinence may seem to be a likely goal of treatment, experts have suggested that lifelong abstinence from alcohol or other drugs on the first try should not be the measure of success. Indeed, treatment goals are not restricted to simply reducing the consumption of drugs, but also to reducing the demand for drugs, cutting down on related street crime, and improving the user's overall physical and mental health. Furthermore, clinicians have argued that the ultimate goal is to allow people to return to a normal, productive life—however that can be accomplished. Once again, this leads us back to the issue of gauging the "effectiveness" of treatment. However, as discussed earlier, a full recovery from drug dependency is not only unlikely but unrealistic. Complicating factors include the length of time that may be required for detoxification, as well as the patient's inclination for relapse.

We do know that some treatment programs seem to have more positive outcomes than others. For example, the methadone maintenance program, which has been intensely studied since it originated in 1964, has the best documented success record. In the program, addicts are given a daily dose of methadone, which is designed to block the craving for heroin and other opiates. More than three decades of experience with methadone maintenance programs show that drug users tend to be less prone to drug consumption and criminal activity when maintained on the drug. Some controversy exists as to whether methadone simply substitutes one addicting drug for another [8]. Furthermore, drug addicts graduating from both therapeutic communities and methadone programs seem to perform better than addicts who fail to complete these treatment programs. Length of stay seems to have a high correlation with better patient outcomes.

Most people who enter drug treatment do so reluctantly, often under pressure from family, friends, or the government. One of the most important observations regarding drug treatment is the positive effects of court-imposed treatment. From time to time, judges will impose treatment as a condition of probation. In addition, corrections institutions will sometimes offer treatment programs for inmates. Studies have shown, however, that legal pressure from the criminal justice system tends to keep people in treatment longer. One such study is the Treatment Outcome Prospective Study (TOPS), a 1989 comprehensive study conducted at the Research Triangle Institute. The study showed that one of every two addicts seeking treatment did so because of an encounter with the criminal justice system, and not just because of a personal desire to kick the habit. Ironically, another TOPS study concluded that those addicts required to undergo treatment by court order do as well as those who do so under their own volition. Such studies therefore support the role of the criminal justice system in drug treatment and control.

Drug Treatment in Lieu of Prison

It is in many ways ironic that the overwhelming proportion of funds allocated at local, state, and federal levels to combat the problem of drugs has been directed at law enforcement efforts, such as interdiction and intensive enforcement, which have shown little hope of positive results. Trying to solve what some perceive as a public health problem with punitive enforcement policies not only antagonizes the problem, but also ignores policies that show great promise of actually doing something about drug use and its ancillary problems. Law enforcement tactics spread a wide net that targets a majority of people who are engaged in behavior that is problematic for society, but it misses an enormous number of people whose behavior and health problems should be specifically addressed. It is important to note that more than 40 million United States citizens use illicit drugs, but only about 6 million of those drug users are classified as drug abusers or drug addicts [9].

Compounding this irony is the fact that those 6 million problem drug users are denied access to a policy initiative that would benefit them: drug treatment. Drug addiction and drug abuse are health problems that can be both treated and managed. The diversion of funds away from treatment programs to interdiction and enforcement assures the continuation of a stable population of individuals who are social problems, while arresting and incarcerating large numbers of people who pose little or no social threat.

No single type of drug treatment works for all drug abusers. As with cigarette smokers, users of other drugs often have to attempt several different approaches before finding one that works. Social factors, lifestyle factors, patterns of drug use, and available support networks in the family and community all combine to impact the effectiveness of drug treatment and the appropriateness of treatment styles for individual users. Nonetheless, the fact remains that treatment works in reducing drug use and in ameliorating most of the troublesome ancillary behaviors associated with drug abuse. The only thing necessary for treatment to work is that it be available, and that drug abusers be given sufficient opportunity to try different modalities until they find the one that works best for them.

Many drug abusers are able to manage their problem through programs similar to those of AA. NA and other similar groups are voluntary self-help associations of drug abusers who follow a structured program that makes extensive use of member support as they progress through the several stages of recovery from drug abuse. Because these self-help groups protect their members' confidentiality and do not keep attendance roles at their meetings, it is impossible to measure their effectiveness statistically. There is, however, considerable anecdotal evidence for the effectiveness of this approach, and many other treatment programs have incorporated parts of the self-help regimen into their treatment plans.

Often, when we think of drug abuse treatment programs, we think in terms of highly structured, long-term residential inpatient programs referred to as therapeutic communities. As a general rule, patients spend up to a year in a TC, both living and working in the facility. Individual counseling and group therapy programs are used to help patients identify and deal with the causes and effects of their drug abuse and the other problems in their lives impacting on their drug abuse. Counselors and social workers work with the patients to help them rebuild their lives through education, vocational training, and work experience. The educational and training components are particularly important features of the treatment program, because many drug abusers lack the necessary skills for attaining and holding on to decent jobs. As the therapy progresses, patients who are judged to be progressing and showing patterns of success are reintroduced to the outside world, first through jobs and then through halfway houses outside the residential community.

For drug abusers with available financial resources or private health insurance, a less demanding and restrictive alternative to therapeutic communities is available. Inpatient programs of much shorter duration are available for people of means. Probably the two best-known private inpatient treatment programs are at the Betty Ford Center in Palm Springs, California, and the Hazelden Foundation in Center City, Minnesota. In these programs, patients typically commit to 4 weeks of in-residence care involving intensive individual counseling, group therapy, and NA or AA meetings. Patients are then discharged to aftercare programs in which they receive continuing outpatient treatment.

The most commonly used outpatient treatment for narcotics (heroin and opiate) addiction in the United States is the methadone maintenance program. Methadone is a long-lasting synthetic opiate. When it is administered to heroin addicts, the addicts do not experience withdrawal symptoms, and they lose the desire to use heroin. In addition, unlike heroin, methadone does not impair normal physical functioning or interfere with the ability to maintain a job and perform normal tasks such as driving. Initially, methadone patients receive daily doses. As the treatment progresses and the patient demonstrates that he or she is free of heroin and is maintaining steady employment, the dosage schedule becomes more flexible. Methadone maintenance programs also provide counseling, health care services, vocational rehabilitation, and educational services. Many methadone patients remain in the programs for many years at reduced doses, and some leave the treatment program entirely.

Finally, for some drug abusers who are unable to commit to residential treatment, and who either do not want to be maintained on methadone or are abusing a drug other than an opiate, a wide variety of drug-free therapies are available. Some involve "talk therapies," but others involve treatments such as acupuncture, which is used to reduce the craving for drugs. An innovative program in this regard is found at Lincoln Hospital in New York City, which for the past 15 years has administered an acupuncture program designed to control withdrawal symptoms and reduce drug cravings. Like methadone treatments, acupuncture involves daily procedures in the beginning, gradually moving to less frequently scheduled treatments.

Critics of drug treatment programs argue that the failure rate is high and relapses are common, thereby ostensibly justifying a law enforcement approach to drug control. Herbert Kleber, former deputy director of the Office of National Drug Control Policy, and now medical director of the National Center on Addiction and Substance Abuse and lecturer in psychiatry at Columbia University College of Physicians and Surgeons, identified the basic fallacy in this pessimistic outlook:

> *Drug dependence has been viewed as a chronic relapsing illness with an unfavorable prognosis. However, there are thousands of formerly dependent individuals in the United States and elsewhere who have remained off both illicit drugs and excess use of licit drugs like alcohol for decades, functioning as productive citizens.... [T]here are already effective methods of treatment if the right approach [and] the right person can be brought together [10].*

As most people know, efforts to stop smoking cigarettes and to stop drinking alcohol often require several treatment efforts before they are effective. Similarly, few people are able to manage and overcome addictions to other drugs in an initial effort. Relapses are likely, primarily because several treatment regimes may have to be tried before finding the one that will best help a particular person in his or her particular social setting [11]. On the other hand, there is one possible "bullet" that has not been fully tested because of the drug laws themselves. Ibogaine, a mild hallucinogen prohibited from use by federal law, has, in preliminary studies, shown a remarkable ability to break heroin addictions and addictions to other drugs after one administration. Drug prohibition probably has slowed down medicine in trying to assess the effectiveness of this therapy.

Beyond questions of resource allocation and possible relapse, one key statement about drug treatment can be made with certainty: drug treatment works. Drug treatment not only can successfully break patterns of addiction and abuse, but also, much more importantly, impacts positively on ancillary social problems linked to drug abuse. Virtually every evaluation study done in the past 2 decades has shown conclusively that the most commonly utilized modalities of drug treatment work. Whether the studies have evaluated methadone treatment programs, inpatient residential programs, or outpatient drug-free programs, they all produce evidence of dramatic and positive results [12].

As mentioned in this chapter, TOPS, which is funded by NIDA, is the most comprehensive evaluation study of the effectiveness of drug treatment done in the United States. TOPS found drug treatment programs to be extremely effective in reducing drug use [13]. The researchers tracked 10,000 drug abusers for a 5-year period following their admission to one of the 37 treatment programs being evaluated. Heroin and cocaine use declined markedly for patients in all three treatment modalities. After only one year in methadone maintenance programs, patients found that heroin use had declined by 70 percent. Heroin and cocaine use dropped by 75 percent for patients in outpatient drug-free programs, and by 56 percent for patients in residential treatment. By the end of the 5-year tracking period, less than 20 percent of the patients used any illegal drug except marijuana, and 40–50 percent of the patients abstained from all psychoactive drugs—legal or illegal—altogether [14].

Other evaluation studies have shown strikingly similar results. A NIDA-sponsored study looking at the risk of AIDS infection for intravenous drug users found that methadone maintenance reduced intravenous drug use by 71 percent [15]. An earlier NIDA study, the Drug Abuse Report Program (DARP), followed the drug use patterns of 44,000 opiate addicts from 1969 through 1974. The DARP study found that most patients stopped using opiates daily upon the inception of treatment, and had not resumed daily use after discharge. Seventy-six percent of the patients in methadone therapy, 74 percent of the patients in therapeutic communities, and 72 percent of the patients in outpatient programs did not resume the daily use of opiates [16]. Much more importantly, a follow-up study found that 74 percent of the patients were not using heroin on a regular basis 12 years after their treatment had ended.

What is remarkable about the evaluations of the three most common drug treatment modalities is that researchers have found them effective despite the many personal problems impacting clients, such as clients' long histories of deviant lifestyles, clients' long absences from medical care, and a lack of support for clients' efforts in their communities [17].

Although pessimistic appraisals of the efficacy of drug treatment programs in reducing drug use seem to be overstated, evaluations of the impact of drug treatment programs on problems ancillary to drug use offer even stronger evidence for a commitment to drug treatment rather than drug enforcement. For example, studies evaluating the impact of drug treatment on the transmission of HIV and other diseases carried in the blood show remarkable results. The rate of HIV infection for addicts living in New York City (46–47 percent) is twice that of addicts in methadone maintenance programs (23–27 percent). Even more notable is the fact that a study tracking the history of methadone patients with 10 or more years in treatment found that none of them tested positive for HIV [18].

Drug treatment also appears to reduce criminal involvement by drug abusers and drug addicts. The TOPS study showed that in the first 6 months following treatment, 97 percent of the residential TC clients and 70 percent of outpatient clients who had self-reported participation in predatory crimes during the previous year engaged in no criminal activity at all. Three to five years after treatment, the proportion of addicts involved in predatory crimes fell between 50 and 67 percent [19]. In looking at all treatment modalities, the DARP study found that arrest rates fell by 74 percent after treatment for all patients and clients.

In addition to reducing levels of criminal involvement and reducing high-risk health behaviors, drug treatment programs also show success in helping clients stabilize their lives. Only one-third of the 44,000 patients in the DARP study worked in the year prior to entering drug treatment. However, in the year following their discharge, 57 percent were holding jobs. More than two-thirds of the patients who had been involved in therapeutic communities were employed after ending treatment. The TOPS study found the same pattern. Three to five years after patients left treatment, the employment level of residential program patients had doubled, and the outpatient program participants increased employment levels by more than one-half.

The other benefits of shifting priorities from law enforcement to drug treatment are equally important and less subtle. For example, addicts develop a wide range of health problems, including chronic illnesses such as hepatitis and tuberculosis, as well as lifestyle maladies such as malnutrition and psychological difficulties [20]. Addicts in drug treatment programs have access to regular medical care, nutritional counseling, and psychological services. The cost of supplying emergency and outpatient services to drug addicts is considerable. Drug treatment not only helps in diagnosing and treating existing conditions, but also places clients in programs in which health maintenance is easier. In addition, drug treatment programs reduce the spread of diseases from drug addicts to others, thereby lowering medical costs even more.

One research study calculated that when the costs of crimes committed, unemployment, and medical treatment for drug addicts are combined, they exceed the cost of supplying drug treatment by a factor of 10–25 times, depending on the treatment modality chosen. The most cost-effective of the modalities was treating addicts in long-term residential programs, which amounted to only 4 percent of the cost to society of not treating the addict. Drug treatment is clearly much more cost-effective than incarceration. In New York City, residential drug treatment costs about $17,000 a year per client, and outpatient treatment costs $2,000–$4,000 a year per client. Putting that addict in a prison cell costs $40,000 a year, and the cost of building that cell is about $100,000 [21]. Recalling that the evaluation studies have also strongly suggested that drug treatment reduces the frequency of criminal behavior and recidivism, this is a savings that would accrue many times over for each addict treated.

The research clearly indicates that drug treatment works and works well. Not only is it less expensive than using a law enforcement strategy against drugs, it also does something prison cannot: it produces healthier, more productive individuals who engage in less criminality and make fewer demands on public coffers for social and medical services. Drug treatment also does what law enforcement has been unable to do—that is, it successfully reduces the overall demand for drugs.

Social Reintegration

Social reintegration is the process whereby the benefits gained from treatment and rehabilitation are sustained, and drug users adapt to a drug-free, productive existence within the community. This can happen in several ways: they can return to their families, they can complete or further their education, they can learn new skills, they can become employed on a full-time or part-time basis, they can continue participation in self-help groups, or they can develop friendships in non-drug-using environments.

FIGURE 14.2 The Talbert House in Cincinnati, Ohio, offers a variety of treatment services for offenders with substance abuse histories. This residential substance abuse program provides assessment, employment, and chemical dependency services, and reintegration for drug-dependent men. *Source: Ellen S. Boyne.*

Statistics show that most drug addicts lack a formal education. In many cases, they drop out of high school, and when they attempt to get jobs, they find themselves at a serious disadvantage. For those who do get jobs, frequently they are fired because of absenteeism due to drug abuse. Unemployment contributes to the drug-using cycle, and social reintegration then becomes difficult and sometimes impossible. Halfway houses were developed, in part, to help bridge the transition between drug abuse and reintegration back into the community. In these houses, residents have responsibility for their own lives, preparing food, cleaning their rooms, and managing their own money matters. Other members, as well as therapeutic staff members, offer the residents support and assistance in coping with the stress of learning to live independently.

Relapse

Over a period of years, drug misuse may be somewhat cyclical, and many people grow out of their drug dependence over time. Studies have revealed that even during the course of abusing drugs, periods of abstinence occur. Thus, it is not uncommon for drug users to drop out of a program before its completion. Programs, therefore, must be prepared to readmit patients who have dropped out so that those patients have an opportunity to achieve control over their own drug use.

Research has shown that many drug users experience a temporary *relapse* (i.e., recurrence of drug misuse) at the end of treatment and rehabilitation. In many cases, however, after a period of a few weeks or months, these same users often achieve long-term stability and, eventually, abstinence. This finding strongly suggests that treatment opportunities offered by rehabilitation and social reintegration can be an important means of reducing the demand for drugs at early stages of abuse.

Problems with Drug Treatment

Factors that complicate the treatment process are attributed to both the psychological and the physiological characteristics of drug addiction. Addiction differs from diseases that are considered treatable through conventional medical methods. One major logistical problem to overcome is the lack of treatment capacity. Many publicly funded programs, particularly those in large cities, maintain long waiting lists. If addicts realize they may not get treatment for several months, their drive to seek help may greatly diminish.

Unfortunately, many treatment centers are not located in towns, cities, or neighborhoods where the need for treatment is greatest. For this reason, some programs have vacancies and others have waiting lists. Moreover, new drug treatment programs are difficult to begin, since funding is sometimes hard to secure, and residents are frequently opposed to treatment centers being located in their neighborhoods.

Another problem in the drug treatment process is the soaring cost of health care. Drug treatment in the United States is a big business and accounts for millions of dollars in private, corporate, and insurance monies. For some employers, for example, costs of inpatient treatment may run as high as $1,000 a day for a 28-day treatment program.

Today, trends indicate that fewer patients are referred to inpatient care in lieu of the readily available, lower-cost outpatient programs. The dilemma becomes manifest when one tries to balance the cost of treatment with the quality of treatment—a frustrating and difficult task. Studies show that many people gravitate toward "brand-name" hospitals or rehabilitation services, regardless of their recovery rates.

When searching for a treatment solution, drug counselors tend to look for variables such as whether the hospital is approved by the Joint Commission on Accreditation of Hospitals, the availability of extended outpatient aftercare, the quality of the staff, and the institution's recovery rate.

As we have seen, many treatment programs exist for the drug-dependent person. The most effective programs insist on a sound code of conduct, individual responsibility, personal sacrifice, and sanctions for misbehavior. The evidence is mounting to support the contention that when these elements exist, the best results are attained.

The Cost of Drug Treatment

When considering the great need for drug treatment programs, one should first consider that the largest proportion of drug addicts is white males between the ages of 18 and 40. Many such individuals have the financial means or health insurance with which to pay for treatment. However, many do not. At private institutions, where these addicts most commonly seek treatment, it is not uncommon to have vacancy rates of up to 45 percent. Publicly supported facilities were financially strapped during the 1970s and 1980s, and were unprepared for the great influx of addicts generated by the crack epidemic. Federal funding increased in the late 1980s and early 1990s to compensate for this rise.

If a single variable that most greatly impedes the improvement and expansion of treatment were identified, it would be the lack of trained, qualified personnel. In many cities, salaries are often too low to attract or retain people with proper training. Indeed, many starting salaries for drug treatment counselors begin at or below $14,000 per year, a figure that is unrealistically low for a professional position. Although improvements are slowly being made in this area, it will be some time before the competency and responsibility of treatment meets the needs of most communities.

Drug Prevention

Although as a rule most drug abuse begins during one's teenage years, many young people start using drugs much sooner. For that reason, most prevention programs focus on younger people. The goal of prevention is to ensure that Americans, especially children, never begin the cycle of drug abuse, even through experimentation.

Unquestionably, drug prevention should begin in the home, with the parents of the potential drug user as the primary facilitators. After the home, school is probably the most effective place for the drug education process to take place. School is where children spend a majority of their time, and where they are subjected to peer groups. Additionally, it is at school where first-time drug users frequently acquire their drugs.

Drug prevention through education is designed to reach people who are not yet personally affected by drug abuse, to inform people about the hazards of drugs, and to reduce curiosity about drugs. Prevention strategists have identified two ways to influence young people against taking drugs. The first is to make people not want to use them, and the second is to warn of severe penalties, to convince potential users that the consequences of drug abuse outweigh the advantages. One of the more disturbing trends revealed by surveys on drug abuse is the decline in the average age of first-time substance abusers. In numerous studies, substantial numbers of school-age children have reported initiating the use of alcohol, tobacco, and marijuana by the time they reach junior high school.

Schools are also primary sources of drug prevention programs, and are well equipped for such undertakings. In addition to many community resources being housed within local schools, young people are required to spend much of their time there and are thus more accessible to prevention programs than are other people. As a rule, students in their final year of elementary school are targeted for prevention programs because the junior high school years are thought to be the time in which many students begin their drug experimentation. In addition to drug education classes, many schools have sponsored other types of prevention programs. For example, schools employ counseling and guidance for students in addition to sponsoring substance-free extracurricular activities and peer support groups. Each is thought to show promise in enhancing the quality and effectiveness of drug prevention.

Communities and neighborhoods also play a role in developing drug-related prevention programs. Many of these programs are sponsored by churches, civic organizations, or parent groups; their content, educational focus, and financial backing may differ greatly. An example of a community-based prevention program is Skills Mastery and Resistance Training (SMART) Moves, which is associated with the Boys and Girls Clubs of

America. Trained staff involve youths in addressing problems of drug abuse, alcohol, and teen pregnancy. Other community-based prevention programs include a school-based program called the Midwestern Prevention Project, which interfaces with community groups and parents, and Fighting Back, which requires all participating communities to establish a task force of community representatives to join forces in drug prevention activities.

Various prevention efforts have also been implemented by law enforcement agencies to address the drug abuse problem. Conventional wisdom in recent years has held that the most effective initiatives should focus on building the self-esteem of young people, improving their decision-making skills, and enhancing their ability to resist peer pressure to use drugs.

Prevention Programs

An important part of drug prevention is the development of programs that prevent illicit drug use, keep drugs out of neighborhoods and schools, and provide a safe and secure environment for all people. Examples include the following:

- *Boys and Girls Clubs of America.* Boys and Girls Clubs programs and services promote and enhance the development of boys and girls by instilling a sense of competence, usefulness, belonging, and influence. Their program areas include education; health; arts; careers; alcohol, drug, pregnancy, and gang prevention; leadership development; and athletics.
- *Centers for the Application of Prevention Technologies (CAPT).* The primary mission of the national CAPT system is to bring research to practice by assisting states and jurisdictions and community-based organizations in the application of the latest research-based knowledge to their substance abuse prevention programs, practices, and policies.
- *Center for Substance Abuse Prevention (CSAP) Model Programs.* The CSAP model programs offer a website that serves as a comprehensive resource on preventing substance abuse and creating sustained positive change in our nation's communities. The featured model programs have been tested in communities and schools across the United States, and have proven to prevent or decrease substance abuse in youth.
- *Division of Workplace Programs.* The Division of Workplace Programs' drug-free workplace initiatives include a clear policy of no use; employee education about the dangers of illicit drug use and the workplace consequences of drug use; supervisor training about their responsibilities under the policy; access to employee assistance programs (EAPs) and treatment referral; and accurate and reliable drug testing, consistent with the policy.
- *Drug-Free Communities Support Program.* The Drug-Free Communities Program is designed to assist community-based coalitions' efforts to reduce alcohol, tobacco, illicit drug, and inhalant abuse by youths. The program enables the coalitions to strengthen their coordination and prevention efforts, encourage citizen participation in substance abuse reduction efforts, and disseminate information about effective programs.

Prevention through Education

School- and community-based drug educational programs should be designed to educate children about drugs and the potential for drug abuse, and provide children with alternatives to socialization experiences that might lead them to drug use. Both experience and logic convince us that if educational programs are realistic and credible, they should divert children from initial experimentation with drugs.

Education has been demonstrated to be an effective tool in preventing the initiation of tobacco use. Similar school- and community-based programs should be effective in preventing and reducing alcohol and other drug use among young people. Attention must be paid to what types of educational programs work and what types are less effective. There is a common public assumption that any form of "education" must be good. That assumption is incorrect; not all forms of drug education are equally effective [22].

Evaluation research directed at drug education and prevention programs strongly suggests that long-term programs emphasizing the social influences leading to alcohol, tobacco, and other drug use are far more successful in diverting and reducing subsequent use than are other types of programs. These educational programs are typically conducted in concert with community prevention and home education programs. The short-term education programs, conducted outside overarching community programs, have proved ineffective in actually reducing drug use. Among the most successful drug education programs are the following:

- *Life Skills Training Program* is a 15-session program for junior high school students that emphasizes personal coping skills that will lead to better decision-making and greater confidence in social settings. The program has been used for the past 10 years in 150 schools in New York and New Jersey. Evaluations of the program have demonstrated that rates of tobacco and marijuana consumption are one-half to three-quarters lower among program participants than among their peers.
- *Students Taught Awareness and Resistance* is a 13-session program for first-year high school students, coordinated with community, media, and family programs, and emphasizing resistance skills and the social undesirability of drugs. The initial program is followed by a five-session refresher course the following school year. A 5-year follow-up study to this program determined that it resulted in reductions of marijuana, tobacco, and alcohol use by between 20 and 40 percent, and in cocaine use by 50 percent [23].
- *Project Healthy Choices* is a program directed toward sixth and seventh graders that integrates discussions about alcohol and other drugs into the everyday curriculum of all students in all subjects. The program is being utilized in about 100 New York City schools.
- *Student Assistance Program* (SAP) has been implemented in high schools in more than 20 states. The program's primary focus is making available voluntary confidential counseling to students during the school day. A study of the program's effectiveness in the Westchester County, New York, school system found a significant reduction in alcohol

and marijuana use. In addition, the study found that overall levels of drug use, drinking, and tobacco use were 30 percent lower among students at schools that had initiated the SAP program.

- *SMART Moves (Skills Mastery and Resistance Training)* is a program run by Boys and Girls Clubs in inner cities, particularly targeting children in high-crime neighborhoods. SMART Moves offers after-school prevention programs, along with recreational, educational, and vocational programs. The program teaches children to recognize the social pressures to use drugs and to develop the requisite verbal and social skills to resist those pressures. Evaluation studies have shown significant reductions in cocaine and crack use among participants, as well as marked improvements in behavior at school.

- *Seattle Social Development Project* is a comprehensive program that tries to strengthen the bond between children from high-crime neighborhoods and their families and schools. The program teaches parents various techniques for monitoring their children, it instructs teachers in how to maintain order and resolve conflicts in schools, and it teaches children how to resist peer pressure.

Finally, a number of cities are attempting to develop prevention programs geared toward the children of drug addicts. These programs attempt to teach parents communication and parenting skills, and provide children with support and social skills.

These education programs are already available in communities throughout the country. Successful programs are those in which the school and the community have demonstrated a commitment to implementing comprehensive programs directed not just at children, but also at parents and teachers. The most successful programs clearly demonstrate the need for education that goes beyond simple warnings about the dangers of drugs and alcohol. They also provide additional support structures that assist children in resisting the pressures of peer drug use.

Two additional prevention approaches are Drug Abuse Resistance Education (DARE), which originated in Los Angeles, and School Program to Educate and Control Drug Abuse (SPECDA), which began in New York City.

Project DARE

One of the main points of this chapter is that many different organizations and agencies, both private and public, are involved in drug prevention efforts. Project *DARE* is one such example. It began as a joint project between the Los Angeles Police Department and the Los Angeles Unified School District. Its purpose is to equip fifth-, sixth-, and seventh-grade children with the skills and motivation to resist peer pressure to use drugs, alcohol, and tobacco. A particularly innovative aspect of the program is the use of full-time, uniformed police officers (selected and trained by DARE's supervisory staff) as instructors. The project uses a variety of educational techniques, including lectures, videotapes, and exercises, to teach students how to resist drugs. The community policing philosophy is also used in that attempts are made to develop positive attitudes toward police officers.

DARE programs send full-time, uniformed police officers to schools to teach grade-school children self-management techniques for resisting peer pressure.

The core curriculum consists of a 17-lesson program, each of which consists of a 45- to 60-minute lesson that teaches children various self-management skills and techniques for resisting peer pressure. The focus of the training rests on the premise that children who feel positive about themselves will be more successful in resisting peer pressure. Other lessons emphasize the physical, mental, and social consequences of drug abuse, and still others identify the different methods of coping with stress and having fun.

The scope of the 17-lesson DARE program core curriculum is as follows:

1. *Practices for personal safety.* Students are acquainted with the role of the police officer and methods to protect themselves from harm. The thrust of the lesson is to explain to the students the need for rules and laws designed to protect people from harm. The instructor and the students review a list of students' rights, which is contained in a notebook provided to each student. Finally, teachers instruct students in using the 911 emergency system to summon help.

2. *Drug use and misuse.* This segment explains the definition of drugs, and the positive and negative effects of drugs on the body and mind. Each student then takes a true-false test that assesses understanding of the lesson. The teacher defines the word *consequences*, and the class considers the consequences of various actions. The students then discuss the consequences of using and not using drugs.

3. *Consequences.* The class discusses both negative and positive consequences of using drugs during this lesson. The students fill out a worksheet that directs them to list positive and negative consequences of using marijuana and alcohol. The officer points out that those who try to persuade others to use drugs will emphasize positive consequences, leaving the many negative consequences unstated.

4. *Resisting pressure to use drugs.* A key component to this lesson introduces students to the different types of peer pressure to take drugs that they may face. It teaches them to say no to such offers by considering the negative consequences of drug use. DARE instructors introduce four different sources of influence on people's behavior: personal preferences, family expectations, peer expectations, and the mass media. After defining *peer pressure*, the DARE instructor explains different types of pressure that friends use to get others to use alcohol or drugs. These methods include threats and intimidation.

5. *Resistance techniques: Ways to say no.* This lesson reinforces the previous lesson by teaching students different ways to respond to peer pressure. Instructors write various techniques of resisting pressure on the chalkboard and discuss them with the class. These include giving a reason or excuse, changing the subject, walking away, and ignoring the person. The instructor also stresses that people can consciously avoid such confrontations by choosing to avoid associating with drug users. Because noting long-term consequences for not taking drugs is usually not as effective as citing short-term consequences, an emphasis is placed on explaining short-term consequences such as "I do not like the taste."

6. *Building self-esteem.* In this lesson, DARE instructors explain that self-esteem is created out of positive and negative feelings and experiences. Students learn to identify their own positive qualities. They discover that drug use stems from poor self-esteem, and that those with high self-esteem think for themselves and have accepted their limitations as human beings. In short, when people feel good about themselves, they can exert control over their behavior.

7. *Assertiveness: A response style.* Instructors teach assertiveness as a technique to refuse offers of drugs. The lesson begins with the DARE officer asking the class what occurrences happened during the previous week to heighten their self-esteem. They then emphasize that once people achieve self-esteem, they can more easily think for themselves without being pressured to do what they believe is wrong. The instructor defines the word *assertive* and stresses that people should learn how to assert their rights confidently without interfering with the rights of others. Role-playing occurs in which each student and his or her partner practice good posture, strong voice, eye contact, calm manner, and other elements of assertiveness.

8. *Managing stress without taking drugs.* This step helps students recognize stress in their lives and how to relieve it without taking drugs. The teacher presents the "fight-or-flight" response to danger along with the physiological changes that accompany that response. The instructor notes that modern-day stressors, such as taking a test, fail to provide the individual with a means to "flee" or "fight," and alternative ways of coping with stress must be learned. Students then work in groups and devise ways of dealing with two types of stressors (from a class list) in their lives. They then share their strategies with the rest of the class and discuss them. Methods include ways to relax and exercise, talk out problems with a family member or a friend, and so on.

9. *Media influences on drug use.* This lesson focuses on ways to resist media influences to use alcohol and drugs. The class discusses various advertising strategies to promote certain products, and the DARE instructor explains how to see through the strategies. For example, by showing a product being used by people who are enjoying themselves, the advertiser suggests that people who actually use the product will indeed have more fun. The students then work in groups to create an anti-alcohol or antidrug commercial while using the techniques employed by professional advertisers. Next, each group performs their own commercial before the class.

10. *Decision-making and risk-taking.* The objective of this lesson is to teach students to apply decision-making skills in evaluating the results of various kinds of risk-taking behavior, including drug use. First, the class generates a list of risk-taking behaviors, including the many everyday types of risks commonly encountered. Although many risks are worth taking (e.g., making new friends, trying out for a play, etc.), many are not and can result in harm (e.g., swallowing an unknown substance, riding with a drunk driver, etc.). Students learn that any assumption of risk involves a choice. The choices that we make are influenced by several factors, including family, friends, the mass media, and personal values. The key to intelligent decision-making is to think through the likely outcomes of various alternative actions.

11. *Alternatives to drug abuse.* This lesson examines rewarding alternative activities that do not involve taking drugs. Students recount the reasons that people take drugs and what basic needs people have. They also learn that these needs can be met in healthier ways than taking drugs (such as playing games or exercising). The students then fill out a worksheet titled "What I Like to Do." They write down their favorite activities and explain to the class why these are better than taking drugs.

12. *Role modeling.* This phase involves older students who have resisted peer pressure to use drugs. The younger students ask the older students questions that they have previously prepared.

13. *Forming a support system.* Students discover that positive relationships with different people create a support system for the student. In this lesson, two fundamental questions are posed: why do people need other people? What do other people do for us? The DARE instructor explains that everyone has needs that can be met only through positive relationships with other people. The students then complete a worksheet titled "Choosing Friends," which requires them to indicate the qualities they look for in friends (e.g., people who are honest with me, people who will not get me into trouble, etc.). When they are finished, students share their responses and discuss barriers to friendship and how to overcome them.

14. *Ways to deal with pressure from gangs.* In this lesson, students learn how to deal with pressure put on them from gangs, and how to evaluate choices available to them. The students begin with naming the social activities they most enjoy and with whom they like to share these activities. These relationships help satisfy needs for recognition, acceptance, and affection. It is also recognized that people join gangs to satisfy these same needs. Students see that gangs use strong-arm tactics to get what they want. The students then learn to cope with bullying and intimidation by first avoiding places where gangs hang out, and by leaving money or other valuables at home. Other techniques include keeping busy with constructive activities that meet the needs for friendship and love.

15. *Project DARE summary.* This lesson is a summary of what the student should have learned through Project DARE. The class divides into competing teams, and the officer reads a series of questions about DARE, giving each team an opportunity to earn points for each correct answer. Scores are then computed, and a winner is announced. Each student then individually completes a true-false questionnaire titled "What Do You Know about Drugs?" The officer reviews the answers.

16. *Taking a stand.* As homework, students must complete a worksheet, "Taking a Stand," which asks them to articulate how they will (1) keep their body healthy, (2) control their feelings when angry or under stress, (3) decide whether to take a risk, (4) respond when a friend pressures them to use drugs or alcohol, and (5) respond when they see people on television using drugs or alcohol. This document represents the student's DARE pledge.

17. *DARE culmination.* The author of the winning DARE pledge reads his or her pledge in front of a school assembly. Each student who has completed the DARE

curriculum receives a certificate of achievement signed by the chief of police and the superintendent of schools.

Concerns about DARE

The U.S. Department of Education concluded in 2003 that the DARE program is ineffective and now prohibits its funds from being used to support it. The U.S. Surgeon General's office, the National Academy of Sciences, and the Government Accounting Office also concluded that the program is sometimes counterproductive in some populations, with those who graduate from DARE later having higher rates of drug use. Studies by Dennis Rosenbaum and by the California Legislative Analyst's office found that DARE graduates were more likely than others to drink alcohol, smoke tobacco, and use illegal drugs [24].

Other research supports these concerns, suggesting that the popularity of the DARE program camouflages the fact that it does not work. Furthermore, evidence from more than 30 studies concluded that DARE "does not prevent drug use" among students, and that DARE graduates "are indistinguishable from students who do not participate in the program." A peer-reviewed, 6-year study published in 1998 concluded that suburban students who participated in DARE reported a 3–5 percent higher rate of drug use than suburban students who did not participate [25]. Moreover, of more than 500 parents of teens surveyed in 2006 by the Center on Addiction and Substance Abuse, only 5 percent believed the DARE program was responsible for keeping kids drug-free, ranking this method of prevention below parents, schools, church, and law enforcement. Finally, in 2003 a Government Accounting Office report concluded, "...the six long-term evaluations of the DARE elementary school curriculum that we reviewed found no significant differences in illicit drug use between students who received DARE in the fifth or sixth grade...and students who did not..." [26].

Administrators of the DARE program have tried to suppress unfavorable research that found that DARE "simply didn't work." A federal judge ruled that DARE had sought to "suppress scientific research" critical of its program and had "attempted to silence researchers at the Research Triangle Institute," according to editors at the *American Journal of Public Health* and producers at *Dateline NBC*. Some reporters, like those at *Rolling Stone* magazine, who have written negative stories on DARE have claimed that they were the victims of harassment and intimidation as a result. Critics such as Students for Sensible Drug Policy, DRCNet, and Drugsense have exposed the DARE program for teaching misleading and inaccurate information about drugs and drug use.

Critics of DARE have the opinion that abstinence or "Just Say No" messages mislead students by treating recreational drug use as substance abuse or by labeling alcoholic beverages as gateway drugs. Supporters of DARE believe that educating students that alcoholic beverages and cigarettes are illegal substances is appropriate, because underage drinking in the United States and cigarette purchasing are illegal for those of primary and secondary school age. In 1998, the DARE program failed to meet federal guidelines that they be both research-based and effective. As of 2013 they had not met those guidelines, DARE was disqualified from receiving further federal grant money.

■ ■ Critical Thinking Task ■

Assume you are a DARE officer working in a sixth-grade classroom. Create a role-playing skit by which children may learn methods of resisting peer pressure to experiment with illicit drugs. The characters and dialogue in your skit must be realistic yet suited for the age group.

Summary

We have discussed many ways to deal with drug abuse in our society, and because of the social dangers of drug abuse, increasingly more attention is being given to this critical issue. In addition to education and law enforcement initiatives, treatment remains one of the most viable options. The immediate objectives of most treatment programs are to control or eliminate drug abuse, give the drug user alternatives for his or her lifestyle, and treat medical complications associated with drug use.

Treatment programs are varied in nature because of the personality type of the drug-dependent person, as well as the specific drug of abuse for which the person is being treated. Options include detoxification, chemical dependency units, outpatient clinics, methadone maintenance programs, and residential therapeutic communities. After treatment, social reintegration is an important step in making the patient a productive member of the community. The halfway house is often used for this purpose; it permits members to assume some responsibilities in maintaining the operation of the house.

Drug prevention is another essential component to fighting drug abuse. The two ways most likely to achieve the drug prevention goal are to make potential first-time users not want to use drugs, and to impose severe criminal penalties to deter first-time drug abuse. DARE and SPECDA prevention programs focus on children to teach them fundamental basics of individual thinking, decision-making, and personal choices when faced with the prospect of using illicit drugs. Many experts believe that treatment and prevention programs offer the most hope for successfully dealing with the nation's drug problem.

Do you recognize these terms?

- DARE
- detoxification
- maintenance
- methadone treatment programs
- narcotic antagonists
- relapse
- therapeutic community

Discussion Questions

1. List three characteristics of treatment and rehabilitation programs.
2. Compare and contrast the five categories of drug treatment.

3. Describe the detoxification process and its role in drug treatment.
4. Explain how the methadone maintenance program operates in treating opiate addicts.
5. Explain how the therapeutic community program treats drug addicts.
6. What are some problems with drug treatment in our communities?
7. List and discuss the two goals of drug prevention.

References

[1] National Institute on Drug Abuse. (2007). *NIDAInfo facts: Treatment approaches for drug addiction.* Found at: www.nida.nih.gov/infofacts/TreatMeth.html.
[2] National Institute on Drug Abuse. (2013). Organizational web site located at: http://www.drugabuse. gov/publications/principles-drug-addiction-treatment-research-based-guide-third-edition/ frequently-asked-questions/drug-addiction-treatment-worth-its-cost. Accessed May 5, 2013.
[3] Ibid.
[4] Office of National Drug Control Policy. (1989). *The national drug control strategy, executive summary.* Washington, DC: U.S. Government Printing Office.
[5] Office of National Drug Control Policy. (2006). *The President's national drug control policy, February 2006.* Washington, DC: Executive Office of the President of the United States.
[6] Apsler, R. (March/April 1994). Is drug abuse treatment effective? *The American Enterprise*, 48.
[7] Ibid.
[8] Ibid.
[9] Association of the Bar of the City of New York. (1994). A wiser course: ending drug prohibition. *The Record, 49*, 5.
[10] Kleber, H. (1989). Treatment of drug dependence: what works. *International Review of Psychiatry, 1*, 81–100.
[11] Falco, M. (1992). *The making of a drug-free America: Programs that work.* New York: Times Books.
[12] Hubbard, R., Marsden, M., Rachal, J., Harwood, H., Cavanaugh, E., & Ginzburg, H. (1989). *Drug abuse treatment: A national survey of effectiveness.* Washington, DC: National Institute on Drug Abuse.
[13] Ibid.
[14] Ibid.
[15] Ball, J. C., Lange, W. R., Meyers, C. P., & Friedman, S. R. (1988). Reducing the risk of AIDS through methadone treatment. *Journal of Health and Social Behavior, 29*, 214–226.
[16] Hubbard, R., Marsden, M., Rachal, J., Harwood, H., Cavanaugh, E., & Ginzburg, H. (1989). *Drug abuse treatment: A national survey of effectiveness.* Washington, DC: National Institute on Drug Abuse.
[17] Ibid.
[18] National Institute on Drug Abuse. (2007). *NIDAInfo facts: Treatment approaches for drug addiction.* Found at: www.nida.nih.gov/infofacts/TreatMeth.html.
[19] Hubbard, R., Marsden, M., Rachal, J., Harwood, H., Cavanaugh, E., & Ginzburg, H. (1989). *Drug abuse treatment: A national survey of effectiveness.* Washington, DC: National Institute on Drug Abuse.
[20] Tabbush, V. (1986). *The effectiveness and efficiency of publicly funded drug abuse treatment and prevention programs in California: A benefit–cost analysis.* Los Angeles: Economic Analysis Corporation.
[21] Clines, F. (January 20, 1993). Dealing with drug dealers: rehabilitation, not jail. *The New York Times*, B2.
[22] Office of Substance Abuse Policy. (1991). Promoting health development through school-based prevention: new approaches, in U.S. Department of Health and Human Services. *Preventing adolescent drug use: From theory to practice*, OSAP Prevention Monograph-8, DHHS Pub. No. (ADM). pp. 91–1725.
[23] Falco, M. (1992). *The making of a drug-free America: Programs that work.* New York: Times Books.

[24] Rosenbaum, D., & Hanson, G. (Nov 1998). Assessing the effects of school-based drug education: a 6-year multilevel analysis of project D.A.R.E. *Journal of Research in Crime and Delinquency.*

[25] Ibid.

[26] Government Accounting Office. (2003). *Youth Illicit Drug Use Prevention: DARE Long-term Evaluations and Federal Efforts to Identify Effective Programs.* Found at: http://www.gao.gov/products/GAO-03-172R. Accessed May 8, 2013.

Appendix I
Drug Scheduling

This document is a general reference and not a comprehensive list. This list describes the basic or parent chemical and does not describe the salts, isomers, and salts of isomers, esters, ethers, and derivatives, which may also be controlled substances.

Substance	DEA Number	Nonnarcotic	Other Names
Schedule I			
1-(1-Phenylcyclohexyl)pyrrolidine	7458	N	PCPy, PHP, rolicyclidine
1-(2-Phenylethyl)-4-phenyl-4-acetoxypiperidine	9663		PEPAP, synthetic heroin
1-[1-(2-Thienyl)cyclohexyl]piperidine	7470	N	TCP, tenocyclidine
1-[1-(2-Thienyl)cyclohexyl]pyrrolidine	7473	N	TCPy
1-Methyl-4-phenyl-4-propionoxypiperidine	9661		MPPP, synthetic heroin
2,5-Dimethoxy-4-ethylamphetamine	7399	N	DOET
2,5-Dimethoxyamphetamine	7396	N	DMA, 2,5-DMA
3,4,5-Trimethoxyamphetamine	7390	N	TMA
3,4-Methylenedioxyamphetamine	7400	N	MDA, love drug
3,4-Methylenedioxy-methamphetamine	7405	N	MDMA, ecstasy, XTC
3,4-Methylenedioxy-N-ethylamphetamine	7404	N	N-ethyl MDA, MDE, MDEA
3-Methylfentanyl	9813		China white, fentanyl
3-Methylthiofentanyl	9833		Chine white, fentanyl
4-Bromo-2,5-dimethoxyamphetamine	7391	N	DOB, 4-bromo-DMA
4-Bromo-2,5-dimethoxyphenethylamine	7392	N	Nexus, 2-CB; has been sold as ecstasy (i.e. MDMA)
4-Methoxyamphetamine	7411	N	PMA
4-Methyl-2,5-dimethoxyamphetamine	7395	N	DOM, STP
4-Methylaminorex (cis isomer)	1590	N	U4Euh, McN-422
5-Methoxy-3,4-methylenedioxyamphetamine	7401	N	MMDA
Acetorphine	9319		
Acetyl-alpha-methylfentanyl	9815		
Acetyldihydrocodeine	9051		Acetylcodone
Acetylmethadol	9601		Methadyl acetate
Allylprodine	9602		
Alphacetylmethadol (except levo-alphacetylmethadol)	9603		
Alpha-ethyltryptamine	7249	N	ET, trip
Alphameprodine	9604		
Alphamethadol	9605		
Alpha-methylfentanyl	9814		China white, fentanyl

(Continued)

459

Substance	DEA Number	Nonnarcotic	Other Names
Alpha-methylthiofentanyl	9832		China white, fentanyl
Aminorex	1585	N	Has been sold as methamphetamine
Benzethidine	9606		
Benzylmorphine	9052		
Betacetylmethadol	9607		
Beta-hydroxy-3-methylfentanyl	9831		China white, fentanyl
Beta-hydroxyfentanyl	9830		China white, fentanyl
Betameprodine	9608		
Betamethadol	9609		
Betaprodine	9611		
Bufotenine	7433	N	Mappine, N,N-imethylserotonin
Cathinone	1235	N	Constituent of "khat" plant
Clonitazene	9612		
Codeine methylbromide	9070		
Codeine-N-oxide	9053		
Cyprenorphine	9054		
Desomorphine	9055		
Dextromoramide	9613		Palfium, Jetrium, Narcolo
Diampromide	9615		
Diethylthiambutene	9616		
Diethyltryptamine	7434	N	DET
Difenoxin	9168		Lyspafen
Dihydromorphine	9145		
Dimenoxadol	9617		
Dimepheptanol	9618		
Dimethylthiambutene	9619		
Dimethyltryptamine	7435	N	DMT
Dioxaphetyl butyrate	9621		
Dipipanone	9622		Dipipan, phenylpiperone HCl, Diconal, Wellconal
Drotebanol	9335		Metebanyl, oxymethebanol
Ethylmethylthiambutene	9623		
Etonitazene	9624		
Etorphine (except HCl)	9056		
Etoxeridine	9625		
Fenethylline	1503	N	Captagon, amfetyline, ethyltheophylline amphetamine
Furethidine	9626		
Gamma hydroxybutyric acid (GHB)	2010	N	GHB, gamma hydroxybutyrate, sodium oxybate
Heroin	9200		Diacetylmorphine, diamorphine
Hydromorphinol	9301		
Hydroxypethidine	9627		
Ibogaine	7260	N	Constituent of *Tabernanthe iboga* plant

Substance	DEA Number	Nonnarcotic	Other Names
Ketobemidone	9628		Cliradon
Levomoramide	9629		
Levophenacylmorphan	9631		
Lysergic acid diethylamide	7315	N	LSD, lysergide
Marijuana	7360	N	Cannabis, marijuana
Mecloqualone	2572	N	Nubarene
Mescaline	7381	N	Constituent of peyote cacti
Methaqualone	2565	N	Quaalude, Parest, Somnafac, Opitimil, Mandrax
Methcathinone	1237	N	N-methylcathinone, "cat"
Methyldesorphine	9302		
Methyldihydromorphine	9304		
Morpheridine	9632		
Morphine methylbromide	9305		
Morphine methylsulfonate	9306		
Morphine-N-oxide	9307		
Myrophine	9308		
N,N-dimethylamphetamine	1480	N	
N-ethyl-1-phenylcyclohexylamine	7455	N	PCE
N-ethyl-3-piperidyl benzilate	7482	N	JB 323
N-ethylamphetamine	1475	N	NEA
N-hydroxy-3,4-methylenedioxyamphetamine	7402	N	N-hydroxy MDA
Nicocodeine	9309		
Nicomorphine	9312		Vilan
N-methyl-3-piperidyl benzilate	7484	N	JB 336
Noracymethadol	9633		
Norlevorphanol	9634		
Normethadone	9635		Phenyldimazone
Normorphine	9313		
Norpipanone	9636		
Para-fluorofentanyl	9812		China white, fentanyl
Parahexyl	7374	N	Synhexyl
Peyote	7415	N	Cactus that contains mescaline
Phenadoxone	9637		
Phenampromide	9638		
Phenomorphan	9647		
Phenoperidine	9641		Operidine, Lealgin
Pholcodine	9314		Copholco, Adaphol, Codisol, Lantuss, Pholcolin
Piritramide	9642		Piridolan
Proheptazine	9643		
Properidine	9644		
Propiram	9649		Algeril
Psilocybin	7437	N	Constituent of "magic mushrooms"

(Continued)

Substance	DEA Number	Nonnarcotic	Other Names
Psilocyn	7438	N	Psilocin; constituent of "magic mushrooms"
Racemoramide	9645		
Tetrahydrocannabinols	7370	N	THC, delta-8 THC, delta-9 THC, and others
Thebacon	9315		Acetylhydrocodone, Acedicon, Thebacetyl
Thiofentanyl	9835		China white, fentanyl
Tilidine	9750		Tilidate, Valoron, Kitadol, Lak, Tilsa
Trimeperidine	9646		Promedolum
Schedule II			
1-Phenylcyclohexylamine	7460	N	Precursor of PCP
1-Piperidinocyclohexanecarbonitrile	8603	N	PCC; precursor of PCP
Alfentanil	9737		Alfenta
Alphaprodine	9010		Nisentil
Amobarbital	2125	N	Amytal, Tuinal
Amphetamine	1100	N	Dexedrine, Biphetamine
Anileridine	9020		Leritine
Benzoylecgonine	9180		Cocaine metabolite
Bezitramide	9800		Burgodin
Carfentanil	9743		Wildnil
Coca leaves	9040		
Cocaine	9041		Methyl benzoylecgonine, crack
Codeine	9050		Morphine methyl ester, methyl morphine
Dextropropoxyphene, bulk (nondosage forms)	9273		Propoxyphene
Dihydrocodeine	9120		Didrate, Parzone
Diphenoxylate	9170		
Diprenorphine	9058		M50-50
Ecgonine	9180		Cocaine precursor; in coca leaves
Ethylmorphine	9190		Dionin
Etorphine HCl	9059		M 99
Fentanyl	9801		Innovar, Sublimaze, Duragesic
Glutethimide	2550	N	Doriden, Dorimide
Hydrocodone	9193		Dihydrocodeinone
Hydromorphone	9150		Dilaudid, dihydromorphinone
Isomethadone	9226		Isoamidone
Levo-alphacetylmethadol	9648		LAAM (long-acting methadone), levomethadyl acetate
Levomethorphan	9210		
Levorphanol	9220		Levo-Dromoran
Meperidine	9230		Demerol, Mepergan, pethidine
Meperidine intermediate—A	9232		Meperidine precursor
Meperidine intermediate—B	9233		Meperidine precursor

Substance	DEA Number	Nonnarcotic	Other Names
Meperidine intermediate—C	9234		Meperidine precursor
Metazocine	9240		
Methadone	9250		Dolophine, Methadose, Amidone
Methadone intermediate	9254		Methadone precursor
Methamphetamine	1105	N	Desoxyn, D-desoxyephedrine, ICE, crank, speed
Methylphenidate	1724	N	Ritalin
Metopon	9260		
Moramide intermediate	9802		
Morphine	9300		MS Contin, Roxanol, Duramorph, RMS, MSIR
Nabilone	7379	N	Cesamet
Opium extracts	9610		
Opium fluid extract	9620		
Opium poppy	9650		*Papaver somniferum*
Opium tincture	9630		Laudanum
Opium, granulated	9640		Granulated opium
Opium, powdered	9639		Powdered opium
Opium, raw	9600		Raw opium, gum opium
Oxycodone	9143		OxyContin, Percocet, Tylox, Roxicodone, Roxicet
Oxymorphone	9652		Numorphan
Pentobarbital	2270	N	Nembutal
Phenazocine	9715		Narphen, Prinadol
Phencyclidine	7471	N	PCP, Sernylan
Phenmetrazine	1631	N	Preludin
Phenylacetone	8501	N	P2P, phenyl-2-propanone, benzyl methyl ketone
Piminodine	9730		
Poppy straw	9650		Opium poppy capsules, poppy heads
Poppy straw concentrate	9670		Concentrate of poppy straw (CPS)
Racemethorphan	9732		
Racemorphan	9733		Dromoran
Remifentanil	9739		Ultiva
Secobarbital	2315	N	Seconal, Tuinal
Sufentanil	9740		Sufenta
Thebaine	9333		Precursor of many narcotics
Schedule III			
Amobarbital—noncontrolled	2126	N	Amobarbital and ephedrine capsules' active ingredients
Amobarbital—suppository dosage form	2126	N	
Anabolic steroids	4000	N	"Body-building" drugs
Aprobarbital	2100	N	Alurate

(Continued)

Substance	DEA Number	Nonnarcotic	Other Names
Barbituric acid derivative	2100	N	Barbiturates not specifically listed
Benzphetamine	1228	N	Didrex, Inapetyl
Boldenone	4000	N	Equipoise, Parenabol, Vebonol, dehydrotestosterone
Buprenorphine	9064		Buprenex, Temgesic
Butabarbital	2100	N	Butisol, Butibel
Butalbital	2100	N	Fiorinal, Butalbital with aspirin
Chlorhexadol	2510	N	Mechloral, Mecoral, Medodorm, Chloralodol
Chlorotestosterone (same as clostebol)	4000	N	If 4-chlorotestosterone, then clostebol
Chlorphentermine	1645	N	Pre-Sate, Lucofen, Apsedon, Desopimon
Clortermine	1647	N	Voranil
Clostebol	4000	N	Alfa-Trofodermin, Clostene, 4-chlorotestosterone
Codeine and isoquinoline alkaloid (90 mg/du)	9803		Codeine with papaverine or noscapine
Codeine combination product (90 mg/du)	9804		Empirin, Fiorinal, Tylenol, ASA or APAP with codeine
Dehydrochlormethyltestosterone	4000	N	Oral-Turinabol
Dihydrocodeine combination product (90 mg/du)	9807		Synalgos-DC, Compal
Dihydrotestosterone (same as stanolone)	4000	N	See stanolone
Dronabinol in sesame oil in soft gelatin capsule	7369	N	Marinol, synthetic THC in sesame oil in soft gelatin capsule
Drostanolone	4000	N	Drolban, Masterid, Permastril
Ethylestrenol	4000	N	Maxibolin, Orabolin, Durabolin-O, Duraboral
Ethylmorphine combination product (15 mg/du)	9808		
Fluoxymesterone	4000	N	Anadroid-F, Halotestin, Ora- Testryl
Formebolone	4000	N	Esiclene, Hubernol
Hydrocodone and isoquinoline alkaloid (15 mg/du)	9805		Dihydrocodeinone + papaverine or noscapine
Hydrocodone combination product (15 mg/du)	9806		Tussionex, Tussend, Lortab, Vicodin, Hycodan, Anexsia
Ketamine	7285	N	Ketaset, Ketalar, Special K, K
Lysergic acid	7300	N	LSD precursor
Lysergic acid amide	7310	N	LSD precursor
Mesterolone	4000	N	Proviron
Methandienone (see Methandrostenolone)	4000	N	
Methandranone	4000	N	
Methandriol	4000	N	Sinesex, Stenediol, Troformone
Methandrostenolone	4000	N	Dianabol, Metabolina, Nerobol, Perbolin

Substance	DEA Number	Nonnarcotic	Other Names
Methenolone	4000	N	Primobolan, Primobolan Depot, Primobolan S
Methyltestosterone	4000	N	Android, Oreton, Testred, Virilon
Methyprylon	2575	N	Noludar
Mibolerone	4000	N	Cheque
Morphine combination product (50 mg/100 ml or g)	9810		
Nalorphine	9400		Nalline
Nandrolone	4000	N	Deca-Durabolin, Durabolin, Durabolin-50
Norethandrolone	4000	N	Nilevar, Solevar
Opium combination product (25 mg/du)	9809		Paregoric, other combination products
Oxandrolone	4000	N	Anavar, Lonavar, Provitar, Vasorome
Oxymesterone	4000	N	Anamidol, Balnimax, Oranabol, Oranabol 10
Oxymetholone	4000	N	Anadrol-50, Adroyd, Anapolon, Anasteron, Pardroyd
Pentobarbital and noncontrolled	2271	N	FP-3 active ingredients
Pentobarbital suppository dosage form	2271	N	WANS
Phendimetrazine	1615	N	Plegine, Prelu-2, Bontril, Melfiat, Statobex
Secobarbital and noncontrolled	2316	N	Various active ingredients
Secobarbital suppository dosage form	2316	N	Various
Stanolone	4000	N	Anabolex, Andractim, Pesomax, dihydrotestosterone
Stanozolol	4000	N	Winstrol, Winstrol-V
Stimulant compounds previously	1405	N	Mediatric excepted
Sulfondiethylmethane	2600	N	
Sulfonethylmethane	2605	N	
Sulfonmethane	2610	N	
Talbutal	2100	N	Lotusate
Testolactone	4000	N	Teslac
Testosterone	4000	N	Android-T, Androlan, Depotest, Delatestryl
Thiamylal	2100	N	Surital
Thiopental	2100	N	Pentothal
Tiletamine and zolazepam combination	7295	N	Telazol product
Trenbolone	4000	N	Finaplix-S, Finajet, Parabolan
Vinbarbital	2100	N	Delvinal, vinbarbitone
Schedule IV			
Alprazolam	2882	N	Xanax
Barbital	2145	N	Veronal, Plexonal, barbitone
Bromazepam	2748	N	Lexotan, Lexatin, Lexotanil
Butorphanol	9720	N	Stadol, Stadol NS, Torbugesic, Torbutrol

(Continued)

Substance	DEA Number	Nonnarcotic	Other Names
Camazepam	2749	N	Albego, Limpidon, Paxor
Cathine	1230	N	Constituent of "khat" plant
Chloral betaine	2460	N	Beta Chlor
Chloral hydrate	2465	N	Noctec
Chlordiazepoxide	2744	N	Librium, Libritabs, Limbitrol, SK-Lygen
Clobazam	2751	N	Urbadan, Urbanyl
Clonazepam	2737	N	Klonopin, Clonopin
Clorazepate	2768	N	Tranxene
Clotiazepam	2752	N	Trecalmo, Rize
Cloxazolam	2753	N	Enadel, Sepazon, Tolestan
Delorazepam	2754	N	
Dexfenfluramine	1670	N	Redux
Dextropropoxyphene dosage forms	9278		Darvon, propoxyphene, Darvocet, Dolene, Propacet
Diazepam	2765	N	Valium, Valrelease
Dichloralphenazone	2467	N	Midrin, dichloralantipyrine
Diethylpropion	1610	N	Tenuate, Tepanil
Difenoxin (1 mg/25 ug AtSO4/du)	9167		Motofen
Estazolam	2756	N	ProSom, Domnamid, Eurodin, Nuctalon
Ethchlorvynol	2540	N	Placidyl
Ethinamate	2545	N	Valmid, Valamin
Ethyl loflazepate	2758	N	
Fencamfamin	1760	N	Reactivan
Fenfluramine	1670	N	Pondimin, Ponderal
Fenproporex	1575	N	Gacilin, Solvolip
Fludiazepam	2759	N	
Flunitrazepam	2763	N	Rohypnol, Narcozep, Darkene, Roipnol
Flurazepam	2767	N	Dalmane
Halazepam	2762	N	Paxipam
Haloxazolam	2771	N	
Ketazolam	2772	N	Anxon, Loftran, Solatran, Contamex
Loprazolam	2773	N	
Lorazepam	2885	N	Ativan
Lormetazepam	2774	N	Noctamid
Mazindol	1605	N	Sanorex, Mazanor
Mebutamate	2800	N	Capla
Medazepam	2836	N	Nobrium
Mefenorex	1580	N	Anorexic, Amexate, Doracil, Pondinil
Meprobamate	2820	N	Miltown, Equanil, Deprol, Equagesic, Meprospan
Methohexital	2264	N	Brevital

Substance	DEA Number	Nonnarcotic	Other Names
Methylphenobarbital (mephobarbital)	2250	N	Mebaral, mephobarbital
Midazolam	2884	N	Versed
Modafinil	1680	N	Provigil
Nimetazepam	2837	N	Erimin
Nitrazepam	2834	N	Mogadon
Nordiazepam	2838	N	Nordazepam, Demadar, Madar
Oxazepam	2835	N	Serax, Serenid-D
Oxazolam	2839	N	Serenal, Convertal
Paraldehyde	2585	N	Paral
Pemoline	1530	N	Cylert
Pentazocine	9709	N	Talwin, Talwin NX, Talacen, Talwin compound
Petrichloral	2591	N	Pentaerythritol chloral, Periclor
Phenobarbital	2285	N	Luminal, Donnatal, Bellergal-S
Phentermine	1640	N	Lonamin, Fastin, Adipex-P, Obe-Nix, Zantryl
Pinazepam	2883	N	Domar
Pipradrol	1750	N	Detaril, Stimolag Fortis
Prazepam	2764	N	Centrax
Quazepam	2881	N	Doral, Dormalin
Sibutramine	1675	N	Meridia
SPA	1635	N	1-Dimethylamino-1,2-diphenylethane, Lefetamine
Temazepam	2925	N	Restoril
Tetrazepam	2886	N	
Triazolam	2887	N	Halcion
Zaleplon	2781	N	Sonata
Zolpidem	2783	N	Ambien, Stilnoct, Ivadal

Schedule V

Substance	DEA Number	Nonnarcotic	Other Names
Codeine preparations (200 mg/100 ml or 100 g)			Cosanyl, Robitussin A-C, Cheracol, Cerose, Pediacof
Difenoxin preparations (0.5 mg/25 ml)			Motofen ug AtSO4/du
Dihydrocodeine preparations (10 mg/100 ml or 100 g)			Cophene-S, various others
Diphenoxylate preparations (2.5 mg/25 ug AtSO4)			Lomotil, Logen
Ethylmorphine preparations (100 mg/100 ml or 100 g)			
Opium preparations (100 mg/100 ml or g)			Parepectolin, Kapectolin PG, Kaolin Pectin PG
Pyrovalerone	1485	N	Centroton, Thymergix

Appendix II
Gangs Highlighted by the National Drug Intelligence Center

Street Gangs

18th Street (National)

Formed in Los Angeles, 18th Street is a group of loosely associated sets or cliques, each led by an influential member. Membership is estimated at 30,000 to 50,000. In California, approximately 80 percent of the gang's members are illegal aliens from Mexico and Central America. The gang is active in 44 cities in 20 states. Its main source of income is street-level distribution of cocaine and marijuana and, to a lesser extent, heroin and methamphetamine. Gang members also commit assault, auto theft, carjacking, drive-by shootings, extortion, homicide, identification fraud, and robbery.

Almighty Latin King and Queen Nation (National)

The Latin Kings street gang was formed in Chicago in the 1960s, and consisted predominantly of Mexican and Puerto Rican males. Originally created with the philosophy of overcoming racial prejudice and creating an organization of "Kings," the Latin Kings evolved into a criminal enterprise operating throughout the United States under two umbrella factions—Motherland, also known as King Motherland Chicago (KMC), and Bloodline (New York). All members of the gang refer to themselves as Latin Kings, and, currently, individuals of any nationality are allowed to become members. Latin Kings associating with the Motherland faction also identify themselves as "Almighty Latin King Nation" (ALKN), and make up more than 160 structured chapters operating in 158 cities in 31 states. The membership of Latin Kings following KMC is estimated to be 20,000 to 35,000. The Bloodline was founded by Luis Felipe in the New York State correctional system in 1986. Latin Kings associating with Bloodline also identify themselves as the "Almighty Latin King and Queen Nation" (ALKQN). Membership is estimated to be 2,200 to 7,500, divided among several dozen chapters operating in 15 cities in five states. Bloodline Latin Kings share a common culture and structure with KMC and respect them as the Motherland, but all chapters do not report to the Chicago leadership hierarchy. The gang's primary source of income is the street-level distribution of powder cocaine, crack cocaine, heroin, and marijuana. Latin Kings continue to portray themselves as a community organization while engaging in a wide variety of criminal activities, including assault, burglary, homicide, identity theft, and money laundering.

Asian Boyz (National)

Asian Boyz is one of the largest Asian street gangs operating in the United States. Formed in southern California in the early 1970s, the gang is estimated to have 1,300 to 2,000 members operating in at least 28 cities in 14 states. Members primarily are Vietnamese or Cambodian males. Members of Asian Boyz are involved in producing, transporting, and distributing methamphetamine, as well as distributing MDMA and marijuana. In addition, gang members are involved in other criminal activities, including assault, burglary, drive-by shootings, and homicide.

Black P. Stone Nation (National)

Black P. Stone Nation, one of the largest and most violent associations of street gangs in the United States, consists of seven highly structured street gangs with a single leader and a common culture. It has an estimated 6,000 to 8,000 members, most of whom are African American males from the Chicago metropolitan area. The gang's main source of income is the street-level distribution of cocaine, heroin, marijuana, and, to a lesser extent, methamphetamine. Members also are involved in many other types of criminal activity, including assault, auto theft, burglary, carjacking, drive-by shootings, extortion, homicide, and robbery.

Bloods (National)

Bloods is an association of structured and unstructured gangs that have adopted a single-gang culture. The original Bloods were formed in the early 1970s to provide protection from the Crips street gang in Los Angeles, California. Large, national-level Bloods gangs include Bounty Hunter Bloods and Crenshaw Mafia Gangsters. Bloods membership is estimated to be 7,000 to 30,000 nationwide; most members are African American males. Bloods gangs are active in 123 cities in 33 states. The main source of income for Bloods gangs is street-level distribution of cocaine and marijuana. Bloods members also are involved in transporting and distributing methamphetamine, heroin, and phencyclidine (PCP), but to a much lesser extent. The gangs also are involved in other criminal activity, including assault, auto theft, burglary, carjacking, drive-by shootings, extortion, homicide, identity fraud, and robbery.

Crips (National)

Crips is a collection of structured and unstructured gangs that have adopted a common gang culture. Crips membership is estimated at 30,000 to 35,000; most members are African American males from the Los Angeles metropolitan area. Large, national-level Crips gangs include 107 Hoover Crips, Insane Gangster Crips, and Rolling 60s Crips. Crips gangs operate in 221 cities in 41 states. The main source of income for Crips gangs is the street-level distribution of powder cocaine, crack cocaine, marijuana, and PCP. The gangs also are involved in other criminal activity, such as assault, auto theft, burglary, and homicide.

Florencia 13 (Regional)

Florencia 13 (F 13 or FX 13) originated in Los Angeles in the early 1960s; gang membership is estimated at more than 3,000 members. The gang operates primarily in California and increasingly in Arkansas, Missouri, New Mexico, and Utah. Florencia 13 is subordinate to the Mexican Mafia (La Eme) prison gang and claims Sureños (Sur 13) affiliation. A primary source of income for gang members is the trafficking of cocaine and methamphetamine. Gang members smuggle multikilogram quantities of powder cocaine and methamphetamine obtained from supply sources in Mexico into the United States for distribution. Also, gang members produce large quantities of methamphetamine in southern California for local distribution. Florencia members are involved in other criminal activities, including assault, drive-by shootings, and homicide.

Fresno Bulldogs (Regional)

Fresno Bulldogs is a street gang that originated in Fresno, California, in the late 1960s. Bulldogs is the largest Hispanic gang operating in central California, with membership estimated at 5,000 to 6,000. Bulldogs is one of the few Hispanic gangs in California that claims neither Sureños (southern) nor Norteños (northern) affiliation. However, gang members associate with Nuestra Familia (NF) members, particularly when trafficking drugs. The street-level distribution of methamphetamine, marijuana, and heroin is a primary source of income for gang members. In addition, members are involved in other criminal activity, including assault, burglary, homicide, and robbery.

Gangster Disciples (National)

The Gangster Disciples street gang was formed in Chicago, Illinois, in the mid-1960s. It is structured like a corporation and is led by a chairman of the board. Gang membership is estimated at 25,000 to 50,000; most members are African American males from the Chicago metropolitan area. The gang is active in 110 cities in 31 states. Its main source of income is the street-level distribution of cocaine, crack cocaine, marijuana, and heroin. The gang also is involved in other criminal activity, including assault, auto theft, firearms violations, fraud, homicide, the operation of prostitution rings, and money laundering.

Latin Disciples (Regional)

Latin Disciples, also known as Maniac Latin Disciples and Young Latino Organization, originated in Chicago in the late 1960s. The gang is composed of at least 10 structured and unstructured factions with an estimated 1,500 to 2,000 members and associate members. Most members are Puerto Rican males. Maniac Latin Disciples is the largest Hispanic gang in the Folk Nation Alliance. The gang is most active in the Great Lakes and southwestern regions of the United States. The street-level distribution of powder cocaine, heroin, marijuana, and PCP is a primary source of income for the gang. Members also are involved in other criminal activity, including assault, auto theft, carjacking, drive-by shootings, home invasion, homicide, money laundering, and weapons trafficking.

Mara Salvatrucha (National)

Mara Salvatrucha, also known as MS 13, is one of the largest Hispanic street gangs in the United States. Traditionally, the gang consisted of loosely affiliated groups known as cliques; however, law enforcement officials have reported increased coordination of criminal activity among Mara Salvatrucha cliques in the Atlanta, Dallas, Los Angeles, Washington, D.C., and New York metropolitan areas. The gang is estimated to have 30,000 to 50,000 members and associate members worldwide, 8,000 to 10,000 of whom reside in the United States. Members smuggle illicit drugs, primarily powder cocaine and marijuana, into the United States and transport and distribute the drugs throughout the country. Some members also are involved in alien smuggling, assault, drive-by shootings, homicide, identity theft, prostitution operations, robbery, and weapons trafficking.

Sureños and Norteños (National)

As individual Hispanic street gang members enter prison systems, they put aside former rivalries with other Hispanic street gangs and unite under the name Sureños or Norteños. The original Mexican Mafia members, most of whom were from southern California, considered Mexicans from the rural, agricultural areas of northern California weak, and viewed them with contempt. To distinguish themselves from the agricultural workers or farmers from northern California, members of the Mexican Mafia began to refer to the Hispanic gang members who worked for them as Sureños (Southerners). Inmates from northern California became known as Norteños (Northerners) and are affiliated with NF. Because of its size and strength, Fresno Bulldogs is the only Hispanic gang in the California Department of Corrections (CDC) that does not fall under Sureños or Norteños, but remains independent. Sureños gang members' main sources of income are retail-level distribution of cocaine, heroin, marijuana, and methamphetamine within prison systems and in the community, as well as extortion of drug distributors on the streets. Some members have direct links to Mexican drug-trafficking organizations (DTOs), and broker deals for the Mexican Mafia as well as their own gang. Sureños gangs also are involved in other criminal activities such as assault, carjacking, home invasion, homicide, and robbery. Norteños gang members' main sources of income are the retail-level distribution of cocaine, heroin, marijuana, methamphetamine, and PCP within prison systems and in the community, as well as extortion of drug distributors on the streets. Norteños gangs also are involved in other criminal activities, such as assault, carjacking, home invasion, homicide, and robbery.

Tango Blast (Regional)

Tango Blast is one of the largest prison and street criminal gangs operating in Texas. Tango Blast's criminal activities include drug trafficking, extortion, kidnapping, sexual assault, and murder. In the late 1990s, Hispanic men incarcerated in federal, state, and local prisons founded Tango Blast for personal protection against violence from traditional prison gangs such as the Aryan Brotherhood, Texas Syndicate, and Texas Mexican Mafia. Tango Blast originally had four city-based chapters: Houstone, Houston, Texas; ATX or La Capricha, Austin, Texas; D-Town, Dallas, Texas; and Foros or Foritos, Fort Worth, Texas. These founding four chapters are collectively known as Puro Tango Blast or the Four Horsemen. From the original four chapters, former Texas inmates established new chapters in El Paso, San Antonio, Corpus Christi, and the Rio Grande Valley. In June 2008, the Houston Police Department estimated that more than 14,000 Tango Blast members were incarcerated in Texas. Tango Blast is difficult to monitor. The gang does not conform to either traditional prison or street gang hierarchical organization or gang rules. Tango Blast is laterally organized, and leaders are elected sporadically to represent the gang in prisons and to lead street gang cells. The significance of Tango Blast is exemplified by corrections officials reporting that rival traditional prison gangs are now forming alliances to defend themselves against Tango Blast's growing power.

Tiny Rascal Gangsters (National)

Tiny Rascal Gangsters is one of the largest and most violent Asian street gang associations in the United States. It is composed of at least 60 structured and unstructured gangs, commonly referred to as sets, with an estimated 5,000 to 10,000 members and associates who have adopted a common gang culture. Most members are Asian American males. The sets are most active in the southwestern, Pacific, and New England regions of the United States. The street-level distribution of powder cocaine, marijuana, MDMA, and methamphetamine is a primary source of income for the sets. Members also are involved in other criminal activity, including assault, drive-by shootings, extortion, home invasion, homicide, robbery, and theft.

United Blood Nation (Regional)

Bloods is a universal term that is used to identify both West Coast Bloods and United Blood Nation (UBN). While these groups are traditionally distinct entities, both identify themselves by "Blood," often making it hard for law enforcement to distinguish between them. UBN started in 1993 in Rikers Island GMDC (George Mochen Detention Center) to form protection from the threats posed by the Latin Kings and the Ñetas, who dominated the prison. UBN is a loose confederation of street gangs, or sets, that once were predominantly African American. Membership is estimated to be between 7,000 and 15,000 along the United States eastern corridor. UBN derives its income from street-level distribution of cocaine, heroin, and marijuana; robbery; auto theft; and smuggling drugs to prison inmates. UBN members also engage in arson, carjacking, credit card fraud, extortion, homicide, identity theft, intimidation, prostitution operations, and weapons distribution.

Vice Lord Nation (National)

Vice Lord Nation, based in Chicago, is a collection of structured gangs located in 74 cities in 28 states, primarily in the Great Lakes region. Led by a national board, the various gangs have an estimated 30,000 to 35,000 members, most of whom are African American males. The main source of income is street-level distribution of cocaine, heroin, and marijuana. Members also engage in other criminal activity, such as assault, burglary, homicide, identity theft, and money laundering.

Prison Gangs

Aryan Brotherhood

Aryan Brotherhood, also known as AB, was originally ruled by consensus, but is now highly structured with two factions—one in the CDC and the other in the Federal Bureau of Prisons. The majority of members are Caucasian males, and the gang is active primarily in the southwestern and Pacific regions. Its main source of income is the distribution of cocaine, heroin, marijuana, and methamphetamine within prison systems and on the streets. Some AB members have business relationships with Mexican DTOs that smuggle illegal drugs into California for AB distribution. AB is notoriously violent, and is often involved in murder for hire. Although the gang has been historically linked to the California-based Hispanic prison gang Mexican Mafia (La Eme), tension between AB and La Eme is increasingly evident, as seen in recent fights between Caucasians and Hispanics within the CDC.

Barrio Azteca

Barrio Azteca is one of the most violent prison gangs in the United States. The gang is highly structured and has an estimated membership of 2,000. Most members are Mexican national or Mexican American males. Barrio Azteca is most active in the southwestern region, primarily in federal, state, and local corrections facilities in Texas, and outside prison in southwestern Texas and southeastern New Mexico. The gang's main source of income is derived from smuggling heroin, powder cocaine, and marijuana from Mexico into the United States for distribution both inside and outside prisons. Gang members often transport illicit drugs across the United States–Mexico border for DTOs. Barrio Azteca members also are involved in alien smuggling, arson, assault, auto theft, burglary, extortion, intimidation, kidnapping, robbery, and weapons violations.

Black Guerrilla Family

Black Guerrilla Family (BGF), originally called Black Family or Black Vanguard, is a prison gang founded in the San Quentin State Prison, California, in 1966. The gang is highly organized along paramilitary lines, with a supreme leader and central committee. BGF has an established national charter, code of ethics, and oath of allegiance. BGF members operate primarily in California and Maryland. The gang has 100–300 members, most of whom are African American males. A primary source of income for gang members comes from cocaine and marijuana distribution. BGF members obtain such drugs primarily from NF and Norteños members, or from local Mexican traffickers. BGF members are involved in other criminal activities, including auto theft, burglary, drive-by shootings, and homicide.

Hermanos de Pistoleros Latinos

Hermanos de Pistoleros Latinos (HPL) is a Hispanic prison gang that formed in the Texas Department of Criminal Justice (TDCJ) in the late 1980s. It operates in most prisons and on the streets in many communities in Texas, particularly Laredo. HPL is also active in several cities in Mexico, and its largest contingent in that country is in Nuevo Laredo. The gang is structured and is estimated to have 1,000 members. Members maintain close ties to several Mexican DTOs, and are involved in trafficking quantities of cocaine and marijuana from Mexico into the United States for distribution.

Mexikanemi

The Mexikanemi prison gang (also known as the Texas Mexican Mafia, or Emi) was formed in the early 1980s within the TDCJ. The gang is highly structured and is estimated to have 2000 members, most of whom are Mexican nationals or Mexican American males who were living in Texas at the time of their incarceration. Mexikanemi poses a significant drug-trafficking threat to communities in the southwestern United States, particularly in Texas. Gang members reportedly traffic multikilogram quantities of powder cocaine, heroin, and methamphetamine; multiton quantities of marijuana; and thousand-tablet quantities of MDMA from Mexico into the United States for distribution inside and outside prison. Gang members obtain drugs from associates or members of the Jaime Herrera-Herrera, Osiel Cárdenas-Guillén, and/or Vicente Carrillo-Fuentes Mexican DTOs. In addition, Mexikanemi members maintain a relationship with Los Zetas, a Mexican paramilitary-criminal organization employed by the Cárdenas-Guillén DTO as its personal security force.

Mexican Mafia

The Mexican Mafia prison gang, also known as La Eme (Spanish for the letter M), was formed in the late 1950s within the CDC. It is loosely structured and has strict rules that must be followed by its 200 members. Most members are Mexican American males who previously belonged to a southern California street gang. The Mexican Mafia is primarily active in the southwestern and Pacific regions of the United States, but its power base is in California. The gang's main source of income is extorting drug distributors outside prison and distributing methamphetamine, cocaine, heroin, and marijuana within prison systems and on the streets. Some members have direct links to Mexican DTOs and broker deals for themselves and their associates. The Mexican Mafia also is involved in other criminal activities, including controlling gambling and homosexual prostitution in prison.

Ñeta Association (Ñeta)

Ñeta is a prison gang that began in Puerto Rico and spread to the United States. Ñeta is one of the largest and most violent prison gangs, with about 7,000 members in Puerto Rico and 5000 in the United States. Ñeta chapters in Puerto Rico exist exclusively inside prisons; once members are released from prison, they are no longer considered part of the gang.

In the United States, Ñeta chapters exist inside and outside prisons in 36 cities in nine states, primarily in the northeast. The gang's main source of income is retail distribution of powder and crack cocaine, heroin, marijuana, and, to a lesser extent, lysergic acid diethylamide (LSD), MDMA, methamphetamine, and PCP. Ñeta members commit assault, auto theft, burglary, drive-by shootings, extortion, home invasion, money laundering, robbery, weapons and explosives trafficking, and witness intimidation.

Outlaw Motorcycle Gangs

Bandidos

Bandidos Motorcycle Club, an OMG with 2,000 to 2,500 members in the United States and 13 other countries, is a growing criminal threat to the nation. Law enforcement authorities estimate that Bandidos is one of the two largest OMGs in the United States, with approximately 900 members belonging to more than 88 chapters in 16 states. Bandidos is involved in transporting and distributing cocaine and marijuana, and producing, transporting, and distributing methamphetamine. Bandidos is most active in the Pacific, southeastern, southwestern, and west central regions and is expanding in these regions by forming new chapters and allowing members of support clubs to form or join Bandidos chapters. The members of support clubs are known as "puppet" or "duck" club members. They do the dirty work of the mother club.

Hells Angels

Hells Angels Motorcycle Club (HAMC) is an OMG with 2,000 to 2,500 members belonging to more than 250 chapters in the United States and 26 foreign countries. HAMC poses a criminal threat on six continents. United States law enforcement authorities estimate that HAMC has more than 69 chapters in 22 states with 900–950 members. HAMC produces, transports, and distributes marijuana and methamphetamine, and transports and distributes cocaine, hashish, heroin, LSD, MDMA, PCP, and diverted pharmaceuticals. HAMC is involved in other criminal activity, including assault, extortion, homicide, money laundering, and motorcycle theft.

Mongols

The Mongols Motorcycle Club is an extremely violent OMG that poses a serious criminal threat to the Pacific and southwestern regions of the United States. Mongols members transport and distribute cocaine, marijuana, and methamphetamine, and frequently commit violent crimes, including assault, intimidation, and murder, to defend Mongols territory and uphold its reputation. Mongols has 70 chapters nationwide, with most of the club's 800–850 members residing in California. Many members are former street gang members with a long history of using violence to settle grievances. Agents with the Bureau of Alcohol, Tobacco, Firearms, and Explosives (ATF) have called the Mongols Motorcycle

Club the most violent and dangerous OMG in the nation. In the 1980s, the Mongols OMG seized control of southern California from HAMC, and today the Mongols club is allied with the Bandidos, Outlaws, Sons of Silence, and Pagan's OMGs against HAMC. The Mongols club also maintains ties to Hispanic street gangs in Los Angeles.

Outlaws

The Outlaws Motorcycle Club has more than 1,700 members belonging to 176 chapters in the United States and 12 foreign countries. United States law enforcement authorities estimate that the Outlaws OMG has more than 94 chapters in 22 states with more than 700 members. Outlaws also identifies itself as the American Outlaws Association (A.O.A.) and Outlaws Nation. Outlaws is the dominant OMG in the Great Lakes region. Gang members produce, transport, and distribute methamphetamine, and transport and distribute cocaine, marijuana, and, to a lesser extent, MDMA. Outlaws members engage in various criminal activities, including arson, assault, explosives operations, extortion, fraud, homicide, intimidation, kidnapping, money laundering, prostitution operations, robbery, theft, and weapons violations. It competes with HAMC for membership and territory.

Sons of Silence

The Sons of Silence Motorcycle Club (SOSMC) is one of the largest OMGs in the United States, with 250–275 members among 30 chapters in 12 states. The club also has five chapters in Germany. SOSMC members have been implicated in numerous criminal activities, including murder, assault, drug trafficking, intimidation, extortion, prostitution operations, money laundering, weapons trafficking, and motorcycle and motorcycle parts theft.

Source: *National Gang Threat Assessment (2009)*.

Index

Note: Page numbers followed by "f" denote figures; "t" tables; and "b" boxes.